"BARRELS ALONG LIKE A RUNAWAY FREIGHT TRAIN . . . MAKES YOU ACHE FOR THE INNOCENCE OF AN ERA THAT QUICKLY TURNED. . . ."

—*People*

Papa John
An Autobiography by John Phillips with Jim Jerome

"HE HOLDS NOTHING BACK . . . from his exploits in adolescence to his sexual kinks as an adult to the time he shot cocaine into daughter Mackenzie's arm."

—*The Plain Dealer* (Cleveland)

"ALL THE DEBASED DREAMS, DESPOILED BEAUTY, AND DASHED PROMISE . . . *Papa John* makes *Up and Down with the Rolling Stones* read like a parson's desk diary."

—Timothy White, author of
Catch a Fire: The Life of Bob Marley

"JOHN NAMES NAMES, FILLING IN THE RAUNCHY DETAILS. . . . His book is a hard and honest account whose glamor is tempered with grimness."

—*Library Journal*

"A WHO'S WHO OF ROCK 'N' ROLL IN THE '60s."
—*The Denver Post*

Papa John

AN AUTOBIOGRAPHY
BY JOHN PHILLIPS

WITH JIM JEROME

A DELL BOOK

Published by
Dell Publishing Co., Inc.
1 Dag Hammarskjold Plaza
New York, New York 10017

Dell ® TM 681510, Dell Publishing Co., Inc.

ISBN: 0-440-16783-3

Reprinted by arrangement with Doubleday & Company, Inc.

Printed in the United States of America

July 1987

10 9 8 7 6 5 4 3 2 1

WFH

This is dedicated to the ones I love, my children:

> *Jeffrey*
> *Laura*
> *Chynna*
> *Tamerlane*
> *Bijou*

—PAPA JOHN

ACKNOWLEDGMENTS

I would like to express my deep gratitude to those members of my family and friends, among others, who gave most generously of their time and recollections: Rosemary Throckmorton, the family matriarch whose unique fifty-year perspective proved to be nothing short of indispensable; Susan Adams Phillips; Michelle Phillips; Jeffrey Edmund Andrew Phillips; Laura Mackenzie Phillips; Billy Throckmorton; Nancy Throckmorton Neiers; Scott McKenzie; Denny Doherty; Marsia Trinder; Lenny Holzer; Chris Thurlow; Steve Thurlow; Mike McLean; Dick Weissman; Bill Cleary; Jimmy Shortt; Peter Pilafian; Marshall Brickman; D. A. Pennebaker; Harvey Goldberg; Arthur Stead; Paul Morrissey; Russell Gilliam; Dottie Ross; Sue Blue; Paul Simon; and, of course, Jane.

Certainly, neither this book nor my life of the last fifteen years would have been complete without the presence of my wife, Genevieve Waite Phillips, and to her I am especially indebted.

Others offered invaluable assistance when I needed to tap their expertise: Mark S. Gold, M.D.; A. Carter Pottash, M.D.; Robert Millman, M.D.; Richard Schaeffer; and Robert Tucker. I would also like to thank *Billboard* and Joel Whitburn for keeping track of all those hits and misses through the years, and Mary Vespa of *People.*

Jack Bloomfield of Tailored Typing and Pat Ambrose of the QED Transcription Service deserve praise for fine work under pressure. Copy editor Mark Hurst handled the manuscript with great care and intelligence and Wilma Robin designed the book beautifully.

I thank those special individuals whose faith and unswerving commitment lifted—and kept—the project off the ground: my agent, Amanda Urban of International Creative Management, and my patient editors at Dolphin Books, Jim Fitzgerald and Casey Fuetsch.

Much of this book was written in an isolated cabin on Lake

George in the Adirondack Mountains. Jim Jerome and I virtually locked ourselves in and recreated—and, for my part, relived—the stories of this book, some painful, some funny. The cabin had an enormous fireplace and we often worked all night against the backdrop of phantoms of friends, wives, lovers, and family playing out their stories in the flames—or in the shadows cast on the walls. Jim Jerome's moral support, encouragement, and friendship got me through it, and this book emerged from that dark cabin into sunlight. Thank you, Jim.

Contents

Contents

I

NAILED

1

EARLY JUNE 1980. Another groaning, semiconscious, midafternoon reawakening into oblivion that told me it was time again to split for Manhattan. I had crashed sometime in the dark, wearing jeans, a tennis shirt, and sneakers. Only the relative clarity of dreams broke up the opiated haze of reality back then. I rubbed my eyes clear and scanned the sprawling ground floor, listening for signs of life upstairs. I could have been alone. It felt as if it were probably the next day; maybe not. Maybe tomorrow had come and gone without me. It wouldn't have been the first time.

I shook my head. My face was creased and flushed from its burial in the sofa cushion. Was it the day after tomorrow? *Had* I missed a whole day again? I walked to the kitchen door and saw the paper rolled up between our house and the neighbors'. I could check the date. What did it matter back then? I wasn't keeping time to the front pages, to the sun and moon, to light and dark. In those days, I measured time and set my gaunt six-foot-five-inch frame to an inner hourglass loaded with a pure and deadly white powder.

I was renting a huge rambling house on Long Island Sound in the quaint and classy village of Old Greenwich, Connecticut. My son Tamerlane was still in grade school, the babysitter was taking two-month-old Bijou for a walk, and, in my stumbling inspection of the upstairs, I discovered that my wife Genevieve was asleep in the bedroom. Her hourglass, like mine, needed turning.

I shuffled into the bathroom, splashed my face with cold water, stared into the mirror, and took a preloaded syringe from my green Gucci stash bag. I shook the syringe to make sure the high-grade cocaine dissolved in its water solution. Then I held my arm down and made a fist until I raised a vein on the back of my hand.

I jabbed the needle in and pumped the shot. Seven seconds later, I was soaring. My heart and lungs went wild. There was no better way to kick off a day than a wake-up blast of intravenous coke—the breakfast of junkie champions.

Then I found the car keys. I stepped outside and shaded my sore eyes from light. It wasn't sunny, just one of those hazy, humid suburban afternoons that seemed to drop out of the weather system altogether, to belong to a season of its own: low and dense fishy breezes off the Sound; air neither warm nor chilly; faint shadows but no sun; a soggy light that faded the colors of coming summer to a throbbing sepia glare. The humidity made it feel hot and sticky as soon as I wiggled into the driver's seat of my beat-up white Cadillac. The next-door neighbor spotted me from her kitchen window just a few yards from the common driveway between our houses. She waved. She couldn't have had any idea what was going on. An hour later, I would learn that I didn't either.

I sped past the homes and hedges on tranquil, swanky Shore Road, assuming as usual that once I got to my Manhattan destination, none of this—the time, weather, Coast Guard small-craft warnings, pollution—would matter. Within minutes I was on I-95. The euphoric I.V. rush was wearing off. Manhattan was a long way off.

I knew this well-traveled trade route like the back of my hand. The back of my hand was the last stop. I reached inside the Gucci bag on the floor and felt for another loaded syringe. By the time I tossed a quarter into the machine at the Greenwich tolls, I was flying again.

It was risky to drive myself, in a fancy car that didn't

seem to belong to someone so wasted and scruffy. I usually
called my limousine service instead. That way, I could cook
a shot of heroin in the backseat between toll plazas and peer
out the tinted windows. Even then I didn't exactly look the
part. But I could have passed.

I had it made in the heart of Cheever Country: the big
house on the Sound, a beautiful wife, two stunning children,
the luxury car, a Little League team to coach—the whole
shot, as they say. But no country club, just a $1,000-a-day
drug frenzy.

I had been living off ASCAP royalties that came to about
$150,000 a year. The trade route took care of the rest. There
were always wads of cash here and there. The views over the
water were gorgeous, but the house was sparsely furnished
and a mess inside. I was a Connecticut Junkie. My life
wasn't defined by acquisitions but by trade-offs and I had
thrown everything away to keep the powder flowing through
the hourglass.

When it came time to invert it and start over, I traveled
fast and recklessly. I didn't see it then, but I was inviting
disaster, begging for restraint. I dispensed with license
plates, registration, insurance card, or personal I.D. No
socks or coat. I wore shoulder-length hair, an unruly long
beard, T-shirts, jeans, sneakers, and a long-sleeve open shirt
or jacket to cover the tracks.

I never left home without the Gucci bag with the three-
digit metal lock on the zipper. I was sweating as the needle
slid past eighty; I had to score and head back before my
fellow commuters. My trips into town gave new meaning to
the term "rush hour."

I had run this course along 95 a hundred times—a bleak
tableau of freight and junk yards, stranded rail cars, power
stations, and the deadening brick façades of faceless corporate headquarters. I opened all the windows for a deafening
blast of air mixing country and city, natural and industrial,
honeysuckle and incineration. The radio howled over the
violent gusts inside the car. I didn't feel right if I wasn't
pushing it to the edge. Drugs and risk elevated this numbing
ritual to supreme exhilaration. I had learned to make I-95

disappear. I meditated instead on my destination, locked it in my mind as the broken white lines pulled me nearer.

81st and Madison.

Corner of Panic and Euphoria.

K & B Drugs.

Inside the bag were syringes, assorted dwindling stashes of barbiturates, clumps of foil, spoons, vials—the junkie's tool kit for shaky day trips between buys. I was going to the drugstore about once a week. I'd walk in, shoot the shit with Sidney Korn and Alvin Brod. Wait until the place was quiet, then take the shopping bag from them, full of large pharmaceutical bottles, boxes of syringes, whatever I needed, whatever my dealers on the street could move for cash and coke. It had been going on for three years now. For all I knew, I was set for life.

My trips to K & B in 1977 began innocently enough, to fill valid prescriptions for Percodan from an Upper East Side quack who was shooting me up with coke and vitamins to get me off heroin.

I went back to buy some Tylenol and toothpaste for my daughter Laura Mackenzie and myself. I got to know Al and Sid more casually. I had been shooting smack into my veins for a year or more. The habit took hold while I was living in London, spending a lot of time around Keith Richards, the lead guitarist for the Rolling Stones, and Anita Pallenberg. They were both on drugs and I let myself slide into mainlining. There was no one to blame but myself. They knew what smack could do.

The habit intensified for Gen and me while I recorded tracks in London for a solo album which Keith and Mick Jagger, both longtime friends, helped produce and performed on. When I returned to New York to resume the album, I wanted to get off heroin and ended up seeing the quack. I was soon cross-addicted to cocaine and heroin.

I had always enjoyed a peculiar, almost mystical knack for running across people in my life just when I needed to find them. And they always end up having a profound impact on me.

It didn't seem too strange then that I was befriending a

pair of licensed pharmacists in early 1977. Looking back, it
now seems somehow fated that I found K & B.

It's boggling to contemplate how my life would have been
different had I bought toothpaste that day at Duane Reade
or Pathmark instead.

I scanned the shelves. They asked me if I wanted anything
else. "Yes," I said. "I could use a box of syringes." I gave an
excuse—diabetes or something. Soon boxes of syringes and
prescription drugs were being delivered to my hotel suite. It
wasn't long before I offered to buy the pharmacy from them.
They refused. I made them a counteroffer: a quarter million
in cash, up front, and total access to the inventories. They
refused.

But the door was always open and I could walk in there
like I owned the place. Ironically, the place soon owned me.
Through dealers, I began scoring hot books of empty state-
controlled triplicate prescription forms, required by doctors
and druggists for heavy-gauge painkillers and Schedule II
narcotics. This was done so Korn and Brod could try to
match their drug outflow with bogus Rx's.

I'd walk in with new scrip books, walk out with giant
bottles filled with thousands of prescription drugs—uppers,
downers, Quaaludes, Percodans. For my own habit, I kept
only Dilaudid, a synthetic morphine derivative, and
Desoxyn, which is pure, synthetic Methedrine.

Both were astonishingly powerful. Keith had always said
pharmaceuticals were for wimps. He was wrong. Dilaudid
was far more potent, longer-lasting, and got you much
higher. Half of one after major surgery kills pain for terminal cancer patients. Gen and I were melting down eight, ten
of the golden four-milligram pills and shooting them into
our veins every day, once it began to rule our lives. Those
doses weren't for killing pain—just killing.

But we didn't know any other way to live, and we
couldn't get enough.

The other K & B drugs served as my chemical currency
among my high-level drug dealers. Their coke was better
than the best coke money could buy because I wasn't buying
it with money. I was swapping my illicit prescription drugs
for it. The K & B pills worked like American dollars in a

Third World black market. They got you anything you wanted and multiplied your purchasing power in the local economy.

There was no stronger exchange rate than when I had "pharmaceutical"—unadulterated narcotics right from the drug multinationals' factories to the drugstore—rather than chemically unreliable and, hence, potentially deadly bootlegs. Even the common street junkie knows the FDA is looking out for his pharmacological welfare.

Using the K & B bottles instead of cash, I became a top slugger in the pharm league of dealers—bartering my pills for their powders—and unfailingly copped the highest-grade unstepped-on coke this side of the Andes. Remarkably, this system had worked to perfection for three years.

I spotted a parking space on the side street, screeched to a stop half a block from the corner of 81st and Madison. I checked the sidewalk for anything out of the ordinary. Regular afternoon street energy: grade-schoolers, high-schoolers yelling in clusters, Madison Avenue matrons, nannies pushing strollers, art buffs peering into gallery windows, deli delivery boys on bikes—nothing at all out of place.

I couldn't possibly see it coming, but I was living out the final seconds of a life I would never again know.

I reached for the door, and at that instant everything changed. The knob didn't twist. I had been locked out. I felt a twinge of anxiety. I could see my partners inside. Something *was* wrong. Maybe they had had a business disagreement, or there was a sudden personal crisis, and they closed the store for an hour. They were both family men from the suburbs and real decent guys. I backed away and kept looking around, behind, across the street. I tapped on the door. They ignored me. Then Sid walked to the door and gave me an almost imperceptible shake of the head, as if to ward me off. His face was stony and sullen.

I tapped on the door and grinned. "Heyyy, Sid, lighten up."

He held a small handwritten sign against the window: PHONE ME. Our eyes met, but it was the blankness of his expression that said it all, that first omen of danger. He walked away. I tapped the window to get his attention.

"Come on, boys, I didn't put any quarters in the meter. I haven't got all day. Open up." But they vanished to the rear of the store.

My mind and heart both began to churn and I came down hard off the coke rush. I staggered backward on the crowded sidewalk, brushing several pedestrians. I fumbled through my pockets for a dime, reeling weakly, trying to maintain balance. This was not good, whatever was going down in there. I broke into a nervous trot, realizing that I might be in some kind of trouble.

I darted out between two double-parked cars and nearly got hit by a swerving, honking cab. In the phone booth my hands were trembling so crazily I had to hit the touch-tone buttons twice. I heard my labored breathing amplified through the mouthpiece to the earpiece. I was gulping in filthy city exhaust. I flashed on my stately retreat on the Sound, my family. This was unreal, it couldn't be happening. It was a sick prank, a junkie fever dream.

I'd wake up any second now in Old Greenwich. For years I had been shooting drugs into my body, but only now did I feel terrifyingly vulnerable. I covered the mouthpiece with my palm to muffle the panting of mounting panic. I stared at the tracks and scars on the back of my hand, spotted the swollen fresh puncture from an hour earlier. I was sick and faint. Sid knew it would be me on the other end. I should be waking up right about now—if only this was a nightmare.

"Yeah, what?" he said.

"What the hell is going on?" I asked him. "What is this 'phone me' shit?"

His voice was dead. "Come in again, but be very quiet," he said. There was an eerie, resigned calm in his voice. This dream kept getting worse.

The door was now open. I walked through. "All right, guys, so the new security system works. What's going on?"

Sid held a finger to his lips, urging silence. I glared incredulously at both of them. *Gen should be calling me now, shaking me awake.*

"May I help you with something, sir?" he asked, as if I were a new customer. This charade was clearly for the benefit of the half-dozen legitimate customers. My mind was racing in a dozen directions, all of them roadblocked with paranoia. Was this gentle sixty-year-old recent stroke victim who leaned on an aluminum walker actually a heavily armed narc poised to nail my ass if I took the shopping bag out to the sidewalk? The tension was getting thick. I killed time by pretending to examine the condoms and decongestants. Then, when the others had cleared and we were momentarily alone, Sid handed me a crudely scrawled message: THE DEA WAS HERE THIS MORNING. THEY HAVE YOUR PICTURE AND THEY WANT ALL OUR RECORDS BY MONDAY MORNING. He balled up the note and chucked it. We stared at each other in icy disbelief. Now my heart was kicking.

"I don't get it," I said. "How the fuck . . ."

"*I* get it, man," he said, inching closer to me, keeping an eye on the front door. Was he whispering because the store was bugged? He rapped the counter with his knuckles. "And you *better* start getting it. They were *here,* John, in my store. They have pictures of you. Do you get it now? You—we—are in deep shit."

"You gotta be joking. Right? They've got my pictures?" He stared back at me silently. "John, they want thousands of scrips in forty-eight hours. Does that sound like a joke to you?"

My body went cold and numb, my blood drained to my feet. I heard what he said, but it didn't sink in. It was no dream. I looked around for the hidden camera. I suddenly saw in my mind photos of me coming, going, the bag, the Caddie, the limo. Or was it a movie, a scratchy, flickering black-and-white peep show for the prosecution? My mind played games to escape the truth. And what crime could they have captured on film—criminal possession of a Gucci bag? It just wasn't sinking in.

"I'm running down on things. I've gotta . . ."

"No fucking way, man. It's finished. Over. Are you out of your mind?" His clenched whisper was full of anger and pain. "Don't come back, you understand now? You *can't* come back, John. *Ever.* It's over."

"But . . ."

"Look," he said, fuming at my inability to grasp the seriousness of it all. He stopped abruptly as a customer entered, smoothly changed gears, and dealt with the sale. Then he locked the door and led me to a corner of the store.

"John," he said more evenly, "I'll try to be diplomatic about this. I don't really give a shit about your problems right now. I care about our two families staying up for two days and nights going through phone books, obituaries, making up names from their school friends, just to be able to give them something that vaguely *resembles* a stack of scrips. Look, I don't know *how* this happened. I realize you might have a problem with, you know, getting stuff. But this is my whole life here, this store. It's our families, our kids, our homes. Do you know how bad this could get for us? Don't you *see?* We're in this way over our heads too. It's totally *fucked.* We're all scared *shitless."*

My hands went to cover my face. "Ohhh my God," I kept mumbling. "How'd they get my picture?"

"I don't know, but they got it and they were here." I couldn't even bring myself to nod. "You better leave now," he said.

"Okay, okay."

I started out and stopped, as my eyes lingered on the large pill bottles on the shelves behind the counter. He pushed me forward from behind. "Uh-uh, man, not now. No more. Don't even call."

I balked. "Come on, Sid. I could load up in a second. Just one last time, please. *Please.* What's the diff . . ."

"OUT!" he shouted, forcefully nudging me toward the door. I pulled the door open and stepped outside, a marked man.

The DEA has your picture. Those words echoed in my head all the way home. I knew by then there was trouble coming down. I gripped the steering wheel like a lifeline, and sweated. Somewhere on the FDR Drive, though, I let go a wild, lunatic shriek. I saw Sid's face, the two notes he wrote, I heard our conversation. I kept seeing shelves of drugs not taken, never to be taken. It was over, all right, but I had no idea what was coming next. I repeatedly checked the rearview mirror for an unmarked speeding car on my tail.

"I think the Feds may be after me," I announced when I arrived home. I sat down with Gen and explained what little

I knew. In the refuge of my home, I felt less exposed, harder
to find. They'd never catch me again at 81st and Madison
and because we were renting, it would be hard for them to
track me down—unless they already had. The *bastards*. She
was alarmed and stunned into long silences. She leaned
against me on the couch in the living room and sighed.

"What does this mean, darling?" she asked, clasping her
hands around mine.

"It means Demerols, Tuinals, and street heroin," I said.

In the next three or four days, we ran through the Demerols—another morphine substitute—and the barbiturate
Tuinal. Neither of us realized that barbiturate withdrawal is
more hazardous and painful than opiate withdrawal. One
morning at six-thirty, I heard crashing and thrashing in the
bedroom from the bathroom. I ran in and Gen was purple
and stiff, propped up against the headboard. Her jaws were
clenched and she was heaving and hissing fiercely. Her eyes
glared wildly and her face was turning purple. It looked like
a scene out of some scary movie about demon possession. I
realized she was having a seizure. She had no idea where she
was and her eyes were glazed over.

"Jesus Christ, no, no, she's dying," I said under my
breath. Tamerlane, who was nine, was getting ready for
school and Bijou, barely two months old, was sleeping.

"Come on, baby, talk to me," I said, squeezing her jaw,
peering into her vacant eyes. "Let's go, let's go, talk, I'm
here, everything's okay." Just then, I heard Tam knock.

"What's that noise, Daddy?" he asked. "Is everything
okay?"

"It's nothing, son. Just go downstairs. I'll be right down."

"Is Mommy all right too?" he asked. "Are you fighting
with Mommy? Mommy isn't sick, is she?" I knew he was
pressed against the bedroom door and worried. I went to the
door, cracked it open, and blocked his view of the bed.

"No, Tam, she's fine." I tried to sound as reassuring as I
could. "She's just awakened with a bad cough is all. You fix
some cereal and I'll be down and make your sandwich in a
sec."

I stayed with Gen another seven or eight minutes, lightly
slapping her cheeks and coaxing her back to reality until she

relaxed a bit and lay down. It was the most frightening thing I had ever seen in my life. I was afraid she would swallow her tongue. I forced her jaws open and kept them apart with a pencil. I grabbed her tongue and she bit a gash out of my finger. It bled so heavily into her mouth that I thought she'd gag and choke on the blood. Her color and breathing slowly returned to normal. She had no idea what had happened.

"Where am I?" she wondered, sounding real spacey.

"You are right in our home. You had a seizure. You're all right now. You just lie here in bed," I assured her. "I'll be right back. I've got to go downstairs and make Tam his sandwich for lunch and see that he gets off to school." I saw her nod vaguely and thought she was coming around fine as I moved for the door.

"Who's Tam?" she asked in that same slow, faraway voice. I froze in my steps and wheeled around. *My God,* I said to myself, *she's totally out of it.*

"Tam's our son," I explained at her side, "and the school bus will take him to school. We do this every day. You know that."

She had no memory of who she was, which is typical of patients with seizures or shock treatment. I sent Tam off and called a doctor at New Milford Hospital. A private ambulance service rushed her over and she was checked into the drug ward. We had been taking barbiturates by the handfuls for years and were so out of it we never realized we were addicted to *them* too.

The doctor examined me and found me out of immediate danger. But he saw the arms and hands. "I can't believe what happened," I told him. "That was one helluva close call."

"You two are extremely lucky," he said solemnly. He didn't know the worst of it. Gen had been addicted through the first few months of pregnancy with Bijou, then courageously went to London and detoxed for the birth. Still, little Bij was born in our Old Greenwich home while I was stoned out of my mind and my daughter Mackenzie was asleep upstairs.

Bijou very nearly died, but somehow survived after six

weeks in intensive care. I was still too upset to discuss it with the doctor. One close call was enough for that day.

"But what are you going to do?" he asked. He knew the situation. Gen was in for at least two weeks. Two young kids at home, an infant and a nine-year-old. I groaned at the ridiculous complexity of the situation.

"I sure can't check *my*self in. We've got no relatives in the area. I've got to stay at home." I explained that we just couldn't bear much more anguish. And he didn't even know about K & B. "It's funny," I said. "We have rented this great summer place in the Hamptons beginning the end of the month, to get away from it all. I hope nothing gets in the way of that. Gen and I really need to hold it together." I had given him little choice.

"Okay," he said reluctanctly. "I'm giving you a prescription for sixty Dilaudids and that's as many as I will ever give you. Just to get you over this period because Gen's going to have to stay in the hospital at least two or three weeks. I know you're used to going through sixty in two or three days, but these will just have to last you. Somehow you'll have to detox yourself at home and take care of the kids while you do."

I tried just that—two milligrams every four hours. About one sixteenth of my usual daily dose. It was very painful. I missed the big shots and hated rationing. I was pretty shaky, couldn't sleep, felt afraid I'd have a convulsion. If I dozed off, I'd catch myself and wake up again, wondering if I had just had a petit mal seizure.

I visited Gen every day at the hospital and saw she was doing much better. "John," she would say every day as I arrived, "please bring me some Dilaudid, would you? Please. I beg of you." And every day I refused. And she'd beg again, desperately clutching my hands.

"I won't do it," I insisted. "You've got to be strong. We've both got to hang tough through this together." And her craving slowly gave way to a building faith.

On the tenth day, I broke down. I kissed her as I arrived and slowly, ceremoniously unfolded my hand to reveal a couple Dilaudids, which she promptly swallowed. She came out around June 20 and we made it to the Hamptons a week later.

I regularly cheated on my detox regime and was out of drugs altogether by the time we had to move. By the end of June, DEA agents were quizzing our Connecticut neighbors about us, our dog, car, habits, movements. We were already gone.

We found a beautiful Bavarian-style cottage hidden behind high hedges on Rose Hill Road in Water Mill, right off the Montauk Highway. Our possessions remained scattered all over the house for a few days. I knew of a local heroin source, a black bootlegger who'd sell me awful nickel and dime bags of street heroin that was stepped on so badly we couldn't even get off on it. We could barely maintain. It wasn't even worth it. So Gen and I decided—for maybe the dozenth time—to stay totally cleaned out by ourselves.

We had tried all the cures. The one we tried over the July Fourth weekend was one of the most excruciating. Our timing couldn't have been worse. Mick Jagger and his girlfriend Jerry Hall were coming to visit. We were so out of it we prepared nothing for our guests by their arrival July 3. The house was a shambles. Tam had somehow talked me into buying him a noisy go-cart and he was tearing up the front lawn with it. Gen and I were barely able to stand and converse at the same time, drinking heavily and smoking a lot of grass to anesthetize ourselves.

It was a hard way to learn that for a big Hamptons weekend, a good host should serve—not *go*—cold turkey. When you clean out on your own, you just go completely crazy. Your whole body aches, especially your joints, you get fevers, you get an incredible case of the farts, you get the runs. In short, you are in no condition to play host to a man of wealth and taste.

Mick and Jerry came out in a limousine, but once they picked up on what was going on, they took off. They went straight to the home of some mutual friends: Lenny Holzer, a real estate tycoon who had produced *Gimme Shelter,* and his wife, Marsia Trinder, a designer of chic and outrageous custom outfits. We had introduced Marsia and Lenny years

before. Their house was several miles away on Mecox Bay
and they had a pool. Mick and Jerry settled there instead.

Once the four of them saw the condition we—and our
house—were in, Jerry and Marsia stayed on to unpack
boxes, hang clothes in the closets, and look after our two
young kids. Mick and Lenny must have stayed over at Lenny's. They weren't around. I was restless, hyper, pacing, and
irritable.

Everything hurt and I started to feel violent urges. Marsia
was the first to figure it out. I kept asking her for drugs,
though I knew she was straight.

"John," she said to me, as she came downstairs from
Gen's bedroom, "could I have a word with you?"

"Sure," I said. My first assumption from her tone of voice
was that Gen may have been acting strangely, or, worse,
experiencing a side effect from the barbiturate withdrawal.

"What's going on?" I asked, once we were alone.

"Jerry and I were going through Gen's clothes, so we can
hang them up, you know—"

"It's incredibly thoughtful of you two to be doing this for
us on a big summer weekend and all."

"Don't mention it. But what I was about to say was that I
came across several of my own original designs among her
things, like the Carly Simon dress with a leopard belt."

"I know she loves some of your work. She looks great in
them, doesn't she?" I clearly had missed the point.

"John," she said, with a sharper edge that managed to cut
through my stony haze, "these dresses have been *missing*
from my private collections for six weeks."

That straightened me right up. "Are you suggesting Gen
stole your dresses?" I was indignant.

"All I'm saying is . . ."

"All I'm saying is that, one, Gen has absolutely no need to
steal anything, two, probably didn't even know she had
them, and three, she's been through a pretty fucking rough
eight weeks—"

"John, I just . . ."

". . . and if you think she's had your designer dresses on
her mind, you're way off base. With all due respect, Marsia,
your dresses would have been the last thing on her mind,

considering what she's been through. Besides," I added, just
to twist the knife a little, "who could afford hotshit stuff like
that anyway? Was it possible you loaned the dresses to
Gen?" I asked.

We had recently visited Lenny's place on Central Park
West in the 70s. She shrugged: Yes, possibly. Well, I concluded, then maybe Gen had worn them sometime and forgotten about them. "But, hey, Marsia, that's still awfully
little to go on. I have to tell you I resent your suspicion,
especially considering the shape Gen's been in."

Mick and Jerry decided to stay the night at Lenny's after
we managed to get through a late party there.

"It really upset me that Marsia would accuse me of taking
her dresses," Gen said to me before falling to sleep. "I can
see why you would feel that way," I said. "Just relax. Don't
let it get to you. It's over. There was some misunderstanding, that's all. It was hardly fair for her to pick on you that
way." I could feel Gen's hurt and fragility. Marsia was one
of our dearest friends. "Thanks for supporting me, John,"
Gen said.

Mick and Jerry came over the morning of the Fourth to
finish putting the bedrooms in order. Mick and I went to
lunch in Southampton while the women worked on the
house.

"What the hell is going on?" Mick asked me right away as
we sat down. He was always one to get right to the point.

"We're cleaning out." He knew I meant drugs, not mementos. He shifted uneasily. His face is always remarkably
expressive and he hides nothing. "Since when?"

"We started yesterday," I told him.

"Are you crazy?" he exploded.

"What do you mean?" I had known Mick for many years
and he was one friend who had always tried to help me get
off the hard stuff. He had confronted me and let me know
how dangerous the whole thing was. I thought he would
admire my determination.

"You can't just stop taking drugs like that. You'll die.
You're crazy. This is the *Fourth of July*. *No one* cleans out on
their own on July Fourth. Why didn't you tell me? I could

have brought something out to you, to let yourself down easy, man."

"Oh, come on, Mick," I said, whispering so our neighboring tables couldn't overhear. We had already attracted the local paparazzi. "I'm not going to set you up as my courier. I know how you feel about it, and I know you care about me and it would be an insult to our friendship."

"But you just don't kick like that. As a friend, I would have tried to help you get off somehow, certainly more easily than this." He looked away, half-disgusted, half-worried for me.

"I'm never doing it anymore," I boasted.

Mick had been trying for years to help. He always hated the fact that Keith Richards and I had let ourselves get so messed up on smack. Mick is different. He's so damned smart. He always finds a way to get around a wall; I try going through it. He's never really gotten himself addicted to anything.

"I'm not going to do it anymore," I repeated. He was still distressed.

"By nightfall, man, you'll be fuckin' insane. By the time the sun comes up, you'll be a maniac."

He was right—though I beat his prediction by several hours. I would be a madman long before dawn's early light.

"Look," he said after lunch, "at least let me help you through it somehow." We went to a liquor store and he bought cases of booze—rum, vodka, scotch.

Back at Lenny's, Gen had been swimming with the kids and the women. Jerry met Mick with a worried grimace.

"Mick, darlin'," she said in her Texas drawl, "I can't find one of the new earrings you gave me."

"What earrings are they?" I asked. "Sounds like the old boy's splurgin' a bit." I figured he could use a little needling.

"I got Jerry these really fabulous earrings with diamonds in 'em and they did cost a bit."

"A bit?" I coaxed.

Mick grimaced sheepishly. "Twenty-five grand's a bit, 'innit?"

"Well, what was the occasion?" I asked.

"Mick gave them to me," Jerry answered, "to celebrate

the beginning of our living together as boyfriend and girl-friend."

"Nice touch," I said.

"They were in my bag down by the room near the pool."

"Now, where do you think it may be, Jerry?"

"Well, see Gen was down by the pool too, and . . ."

She stopped herself, then said to Mick, "Honey, can I talk with you a sec?"

I could hear this one coming. By now, of course, at least half a dozen people had been in and out of the room all afternoon. But Jerry seemed to be jumping to an inescapable conclusion and related it to me through her boyfriend.

"John," Mick said quietly to me out of earshot of the women. "Jerry has the vague suspicion that Gen may know where the earring is."

"In English, Mick, let's hear it."

"She *thinks* Gen stole it. As far as she *knows,* only she and Gen were in the room when she took them off today. And she *thinks* Gen's a little off the wall and not totally responsible for her actions."

I was enraged. Mick tried to calm me down. Gen denied knowing anything. "Just talk to Gen about it," Mick asked. "It would mean a lot to get the earring back."

"Gen," I said, "have you seen Jerry's diamond earring? She thinks . . ."

"Yes, I know what she thinks," Gen snapped back, on the verge of tears. "She thinks I stole it. My God, what is going on around here? I can't take this anymore."

"So you don't know anything about the damned earring."

"Right." I believed her and went back to Mick. "What the fuck would she do with just one earring, Mick?" I said. "You don't steal *one* earring."

"Well, you know Genevieve," he answered. "She could do *anything.* I mean, after all, she stole Marsia's dresses, didn't she?"

"Ahh-ha," I said, suddenly getting the picture. Everyone was picking on Gen. Jerry was sobbing in the bathroom over the sentimental value of the earring. I was going through withdrawal. Mick was looking all over the house for his

diamonds. I felt the house undulating on me, as if it might
detonate any minute.

And Gen, feeling betrayed by her two friends' accusations, began screaming. Her wild, frizzy hair stood on end.
In my condition—even given my ridiculous height, weight,
and reach advantage over sinewy Mick—I wasn't about to
try to knock him out, so I went to work on myself. I took a
huge swig of booze and started to black out from lack of
drugs.

"We're keeping the kids here," Mick said. "They're just
not safe around you with you in this condition and Gen
overreacting so badly."

He was being so considerate, so *mature* about the whole
mess. I'm sure this wasn't how he had counted on spending
the weekend.

"Oh yeah," he said as an afterthought. "If you still want
me to cop some heroin for you, I will. I just want to see you
make it through the night. Alive."

"No way," I sneered. "I'll make it. I wanna see *you* make
it through the night with an infant."

I got pissed for no reason, except that I gradually got the
point that they had taken our kids away from us and Gen
and I were lying around the house like zombies. Back home,
I set a trash bonfire against a wall in a crazed attempt to
burn down the house. I was way out of control. I wanted to
burn something down. The fire snuffed itself out, though
Gen's screaming at it may have helped.

I stormed back over to the Holzers'. "Who the fuck do
you all think you are, taking my kids?" I shouted belliger-
ently. In a few hours my gratitude had dissolved into rage
and humiliation.

"You can't have them," Mick said. "Look at you," he
glowered. "You're totally wacked out of your mind. I'm not
letting these kids go home the way you are and that's that."

"Where are they?" I insisted.

"It doesn't matter," Mick shot back. "But they *are* safe."

"Who the hell are you all of a sudden, dictating who gets
whose kids and when? Who ever voted you Father of the
Year?"

"John, you can't handle it is all. Cool out. It's crazy to

come off junk like this. I told you it is. I'm doing this for you, dammit, and Gen. I refuse to sit there and watch these kids endangered by this insanity. When you're more together, they'll come home." I stood there panting, trying to come to my senses.

"You don't want your *kids*, John," Lenny suddenly piped in. "You want coke." He handed me a stash.

"Wouldn't hurt the situation," I half-joked, taking the small brown vial.

"I don't know what to do with you," Lenny said. I tossed the coke vial up and snatched it with a happy grin. "Sure, you do, Len." He watched me walk away and shook his head helplessly.

"This is all so crazy," I heard him say.

The sun rose, I went home, shot the coke, and felt a surge of heat and delight that nearly ripped my head off. I felt like I might have an orgasm. I was totally gone.

A hit of coke is a potent magic when you're coming down off heroin. You feel almost human again—for twenty minutes. Then in twenty minutes you crave more coke in the most inhuman way. I felt that crash coming. I had to get out of there. I started out for the car. "Come on," I said to Gen. "I'm going to the hospital."

"No way," she pleaded. "I'm not getting in a car with you the way you are. Mick's right. You'll never make it. I'd rather die here. Please, darling, don't go."

I took off like a madman on Montauk Highway, which was fortunately deserted at dawn. I beat all the beachcombers and surfers. It was quite a race: man against drug. Southampton Hospital was only fifteen minutes away, but she proved right. I never made it. At least not in my vehicle.

I was so out of control I totaled the car, crashed it somehow into the side of the road. I never saw it coming. My knee ended up somewhere in the local Top 40 countdown in the dashboard, my head got bashed in, I heard glass shattering, and I lost consciousness. I finally got there in an ambulance and took a bunch of stitches to the head.

"I have a pretty serious drug problem," I said to the nurse who attended me. Staffing was down because of the Fourth.

"You really are very lucky," she said. "Unfortunately, our

drug treatment specialist won't be in until later this morning. For now, I'll give you some Thorazine, but you should wait here and see him to get into a counseling program."

"Sure," I promised. They shot me up, a real megadose of the heavy-duty tranquilizer and antipsychotic drug. I immediately went to a pay phone, called a radio cab, and split—walked right out of the empty lobby with my head all bandaged up and wearing a hospital gown.

The shock of the near-fatal crash and the shot of Thorazine had brought me pretty well around. I figured even Mick would reinstate me as a father. I knocked on the door and I saw Gen rise from the couch. She pulled the door open and nearly collapsed with fright. "Ohhh my God," she gasped. "What happened to you? I was so worried."

"Oh," I shrugged, realizing I might have looked a little weird. "The car is history. I *said* I was going to the hospital."

"But . . . but your clothes . . . your head . . . What happened to . . ."

"They wanted to keep me there for a drug program, but they only had Thorazine. So I said, 'Look, miss, it's July Fourth, I need to *clear* out, not *clean* out.' Then I dressed up as the Invisible Man and split."

Her mouth just hung open as she looked me over, studied my stitches. "I don't know how you're still *alive.*"

"Blame it on the Thorazine, baby. Sorry."

Back at the Holzers', Mick was getting more than he had bargained for with the kids. They were driving him nuts.

"I want my kids," I announced.

I think I had awakened Mick. He looked pretty run-down —if he had slept at all. He saw my bloody turban and robe and just shook his head. "What the fuck 'appen a you? I told you you wouldn't make it alive."

"You were almost right."

"Are you all right?" he asked with groggy concern. Then he started to laugh at the whole sick spectacle.

"I'm gettin' by. They're doing an autopsy on the car right now. You better start looking for another ride out to the seaplane. Look, man, I want my kids back, okay? They popped me with some Thorazine and I'll be fine, unless you feel a dry mouth should disqualify me as a parent."

"You can 'ave 'em," Mick grumbled. He and Jerry stayed another day or two at the Holzers', then were rescued from our madness by their seaplane.

"You should've seen them," Marsia told me later when she returned from seeing them off. "The plane couldn't come in to the beach, so Mick and Jerry had to roll up their pants past their knees, tie their shoelaces together and hang the shoes around their necks, and wade out in the surf with their suitcases balanced on their heads. It looked like it could have been Bogie and Hepburn in *The African Queen.*"

"Did Mick say anything to you?" I asked.

"He kept yelling, 'I 'ate you, John. I fuckin' 'ate you.' "

Gen and I figured we could maintain with the awful heroin from Bridgehampton. We had no choice. The drugstore closed down for me and we tried to clean out again. Gen had almost died in a seizure. I tried to burn the house down and then almost killed myself in the car. It was beginning to feel like the end of the line. We were in a bizarre vacuum. Life with the pharmacists had ended; life with the Feds hadn't begun. Where *were* they? It just hadn't hit me yet. For weeks I had seen the same police car staked out near our house and kept convincing myself it was a speed trap.

About three weeks later, at the very end of July, I started getting some peculiar phone calls from friends. They had all seen a headline in the New York *Post* and called to get my opinion of the piece. They said the headline read something like: FAMOUS ROCK STAR FACING DRUG BUST. Informed DEA sources were speculating about an imminent arrest. They couldn't identify the rock star for fear he might blow the country.

"Have any idea who it may be?" they all asked.

"Beats the hell out of me," I told them. I couldn't figure it out. We threw names around over the phone. David. James. John. Mick. Don. No one really fit. No one knew. I never really did catch on that they weren't calling to ask me but to *tell* me.

Twenty-four hours later, on the afternoon of July 31, 1980, the mystery of the famous pop star druggie was over. I was stoned, staring vacantly at "Live at Five" on the TV in the upstairs bedroom. I was lying on the bed with my hands clasped behind my head when the answer came. I had stared at soap operas all afternoon and was fading out.

Through my stupor, I heard several cars pull in close to the house. I tried to push them out and doze off, but a bunch of car doors opened and slammed shut. My golden retriever started barking. My eyes couldn't focus on the TV screen any longer. I had already slipped halfway inside a dream.

I picked up indistinct male voices downstairs. A couple of repairmen, possibly. My eyelids closed.

Then silence. I drifted off peacefully until, seconds later, I heard Gen's voice with an edge of tension.

"John," she called upstairs from the kitchen. I said nothing and waited. "There are some men here to see you and they've all got Hawaiian shirts and guns."

I shook my head and smiled.

Then all hell broke loose. The first sound was the door to the bedroom getting kicked open. They burst through and moved in around the bed. A surge of adrenaline caused my body to jerk up in bed before I could even feel fear.

The ones closest to me had their guns drawn and they weren't fucking around. And some of them wore Hawaiian shirts.

"Stay right there. Don't move. Keep your arms over your head," I heard the leader say. My body instantaneously became one giant pulse. I could feel my temples and neck bulging with blood.

"Are you John Edmund Phillips?" the leader asked.

"Yes, I am." I answered before I knew what I was saying. My throat was parched. My heart felt lodged in my neck.

"You are under arrest." I was very close to losing it right there in my pants. I had been invaded. The main man identified himself as a DEA agent named Len Curran. The others —a dozen or so—were local and federal agents.

They told me I had the right to remain silent.

Gen was led in by one of them and told them they had the right to take their coffee black, with cream, or with sugar. She was wild-eyed and freaked. "They just came in and told me to be quiet, asked me where you were, and said to keep

Tam and myself out of the way," she blurted out. "It was awful. I was so afraid."

"And where's Bijou?" I asked her.

"She's out with the nanny. That's how they finally located our house. These men spotted her with the carriage and asked her if she knew the Phillipses. She pointed over the tall hedges."

Tam locked himself in his room with the TV blaring. His way of dealing with this was to deny it was happening. I didn't have that option; they made that clear.

"Conspiracy to distribute drugs in the Southern District of New York." That was the count that counted the heaviest.

"Can I call my lawyer?"

They nodded and acted as decently as can be expected, under the circumstances.

"Can we search the house or not?" Curran asked.

"Are you giving me a choice?" I asked.

"If you say we can't search," he said, "then we will have to get a warrant and that'll take one call back to the city and we'll have it in an hour. And we'll search. If you say we can search right now, then chances are we probably won't search at all. What do you say?"

I thought it over a few seconds. I knew the green Gucci bag was loaded with at least five years' worth of prison time —dope, syringes, paraphernalia, barbiturates, what remained of our ups and downs. It was sitting right there over their heads on a storage ledge off the kitchen. I took a deep breath—and a gamble. "Go right ahead. Search all you want."

"Fine." He nodded to the others around the kitchen. I held my breath and watched Curran closely as he mulled over the next move. Nothing was said. Glances were exchanged. "Okay, men," he said, as adrenaline shot through me again, "we won't bother."

I nearly fainted with relief. I got my attorney and close friend Bob Tucker on the phone, and broke the news to him. Curran, a blustery, red-faced, middle-aged Irishman, took the phone and vaguely set Tucker straight. I grabbed the phone back to get his reading of the situation.

"We are not talking, John, about being out on the dunes

with a couple of loose joints," Tucker said solemnly. He said he would arrange bail once it was set and would see to it I was freed after my arraignment the next morning. Though he admitted being stunned, he reassured me: "Don't do anything crazy. I'll take care of it, figure something out."

The real purpose of my call wasn't legal advice but to have an excuse to turn my back on the agents, walk over to the telephone alcove near the kitchen, and get the three dime bags of street heroin out of my shirt pocket before being frisked for concealed weapons. As I spoke, I nonchalantly slipped them out of my pocket and under the fat phone book on a small corner table.

Trelawny, my trusty ten-year-old golden retriever, paced and sniffed around. He knew something was up and wasn't liking it. We got out to the porch. The evening summer air was warm and sweet with honeysuckle. It was time for us to drive in to a holding facility in Queens for fingerprinting, mug shots, and official registration as an alleged narcotics felon.

"We're gonna have to cuff ya," Curran said. He was blunt, but put a softening apologetic edge on his voice. "It's the law."

"Can you please wait until we get inside the car?" I asked. "I'd hate if my son was looking out the window and saw me in cuffs." They went along with that and the sedan door opened. I looked over my shoulder and, sure enough, Tam was wedged against the window upstairs, staring out. I waved. He shouted, " 'Bye, Daddy," and I saw his little hand wave. My heart broke. He had no idea what was happening. Trelawny did. He immediately hopped in before me, all eighty pounds of him, and refused to leave. The agents were too afraid to deal with him. Mr. T bared his teeth.

"You gotta get your dog outta the car, Mr. Phillips," one of them told me.

"Mr. T wants to come with us. He won't let you take me away." It really was touching. I think I was more heartbroken for Mr. T than for myself.

"He can't go. If he doesn't leave the car, we may have to plug him." They were losing their sense of humor and wanted to get back to town. They told me reporters had been staking out the Metropolitan Correctional Center since noon, when press releases about my arrest had been distributed. I wondered if, instead of a rap sheet, there would be a complete discography.

I patted Mr. T on the head, calmed him down, and explained that I had to go away for a little while and that Gen would be taking care of him. I think he finally understood after thinking it over. Then I gave him a little slap and he ran to Gen. They cuffed me behind my back between two beefy guys in the backseat. I was down to about 135 pounds from 220, but it was still really packed back there with all that weight on my manacled wrists. So they agreed to cuff me in front.

"You want us to call ahead for anything at MCC, anything you'll need to get you through the night?" Curran asked. It was a generous and humane offer. I said no, I wasn't that heavily addicted. Street shit didn't get me off anyhow, I said.

"What are these all about?" one of my backseat companions asked, turning my hands over in his. He had noticed the crisscrossed scratches, tracks, and scars on my hands from where I had hit myself scores of times.

"Tried to break up a fight between two cats," I said. "Cat scratch fever."

I thought they'd book me for possession, I'd pull a suspended sentence, a little fine, max out at three years, do no time. I was so junked out I didn't realize how serious a crime I had committed. I didn't understand tens of thousands of ludes and other controlled substances had made their way out of K & B over three years and circulated through the Southern District of New York. I just never grasped the concept. But it was all beginning to filter through now, as we headed west toward the early night sky.

Curran and two others tried to grill me in the car about the store, about drug dealing. "Look," I said, "I know this is your job, to play good cop, bad cop with me. But I'm not saying anything pertaining to this case."

"We've got a long drive ahead," one of the agents said. "Let's talk about show business. How's your daughter Mackenzie doing? How is that show 'One Day at a Time' going?"

By the time my fingers were being pressed and rolled through the tarry black ink in Queens, I was more fatalistic about my status. Caught between the past and the future, I told myself that all this *had* to happen. My life had been hurtling out of control and people close to me were getting hurt. Perhaps this was the inevitable climax toward which my life had been speeding. The message was clear enough now, after several brushes with tragedy: Bijou's harrowing birth; Gen's seizure; the July Fourth car wreck; my deranged attempt at arson.

There's nothing quite as sobering as the sight of your own fingerprints and mug shots as an alleged federal drug felon. There was also an undeniable sensation of security now: I couldn't do any harm to myself or my family now.

When we arrived at MCC down in Chinatown, a pack of zealously competitive reporters, camera crews, and photographers swarmed near the cars. They had been staking the place out since noon. It was now ten o'clock. They were frantically jockeying and shouting. "Sorry about this," Curran said sympathetically as we got out of the sedans. "We thought we'd have you back here by noon and sent releases to that effect. We got lost way out in Montauk."

"So that's where your pal's matchbook from Gurney's Inn came from." Curran grinned wryly. "Good eye you got." He raised his eyebrows and softened his face self-consciously. "Even guys like us get a nice lunch out every now and then." Before he could tell me how great a cop I would have made with my powers of observation, the circle of press bloodhounds tightened around us. The strobe flashes exploded out of the dark, blinding me. I felt Curran's iron grip on my bicep as the others cleared a path. Just like on TV. I felt helpless with my hands in cuffs, unable to protect myself. It's too much work to even flip the bird when you're in federal custody.

"Are you guilty?" they shouted, running alongside us.

"Did you do all this?" "Do you have any statement to make?" "Is this a DEA witch hunt?" "Will your celebrity status get you off light?" "Were you set up?"

They fired questions and shoved mikes at me. The wheezing motorized cameras sounded like asthma patients cracking up from the funniest joke they ever heard. Curran mumbled helpfully, "Just don't answer. Don't say anything to them." I raised my cuffed hands over my face, covering it with the sleeves of my jacket. It was right out of *The Godfather*. MOB BIGGIE BUSTED.

They issued me gray prison clothes, the penal leisure suit, robe, slippers, crummy pillows, and threadbare blanket. It was midnight and I was starting to nod out. The hallways were full of real hard criminals—bank robbers, drug dealers, violent types. It was still "them" and me. I was scared shitless.

While waiting to give urine and blood tests, I met four guys from Georgia who had gone to Florida to score four kilos of coke. Then they drove it back north to unload in New York.

"How did you fuck up?" I asked.

"We had a broken rear taillight," one of them told me. He shook his head, still unable to believe what went down. "Cop pulled us over, saw the Georgia plates, the busted taillight, and came over. I saw him and said, 'Ohhh shit, this is it. Let's get the fuck outta here.' So we sped off."

"Where were you?"

"The Village."

"The Village? Greenwich Village?"

He nodded with embarrassment. "Uhhh-huh."

I was stupefied. "You started a car chase with a cop in *Greenwich Village?* What did you guys think—you'd do the Cannonball Run between Bleecker and MacDougal streets?" Real cocaine crackers. "How far'd you get?"

" 'Bout a half a block. Cain't drive innywhere down there without hittin' a bunch a queers. Course, once we tried to outrace the bastard, he could search the car and found the blow."

Everybody had a story and they all ended with fingerprinting and pissing in the urine sample bottle. I just kept saying I was busted for a couple of joints in the park.

I put a little urine in my bottle and filled the rest with

warm tap water. It seemed better to go to my arraignment clean.

They herded us to the real lock-down area, an endless corridor with steel cages on both sides and a walkway above for prowling guards. We walked past the huge circular dayroom with Ping-Pong, TVs, chairs, card tables. It felt depressing and empty. There are haunting echoes on the inside. The sound of the heavy gates shutting behind you is one of the scariest sounds you can ever hear.

I shared my cell with one of the Georgia boys and took the top bunk. The room was five feet by ten, eight feet high. My nose almost scraped the ceiling when I lay down in the shabby bunk. There was a noisy, filthy air vent directly over my face with soot and grease hanging off the grate. Cold stinking air was belching right into my face and I was freezing in my cheap torn-up blanket. I twisted, wrenched, covered my face. But it just kept blowing putrid air from the bowels of the prison. It was impossible to sleep. It was beginning to hit me that I was, in fact, under arrest.

We all got awakened at 6 A.M., but I couldn't eat. I had smelled the air; food was out of the question. Later in the morning I was led to an open and instantly gloomy waiting room for my arraignment. Fluorescent tubing, gray cinder blocks, and stir-crazy alleged perpetrators. All my new friends were there, dressed again in the clothes they wore when they were apprehended. Others were zonked out in the halls, snoring away on their little bundles of clothes. I was dressed for backgammon and frozen margaritas in the Hamptons—alligator shirt, sockless, sneakers, and jeans.

I milled around restlessly. There were no windows, just long vertical slits in the wall of the holding room, overlooking a Chinatown air shaft. The slit wasn't more than two or three inches wide. To see out I twisted my head ninety degrees sideways. Down this winding, narrow Chinatown street I could see the Golden Age Rest Home. Bustling groups of Chinese were going in and coming out. I imagined them all inside, playing Chinese checkers, marbles, families feverishly poking chopsticks into take-out food containers, animated, chattering wistfully about Shanghai in the good old days. The groups going in all brought flowers, lunch boxes, gifts, plants; the happy little grandchildren toddled along.

I had already been told by the assistant district attorney prosecuting my case that the conspiracy to distribute rap and the counts of selling Quaaludes might get me forty-five years in jail. I thought of all those free people in Chinatown.

While I waited, I was amused by the bickering among four Caribbeans who had knocked over a bank in Connecticut and made a clean getaway with something like fifty grand. They weren't any smarter than the four Georgia crackers. They were driving down the Connecticut Turnpike with the loot in the trunk when a tire blew. The car overturned, the trunk blew open, and all the bills flew out and scattered in the wind. Now they were up to the point—I was sure they had argued over this issue already a hundred times and would have plenty of time inside to settle it—when they needed a scapegoat for the blowout.

"I toll you, mon, to check the tires first," one of them said.

"No whay, I toll *you* to get that tire feex, mon. Whatchou wanna do 'bout it? I rotate 'em yust last month, whatchou sayin'?"

They started jabbing at each other, lapsing into native Caribbean epithets. "Fuck dasshit, mon, I toll you a hunner time, mon, you were espeeding."

"I wass *not* espeeding, you too estoned to check the tire, mon, iss you fault."

Then their cool macho leader stood, spreading his long arms out and wincing with nonchalance as he walked to the driver of the getaway car that got away from them.

"My man," he said, planting his palms on his buddy's chest to end the discussion, "it don't matta, y'hear what I say? We blow the crime, we do the time. We be outta the joint in three, four years, we go back on the street. No problem."

I stared out again over Chinatown, suddenly aching for my freedom. I thought of life among these criminals in the Rikers Island slammer. No problem. *You have really fucked your life up this time,* I thought. I punched the wall with a tight fist and clenched my jaws. "SHIT!" I was seething and felt overcome by a cold gray wave of despair.

I tried to fall asleep on a hard bench in the holding room. I was last of the twenty or so guys who were to be arraigned and for the first time there was some calm around me as the others had come and gone. I lay down on the bench, facing the wall for privacy. I was nearly out when some guards came over to me—they must have been waiting for me to be alone—and asked for my autograph. One guard goosed me with a billy club and I wrenched violently to face forward. I was furious and twisted away.

"Hey, Johnny, tell me. Did Mama Cass really choke on a ham sandwich or what?" one asked. I was nauseous and exhausted. "Hey," I said, "read my lips. FUCK YOU." Time seemed to have just stopped moving on the inside.

Late that morning, I finally spotted Len Curran, the DEA agent who had headed the arrest squad in Water Mill. He would accompany me to the arraignment room. "Come on, Johnny," he said in a voice that bordered on cheerful: "You're on."

He asked me how the night had gone, if everything was okay. Somehow the mere sight of Curran—a man who had burst into my bedroom not twenty-four hours earlier with a gun and a warrant for my arrest—immediately lifted my spirits. He had been decent and mild-mannered throughout, a real pro. Now, ironically, after a night in the pit among hard-core cons, Curran represented familiarity, security, and friendship to me. He was, after all, the last human I spoke to before my imprisonment, and I suppose I associated him rather affectionately with the precious gift of freedom.

Charges were filed against me at the arraignment on the prosecutor's information. Tucker had, in the meantime, contacted a friend of his named Richard Schaeffer, a former assistant district attorney with much more experience in drug and criminal cases than Tucker. Tucker's specialty was business law. But Schaeffer was away and when I introduced myself to the attorney it wasn't Schaeffer. He had sent *another* attorney just for the arraignment.

He explained that I could always change a not-guilty plea, in the event of a plea-bargaining deal, anytime prior to a trial date. It all depended on the case the government had. "If you plead guilty," he said, "you might just find some way out of this on a bargain."

It disturbed me to talk in such sweeping, strategic ways with a guy who wasn't even going to be my attorney *after lunch.* I called Tucker for advice. He said stay cool, plead not guilty. "You can change your plea to guilty," he reassured me, "and, besides, at this point you don't know how the prosecutors will make their case and prove their allegations, or if they have witnesses or what case they plan to make." That gave me hope.

I pleaded not guilty, bail was set at $50,000, Tucker came up with five grand—the required 10 percent—and the trial was scheduled for September 15.

I went to Tucker's midtown office and at the end of the day he put me in a radio-dispatched cab for Penn Station and loaned me $400. It was a scorching hot Friday evening in August. The information window at Penn Station, the starting line in the frantic weekly race to the Hamptons for tens of thousands of New Yorkers, was jammed. The place felt like a furnace, swarming with young sportily dressed weekenders and dark-suited commuters all sprinting to catch trains to Long Island retreats at the end of their pressured week. Hundreds shifted tensely in ticket lines while masses of others just stood, trapped in the stinking subterranean heat, straining to catch announced train departures and track assignments out of the sweltering chaos.

I squeezed into the crammed train bound for Southampton. Everyone on the train was heading for the beach. Lawyers and CPAs and ad execs and secretaries and doctors and flirty singles—all trying to cool off, relax, and recharge for another hot, fabulous weekend.

It was easy to figure out what each class of weekender had in store: drugs, sex, and romance at the singles' bars and lawn parties; artistic inspiration in the oceanfront or woodsy garrets; gardening, puttering, and Quality Time with the wife and kids in the phoneless saltbox two blocks from town; getting high and cruising the slinky, sun-tanned chicks in their sexy swimsuits.

But for now, as the train rumbled out of the sooty tunnel

and into the late-afternoon sunlight, all eyes seemed riveted
on copies of the Friday late-edition New York *Post* with a
front-page picture of me as I was being whisked into MCC,
hands over my head in cuffs. I stood in the crowd and saw at
least two dozen identical headlines, lined up like a mirror-in-
a-mirror reflection: ROCK STAR NABBED IN DRUGS SWOOP.
"John Phillips," the article began, "founder of the Mamas
and Papas rock group, was arrested in Southampton last
night as part of a jet-set pill-pushing ring." I was wearing the
same shirt and light jacket I had on when I got busted—and
photographed.

I felt disgust for what had happened. I had been living in a
void of unreality. I had thrown it all away.

Fortunately, the passengers were too busy reading about
the bust to notice the alarming resemblance between the
front-page Papa and the emaciated weirdo squirming toward
the rear corner of the car, averting everyone's gaze. I was in
no shape to oblige autograph hounds.

I walked in the house and greeted Gen and Tam. There
was so little to say, really. I was wilting from the heat and
ordeal. I couldn't even begin to tell Gen and Tam about the
previous twenty-four hours. Besides, I had no idea what lay
ahead and my nerves were still raw over the bust, the night
in prison, the weaning from drugs.

I couldn't deal with the issues of rehabilitation, leniency,
and redemption. I thought immediately of the three dime
bags I had slipped under the phone book. It was at that
precise moment that I finally saw how morbid and reckless
and fucked-up I was: I was looking at forty-five years behind
bars and all I wanted to do was shoot up three bags of street
shit. Nothing could stop me.

The smack was still there. I gave one bag to Gen and kept
the two other "spoons" for myself. We shot up, but hardly
got off. The street stuff was mostly cut, probably lactose or
laxative. I knew it as soon as my thumb went down all the
way on the syringe. "Gen, this is it, baby, the end of the line.
It's over." No. Wait. There was one more shot.

"Where's the green bag?" I asked her. There was always a
little *something* left over in the Gucci—some dust, a loose
Dilaudid, a tiny rock of coke.

"Tam and I tried to sink it in the water out by the Sisters of Mercy convent," she said calmly, in her delicate, lilting South African inflection.

"What? You're kidding." At least it was soaking in holy water.

"No. We were scared they'd come back and find something, so I took it. We walked down to the water and tried to sink it with the needles and stuff inside. There wasn't much of anything in there. We tossed it in and ran back toward the house," Gen said with a faint smile. "Then I looked back, but it floated up to the surface. We tried again." It was, fittingly enough, like an uncooperative corpse in gangster flicks. They did what anyone would have done. "Tam had to go in there and swim around with his little arms and fish it out," she said. "He didn't really understand what was going on, but he was so brave and helpful. So then I filled it with large stones and tried again. I was so scared I left the bag open and the stones fell out and it surfaced once more. Finally, I got crazy and just flung it in the reeds by the water so no one would ever find it."

Over the next couple of weeks, I met several times with Tucker and his handpicked criminal lawyer, Richard Schaeffer, to map out the defense strategy. It didn't take long for Schaeffer, the more expert of the two in drug felony cases, to lay it out in plain English. Tucker assured me Schaeffer was the best. Still, as I sat on the couch in Schaeffer's office high over midtown, watching the young, well-dressed, upwardly mobile staff hotshots come and go through the carpeted halls, it was painfully clear there *was* no defense available to prove my innocence. I had the best and it felt like it still wasn't going to be good enough to save my ass. The issue now was staying out of prison—or going in for the least possible time. I was forty-five years old. Another forty-five behind bars made ninety. I was going to die in jail if I maxed out. I brooded over the sadness and waste. Why had I done it? Where had it all gone wrong? How could I have let my family suffer this way?

"They just have you," Schaeffer said flatly. "There's absolutely no way to pretend they don't. I've met with the U.S.

Attorney's office and reviewed the case. It is a clear winner for the government."

I listened without responding and squirmed in agony. I desperately wanted it to not be true. I propped my elbows on my knees and leaned forward, dropping my head into my hands.

"Of course," Schaeffer added, to soften the blow, "you never *really* know what's going to happen. But as far as their evidence goes, and what sort of case they are in a position to make at trial, I'd be less than totally honest and forthcoming to you as your attorney if I didn't let you know that, basically, John, they've got you nailed."

II

TAKING OFF

2

EVERY KID GROWS UP hearing the stories and myths that account for how he or she actually made it into this world. It always seems like we have to beat ridiculous odds just to get here, let alone survive half a century. I certainly did. In my case, if the Cherokee Nation hadn't been forced by the U.S. Army to march at gunpoint from its homelands throughout the southeast and resettle in a hostile, barren wasteland of northeast Oklahoma in the late 1830s, I *know* I'd never have made it. Nor would I be here if, about half a century later, a young Canadian-born architect hadn't leaped—or been pushed—to his death from a construction site in Watertown, New York. But here I am.

The ancestors of the architect, my paternal grandfather, John Andrew Phillips, were English immigrants in Canada in the 1800s. He was born in eastern Canada and grew up in upstate New York. I never knew him. In fact, my father, Claude Andrew Phillips, never really knew him. John Andrew Phillips became an engineer and architect and helped build up Watertown. He married a young red-haired Watertown girl named Anna Moran. She was born in County Cork, Ireland, but settled in Watertown with her brother during the massive Irish immigrations of the 1850s.

They had a respectable and prosperous life ahead of them. They lived on the same quaint street as the mayor with two children. That John Phillips was a young, dynamic dreamer with the drive and vision to build a city. Then he mysteriously fell to his death from one of his project sites. His widow, Anna Moran Phillips, raised their children, Claude Andrew and Marcia, alone.

Marcia was ten years older than young Claude. She was a schoolteacher and helped support the family. She and her mother were devout Catholics who attended Mass every day. Claude was an altar boy and sang in the church choir. He was like an only child, with Marcia always out working. He was lonely and restless and missed his father very deeply. He created a rich fantasy world and became an adventurous and rather cunning teenager.

After finishing high school, Claude worked around town for several years before traveling to Buffalo to join the Marines in 1913. He learned engineering as he rose through the ranks, and spent three years on the battleship *Virginia*. Then he was transferred to Parris Island, South Carolina, and became a drillmaster and field sergeant major.

While at Parris during World War I, he trained recruits and developed a passion for gambling, booze, women, and camaraderie among his marine buddies. He would drink his whiskey and play cards and show off his soulful Irish tenor to blow off steam. His voice brought tears to people's eyes.

His overseas commission came through just in time—two days before the signing of the armistice in November 1918. The timing was perfect. He was stationed in France, and if he saw any action, it was more likely in boudoirs than on any battlefields. Later in life, he said he fathered an illegitimate daughter by a French woman he had loved but left behind after the war.

Claude was "mustered out" of the Marines a year later as an enlisted man and, on the troop ship sailing home, he and his buddies went on one last binge of craps and booze. One of the guys was broke and staked his final pass on the only currency he had left—the deed to a small family-run hotel and saloon in eastern Oklahoma.

"All right, you bastard," he said to my father, "I'm out—

except for this. Whattaya say I roll for all your money, you roll for this." He took out a crusty, torn-up paper, squinted down, and read it in a rambling slur. "Henryetta?" my father squealed. "Who the hell is Henryetta?"

"Not 'who,' Lieutenant Phillips. The question is 'where.' "

"All right, *where* the hell is Henryetta? And what the hell is this, anyway?" Everyone curiously peered at the deed and started laughing.

"Why, Henryetta's right near Okmulgee, fool."

"Okay—what? If it's so great, how come you ain't so hot to go out there?" Claude was in his early thirties, the year was 1919; there was no family, woman, or career to come home to in Watertown. The family had always hoped Claude would enter the priesthood but, somehow, the out-of-wedlock baby and his prowess at gambling, booze, and broads didn't exactly qualify him for that sort of cloth. He had $1,000 from gambling and nothing to go home to. He swigged on his bottle and eyed his pals. The kid saw the lieutenant was balking and picked up the deed. He shook it before Claude's wary, sideways glare.

"Just think, it's all yours, right in the heart of Cherokee country." The guy was making his last desperate pitch. "My brothers say the place is *crawlin'* with awful pretty Indian squaws hungerin' for war heroes."

Now the kid had said something Claude wanted to hear. Squaws. Visions of nubile, bronzed Indian princesses with dark, inviting eyes and waist-length black braids floated out of Claude's whiskey bottle. He squirmed with new interest, drank some more, and swept up the dice as a sly grin curled from the corner of his mouth. He scanned the table littered with glasses, bottles, cards, dice, and dollar bills, tipped back his hat, then pounded his fist on his pile of winnings.

"Let's roll 'em," he said.

When Claude Phillips stepped off a steamy, dusty railroad car near Okmulgee several months later, he peered around at the flattest, driest, most barren land he had ever seen and must have shuddered to know that he was home. He moved into a ground-floor room of the six-room hotel that housed migrant oil laborers, cowboys, prospectors, and gun-wielding train robbers. Short and stocky, with a ruddy Irish complexion and red hair, he stood out from the swarthy, rugged, crustier western types who worked the oil fields and cattle ranches. He wasn't likely to be taken for a Cherokee, either. With "Cap" holding court each night, the hotel saloon soon became the hub of life in Okmulgee.

The Cherokee Nation had rebuilt its culture, economy, and way of life in the decades since the Great Removal, or the March of Tears, as their tragic resettlement was known. Close to three fourths of the sixty thousand Cherokee had perished during the March. Among the hearty survivors were the ancestors of my mother, Edna Gertrude Gaines.

Local gossips and wary Cherokee soon realized Claude was not there on a peacekeeping mission. The feisty Irishman had a weakness for Cherokee maidens. But only one truly made his body ache and his blood boil with temptation —Edna Gertrude Gaines.

She was the daughter of the hotel's housekeeper, Zora Hardgrave Gaines. Zora bore thirteen children and was revered as a matriarch and faith healer. Her people believed she possessed mystical healing, psychic and telekinetic powers. Claude took a look at her daughter and was not about to disagree. Zora was a woman of great spiritual and physical strength. She took on manual jobs to help clothe and feed her family. And her eldest daughter, Edna, then fifteen, often arrived with her to help out with the housekeeping. Zora's husband, Edmund Pendleton Gaines, had fought in the Civil War and taken his general's Christian name. He was a laborer in the oil fields surrounding Okmulgee.

Claude adopted enough Cherokee mysticism to convince himself he was put on this earth to lust after the young, striking Edna Gaines. Not even the evil eye from the strong-willed Zora could deter the stubborn, smitten ex-marine. He would wait for Zora to leave Edna alone, then stroke her long thick black hair. She'd stare, then unload a left hook at him.

"You are the most beautiful little girl I have ever laid eyes on," he would whisper anyway. He loved to tease her. There was no doubt about it. "It happened immediately and when I felt it, I never once considered it taboo or impossible," he said years later. And he was quite the romantic. "The very first time I saw that young gorgeous girl bend over and tuck in a sheet, I knew I had to have her."

Soon a scandal swept through Okmulgee. Even the Cherokee priest, who had become Claude's drinking buddy at the saloon, warned him. "Claude," he once asked, "what exactly are your intentions with regard to that young Gaines girl?"

"Intentions?"

"They're telling stories of you grabbing her from behind, chasing her around the beds and up and down the stairs, wrestling the poor girl down to the ground like some panting dog in heat. Are you crazy, man? Guests at the hotel have seen you groping and lusting after her—and she's but half your age."

"Then I'll lie about my age, if that's the issue."

The priest was in no mood for jokes. "If you want to court the girl and marry her, then you better come right out and say so. I'm not so sure the Gaines Boys love the talk going around town about young Edna."

"The Gaines Boys, huh?" Claude repeated.

The priest nodded slowly. "Yup," he said.

The Gaines Boys were Edna's older brothers, mean gunfighters and bandits who had outrun and outshot their share of posses in their time. They were in and out of jails for years.

"What can I do? She's the first woman I've really loved."

"Are you mad, man? She's but sixteen. If you feel that way, then you'll have to marry her, Claude."

"And if I don't?"

"If the Gaines Boys find out you lay a hand on her, violate her in any way, they'll string you up by your toes—or something worse."

Claude proposed marriage and the reaction was a mixture of reluctance and enthusiasm. Edna, the first of six daughters born after the three most notorious Gaines Boys, would be running off with a white man. But there would be one less mouth to feed and she might come to prosper in the white man's world. There were, however, other reasons the family and young Edna consented. Dark tightly held family secrets suggested why.

Zora, on her deathbed, told her twin daughters that when Edna was one year old she had been kidnapped by a band of gypsies who had camped near the reservation. Her father, Edmund Gaines, searched for her whenever a band of gypsies was in the area. He finally found her a year or so later in Mexico. On the trip back to Okmulgee, baby Edna developed a high fever. Her mother, Zora, nursed her back to amazingly good health.

Edna and Claude were married twice, once according to colorful and elaborate Cherokee rituals and again in the local Catholic church. He had the blessings of his mother and sister back east, with the condition that Edna, who had a cross seared into her arm when she was Christianized, convert to Catholicism.

Claude and his new bride lived at the hotel for a year and she studied hard to improve her English and religious knowledge. Then the Marines sent a telegram that brought some welcome news. "We're going east," he announced immediately. He was delighted.

"What for?" Edna was stunned. There had never been plans to leave Okmulgee. "The Marines are offering me a commission back at Quantico in Virginia."

Claude was ready to leave the parched prairie behind, but Edna knew she might never be back. It was ironic. Her people had already been ordered once by the military to march from the eastern seaboard to Oklahoma; now the military was uprooting Edna from the new Cherokee homeland *back* east.

There was little holding her. Her whole life she had cared for the younger children and never had a life of her own. A move would give her that, though she would be enduring her own private Great Removal—as an officer's wife. The conflict cut sharply through her but the family never stood in her way. They knew she loved Claude, was proud for him, and would make a lovely military wife and mother. The Gaines family gave them a hopeful, bittersweet send-off. Edna felt special now; she was the one who may not have been full-blooded after all, the one who may not have been born on Cherokee earth. And now, she was the one chosen to leave that hallowed ground to discover the new world.

Months later, the conflict erupted in her. "I'm leaving, to go back home to my people," she said sadly.

Claude denied her. He needed her too much. Claude fit right back into the military base life but Edna felt out of place, socially rejected by the other wives. "The women here will never accept me as I am," she explained to him tearfully. "They laugh and whistle at me in the street, the marines make me sick, they tease me, call me names. I'm an officer's wife, not some cheap pickup. I need to go home."

He could hardly deny her pain and loneliness. Twice, he gave her the train money and twice he went out to retrieve her. He could not bear to live without her. But Claude didn't know what was really best for his young wife. He went to old man Gaines in Oklahoma and got one word of advice.

"Pregnant, my boy, get the girl pregnant. If you want to keep her in your world, let her bear your daughters and sons. She will not come back home then. Go. You'll see. She'll stay."

Claude took the old man's wisdom to heart and Edna to bed. My sister Rosemary was born back at the base on New Year's Eve, 1922. Gaines was right. Edna, who was then known as Dene, was a doting eighteen-year-old mother. Within two years later, my brother Tommy was born. As the children grew up, they enjoyed a comfortable life with a yard boy, cook, and housekeeper. During the 1920s, he was elevated to lieutenant and placed in charge of all engineering and construction projects at the base. My mother's confidence grew in the community. Now that she was a military wife and mother—two patriotic roles for a woman—she earned acceptance and respect around the base.

Claude was commissioned to Haiti for four years, and after a brief respite back at Quantico, the family shipped out to Managua, the capital of Nicaragua. On the morning of March 31, 1931, a devastating earthquake leveled the city. Two thousand people died and the entire central market was demolished. More than twenty-five thousand people were left homeless.

Dene must have been the best-dressed woman shrieking through the debris. When the quake hit, she was having a frilly, yellow organdy gown fitted for an officers' ball. Terror-stricken, she groped and screamed through the smoking, burning rubble, trying to make it to Rosie's grade school. The pins were still stuck in her dress. Neither Rosie nor Tommy was hurt, but the family's house was destroyed. The officers' families were evacuated to Panama City and Captain Claude helped coordinate the Marines' relief effort. "Cap" Phillips was cited for his heroic duty in helping to dynamite the marketplace to create a fire wall that spared much of the downtown area.

The family settled on Parris Island and life settled down for Dene. She read avidly, studied Catholicism, and learned to play bridge—the quickest entrée into officers' wives' clubs. "Cap" took up fishing in the bay off the island, filling enormous baskets with oysters and clams and hosting wild, jolly parties. He'd drink himself silly, then thrill guests with the sweet, lilting Irish folk ditties.

By early 1935, America was caught in the Depression, but the family was insulated from much of it on the base. In February, my father became a major. For once, life had settled down comfortably and contentedly for Claude, Dene, and the children. They were twelve and ten. Then came a rather shocking piece of news. "You'll never guess what's happening," he teased the kids. They begged to know. It wasn't exactly a seismic tremor, but Claude called it an act of God.

The kids pleaded to know the secret that was making Daddy so happy and Mommy so sick in the morning. He was forty-eight. Edna was thirty-one. The kids couldn't imagine. A new house? Another adventure in a weird country?

"It's our own little gift from heaven," he explained. "Your mother's going to have another baby."

Two hurricanes collided along the eastern seaboard at the end of August and early September 1935. One was called the Labor Day Hurricane and it was the most violent tropical storm on record, with winds up to 160 miles an hour and swells of twenty feet off the South Carolina coastline. Damage was estimated, in mid-Depression terms, at $6 million and several hundred lives were lost.

The other storm was Hurricane John—and I hit Parris

Island on August 30 that year. My full name—John Edmund Andrew Phillips—paid respect to both my grandfathers.

The Labor Day storm that first week of my life now looks like a ferociously destructive omen of Hurricane John's later path. Beaufort Sound flooded over, streets and homes disappeared underwater, winds battered the entire island, trees collapsed across roads and highways, and mighty gusts blew out windows and scattered glass everywhere. Power went out all over the area, but I managed to make it through the first few crazy nights as a healthy newborn infant.

My father tried driving all over town to announce the blessed event to friends, but they were afraid their doors would be blown off if they opened them to him. Claude must have been sloshed real good, since Rosie, who had learned to drive at twelve, steered the car home and friends used to jokingly veer off the road in self-defense whenever they saw *her* barreling along.

When my mother came home with me from the hospital, my father threw a wild seventy-two-hour party. "Isn't my son beautiful?" he'd tell every guest over and over. "Look at those little eyes, that pink skin." He was so proud. Rosie adored me; Tommy was ten and ran away. He didn't like being upstaged.

I apparently was a sweet, happy infant. I was never put down, was always held, and if I cried, my mother, Rosie, or our housekeeper would immediately comfort me. Our garden boy, Ezekiel, a young black kid, took me for walks in my pram, singing me songs and decorating the carriage with flowers.

"Captain" Phillips was assigned to the Brooklyn Navy Yard when I was two years old, working in the Quartermaster Corps for the Marines. He was awarded a medal for having helped to save Managua during the earthquake. Then he suffered the first of several heart attacks. He was a rather heavy—if not constant—drinker, fifty years old at the time, and he just collapsed at work after feeling sharp pains in his chest.

"He could go at any time," the doctor told my mother. She was petrified. "We can't get a positive EKG on him.

He's got arrhythmia—an erratic heartbeat—and he could have another attack anytime." He was in and out of hospitals, both in Brooklyn and at Bethesda Naval Hospital after the family moved back to Quantico.

Then we moved to Alexandria, Virginia, to be nearer the big hospital complex, and he had a second attack. When I was about four, in 1939, my father was discharged from the Marines after a career that stretched more than three decades. Life went downhill immediately; the perks were gone and, with plenty of tension and sadness in the air, I was no longer the center of attention in my parents' lives. Some drastic changes were ahead at home.

My father's medical discharge with total disability enabled him to receive three quarters of his current salary—which came to some $600 a month. My mother started her own business. He helped set her up in a dress shop down the block from our house with their savings. She was a hard-working, talented seamstress and so they would buy vintage clothes and strange knickknacks at auctions when other businesses would go under. My mother began spending all her time there. My father, though, fell apart, isolating himself in a small room in the cellar which he had built next to the blast furnace. Captain C. A. Phillips all but ceased to exist as a man once out of that marine uniform.

Like my father, I grew up feeling like an only child. Rosie went off to Mary Washington College in Fredericksburg, Virginia, and Tommy, who my father constantly picked on, quit high school just before graduating to enlist in the service at the outset of World War II.

It destroyed my father not to be in uniform. "Just leave me alone," he'd grouch at my mother before she left for her dress shop. "Put a bottle of Four Roses on the steps to the cellar before you leave." So every morning, she'd leave the bottle there for him, and he'd head on down to the dark, dank cellar and just drink himself into a stupor every day for months at a clip. It was like I didn't really have a father much of the time. If I wasn't clinging to my mother's dress at her store, I was alone with him in the creepy, quiet house.

"Daddy, are you all right?" I would call down to him from the top of the stairs off the kitchen. I couldn't hear him and assumed he was asleep. I could only hear our half-dozen Boston bulldogs down there and I was afraid to go down the stairs. They were nasty dogs, particularly Buck. I thought they were all named Buck. My father would call, "Buck, come on down, Buck," and they all would race down in a thundering herd. They were my father's best friends.

Once, feeling scared and alone, I decided to go downstairs. Halfway down, I stopped, and heard Buck growl. The dogs then raced upstairs past me and went out. I shut the door tight, so they couldn't come down after me. I went down slowly, landing and stopping on each step. When I got down there, the furnace was rumbling and hot and it smelled awful and stale. I was in another world—strange and menacing, directly beneath the living room.

My mouth dropped open. What I saw was like out of a scary film. He was in his marine dress uniform, but his coat was unbuttoned and his hat was almost off his head—a once-proud marine hero slumped over and limp. The stench of dogshit and urine stung my nostrils. There were old whiskey bottles, newspapers, and smelly clothes littered all over. I trembled. He looked so bizarre. I was sure he was dead.

I walked up to him slowly and touched his shoulder. "Daddy?" I whispered. My heart was pounding. I poked him harder and placed my face right under his mouth. I could see—and smell—that he was breathing. My first intense whiff of an alcoholic's breath. He smelled so sick and dirty.

I leaned over to shake him again. "Daddy," I said, thinking he might hear me, "can we go out and play catch?" He didn't move. I shook him again and this time my foot knocked over a bottle of Four Roses between his feet. The noise of glass against concrete jolted me, but he didn't even twitch. I stared. I felt invisible. I heard the dogs barking inside and got scared they'd rip me to pieces if they found me. I quickly straightened Captain Phillips's hat on his head, pulled the jacket over his rounded gut, backed away, raced upstairs to my bedroom, and began to cry.

I missed my mother. By now the store had folded, they had lost all their life savings, and she was working at Woodward & Lothrop's department store in downtown Washington. One summer day I felt alone and bored, so I began to ride my new bicycle. I had no idea where I was, but before I knew it I recognized the words on a sign that said LEAVING THE STATE OF VIRGINIA. ENTERING THE DISTRICT OF COLUMBIA. Suddenly a fantastic shiver of adventure, escape, and freedom swept through me. I recognized the different-colored bus lines from trips in town with my mother and I figured out the route to D.C. Whenever I could, I grabbed on to the rear fenders of buses and cars to speed up and rest my legs.

I crossed the Potomac over a long bridge and just kept pedaling. I never got tired. I was sure she'd be surprised and delighted to see me. Six hours and a lot of miles later, I was at the corner of 14th and G. I went up to the eighth floor.

"Hi, Mom, look who's here," I said, catching her from behind. She spun around behind her counter and I saw she was stunned and speechless. Then she gasped and bent down to kiss me.

"John, darling, how on earth did you get here? Is everything all right? Is Daddy sick?" She was more worried than delighted.

"I rode my bike." I hugged her and kissed her. I almost started to cry. "I was lonely and bored at home and I needed to see you. I missed you."

"Ohhh, sweetheart," she whispered as she hugged me. "You know your mother loves you, but she can't be at home all the time because she has to work so you can eat and have nice clothes. And your father gets sick sometimes and can't really be with you like other boys' daddies." She gently pushed me away and looked at me. She smiled full of love and the touch of her soft hand through my messy hair and across my sweaty forehead was so soothing that I had to try hard not to start crying. But I saw there were tears in her eyes. "Do you understand, honey?"

I nodded silently and bit my lip. "Come on, now," she said, "you'll have to go all the way home now in a taxi because I have lots of work and that way I can come home earlier and make you a nice dinner."

At the elevator, she squeezed my hand and smiled. I was sniffling. "I'm okay now, Mommy, I really am."

I always got a lot of help learning to read and write from my sister Rosie at home, so my grades were very good without trying. Then I had to deal with *sisters*. Until ninth grade, I always attended Catholic or military schools. At St. Mary's Academy, the nuns who taught first grade were severe disciplinarians; they were in the habit, you might say, of corporal punishment. The obvious and sensible reaction to that situation was not to go to school. Any idiot could have figured that out.

I'd ask for extra lunch money from my mother—explaining there was some sort of special collection for some Mass —and head off to school. Then I'd detour and go to the Richmond Theater for matinees in downtown Alexandria. When I had seen a movie five times, I'd fake a fainting spell in the schoolyard, so the nuns would have to carry me out and send me home. I was pretty neurotic as a kid, but it was worth acting weird to escape the tyranny of the sisters.

The summer between first and second grades in 1942 was a dramatic turning point at home. My father's spirits picked up after Pearl Harbor with the prospect of more action. He once dressed up in full uniform, saber at his side, and staggered down the street to the post office, where young men enlisted. He was pissed out of his mind, drew his saber, and demanded to be taken back into service. He got as far as the local hospital, where he was held for psychiatric observation and released.

Then the Marines needed any male who was breathing and under sixty and now even *he* had a chance. Captain Phillips was a reborn man when they contacted him, filled with hope and a sense of purpose. Another war. He'd have done anything to suit up again—even for limited service. But my father knew he'd have trouble passing a physical, so he put himself on a courageous regimen to make it back into the service. It meant everything to him. He stopped drinking, he cooked and ate healthy foods, and returned cheerfully from oblivion to putter around the house for several months. It was a phenomenal change. We played ball, went to movies. I had a dad like the other kids in town. It was amazing what a war did to his spirits. When the day came for his physical, Rosie was home and we waited and prayed.

The moment he walked through the door, we knew it was all over. He failed. His heart just wasn't strong enough. He grabbed a bottle of booze, said nothing, stormed through the living room, and slammed the door behind him as he descended the stairs. "That's it," Mother told us, following him in. "That's the end. He's crushed. He has nowhere else to go now."

A couple of weeks later, there was another failure at home. "John, darling," my mother said, holding a letter in her hands, "St. Mary's says it might be better if you didn't go back there for second grade."

"How were my grades?"

"Well, you did get all A's. But you were never there. You never learned the alphabet or the months of the year in the right order."

That was right. I knew June–July–August; the rest of the year didn't matter.

I worked hard at getting on people's nerves. My mother always made Rosie take me along on her dates during high school and when she was home from college. She hated that, and I couldn't blame her. She was twelve years older than me and I loved to call her and her boyfriend Bill Throckmorton "Mom and Dad" because it really embarrassed the hell out of them. Once, I ran out to the field during the George Washington High School football game and made her chase me all over the field at halftime in front of the big crowd.

I used to ride buses with her and Bill and swat people's newspapers as they read them, step on their toes, and generally disrupt life and attract attention with irritating stunts.

Once, at home, I was alone playing with a new litter of bulldog puppies. One of the little pups was whimpering, so I tried to feed it a small bowl of white liquid spread-on shoe polish for saddle shoes and white bucks. The dogs were named Buck, anyhow. I thought it was milk of magnesia, which mother always gave us when *we* were sick. Another time, the pups were outside and cold and shivering and so I picked two of them up and tried to warm them by putting them inside my heavy wool socks. I closed my top drawer and forgot about them. So did everyone else. When I went back into the drawer for my socks, they had suffocated. I can now understand why it made sense to get me out of there for a while. I was a lot to handle.

For the next four years I attended Linton Hall Academy in Manassas, Virginia, a military school run by nuns that was close to an hour's train ride from Alexandria. The first week I was there, I was having my first serious talk in the dark with my bunkmate. There was a wonderful feeling of intimacy and confidentiality about it. "You know, Johnny," he said in a conspiratorial whisper, "when the sisters take you to the office and beat you here, did you know they do it to you naked?"

My eyes widened in shock and my mouth fell open. What I pictured in my head would have cost me an eternity in hell. "Wow," I said, "I'm glad I switched schools. That's amazing. I can't wait to get it. I always wondered what they looked like without any clothes on."

I stopped and heard him trying to stifle his wild giggle in his pillow and not wake anyone. I wondered why he was laughing so hard. Suddenly I felt real stupid. "You idiot," he said. *"They're* not naked, *you* are. So it hurts more. The paddle comes down hard right on your ass and stings like the devil."

"Shit," I whispered back.

What a terrible disappointment. But it hardly kept me out of trouble. The more I misbehaved, the more shots I took on the rear and the more intense was my aversion to any and all forms of authority. When you're in grade school and you are awakened by a nun blowing "Reveille" on a bugle at 6 A.M. and you have a half hour to prepare for a full military room and uniform inspection, you start not giving a shit to protect yourself. The nuns even watched us take showers to screen us for fags. Of course, that just flushed them out to the gym, the bedrooms, and the woods. I hated the place but earned good grades without doing anything except getting my red, raw buns whacked by the nuns. But I made lots of friends, I played sports, and I gradually came to see that home was nowhere to go back to, either.

If my father was most often beyond reach, my mother spared nothing to make me feel loved. For the years I was at Linton Hall, she visited me just about every Sunday. By midweek, I was filled with anticipation of her visit. I once wrote a note home reminding her to "bring my potato"—a favorite treat stuffed with cheese and chopped meat.

She always brought a delicious picnic lunch and we would take long walks over the rolling, lush grounds or through the woods and spread out a blanket and just sit there and talk all afternoon when it was warm. Rosie was already married and her husband Bill was in combat; Tommy was fighting in the Pacific and my father was fighting his private war in the cellar. She worked hard all week and I imagine she could get pretty lonely at home. I know she looked forward to these picnics, but it wasn't easy to get there. Still, she always made me feel it was very important for her to come. She had to train from Washington, then ride a bus provided by the academy. I was always there waiting for her to step off the bus and she always looked so beautiful. I hated the place and the discipline, but those Sunday afternoons with my mother let me forget about the inspections, the beatings, the dreary schoolwork. I lived for those picnics.

There were novels and books of poetry to read to me. I would lie there on my back, staring up at the big sky, listening to her soft, soothing voice. Then we would sit up and talk about the war and events around the world. We'd go to chapel together and sit serenely for hours. I know I asked her many times if I could come back home and go to public school and she always explained why I had to stay at Linton Hall.

"Your dad has a big problem with alcohol, Tommy and Rosie's husband are at war, the whole world's on fire, and this is a very safe place to be," she would say. "I don't want you in Washington. It wouldn't be safe if the enemy decided to attack us. I go to work at seven, I come home at seven at night, and no one is home. I hate your being here, I know you hate it. But you know I love you and that this is the best thing to do. And you are doing very well in school, even if you don't exactly love it. But you know, darling, that I am not abandoning you."

I always felt sad and alone when she got on the bus at five sharp every Sunday afternoon. I would stand straight and stoic and give her a little salute. Then it was back for one more week of life with the four-star nuns.

During the summers, I participated in Catholic Youth Organization activities. By the time I was eight, I was, like my father before me, an altar boy at St. Rita's parish. Anything to keep me busy and out of the steamy house, where my father's drunken blackouts seemed more frequent. Weeks could go by without seeing him. I never remember my parents sharing a bed. He slept and drank alone and fed himself in the cellar. Once I tried to go downstairs during a break from school and show off my crisply starched, spiffy military uniform and toy gun—all part of the toy soldier act at school. He reached for a bottle. Then he just slumped back, glazed and snarling. "Get out of here, son," he bellowed.

Father McKinley appreciated my CYO work so much he took me under his clerical wing. But the poor man underestimated the extracurricular program at Linton Hall. One day during my last summer—I was twelve—he pulled me aside. "Some things I think you altar boys ought to know about sex," he said. "Like about that white stuff that comes out of your little things."

I smirked with embarrassment. "Father," I said, "I've been at a school where we've been whacking off for four years now. We know all about the white stuff. And my *thing's* not that little anymore, either, Father."

Father McKinley was all set to swing a scholarship to a local seminary on my behalf. He saw a clear path to a life in the priesthood for me. It was a uniform, but at least a different kind—and no guns. I proudly went down to the cellar to break the good news to my father. He took a wild swing at me and knocked me across the room. He flew into a red-faced rage. "No son of *mine's* going to be a priest," he roared. "Don't you dare mention the word around here again. Tommy's the priest, you're the bartender, that's it. No more priests!"

"Dad," I answered, "Tommy's become a *cop* in Washington. He's no priest. And I'm not going to be any bartender."

"Get out of here," he snapped. "Just get out."

I came home for junior high parochial school. I still had trouble with the nuns. At the end of one year, a sister asked me why my parents hadn't come to any parent-teacher conferences. "They work very hard," I said, or something like it.

"No, John," she said, "it's because they don't really love you."

I was really hurt. I stared up at her and made a mean face. I wanted to cry. Then I decided not to cry. I stepped forward and slapped her across the cheek.

Still, after the rustic isolation at Linton Hall, I was happy to be back in my Del Ray neighborhood with a new set of rough and tough pals. My social life still revolved around CYO. My altar boy work during the summer before junior high still gave me plenty of pleasure—until I realized what pleasure was.

Her name was Jeannie. She was the neighborhood tomboy and she had big blue eyes, curly blond hair, and freckles. She was mischievous and wore tight short-shorts that made her legs look long and lean. And she was more stacked than any girl I had ever seen. And she wanted you to know it.

I thought she was older, but we were the same age. She had been away at a girls' Catholic school and by midsummer I began to realize her Catholic school was real different from mine. She was in heat with a vengeance.

She was athletic and was always moving by on roller skates, churning her tanned legs on her bike, or strutting to the community pool in her bathing suit. God was she ever built. There were all kinds of stories going around about her doing it for quarters. I never believed it but, just in case, I got a paper route and saved up coins. It was almost impossible to watch her hands slide up and down a softball bat and not drop dead from desire in the left-field sun. She knew one sport I didn't and it drove me nuts.

That summer, her tough older brother saw me walking down the street and came up to me. "Jeannie wants to play ball with you," he said. I looked skeptically up at the sunset. "It's getting dark. And my mitt's back at the house." He gave me this wicked smirk and steered me toward their street. "Don't be a schmuck, Johnny. Forget the mitt. All you need is the Louisville Slugger between your legs. It'll cost you a quarter, but everybody hits a homer."

Their garage was empty. The parents were away, he said. He followed me up a ladder that led into a dark attic above the garage. I was shaking nervously and paused halfway up. I had no idea what this trick was all about. I was bigger than he was and could have taken him in a second. Maybe those stories were *true.* "Where's Jeannie?" I asked. "If this is some goddamn lemonade stand up here," I threatened him, "I'm gonna beat the shit outta you."

"Keep going."

I poked my head around the musty attic and there she was, in the corner, lying on her side on an old mattress in nothing but her underwear and candlelight. "Holy shit," I whispered to myself as my body flooded with adrenaline.

"Come on up," she said, rolling over on her stomach. I crawled next to her. She was smiling, relaxed, breathtakingly sexy. Her breasts were gorgeous and freckled and looked huge inside her bra. She had on white nylon panties that went way up—almost to her belly button. My mouth was so dry I couldn't swallow. Her brother was still standing on the ladder. I could see only his head sticking up out of the attic opening. Jackie slid over on the bare mattress and put her hand on my zipper.

Her hand touched me. I was sure this was all a dream and I'd wake up any second with white stuff all over the sheets and three sisters fiercely pounding me senseless. I was distracted by her brother. "It's only a quarter if you let me watch," he said matter-of-factly. "Plus, I stand guard in case the old man comes home. It's an extra quarter if you don't want me to watch."

I reached into my pocket and tossed back a dollar. "Keep the change," I said. "Great," he said. "Don't worry, you won't notice me once Jeannie gets goin'."

This was impossible. It wasn't happening. I was going to hell for this someday. And what about her? What about catechism, confession?

Jeannie slipped her hand inside my pants and I forgot about her brother. In fact, I forgot about everything. Before

I knew it, my hands were all over her breasts, her tan
tummy, and warm bare thighs. She kneeled, unfastened her
bra, and peeled down her panties. In about two minutes, I
had already gotten my first quarter's worth. It was the most
exciting thing that had happened to me since the bike ride
into Washington years earlier—only this was better, much
better. I could hear her brother moaning and grunting. I also
picked up that unmistakable slapping sound that had been a
nightly feature of life in the dark at Linton Hall. I pulled
back nervously. "I'm getting out of here," I said.

"He's okay," she whispered as she kissed me and pulled
me on top of her. "He says those stories about going blind if
you do it too much aren't true."

"No, they are. Look." I fumbled clumsily for my pants,
staring away, pretending to be blind. She started to laugh
and fell back as I reached inside my pocket for another dollar. I threw it back to her brother.

"Come on, you guys," her brother said, annoyed at the
interruption. "We haven't got all night."

He got off the ladder and Jeannie and I picked up where
we left off; now her self-flogging fan club president and business partner was gone. She was terrific, showed me how to
do everything. She made it so easy that I never felt sneaky or
dirty or guilty. In fact, I loved every second of it. I had been
inducted into the world's most exclusive men's club. I had
always heard there were only two kinds of females in the
world—nuns and nymphos. I knew where the nuns were; I
never dreamed I'd find my own nympho.

"How old are you?" she asked softly, right in the middle
of the most important part.

"Thirteen, sort of."

"You're bigger than most guys your age, you know that?"

"I don't think I'm so tall," I said. "You should see the
guys on my basketball . . ."

"Nooooo," she whispered, "I don't mean *that.*"

I stopped moving for a second to think over just what she
did mean.

"Jesus! So what do I do now, just keep going like this?" I
asked her. She nodded slowly, smiled, and closed her eyes.

"You're doing just fine. Doesn't this feel *great?*" she whispered. I never wanted to wake from this dream.

"It feels incredible. And you *know* it beats lighting the candles on the altar during Mass at St. Rita's."

3

AFTER THE SUMMER, I gave up on sex and saved all my
energies for doing poorly at school. This required concentration, since I was used to getting 80s and 90s in everything
but arithmetic without trying. I couldn't risk pulling A's. I
enrolled for ninth grade in a public school, George Washington High. At G.W., I hit my stride and rarely came anywhere close. A's just didn't fit the image. A top average
would have convinced my father that I was, as he had begun
to boast during wild, slurring harangues, Annapolis material. I took no chances and never—*never*—handed in homework. My aversion to schoolwork was exceeded only by my
dread of military uniforms.

I shot past six feet and played varsity basketball. I loved
the rugged ambiance of sweaty socks, wintergreen muscle
oils, post-practice b.o., slamming lockers, and jock talk. I
loved taking showers with no nuns around. In school, I hung
out with a bunch of rowdy, action-loving hoods who called
themselves the Del Ray Locals. I worked hard to fit in with
my own style. I wasn't by nature a hitter, so I became a
popular cutup, the tall skinny one who was much too cool to
be caught dead taking anything seriously—least of all himself.

I towered over most everyone in the halls. G.W. was like a nonstop party compared to Linton Hall. Sadly, school was also a nonstop party compared to home. For four years I had dreamed of living home again. The leaves hadn't even changed color before reality intruded upon that dream.

One chilly late summer night, I was awakened by hysterical screams upstairs. My body jackknifed up in bed. Rosie was shrieking at Buck. I could hear her daughter Nancy's squeals and the bulldog's ferocious growling. I was paralyzed in the dark, but I knew what had happened.

Nancy was about three and, while wandering to the bathroom in the darkness, startled Buck. The monster went berserk and tore into her. Rosie's husband, Bill Throckmorton, was in the service and away from home. Rosie and Nancy were staying with us. I stood in my bedroom doorway; the light hurt my eyes. My mother was pulling the car around front to go to the emergency room. Buck had ripped Nancy's cheek open. Rosie kicked Buck down the stairs. If she hadn't, Buck could have devoured the helpless girl alive and buried her bones. Rosie washed the blood off Nancy's face, cleaned the cuts, and tried to quiet her first daughter's wailing. Then she bundled Nancy up in a blanket and dashed out.

"Tommy, goddammit," my father yelled from the basement, "Tommy, get down here right now." My brother was still living with us and working as a cop in D.C. They talked a few moments, then Tommy rounded up the dogs in his pickup truck and peeled out. It was well past midnight. Moments later, the phone rang. I waited until my father answered. I tiptoed into the hallway and carefully lifted the receiver to eavesdrop. It was Rosie. She was at the emergency room and wanted to know if my father had ever bothered to get rabies shots for the dogs. He kept repeating that he couldn't remember, and she kept demanding that he look at their tags. "You don't get it, Rosie, do you?" he snapped angrily. "I can't look. They're gone. The dogs are *gone,* dammit, and it's your girl's fault."

"Gone?" she shouted. "Just go out and look, for God's sake."

There was a long pause and then my father's voice came

back, sad and flat. "Gone. Buck's been shot. Tommy's taken
them all out and shot them. My Buck's gone."

I staggered back into my dark room, dropped to the bed,
and covered my eyes. Horrifying images flashed through my
mind. I saw Tommy lead the dogs to a remote bank of the
Potomac, vapor streaming from his mouth in the crisp night
air. The dogs were shivering; their eyes were red and full of
fear in the glare of the headlights. Tommy marched toward
Buck and raised his service revolver at the ugly beast's head.

My body shuddered as I opened my eyes. Dad had lost his
best friends in the world. I cried but felt no sadness, only
relief. It was hard to mourn the loss of a dog like Buck, who
had once launched himself from the top of the couch
through a thick two-pane storm window to go after the
newspaper boy and his fluffy little terrier. I wasn't crying for
Buck, the other dogs, or for my father. I was crying because
I was home. My sentence at Linton Hall had been com-
muted; but now another one, longer and with no hope of
parole, had begun.

I pitched for the Alexandria team that made it to the
second Little League World Series in the late summer of
1948. I was almost thirteen. Playing hardball in the Wil-
liamsport, Pennsylvania, stadium—with its official batters'
boxes, foul lines, and pitcher's mound—was every kid's
dream. On the bus ride from Alexandria, I was weak with
butterflies. We stopped at a gift shop/cafeteria and I wandered around, buzzing on adrenaline. For no apparent reason, I impulsively shoplifted a worthless penknife and got
caught by my coach. He made me return the knife. Then he
benched me, ordering me to stay in the motel room during
the game. I was furious. I pleaded with him, I begged for-
giveness, I cited my earned-run average. I promised a
shutout.

Nothing worked. As my team took the field in the Wil-
liamsport sun without me, I suited up anyway and fumed
inside the room. I punched the table and walls and noisily
cursed myself for getting caught. I rolled up wads of toilet
paper, soaked them in water, squeezed them into hardballs
and hurled them against the door. I swiped a dozen rolls

from the housekeeping girls' cart and drove them nuts. That was my World Series. I really had my stuff that day.

When I turned thirteen, I left the Little League behind—in knife-stealing, anyway. Now it was ten shiny penknives from a hardware store display in downtown Alexandria. I hid them inside my pillowcase. My mother dumped them all on her feet the next morning when she made my bed before work. She confronted me a day later and I told her the Locals had turned their knives over to me for sharpening.

"If you boys throw these knives, you'll cut your fingers with the price tags," she said, full of teasing sarcasm. Now I was 0-for-2. She drove me back and made me return the knives, with a confession and apology, a pretty stiff penalty for a Local. Humility was not a prereq for admission into the Locals. While my mother waited in the car, I slipped the knives back into the display case without detection, spun around, walked past the owner without a word, and left.

"What did he say?" she asked me as I got back inside the car. I shrugged nonchalantly and gazed out the window. "It's all taken care of," I reassured her. "He was real cool. He thanked me for being honest, not like those other Del Ray Locals."

She smiled and patted my leg. "I'm proud of you, son."

I was learning there was a way out of any situation and that *was* a prereq for the gang.

The only way out of the craziness at home was to stay away. After the Buck episode, life deteriorated. There were new dogs, more crusty white dogturds left for weeks underfoot, rooms littered with rancid food, old magazines and papers strewn all over. Friends never came by. I didn't want anyone to see this part of my life. I was ashamed. I spent many nights at Rosie's or just slept in the car. I began dating a sweet, good-looking girl named Maggie Lee. We had met through CYO summer activities. Her home and family were warm and secure and I often shared a room with her brother. Her parents were generous and understanding people and that's why it was basically all right with me that Maggie, who went to a local Catholic school, was saving it for marriage. It just didn't matter. I valued her companion-

ship right up there with her body and could never get
enough of either. I tried extra hard to behave myself around
her parents, which meant not being anywhere near her room
when she was getting dressed or undressed. I couldn't risk
getting tossed out. My father was in and out of hospitals
with heart problems. My mother worked all the time and set
up charge accounts at local drugstores and luncheonettes so
I always had a meal. But, aside from Rosie's or Maggie's, I
had no home.

Instead of a typical early fifties high school kid's bedroom,
I had my canary yellow '48 Plymouth convertible. That was
home. It had everything I needed: two-tone top, whitewalls,
G.W. High pennants taped to the antenna, radio, ice bucket
for six-packs. I hot-waxed her so often that the Locals used
the gleaming hood to comb their hair, dress, and shave. One
Local named Duck dressed in skintight pants, T-shirts, and
cheap shoes painted aluminum with pinholes punched in to
make them look like wingtips from outer space. We all
slicked back our hair with grease and wore as much black as
possible. We looked like Elvis three years before *Elvis* looked
like Elvis. We would spend hours every evening tooling
through town with beers on the floor. We roamed the halls at
G.W. in a pack. For most kids there, school was an end in
itself; for the more worldly Locals, it was the means, the
jumping-off point for a life of cruising, a base of operations.
Schoolwork, however, was a never-ending drag.

"Mr. Phillips," the math teacher would say, "please complete the equation on the board." "Two x plus two x equals
Purex," I'd say. Anything for a laugh. Math was the worst. I
knew enough math to figure out I made 70 percent of my
foul shots. Tenth grade English was an exception. The
teacher turned me on to poets like Blake, Shelley, Keats,
Byron, and Poe. He also worked hard to turn me on to
myself. "It really pisses me off," I remember him saying,
"that your IQ is higher than mine and you're failing everything. You're determined to be like all these tormented souls
whose poetry we're still reading today. Artists who never fit
in, misfits, outcasts who had vision but were never understood."

I could relate to that, to images of noble artistic suffering and martyrdom. It made sense. He read my essays. Behind the goofball extrovert, he saw a sensitive, brooding, angry malcontent. He saw through the posturing and the façade.

I wrote one paper called "The Good Life," a dark, sardonic assault on Christian hypocrisy and the haves' indifference to the have-nots' suffering. "How can anybody be happy in a world like ours?" I wrote. "A world where people starve in one part, and in the other are the fat and indolent? We call ourselves Christians, yet we stand by while all over the world people are being enslaved and treated like medieval serfs." Toward the end, I laid it on thick: "The homeless, starving child in India has emotions as real and poignant as those of the chubby daughter of a nine-to-five married man. She too wants a doll to put to bed every night, wants to be loved and cared for, go to parties in new dresses . . . Eventually, the pestilence, hunger, and hopelessness conquer even the bravest spirits."

The teacher wasn't afraid to praise my writing—"Another grim and cynical but realistic interpretation"—and still lecture me about the need to pull good grades. He sparked an intellectual quest and I began to devour literature and poetry.

"Just don't throw it all away," he was warning me. "I wasn't trying to waste it," I told him. I just had to learn to block things out, pretend a bad situation didn't exist. I made myself not give a damn. That way I could never be hurt or disappointed. My driving passion then wasn't success but escape.

"I know I can succeed if I just try," I told him. "Here, watch this." I took out two orange Duncan yo-yos and started doing tricks with them. I could never stick to a heavy discussion for too long. "See?" I said. "I'm the Duncan yo-yo champ of Alexandria. A real natural athlete." We both cracked up. I got so good I actually sold yo-yos around town for them. "I can do it all," I bragged jokingly as his eyes followed my yo-yo repertoire with bewilderment. "Shoot the Moon," I called out before one trick, then tried another: "Walk the Dog. Rock the Cradle."

Slash the Tires was another trick. The Locals and I did that one with knives. One Halloween night a crabby neighborhood hermit caught us in the act and he blasted us with a shotgun from the porch as we ran off. I took about a dozen birdshot pellets in the ass, but it was worth it. We were terrific car thieves, too, but we always drove the cars back after our joyrides. Sometimes we left them with new license plates, which we would remove from other cars. I only stole a car once on my own, and that was to visit Maggie Lee for a date over a sorority weekend in Ocean City, Maryland. I had no money for tolls. When I got to the immense Chesapeake Bay Bridge, I told the toll collector my mother was very sick, that it was an emergency trip. "Look," I said, "why don't I leave the spare tire with you as collateral and my father—he drives here every day—can reclaim it and pay the toll tomorrow. Whattya say?" I couldn't believe the guy went for it. There was a way out of everything. I was sure there'd be an APB out on me for a stolen car. I had a great date with Maggie Lee, then ditched the car in Ocean City and borrowed bus money from her.

My mother gradually began staying out all night for joyrides of her own. Men still found her quite attractive. Her life with my father left her empty and angry and she still had plenty of partying to do.

She led a double life. She belonged to Officers' Wives clubs and made lots of women friends; she joined VFW groups and was president of the church Sodality, entrusted with making sure linen and flowers were on the altar. Then, at night, she'd stay out late at bars cruising for men. She had a weakness for the rugged construction worker type. If I saw her at home, it was in the evening and she'd be all dolled up in a dress, hair sprayed and stiff, perfume filling the room. It confused and hurt me to picture my beloved mother out looking for action. There were flings and one-night stands.

But then she got involved with an army colonel named George Lacy and I hated him. He was a tall and sickly boozer and he had a wife and children back home in the midwest. He must have offered her security, companionship, respect—even romance. Whatever it was, it was beyond me.

One night she came home just before sunrise, so smashed

she was mumbling incoherently to herself. She slipped on the stairs and almost rolled down them. I had to help her to bed. She didn't even know where she was.

"Rosie," I said to my sister the next night, "the bastard leaves her in that condition every time and it makes me furious." Rosie—strong, responsible, and mature—was shaken. "Have you said anything to Dad?"

"Sure. He just said, 'I don't care. Pass me the bottle of Four Roses over there, Johnny.' "

"She's worked hard her whole life since she left her people," Rosie explained to me. "Living with Dad's been quite painful and difficult, wouldn't you say?" I shrugged in agreement and she went on: "Way down deep, she must be very angry. She has her own life, she's successful at the navy job, and she has her friends. All her life she's taken care of other people—her baby brothers and sisters, us, Dad. And Dad treats her like a slave. So now she's got to start taking care of herself."

"Well, Christ, Rosie, falling down drunk after a wild night with the colonel isn't exactly taking care of herself."

Rosie cut me off with a shake of her head. "That's not for us to decide." She took my hand and I thought back to picnics with my mother at Linton Hall, to the warmth and security that were now missing from my relationship with my mother.

"Rosie," I said, "I have to confess something. I followed them from her office to a seedy motel downtown the other night. It was sick, what I did." She shook her head disapprovingly. "They've been doing this for months. Lacy must have already checked in alone because he had the key and they entered from the parking lot. I wanted to bust in, break it up, get Mom out of there, and pound the crap out of him. I didn't know what I'd be saving her *from,* exactly. I waited a quarter hour, guzzled three beers, and walked right up to the window. But I couldn't move. I felt helpless. So I split."

"Good thing," Rosie sighed, relieved. "It's none of our business anymore. It's her life."

I stood up and exploded. "Yeah, well, it's easy for you to say because you're here all the time in your own home and you don't see what's happening. Her life is also bill collectors calling all the time. No one's paying any bills, there's crap all over the house, Dad's dying in the fucking basement. He took a swing at me the other day and pushed me around. He won't have to go to hell, the old bastard. His furnace is right there next to his mattress. Every morning he rolls up another paper and lights it and tosses it into the fumes. It scares the shit out of me. One of these days, he'll blow me and the whole place up. There are rats all over down there. The only good thing is that the dogshit's so hard and old that it cracks when you step on it . . ."

"I know, I know."

"There's no food in the icebox."

She was grinning slightly. "And we *know* it's no place for you to do your studies."

I caught my breath and gave Rosie a mock scowl. The humor in that remark was most welcome. "Rosie," I said, "there *is* no place for *that*. Don't you know me by now?"

Between Rosie's house and Maggie Lee's, I discovered a new form of escape that didn't offend, disappoint, or hurt anyone else—music. Maggie had a sweet, fluttery voice and dreamed of singing professionally. We'd dust off and sing along to scratchy 78-r.p.m. standards her family had stored away. Sometimes we'd clutch hairbrushes as our microphones and imitate Ella Fitzgerald scat jazz improvisations or create harmonies as we went along. Our favorite was "Goodnight Sweetheart," which was always the last dance at CYO summer dances. It reminded us of me trying to cop feels before saying good night.

Then, during the fifties, a new pop music came along out of Big Band and Bebop. The hit tunes had bouncy rhythms, singable melodies, and upbeat lyrics and they were always being played on the radio. The big hits were songs like "Ghostriders in the Sky," by Vaughn Monroe, Tony Bennett's "Rags to Riches," "Ricochet" by Teresa Brewer, "Hey There" by Rosemary Clooney, "Old Cape Cod" by Patti Page, and Perry Como's "Catch a Falling Star." We also listened to Jo Stafford, the Hi-Los, the Four Lads, Les Paul and Mary Ford, Eddie Fisher, and Frank Sinatra. Some songs made us swoon with both romance and sexual urges. My brother-in-law Bill Throckmorton introduced me to a lot of fine jazz-oriented pop music. He was a weekend drummer and had a great collection of records. He and Rosie set aside one small room of their house downstairs just for Bill's music. He would take me in there on weekends and wail on his drums and piano to Gerry Mulligan and Dave Brubeck. We would just lose ourselves for hours. I could tell he loved music even when he couldn't get any weekend gigs. He needed to bash around on those drums just to blow off steam. He also had a flute, a ukulele, and other instruments down there. It was the one place I could go and never get bored or restless. One dreary, rainy Saturday in winter, as we noodled around importantly in our own little world, he pulled a cardboard guitar case out from under a couch. "Here," he said, "I've got something for you and you better learn to play with it soon."

My eyes bugged; I had my own guitar. I held it against my side and ran my fingers up and down the steel strings until they creased my soft, stinging fingertips. The guitar was grainy and smooth and had a rich, woodsy odor from some sort of finish. Bill sat beside me and pressed three fingers of my left hand into position against the hard fingerboard. "Okay," he said, "now strum with the right hand."

I did and it sounded amazing. I felt the vibrations of the strings go right through the bottom curve of the guitar and into my right thigh. I kept strumming, fingers pressed firmly in place. "It sounds great. What song is this?" I asked naïvely over the droning guitar.

He laughed. "It's not a song. It's a chord, a G."

"Wow," I said. "I like G. What comes after G?"

After G came C. Now I had those two chords down, G to C to G to C. "You're really cookin' now, man," he said, slapping my leg and exaggerating his jazzman jargon to make me feel hip. Pretty soon he had me "groovin' " on G and C. I never looked up until he had moved my fingers around for D-7th and E-minor, A-minor and B-7th, E and A, C-7th and D-minor. My fingers were scraped raw, but we were making music. I was flying. There were other songs, new sounds, stranger contortions for my quivering fingers.

Bill played piano and drums to my crude chord progressions. I began to hear how it all fell into place—chords and rhythm, melody and harmony, major and minor. That first afternoon I was mesmerized and stayed down there with my guitar for hours. I lost track of time, of food, of girls.

I emerged from the room as if I had come out of a trance. My head and body felt weightless. Only then did I notice it was dark outside and the house was empty. I was hooked. I was spending more and more time down there with the guitar, trying new tricks, playing along to a variety of sounds, strengthening my fingers, tuning my ears for pitch. Music became a refuge, an outlet of self-expression. With the guitar, I could create and explore my own world of images and sounds without any hassles from the outside. No one could touch me; I felt safety, privacy, strength, and beauty through music. I felt *alive* with discovery and in control. No one could rob me of that. If my '48 Plymouth was my home in the outside world, music was my shelter on the inside.

Bill's guitar helped keep me out of trouble; the Locals kept me in. During senior high, our headquarters for hanging out after school and on weekends was the Hot Shoppe, a downtown dive with 35¢ burgers, 25¢ fries, and giant milkshakes. I'd cruise by and pick up some of the Locals in my top-down yellow wheels and whitewalls and crank up the radio good and loud.

We'd meet the others at the Hot Shoppe, bop through the joint like we owned it, check out the action, split some burgers, fries, and shakes, then cruise some more through town. We'd have to pay some guy to get us beer because we were underage.

The Locals started singing doo-wop harmonies on street corners. Usually, my closest pal, Bill Cleary, a handsome, wiry guy with a drawling voice, sang lead. Soon, we made room for an honorary Local, a more refined, blond-haired kid named Phil Blondheim who went to St. Stephen's. If it was basketball night, we'd have to interrupt the singing to throw a few punches with the rival school's gang, then go back to the music.

We took our dates to the banks of the Potomac and necked in the cars. We sat through drive-ins and hopped into and out of everyone else's cars. We'd build bonfires at the shore and drink beer all night until daybreak. Just for kicks,

Bill and I tried getting into this one all-black dive just over the 14th Street Bridge in Washington, at 7th and O Streets. Two white kids from Virginia checking out the Cajun and blood music. We kept going back until they let us in—at our own risk. There were so many cop cars outside this place all the time, they needed valet parking just to make room for all of them. We always made it in—and out—alive. We not only heard great music, the fear and risk made it exciting. We got to see plenty of fights that way.

During the summers, I worked as a lifeguard at local pools. At night the Locals would drill holes in the walls between the boys' and girls' dressing rooms. This was what you had to do in the early fifties, in Eisenhower's America. That way, even if we couldn't *have* it, at least we could *see* it anytime we wanted.

I tried a job on a fishing charter but, as usual, couldn't fit in. It was just the captain, a retired navy officer who hated the Army, and me—with four retired army generals who had hired the boat from Ocean City. I got the job through my father, but I hated everything about fishing—hooks, gushy bait, dead fish eyes, seasickness, the stench. We ended up miles offshore in a vicious squall. I was terrified. I had been on a three-day bender at the beach and was hung over. The captain was in his element, yelping and howling with every violent pitch of the boat. He loved watching the land-lubber generals barfing over the side and turning white.

"Keep the arrow pointed in this direction," he shouted to me on the flying deck over the wind and blinding rain, "and we'll get back to shore." I grasped the prongs of the helm, in my clammy slicker and plastic foul-weather sombrero. I saw nothing but gray ahead and I knew we were dead. I guzzled a pint of whiskey hidden in my pocket.

By the time he came up to check our progress, I had passed out. My hands still gripped the helm and my body lurched from side to side as the boat's momentum turned the wheel in my hands. He must have seen the bottle and smelled my breath.

He was furious and tried to wake me up. I was semiconscious when he returned with a live bluefish in his hands. He stuck it down my shirt and snapped my collar to lock the nasty, thrashing fish in. The stench and the scratching of the scales against my back made me want to die. I rolled over, felt the fish squirm under my weight, then slide to my side. I heaved a couple times and decided I would kill this man.

I ripped my coat and shirts off and stalked the bastard half-naked on the deck. I picked him up by the collar and the belt and held him over the side as the boat rose and dipped. The generals begged for his life. "We'll never get back," they screamed. They were right, so I dropped him on deck. We were fifty miles off course. The storm passed. We made it back. I went back to lifeguarding and reeked for a month.

The Locals in the summer had too much time on their hands. They moved up from stealing cars to break-ins at local country clubs for sodas, Cheez Whiz, and whatever was in the register. There were weekly gang bloodbaths with chains and crowbars. I hated that, but I didn't dare miss any of it. I had to belong. Luckily, my long reach kept most hoods away.

The Locals took to hanging out in Lafayette Park across from the White House because we had moved into rolling fags there. We hassled them until they forked over money or cigarettes. The Locals' antisocial activities were always escalating and this made me uncomfortable. Tommy was a D.C. cop and I was afraid we'd end up in his station house.

Lafayette Park was always crawling with army fags, elected fags, white-collar fags. We could have made a fortune back in the height of the McCarthy era just by blackmailing three-star or Commie queers for hush money. But we weren't in it for the trade, just the kicks. One night one of the truly dangerous and volatile Locals, known as Ronald McShae the King of Del Ray, asked this gorgeous blond drag queen for a light, just to get things started. The blond whipped out a crowbar and stomped on his foot. The queen turned out to be a decoy cop assigned to bust us. The cops were mean and wouldn't even let Ronnie smoke back at the station house. "You better lighten up," I warned the arresting officer. "My brother's a cop here."

I told them who he was. "Crazy Tom, ehh?" the decoy cop sneered. This hurt. My brother had been messed up psychologically by combat in the Pacific as a marine. He was never the same after that. We always fought. I couldn't reach him after the war. He withdrew into himself and was becoming more and more like my father. He had once been suspended from the Alexandria police force for violence toward blacks. He had no money, but married a widow with four kids, Rosie's closest sorority sister from college. He now lived over a bowling alley and drank heavily. Tommy was a D.C. cop, temperamental and unstable. In his mind, he was still at war, haunted by invisible enemies everywhere.

"Hey," the cop shouted, "tell Crazy Tom his kid brother's been busted for rolling fags."

That cop should have realized that you don't deny Ronald McShae the King of Del Ray permission to smoke a second time. Ronnie was tough. Five-seven, 150, all coiled brawn. Insanely tough. Not a happy, stable home life, but no one asked.

A week earlier, he had proved just how dangerous he was. We were chasing some girls around Washington and ended up facing half a dozen buzz-cut marines in front of a hotel lobby where the girls—and the grunts—were staying. Their leader was six-foot-four and about 240. Ronald opened the trunk of the car, where we kept all our baseball equipment for games and fights. He grabbed a Louisville Slugger and tossed a pair of cleats to Duck. Duck slipped his hands inside, ready to come out clawing. I ended up with a catcher's mask and mitt.

These marines were on leave from Korea and I had the feeling that they missed combat. The guy taunted Ronald once too often. "You know you can't hit me. You just don't have the guts to take a swing, do you?" I sure didn't think he did. I was wrong.

Ronald suddenly unloaded on the guy, really mashed him on the side of the head with a mighty cut. Nobody could believe he did it. The guy dropped, with blood and teeth everywhere. We ran like hell for the car and sped off. Ronald tossed the bat through a window and set off an alarm. I could never be that nuts.

Now he sat there facing four smug cops who wouldn't let him smoke. He was seething and didn't give a shit. He stood slowly and walked to the arresting cop. Without warning, he decked the cop, knocked him right off his chair. Made him puke all over the floor. Then another cop clocked Ronnie. That was it. Four of us against the whole precinct. A wild brawl erupted and I hit the deck, scrambling for cover under a desk. *This is fucking ridiculous,* I said to myself—fingers in the ears, waiting for the fatal gunshots. I didn't catch any fists or clubs, but I did catch on at that instant that not only did I hate fighting and violence but I was also scared. Who was I kidding? This wasn't me. I was going along for the ride. I needed to fit in, be one of the guys. But not to destroy. My days as a gang member were over.

I heard gunshots and I buried my face. I was dead. Then a familiar, booming voice. "All right, everybody freeze." It was Tommy. He had blasted two warning shots through the ceiling. "Okay," he said to all the cops, "which one of you bastards hit my brother?"

I crawled out and looked at Ronnie. He and the two others were battered. The place was a mess. Ronnie looked at the cop he decked. Tommy, good Irish cop that he was, looked at me for confirmation. I gave him just a half nod, though it was a lie. "He's the one?" Tommy said threateningly. I felt bad for the cop, but worse for Tommy as he stood up for me. Tommy calmly put his gun away and punched the guy's lights out right there. The other cops brought Tommy to the ground and roughed him up. We were released without being charged. We were warned to stay clear of the park; Tommy was suspended for three months without pay.

The Locals had a more sociable side. It was our last year of high school, 1953–54, and it was time to party. We were always out lindying and jitterbugging. I dressed up for these dances in baggy cardigans and pleated slacks, slicking my hair back real neatly. The girls wore swishing hoopskirts or straight skirts with kick pleats in the front, white blouses or tight sweaters. They piled their hair up high on their heads, held stiffly in place with spray.

I still dated Maggie Lee, but I often danced with an aspiring ballerina named Susan Adams, whose well-bred and well-off family was descended from President John Adams.

Susie dated a Local named Gus and was a foot shorter than me. She made it clear that she had a wild crush on me, but promised never to try to break Maggie Lee and me up. Susie was a year behind me at G.W. and because Maggie Lee went away every day to school, she was jealous of Susie's daily contact with me. Maggie watched our every move on the dance floor, but there was nothing more than a few sneaky kisses. Susie's family left for Europe and she studied ballet in Vienna.

Maggie Lee and I hit a sexual plateau early and got stuck. She had a tongue that wouldn't quit and hands that wouldn't start. She let me go under her sweater and that was about it. It still beat the circle jerks in dark bedrooms with the Locals.

And yet it was a long way from the occasional gang bangs the Locals pulled off with a hot-looking neighborhood nympho who just wouldn't quit. We'd pick a house that we knew would be empty after school and agree on a batting order. Then she and the leadoff hitter would disappear to a bedroom. The rest of us waited in the kitchen or living room. We had to keep the action flowing. We never knew when Mom or Dad or little brother would be coming home. So we always set an egg timer to ten minutes and left it outside the bedroom door. That tended to separate the men from the boys.

Of course, the rest of the time, I didn't even get close with the love of my life. But we did get to see a lot of movies at the drive-in.

"Come on, what about *now?*" I would plead with her over and over in the car. She'd smile, plant her hand in the middle of my thigh, kiss me, and say no. The cramps from blueballs were deadly, but I was crazy about her and always limped back for another night out of turgid torture.

We petted and panted our way through such classics as *It Came from Outer Space, The Thing, High Noon, Crimson Pirate, An American in Paris, Shane, The Wild Ones,* and *The Day the Earth Stood Still.* More than anything, I wanted to be there with Maggie the day the earth moved.

My mother's ongoing affair with Colonel Lacy had turned her marriage and home life into a sham. Rosie, Tom, and I met to discuss the situation with her at home. It was the only time I remember the four of us meeting like that. I told her she should quit her charade, divorce Dad, and marry Lacy. She stiffened and looked away. Tension in the living room was sharp. "You can all go to hell," she said nastily. "You all clearly have no compassion for me and I've got none for you." Her anger made me shudder, and for the first time I felt she was abandoning her family.

"We understand living with Dad is impossible," I said. "Marry Lacy if you want . . ."

"You have nothing to do with this," she snapped. "I have to live for me. Besides, I still need his monthly paycheck and have no intention of giving it up. Why should I? I'm as free now as if I were divorced and I'd lose the check if I remarried."

Her bluntness left us silent. I stormed out, jumped into my Plymouth, and screeched away. The meeting had failed and only thickened the wall between my mother and us.

I had begun to feel compassion for my father. He had retreated deeper into his own world downstairs in between dry-outs at the hospital. He had become so obsessed by Annapolis that I told him I would apply. I was doing it for him alone. Nothing else I had ever done seemed to matter to him, but he still harbored dreams of me in dress whites at the Naval Academy. I felt that I at least owed him my best shot. By the end of my junior year in the summer of 1953, though, the truth about my grades was that I could play them as a chord progression on the guitar for the Loca to F to C to D to F to D. There was no way I'd put a diploma out of all that.

The dream vanished when I dropped a typewriter on the foot of a swishy European teacher who had groped me from behind, just slid his hand down there and I got wild. The class was in hysterics. The principal was not. It was an excuse for the principal to review my absentee and discipline record and my grades.

"Phillips," he said, suddenly standing tall, "you're expelled. I want you out of this school for good and don't you ever come back."

I drove a Coca-Cola truck all around the area to make beer money and played basketball in an industrial league. With the help of some scouts, my father's name and pull, and some uncharacteristically high test scores, I got accepted to the Bullis School, an Annapolis prep school in Silver Spring, Maryland. I would get my diploma there, then join the Navy and see the world. I also hoped I would see my father happy. I was wrong.

Weeks after my expulsion, my father became unusually hostile with my mother. He was raving like a maniac; she tried to calm him, but he threatened to burn the house down. I heard some pushing, slapping, and screaming.

My mother came into my room an hour later, shaken and soused. She had been crying. "John," she said, "there's something you ought to know that I must tell you." Her voice was flat and sad. My heart began to pump. "John," she said, "do you really believe for a second, knowing me as you do, that I would ever marry a drunk like that man downstairs and then bear a third child by him after ten years? Do you?"

I sat there bewildered and worried. "I don't understand," I said. I flashed on: *A gift from heaven.* I waited. She gained her composure.

"I hope someday you can understand all this—but that man is not your father. He's not your father, John."

She broke down and started to cry, resting her head on my lap. I felt the warm moistness of her tears on my leg. I shook my head in silence, betraying no reaction. I thought of Maggie Lee, my car, the Locals, a new guitar, anything. I tried to feel nothing, but it was impossible. I was crushed, then enraged. It was a joke, all right. My whole life was the joke and this incredible confession was her punch line. She straightened up and I wiped her tears with the sleeve of my shirt. "Haven't you wondered," she continued, sniffling and shaky, "why you don't look anything like him?" I shook my head. I couldn't speak. I was loaded with conflicting emotions—sadness, bewilderment, rage, sympathy, betrayal. After a silence, she grew more composed.

"Your real father is, was, a man named Roland Meeks and he was a wonderful, sensitive, brilliant man. He was a doctor in the Marines back on Parris Island—a Jew, a poet, and he knew your fa—he knew Claude. I'd see him at the beach and tried so hard not to . . ." Her voice broke off, then she resumed, stronger, more in control. "I tried hard not to fall in love with him, but I did. He was everything I was looking for in a man. We had a wonderful, exciting love affair, and I was totally swept away."

"Where is he now?"

"He was shipped out to the Pacific right after that Christmas in 1934. I remember so clearly. Weeks later, I found out I was pregnant with you and I wrote him letters."

"Did you ever see him again?" The reality was settling in on me now. She wiped away more tears and clutched my hands. "We wrote for years, but he died in a Japanese prison camp."

We sat quietly for a long time. There was nothing more to say. *He's not my father.* The words played over and over in my head. I was at once elated and heartbroken. I knew I could ask a hundred questions but I chose to ask none. Suddenly, at eighteen, I had a hot 1948 canary yellow convertible but no father. I didn't know who I was, where I had come from. Everything was an illusion. The person I had always been never really existed, or he had just died and been recreated as someone new. Good ole Johnny Phillips— the varsity center, class clown, the tall skinny guy with the guitar, the virgin, and the D average—suddenly wasn't real. Could I take after a man who didn't exist? It hardly mattered now whether I really went to Annapolis or not. Who would I do it for? Now at least I might understand why Captain Phillips preferred to live in a fantasy world beside his private inferno.

It was overwhelming. I had to get the hell out of there for good. I thought back to that night of violence and chaos and insanity when Buck and the bulldogs were hauled off and executed. That had been a warning sign for me. I caught a glimpse of it then in the darkness of my room, but only now could I allow myself to feel its devastating impact. We were all dying in that house. To survive, I had to leave. My

mother must have read my mind; of course, she had known
it all along. Only she never really left. She and Lacy had
their trapdoor to that wretched motel room. But now I was
flattened under the weight of the truth. And so was she. It
was time for us to let go.

"Let me tell you one thing," she said. "I love you, John.
No matter what happens, don't forget that." There was a
soft, whispered hint of finality in her voice, as if this might
be the last time we would speak. In another sense, it was the
first. "You just have to go where you want to go, do what
you want to do. Don't let others rule your life. Please remember that."

I spent the day aimlessly driving my car, switching radio
stations, offering rides to anyone I passed, and guzzling
beers. I tried to picture Roland Meeks in my mind, but I
couldn't. *This isn't happening to me,* I said to myself behind
the wheel. *It just isn't fucking happening to me.*

That night I went to Rosie's. I had to unload my shock
and pain on someone and did so standing up, pacing around
her living room. She took it all remarkably well. "Mom
must be very angry with all of us for pressuring her about
Lacy," she said. "And she doesn't see why Dad suddenly
deserves all this loyalty. Sometimes she says things she
doesn't mean, especially if she's been drinking."

"What the hell does that mean?" I asked. "You mean she
made that whole Meeks story up?" My arms dropped to my
sides and I felt limp.

"I didn't say that."

"Rosie, it's true. Let's face it. I don't look a helluva lot
like the old man, do I?"

"And I do?"

"You *never* looked like him. What does that prove?"

"Well, see, not long ago Mom and I sat down for *our* own
little tête-à-tête. And she stood right there where you are
now and told me that Dad wasn't *my* father, either." She
flashed a wacky, can-you-believe-it smirk.

"Holy shit." My mouth dropped open, then curved into a
sly smile. "I don't fucking believe this. This is CRAZY. Was
it Meeks?"

"Oh no," she said. "Remember the stories about Mom

leaving Dad and riding back to Okmulgee?" I nodded, eager for Rosie's punch line. "Turns out during one of those trips she met this handsome, rugged rodeo rider . . ."

"Jesus Christ," I shouted, "Rosie, are you telling me you're half cowboy, half Indian? Holy shit."

Rosie laughed and shrugged. "I guess so, because by the time Daddy fetched her from out there and brought her back for good, she was pregnant with me. And she told me that Daddy knew right from the start and that he didn't care. He still adored Mom after I was born. She also said that everyone at the base knew Meeks had gotten her pregnant with you, but no one would tell him because they were sure he'd kill him."

"This is too much to believe. What about Tommy? He's the spittin' image of Claude."

"Tommy's all his."

I just shook my head. "One out of three. Can you believe that?" I said.

"Try one out of four, sweetheart."

"Oh SHIT NO!" I yelled.

"She didn't tell you about the first baby she had?"

"Before you? Before . . ."

"Before Claude even got to Okmulgee."

"Oh Jesus, oh Christ."

"She claims she had a baby when she was about thirteen or fourteen by one of her distant relatives on the reservation. She gave the child up to the wife of one of her brothers who couldn't have babies."

I slumped over. "I'm exhausted," I said. "Rosie, how much do you really believe?"

"Everyone believes what they want," she said. "There are all kinds of stories in this family. Mom's stories always change. She's quite a spinner of tales and tells different people different things. Maybe now if she tells us we all have different fathers, then we won't all gang up on her and defend Dad."

"But Rosie, do you *believe* it?"

"Mom tells stories. *Her* mother told stories. But it's possible. Even the supernatural was possible where they came from."

"Yeah, right, like the time Uncle Orbie came out to the house and did that crazy rain dance in his big headdress on Dad's tomato patch in his Victory Garden? Then it started to pour and the guy almost had a stroke right there in the mud he was so shocked."

"Well, that's what she came from. Anything can happen. What do you think?" The laughter died down. I shook my head the longest time, searching in vain to say something clever. "This isn't a rain dance, Rosie. I just want to know who my father is. Mom dropped this on me like an afterthought. I just want to know the truth. Why should I spend the rest of my life wondering who the hell my real father is? Dammit, Rosie, it makes me furious. I just want to *know the truth.*"

"Well, honey," she said sympathetically but with an edge of toughness, "in this family, that just may be asking too much."

By the time I got to Bullis, my mother's bombshell had strengthened my drive to wear the middy whites—for Dad. But Bullis turned out to be a grueling, regimented bore. I survived only to prove something. I hated the place—no girls, no dances, no Locals, no cruising. I wasn't allowed to keep a car on campus, so I kept mine three blocks away. I was usually grounded on weekends for disciplinary reasons, but I often managed to get away and sneak off to see Maggie Lee at her school. I once tied some sheets together and dropped them out the window for a prison-type escape. My room was only on the second floor, but I had to give it a shot. I spent dozens of hours alone, in my room or out on the grounds, playing guitar and singing. My roommate was a hulking German kid from Minneapolis whose accent was so thick I always expected to find him playing with toy U-boats in the sinks. But a common enemy brought us together.

Every morning at 5 A.M. a woodpecker started hammering away at a tree outside our window. We'd curse and turn over, but never fall back asleep. The bird enraged us both. Then, shortly before Christmas, Hans cheered up after receiving a box from home.

"Vood you mind sleeping in uzzer room yust one night?" he asked. It was a mysterious request, but I went along. That month I had bought the premiere issue of *Playboy* magazine with Marilyn Monroe on the cover at a newsstand. All the cadets guarded their own copies under pillows and in closets. Bullis was a less lonely place with Heff looking out for us. I assumed Hans had a sympathetic brother who had sent him a copy and now the horny kraut needed to be alone with the world's first Playmate.

At 5 A.M. the next morning, the woodpecker's drilling woke me in the next room down the hall. Hans stirred and I could hear him shuffling around the room, mumbling German curses to himself. A smile spread across my face as I lay awake, staring up at the ceiling. I heard a rhythmic, sliding sound and felt embarrassed for the kid, who was such a lonely, modest farmboy he had had to ask me to sleep elsewhere so he could whack himself off in peace at dawn.

Then I heard the gunshot, a blast as powerful as a grenade, resound through the woods. The windows rattled and everyone sprang from their beds. Instinctively, I rolled off the mattress and covered my head. There was silence. I raced to the doorway, beating the other frantic students.

Hans stood at the open window, turned, and casually tossed a giant silver handgun to the bed. The smell of gunpowder stung my nose. The gift box lay near the pillow, with the foam casing, cleaning rods, oil and cloth inside. That explained the rhythmic sliding sounds. A dozen of us crammed into the doorway. I looked out and saw a huge splintered branch dangling off the trunk and feathers plastered into the bark. "Hans," I said, "what the hell's going on?"

He grinned at his stupefied friends. "Vat you hear now?" he asked with a wacky, cockeyed gleam in his eye. He craned his head toward the still woods. "You hear nussing, right? Dat muzzerfokking bird vass drifing me upza vall, ya?"

He then stooped, picked up a shell off the floor, and hoisted a beer stein in his other hand. "Only von shot Hans's fazzer send viss gun," he boasted. "Von shot, von dead fokking voodpecker."

I somehow passed the exam for Annapolis and, with my father's distinguished marine record on my side, earned an appointment to the Academy. But whatever desire I once had to excel in the armed services was gone. I had straight D's on the final report card, ranking 136th out of 145 students. I thought I had a rejection all sewn up. I had dreams of getting a basketball scholarship to a Southern Conference school, where I could just party and play ball. I was heartbroken when I passed. I had made a commitment to my father and Maggie Lee. But I still didn't act like armed forces material. During a history class, our British teacher was once explaining the Marshall Plan to rebuild postwar Europe with huge amounts of American foreign aid.

"There'll always be an England," he said proudly.

"Sure," I blurted out, "and I hope the U.S. can always afford it."

There was only a month between Bullis and Navy and my family and friends were indeed excited for me. The Locals could not believe that I had actually gotten in, so they made sure that there was enough partying and cruising to last me a year. Maggie Lee's prom was a real blast, with tuxedos, gowns, corsages, gloves to the elbow, bouffant hairdos for the girls, the works.

We did a mean grind to a slow song and I was ready to explode. The costumes felt so awkward—my suspenders, her wire supports—but it was definitely us underneath.

"I'm so proud," she whispered, "and I know the Academy's just right for you. You'll straighten out and start making something of your life. You'll get a commission and find some purpose." She had so much faith in me, but when we talked about getting engaged, my capacity to screw up left her wondering. Now that Annapolis was the real thing.

"What about tonight?" I whispered. "I can't think of a sweeter send-off for Fourth-classman Phillips."

She stiffened and pulled back. "Uh-uh, sweetie, not yet. Only when we're married."

Jesus, I thought, *you're harder to get into than the goddamn Navy.*

My father went through a healthy phase and was delighted for me. We managed to get out to Griffith Stadium to

watch the awful Washington Senators get blown out by the
league-leading 1954 Indians. We ate hotdogs and peanuts,
drank beers, hooted and hollered at every Senator error and
strikeout. During the lulls we just sat and talked, like two
guys who had never met before but who wanted to get to
know each other. It was the first time he opened up about
his childhood, the war stories, meeting my mother, the depression that wiped him out after his heart attack and discharge, and his struggle to kick booze. He admitted he was
sorry for what he had done to the family and sad that he had
let me down. He didn't seem to give a shit about my mother's life-style. The only battle Dad was fighting anymore was
his own battle about taking the next breath or not. That's all
he cared about and it was enough. Before he could lapse any
further into melancholic ramblings, I put an arm around
him and assured him it would all turn out okay.

Afterward, we hit a few saloons on 7th Street in Washington, went to a movie, hit another bar, and played pool. He
ran the table four times. It was quite a revelation. He was,
down deep, a tough Irish street punk and I was sorry we
hadn't hung out more often. We could have been real close
buddies.

It only took a week on campus for me to prove that I was
not, after all, Annapolis material. There was no way I would
ever steer an aircraft carrier. I used so much cunning just to
get in and out of the place that I had nothing left while I was
there. I slouched to pass the height requirement and covered
the same 20/40 eye with two different hands so I could fool
the eye doctor and pass the vision test. Then I tried to *fail* an
eye test by claiming I had no peripheral vision past forty-five
degrees. "Can't track subs or stand watch with *these* eyes," I
warned the doctor. It didn't matter what the system was; the
game was to find a way to beat it. Then I launched my
campaign to rack up demerits during plebe summer. I got
them for failing inspections, talking back, not saying "sir,"
not standing straight, eating round, not square, meals, dressing against regulation; I was caught jacking off in my room,
which was against the law. I brought my guitar to school
and every night I played and sang for the plebes. They loved
it and most summer nights we had scores of kids hanging

around the barracks joining in. This was the main entertainment until the goons came one night and confiscated the guitar. From then on, plebes were not allowed instruments in their barracks. Every time I moved, it seemed I tacked on a few more D's.

The night before the final summer inspection, every plebe gummed up his black shoes with dull polish for a whip-'n'-spit shine in the morning. I did the same, only I forgot the whip-'n'-spit part when I awoke. My shoes looked like they were smeared with dogshit. As I stood in formation, the admiral looked down and glowered. "Seventy-five demerits, plebe!" Annapolis was exactly what I dreaded: Linton Hall for adults, except the nuns were vets who wore starched uniforms with colorful rows of combat medals. I hated being back in uniform, regimented every second of the way. There *was* a way out of this one, too, I realized: 300 demerits.

In November, Britain's Queen Elizabeth, the Queen Mother, visited the Academy for a full dress parade and an address before the entire school. There was talk at breakfast that morning that any visiting royalty or chief of state had the power and privilege of granting amnesty for all demerits, just like that. I almost choked on my food. "That's the worst news I've heard in years," I said. "That's impossible." No, my buddies said, it was true. They were praying to have their demerits wiped off their records. "How can they do this to me?" I blurted out, pounding my knife and fork into the table. "Is there no justice? I'm only three D's short of a dishonorable discharge. I could jerk off right here and be *gone* before lunch. I've worked my *ass* off piling them up. And she can just take 'em all away? Shit." I had managed to pull 297 demerits faster than anyone could remember.

The Queen's address droned on and on and I grew nervous. The Academy presented her with an aerial photograph of the campus, then suddenly she mentioned demerits. "No," I mumbled in the rear of the assembly hall, "don't do it, Liz, have a heart." My buddies yanked my arm to calm me. Then she did it. It was with a great sense of honor and humility, she said. I tried to get her attention by waving my white hat. Again I was restrained. "No, for God's sake, Elizabeth, you can't do this to me," I muttered. But she did.

Britain's Queen Mother had stolen all my demerits, tons of them, undoing months of shrewd misbehavior.

Not even Queen Elizabeth could keep me in line outside the Academy. My father suffered another serious heart attack and was rushed to Bethesda Naval Hospital. I took emergency leave to visit him. I had been working out and looked great in my whites. My father reached out to grab my hand from inside the plastic oxygen tent. "My golden boy," he mumbled. It deeply moved me that he was so happy with me in my clean crisp whites. He mumbled for half an hour and didn't make much sense. He told me how proud he felt, how he had always hoped he'd see the day. He asked me about plebe life and I said it was great. There was no need to mention my flair for pulling demerits. For the first time I let myself feel—and say—that I loved him as a father. It was an awkward, moving moment, but one filled with pleasure and a sense of completeness. I squeezed his hand, stood, and backed off slowly, keeping my eyes fixed on his. I wondered to myself whether I would ever see him alive again.

On my way out I brushed into Colonel Lacy, who was with my mother. They had waited for me to leave before she would go in. Lacy stayed outside and made conversation about Annapolis. I had never spoken with him face-to-face. He was weak-looking and flushed and he stank from booze. The man looked thoroughly spent. I imagined them interrupting a motel tryst so Mom could see Dad in his oxygen tent. "You know," he said in his gravelly slur, "your father's probably going to die soon, but I want you to know that I'm going to take care of your mother, I really am. Much better than he ever did."

I didn't think first; I just clamped the spindly-limbed, arrogant son of a bitch by the armpits and mashed him against the cinder-block wall outside my father's room. He gasped as I dropped him, then I did it again. "You can't take care of anybody, you rotten bastard," I said. "If anything, she's taking care of you, just like she took care of Claude. She buys you booze. Isn't that it, *sir?*" I dropped him again. He was moaning and groggy as he slumped to the floor. Nurses and doctors came by to pull me off him. I straightened my uniform, gave Lacy one last ugly scowl, and walked off.

Aside from heavily chaperoned afternoon tea dances with
girls bused in from all the proper finishing schools and junior colleges, the only way I was allowed a woman visitor
was if Maggie Lee posed as my cousin and came with my
mother. Maggie grew angry with me during one visit when I
boasted of my demerits. I was throwing away yet another
opportunity for a life of patriotic service and discipline.

"He must be out of his mind," Maggie said to my mother.

"It was probably that time," she said, laughing, "when
Johnny was three and he got dropped on his head."

She had unwittingly mapped my escape. The next day I
was in sick bay complaining of mysterious blind spots. I was
tested over and over, but the doctors were baffled. They sent
for my childhood history and asked me about a week-long
hospitalization when I was three.

"You mean for the severe head injury?" I asked. "Yes,"
they said. "That could very well be the cause of the blind
spots." "I don't remember it," I said. "Better call my
mother." They summoned my mother and she gave them
the whole story.

A drunk neighbor of ours back at Parris Island was
throwing me up in the air, she told them, when his wife
called his name and he absentmindedly spun around and
said, "Whaaah?" I dropped right through his hands and
struck the concrete sidewalk with my head, fracturing my
skull. I had nausea, headaches, and fatigue, but she didn't
suspect anything until I started blacking out. She tried
mudpacks, she told them, the old Cherokee cure. Mysterious
invocations and herbs shaken over my head. Then she
brought me in. "It was Halloween and he was miserable in
the hospital," she said. "I had to bring Johnny's ghost costume to his room, just so he could wear it there. He was
quite upset because it was his first Halloween and we were
planning to go trick-or-treating."

"Was he able to recognize you?" the doctor asked her,
probing the gravity of my head trauma. "No, of course he
didn't recognize me," she said. "I was the Big Bad Wolf."

The next morning I hit the library. I researched fractured
skulls and concussions and saw with dazzling clarity that I
should stick with my imaginary blind spots. The Navy did

not want its officers piloting carriers with chronic blind spots. The tactic worked. The doctors told me that they were caused by the fall. I probably had always had them, but never noticed until my rigorous physical training. By March 1955, I was liberated on a medical discharge.

I came home and knew right away that Maggie could never forgive me for blowing it at Annapolis. She gave me a dishonorable discharge. She needed a man with a future, with a game plan. I seemed to have only the game, not the plan. In no time at all, she found herself a navy officer and married him.

I was just beginning, though, with higher education. For the next year and a half, I managed to enroll in and leave American University, George Washington University, the University of Virginia regional branch in Arlington, and tiny Hampden-Sydney College in rural Virginia. I attended classes for only a couple of weeks at American, but became an honorary member of the Sigma Alpha Epsilon fraternity. I made plenty of friends and moved into the frat house for half a year. I loved fraternity life. I always played guitar and sang for the brothers at parties. I was getting more intrigued by music and by now the first wave of rock and roll and rhythm and blues hits had made their impact.

The range of musical styles during that period was extraordinary. I didn't listen to the radio; I studied it, memorizing lyrics, charting chord progressions, trying out harmonies with anyone who walked past my room. This became the new passion in my life. I was open to every different style along the spectrum of pop. There was Sinatra's "Love and Marriage," Pat Boone's "Ain't That a Shame," Bill Haley's "Rock Around the Clock" and "Burn That Candle"; Georgia Gibbs had "Dance with Me, Henry," Chuck Berry had "Mabelline," Teresa Brewer did "Let Me Go, Lover!" the Four Aces crooned "Love Is a Many-Splendored Thing," the Four Lads harmonized so tightly on "Moments to Remember," and the Penguins gave us rock and roll's first horny slow dance, "Earth Angel." I must have performed that one a thousand times in hallways, acoustically resonant tiled shower stalls, and bedrooms, always with an impromptu trio of backup vocalists. There were hundreds of great songs to hear on the radio by performers as diverse as the McGuire Sisters, the Platters, LaVern Baker, Gogi Grant, Fats Domino, and the Moonglows and suddenly rock and roll was not just a sound or a style, but a cultural revolution.

By the time I wangled myself into Hampden-Sydney College on a basketball scholarship in the fall of 1956, Elvis Presley owned the airwaves and rock ruled the world. The first time I saw Elvis on "The Ed Sullivan Show," I called one of my buddies from home and learned he had seen the Pelvis too. We couldn't believe what we had just seen. It was phenomenal. The first thought that went through my mind was, "Jesus, they got Del Ray Locals out there in Memphis, too." Now, finally, there was a look, a sound, an attitude that defined who and what we had already been for years. And it was sweeping away American youth. The social and sexual energy generated by the new rock culture was electrifying. If you played half a dozen chords on the guitar, you were one cool guy, a center of attention. That's what had happened at every campus. The guitar was *the* rock instrument, the ticket into all kinds of social connections and parties that might otherwise have been beyond reach. I would sit under a tree or against a building and play and girls always came by to sit and listen or sing along. I went nowhere without my guitar and started saving money for a better one.

The Hampden-Sydney setting was serene and rustic and the student body was mainly old Virginia money, genuine blueblood conservatives. I was at Hampden-Sydney for my hook shots, not my trust funds, and I might have been the first student ever to cruise into campus with his own yellow convertible, wet bar, stack of 45s, guitar, and flashing polelamp lights. I was ready to rock, but I was in Perry Como Country. "Slippin' and Slidin'," "In the Still of the Night," "Blueberry Hill," and "Love Me Tender" were on the radio.

At orientation, I knew it was over. I couldn't have Elvis as a hero and wear a beanie with a pinwheel on top. Not at twenty-one. I cracked up. I thought hazing was a joke. I refused to go through it. I went up to the sophomore class president and calmly explained that twenty-one-year-old freshmen did not wear pinwheel beanies under any circumstances. "There are no exceptions," he warned.

I tried to rally the class against hazing, but they all went along whenever the sophomores woke them in the middle of the night to duck walk around the football field while they sprayed them with water and mentholated shaving cream.

The next time the sophomore Gestapo raided my room, I swung at one of them. Minutes later, as all the freshmen scurried obediently to the field, three goons raced in and beat the crap out of me. After they left, I was bleeding and numb, with a swollen lip and headache. But at least I wasn't out there freezing my ass off in juvenile humiliation. I was all alone in my dorm and picked up my guitar. My hands and lips hurt so badly that I could hardly finger any chords or sing. But the guitar was my comfort. I had no idea anymore why I was even trying to fit in. It was time to make my own way, on my terms. I always felt out of place. And I burned with anger.

I collected a dollar from all three hundred or so members of the class. I said it was time to get even. "The technique," I explained conspiratorially, "is called abduction." We took in quite a bit of money.

Two of us forced Chuck, the sophomore hazing leader, into a car and drove four hours to National Airport. We bought a one-way plane ticket to Miami, removed his shoes, gave him a dime for a phone call, and said good-bye. He took it all pretty well. He contacted the local chapter of his fraternity and borrowed plane fare home. We posted signs all over campus with Chuck's face on them, asking WHERE IS YOUR LEADER? or WHERE'S CHUCK?

I knew the moment Chuck got back to school that the story would go around and that eventually I would get a call. When it came, weeks later, I put on my beanie to face the music. "Mr. Phillips," the dean began rather gravely, "is it true that you are on a basketball scholarship?" I nodded. "So," he said, like a cross-examining trial lawyer, "in effect, we are *paying you* to attend our college, is that right?" I nodded, then slipped the beanie off my head. I blew hard into the pinwheel, making it spin. "But not," I said, "to wear a fucking pinwheel beanie."

"Keep quiet, Mr. Phillips." He glared. "It is October. The season doesn't start for another month, is that right?" I nodded.

"I'm afraid we are going to have to expel you, Mr. Phillips, before opening game. You are not exactly the element we want around here. I have *every* confidence we will find a way to win without you."

As a student, I was dead meat; history. I felt the bitter rejection of an outcast looking in, but I knew I had never made it easy for myself. Hadn't I, ever since junior high, been asking—begging—for this moment? Then something snapped inside me at that instant. I felt a powerful surge of relief wipe out my stinging bitterness. Who was I trying to fool? I had always wanted out and now the dean was kicking the keys to me under the jail bars. At last I was free. The truth was that the only thing I had enjoyed about college *anyway* was playing the guitar and singing for people. And I could do that anywhere.

I stood, flung the beanie into the dean's wastebasket, and cleared my throat for one last remark. "And I have every confidence," I proclaimed sternly, "that *I* will find a way to win *without you.*"

4

When I returned home from Hampden-Sydney in the fall of 1956, I took a small apartment in downtown Alexandria and did what any twenty-one-year-old man with no career would do—I began a career in sales. I sold encyclopedias by phone and door-to-door; I sold sewing machines; I worked in a Kinney shoe store. Then I got a sales job in an area that offered challenge and human drama: graveyard plots for a local cemetery. I used dioramas depicting grieving widows and stunned, fatherless kids in a lushly landscaped graveyard. Sometimes, I took black families on a stroll through the cemetery and, at the urging of my boss, explained as sensitively as possible that the state of Virginia was permitted by law to bury in a dump or shallow grave any deceased blacks who did not own a plot. This sick tactic loosened up quite a few cash down payments.

The work was morbid and depressing, which justified using some of those cash down payments at a local bar. Hanging out wasn't what it used to be. The Locals had disbanded; Maggie Lee had surrendered her virginity to a Navy lifer and started a family. My parents had finally split up and my father was living alone in the house or at hospitals. I was alone and often drawn to a fancy lounge on the ground floor of the Huntington Towers complex. The high rise was crawling with stewardesses based out of National Airport. Every night scores of them lined up at the bar to blow off steam and pick up guys, but I quickly got the point that a stewardess is not looking for a graveyard plot salesman.

"And what about you?" they'd invariably ask, after the unbearably upbeat banter about how safe and fun flying was.

"I sell graveyard plots." A real man on the move. Women who spend most of their time being jostled by air pockets, smiling through fear, and wondering if they would ever sip another whiskey sour and grind a new pickup to "Love Me Tender" did not want to hear about burial plots. If they didn't shove off right away, they'd roll their eyes and come back with a crack like "I bet people are just *dying* to do business with you."

"It's quite an undertaking" was my preferred exit line.

I was feeling as uprooted in my hometown as I had on campus. I'd go home, strum guitar, drink, then sleep. In the morning, I was back on the job, burying people alive.

After work one night, I was at the bar and saw a man and a woman walk up and order drinks. I stared in the mirror behind the bar and realized that the woman looked familiar. I had never been on an airplane, so I knew she wasn't a stewardess. Finally, I had a chance. She caught my eye and came over. She was short, with a tight, compact figure and brown hair in a pageboy. I saw that she walked with the brisk turnout of a dancer in her snug slacks.

"You *can't* be Johnny Phillips, can you?" she asked. I smiled and shook my head. "That's true. I can't. No one can be Johnny Phillips. Believe me, I've tried." She threw her head back and roared with a low, hoarse laughter that I couldn't possibly mistake.

"Susie Adams, right?" I asked. We clinked glasses.

"What a memory!" she said.

"What legs," I answered. She threw me a sly, foxy smile. *Shit,* I thought. *She's got a boyfriend hanging on to her.* "You're Johnny Phillips, all right."

The guy was her brother Tom. For once, my luck seemed to be turning. She told me she had been in Europe again

with her family and had just come back from a London
finishing school.

"Yeah," I said, downing my screwdriver, "it took five
schools to finish me off." I ordered a round of drinks and
pulled out my wad of cash. Susie noticed the thick roll,
mostly singles. "Looks like you're doing okay for yourself,"
she said admiringly. I explained my work. "Sounds pretty
interesting," she said.

"People are just *dying* to do business with me."

She rolled her eyes. "Very cute."

We broke up laughing, then went through all the high
school names we knew in common. Susie explained that
when we were still at G.W., her family moved to Vienna.
She studied ballet for two years and danced with the Vienna
State Opera Ballet. Then, while I was away at college, she
came home for eight months and left again, this time for two
years in London. She had just come home again and was
living with her sister three blocks from the Towers. Her
brother had a house in the Ramsey Alley seaport section of
town.

She came from an interesting family. Her grandfather, Dr.
James F. Adams, was a surgeon and professor at the University of Maryland. The family raised horses at Glenwilde
Farms in rural Maryland and one of them, Adamite, hit the
jackpot by winning the Maryland Futurity in the early
1930s. Susie's father, James Adams, Jr., got a doctorate in
engineering and did consulting work on the diplomatic circuit. As she put it, in a whisper, "It was cloak-and-dagger
stuff with the Air Force in Vienna."

We talked about Annapolis, the guitar, fraternity life. I
told her I had disappointed my father and Maggie Lee with
my performance at the Academy and we ordered another
round.

Susie was sympathetic when I told her that Maggie had
given up on me and married. "It obviously was not the life
you wanted," she said. People were selfish, we agreed, when
they imposed *their* values and didn't give you the freedom to
find yourself, to make it or fail on your own terms. Susie let
me know that she was the kind of woman who would back a
guy up in whatever he wanted to do. "Didn't she encourage

you in music?" she wondered. "She always sang so well. It's surprising she . . ."

"She never thought I'd do anything with it," I abruptly cut in. "She wanted me to have a job, money, status, success —they were all much more important to her than they were to me."

Susie cocked her head sideways and smirked. "We all knew what was important to you, Johnny Phillips."

I paused guiltily. "Well, all right, so I wasn't the most faithful boyfriend in the world after I went away to school."

She sighed wistfully and looked away. "God, John, I had the wildest *crush* on you." I shrugged uncomfortably. We were both getting loaded. Tom cruised the bar. We were heating up. She edged forward with a seductive glance. "The poor girl," she whispered, "really blew it. She didn't know what she had. You've got so much talent and you were such a great dancer."

Susie halted, swirling her drink in the glass as we recalled Maggie's jealousy when we danced. "Remember how ridiculous we looked out there, with you standing a foot taller than me, and me trying to do the turns?" I shook my head. "God, that seems like a long time ago, huh?"

I liked Susie's girlish, spunky exuberance. By now we were both plowed, but we ordered a last round of screwdrivers.

"So what do you want to do now?" she asked.

I crossed my eyes and peered down into her big brown eyes.

"Become an air force pilot." She shook with a laugh and looked at her watch. "Right now?" she asked. "It's pretty late. I'm sure the Air Force is closed for the night."

"Okay," I said. "Fuck the Air Force. Let's go dancing."

We still made a great team, dancing to all the new rock hits stacked in the jukebox at the SAE House at George Washington, where I was always welcome to crash. By dawn we were lustily contorted in my '49 Ford convertible at the docks in Ramsey Alley. Only the nosey blinding flashlight of a town cop brought the evening to a riotously awkward end.

Susie and I dated through the fall and right up until the holiday season. We had some great times around music. I'd play guitar and we'd make up new rock songs. One night, we got smashed at her apartment and I did my version of Harry Belafonte's "The Banana Boat Song." We created a new genre right there—Del Ray Calypso. I flipped up the collar, twisted the long tails of a pink-and-black checkerboard shirt into a knot, and rolled up my black slacks to midcalf. I took off my shoes and socks, balanced Susie's tiny straw sombrero on my head, strummed the right chords, and shouted perfected harmonies with her to the top hit of the day. We behaved like maniacs, but had the time of our lives. "DAY-O!" we shouted out the window, "DA-AY-AY-O! DAYLIGHT COME AND I WAN' GO HOME!"

My father moved in with me for several weeks in a small apartment, but this caused bitter family squabbling over his monthly checks. My mother and sister accused me of taking Dad in so I could live off his pension. I felt my mother was angry because she still wanted that check. I felt guilty that I had let him down at Annapolis and tried to take care of him. It didn't work. He was alone much of the time and bombed out of his mind.

One night Susie and I went back there after a date. I was nervous because none of my friends ever came over all through high school. Susie saw Dad sprawled out on the couch, the bottle of whiskey spilling on the rug beneath the couch. The TV was on. "Don't sweat it," I whispered, turning the TV off, "he's not dead, he's just *Dad.*" Immediately, I was defensive and apologetic. *It was a bad move to bring her here,* I thought.

She shook her head. "God, John, this place is a shambles. You can't live this way."

Those were the words I feared hearing the most while growing up. For that reason, no one ever came over to see my house.

"My father can." I shrugged, but it hurt. The place was a window into my past, into the person I really was. To Susie, to anyone raised in a proper home, the apartment was a degenerate mess. But Susie was great. She insisted on helping me clean up, so for two hours we danced around to the rock radio station, mopped, swept, straightened up, did the dishes, and got blasted together on wine. We hardly spoke, but I was never tense with the silence. Instead, we took breaks to kiss and hug; it was as much fun as any other date. I had never been *home* with anyone. Susie had so much energy and she never sat in judgment over me.

After about a month, my father's heart acted up again and he went to Bethesda Naval. Susie and I went to visit and I introduced her to my mother and Colonel Lacy. I couldn't stand the sight of him anymore and ignored him. My mother was pleasant to Susie, but refused to let me see my father. It was a dismal Christmas season with all the family feuding.

It was not a great time to sell graveyard plots. One day between Christmas and New Year's, while I was out on my sales pitch rounds, the grieving members of a black family came in claiming they had made a down payment. Gramps had just died and they now needed the burial site. My boss couldn't find any record of the payment and wouldn't assign them the plot. When I returned to the office, they were all sobbing and following the boss around the office. Then they spotted me.

"There," they said, "he's the one who took our money at the cemetery. Ask him." All heads turned to me and I raised my eyebrows in fake bewilderment. "He knows where the down payment and receipt are." My boss glared at me like he wanted to drop me in the ground right there.

By nightfall I was unemployed. The boss gave the family their plot and I agreed to pay him back for two other down payments I admitted were missing. What I did was cruel, but the way I looked at it, the money got me to Susie. I asked her out for New Year's Eve but someone had beat me to it. I was much more upset than I expected. We ended up at the same fraternity party and checked each other's dates out real closely.

On the next date with Susie, we wound up in her bed and had ourselves one fantastic time.

"It was worth the wait," I told her in the dark afterward.

"Yes," she said softly, "the time was just right. It never would have worked as well in high school."

I peeked under the sheet. "It *always* worked well in high school," I joked. She slapped me playfully.

"There was so much growing up to do in Europe," she said.

"That's a lovely way to put it," I said, stroking her long brown hair. She rolled over to face me and frowned.

"What the hell does that mean?" she asked.

"Losing your virginity," I told her.

She buried her face in the pillow. "Hey, it's okay," I assured her. "It doesn't matter to me. You were fabulous."

"What about you?" she asked.

"I was fabulous too, wasn't I?"

Music brought us closer together. The Belafonte act turned into a Presley act. His songs were heard everywhere by the early months of 1957 and if you played guitar you had to do a Presley. If you played piano it was Jerry Lee Lewis or Little Richard. If you didn't play anything, you had to learn how to scream and wiggle anyway. Rock and roll had everyone moving their bodies and singing. I must have told Susie a hundred times that one day I would give it a shot. Unlike Maggie, she didn't doubt my conviction or try to steer me away from music toward an office job. Susie gave me confidence to be what I had to be.

I switched from selling grave sites to Corvettes. This was a major step up. After all, you couldn't test drive a graveyard plot. 'Vettes were *the* sexy cars to have in the late fifties. In the spring, Susie came over to my apartment to break the news: She was pregnant. There was very little discussion, no hysteria. It all seemed to fall into place rather easily. "I guess we'll do what anybody else would do in this situation," I said.

"It's probably what we'd have gone ahead and done anyway," she said. "I *know* how I feel. I'm happy with you."

"Great. Then let's go and do it and give it our best shot. It's the right thing—the only thing—to do."

In May we were married by the justice of the peace in Arlington and I paid him with a $25 check that eventually bounced. The ceremony was brief, as was the honeymoon. We spent a blustery chilly night in a local motel with take-out sandwiches from a deli and a bottle of champagne. But we were relieved and happy.

Susie's parents disapproved of her impulsive act. They

were very proud of the Adamses' presidential lineage and believed their classically trained ballerina daughter deserved more than an Annapolis dropout and salesman of encyclopedias, graves, and Stingrays. But she assured them I was able and willing—ready was another issue—to take care of her in a proper manner. Susie hadn't gotten on well with her parents for a long time and their disapproval only made her more rebellious.

My mother was delighted and the marriage had a unifying effect on all of us. "John," she said in the kitchen of her new apartment, with Rosie, her kids, and Susie on hand for a little celebration, "I wish you both the very, very best. I always wanted you to find yourself a real lady and Susie is just that."

We moved into Tom Adams's quaint little house. While Susie was pregnant, I was a postal carrier; Susie became a $45-a-week contributor to the Washington *Evening Star* society page. She was off to a great start with two byline stories —one about the wife and dog of the Secretary of the Treasury and the other about the children of the Burmese ambassador to the United States. I loved to visit her at her cluttered desk in the busy, brightly lit newsroom. When she took calls from sources, I'd flirt with her cute secretary named Marcia.

It didn't take long for me to get into trouble on all fronts. The U.S. Mail bags were so heavy in the summer—and I hated my uniform. I tilted back my hat, strapped a transistor radio to my cart, and sang and danced along my route to all the hits of the day and that helped make time go. But there was just too much mail to deliver.

Every day I'd take a few fistfuls of mail from the bags and dump them into the well behind the backseat of my Ford convertible. I was so tired and bored, once I dumped a whole bag down a sewer. It never occurred to me that the residents in my district would all complain to the local post office about missing bills and checks.

One afternoon I was at a body shop to repair my convertible top. Suddenly from behind, as I waited to speak to the mechanic, a hefty middle-aged man clamped handcuffs on my wrists. He was a postal inspector who "happened to be

waiting" behind me in his car. He noticed the pile of mail
overflowing from the well and became suspicious. That same
day, it turned out, a man came to the house and told Susie
he was from the FBI. So many Social Security checks were
missing from my area that they had investigated. I was inter-
rogated at the regional post office and dismissed on the spot.
But I got away light, with no charges filed against me. The
Locals would have been proud.

I got back my job as a sports car salesman but immediately got into trouble there, too. Friends of Susie's kept calling to ask her if we had bought a new 'Vette. "Of course
not," she'd say, "we're practically broke." I had been seen
cruising around town on a few too many test drives with
young, attractive women. Then the women started calling
me at home. And I left a couple too many cocktail napkins
with phone numbers on them around the house. "I must be
a real idiot," Susie said to me one night at Ramsey Alley.
"Here I am, carrying your child, holding down a job, trying
to make the rent and not get us evicted, and you're out
carrying on with these chicks. It stinks."

I denied everything, apologized for the misunderstand-
ings, and tried to smooth over these disputes with Susie in
bed or by singing a song together. I'd tell her she was overreacting because of the pregnancy, that I really did want to
make it work, but I was scared to death about becoming a
parent and settling down. She understood that and tried to
assure me it would all work out. We'd stay up and read to
each other by candlelight while I'd pat her bulging tummy,
or I'd play guitar and sing to her. But that wasn't enough.

Susie needed some time to sort out her own complex feelings about impending motherhood. She quit her job, moved
out, and lived with her sister for about a month toward the
end of the pregnancy. I was miserable alone and unable to
talk to Susie. My father had had a severe setback and was in
a nursing home. I had only one true ally and I broke down
in front of her. "I've lost Susie," I told my mother. I was
upset. "I've hurt her too many times and I've screwed everything up—for nothing."

"Go pick her up," she said, "and bring her here to me.
The two of you can have my bedroom. Lacy's out west with

his family and I'll sleep on the pullout sofa. I'll take care of
Susie while you work. But just go and do it. And if she gives
you a fight, insist! Do what your father did to me when he
came out to the reservation and brought me home again."

"I already *got* her pregnant."

"I don't mean that. Just don't take no for an answer."

Susie was skeptical at first, but she relented and came with
me to my mother's. "I may be young and foolish," she said,
"but I still love you enough to go ahead with this."

My mother helped Susie make it through the birth. At five
feet four, Susie looked enormous. We had to be very careful
in crowded department stores and on icy sidewalks with our
Christmas shopping. Having grown apart from her own parents since our marriage, Susie became like a daughter to my
mother. Like all her friends, Susie called her Dene.

On Friday, December 13, 1957, our son Jeffrey was born.
There were a lot of elbow-poking jokes about bad luck, but
as far as his and Susie's health went, we could not have been
more blessed.

A gift from heaven. My father's words upon my birth
came back to me over and over again.

They came home from the hospital in time to do some
last-minute shopping for baby-boy outfits, toys, rattles, and
assorted necessities. I was thrilled at the sight of my infant
son. Susie never looked more beautiful or content. But, despite the outward pride and elation, I could not deny that, at
twenty-two, the maturity, responsibility, and commitment
that went with fatherhood were beyond me.

I loved my baby son. But nothing brings out a young
father's fears and insecurities like the sound of a newborn
baby's cry in the darkness. I would lie awake at night, as
Susie would hum and nurse Jeff into silence, and wonder
what the hell I was doing with my life. It was Linton Hall, it
was CYO, it was high school, Maggie Lee, Bullis, Annapolis,
Hampden-Sydney, marriage, it was selling books and graves
and cars all over again. I wasn't *there*. I wasn't ready to
handle it.

By the first week of the new year, I split.

Susie stayed on with my mother and packed my bags. She
wrote me a note: I HOPE YOU AND MAGGIE WILL BE VERY

HAPPY. I didn't go to Maggie's. She was already married. I went to Susie's former secretary at the newspaper, Marcia. We had to sneak around town to avoid being spotted. I lost interest in Marcia after a few weeks. She chose a bizarre way to get back at me.

Several weeks later, Marcia called Susie to chat all about how baby Jeff was doing, how life at the paper was going. Then she asked Susie what she had done with all her maternity clothes.

"I still have them. Why?"

"Would you mind terribly if I borrowed them?"

"Borrow them? My God, Marcia," Susie said, "are you pregnant?"

"Yes," Marcia said. The subject of marriage hadn't come up. "Honey," Susie said, "I don't understand. You didn't tell me the good news. When did you get ma . . ."

"It's John's baby, Sue."

During my next visit to see Jeff, Susie backed me against the wall. I copped a plea: Yes, I had dated her; No, she couldn't be pregnant by me. I admitted I was wrong and that I was sorry I had hurt Susie. The time apart—once I got the flirtation out of my system—convinced me that I missed my family and wanted back in. As usual, one night in bed together proved it, erasing for the moment Susie's anger and doubt. By spring, my mother had loaned us money for an apartment and we gave it another try.

I worked away at songwriting and practiced breathing and pitch in front of a full-length mirror. Susie gave up her writing career and took a job at an aerial photography firm, first as a receptionist and then as a PR director. I still sold cars on a commission basis and had full-time use of an Austin-Healey demo car, but we were struggling. Susie's shoes had holes in the bottom that she plugged up with cardboard. Much of the furniture—a green plastic chair, a three-legged couch delicately balanced on a cinder block, a roll-away bed with a lumpy, mildewed mattress, a stained, shredding oriental rug—had been borrowed from friends or hauled from sidewalks. Susie wrote her high-brow parents a long heartfelt letter explaining what had gone on and they refused to help us at all. Her father's answer was condescending and blunt: "Leave John once and for all and we will set you up in a house of your own, with a car, maid, job, the works." Susie's answer: "I'd rather go it alone and leave open the possibility of working it out with John."

I was proud of Susie's tough, independent stance. She was burning a bridge back to her family and that made me feel worthy of her love and commitment. It also made me feel hopelessly inadequate to match it. But I never had the heart to reveal this gnawing sense of futility. Instead, I acted it out, usually by coming home in the middle of the night, disappearing for a day or two, or by having a brief, senseless fling. I was always drawn back home again. But during the summer of 1958, I couldn't keep from feeling trapped. It was time to hit the road.

5

ONE STEAMY JULY NIGHT I dragged myself home from a long day at the car dealership. Susie was in an exuberant mood and the apartment had a homey, feast-in-the-works smell. "Dene came by to cook us dinner," she said. "She bought us all filet mignon for dinner. God, wasn't that fabulous of her?" I hugged Susie, bent down to nuzzle Jeffrey, and mumbled, "Yeah, fabulous."

"What's wrong with you?" she snarled. Before I answered, I kissed my mother over the stove. The kitchen was an inferno, so I moved back to the living room and slumped to the couch.

"This heat's killing me. Don't we have a fan or something?"

"Fan?" Susie said. "Sweetheart, we've got $35 in the checking account."

I wiped my forehead dry with my sleeve and sighed. Susie saw that I was perturbed and curled up beside me. "What happened?" she asked. "Bad day at the lot?"

"I just wish you had let me know about all this," I said. "I feel terrible. I told this friend of mine, Mike Johnson, that I'd run him out to the airport."

"Mike Johnson?" she asked. I told her I had only known him a couple of weeks, that he and I sold cars together.

"Not tonight," she said.

"Yes, tonight. His father just died and Mike asked to borrow some suitcases. He also needed a ride to National, so I offered. He was real broken up. I guess he and his old man were pretty close."

Susie was upset and didn't know what to say. My mother overheard us and walked into the living room. "So?" she shrugged cheerfully as she wiped her brow. "I'll take the steaks out and we'll just wait until you come back."

When Mike came over, he apologized for interrupting our dinner plans. Susie and my mother conveyed their condolences. I solemnly led Mike into the back bedroom and shut the door. We emerged a while later with two suitcases. "Be back in a flash," I said, kissing Jeffrey, Susie, and my mother. We drove off.

I wasn't back in a flash. I wasn't back in two hours, or three. I felt horrible. Mike felt worse. First, he phoned his father and broke the news. Then I called Susie and had to yank the phone from my ear, she was screaming so hard.

"Will you please tell me where in hell you are, goddamn you, John Phillips. This is the most disgusting stunt you have *ever* pulled in your life. Three goddamn steaks! Your mother is furious. How long are you going to be?"

I worked up my nerve. "You and Mom better go ahead and start dinner without me. I'm in Havana. We're fighting for Castro."

The idea just came to Mike and me one day while hanging around the lot. We were bored. We needed adventure, a mission. Fidel and his raunchy band of *guerrillistas* were encircling Santiago, preparing to rout the despot Battista from power. We didn't know what to expect down there. Mike brought down all his records and I took my guitar. We never made it out of Havana because we were having too much fun. The closest we came to combat was fighting with Customs over Mike's bulging suitcase. They were immediately suspicious.

"What you hab in the suitcase?" the agents asked us.

"45s," Mike said.

"Cuarenta-y-cincos," they mumbled contentedly among themselves. Battista's Customs goons eyed each other and shook their heads, as if they had been trying to break up our arms-smuggling ring for months. "Jankees smuggle guns into Habana, berry, berry bad. We choot Jankees who fight with the *Fidelistas.*"

"Not guns, *capitán,*" Mike said, smiling calmly as he tried to clear up this confusion. "Records. *Discos.* Rock and Roll."

They ripped open the suitcase and out slid scores of 45s. The chief agent gave us another cold, menacing glance. I picked one out of the pile. "Look," I said. "Elbis Presley. 'All Chook Up.' "

They made us wait an hour while a small record player could be brought in. For three more hours, the agents stared at us and grimly listened to every 45 we had, making sure they concealed no coded military secrets. They gradually became less surly and offered us shots of Cuban rum. Once we were free, a mysterious taxi driver brought us to a decaying, squalid hotel in downtown Havana. We assumed he was a police informant assigned to watch us. The overhead fan in our room was too rusty to spin. The heat sapped our energy despite the breezes off the Caribbean, but we loved every moment of dark, sweltering intrigue. There were tanks rolling through the city and armed patrols snaking down every street. From our stuffy room, we smelled fires and gunpowder and heard casino windows and slot machines being hatcheted by bands of guerrillas.

I had brought my guitar to Mike's the day before we left so we would have it in Havana. During the day we'd make the rounds of the waterfront cafés and sing duets of every folk or rock song we could remember. The audience always included wary armed militiamen. We needed no rhythm section, with incendiary devices going off all around Havana. We put together a repertoire of songs by Presley, Ricky Nelson, Chuck Berry, and Carl Perkins. The Cubanos particularly loved our harmonies on a song by "Los Eberlys" they called "Bye Bye Lubb" and we didn't mind the hundred-degree sun as long as they graciously thanked us with free rum after sets.

We kept planning to visit Castro in the foothills and sell him some 45s but always got sidetracked. We were once whisked off the street by a director, straight into a TV studio to appear on a live Havana variety show. Usually, our driver/spy would take us to a bar, get us drunk, and then tell us it was siesta time. After siesta, we'd ask him to take us to see Castro. "You see dirty pictures instead," he'd say and drive us to a filthy, suffocatingly hot theater on the outskirts of Havana. There, we would watch crude, flickering stag movies and pass out. This happened every day for a week. Our revolutionary fervor was soon sapped.

The second week we were in Havana, I fell in love with an exotic Cuban-American hooker named Rita at the hotel. I used to watch her go up and down the stairs with a different guy every half hour. One night she hustled me for an hour, then said she'd go upstairs for only twenty bucks. " 'Only' twenty? You do it with every other guy for ten. I don't have twenty."

"Okay, man, ten, and I'll be yours for the night."

"I don't have ten. How 'bout five for half the night?"

She walked away. One lingering gaze at her long-legged strut and I was out on the street with my guitar. I sang "That'll Be the Day" and "Peggy Sue" until I had ten dollars in my guitar case. Back at the bar, I gave Rita the money and minutes later we were soaked and naked on a bed in a stuffy, windowless room over the bar. Rita was an animal: tireless, uninhibited, and full of tricks. "Here," she said, suddenly sitting up in the dark. She handed me what I thought was a Havana cigar. "I don't smoke," I said.

"You'll smoke this. This is mari-hwana, the tobacco of the *Revolución.*" I smoked. It was my first hit of dope and I was a stoned goner within thirty seconds.

She raised herself up on her elbows and slid over me so her large breasts brushed lightly against my chest. "You like?"

"I like." Rita grabbed the roach from my fingers, finished it off, flicked it away, and began rocking over me. "How you feel now?" she asked. *"Muy bien,"* I muttered, *"muy bien."*

As I left, Rita handed me back my ten dollars. "You're a

good kid," she said. "Save this for the trip home. And get your asses out of Cuba before the chit hits the fan."

"This is nothing," I said, "compared to what'll happen when I get back to Alexandria."

Susie wasn't furious back home, but she wasn't very friendly either. "A woman called and told me that she was pregnant with your baby," Susie said wearily. We had been through this before. I waved my hands through the air in exasperation and sat down in the living room. Susie stood over me, tapping her foot. "Oh Christ, is Marcia still at it?" I answered casually. "We already dealt with her."

"Uh-uh," Susie said. Her body tightened with building fury. "Try Donna."

"Donna? Hmmm, doesn't ring a bell."

"Try Hampden-Sydney. Did you go back there for a little class reunion? Ring a bell now?"

"Honey, I was at Hampden-Sydney for twenty minutes and got tossed out."

"Try two months ago, on a little weekend quickie with some ex-stewardess slut. Ring a bell now?"

"Ahh. The bells. Yes. Well, so I drove down there to get away from it all . . ."

"No, honey, sorry. The dirty deed was done here, then she went back to school and found out she was . . ."

"Pregnant? That's bullshit. Forget it."

"Her father can't forget it, John, and he was real thrilled to learn his daughter's been knocked up by a man with a wife and baby. He wants to see you in court."

I was getting angry now, too. "Did it ever occur to you, sweetheart, that these little chicks go around screwing anything in pants and then try to nail the one guy whose phone number they can find? Huh? I can't believe you're so quick to put their word over mine."

Susie wanted to trust me and decided to back off. Donna's father decided to back off too. He called days later and apologized for the messy misunderstanding. Donna was not, it turned out, having my baby, or anyone else's. I was relieved it blew over, but tension was still high at home.

The car sales job was erratic and money was always a

struggle. I couldn't take the pressure. I was too restless to be
the husband and father I wanted to be. I dreaded the routine
and missed the excitement of Cuba. For the first time, I also
missed those waterfront performances in the blinding sunlight of Havana. I wanted to run away again. In the fall of
1958, without telling my wife where I was headed, I got in a
cab, rode to National Airport, wrote a check I knew would
bounce, and for no particular reason caught a plane to Los
Angeles.

L.A. was rough to take the first few days. There were no
buildings higher than three stories and no pedestrians. Every
day felt like a Sunday. Sunset Strip at midday made downtown Alexandria look bustling. I crashed in sleazy flop-
houses and dingy motels with hourly rates. I was hungry all
the time. I had to hitch around with my guitar and suitcase
and look for day jobs. I never even spotted any movie stars.
In fact, agents were always accosting me on Sunset Boulevard and saying, "Aren't you Tony Perkins?" I'd say no and
they'd ask me if I wanted jobs as his double. "His double
what?" I asked. I couldn't be bothered.

At one point I traveled over Laurel Canyon into the San
Fernando Valley and got a job selling Chevys in Van Nuys.
Then one day a remark to a customer about being a strug-
gling musician led to a tip: A folk club on the Strip called
Pandora's Box had amateur-night-type auditions and I
could get a gig there if I was good enough.

I got up onstage at the club and sang some folk songs I
had taught myself. I wasn't good, but I was loud and ener-
getic and caught the eye and ear of Theodore Bikel. Bikel
was a regular performer at Pandora's and he liked what he
saw. He introduced himself to me and said he could swing
me a job if I wanted it. I couldn't believe it. For a month, I
shared the stage at Pandora's Box with a bongo player from
the Indies and made just enough money to stay alive.

The rush of performing kept me going night after night. I
slowly grew more confident onstage with the vocals, the
storytelling patter between songs, and the diversionary wise-
cracks while retuning the guitar. Folk music was beginning
to catch on as a soothing, more intellectual alternative to
loud, lyrically inane rock. It was simple enough to perform

and folk clubs were popping up all over, mixing this revived traditional music with beatnik poetry readings, esoteric teas, and avant-garde hipness. The movement was catching on. I had finally found my groove. The instant that spotlight hit my face onstage, I became a new person, utterly free to create my own world and exist purely in that moment with no past or future to weigh me down. I was reliving those afternoons in my brother-in-law Bill's music room again—that sense of privacy and pleasure. I quickly learned in L.A. that when you are a performer, there are always young female fans who are more than happy to give some pleasure back.

I fell in with the regulars at Pandora's, an eclectic bunch of hipsters and aging beats with their "way-out" tastes in literature, food, drink, and clothes. As for the young, long-haired ladies, their tastes for casual sex suited me fine and several of them let me crash at their apartments just like that for free. Connections with women just sparked, effortlessly, without tension. My own domestic turbulence was fading from memory, a fact that made L.A. seem far more seductive than it was.

After a month, the scene grew shallow and impersonal, the air was smoggy, and the town itself felt flat and lifeless. Despite my success as a rookie folksinger and a new circle of friends, I was restless and homesick. I missed the east— Susie and Jeff and the late-fall colors and change of seasons. I overheard two brothers at Pandora's discussing a cross-country jaunt to Florida in an old Studebaker. It sounded like my kind of adventure on the road home to stability. I offered to split gas and food expenses and won a seat in their car. It was exhilarating to hit the road again. I left the West Coast convinced I could make it in music and delighted to be going back for Jeff's first birthday and Christmas.

We took turns driving around the clock. Our fuel pump broke in New Orleans and we had no money. We saw a billboard for the Shriners' Circus and headed straight to the tent in a cab. We all got hired and worked the next several nights at the circus in New Orleans and Baton Rouge, running up and down concrete steps, tossing peanuts and popcorn to kids.

I broke down and called Susie. I told her about my break-

through in L.A. and the decision to make it as a folksinger,
to put together a local singing group and try to sell songs in
New York. "I want to come home again, Sue, I really do. I
want to make it work."

"Johnny," she said, "I'm thrilled for you and I know you
can be great at it. I've always said so. But you can't just walk
out and back into my life like that. Not after some of the
crap you've pulled." I wasn't prepared for such firm resistance. I had to really pour it on to make myself understood.

"Sue, I miss you. Doesn't that mean anything? Is the carpet still red at home? I miss that ugly carpet, too."

"Johnny, you know I miss you and want you back here
more than anything. I still love you. I can't believe I'm saying this, but it would be a lie if I told you I didn't. But I
don't think you know how much you've hurt me. I'm working to support your son, your mother's trying to help take
care of us because you're nowhere to be found, and you've
left twice for weeks at a time without even letting me
know . . ."

"I'm coming home," I insisted, almost in tears. "I'm
sorry, Sue, for what I've done. I had to do some growing up,
find myself. I want us to give it another . . ."

"No, Johnny, please. Not now. I can't handle it."

The brothers abandoned the Studebaker in the garage and
we all flew to Miami on bad checks. I didn't realize how
messed up and alone I felt until I took a job as a bellhop and
trampoline instructor at one of the splashy hotels on Collins
Avenue in Miami Beach. I had never bounced on one in my
life. I bought a book about trampolines so I could stay fifteen
minutes ahead of my students.

The hotel lodged and fed me in return for the work, but I
ended up spending most nights in the satin sheets of the
hotel's voluptuous, hot-blooded ballroom dance instructor
from Puerto Rico.

Her name was María and her homicidally jealous husband
had just moved out. She could have been Rita's younger
sister, except that María's foreplay didn't involve smoking
dope. Instead, she tangoed. The ritual always began by getting blasted on rum or tequila. María would shimmy and
writhe out of her brightly colored dress and throw my igno-

rant, passive body around the room to pounding Latin percussion music. She'd toss her head back while her smooth, olive body slithered against my skinny white-boy frame. Her wild black eyes would slowly glaze over, then she would sink into a deeply eroticized trance and pull me down hard on top of her. After making love, María would pass out and I would lie awake until I could limp home at sunrise. That was the dangerous part. I was constantly whipping my head around, ready for an assault from out of the bougainvillea by her maniac husband. Once home in my tiny room at the hotel, there was barely enough time and strength to shower, swim a few laps, and drag myself over to the early trampoline class.

By early December, Florida was beginning to get on my nerves and I came to my senses. I wasn't advancing in music. It seemed wrong to hear Christmas carols while rubbing on Coppertone. My son was almost a year old and I hardly knew what he looked like now, if he was walking or talking yet. My sex-zombie María had unknowingly clawed half the skin off my back and I was sure her husband would rip off the rest if he ever saw me leaving her house. A woman like that should make you forget your marriage, but María made me welcome it. Alexandria was looking better every day.

One hot, humid morning, only two kids showed up for class. I couldn't do it anymore. I had to go home. I bounced right off the mat in the middle of the lesson, ran to the manager's office, announced my resignation, and phoned Susie.

"I've had it with Florida," I said, "and I'm coming home whether you like it or not. It's where I belong. Just give me another chance." There was no mistaking the urgency and sincerity in my shaky voice, and this time Susie was right there. "I'll be waiting at the airport with open arms."

6

SUSIE GREETED ME with open arms and closed mouth. Her conciliatory stance threw me. "Aren't you going to grill me?" I asked on the way home. It was a lighthearted, needling approach to defuse the tension. "Or are you waiting to go in for the kill at home?"

"It doesn't do any good to rehash and rehash and pound a man to death over something that's finished," she said. I could hear wisdom mixed with resignation in her low, throaty voice. I watched her warily as she went on. "That's what destroys trust. We don't want a love-hate marriage."

I nodded my head in agreement. "Besides," she continued, "you're going to be a good boy, right?"

"Right. I'm sorry for leaving the way I did. You're being incredibly fair. But you know I had reasons for leaving."

"I don't want to know everything that went on. I want to start over with a clean slate."

"Deal."

After all the wandering among strangers and crashing in hotels, it was good to be home with Susie and Jeffrey. My mother, Rosie, and Rosie's four kids lived in the neighborhood, so we were like one family between Jeffrey's first birthday, Christmas, and Rosie's birthday on New Year's Eve.

Susie was part of my family now and spoke with my mother every day. That had helped cut her loneliness while I was gone.

I put together a quartet and worked out harmonies for my own songs during numerous rehearsals at home. I was fascinated by groups with intricate four-part mixes like the Four Freshmen, the Four Lads, the Four Aces, and the Hi-Los. My group *had* to harmonize with the best of them and get along smoothly, in case there ever was a road act. Once the lineup was decided, the chemistry worked just right: my old Del Ray Local buddy Bill Cleary, the handsome ladykiller with a deep, mellow voice; Mike Boran, a tall, younger kid who had played piano in a notorious D.C.-area party band called the Capitol City All-Stars; and Phil Blondheim, the St. Stephen's kid who had sung doo-wop with us on street corners. His style was much more polished now, since he had been listening endlessly to Johnny Mathis's early songs. Phil did "Chances Are" almost as beautifully as Mathis did it.

Phil and I became buddies again because our mothers were friends in their new apartment building and he lived there after spending six months in the Army. Any escapee from a military academy or the armed services was a friend of mine. Phil had been a bank teller, but wanted to break into music. Susie and I often had him over to the house for dinner and we spent hours fooling around on our guitars with two-part harmonies.

He and Susie had become even closer during my absence —keeping nighttime vigils beside flickering black candles, wondering whether I'd call in or show up. Phil was a good companion to her during the confusing separation.

He had curly blond hair, big blue eyes, and a cuddly, sheepish look that softened the group's image. More importantly, Phil's rich, feathery tenor would have been sadly wasted behind a bank teller window, and by the spring of 1959 he became the lead singer of a new group I named the Abstracts.

Around the same time, Susie told me she had her own project to look after: a second baby. She was exhilarated right off the bat; it took some time for her to break down my

ambivalence. We were still working on a reconciliation. I
didn't know if I was ready. The timing was wrong. The new
group was already demanding my time and energy and making more and more trips to New York to get contracts for
session work and song publishing. I was afraid, I told her,
but I was already beginning to believe that the best way for
us to stay together was to stay apart much of the time and
look forward to the homecomings. That wasn't going to be
enough for her, not with a second child on the way.

The one obvious "option"—abortion—was not only taboo
but illegal and dangerous. Back then, everyone had heard
their share of horror stories about coathangers, stirrups, rip-
offs, and rape. The stigma, the shame, the risks were horrifying for a woman or teenage girl. As confused and fearful as I
felt, I drew the line and never brought it up.

"Well," she said, "what exactly do you expect me to do?"

I felt stuck. "You could drink cod liver oil. Drive over a
bumpy road. How 'bout moving some heavy furniture?" In
those days, the abortion nightmare included scenes of gruesomely induced miscarriages. Susie knew I wasn't entirely
serious and didn't budge. "It's your baby as much as it is
mine," she reminded me. "There's no way I'm not having
this baby. No one, not you, not God, *nothing's* going to take
this baby from me."

Her sureness won me over. The prospect of a real family
suddenly lifted my mood. The truth was, I loved the idea of
a large, happy family—but not like the one I grew up in.
And yet I dreaded living alone. I was better off gambling on
family life.

Weeks later, we learned that my father had suffered a massive heart attack that had left him near death. We all visited
him at Bethesda Naval Hospital, but he was barely able to
recognize us or speak. I sat alone with him at his bedside. It
was clear that I would never see him alive again. I wanted to
share some final words with him, but he muttered nonsense.
I clasped his hand in mine for a long time, looking away.
Occasionally, his fingers twitched and tightened in response
to my grip. A dark, stinging sorrow swept through the small
room like a cold wind. I remembered how I had always
wanted to connect with him, like other kids and their fa-

thers, to have him accept and guide and love me as a son.
But it wasn't meant to go that way. Then my mother had
her wild, drunken tirade and told me another man was my
real father. It didn't matter anymore. I had long since refused to let that mystery haunt me. At that instant, it was
my father whose life was now slipping away as I sat in the
spooky silence of intensive care. I felt no anger or blame—
only deep loss and unspoken love.

I walked slowly from the room and was met by my
mother and Susie. It was a moment of painful awareness and
sadness. "What did he say, John?" they muttered, closing in
around me.

I paused and thought of a clever reply to lighten things.
"You mean, did he impart any final words of wisdom for the
living as his soul was leaving his body?"

There was one of those "you're-such-an-asshole" silences
and they asked again. "He said, 'Son, don't you ever forget
this. Never use a plain bar of soap under your arms for b.o.,
okay? Always use shampoo. It works better.' "

They were dumbfounded. "That's it," I reassured them.
"Captain Claude A. Phillips's secret of the meaning of life,
spoken from the brink of Eternity. Use only shampoo for
your pits."

I kept a straight face; they couldn't tell if I was bullshit-
ting them or what. "*That's* what he said?" Susie asked.

"That's *all* he said?" my mother piped in. "What the hell
does that mean?"

"It means buying a shitload of shampoo from now on."

Back home in Alexandria, I was lucky to have the Abstracts to distract me from the deathwatch. My father was
soon transferred to a V.A. hospital in Martinsburg, West
Virginia, and we all figured it was just a matter of time.
Meanwhile, the group got down to business. We bought
matching cardigans with large, varsity-letter A's on them.
We ordered blazers and tux jackets. We'd pile into a station
wagon, guzzle a few six-packs, practice pop harmonies, and
drive up to New York week after week. Hawking tunes
around the Brill Building in midtown led only to frustration,
rejection, and exhaustion. We would return home for week-

ends, then drive back up Sunday night and start all over in
the song-hustling jungle. We sometimes slept in the car,
sometimes crashed in the Albert Hotel. We were desperate to
break into the tight and talented Brill clique of songwriters.
I met with Freddie Bienestock of Hill & Range, I met with
Doc Pomus and Mort Shuman. I pitched secretaries and
janitors and found out *they* were pitching tunes.

Back home, we had played some local proms, but folk-
jazz quartets who kicked off their sets with "How High the
Moon" just didn't cut it on Prom Night 1959. No one could
dance to us. Schools that couldn't afford to hire real bands
hired us.

I knew we worked better on tape and it was time to cut a
demo. We finally had some luck. George Wilkins, a co-
owner of Edgewood Studios in Washington, gave us a break
on studio fees and let us record there. George had sung in a
group called the Spellbinders and was still in the U.S. Army
chorus in Washington. He knew plenty of musicians, singers,
arrangers, and agents. But they were bland. George wanted
to find the raw, native talent of Alexandria. He was sure he
had found it in the Abstracts.

George promptly put us in touch with a New York agent
named Charles Ryan. Charlie had once been George's manager and enjoyed some pop success of his own in the late
forties as part of a group called the Smoothies. He agreed to
audition us. To my amazement, Ryan was impressed enough
to urge us to stay up in New York and work up more material. We moved downtown to the Albert Hotel, just off Washington Square in the Village.

Ryan had us running around so much that, before I knew
it, Susie was calling me home from New York. She was going into labor. Our daughter, Laura Mackenzie, was born
the night of November 10, an effortless cinch of a birth. We
were overjoyed. Days later, we got more incredible news.
Ryan was on the line from New York.

"I got you guys a real booking, a class act," he said. "The
Elmwood Casino. You're a working group now and it's some
gig. I pulled strings to get you on the bill. A month at the
Elmwood over Christmas season. It's one of the top clubs on
the circuit."

"The circuit?" I asked. "I've spent my whole life around Washington and never even *heard* of the Elmwood."

"The Elmwood's in Windsor, Ontario, schmuck. Jimmy Durante headlines there. Sophie Tucker, Sammy Davis, Jr., they headline there. You're in pretty damned good company. You'll sing, do some production shtick with half-naked chorus girls, you'll love it. Trust me."

Windsor, Ontario, was a slapshot across the Detroit River from the Motor City. By the time I hung up the phone, we were international stars. I fought off visions of us onstage, surrounded by spectacular bare-titted beauties jiggling their way through a Nativity dance number.

I wasn't too far off. At one of our first production meetings, I helpfully pointed out that we brought our own sweaters and tuxes. One staffer was confused. "John," he said, "didn't your agent explain the date to you? I don't know how much time the Abstracts have spent up here in Canada, but the RCMPs don't wear cardigans and tuxes."

"The RCMPs?" I asked, looking over at Phil, Bill, and Mike.

"The Mounties."

"I don't get it. There aren't any Mounties in our group."

"John, for 'Winter Wonderland' the Abstracts *are* the Mounties, eh? Can you guys pretend to skate and sing at the same time?"

"I know we can pretend to sing. We've been doing that for months." My cronies cracked up. Phil decided to play straight man in this act and clue me in.

"John, he means we sing and pretend to *ice-skate.*"

"You mean with our hands clasped behind our backs, sliding our feet on the floor?"

"There you go," one of the production people said, "you *have* done this kind of number before, eh?"

The shows were a riot. The joint was packed on weekends —a thousand or more a night. The wildest audience was a house full of assembly-line roughnecks on a convention junket who were there strictly for the tits-'n'-ass revue.

We came out, sang "The Birth of the Blues," and ducked cigars and ice cubes for ten minutes. We had to wear mittens and ski caps with big pom-poms and do "Let It Snow!"

while pretending to sing and skate at the same time. Charlie was right: This was one class gig.

During our short set, I once announced the folk standard as "Purple Ribbons." It had been re-recorded by the Browns and was a current hit. Phil corrected me to the crowd. "He means scarlet. John's color-blind."

I leaned into the mike. "So *that's* why people look at me funny when I tell them my favorite heroine in movies is Purple O'Hara." We had to keep it moving, send them back to the auto plants smiling.

Ryan got reports back to New York that we were going over well and drawing crowds. We didn't care if the crowd was going more for the harmonies or the mammaries. We were making music and money at the same time and we were on the Circuit.

Life warmed up for the last week or two in frigid, windy Windsor. There was plenty of New Year's partying, slot machine gambling, and lusting after the snow bunnies in the chorus line. We were the casino's token low rollers, with a total monthly paycheck of $1,500—split four ways. We shared everything—the dough, the gambling wins and losses, the booze, and a dormlike suite in the casino hotel, directly below the girls. At times, we even shared them.

One dancer, a gorgeous dizzy blonde with honey-colored curls from Switzerland, had been driving all four of us wild with her frisky cock-teasing. "Tell me," she asked me at the bar after a show, "are you a werchin? Because I want to make it widda werchin."

"What is a werchin?" I had no idea what she was talking about, but the way she looked in her skintight white sweater and red slacks, I knew I wanted to become one immediately. She widened her pale-blue eyes and inched forward to whisper. We each held a drink along the edge of the bar. "You don't know what means 'werchin'?"

"No," I whispered back. She pressed her ribs against the bar. My fingers were two inches from her left tit, and it was no accident. "What means 'werchin'? I don't speak German."

"'Werchin' is English langwich. Do you speak French?"

"No, I speak Mountie. You must mean 'urchin.' You want to make it widda *urchin,* a little kid who lives in the streets?"

She laughed and moved closer until her tit grazed the back of my hand. My jaws clenched so hard that I thought my teeth would crumble into dust. "No, a *werchin,*" she insisted. She giggled and covered her pouty red lips in embarrassment when others at the bar heard her. "A werchin," she whispered, "is somebody who has not yet, howyousay, made the sex."

"Ohhhh, a *werchin.* Baby, this is your lucky night. I am a total werchin. I have never made the sex with anyone."

"Ahhh, good."

The final days in Windsor flew by once I had a crack at losing my werchinity all over again with the leggy dancer. We got back to New York and Ryan started lining up gigs. We signed a recording deal with Decca in early 1960 and cut some tracks. The sessions gave us a rush. For the first time, we felt like pros with a chance to make it. Momentum was building by the end of February when I got a call from Susie late one night in a hotel room somewhere on the road. I knew something was wrong.

"It's Dad," she said. "He died last night."

I flew home for the full-dress military funeral at Arlington National Cemetery. The day was raw and colorless. I watched the marine pallbearers fold up Old Glory, heard the lone bugle and gunfire salute. I felt my empty stare move across the endless rows of grave sites as large twirling snowflakes floated softly to his casket and melted down the sides. He had had several paralyzing strokes, leaving his left arm bent across his chest. Toward the end, Rosie told me, doctors had to sever tendons in the arm to straighten it so they could perform the futile last heart surgery.

We came back to my mother's home and recalled my father's war stories, the tales from the Okmulgee saloon among the Cherokee, the stint in Haiti and the Managua earthquake, the Medal of Merit he received at the Brooklyn Navy Yard, the sadness of his forced retirement two years later and the long, agonizing retreat into alcoholic madness. Hearing all the tales from my mother, Rosie, and Tom, I wished I had known him better. There was now only relief and comfort, knowing that the storm that devastated him during his later life had finally passed.

It was soon time to head north to work in New York. Ryan suggested we take over his old group's name and we became the Smoothies. Then Phil Blondheim, who was my daughter Laura Mackenzie's godfather, became Scott Mc-Kenzie. He took her middle name as a last name and Scott from nowhere in particular, just to get rid of Phil. We played industrial shows in the northeast, the Town Casino in Buffalo, the Town and Country in New York, we headlined at the Cotton Carnival in Memphis. We played USO dates on army bases. We were even invited back to the Elmwood in the spring. "No water-skiing numbers," I warned Ryan. When we weren't driving between gigs or running around town to rehearsals, meetings, and studio sessions, we were holed up in a cramped suite in the Albert Hotel. Scott and I were by then gravitating more and more toward the Village folk scene and were hanging out at clubs every chance we got.

Ryan had the Smoothies on a weekly dole and we lived on baloney-and-mayo sandwiches. He must have thought we'd starve, so he booked modeling jobs for Scott and me in pulp magazines like *True Detective* and *Personal Romances*. I usually got the "lying and dying" assignments or played a corpse sprawled on the floor or a mass murderer coming through a window. The jobs usually lasted a couple of hours, paid between $25 and $60, and were done in Upper West Side Manhattan apartments. As the Smoothies got busier in summer and early fall, though, we had to cut back on the modeling. After about two dozen bookings, we retired from pulp to work full time in pop.

Our first single "Softly," which I wrote, was recorded in March and released by June. There were articles in fan magazines and the airplay was good enough to land us on Dick Clark's "American Bandstand" in July. "Softly" was hardly rock and roll, with seven violins and an eighteen-piece orchestra behind the harmonies. But we weren't alone out there. The biggest song of the year was Percy Faith's lush "Theme from *A Summer Place.*" The record charts and radio playlists were still wide open, eclectic mixes of rock, early folk, R&B, doo-wop, country, girl groups, and heavily arranged pop. Everybody had a shot. There was no formula that dominated the market. Doing "Bandstand" was the ultimate at the time. Lip-syncing had become a genre unto itself and we weren't up to it. When we did "Softly," none of us wanted to do the lead, even though it was only a mime. Scott finally volunteered, but was so terrified to lip-sync on camera that he shut his eyes for the entire song.

Conway Twitty was on the show with us and he had no problem handling his shot at the top. He had had a giant hit with "It's Only Make Believe" two years earlier. His most recent effort had been "What Am I Living For?" The answer was right there when he pulled up in a long black limousine and strutted into the studio flanked by two monster bodyguards. He was hidden behind dark shades, with his starchy pompadour piled high and swept back. Girls swooned and collapsed. Conway had charisma. Conway had star quality, power. Conway had *bucks.* And what were *we* living for?

Later in 1960, our first album, which was mostly folk, came out and we released a couple more singles, "Lonely Boy, Pretty Girl" and "Ride, Ride, Ride." I was only able to see Susie and the kids once or twice a month. Scott and I found the folk crowd around Washington Square seductive and inspiring as we took in the loosely flowing, funky atmosphere of the clubs on Bleecker and Macdougal streets.

I was being pulled from home and toward a new, wide-open creative milieu. The political and cultural tone of the day was more liberal and youth-oriented. John F. Kennedy was on his way to being elected President with his New Frontier. Kennedy was a dynamic, pioneering force of social and racial conscience, a troubleshooter for the poor, the minorities, the working class, and the Third World. The music that embraced his liberal social vision was folk, and Scott and I immersed ourselves in it.

The Smoothies' singles didn't exactly scorch the charts. There was a dreary Thanksgiving break from the road. The bookings had dwindled. Christmas was coming and there were calls from Ryan. Could Windsor be far behind? We were back for "Winter Wonderland" at the Elmwood. But the Smoothies' party was over.

It had been quite a year. We had grown up under Charlie
Ryan and broken the ice as a performing and recording act
in the music business. I was confident that I could make it as
a songwriter. Mike and Bill had had their shot at singing
and were ready to leave it behind. Scott and I made a pact to
stick together and explore the folk scene for new artistic
directions. Our Alexandria quartet harmonized its way
through the closing Christmas season show at the Elmwood
and, with no regrets, agreed it was time to hang up the
Mountie hats and invisible skates.

I returned from Windsor after New Year's, 1961, with a
Norwegian ski sweater for Susie and a strong desire to get a
folk act off the ground in the Village. Back in the City, Scott
and I made it known among our friends that we wanted an
accompanist to play with us on demos. Through Israel
Young at the Folklore Center on Macdougal, we started jamming with a wiry, curly-haired bohemian banjo and guitar
picker named Dick Weissman.

Weissman was only about twenty, but he was already a
brilliant folk instrumentalist. As a Philadelphia teenager, he
had focused all his energies on fifties folk and Ping-Pong
tournaments. He must have been the only kid in America
caught up in the music of Pete Seeger, Woody Guthrie, and
Leadbelly and ranked among the Top 10 in under-eighteen
national table tennis competition. He exuded an ethno-musi-
cologist's love of obscure bluegrass, blues, and mountain
music. He had learned 5-string banjo at Goddard College in
Vermont, taught himself blues on piano, studied folk music
at the New School in the Village, and bummed around New
Mexico to hone and expand his banjo repertoire among authentic rural folkies. Dick was happy when he found a new
Library of Congress anthology of scratchy chain-gang
chants recorded out there in the rock pile. He was a folk
purist.

The chemistry was right. Dick's dazzling musicianship
helped anchor my more commercial songwriting and
rhythm guitar, Scott's smooth vocals and tight harmonies.
We became the Journeymen.

I moved into Dick's seven-room $105-a-month apartment

on 116th Street and Amsterdam, in the no-man's-land between Columbia University, where he was studying sociology, and Harlem. Scott took a ratty, closet-sized room at the Albert Hotel near Washington Square. The life-style suited us all fine: the funkier the better. There were hundreds of aspiring folkies playing and milling through the Square on Sundays or loitering along the narrow Village side streets with their guitars and poetry paperbacks outside all-night coffeehouses like the Cafe Wha? and Le Figaro. The folk uniform was in: worn-in cowboy boots, denim jackets, turtleneck sweaters, and wool caps. The more down-and-out you dressed, the more up-and-coming you looked.

The Journeymen rehearsed for two months until we had an album's worth of material that blended folk harmonies and pop melodies. Dick and I thumbed through the Schwann record catalogue and picked nine labels to contact. We insisted on a live audition, not on a demo. Eight passed; MGM gave us a shot.

The Artists and Repertory guys said they "dug" our vocals and Dick's 12-string guitar sound. But they didn't hear a surefire hit single among my songs. Soon the A&R department tried mating us with Broadway songwriters to create a formula hit that would promote albums. We never signed. The songs all fell in the cracks: "too artistic" for the label, "too commercial" for us.

After failing to get an agent from the Yellow Pages, Dick used some contacts from his TV jingle sessions and got us an audition with the International Talent Associates booking agency. ITA handled the most popular folk groups of the early sixties, including the Kingston Trio and Brothers Four. Our audience at ITA grew from a couple of low-level agents to the whole floor as our harmonies filtered down halls and into offices and lured curious staffers into the small rehearsal room. Among the newly won fans was a manager named Rene Cardenas.

Cardenas liked what he had seen and wanted to sign us to a deal with him and his partner, Frank Werber. They also happened to manage the Kingston Trio out west; they had clout with their label, Capitol, and ITA, which booked Werber-Cardenas acts. He was concerned that Scott and I might be held to our recording deal, as the Smoothies, with Decca.

"No sweat," I said.

"What do you mean, 'no sweat'?" Cardenas asked.

"You'll see."

We went to our chief backer at Decca, Milt Gabler, to audition as the Journeymen and see if he would, in fact, hold Scott and me to our contract. He had liked the Smoothies. As we walked toward Gabler's office, I told Dick, "Just play as loud and fast as you can on the banjo. And stand out front this time, right in the guy's face." Dick looked to Scott and they shrugged. "Milt *hates* hillbilly and banjo music," Scott said. "It drives him up a wall. There's no way he's gonna go for that."

"Now you're catching on," I said with a wink and a thumb in the gut.

Dick's banjo twanged loud and fast and by the end of our first song, we were ex-recording artists at Decca. I knew Gabler would hate the new sound. The Journeymen were soon signed to Werber-Cardenas and Capitol. By March, we were booked at Gerdes Folk City, a genuine folk mecca in the Village. Werber had us believing we couldn't fail to make it. We soon learned that he planned to sign us as insurance against the imminent—but still secret—breakup of the Kingston Trio.

We played Folk City for six weeks in the spring and each of us pulled down $125 a week. We *were* making it in the folk mecca. We shared the stage with great acts like the Clancy Brothers and the venerable Mississippi Delta blues legend Lightnin' Hopkins.

In mid-April, we were on a bill with a scruffy, anemic-looking kid who had been kicking around the Village. This was his first paid gig. He looked pale and fragile, like he had just gotten over mononucleosis, but his audiences were spellbound. He sang with an angry, nasal whine and seemed to work at his "look": tousled hair, rumpled shirt, jeans, boots, cap, the watchful, restless squint. When we had met him backstage before the show, Lightnin' was helping him tune his guitar. There were all kinds of wild stories going around about the guy. All we knew was that he was from Minnesota and went by the name of Bob Dylan.

The Folk City stint lasted through April. By the end of May we had cut an album for Capitol, received $250 advances against royalties, and done a CBC variety show in Toronto. In early spring, Werber called and sounded real up.

"The Journeymen are definitely going to make it," he said firmly. "I've got you guys the best booking you can have now—the Hungry i in San Francisco for *a month.*"

We were on our way. The club was part of the thriving West Coast hip folk scene and we had it for a month. It was a terrific break. I convinced Susie she should give up her apartment in the suburbs of Washington, D.C., for the adventure of a new life-style with the kids in northern California. I put the best possible spin on my pitch. I didn't want to be alone and that far away for so long. It would help save our fading marriage. We had to do the gigs for the group's future. She knew that the last time I went west it almost killed our marriage. Only Susie's restraint and patience kept it going. This time she said she would go along with me—*if* there was reason to believe I'd be staying for good. It was going to be a major move now with two young children, but she agreed to come and we began to pack up the apartment.

The adventure west pulled everything into place for once —the career, the family, better money—and gave us an exciting lift. I couldn't have possibly seen it coming. It wouldn't take long for everything to fall apart for Susie and me once we got out to the coast—once I caught a glimpse of the California Girl.

III

CALIFORNIA SCREAMIN'

7

THE HUNGRY i was *the* avant-garde nightclub to play in the post-beat, pre-hippie era in North Beach. Mort Sahl headlined our shows with an offbeat, satirical sense of humor. Dick Gregory and Shelley Berman were also working the club. The hipsters took drugs, slumped down and read poetry, or played chess during shows. The mood inside was loose and cool. Unlike the previous trip to L.A., we felt like we belonged in California. Political and cultural changes were in the air. Kennedy was in the White House. Lenny Bruce was in the Purple Onion and Dylan had made it into Columbia Studios for his first LP. It was a real scene—the Fox and the Hounds coffeehouse, the Enigma, a hip jazz hangout with John Coltrane cuts on the jukebox, and the Smothers Brothers at the Onion. Beat literature groupies got to mingle with Jack Kerouac, Lawrence Ferlinghetti, and Allen Ginsberg at the City Lights Bookshop. Scott, Dick, and I even met Lenny Bruce at our dingy hotel in Chinatown, a place run by and filled with mysterious Koreans.

After the first few shows, we knew we were going to make it. Werber's master plan was for me to write songs and join the Kingston Trio, Scott to open for them as a solo act apart from the Journeymen, and Dick to add his instrumental virtuosity to the Trio's mellow sound.

Within a week or so, Susie, the kids, and I were in an apartment in Mill Valley that was owned by Bob Shane of the Trio. She came to the sets at the club and we would stick around afterward, then drive back home. By that time, I had seen the quintessential California Girl at some of the shows and couldn't take my eyes off her. Susie noticed me noticing.

She was sleek, graceful, and gorgeous. She stepped out of a dream: long blond hair; blue eyes; high, chiseled cheekbones; sensuous mouth; great skin. They didn't grow 'em like that in Alexandria. She did wonders for tight jeans and skimpy tops. She could look innocent, tough, pouty, girlish, aloof, and fiery. And she was just seventeen.

She and an older girlfriend named Dawn came to catch Dick Gregory's headline act, but one night they stopped backstage to meet us. They heard we had a cute lead singer —Scott. Her name was Holly Michelle Gilliam. They were sharing Dawn's place. Dawn was sexy and sultry; she was getting divorced from a local folksinger and raising a young daughter. Michelle was sharp, a real live wire. She had just been expelled at the end of her junior year from John Marshall High in L.A. for forging one too many absence slips from her father, so Michelle came north to visit Dawn. They had been friends ever since, years earlier, Michelle's sister, Russell, a year older, had dated Dawn's brother and the two of them would baby-sit for Dawn's daughter.

The ten-year age difference didn't bother me. The term "jailbait" never crossed my mind. We all sat around, drank, checked each other out. I had the hots for Michelle, but I sensed that Michelle and Dawn both had their eyes on Scott. Dawn and Scott seemed to share an interest in getting high and wasted no time going off together that first night. I decided to make my move.

The timing for a torrid affair couldn't have been worse. I had just lured my devoted, understanding wife three thousand miles from her home to try to work things out under one roof. Now I was filled with lust and temptation for a slinky California fox who should have been back home in L.A. picking out her junior prom dress.

For the next few nights, I couldn't wait to get offstage and be with Michelle. Going right home to a wife and kids after shows was a drag. I'd drive across the Golden Gate, obsessed with Michelle—what she was doing, who she was with, how she looked. Scott and Dawn were hot and heavy and in her place most nights. Michelle and I went more slowly. She was a kid. With Michelle beside me backstage, I lied to Susie on the phone about being late.

Michelle grew up in L.A. until her mother, Joyce Gilliam, died unexpectedly of a cerebral hemorrhage at a young age. Michelle was five, her sister Russell was six. Gardner Gilliam had been in the service and ran a liquor store in downtown L.A. He and the girls were devastated. He moved the girls with him to Buffalo. He decided to get a college education. He had little money, so he lodged his daughters with a family and moved into a boardinghouse nearby. The parents of this family were nasty and temperamental and threatening. Rusty got strapped by a belt once. By 1951, Gilliam had taken them to Mexico City. Rents were cheaper; they could all stay together.

Michelle spent six years there and became fluent in Spanish while her industrious father got a college degree. When they returned to L.A., the two girls and their father eventually settled into a small converted apartment in a stucco bungalow in Griffith Park. Michelle and Rusty attended John Marshall High. Both were knockouts. Russell was dark-haired, an inch taller, more studious and voluptuous—a bookworm who filled her first bra before she was thirteen. Michelle was a skinny late-bloomer who wanted to goof around. She didn't develop until she was fifteen—an untouchable dream prude. Russell kept a low profile, got high grades, went all the way with older boyfriends through high school, and still had the spotless rep as the good girl. Michelle had the flair for mischief and forging her father's signature on report cards and absentee slips. She was always in and out of trouble. In her tight skirts and sweaters, Michelle's long legs and girlish, athletic body drove guys up the walls. She wore plenty of makeup and looked like a girl who was always ready for a good time, but the image was misleading. Behind the front, she was socially shy and vulnerable. She worked hard to keep her guard up. Guys all lusted after her, but couldn't get close. Marshall High was one of L.A.'s top schools, with plenty of rich kids, but Michelle fell in with a tougher crowd of Chicano kids who lived in the neighborhood.

Gardner Gilliam was a loving, caring father and a hard-working probation officer for L.A. County. But his work often required him to go out of town. He had to leave his teenage daughters in the house three days each week. By the time Michelle was a junior and Russell a senior, he was gone every weekend and the place was party headquarters. They ran wild. Michelle finally discovered her first love that spring.

After being expelled, she landed at Dawn's and they were soon among the regulars hanging around the Hungry i. Once we got to know each other better, I saw in her keen, quick eyes that she was ingenuous but tough too—a kid who knew what she wanted and how to get it.

I knew what I wanted. One night when Michelle and I knew that Dawn and Scott wouldn't be back at her place, we headed there after a show. Dawn's apartment was the classic all-lavender hippie pad. We took full advantage of being alone and made love for hours. My passion for her was electric and powerful. She was nervous and tentative at first, then things warmed up. I lay there with my arm around her, exhausted and satisfied, knowing this one was different. I wanted to be with the California Girl.

I was moving awkwardly between two very different cultures—my family in a straight, middle-class Mill Valley apartment, and a secret, lusty fling with a wide-eyed teenager based out of a hippie pad. It was a whole new world to me.

Scott and I were driving toward the bridge near Sausalito when he mentioned that Dawn had been quite upset lately. They had been using drugs together. She was having man problems. He said she had made a vague remark about suicide. I turned the car around and headed straight for Dawn's. We found Michelle sitting in the living room. "Dawn's asleep," she said.

Dawn was out cold on her bed. Her eyes were glazed like

marbles. We slapped her face and called an ambulance. Michelle was alarmingly calm and said Dawn had asked her to help her go through with it. Michelle must have been confused and not known what to do next. Before the ambulance came we cleared away all the drugs. Dawn got to the hospital in time and straightened out.

If I was hooked by Michelle, Susie soon had me *skewered* by suspicion. I could neither cover my tracks nor back off from Michelle. A showdown was inevitable. One morning I walked in at eleven-thirty wearing the same blue suit I had left in the evening before.

"Where the hell have you been all night and what is this?" Susie said, picking off some telltale wisps of pink angora wool.

"What's what?" I asked dumbly, looking at her fingers. "You mean this cat fur?"

She waited. "Tommy and Dickie Smothers invited me on their houseboat and I fell asleep on a pink rug."

"Yeah, sure," she said. "That's their color."

There was a booking at the Joker coffeehouse in San Jose down the coast later that same week. The group bought three expensive V-neck sweaters for the date. Michelle came along for the ride. We had a great time, but when I walked in, Susie asked to see the new sweater. I gulped. She had me cold. I had left it somewhere in a moment of lustful distraction.

"It's in the car," I said, stalling.

"Fine," she said. "I'm going shopping. I'll go get it myself." Before I could stop her, she was gone. When she came back, there was no sweater, but she waved Michelle's fragrant silk scarf in my face. "I'll bet you look terrific in this onstage, darling." She was gnashing her jaws she was so angry.

"It was chilly down there."

She was hurt. What was there to say? "All I can tell you, Sue, is that it won't last. They never do. Don't I always come back home?" I tried to assure her. "She doesn't matter to me. It's over. I promise."

When Susie came to the club, she spotted Michelle in her pink angora sweater gazing up at me onstage. She then knew what she was up against. "She's stunning, John," Susie said afterward. "She'll be one tough nut to crack and it may be a losing battle, but she'll fade. I'll see to it."

One of her methods involved voodoo. She summoned all her psychic energy one rainy night and focused it on my teeth for some reason. By the middle of our second set, I had an abscessed tooth. She must have been trying to ruin my affair with Michelle *and* my singing career. I could hardly open my mouth. I was in so much pain I went straight home. When I showed it to Susie, she freaked out. "Oh my God," she said. "I did it to you."

Michelle worked her own brand of magic. While I was on the road, she visited Susie, unannounced. Michelle wore the pink angora and slacks to look as spectacular as she could. She drove up and knocked. Susie was playing housewife-mom in a huge white dress shirt of mine hanging out over red tights. She calmly opened the door. "Hello, Susan," Michelle started, full of self-assurance. "I'm Michelle. Michelle Gilliam. But in a couple of years, my name's going to be Michelle Phillips. You might as well give up now. I love him and he's going to be all mine."

Susie was stunned, then self-conscious. She had a few pimples from tension. Her face had never once broken out during adolescence. She asked Michelle in, then led her into the kitchen and made them tuna fish sandwiches and gin martinis. The kids were asleep.

Susie's genteel breeding and European manners took over. She adopted a cool, knowing stance like that of a protective older sister. "Michelle," Susie said calmly, "you must realize that John has a Michelle in every town. Believe me. They've all called. You're not the first, honey, and you won't be the last."

Michelle was unfazed. "But they're not like me. Anyway, he's only going to have *one* when I'm around."

"I don't know about that," Susie answered. "I've seen 'em come and go and I've stuck by him and I'm still here." She paused. "Of course, you *are* the first with enough nerve to make a house call."

Next time I walked through the door from the road, Susie was seething. "Your pretty blond teenager came over to tell me how happy the two of you are. I think it's time you and I got down to the bottom of this mess. How do you feel about her?"

"I'm deeply in love." The sound of the words shocked me. I couldn't believe that I came out and declared my feelings so honestly. I was ready to give up the charade.

"I knew I shouldn't have asked that question. I'll ask another one. Do you think you want a separation?"

I thought for a while. Susie was great—opening the door for me like that. "Yes, I guess I must. Don't you think that's the only fair way to go? I don't want to keep hurting you, Susie. I'm sorry." She said nothing, but started to cry. "How was she when she came over? I mean, was she decent toward you or . . ."

"Oh, *she* was quite cordial and decent. I was a nervous wreck afterwards." Susie's voice was quaking as she fought back the tears. "She told me I made the best tuna fish sandwich she had ever eaten. Wasn't that sweet?"

When I saw Michelle, I tied into her for going to see Susie. She wasn't exactly contrite. My anger lasted until we hit the sheets. No man could stay angry through *that*.

Susie soon had to endure another kind of anguish. She got pregnant. There was no way we could go ahead and have a third child now. This was the heartbreaking decision we hoped we'd never have to make. But it was unavoidable now. All the fears and horrible images came up to the surface. I asked Cardenas for a $500 loan and Michelle helped arrange an appointment with a doctor she and Dawn knew in L.A. The date approached, but the money never came. We were desperate and frightened. A friend of Dick's in New York bailed us out by wiring the money.

As it was for thousands of other women back then, the "procedure" was a terrifying, lonely ordeal for Susie. She was shot up with morphine in a motel room and had to signal me—by placing her white sunglasses on the windowsill—when it was okay for me to come up. But she was too drugged to remember. I waited on the sidewalk and got worried when no signal was made.

Something must have gotten crossed up because when I arrived the doctor was just packing his black bag. Susie lay there mumbling incoherently. I reached for her shoulder and she said, "Don't touch me. Don't touch me again." Buttons went off in my head. It didn't look right. I had heard the stories of doctors molesting and raping drugged abortion patients. I suddenly *knew* something had happened. My eyes met the doctor's and he hurried to leave. "Did he lay a hand on you?" I asked Susie quietly.

She twisted away, still in a fog. "No no, don't let him touch me again. Please, don't . . ."

I jumped the guy and rammed him against the wall. "You bastard, you filthy son of a bitch," I said. I cracked his nose with my hand and, as blood poured down his face, I shoved him all the way downstairs, out the door, and onto the streets.

Michelle and I moved into our own apartment, but as the group got more bookings, we were spending most of our time driving with Scott and Dick on the road. I was writing songs with John Stewart after he replaced Dave Guard in the Kingston Trio. I had rearranged "500 Miles Away from Home," which Dick's friend Hedy West wrote with Bobby Bare and Charlie Williams and played for us the night I met her at a party in the Village. We put the song on our first Capitol album. The Trio had cut it on one of their albums and I was credited as co-writer, so Werber was after me to write others. I had my credit removed because it was always Hedy's song and I didn't deserve the credit. It's too bad in a way. By the time the Trio, Peter, Paul, and Mary, and so many others recorded it, each mile would have been worth about $1,000 in writer's royalties.

I eventually wrote or co-wrote, "Chilly Winds Don't Blow," "Sail Away," "Miss Mary," and a couple of others. I stopped paying attention to the business side of music and never knew whether there was much money in writing these tunes or not. But I was becoming more inspired. I was also beginning to smoke pot and take an upper now and then. It was tempting to believe that drugs allowed me to create better music. It sometimes felt that way. But whether that was true or not, drugs were certainly fun to get high on back then.

Scott, however, was lapsing further into drugs and drinking while he was hanging out with Dawn. Some of his new friends were druggies and all kinds of stuff—peyote, mescaline, acid, magic mushrooms—was available. We stayed away from almost all of it. But Scott was moving a little out there. In the fall, the Journeymen had to hit the road and play campuses. Michelle and I were facing a longer period of separation.

A tall, rugged man sought me out at the Hungry i one evening before a show and told me he wanted to buy me a drink. "I hear you're seeing my daughter," he said.

"Yes, I am. You must be Gil." That's what they called him. He shook my hand.

"You sleeping with her?"

"Yup."

"In love with her, are ya?"

"Yup."

"Know how old she is?"

"Yup. Seventeen."

"Know what my job is?"

I paused, knowing he would answer for me.

"Juvenile probation officer, County of Los Angeles. So it sounds to me like if you knew what you were doing, you'd be pretty fucking good to my little girl, ya hear?"

"I hear," I said. We shook hands, then he finished his drink and walked off.

I knew where Michelle got her gritty, no-bullshit directness from, anyway. She visited Susie a second time several weeks later. She went for the jugular this time. "I *know* John doesn't love you," she told Susie, "because he's told me that when you married him you were already pregnant."

"Okay," Susie yelled, "out! Get out of here now!"

Susie called her parents and told them she wanted to come back. When I returned from the road, she was in the kitchen, slicing open a knot in Jeffrey's kite string with an unfriendly-looking butcher's knife. "She came back again, your little girlfriend." Susie stopped playing with the string and faced me. She looked mortified. "I can't believe you told her about us getting married when I was pregnant. I was so upset that I saw a doctor in Sausalito and he gave me these pills—Dexa-somethings—and I've been a complete wreck."

"Put the knife down."

"We've got to sit down and get this thing over with," she sobbed. "I can't take it anymore."

"What do you want?"

"I want the car—isn't that all we own?—and airfare home."

"I love you, Susie."

"You can't have it both ways."

"But you lived in Europe. You should know about mistresses."

"I give up. This time I give up. You can have her."

Susie meant it and prepared to go back east. I wasn't about to try to save the marriage and promise her what I could never deliver. I wanted out and she knew it. It was sad. Even though our marriage had started off at a disadvantage, Susie had given it her best shot to make it work. She really had. As a wife, mother, member of my family, and as a friend. But it wasn't ever going to work the way she wanted it to.

We were all back east for some shows around Christmas. Susie was at her parents' home. Laura was sick, Jeffrey was wandering around restlessly. I called. Her father, who had essentially disowned Susie when we married, answered.

"I'd like to come by and see Susie and the kids," I said in my friendliest voice. He was never my strongest supporter, but I hoped he was all caught up in the holiday spirit. And he must have felt vindicated to see Susie so miserable.

"If you set foot on this property," he said with distressing calm, "I will take out my rifle and I will shoot you, you bastard."

Susie knew that any visitation with the kids at the Adams house might end in a bloodbath, so shortly after the New Year she got her own apartment in Alexandria. My sister Rosie helped get her a job at the Pentagon as a receptionist for about $3,500 a year.

One of my first visits to Susie's own place ended in a one-night stand with my estranged wife. It was very confusing for both of us. Susie made it clear she was still in love with me. Sex always smoothed things over. But I told her there was no way we could get back together. Maybe getting into bed was my guilty way of saying good-bye.

Michelle stayed out west and I missed her terribly. I couldn't stop thinking about her. I lost track of her for two days and went crazy trying to find her. Finally, Dawn gave her my hotel number somewhere in New England. When I got a message that she called, I realized I was totally in love with her and needed her with me. I asked her to come out the same night. By sunrise, she stepped off a red-eye and threw her arms around me. It was a sweet romantic moment. "I don't ever want us to be apart again," she said.

In late March, we played the Coffee House Theater in Springfield, Massachusetts, for a week. We got a very positive notice in the *Daily News* as a well-balanced, eclectic group with solid music and an engaging sense of humor. "Thanks to John Phillips' keen mind," the reviewer wrote, "comedy is infiltrated and the audience loved every line."

But the best punch lines were all offstage. Susie found out from my booking agency where we were and called. "John, you're not going to believe this, but I'm pregnant."

This was getting crazy. "God*dammit,*" I said.

The second one was scarier, more paranoid. Susie went to hell and back. It had to be arranged through phone numbers with no names to go with them and secret contacts to get in touch with certain doctors who risked their reputations, their whole careers, to perform abortions. It was all underground and nerve-racking. She finally got an appointment and had to wait for a limousine in the evening to pick her up on a seedy street corner in Washington. She was blindfolded in the backseat so she wouldn't remember how she got where she was going—and lead police there. A husband-and-wife team in the front seat was the intermediary contact and they were abortion advocates who worked to arrange appointments for women with sympathetic doctors. Still, it felt more like an underworld hit to her. Susie was tough and resilient during and after the trip out to the doctor's private home in the countryside. The doctor, they explained, made himself available for the ultrasecret procedures to provide women with the alternative of abortion under controlled, safe conditions. It was still illegal, but if you had the right connections and a fair amount of cash, you could at least assume that you would survive.

The group had dates coming up in both Washington, D.C., and Juárez, Mexico, during the same month. I must have taken this as a sign from the gods. I had divorce papers drawn up in New York, went to Alexandria, and invited Susie out for dinner. I pulled out the papers at the restaurant. We were already fairly looped. Susie must have been expecting to be wined, dined, and seduced. We both got so upset discussing the terms of the separation that we drank way too much. Susie was extremely disturbed. I took her home. My sister Rosie was baby-sitting. Rosie, who had only weeks earlier finalized her own difficult divorce, grabbed the papers.

"This is the cheapest, most underhanded, insulting thing you have ever done. You are really rotten," she yelled. She looked at Susie. "If you sign these papers, you're crazy."

"The settlement is reasonable enough," I said. I wanted free access to the children, I granted Susie primary custody, I expected to have a say in medical, dental, and school matters, and I wanted a clause preventing Susie from taking the kids out of the country without my prior consent. And I agreed to pay alimony and support. "You have no right talking to me that way in Susie's house with my children present," I said to Rosie. "If this were my house . . ."

BAM! That's when Rosie stood on her tiptoes and socked me right in the jaw. Never saw it coming. The punch knocked me over a coffee table. She stood over me and looked more shocked than I was by the power in her right hook.

"It's not so much *what* you're asking," she fumed, "it's the horrible, sneaky way you set her up for it."

Susie signed the separation agreement in late April 1962. Two weeks later the Journeÿmen opened in Juárez. Michelle finally got a chance to prove her fluency and accent in Spanish. In the District of Bravos, State of Chihuahua, I was granted a Mexican divorce.

8

MICHELLE AND I moved to an apartment at 70th and Third Avenue on Manhattan's Upper East Side after San Francisco. When she wasn't on the road with us, Michelle wanted to stay busy. I had her meet with my old manager and modeling agent, Charlie Ryan. Before long, Michelle was doing pulp magazine shoots like *True Romance* and *True Detective*. She quickly worked her way up to the teen lingerie jobs. Her qualifications for that were exceptional. She tried to come out for short trips but when she stayed behind, I often had her stay in the Rehearsal Club, a residence for working teenagers because she was only seventeen, alone, and in the big city.

The Journeymen played mostly campuses during the school year and folk clubs during the summer. The first LP had been released in the fall of 1961 and didn't even recoup our meager advances. The second album was recorded live at the Padded Cell in Minneapolis in mid 1962. That album was a disaster. *We* were "live"; the crowd was dead. The audience reaction was mixed so poorly that it sounded like we were playing to a half dozen fans wearing gloves.

When we played a show at the Virginia Military Institute, there was faint, muffled applause. We couldn't blame this on electronics. Dick played an instrumental and I ran backstage. I told a student officer we needed some gung-ho spark in the crowd.

"What do you mean, sir?" the confused kid asked.

"We're killing ourselves. Can't your cadets generate some enthusiasm? It just sounds like we've got a hall full of guys wearing gloves."

"Sir," the kid gulped, "you *have* got a hall full of guys wearing gloves. VMI cadets are required to attend all functions in uniform—gloves and all." At last, I had a new reason for hating military dress codes.

By the third number, some top-ranked commandant had issued an order authorizing immediate removal of all gloves at VMI for those cadets in attendance. The sound of many hands clapping was music to our ears.

Playing one campus—Hampden-Sydney—provided a special and vindictive thrill. "You *do* look familiar," the dean said in his office, twisting his head skeptically. "Where have we met?"

"You must not recognize me without the beanie," I joked. I told him all about the abduction and explusion and we had a good laugh. When he introduced me onstage and we told the story to the audience, the place went wild.

In July 1962 we played the Shadows in Washington for two weeks. Susie and I were on amicable terms. In fact, I was getting along better with her than with Scott. He thought I was crazy to ditch Susie for Michelle.

My mother and I were on a more even keel now, perhaps because my father was gone and Colonel Lacy was out of her life. Though she and Rosie were Susie's staunch allies—and had felt she had gotten the shaft—my mother slowly took to Michelle. Maybe my mother saw something of herself in Michelle. They had both left home and run off with much older men as teenagers. Still, she opposed our marrying. Rosie's husband had left her to raise four children; she was even less sanguine.

Susie was more conciliatory toward Michelle and had us over for dinner. I was able to see Jeff and little Laura in their own home, playing with their own toys. They were only four and two. Susie worked hard at her Pentagon job and was stronger and tougher as an independent, working single mother. She got help from a housekeeper whom the kids adored. She was resilient and decent enough to see that it would hurt the children if she isolated me from them. After all, it was our first child that kept us together to begin with.

And she knew Michelle was far from my first infidelity, only my favorite. Our problems had existed long before the Hungry i. She betrayed no bitterness. Perhaps her strategy was to hang in patiently and wait for me to tire of Michelle —when I'd come running back to security.

Whatever the tactic, it made our visits to Washington more peaceful. Michelle warmed up to Susie, too, once she was no longer a rival and felt comfortable in Susie's home. Susie was far more self-assured on her own turf than she had been as an insecure, suspicious newcomer in Mill Valley at the time of the Tuna Fish Sandwich Massacre. Plus, her woman's vanity had been wounded. Michelle had caught her at her worst—sporting housewife rags, no makeup, and a few zits.

Eventually, Michelle and I would visit from New York and stay over at Susie's. Susie would sleep with the children and give us her bedroom. It was incredible. Susie seemed as attentive to my needs in divorce as she had been in marriage. Only right-hook Rosie was incensed. "How could you do this?" she would ask. "How could you let that woman in your house—in your *bed?*"

"John needs to see the kids—and I love him so much I'll do anything to be with him." Even so, she got the short end of the stick. One night Michelle and I broke a leg of the bed. I had made a point of trying to be quiet in the sack with Mitch. When she came home after work, Susie had to prop the bed up on a cinder block. Susie was such a good sport. Her anger was tame and short-lived, considering the offense. "It's bad enough you broke the bed," Susie said, "but you could have at least *made* it."

Not even the Padded Cell album could prevent us from enjoying a busy itinerary of campuses during the fall of 1962. The image of the Minneapolis club's name seemed hauntingly appropriate. Scott was burning out.

In late October, we followed the Cuban missile crisis on
TV from a beachfront hotel room in Jacksonville. We had
played in the area and remained there for two weeks of rest
and rehearsals. I was always a perfectionist for harmonies
and worked my partners hard. Scott's voice wasn't in the
greatest shape and he threw tantrums because I was such a
maniac for harmonic precision. I couldn't write music, but I
knew exactly what sound and vocal blend I wanted—the one
I heard in my head. It was painstaking work to get it all to
work just right and Scott was pretty wired. Tension must
have been high, if the main diversion was watching the navy
vessels offshore on their way to blockade Cuba. The two
superpowers were on the brink of a nuclear shootout. It was
no time for a paranoid flash.

"The world may be coming to an end, Scott," I said.

"You and Dick are trying to poison me, aren't you?" Scott
said. "You can't pull the wool over my eyes anymore."

"Wool over your eyes? We're all going to be dead in six
seconds if JFK doesn't stick it to Khrushchev."

"I've seen it coming a long time."

"The Russians are coming," I said. "Ninety miles from
Key West! They're building missile silos."

"It's been cyanide all along, hasn't it?" he said.

This was sad to watch. One of my closest friends was
snapping. Scott's innate shyness and insecurity had degenerated into delusions of persecution. If he had a fragile and
vulnerable ego to start with, the drinking, drugs, and constant pressure to perform as a lead singer had only worsened
his state of mind and lowered his self-image. "You've been
putting little increments of it in my food and it's slow-acting.
I'll never work with you again."

"Hey, if there's a nuclear holocaust, next week's gigs may
be canceled. Cool it."

The world survived Cuba and Khrushchev; the Journeymen survived Jacksonville and Scott's momentary madness.
We hit the road again, intact. We couldn't afford to quit. We
were averaging $1,750 per show and selling no albums. We
did sign a lucrative deal to record a series of jingles for
Schlitz beer out of Chicago. They paid us $25,000 for the
first year of jingles, which I wrote. The account people liked

our buoyant sound. They didn't like our buoyant life-style on the road.

We flew into Chicago and checked into a hotel. All expenses were to be paid by the agency. By the end of the evening there was a traffic jam of room-service carts in our suite and I was sloshing around in the bathtub ordering up shots of tequila by phone. The next day we were put on a per diem allowance.

I missed Michelle when she wasn't around. We had talked about it ever since I moved to break up my marriage, so when we played the Shadows in Washington through Christmas week, Michelle and I decided to get married. We found the justice of the peace in Rockville, Maryland, and tied the knot on December 31, 1962. The ceremony lasted just a few minutes. It was just the Journeymen plus the bride in attendance. Scott was best man. There were so many couples to marry before midnight, the justice never bothered to turn off his radio. We took our vows before God, the state of Maryland, and Muzak in the background. Scott and Dick tried not to crack up laughing at the bland background music. They bought Michelle a Lady Martin guitar as a wedding gift.

I had called Rosie that day. "Happy Birthday," I started. Hers was easy to remember—New Year's Eve. She was pleased that I had taken the time to call. "Rosie," I went on, "Michelle and I are getting married today." She was stunned.

"Did you tell Susie yet?" she asked.

"No. I don't have the heart. I was hoping you would tell her for me."

"You're probably right. She won't be happy. I think she's always thought you'd come back—at least because of the kids."

"I'll call Mom."

"She'll be stunned too, John. I don't think she ever figured you'd do it. She's been giving Susie a lot of encouragement about the two of you getting back together."

"Well, it's time she stopped."

While we were partying, I proudly introduced Michelle from the stage as my new bride. Meanwhile, out in Alexandria, Rosie brought over some Chinese takeout food and a bottle of champagne to Susie's. It was supposed to be a festive evening—New Year's Eve and Rosie's birthday. The kids were asleep and out of the way. Instead, Rosie broke the news to Susie and they spent the evening getting smashed and crying together.

By Easter of 1963, Susie had recovered enough to have us over for a calm traditional ham dinner with my family. Relations within my family were smoother than within the group. Dick wanted to get away from the touring and slickness of the music. He wanted to create serious folk music and build a dream house in the Colorado Rockies. Despite the jingle work for Schlitz, American Express, and a tire company, there wasn't as much money as he needed.

Scott talked about a solo career, but he was having serious medical problems beyond drinking. One day he opened his mouth and produced no sound. He had been complaining of a sore throat for weeks; now we knew why. He was diagnosed as having precancerous tissue on his vocal cords. He had surgery to remove it right away. This shook his confidence even more.

We began smoking grass more often. It was great for making love, bad for making planes. I missed flights to gigs in Ohio and Vermont. Promoters—not to mention my colleagues—didn't appreciate the Journeymen as a duet. And I was resorting more and more on speed to get through it all. I found that I liked drugs and was able to hold it together when I was high—most of the time. Once, when we were rehearsing at our apartment in the City, I went into the bathroom and got so stoned in there that I forgot all about Scott and Dick. I didn't hear them call me. They got pissed off and left before I came out. This hardly restored the group's fading camaraderie.

We decided to take a break that summer. Scott and I needed the rest; Michelle had to get away. The three of us picked Mazatlán on the Pacific Ocean in Mexico. Michelle was in California and called her sister Rusty and persuaded her to join us. "We thought Scott would be happier with a lady companion," she said. They had dated on the West Coast, but had been out of touch.

I bought a beat-up Chevy for $200 in New Jersey and drove nonstop to pick up the sisters. Scott flew down and Mexico was just what we needed. We got some potent grass and turned Rusty on for the first time. We'd get stoned before breakfast and eat freńch toast for an hour. Then we'd lie in a pool and drink brandy Alexanders. Then we'd go fishing. We caught two marlin over nine feet long. At night we'd have dinner by the water and go dancing. We got a taste of the Good Life and we liked it.

The Journeymen were booked at the Shoreham Hotel and the Shadows in Washington, D.C. Whatever our internal and domestic problems were, we did manage to put it all behind us for ninety minutes a day and get down to the basics of making good music. That was what all the other hassles were for. This lesson from the road would serve me well later on. A local reviewer still found us a "dynamic combination" and "imaginative and distinctive" as we "blitzed thru" our set.

The shows had plenty of help from our opening act, a satirical low-key comic who set crowds up beautifully and earned critical raves. "As for Bill Cosby," the same reviewer wrote, "here IS a find. This 24-year-old Negro is destined for the top rungs. Unlike any other Negro comedian on the cafe circuit, he tells no strictly Negro jokes. This fact alone elevates him on the laugh ladder."

For a "24-year-old Negro" like Bill Cosby in the United States of 1963, the laugh ladder was a far simpler climb than the social ladder. Folk's vehement protest songs had provided the soundtrack to the civil rights movement. Race relations were at a breaking point, with Freedom Riders, civil disobedience marches, sit-ins, fiery speeches by charismatic leaders like Martin Luther King, Jr., and Malcolm X, confrontations to desegregate schools, and violent riots down south.

The Journeymen were firmly liberal but never overtly political in our music. Our third LP, *New Directions in Folk Music,* came out in the fall. We had enough trouble tapping into the mainstream *without* political controversy. So when ABC that year aired its nonpolitical "Hootenanny" show, which was designed to cash in on the folk boom, we were invited to appear with Johnny Cash and Judy Collins. Then, when a "Hootenanny Tour" was staged for a month in the late fall to cash in on the TV show, we were on the bill, along with Glen Yarborough of the Limelighters, Jo Mapes, the Geezinslaw Brothers, and the Halifax Three.

Almost twenty of the thirty-odd dates were in the southeast. We traveled by bus to some remote rural venues. The rest were in the midwest, with the finale in Carnegie Hall at the end of November. Michelle came on the bus for a couple of hops along the way. Scott and I passed time harmonizing with guitars in the bus. The lead singer of the Halifax Three —a Halifax kid with Irish blood, a broad grin, and a rich, silky tenor named Denny Doherty—often joined in. His voice, like Scott's, was an instrument of breathtaking delicacy and precision. Once we got ripped and Denny and the three of us staggered through the French Quarter in New Orleans doing Bo Diddley's "Who Do You Love." He wanted out of his group. We usually broke off these jams with promises to keep in touch, maybe get something going someday.

The "Hoot Tour" was never conceived as a political event, but in the south during the end of 1963, if you were white, on a bus, and played a guitar and sang for a living, it didn't matter—you *were* political. Suddenly we found ourselves in the thick of the civil rights movement.

Racial strife was rampant—Greensboro, North Carolina, Greenville, South Carolina, Lake Charles, Louisiana, all-white state college campuses, Georgia, Mississippi, Louisiana, Alabama. At the University of Alabama, I announced a Josh White song and before we could start, we were interrupted by fans chanting, "Nig-GER, Nig-GER." Without thinking, I yelled back, "You people shouting are real crude." There was applause.

In one city, we were met by some white students wielding Louisville Sluggers and shouting, "Nigger lovers go home." Fred Geezinslaw walked off the bus and got socked in the nose. Other musicians and crew got roughed up. The bigoted thugs ordered us back on the bus and out of town. One less show to do. We played to empty halls and angry jeers. Michelle was with us when we decided we would be safer traveling in our own car than on a bus that was a target of such lunacy.

The day we were scheduled to play in Jackson, Mississippi, a telegram arrived at our hotel from the headquarters of the Student Nonviolent Coordinating Committee in Memphis. We were advised that a Jackson city ordinance essentially prohibited blacks from entering the city auditorium. The police were arresting any black within a hundred yards and did not want a test of the local law in the courts. We all got together and by majority vote decided to boycott Jackson and any segregated venue. When word got out by radio, local TV, and the wire services that we had refused to play, the city's rednecks went crazy, smashing hotel windows, baiting us with chants of "Nigger lovers," and surrounding the hotel.

Tension was high, nerves were frayed. Fortunately, I had asked Dick to stash my bag of grass in a bus depot locker because he was straighter-looking. I didn't want either of us getting billy-clubbed or cattle-prodded over a little weed. We considered pulling out, but our New York management didn't want to blow the $2,000 job. At one point, our Schlitz beer people called the tour promoter and offered to buy out two shows completely, just to fly us to the West Indies for some radio spots. Our hopes soared. The "Hoot" promoter refused. We were locked in.

We told SNCC that we would play a free concert instead at Tougaloo College in the heart of the state. Tougaloo was mostly black but officially integrated and a showcase of civil rights advocacy. The campus was in the sticks and none of us could hide our fear. The first thing we saw from inside the bus was a large cross burned into the lawn beside the campus church. We met with a white Tougaloo administrator. He had been beaten by Ku Klux Klansmen nights earlier when he tried to attend a meeting in a black church. His face was still battered and bandaged. We were encountering the racial hatred of the deep south from its violent, lunatic core.

We performed that night in the church. Outside, black and white students milled around campus with walkie-talkies, looking for signs of a Klan attack. We heard occasional gunfire, shattering glass, and shouting in the distance. We were advised to rely on our own security—not the local police—for protection. We were warned to stay inside if there was a riot. It was a profoundly moving night. The young students, with tears in their eyes, walked up to the stage and asked us to sing freedom songs. We ended the show with all of us onstage, holding hands with our arms crossing our chests, a human chain for freedom. And we sang "We Shall Overcome." There were tears in most of our eyes as well. It felt as if our harmonies could carry a hundred miles into the night, soaring together with an emotional power that nearly ripped the church roof off.

With a week left on the "Hoot Tour," we were all looking forward to getting back to New York and the November 30 finale at Carnegie Hall. None of us had ever played there before. The bus was barreling through the midwest when the tour bass player, who had been grooving to music on a transistor radio, suddenly stood. "Hey, hold it, everybody," he shouted, pressing the radio to his ear, raising an arm for quiet. "This is too much. I just heard. Wait. Oh my God, I don't believe it. It's a bulletin. They say Kennedy's been killed in Dallas."

The show that night in Ohio was canceled and the bus drove all afternoon and night toward our next stop in Illinois. We were numb, devastated, eerily insulated from it all by the road.

Michelle went home to L.A. Every few hours we pulled into a motel or truck stop to check the news, shake off the unreality. Wherever we drove, the vacant faces in shock, the inarticulate mourning, the anger, disbelief, and sadness were the same. We had days earlier left one America divided by racist insanity; by nightfall we were pulling into another America united by grief.

The group returned to New York and I soon learned that, as a songwriter, I was inspired by romantic, rather than political, turmoil. I took a cramped but cozy place on Charles Street in the Village that had a large fireplace. The intensity of all our emotions—the pleasure, pain, passion, longing, love—made me deeply vulnerable to Michelle and awakened my muse. I was alone and the City felt cold and dreary. I eagerly awaited Michelle's return. I wrote "Monday, Monday" there in the cold of approaching winter. The song matched a lyrical theme of loss with a wistful melody bouncing around in my head. "Oh, Monday mornin', you gave me no warnin' of what was to be/Oh, Monday, Monday, how could you leave and not take me?"

That very question promptly came up for the first time in our marriage. Michelle called. "I've met a man out here," she said, "and I didn't intend for this to happen, but I like him very much. I've already gone to bed with him." I was stung. Adrenaline shot through me and made my heart thud. "Who is he?" I asked. He was an up-and-coming record producer her own age named Russ Teitelman, a former boyfriend of her sister's. She met him when she went back to L.A.

Anger, hurt, jealous rage—I felt all of it when she returned to Charles Street to patch things up. I couldn't bear to lose her. We were still a month short of our first anniversary. "I'll tear his fucking head off," I said. I tried to lay the guilts on her and she didn't like that. I hadn't grown up myself. In my mind, she did something she was not supposed to do. In my Virgo nature, everything must be perfect all the time. Everything should work properly and people should do exactly what they're supposed to do. Except me. I told her I was very disappointed in her behavior and that I found it inappropriate and indecent. I was very angry with her. I sulked. She didn't say much. She wasn't one for long serious discussions. When she was in a nervous situation, Michelle giggled like a little girl. She showed no remorse or guilt.

My actions more than anything else may have driven her out, caused her to look elsewhere. I needed to be in control, have everything be perfect. She was still growing up, she said; she needed to spread her wings. Russ was less controlling, ten years younger than me. By the time the talk moved to the bed, we were in much better shape. But she said she needed to go back to L.A. and think things over.

The first night she was gone again, I sat home alone, depressed and brokenhearted. I sat up all night and wrote "Go

Where You Wanna Go." My mother had given me that advice as a teenager seeking independence. The words now took on a more bitter, wounded edge: "You've got to go where you wanna go, do what you wanna do/With whomever you wanna do it, babe." I thought of her making love to another man in L.A., and considered heading out there to retrieve her: "Three thousand miles, that's how far you'll go/And you said to me, 'Please, don't follow.'"

I didn't. I stayed home and received postcards from L.A. that were signed by Michelle. She wrote that she missed me and asked me to try to not hold this affair against her. And yet I couldn't seem to get her on the phone at her sister's place. So I finally called Rusty and said, "Tell me where Mitch is, so I can talk to her. I really want her back." I trusted Rusty as a friend and ally.

She started crying on the line. "John," she said, "I can't lie to you. Michelle is not *in* California. She's in New York City. She never left."

"Rusty," I said incredulously, "it's been over two weeks."

"She's in the City." In fact, she was right in the neighborhood at a small hotel around the corner. "Look through your window," Rusty said, imagining, perhaps, that Mitch might be just outside on the sidewalk. I called her at the hotel but didn't reach her. I felt even more alone now, knowing she was that close. I had no one to talk to in all of New York. I had never felt close enough to anyone there. I sat up with my guitar and began writing "Look Through Your Window." I not only felt jealous and lonely, I felt aimless and empty. I was jealous of anyone who had a purpose, a lover, something to do. I felt trapped. The streets were teeming with people whose lives looked so busy and content. Christmas was coming and I was no longer in control of my feelings. "Look through my window/To the street below/See the people hurrying by/With someone to meet/And someplace to go/And I know I should let go."

But I didn't. I finally reached her. She let out a scream. "How did you find me?"

"Rusty told me where you were."

She sighed. "Okay, so what do you want?"

"I want you to come home."

"When?"

"Now."

Half an hour later, I heard a bang at the door and she was home. She dropped her luggage, took off her coat, and our lives went on from there. We made love, fought all night until everything was right, and then never mentioned it again. It wasn't something I wanted to hold over her head for life. I knew Michelle wasn't real big on guilt or remorse, anyway. But that was not the point; I was happy to have her back.

By the time we took the stage at Carnegie Hall, it was the Journeymen who needed the separation. Scott and Dick bought a $15 guitar that day and, with no warning, Scott destroyed it onstage as a prank. This was Carnegie Hall! He really *had* flipped.

We were barely making it to the mike together in early 1964. Scott and I got on each other's nerves so frequently that we found ourselves communicating with each other through Dick. We needed two rented cars to get to dates, just so Scott and I could ride separately. Dick had met a woman he planned to marry and he wanted out. Bob Cavallo at the Shadows was convincing Scott he could thrive as a solo act. I had had it with commuting three times a week from our apartment to shows all over the country.

And by February the music industry was jolted by a sound—a force—that would alter all of our careers. It was a song called "I Want to Hold Your Hand." With little more than two minutes of electric rock music, the Beatles had virtually ended the era of commercial acoustic folk music. Our *New Directions* album pointed us only in one direction: out.

We struggled through a month at the Troubadour in L.A. with country singer Hoyt Axton. At spring semester's end, we had played out our bookings and Scott and Dick split for journeys of their own. But I wasn't finished with folk yet. I knew a dazzling young woman with a sweet, honest voice. She understood my waking in the night to capture a fragment of a melody or lyric that could grow into a song. She had been living with that kind of creative spontaneity for two years now and was beginning to get the hang of it her-

self. And if she were coached to perform live, she could be
part of my act on the road. That way we'd never have to be
apart and miss each other. I discussed it with her and she
was all for it. Michelle and I teamed up to start the New
Journeymen.

9

I TRIED TO IGNORE the British Invasion headed by the Beatles and Rolling Stones that summer and carry on in folk-pop music. I wasn't about to transform myself into a Mod or a Rocker just to keep up and hope for airplay. With the tension of the Journeymen gone, I was less drained and wrote more songs. Scott was in therapy; Dick was in love, preparing to get married and return to studio work.

Michelle and I spent hours each day in our place on Charles Street, working on harmony, pitch, and projection. There was no improving her stage presence. She was a knockout from every angle. Mitch had just turned twenty. She didn't look or act like a teenager anymore. She had changed—she was more self-possessed, independent, and feisty. And she wanted to make it in music.

One of the first songs we worked on was written during the winter, inspired by a bone-chilling walk through the snows of the Village. We were daydreaming of bright sun, blue skies, and palm trees. L.A. was home for Michelle and as winter dragged on in New York it was impossible not to miss the twelve-month California summer.

I started mumbling to some chords. "Hey," I said, "listen to this. 'All the leaves are brown, and the sky is gray/I've

been for a walk on a winter's day.' " To get out of the biting
cold, we had stopped into a church. We tried to look like we
belonged. "There's more," I said. " 'Oh, I got down on my
knees/And I pretend to pray.' " We both thought it worked.
It had a title: "California Dreamin'. "

We hooked up with a banjo accompanist who could also
sing. I had first known Marshall Brickman from hanging
around Washington Square. He and Dick Weissman were
friends and played banjo together in the Square. Later I
heard Marshall's fine folk work on the club and campus
circuit with the Tarriers. The new group would take the
Journeymen's fall bookings.

We rehearsed briefly, then moved to Sausalito to work all
summer with a well-known voice coach named Judy Davis. I
had saved about $30,000 from my three years as a Journey-
man.

We rented a large three-bedroom house overlooking Sausalito Bay. It was a gorgeous setting. Life was disciplined
and feverishly inspired. I declared that the New Journeymen
were in training. Every morning we awoke and launched
into Royal Canadian Air Force exercises on the carpet. Then
we'd drive over the San Rafael Bridge to Judy's. After a
rehearsal back home, we'd have dinner at the Barge or the
Trident restaurant on the waterfront in town. We stayed
away from parties or late nights out. Still, Michelle and I
managed to squabble enough at one point for her to storm
off with the poodle and car and head for L.A.

We were all set to hit the road when we learned that Marshall might get drafted. In the summer, the North Vietnam-
ese attacked a navy ship in the Gulf of Tonkin and LBJ was
thrusting us into an undeclared war in Southeast Asia. Uncle Sam wanted Marshall Brickman. So did the New Journeymen. We needed him more. Vietnam was already a cause
célèbre among intellectuals, artists, and campus radicals.

Some of our "peacenik" friends were classified 1-A by
their draft boards and about to receive induction notices
when they found legal ways to avoid the draft. Suddenly
everyone was an expert on the Selective Service loopholes
regarding deferments. The best one was the notorious 4-F,
which meant that you were sufficiently damaged—psycho-

logically or physically—to make you unfit for service. You couldn't top that one; 4-F was often called "forever." The catch was that a man's draft status would usually come up on job or college applications and having a 4-F rating tended to raise some questions about your fitness for just about everything else. It also eliminated all federal jobs, including some of the cushy post office gigs favored by hippies, from your future.

By that summer, a whole underground folklore emerged around beating the local draft board, as crazy anecdotes circulated from coast to coast about who got out, who didn't, and why. The desperation implied by some of the tactics—shooting off your big toe, taking huge amounts of drugs to simulate psychosis or catatonic depression, paying a woman friend to participate in a sham marriage long enough to become a deferable "husband," refusing to bear arms on religious grounds, refusing to bare ass on homosexual grounds—helped define the antiwar counter culture. So, of course, did burning draft cards and draft-dodging to Canada or Sweden.

But these were extreme solutions that could leave a young man either limping, hallucinating, or writing postcards back home for life. The most common and sensible way of staying out of the military was to apply for a deferment from the local board, whose classification could be appealed at a state and "presidential" level. There were, among others, deferments for graduate students, ghetto teachers, Peace Corps and Vista volunteers, married men, fathers, conscientious objectors, hardship cases, and men in medical, technical, or "critical" war-related fields. Consequently, the dread of getting a 1-A and the draft resistance movement led thousands of men to dramatically improvise some wild decisions that forever altered their lives.

There were, however, no automatic deferments for folksingers. Banjo-picking was not a "critical" industry in the Vietnam Era, at least not at the Pentagon. So Marshall found himself caught in the draft just when the war was beginning to touch more and more lives. Marshall kept his cool, got himself a deferment, and, when it was all squared away, the New Journeymen hit the road through the southeast and midwest. Michelle gradually loosened up onstage and the singing fell into place. We usually traveled together by plane and charged everything on a jointly held American Express card bearing all our names.

Michelle and I only blew one gig. Marshall showed up for a homecoming concert at a large football stadium with his banjo and we never made it. It was awkward sometimes for him to tour in such close quarters with a couple like us; it wasn't that simple for us either. We were finding it tough to work and live together around the clock.

For our Shoreham Hotel dates in Washington for Christmas, I thought the group needed a class lead vocalist like Scott. Marshall and I just weren't in his league. So I tracked down Denny Doherty, who had by now left the Halifax Three. We had always talked about playing together and now Denny could use the work.

Denny was broke and sharing a grungy pad at the Albert Hotel with his musician cronies. They had just spent six months playing electrified folk-rock sets, mostly between New York and Washington, as the Mugwumps. One roommate was the Halifax Three's guitarist from the "Hoot Tour" days, Zal Yanofsky. Another was the Mugwumps' harmonica player, John Sebastian. Those two were trying to get the Lovin' Spoonful going. The third roommate was the Mugwumps' singer, Cass Elliot.

I had heard incredible things about Cass when she led the Big Three out of Chicago with Tim Rose and Jim Hendricks. They had toured extensively on the campus and coffeehouse circuit and had lengthy engagements at the Bitter End downtown.

When Denny walked past the Village club and heard the voice—a gargantuan contralto that powered the noisy band behind her—he wandered in and saw Cass shimmying inside a flowing caftan. They became fast friends and kept in touch by swapping itineraries.

"I told her I was meeting you and she said she had grown up in Baltimore and Alexandria and that they were still talking about you at George Washington High," Denny said.

Cass had gone there, but we were about eight years apart. Her father owned a delicatessen not far from where I had

grown up. Denny had never stopped wanting to work with
her; she had never stopped wanting to sleep with him. "She
lets it all hang out, I'll tell ya that," Denny said. "And that's
about three hundred pounds of hangin' out. She's an amazing chick. When Hendricks was being hassled by his draft
board and given a 1-A, she married him just so he could beat
the draft. Can you imagine that?"

Denny said they were living hand-to-mouth, with no work
in sight. "Well," I said, "we've got two weeks at the Shoreham, fifteen hundred a week, and we're looking for a male
lead out front. Come on over for dinner tonight—just you,
Michelle, and me—and we'll see what happens."

We had moved to a more spacious apartment in a sleazy
area of the Lower East Side—on East 7th Street and Avenue
D. He was in great shape—lean, shaggy-haired, and goateed,
with fragile, angular features and intense blue eyes. To me,
he looked like some lute player in Elizabethan England.
"Cass and Zal are going crazy at the Albert," he said with
his Irish-Canadian gleam. "They went buzzing around the
place, yelling, 'He's got work! He's got work!' "

"Let's hope they're right."

After dinner, we drank wine, smoked grass, and went
across the street to fill a prescription for Eskatrol, a powerful
diet pill. We got a hundred of them and went to work.

Denny's voice blended beautifully with ours and we knew
right away we wanted him with us for the Shoreham a week
later. We went through all twenty-eight New Journeymen
songs and almost as many Eskatrols. After eighteen-hour
marathon rehearsals over several days, Denny had mastered
every vocal arrangement in time for Washington.

We made it through the Shoreham Christmas engagement
as a tight, confident opening act. We had good crowds who
came to the hotel club in good spirits, ready for a lift from
the headliner—Bill Cosby.

In early 1965, Marshall decided to quit the group. Like
Dick, the alienation of the road got to him and I couldn't
blame him. "It's strange," he said. "I was walking across
57th Street the other day and I had this peculiar vision.
There's that storefront that's like a huge mirror, only it's just
slightly distorted like a carnival funhouse effect. Anyway, I

saw myself carrying five instruments in the cold on my way to another gig. I looked at myself in this mirror and heard myself say, 'Is this what my grandfather escaped the Cossacks in Russia for, so I could do *this?*' I came to the conclusion that it would be better if I didn't play banjo anymore."

We hired a friend of ours named Eric Hord on guitar and banjo for the last dates and Marshall got a job as a writer for "Candid Camera" alongside Joan Rivers. But we still had the American Express card. By late winter, the balance was in the high four figures.

We returned to New York and for the first time in years I didn't know what to do next. I was at the end of the line with folk. My taste for it was gone and so was the market. Our money was gone. Mitch and I had matching motorcycles to show for it all. Acoustic music was dead. Electric rhythm guitars, flashy lead solos, and crashing drums were in. Denny had tried to turn me on to the Beatles. I resisted. He was a fanatic, but he told me there was one Beatlemaniac who was *really* hung up on them. "You got to meet Cass," Denny said. "She's dying to meet you."

The afternoon before she was due at the apartment, Denny took us to the East Side loft of an artist friend of his. We had begun to hear incredible stories about an exotic drug called LSD. Very few people seemed to know about it and only way-out artists and musicians could cop it. The talk was always mysterious. "Acid" apparently wasn't like any other drug. "Speed, grass, hash, and ups just make you high," people said. The word on acid was that it made you hallucinate. The stories we heard astonished and lured us. On good "trips," people thought they were Jesus Christ. On bummer trips, people thought they were cockroaches. On weird trips, people spoke with Christ and thought *he* was a cockroach. Acid sounded like a major gamble on your brain chemistry. Denny's pal had plenty for all four of us.

We bought two caps for $10 apiece. They looked like vitamins. We cabbed back downtown and as we pulled up to our corner, I saw this behemoth of a woman dressed in a maroon tent. Our block always had its share of junkie stabbings and comatose, drooling derelicts. But this was a new one. "Jesus, what is *that?*"

"That," Denny said with a grin, "is Cass."

We all came in and small-talked about the folk scene, mutual friends around the Village, the Beatles, Alexandria. Cass was a brassy, self-mocking riot. "I used to work in my father's deli," she said, "but I ate so much behind the counter that I got stuck and couldn't move."

She said she wanted to break out of folk and go into musicals. "But Barbra Streisand's getting all my parts instead."

We chopped up the acid and I snorted my line first. It stung so badly that I drank the second in water. Then Michelle took hers, followed by Cass and Denny. Forty minutes later, we were all rolling on top of each other on the floor in the dark, cackling and howling and shrieking like maniacs. We laughed uncontrollably for what seemed like hours. We were, without question, the four funniest people on earth.

Michelle and I had a giant wrought-iron birdcage with an elaborate filigree design. We turned off the lights and placed a candle inside the cage. We took turns wiggling our fingers just over the flame, so the whole room would glow and shimmer and vibrate. Colors flowed like liquid rainbows into and out of the cage, over my body, into my body and out again. A Chinese fan overhead gently blew waves of air through the walls. The walls and floor were breathing, pulsing membranes. A fluttering, menacing hand would slowly descend over the candle from outside the cage like a giant claw as we all screamed in mock terror.

"NO ONE MUST LEAVE THE CAGE!" the voice of the Hand would announce.

We imagined that we were all birds grooming each other and made up senseless bird jokes that made perfect sense at the time.

Cass and Michelle sat transfixed around a candle on the floor and confided to each other about men. Cass couldn't keep her eyes off Denny. "Is he hot or *what?"* she whispered. Michelle just gazed over and nodded.

I scooped out globs of Red Devil sandwich spread with my finger and stuffed up my ears and one nostril with it.

Denny spent two hours prying it all out. "It's okay," I said. "We'll save it for leftovers."

Then he guided me down to the floor, folded my arms

around two stereo speakers pressed against my unclogged ears, and ordered me to listen to *Meet the Beatles*.

"Okay, man," Denny said sternly. "I want you to listen to these guys once and for all. I know you think they're jive, but you're wrong. I want you to listen and listen and just keep listening."

I sat up and obediently asked, "Then what do I do when I'm finished?"

"I want you to listen some more and then I want you to write songs. Songs that sound like these songs. I want you to write and write and keep writing songs that are as good as these." He crouched down beside me and clamped a fist around my forearm. His face was two inches from mine and he was staring right through me. "No more folk. Folk is dead. You got it?"

I nodded compliantly and fell back to the floor with my head on a pillow. And then, surrendering my consciousness to this awesome, exhilarating maiden flight on acid, I closed my eyes and met the Beatles.

By daybreak we were all still awake but coming down fast. Denny kicked over the cage and I blew out the candles. We made coffee, then slept off the acid for two days. It had been an extraordinary mind-blowing trip. When the four of us tried to start the day, we all knew two things were clear: one, that our lives would never be the same; and two, that we immediately wanted to score more acid. There was no going back now.

Within a month, I had written about thirty new songs. Acid, Denny's hypnotic spell, ambition, Lennon and McCartney—*something* had unleashed my creative energy. Cass had gone home to the Washington area to start a solo career, but she was eager to join us if we started a group again. Michelle, Denny, and I were stoned one night and discussing what we should do next. I had come around to the realization that electric instruments and rhythm sections had to be reckoned with. I understood more about the Beatles revolution. I had a new stack of songs to rehearse and arrange and an idea that two guys and two girls could make a great pop-rock group.

There was a suitcase in our bedroom with about $7,000

cash from savings and the last concerts. And there was the American Express card. Marshall was going to be with us in spirit.

"We can go anywhere we want," Denny said, looking at a world map on the wall of the apartment.

"How do we decide?" Michelle asked.

"Let's blindfold Mitch," I said, "spin her around, and wherever her finger touches, we go."

We spun her around several times. She stepped to the wall, giggling, finger pointing straight. She touched the map and tore off the blindfold, keeping her finger in place. I looked close and sighed loudly. "Phew, you did great, baby. St. Thomas, Virgin Islands."

The three of us found Paradise during our ten days at Villa Fairview. I bought a green Gucci bag for the drugs. The Caribbean was where we wanted to be. We could get a group together there to make new music. When we came back to New York, we knew that we had to get out of there.

"Let's get a family together," Denny said. "Go down to the Islands till the money runs out and swim home."

We got down to work. Mitch and I drove our cycles through an early spring cold snap to tell my mother, Rosie, and Susie about our plans. We got as far as Philly and froze. We rented a car with a U-Haul trailer for our stuff and the cycles. We parked the car around the corner from Rosie's apartment complex, put on our coats, and came roaring in on the cycles. "They're here! They're here!" everyone screamed. I walked in pounding my mittens together, looking frostbitten. I was wearing a thrift-shop raccoon coat. "You must be freezing," they said. "We're tough," I said. "We're rugged and indestructible."

Mitch used the credit card to buy camping equipment and we loaded up on fifty hits of acid in a feedbag. Mitch called Rusty in L.A. After the trip to Mexico with Scott, she should have expected something like this. Mitch told her that we had bought her and her boyfriend, Peter Pilafian, two tickets to the Virgin Islands. They only had three days to make it to New York.

That day they packed, closed up their apartment, and got a Driveaway car that got them to Philadelphia, speeding nonstop for seventy hours. Denny drove down and met them at the car-return office and made it to JFK Airport twenty minutes before takeoff. There wasn't enough time to crate or check Peter's upright bass, so I had to buy an extra ticket for the bass.

We decided to take Laura along and she flew in from Washington. She was five and a half. Denny was there, plus Eric "the Doctor" Hord, our latest New Journeymen picker, and his girlfriend. We looked like spaced-out vagrants. I took a hit of mescaline before boarding the plane. I turned on anyone who wanted to.

When we got to St. Johns, we pitched tents at a campsite we affectionately named Camp Torture. Michelle and I had a large tent with cots inside and candles for light. The mosquitoes were fat enough to be the national bird of the Virgin Islands.

Poor Laura hated insects and was devoured by mosquitoes. At night she often went screaming from her little pup tent and crawled into ours. Denny once killed a scorpion with a piece of driftwood just inches from Laura's bare foot.

We spent our first weeks at Camp Torture snorkeling on acid, barbecuing, skinny-dipping, watching sunsets, and rationing money. Our favorite thing was to get stoned and rent a fifty-foot trimaran and sail around the island through the night. We'd stare up at the stars on a large net just off the water and let the waves splash over us till the sun came up. Laura knew when we were tripping. "Daddy," she'd ask, "are you and Uncle Denny and Michelle going to get funny now?"

We got real funny all the time and tried rehearsing. I offered everyone some acid before starting, to loosen things up. "You mean you can rehearse with that stuff?" someone asked.

"You mean you can rehearse *without* it?" I answered.

It was the first time that we tried playing electric and it went well after a while. We worked on the arrangements to tunes like "Monday, Monday," "California Dreamin'," and "Go Where You Wanna Go." We had little money or acid left, but we felt ready for work. Michelle and I ferried to the island of St. Thomas and met Hugh Duffy, the owner of Duffy's, a sixteen-room beachfront boardinghouse on a narrow street in Charlotte Amalie called Creeque Alley. "The competition's killing me next door," Duffy said. "They got a rock band from Jersey that know every number off the radio."

"We've got a pretty good band ourselves and we're between things for now," I said. He said okay. We went back and closed up Camp Torture to move in to Duffy's. He refurbished his nightclub for us and lent us some equipment to play with—a couple of mikes and a huge Ampeg amp we all plugged into. The Doctor and Peter had scoured the island and found two electric guitars, a Fender bass, and a drum kit. We rehearsed hard, spending hours in our room on the top floor overlooking the water. The late evenings with Michelle, lying together in our bed with the ocean breezes and sunset light coming in—and the drugs—were exquisitely romantic and serene. The feedbag was almost empty.

Just then Cass, who was no longer with Hendricks, and my eighteen-year-old nephew Billy Throckmorton showed up. They were close friends from Washington. Cass still lusted wildly after Denny, and he still resisted her. Cass wanted to sing with us in the worst way.

She flashed a small glass vial filled with a clear liquid. "One drop on the tip of your tongue, honey," she said, "and you're gone!" If that was Cass's way to make friends and become the fourth singer, it didn't hurt her chances. We stayed stoned constantly now as we rehearsed with Cass on the beach by flickering bonfires all night and through the day. But her voice was too low for the range of our material and the sound I wanted. And she kicked in her 2¢ about some of the arrangements. She was stubborn. She and I were dueling Virgos. Besides, Mitch, Denny, and I were three stringbeans and she was huge. The sound was off and the look didn't fit, either. So I kept her out. But she was determined to be part of the crowd and she and Rusty became close. Rusty was pregnant and was going to have the baby, even if it jeopardized her relationship with Peter. Rusty was in her own new world of motherhood and kept her distance from our antics. She needed a confidante and Cass needed an ally.

Billy was good-looking, stoned, a gentle, guitar-playing hippie who read *Siddhartha* and *Journey to the East* by the ocean and meditated before any of us knew how to spell OM. He was also meditating intensely on Rusty and couldn't keep himself from hitting on her. I urged him to stay away, but I could hardly blame him. She was delightful to be around and awfully attractive in T-shirts, white cutoffs, and long dark hair.

Billy was walking Rusty home one night through a bad neighborhood and got beat up. A sailing instructor's girl-friend looked him over for a fraction of a second too long and the guy decided to go after Billy. Rusty, about three or four months pregnant, jumped the guy, yanked his hair, but couldn't get him off. Billy's bruised face bled and he vomited all over the place. Back at Duffy's, Rusty helped him into the shower and lovingly nursed him through the night.

Still, Rusty and Cass swam and hung out together in the daytime. She and Rusty took our Yamaha 120 up the mountain to go swimming in Magens Bay on the other side of the island. Cass sat on the backseat. Who would have thought the little 120 could haul the two of them all the way up? But it did, and they only had to walk it the last couple hundred feet after it finally gave out under the weight. They waited on tables at night by Duffy's lounge. From the stage at Duffy's, it was clear that Cass had great inner strengths to help her survive the jackasses who insulted her. The town was crawling with drunken Marines and sailors on their way home from Vietnam. They wouldn't leave the poor woman alone. "Hey, fatty," they'd call out, "you forgot our orders —or did you eat them all yourself?" She was proud and stoical, but withstood more humiliation in a week than a human deserved in a lifetime. She was somehow able to block out the hurt and rage and rise above them all.

At Creeque Alley, I started hurting a little myself. One night Michelle came up to the bedroom. I had been writing songs for hours. Michelle seemed moody.

"Where you been, baby?" I asked, happy to see her.

"John, I've got something to tell you." I shifted around to

face her. "I was walking along the water and I saw Denny in
the distance, standing near the rocks, staring off at the most
gorgeous sunset. I walked up and joined him. There was—I
don't know—something going on between us, an attraction."

"What are you talking about? You're my wife. He's my
best friend."

"Oh, we didn't *do* anything. Don't get angry. I'm just
trying to be honest. We sat on the rocks and the water came
rushing up and the sun went down and night fell and it was
all so . . ."

"Romantic?" My heart sank again, like in New York,
when she went around the corner to California to think
things through with Russ Teitelman. *Denny?*

She paused. "Yeah, it *was* romantic. I'm very attracted to
Denny. I just wanted you to know that, in case anything
happens."

Our money supply was dwindling fast and the band was
getting killed at the door. And we were doing Duffy in. He
had a mild heart attack but was soon back at work. We *did*
kill the lounge business. The band next door was drawing
big crowds with tacky copy versions of R&B, Beatles, and
Beach Boys tunes. He moved us out so he could at least rent
our five rooms to paying tourists.

We took over an unfurnished hovel of a house nearby and
fell behind with the first month's rent. Community relations
were getting tense. The town was filled with slick tourists,
servicemen, and suave cosmopolitan expatriates. We dressed
in rags, we were rockers, and we stood out. And we owed
everyone in town money, from Duffy to a local seamstress
who embroidered us brightly matching shirts to perform in
to help support her blind son.

I went island-hopping to draw cash or traveler's checks
against my credit card. No luck. Finally, one American Express officer told me he would be happy to help me. He took
my card and said he'd be right back. I was sure I had it
made. When he returned, he pulled out some pinking shears,
mumbled something about a $30,000 unpaid balance, and
smilingly sliced the card in half. That one hurt.

And our "family" now often included new members from

the town who had been drifting in and out of Duffy's, trying to be part of the scene. We were the island's open house and everyone was welcome to our commune. The governor finally ordered us off the island because he thought his nephew was doing drugs with the crazies at Creeque Alley.

Laura took to hustling sailors and tourists for breakfast. I once watched her from across the street as she walked to a sidewalk café on the waterfront. She told a table of sailors that the Styrofoam cup she was holding was loaded with chemicals that would blow the island up if they didn't treat her to her pancakes. These grunts had been to Nam. They were probably shell-shocked and on their way home. They weren't taking any chances. No one has never seen a little kid go through a stack of pancakes so fast. A born actress.

Cass continued to rehearse with us for kicks, but her voice was still too low. Then a lead pipe dropped from a scaffolding at Duffy's and hit her on the head. She was taken to the local infirmary. Denny came to visit her and she tried to seduce him at her bedside. He pulled away. The pipe hadn't hurt her sex drive, but there was one lasting side effect of the blow to her head. When she opened her mouth to sing at our next rehearsal, her voice was a full tone higher. Her harmonies never sounded better. They were perfect now. "Cass," I said, "I've got some good news. You're in. You can rehearse with us."

In midsummer, we knew it was time to split. There was no money for food; a second month's rent was due. Rusty was almost five months pregnant. Susie had become frantic about Laura because it was just too hard for us to keep in touch by phone. Laura missed her mommy and brother. She flew home, riddled with scabs from her bites.

We had our vocal lineup and an album's worth of material that sounded commercial. We were restless. We knew what was on the radio. Some of our Village friends who had lived hand-to-mouth bohemian lives were now conquering the Mainland. Roger McGuinn and David Crosby, who had sung with the New Christie Minstrels, had "Mr. Tambourine Man" with the Byrds; Barry McGuire's antiwar song, "Eve of Destruction," was moving up fast; and we had even started to hear the first release by the Lovin' Spoonful, "Do

You Believe in Magic?" Denny and Cass were filled with envy. The last time we had seen their old Mugwumps buddies, Żal Yanofsky and John Sebastian, they were struggling in the Village. I had a friendly argument with John in my apartment over which notes were in a C-major chord versus a C-major 7th. Then he sang "Magic" for me. "What difference does it make *what's* in a C-major 7th," I told him. "That's a really nice song." Even Frank Werber had a winner after the Kingston Trio and Journeymen faded; he was managing the We Five and their song "You Were on My Mind" was all over the radio. The music business was passing us by, but now we were ready to make our move.

"Incredible, eh, it's all electric now and rock," Denny said one night as "Tambourine Man" drifted in over the radio. "We're all evolving toward the same sound at the same time without really communicating with each other about it."

"We're all obviously taking the same drugs," I said.

We organized a garage sale of most of our camping and musical gear and anything we couldn't take with us. We tried to get off the island quietly. We split up in groups at the airport to look inconspicuous. That wasn't easy with Cass in tow. We went at night so there couldn't be any credit checks done on me. Finally, one airline was willing to accept my last check without a credit card. We had about $150 from the garage sale.

I told Michelle to put on her sexiest dress, a slinky red number, for a quick run through the island casino. Denny couldn't take the pressure. It was our last $150. He stayed outside. Michelle walked to the craps table like it had her name on it. All eyes at the casino locked on the blond vision in red. Within five minutes, she had rolled seventeen straight passes for $1,500. By the end, she had a pair of monogrammed gift dice from the house and a few thousand bucks in a brown paper bag.

And we believed in magic.

10

DAYS AFTER GETTING BACK to the Lower East Side, I came to the conclusion that New York was no longer the place for us to live and make music. Music was happening out west. Michelle was delighted. She and I dressed up as a straight couple—me in a business suit, Mitch in a dress—and went to U-Drive-It to see if they had cars to be driven west. They did—a silver-blue Cadillac limousine with about nine miles on it. Only Denny and Billy Throckmorton were left in the City from our "family" and they decided to make the trek with us. Cass had already gone to L.A. to reconnect with Jim Hendricks; Rusty was in L.A. too, having her baby. Peter Pilafian was off in Paris working with a film crew.

We filled the tank with premium, loaded the stash bag with acid, grass, brown Lebanese hash, and Black Beauties, leaned a couple of guitars on the jump seats, and headed west.

I had driven across America three or four times but never in such style. Never on such drugs. We stuck flowers in the air-conditioning vents and all over the interior. The radio soundtrack for the summer of 1965 was incredible: "Satisfaction," "I Got You, Babe," the *Help!* album, "California Girls," "Like a Rolling Stone," "The Tracks of My Tears."

We all sang along and added our own harmonies and instrumental "hooks." The hits were exciting and varied and I was hungry and determined to be a part of that world.

I was so accustomed to acid by then that I could function reasonably well on it anytime. Except during the initial rush. All I did was laugh. The first hour on acid was always a carnival. Everyone was a clown. I never had a bummer. The trip for me was colors. I'd switch on the wipers if I was driving, and follow them from side to side like a cat. Denny was good enough between Pennsylvania and Illinois to point out every hundred miles or so that it still wasn't raining. But it *was* raining—colors were pouring down from the sky. The wipers were spraying and spreading silky, iridescent ribbons of color across the windshield. They drained off and spilled onto the road. The rhythmic sweep of the blades had me entranced.

Billy played guitar and we practiced our three-part harmonies. We drove in shifts so we didn't have to stop overnight. Michelle and I were entitled to conjugal visits on the plush backseat. With Billy and Denny driving up front, we'd wedge the glass partition closed with a towel draped over it and take full advantage of our eagerly awaited privacy.

We rarely left the interstate system. We needed a repair job in Denver and then took an unscheduled detour into the Rockies. Along a winding mountain road, we pulled into a diner. A biker lady and her teenage son dismounted from their monster chopper and walked up to us. She asked for our autographs. "I *know* who you are," she said politely, "but I'm drawing a blank."

"So are we."

"This is so embarrassing. Aren't you people, like, *somebody?*" she asked.

"Aren't we all?" I smiled, taking the pen from her hand.

We passed the autograph book around, signed, and gave it back.

The terrain and vistas were so spectacular. We hiked down into Bryce Canyon. It was not to be missed on acid. At the bottom, we perched ourselves in the sturdy limbs of petrified trees and stared at the faces in the rocks. The rocks stared back at the faces in the trees. We gazed in wonder at the fleet of cotton-puff clouds sailing through an ocean of sky. The sun would vanish, filling the canyon with shadow, like a cool, dark liquid rushing over our hot skin. A tour group came down after us and their ranger guide almost choked when he saw our bodies. "I don't know *what* they're doing here." We lay perfectly still like mechanical creatures in a theme-park jungle as the tourists approached and clicked away on their cameras.

I was doing eighty across the Salt Flats in Utah one night and everyone else was asleep. Mitch was curled up on the front seat beside me. The window was open and the wind roared into the car and across my face. I had been putting together a melody and lyrics through the night.

I must have been zeroing in on Denny and Michelle and their Caribbean flirtation, how she described the moonrise, the sunset, the sailboats in the water—and sitting on the rocks with Denny. Denny hadn't even tried to *kiss* her, she told me. It was as if Denny's hesitation had bruised her ego. Denny wouldn't be able to hold out indefinitely once Michelle set her mind to breaking him down. I kept playing with lyrics in my head. "Don't get me mad, don't tell me lies/Don't make me sad, just keep me high." I stopped the limo and got out a guitar: "Straight Shooter" was finished and now I had to hear it aloud. "Baby, are you holdin', holdin' anything but me?"

I sat by the road in the middle of a vast, barren stretch of the flats and worked out the chords and harmonies. Then I woke the others up. We smoked some grass and silently grooved on a neon stream of rose light ooze across the deep-blue rim of the eastern horizon.

We dropped off the car in San Francisco and had almost no money left. I called my mother and she was good enough to wire me $100. We all stayed in one room of the same Chinatown dive the Journeymen used and I began to pick up stronger vibes between Denny and Michelle. I tried to block out my suspicions, but it wasn't entirely possible. Not on mind-expanding chemicals, it wasn't.

We tried to get in to see my old buddy Werber. He was too busy for us now. The We Five was breaking big with "You

Were on My Mind" and he made it clear that we were not on his.

Michelle drove our rented car when we got to L.A. because she knew her way around. We hit the Harbor Freeway downtown, but it wasn't the way she remembered it. It was the second week of August, the temperature was up near a hundred, and we drove straight into the nightmare of the 1965 Watts riots. There were police roadblocks, snipers firing at cars, thousands of National Guardsmen in town, gangs on a rampage, and fires everywhere at night. The smell of incineration was hanging heavy in the smog. We were brought way down in a hurry.

We moved into an old folks' home called the Padre. Most evenings we sat in the sauna together. Someone must have been tipped off: Our Mustang was stolen with all our stuff in it and was found days later, stripped and empty, in Mexico.

By this time, I was certain Michelle and Denny were getting it on. It was time to write another heartbreak song. "I Saw Her Again" was done partly in the "other man's" voice. "I saw her again last night/And you know that I shouldn't/ To string her along's just not right/If I couldn't I wouldn't." But apparently, Denny just couldn't help himself. "I'm in way over my head/Now she thinks that I love her. . . . But what can I do, I'm lonely too."

Most of the chorus could have been in either of our voices. "Every time I see that girl/You know I wanna lay down and die/But I really need that girl/You know I'm livin' a lie."

We rehearsed the song for the next few days and it sounded like a keeper. Denny had a sheepish look on his face. He knew what it was about. I felt he deserved some credit for writing—or at least inspiring—the song, so I named him as co-writer.

We caught up with Cass at Hendricks's place in Hollywood and were invited to crash there with them. They were trying to write songs for $25. By now, Hendricks was living with a girlfriend named Vanessa. The pad was crowded and hot, but we didn't mind roughing it. The gas had been turned off, so there was no stove to cook on. Denny figured a way to remove and rewire the heating plate in the bathroom wall so we could cook on it over the toilet.

Cass's status with us was still vague in everyone's mind but hers. She was so determined to be a part of the group that she would iron in the living room while we rehearsed and add her soaring vocals to our efforts. The windows rattled when she cut loose, and her voice drove everyone's energy up. When she sang, the harmonies fell into place and flowed. Cass never even put the iron down in the kitchen and still knew every lick from the islands. There was no keeping her out any longer. "Okay," I told her after one long evening session. "You're one of us."

An old friend from the Village, Barry McGuire, was a frequent visitor. He was riding high. "Eve of Destruction" was becoming a major hit and antiwar anthem. He drove a massive Royal Enfield cycle and wore heavy boots with spurs on them. He came up with a lead for us: Nick Venet. He got Venet to come over to check us out. Venet had played on some early Beach Boys sessions and produced a few L.A. acts. He wasn't really big time, but he hustled. Venet loved what he heard. He wanted to sign us up to a management deal and get us a label. We needed instant cash.

"Okay," he said, "I understand. I'll sell my car and there's about fifteen hundred right there. That'll be like a down payment on a ten-grand advance, which I can get together in a week or so. Whattya say?"

"Sounds okay," I said.

McGuire was recording an album to follow up "Destruction." When he came over from his sessions, he asked how everything had gone with Venet. "Fine," I said. "I never thought a recording deal would hinge on a guy selling his car."

"You know how it is," McGuire said. "There are hundreds of new groups all over this town. Everyone's got an angle." He paused, then said, "You know, it occurred to me last night at the studio, you guys should meet Lou Adler. He's the head of my label, Dunhill, and he's producing the sessions. He's got a real good ear . . . ."

"Of course. He signed *you.*"

"There ya go," he smiled, "and he's a businessman. I think he'd go for your sound."

At Western recording studios in Hollywood, McGuire

walked us past Lou's sleek black Caddie in the parking lot and brought us in to meet him. He was swarthy, dapper, and slight, with a wary, intense face that peeked out from a thicket of dark curly hair. Lou was married to Shelley Fabares of "The Donna Reed Show" and a couple of Elvis movies. McGuire said he was a real tough, uneducated but streetwise Jewish kid from the hard-edged Mexican section of L.A. He had produced some Sam Cooke records. This was the closest we had ever been to a real mogul.

Lou was mild-mannered and cordial. We were dressed in funky jeans and shirts—except Cass. She was draped in one of her magenta muumuus. Denny and I looked scruffy and wasted. Michelle was as ravishing as ever.

Lou had actually heard of us. It never occurred to me that we were "knowns." Acid was a great equalizer. It made you lose things. You could lose your ego; you could lose your keys; you could lose your life on acid. Lou knew my name as a Journeyman and writer of some Kingston Trio songs; he had seen Cass on TV with the Big Three; and he had heard of Denny with the Halifax Three. This loosened us up as McGuire got ready to do a track.

During a break, he asked us to sing. So with me on a 12-string guitar, the four of us went into the cramped sound-proofed Studio 3. We sailed right through "California Dreamin'." Lou came out with his palms against his shaking head. "I can't believe my eyes and ears!" he shouted. "I've never heard anything like this in my life. It's a great track," he said. "Let me hear another."

"No sweat," I said. We broke in right on the money with the hymnlike G-major opening harmonies of "Monday, Monday."

"Baah-daah, baah-daah-daah-daah.

"Baah-daah, baah-daah. . . . Monday, Monday."

We sang our asses off. Our sound could have filled a cathedral. It was the first time we ever achieved what Denny and I called the Fifth Voice: the ringing, resonant overtones that vibrate through the harmonies and into your limbs and chest when they are perfectly tuned. It was like creating an extra voice in the mix. We were flying. Adler emerged more ani-

mated than before. "I'd love Barry to do the lead on it for
his album. You guys have the backing vocals all ready."

After signing, we agreed to do the back-up vocals. Barry
tried to sing the lead to our backing in the headphones, but
it just didn't sound right. Denny recut the lead and we
played it back over the big studio system. It sounded great.
Only Denny was meant to sing that lead.

We went through another half a dozen songs for him. "I
want a single out immediately," he said. "I want you guys
here in the morning and we'll sign the deals."

"Lou," I said, "we don't even have a place to live. And if
we did, we wouldn't be able to get there because we have no
car, no food, nothing."

"Don't worry about a thing."

The next morning we got stoned and went to the label
office. We were so excited that we signed everything that was
put in front of us. We didn't get our own business manager
to check the contracts; we didn't negotiate the percentages
on royalties or anything. We took what we were offered. It
was pretty low—5 percent on 90 percent of retail sales. We
didn't know what hit us. After less than a month in L.A., we
had a deal to cut an album.

Dunhill gave us a $5,000 advance for the album and I got
$5,000 as an advance against songwriting and publishing
royalties. He arranged to buy a used car through a friend
who owned a dealership in East L.A. We picked out a black
'61 Buick convertible with huge fins and a white top and
named it Harold the Bleak. He asked if there was anything
else we needed. We told him a guitarist friend of ours was in
jail back east, busted on a marijuana rap. Lou made one call.
"You'll have your guitarist here tomorrow," he said.

We drove back and showed off our new car to Hendricks,
McGuire, and our friends. It was beginning to sink in. Then
Nick Venet drove up. "Well, guys," he said, "I got your
advance all set. Got a great deal on my car." This was terrible. It now seemed like we had a car and he didn't. I tried to
apologize.

"You're too late, Nick. We're signed. Sorry."

The Beatles played the Hollywood Bowl late that summer
on a hot, tropical L.A. night. We had no tickets, but we had

Harold the Bleak. I took some acid and drove with the top down all across the top rim of L.A. and found a spot near the Bowl. We stopped and looked down at the Bowl, which glowed in the darkness like a jewel. The roar of the delirious fans carried through the night into the stillness of the hills and canyons. We were mesmerized. It was an awesome sight. "Okay, guys," I said, "I'm going to make you a promise right now and I want you to remember it. Two promises. First, within a year, we are going to play the Bowl. Second, we are going to win a Grammy for one of our songs."

Not that the Beatles had to start worrying. We didn't even have a name yet. We solved that problem while watching a TV interview with the Hell's Angels one night as one of their bikers was explaining how they called their women "mamas." Our newest member, Cass, was on a sassy roll, mouthing off to the TV. "Well," she said, "we've got mamas in our gang and we've got papas, too. You can call us the Mamas and the Papas."

Lou opened charge accounts for us around town so we could at least start *looking* like stars. The outfits got brighter, weirder. We started our recording sessions and worked eighteen hours at a time. I was buzzing around on speed and acid and spent dozens of hours getting to know Lou behind the board as our producer. He and I were most involved in the overall musical direction of the album—the vocal and instrumental mix, the overdubbing, the song selection, the album package, the business side, music publishing. He showed me around to all the "in" spots around L.A. I was out much of the time, intensely absorbed in our new career.

Soon after signing, Dunhill opened accounts for us at hip clothing stores and financed a move into a decaying, drab-green house below Sunset on Flores Street. We called it the Green House. I often stayed on in the studio with Lou after recording sessions, so my schedule wasn't the same as Michelle's. We were getting to bed at different times. She sometimes behaved in an aloof way, and I was consumed with our debut album. There was too much on the line now. We were so close. But the vocal arrangements had to be perfect. If we were going to offer anything unique, it would be the intricate harmonies of a mixed quartet.

The control board was like a palette to me. With overdubbing, instrumental tracks, and string arrangements, the studio allows you to build a song tier by tier, until it sounds like fifty people recorded together. I had little time for going out and partying and still too little money to live it up. Michelle and I were growing apart. Sometimes she was hard to find back at the Green House.

It never occurred to me to check in Denny's room.

One late morning I woke up and Michelle was already gone. I looked downstairs in the kitchen and living room; I checked in Cass's room. Then it hit me. I knocked on Denny's door.

Denny was under the sheets and Michelle was dressed and sitting on the covers. My blood turned hot, but I stayed as calm as possible. "All right," I said, "what the fuck is going on with you two? We better sort this shit out now."

They both squirmed very quietly, very uneasily. "Well, as you see, there is something happening here between me and Michelle," Denny said, clearing his throat nervously. "I'm sorry. I tried hard to . . ."

"I can imagine," I said, cutting him off as I glanced at Michelle. "I'd have trouble holding off too. I just wish I had known when we signed the contracts. Who the hell signs a five-year deal to work together when the other guy in the group's got a thing going with your wife? That's insane. I never would have done this to myself. I'm not *that* crazy."

"I always thought we should have come out and said something to head it off, way back at Duffy's," Denny said. "I didn't want you to find out like this." We both looked at Michelle.

"I thought you said nothing really happened back then, Mitch," I said sternly. "I can't believe it's been going on that long?"

"It hasn't, really," Denny said for her, trying to ease through. "Just a couple of weeks—if that. Since we got to L.A., really, I guess, maybe the Landmark."

"Okay, okay, I don't want to hear about it." They saw I was hurt. We needed a way out of this fast.

"What are we going to do?" Michelle asked.

"I'm clearing the hell outta this house today," I said, "that's what I'm doing. If you want to stay here, stay. Fine. It's over. If you're coming with me, then let's forget this whole thing and get our own place."

Michelle looked to Denny for an answer, then back at me. It was a confusing, tense, painful moment for us all.

"Go with John," Denny said. She looked at us both and slowly got to her feet. "Come on," I said, grabbing her hand. "Let's go."

We moved out and got a small cozy red house on Lookout Mountain Road in Laurel Canyon. Cass and Denny stayed on for a while in the Green House. Michelle and I tried to resume life as usual, just as we had in the Village two years earlier.

I did manage to begin a song while living up there—"Twelve-Thirty (Young Girls Are Coming to the Canyon)." It was about how L.A. struck us as being so friendly after New York, especially in the early days of the Flower Children. The title referred to a steeple outside our city apartment where the clock had stopped at twelve-thirty. We had come to the coast to put that world far behind us: "Cloudy waters cast no reflection/Images of beauty lie there stagnant/Vibrations bounce in no direction/And lie there shattered into fragments."

The lyrics were proving to be ironic. I knew there would be some bitter undercurrents, but no one in the group wanted Michelle and Denny's affair to complicate life just as we were taking off. But because of the way our four strong and distinct personalities meshed, some turbulence seemed unavoidable now. Cass had been crazy about Denny from the very start, but he had gently thwarted any romantic advances by acting more like a caring brother. Cass was insecure around Michelle because of Michelle's slim, sexy looks. At one point, Cass even wisecracked to me, "I ain't *never* goin' out there to stand next to her onstage. Are you *crazy?*" And yet Michelle knew Cass could stand at a mike and blow away just about any other female singer around. Mitch was the bombshell, Cass the belter, and I loved that part of each woman. But somehow the two Mamas were going to have to go onstage together and perform side by side.

Denny's infatuation with Michelle only confirmed Cass's insecurities and made her angry. Certainly she sensed that the affair would jeopardize not only my friendship with Denny but the band's very existence.

I was trying to keep everything together, being the obsessive perfectionist that I was. But that was probably most of the underlying problem to begin with: Michelle didn't like seeing me have such total control. By acting on her sexuality, she was clearly going to her strength to shake things up, whether intentionally or not. She knew that was one area where she always retained control—and considerable power over me.

We hadn't even released our first track and the harmonies offstage were strained. My dream of a peaceful "family" of musical artists was crumbling fast.

Lou decided we should put out "Go Where You Wanna Go" as the first single in late fall, once it was in the can. Five thousand singles were shipped to Hawaii to test the market there. There *was* no market there. Three days later, he changed his mind and released "California Dreamin'."

The single took several weeks to get any airplay across the country, but by Christmastime, 1965, the momentum was building. I first heard it on the radio in L.A. while driving up to the house Michelle and I were sharing on Lookout Mountain Road. It was a thrilling sensation. I called Denny and we immediately went out and bought matching Triumph 500 motorcycles. As the record moved higher up the charts, the first album came out—*If You Can Believe Your Eyes and Ears.* Soon other album cuts were getting airplay.

The label rewarded us with bigger advances—and royalty checks for me as writer and artist. We signed a management deal with Bobby Roberts, who was one of Adler's partners at Dunhill. He wanted to get us on the road right away.

David Crosby came into the office one day and said to us, "Hey, you guys see *Billboard?* You're on the charts at number nineteen with a bullet. It's a balls-to-the-wall hit."

"Great," I said. There was so much going on in our private lives already, we could hardly gloat. I looked at Denny.

"Let's get Werber's address up in San Francisco and make sure he gets his copy delivered every week with our chart listings circled."

Michelle and I split again briefly after a fight. Cass wanted to live by herself and get away from it all. Denny moved into a rented house on Woods Drive, over Sunset, and I moved in with him. It was an elegant bachelor pad, with a pool, the tough-looking cycles in the driveway, and a posh sunken living room built around a large fireplace.

The first time Michelle came down from Lookout to visit, she was much friendlier. Our marriage was proving to be—if nothing else—resilient. A little distance always took the heat off. That was becoming our pattern. She and Denny had assured me it was over between them. She and I slept together there several times and it was as good as ever, but she kept her place in the hills.

I was hanging around the Whiskey and Michelle came in late one night with a group of people. Obviously, she had wasted no time creating a new life for herself. Finding male companionship would never be a problem for her. She snubbed me in the Whiskey when I said hello. She was still my singing partner—if nothing else. I felt jealous and frustrated that I couldn't convey to her the depth and power of my feelings through loving, tender thoughts.

So I sulked out of the Whiskey, rode my cycle to Woods Drive, and wrote "Words of Love." "Worn-out phrases and longing gazes/Won't get you where you want to go/Words of love, though soft and tender/Won't win a girl's heart."

Finally, we tried to have it all out with Denny present but didn't get far.

"Okay," Denny said, "which is it going to be: him or me?"

"I can't make up my mind," she said. "I don't want to make up my mind. I don't want to talk about it."

"Well," I said, "we better straighten all this out fast. There's plenty of pressure coming down on me to get us out on the road. We've got big advances to make back and the label wants us to work the album while "California" is getting airplay. Cass is going crazy because she's dying to do her thing onstage. Bobby Roberts is going crazy. He's got dozens of calls coming in for bookings and he can't commit to them because we can't work the road in close quarters."

Nothing was resolved. Michelle was confused. Denny was obviously caught in the middle. I assumed that he would stay clear of Michelle. Cass was at the Sunset Towers. One night after taking a swim in the large pool at Woods Drive, Denny walked out back, nervously jangling the keys to his Triumph. The pool was a refuge where I relaxed and gathered my thoughts at night. The air above Sunset was cool in early spring, but the lush landscaping smelled wonderful and the pool was heated.

"I'm heading down to the Strip to see what's happening," he said. I hopped out of the pool and grabbed a towel.

"Where to?" I asked, drying off. It was unusual for Denny to take off at night to cruise the Strip without asking his bachelor roommate to come along. My mood was lifting for a change.

He shrugged and looked off. "Oh, I don't know. Probably hit a few clubs, shit like that. No big deal. Just wanna get out for a while."

"Want some company?"

Denny shifted from boot to boot. I could see he was tense. "Naww, it's cool. I'd just as soon hang out alone."

"Okay. Whatever you say. See ya later, man."

11

I HAD NO IDEA at the time, but Denny roared off on the Triumph and sped down Woods Drive to the Strip. The drugged-out nightcrawlers all turned to look. He pulled up along the curb in front of the Whiskey and spotted a lean blond beauty in tight jeans. She recognized him right away and walked to him.

"Hop on," he said.

"Where to?" Michelle asked, mounting the rear cushion. She clasped her hands tightly across Denny's stomach. Her head snapped back as the cycle tore off. A purple felt sac of Crown Royal dangled from the handlebar. Denny gunned the Triumph with a vengeance all over L.A. through the cool night. He was restless and disturbed. The cycle climbed up the canyon and came to a stop in front of the small red house on Lookout Mountain. "Why are you taking me home so soon?" Michelle asked.

Denny got off and faced her. "Look, this whole thing is too fuckin' strange and wishy-washy. I got an idea. Just stay on the bike with me and let's split . . ."

"What?"

"Yeah, just split, get the fuck outta here, tonight. I got

four, five hundred bucks in my pocket right now. Yes. That's what we should do. Whattya say?"

"Where do you think we're going to go?"

"Duluth, Memphis, the islands. What's the fucking difference? I don't care. I'll work in a gas station. We're in love, aren't we? I mean, we'll just run away from all this crap and start over, just the two of us. Raise a family together. Isn't this what it's all been about?"

Michelle was dumbfounded. She stared away through the trees, then tried to read Denny's intense eyes to see if this was a prank. " 'We're in love'?" She was stupefied, shaking her head in bewilderment. "I think you're crazy," she muttered solemnly.

"I'm crazy? You wanna keep sneakin' through the bushes and lyin' to John? I say fuck it. Let's just split."

"You're out of your mind, Denny. We agreed to stop it in the Green House, remember? We promised John."

"John can't work or sleep, Cass is crazed, I don't know where the fuck I stand. I thought you and I had something going that . . ."

"I'll see ya around, man," she said, getting off the bike. "I can't handle this anymore. Let's just cool it, okay?"

Denny watched her walk off toward the house. "Yeah, sure," he said. "Cool it."

Through the early months of 1966, "California Dreamin' " gradually turned into a major hit that would launch us as an international supergroup. It was playlisted in radio markets across the country and abroad and could be heard floating through the air from car radios, transistor radios, hippie vans, and hipper Beverly Hills boutiques. It was all unreal. The press was hounding us because we made great copy and we didn't look like any other group in the business. I couldn't believe that it had been that simple.

We knew that we had made it when one promise high over Hollywood Bowl came through for us. We were booked for our first live concert at the Bowl, a benefit show for an L.A. radio station. The headliners were Sonny and Cher. The crowd went berserk when we ran out onstage. It felt like one of those dreams as a kid when your body begins to soar all by itself. The sun had just gone down and the roar of the crowd took our bodies and lifted them into the night. It was that heady. I remembered the way the Bowl had looked from the outside several months earlier. The surge of energy was phenomenal. I was dissolving into the colors of the sunset. The run onstage seemed to take an hour. There was no time, only sound. The acid was just kicking in.

As a group, our appeal cut across all types of fans. Guys had the hots for Michelle, with her flowing blond hair, sleek mannequin beauty, and sexy, subtle motions at the mike. Denny and I were hip and sensitive bearded poets who appealed to the girls. That was the look, anyway. And everyone adored Cass and the free-spirited, let-it-all-hang-out philosophy her stage presence conveyed. Fans screamed out, "CASS! CASS! CASS!" as she shimmied and jiggled all over the stage. Our music was far from political or antiwar, but America's freaks and "heads" in their faded, ragged jeans, sandals, beads, long hair, and hippie headbands had embraced us and discovered Cass as the ultimate Earth Mother for rock's new counterculture. Considering how stoned I was out there before eight thousand kids, and the fact that we screamed into the mikes because the crowd drowned out the monitors, our performance wasn't bad. One critic was moved to write that we were creating "the most inventive vocals since the Beatles." That blew us away. I wish I had been able to hear what we were singing.

In March 1966, our debut song made it to number one on some of the charts in America. It had taken close to four months. We had plenty to celebrate. Indeed, the champagne and money started to flow from the Dunhill offices.

First, the clothes—the wildest stuff we could find in Beverly Hills. Then the cars. Cass bought a Porsche but couldn't fit inside, so she got an Aston Martin. Denny got a red Caddie convertible. We all kicked in and bought our engineer an Alfa Romeo. Michelle and I bought matching Jaguar XK-Es—lavender for me, red for her. It turned out to be a practical investment, since the odds of us going to the same place at the same time were getting longer every day.

In May, "Monday, Monday" hit number one within a couple of weeks of its release. It was amazing. It just came out and there it was. My second promise was fulfilled when the record won a Grammy for best vocal performance by a group.

The melody and harmonies were on everyone's lips wherever we went. More than 150,000 records were sold the day it shipped. We were told only the Beatles and Elvis had ever moved so many records that fast. In the middle of May, with the new single at the top of the charts, the *Eyes and Ears* LP shot to number one. We had the top single and top album in the country. We had replaced Staff Sergeant Barry Sadler's somber anthem about our rugged, fearless heros in Vietnam, "The Ballad of the Green Berets." The controversial hit was an answer to McGuire's "Eve of Destruction," but the rapidly swelling battalions of campus radicals and antiwar counterculture dropouts weren't getting stoned, tuning out, and turning on to Sadler. Clearly, part of America listened to him. Politically and culturally, the country was polarizing fast. "Monday, Monday" got stuck at number one for several weeks and turned out to be one of the biggest songs of the year. For two months, the Green Berets and the Mamas and the Papas fought it out at the peak of the pop-music mountain. No two acts could have been more unlike or more symbolic of what was happening to America in 1966.

If Sergeant Sadler was waving Old Glory, I was waving the white flag at home. Not even the astonishing success of our music could get in the way of our domestic turmoil in the canyons.

Michelle and Denny had by then cooled off. The affair had touched too close to home, but Michelle was hardly about to usher in an era of connubial peace. She wasn't ready for that yet.

Maybe she felt she had been deprived of the normal adolescent flings a gorgeous California Girl could enjoy before she got hitched up with me. She had, after all, jumped from her first boyfriend in high school to the married father of two small children. When we married, she was eighteen; I was nearly ten years older. That same irrepressible spirit of adventure regarding men—the one that got us together—was only growing stronger now and pulling us apart. I sensed that it wouldn't stop with Denny. She had too much fire inside for that and she still had her own place. But now, at least, her quest for excitement was aimed at a different pop group. She started seeing Gene Clark of the Byrds.

I could never accuse Michelle of being devious. Just blunt and defiant. She would call me at home and interrupt herself by saying, "What, Gene?" with her hand over the phone. "Oh, anyway, John," she would then continue, "Gene and I are in bed, but before we go to sleep I wanted to ask you what time the Mamas are supposed to be at the studio tomorrow."

We had a show at Melodyland in West Covina in early June. Our opening act was a tough one to follow: Simon and Garfunkel. "The Sounds of Silence" had carried them to the top of the charts and they now had "Homeward Bound" from their great debut LP. I felt it was important for us to turn the audience on—they were older, straighter, more middle-class than the usual rock fans. Halfway through our set, I looked down in the front row and saw that part of that audience included Gene Clark in a bright red shirt. I was so close to him and so pissed off that I felt like swinging my guitar at his head from the stage.

I stormed off the stage, cutting off the set. I blocked Michelle from getting into her Jag in the parking lot afterward and threatened to fire her from the group if she continued to flaunt her affairs in front of me like that. "Just try it," she said. "You have no right to do that. No one else will back you up."

Lou rode with me in my car after the show. As chief of Dunhill, he was already concerned about our centrifugal energies. He had broken us as a huge new act and didn't want to see us throw it away. But he also saw that I was hurting as a man—and taking it out on the car. "You've got to slow down," he said.

I checked the speedometer. "I'm only going 120."

"We'll all be dead if you don't watch out. Look, John, this whole thing breaks my heart."

"Imagine what it's doing to me."

"Here you guys hit the top with your first two records, the album's a total killer, you've got the brightest future in the business, everything is popping left and right . . ."

"And I'm miserable."

"You don't go out. You're alone all the time—no dates, no parties, nothing. You sit home and write songs all the time."

"We've got to do another album this year."

"Right, but if you don't take the pressure off yourself, there won't be a group to do a second album *with*. It's no good, man. I've seen 'em come and go. It's not worth it. I got to get you out to my place in Palm Springs."

I was heartbroken. Whenever I heard Michelle's name, I popped acid. For eight hours, the psychedelic light show in my head eased the pain and distracted me.

We were getting to a breaking point. The demand for concerts was at a fever pitch, but none of us could stand being together long enough to sustain a tour. We were beginning to rehearse for the second album. This couldn't go on. We'd never make it through the sessions.

I met with Denny and Cass at Denny's place on Woods and offered to quit. They were stunned.

"It's up to the two of you," I said. "I can't decide for all of us. I can't work anymore with Michelle. It hurts too much. I'm in love with her. I can't be around her twelve, eighteen hours a day. I can't go on the road and stay in different hotel rooms and watch guys drool over her. I can't create, my mental health is shot. It's a fucking living hell." I looked at Denny and for once let out my anger. "Why did you set me up for this? You had to know it would come to this. Was it worth it? We've come so damned far and look what's happening to us. We're at the top and we're fucking *depressed*. We were happier starving in the Village, man. Back then, at least we knew where we stood. Everything was so clear-cut. Why didn't you think of this back then? It's turned me into an animal."

He shifted around, visibly shaken but silent. Cass knew I had more to say.

"Look," I went on, "I'll quit, form another group, or do something totally different. Or Michelle can go. One of us has got to go. I'm quitting as of now, unless Michelle goes."

Cass and Denny looked at each other, then back to me.

There was no question. "Michelle goes," they said.

We spoke to Lou, Jay Lasker, his second-in-command at

Dunhill, and our management. Dunhill officially fired Michelle in a letter after the series of meetings.

Michelle thought Denny would be an ally in her fight to stay in the group and came to the studio during a rehearsal one night, hoping to be reinstated. "I thought you said you would vote on my side," she said. Obviously they had been talking. "I thought you *loved* me."

Denny was awkward and impassive, swigging from his trusty bottle of Crown Royal. He wasn't backing her up.

Michelle was livid. "You traitor!" she yelled, and slugged Denny across the chin, knocking him against a wall. Denny was enraged but dazed enough to restrain himself.

Then she turned to Cass. "You're not going to let John and Denny get away with this, are you?" she asked.

She picked on the wrong Mama. Cass was still bitter at Michelle for seducing Denny—when she knew Cass was in love with him. "Frankly, Michelle, you can go leap off a building after what you've done. And I wouldn't give a sweet shit."

Michelle was out of the group during most of the summer of 1966. The album and "Monday, Monday" were both going gold and we couldn't capitalize on that with concerts and hefty guarantees. It was bizarre. All that was happening *out there* and we weren't part of it. Our failure to tour that summer must have cost us hundreds of thousands of dollars. Still, the bucks kept rolling in—close to $60,000 in songwriting and artist royalties and advances on the second album.

If I was getting rich, I still had no home. I left Denny's place and moved into Sunset Towers. I should have been the happiest man alive, but I was angry and disillusioned and retreating into drugs. I began dating a stunning, well-educated woman named Ann Marshall, who had worked for Lou and Phil Spector. Ann was classy and worldly, a daughter of Old Hollywood. Her father was the English actor Herbert Marshall. He had lived with Gloria Swanson for years. Ann had grown up in Hollywood and knew everyone in town. We spent quite a bit of time together at Sunset Towers through the summer. We listened endlessly to the Beach Boys' *Pet Sounds* album and I heard Ann's stories about all the Hollywood legends. She was a good friend and eased my

loneliness. The relationship wasn't bad for my wounded
male sexual pride, either.

Lou worked hard to keep my spirits up. He made sure to
invite me to his desert home in Palm Springs on weekends.
He felt it would be good for my creative energies to stay
busy and put the group's endless squabbling in perspective. I
was working on material for the second album and it *had* to
be good. I wanted there to be no doubt in anyone's mind
that the Mamas and the Papas were for real. I didn't want to
be a flash in the pan and live down a rap about our first two
hits being flukes. The group's soap opera life was threatening
it all.

Denny, Cass, Lou, and I took a trip to London to check
out the music industry's other thriving center of action.
Swinging London was then the home of Beatlemania, the
Rolling Stones, the Who, the Mods and Rockers. Lou
brought along a girlfriend named Jill Gibson, a striking
blond singer-artist. She had dated Jan Berry of Jan and
Dean, one of Lou's big groups, until his near-fatal car accident. We began to talk about replacing Michelle with Jill.
They had the same basic look and Jill could sing. We did
some rehearsing in London and talked about giving it a try
back in the States. The partying in London put some distance between us and our problems, though I did miss Michelle and thought about how much she would love London.
We rented the top half of a big house in Barclay Square and
our first morning we noticed this beautiful, lean blonde in
the ground-floor window. Around noon, Denny, Cass, and I
walked back from a stroll through the neighborhood and
saw her through the lace curtains half-naked, slowly pulling
up her stockings, then wiggling into a tight miniskirt. It was
quite erotic, particularly because we had the feeling she
knew she was being watched—and didn't mind.

Then we heard a knock on the door. I opened and Mick
Jagger was standing there.

"Ahhh, so it really *is* you," he said, smiling.

"Yes, it is," I said. "And it really is you. How did you
know?"

"Chrissie said she thought she saw Mama Cass watching

her through the window," Mick said, walking inside. "I thought it was a joke."

"Chrissie?"

"Chrissie Shrimpton. The model. Yeah. We live right downstairs from you."

"Amazing. So that's *your* Aston Martin out in the alley behind the house, is it?"

"Yeah, it is. Nice little car, innit?"

"Mmmm. Well, tell Chrissie she looks great in white silk stockings and miniskirts and that we'll help her get dressed again tomorrow."

"Why don't you tell her yourself?" Mick said. "We should hang out at Dolly's while you're here. Everybody goes to Dolly's."

All of us but Cass went to Dolly's, the original private London disco for rock stars. Mick and Chrissie introduced us around. We ended up sitting at a table with John Lennon. It was late and we had just arrived. We told him we wanted to get high and asked him if he could help us score some grass. He said he'd have to make a call to a friend who was in a recording studio and planning to come by anyway. He made the call. Twenty minutes later, Paul McCartney walked in with a small bag of grass.

Lennon asked Denny, "Hey, man, have you boys ever heard of a drug called Eskatrol? You can't get it 'ere. It's like speed."

"How many do you need?" he answered.

Lennon's face lit up. "Well, all right," he said. "An American friend turned us on to it a couple of years ago. We been writin' all our songs on it for years."

"That's funny," Denny said. "We've been doing *our* songs on it for years too."

Keith Richards was there. Brian Jones showed up with his tall, statuesque girlfriend Anita Pallenberg. They walked in with matching black eyes. It was some scene. Our heads were spinning. I felt from Anita an unmistakable electrical charge. She was so clever, so European, so built. "Where are you staying?" she asked in her husky Germanic accent. I told her. "You know the Stones have a gig and have to leave town."

"I didn't know that," I said. Brian was spaced out and stared off sullenly.

"Maybe I stop by before we leave and have a drink."

"Yeah, maybe. You got the address. Mick's place. Who does your eye makeup, by the way?"

She laughed. "Oh, Brian got mad last night and took a swing. Then we drank some wine and he passed out. So I take ze telephone receiver and give him black eye to match. I don't sink he ever even awoke. We cannot go around town only one of us having black eye, *non?*"

"Mais non."

I saw that John Lennon and Denny were hitting it off at the table. They almost looked alike in the dimness. "We've got to go get Cass," I said to Denny.

"No, she'll never believe it. I got a better idea. Let's get the Beatles over to the house."

John and Paul were great admirers of our early music and Cass's voice in particular. We all piled into John's famous paisley Rolls-Royce and went to Barclay Square. He had speakers built into the underside of the car, just above the wheels. He used a microphone like CB radio in front, making suggestive and comically vulgar remarks to girls on the street as he moved through traffic.

Cass had gone home early and taken something to help her sleep. Denny whispered in her ear, "The man of your dreams is here!"

She coiled up grumpily and barked in her sleep, "Fuck OFF! There's only one man of my dreams and I know he isn't here, so leave me alone."

"I swear by my mother's fuckin' grave they're downstairs, both of 'em." Cass's eyes opened, rolled back, then shut again.

She rolled over went back to sleep.

Denny brought Lennon to Cass. He playfully leaned over and kissed her cheek. "Hello, beautiful," he said tenderly. Sleeping Beauty stirred and rubbed sleep from her eyes. Her Prince had come. Only one man had a voice like that. She sat up, focused on Lennon, and fell back in shock. She shrieked in delight, leaped into his arms, and started dancing

Lennon around the large bedroom. She was so thrilled, she just stared and gaped at him.

We all sat up through the night and smoked dope and played music. There was a beautiful old out-of-tune grand piano in the living room and McCartney practically crawled inside and started plucking the strings. Cass was deliriously happy and ordered the Beatles to stay at her house in L.A. whenever they came to town.

A little before sunrise, the paisley Rolls pulled away with the greatest songwriters in the world and I got ready to crash for the night. Then there was a loud, insistent clubbing at the door. I expected to see Lennon or McCartney. It was Anita. "Let's go to Morocco" she said in the doorway.

"Where?"

"I want us to go to Morocco. We fly to Paris, then to Casablanca, we rent a car and drive to Marrakesh. Yes?"

She walked in and I closed the door. I didn't quite get it. I didn't want to get involved. "Anita, I have to do some work here. I have appointments, rehearsals, meetings, *responsibilities.*" She wasn't paying attention. She was looking around as she walked to the living room. She tossed her purse to the couch, plopped down, and lit up. "Where is the tall blond one on the album cover?"

"Michelle? It's a long story. She isn't here. She's in L.A." She turned pouty. "So, we don't go to Marrakesh?"

I shook my head and yawned.

"Then we make love anyway, yeah?"

"Yeah," I said, "we make love anyway."

First, we talked a long time, mostly about Michelle. Anita wanted every detail about her background, family, schooling, and life-style. Anita seemed intrigued by the California Girl too. She exuded a stylish and playful decadence that was at once intellectual, sultry, and mischievous. She was so perfectly Continental. She made quite a lasting impression on me that night.

After we returned to L.A., I heard she even got to go to Marrakesh. It seemed Keith, Brian, and Anita were shopping in Harrods. They were in the wine department when Anita turned sharply to Brian with a gasp of surprise and said, "Oh, Brian, love, I left my lingerie and makeup in the

lingerie department upstairs. Would you mind terribly going
up and getting it?"

Brian dutifully headed off, leaving Anita and Keith together. "Let's go to Morocco," she said to Keith. "We fly to
Paris, then to Casablanca, rent a car and we drive to Marrakesh, yeah?"

"Yeah." By the time Brian figured it all out, Keith and
Anita were in the King's Suite at the Mamounia Hotel in
Marrakesh.

We decided to do a few shows together with Jill. One of
them was at the Forest Hills tennis stadium in Queens, just
outside Manhattan. Again, the opening act was Simon and
Garfunkel, but this time they were playing to a home crowd.
They were local boys from Queens and grew up in the immediate vicinity of the stadium. We only had enough time together to rehearse eight of our live arrangements with Jill
before the shows. Paul and Artie did well over an hour of
flawless folk duets that thrilled the fans.

"Okay, guys," I said backstage, "we'll open with 'Straight
Shooter,' then kick right back into it and do it again." I was
stretching the material we did know as thin as I could.

"You're crazy," Cass and Denny said. "This is Forest
Hills."

"Exactly. I don't want to turn it into Forest Lawn. Just
try it."

We did the song twice and no one seemed to care. We
hooked the fifteen thousand fans with "Dedicated to the One
I Love," and tore through our abbreviated set in about
twenty minutes. The sound was clean and Jill handled Michelle's vocals quite nicely. It would have been a perfect set
—as an opening act. There was nowhere for us to go in the
show. A couple of fans rushed the stage after "California,"
maybe to hug Cass or get a better look at the new Michelle. I
took it as our cue to split.

As security guards dispersed the onrushing fans before
they could get to us, I yelled, "Danger, danger, let's go," to
the other singers and band members. They were all confused. Hundreds of fans were now feeling short-changed and
turned nasty.

We ran up a winding path behind the stage and looked

back. We left a small, messy ruckus behind us in Forest
Hills. I saw that, though Jill was a perfectly adequate singer,
she was an artist first. We needed Michelle's stage charisma
and grittier edge.

In June, Dunhill released "I Saw Her Again" from the
first LP and, again, we did almost no touring to help promote it. It was a disappointment that, after two million-
selling gold singles, it never made it all the way. It hit the
Top 5 on most charts but was clearly not "Monday, Monday." We had been charted virtually every week for six
months running, but the third single had a short life span on
the airwaves. I was beginning to feel we had to live with the
volatility, the risks, and go for it as a foursome again. It
would soon be too late. The split from Michelle was dreary
and took away the excitement of writing and playing music
together. The label had a potential moneymaking machine
on its small roster and wanted us to keep going. Our music
was filling Dunhill's coffers and Dunhill in turn was making
us rich. And that was on just 5 percent of 90 percent of
retail. But numbers seemed unimportant when we were pulling apart.

Michelle was up on Lookout Mountain and occasionally
stopping in to see me, first at Denny's place on Woods Drive,
then at Sunset Towers between evenings with Ann.

Denny took a box filled with cash and went home to Nova
Scotia, then to the Virgin Islands with some friends. He had
moved into an elegantly furnished fourteen-room mansion
high up in Laurel Canyon on Appian Way that was once
owned by Mary Astor. He paid about $52,000 for it and it
was jam-packed with antiques, a Chippendale dining-room
set, grand piano, sideboards stacked with gilt-edged Royal
Dalton china, $300 cups and saucers, grandfather clocks,
and enormous vases. He said the living room alone was
worth fifty grand. But what made parties happen at Denny's
was the fact that he found out I had an open account at
Greenblatt's Deli on Sunset. The Crown Royal and Harvey's
Bristol Cream arrived by the case; cold cuts and steaks came
packed in heavy cartons. It didn't take long for the balance
to hit $3,000. Denny made sure the fridge was stocked, then

kept out a large glass bowl full of speed for his party guests
and never ate.

Denny's crowd was macho and rowdy. A few guys lived
there with him—Barry McGuire stayed almost a year with
his girlfriend. They would tear down to Sunset, meet some
familiar faces in a club, and invite everyone back home with
Denny. That was the big lure his pals used to get chicks—
"Hey, baby, let's go hang out with Denny, the one in the
Mamas and the Papas."

It was open house round the clock, with plenty of dope,
sex, and booze. A large round bed covered with a fox bed-
spread took up most of the bedroom built into the corner
tower of the house. Once a party got going, the bed was
rarely empty—and usually crowded. If he wanted to clear
out undesirables, he bought them plane tickets to Europe.

One night I got so stoned I convinced myself that Denny
and Michelle were making love at that instant. I drove to
Denny's and crawled through the bushes beneath his bedroom tower and somehow climbed up the outside of the
house. I hopped over the balustrade and peered through the
french windows. Denny was in bed with a woman. I saw him
stirring. I pushed through the french windows, smashing
glass all over the bedroom floor. I felt like the Wolfman of
Hollywood as I screamed and hurled myself through the air
into the bed. "Okay, Mitch, what are you doing here?" I
shouted. "Goddammit, get out of here!"

I heard the woman shrieking and saw her roll from the
bed, wrapped in the sheet, and take off. Denny slapped me
around until I settled down. "Where's Michelle?" I said.
"Where'd she go?"

"Beats the fuck outta me," he said. "That's Linda you just
scared to death. Get it together, man. And use the front
door next time, eh?"

Denny had the ideal form of punishment for me in his
house. An oversize hammock was ingeniously hung from the
twenty-foot ceiling and beams. It could be lowered and lifted
by a set of pulleys and it could hold twelve people. He asked
me to try it out a few days later and then kept me aloft for
forty-eight hours. Food and drugs were sent up by pulley
every eight hours. There were Crown Royal sacs everywhere

in the living room. A large coffee table was usually deco-
rated with a fragrant mound of cleaned dope. Denny liked
nothing more than to get a raucous, decadent scene going—
then leave it behind for the peace of mind of a stoned, solitary glide on his Triumph.

Cass lived at Sunset Towers for several months before settling on a quaint retreat on Woodrow Wilson in the hills. It
had once belonged to Natalie Wood but now was home to
Cass's eclectic band of stoned hippie worshipers—poets,
struggling musicians, and would-be actors, sun-fried beach
bums, debauched playboys, drug sponges, and bikers.

She treated herself to the most outrageous hippie costumes money could buy. Her lovers all looked like they were
cut from the same handsome, leather-jacketed biker mold,
and they all claimed to be on the verge of the big breakthrough as screen idols. Cass loved to hold court for her
subjects and created, like Denny, a private world all her
own, safe from the draining tension of the group. And, like
Denny, when she had had enough of the hangers-on, she'd
squeeze into her sports car and speed off toward the beach to
be alone with her thoughts.

We came back from another concert with Jill and I called
Michelle to come over and talk. My mind was made up. "I
want you back, baby, in the group, in my home."

"You'd really take me back?" she said.

"You mean you'd really bite the bullet and *come* back?"

She turned her head slightly and scowled. "Don't rub it
in."

"Okay, I won't. We'll get Cass and Denny and go right
into the studio." We did "Dancing in the Streets" that night.
It was wonderful to be reunited. The high-energy sound and
tight harmonies were right there again and we were all high
just from relief through the session. Afterward, Mitch and I
shared a loving, romantic dinner together and headed back
to my place at Sunset Towers. We talked about house-hunt-
ing and creating our own private fantasy world somewhere
special. We had never given ourselves the chance to work
things out in a *real* home of our own. We had either traveled
or shared a home. It was odd. Behind the spirit of reconciliation, I suspected that Michelle would never forgive me for

getting her to come back. There would be times I thought
Michelle wanted to kill me for regaining control, for exerting
that power over her and the others. But for now, the hatch-
ets had been buried—sharpened, perhaps, during the split,
but buried. It was evident that the right move had been
made. We had to go through Michelle's firing to realize how
much we—and I—needed her.

By late August, the sessions were nearly completed for the
second album and we were finally ready to discover America
all over again, this time in a Learjet on a major concert tour.
The Mamas and the Papas were back and a great weight had
lifted.

Then we found our dream house. We spotted it high up a
winding road in Bel Air. We had been through Brentwood,
Westwood, and Bel Air and hadn't found the perfect place.
But as we drove by 783 Bel Air Road, we saw what we were
looking for: a Tudor-style country home, a quaint but spacious monument to the grandeur of Hollywood's Golden
Era. It was a fairy-tale castle perched on a cliff high over Bel
Air. It had once belonged to Jeanette MacDonald and we
bought it from her husband.

Inside, the living-room ceiling must have risen thirty feet
and the room felt large as a basketball court. Off the living
room, there was an English pub that had been brought over,
brick by brick. There was a gray-slate floor, hand-carved
wooden gargoyles over the doors, and old musty stone walls.
A walk-in vault beneath the house had been converted into a
wine cellar. And there was a pool behind the house. We
loved it and wanted it. The asking price was $225,000. I
made an offer: $150,000 for the house, with an immediate
cash down payment of $90,000. To our everlasting astonish-
ment, the offer was accepted and we had our dream house.

Just after closing the deal in mid-September, Michelle and
I took a tour of our grounds. We had been so awed by the
sweep and elegance of the interior that I couldn't remember
if anything was said about the grounds. It turned out that we
now owned five acres of prime Bel Air real estate. The morning smog lifted. The rugged, densely thicketed land beyond
the house dropped steeply to the south and west, giving us a
spectacular vista over Bel Air. There were five small guest

bungalows on the land. We hiked through our new jungle
and garden, along a crumbling stone path, and saw we
owned an avocado orchard, rose and grape bowers, gurgling
springs, and stables. We stood on the terrace and faced
southwest. We had never been happier.

"I guess that's Santa Monica, way off in the distance,
babe," I said, pointing toward a cluster of buildings and
homes in the distance.

"Yeah, it makes quite a difference when the smog lifts,
doesn't it?"

"No shit. Look," I said, pointing again. "See those tiny
white specks out there? What the hell are they? I never noticed them before."

"My God," she moaned in awe. "John, you know what
they are? They're *sails*. Look, they're moving. We can see
clear out to the Pacific from here. I can't believe it. It really
is a dream house."

The changes in our lives were absurd. A year before, we
were starving artists, working out vocal parts, groveling
hand-to-mouth in a seedy hotel suite with no leads. Now we
were the hottest pop group in America with more money in
some days' mail than I used to make covering twenty thousand miles on tour in a year. Much of my hand-to-mouth
motion was still about staying stoned. That hadn't changed.
But we had twin XK-Es, a magical mansion in which we
could live out all our fantasies, accountants and bookkeepers
to keep track of the money as it came in and went out; we
had gold records, a Grammy, notoriety, respect, fame, a
Learjet ready to fly us anywhere we needed to go; and we
had the exquisite and rare freedom to do whatever the hell
we pleased as artists and as celebrities.

It turned out that making the money was the easy part.
The trick now would be discovering the secret to holding on
for the ride.

12

MY PHILOSOPHY about being a so-called "star" was that if you wanted others to treat you like a star, you had to first treat yourself like one. When it came to touring between the late fall of 1966 and early, cold months of 1967, I didn't want to go out on the road too often. My days as a vagrant folkie and Journeyman more than satisfied my wanderlust. But when we had to go now, it would be first-class all the way.

Our management stuck tightly to a policy of strict *under-*exposure. Despite the record sales, we probably played no more than thirty concerts altogether. But we made them count: They were all in major cities and in large venues. And I set the limit at a couple of shows a week. We flew Learjet all the way.

Rock has always had its "road bands" and "studio groups." We were more a studio group. I was an obsessive tinkerer who came alive in the studio. Not even concert guarantees of up to $90,000 could make me enjoy the symptoms of Road Fever.

By then, we had had our fourth and fifth singles out—"Look Through My Window" and "Dancing in the Streets"—from our second album, *The Mamas and the Papas.* Touring *does* stimulate radio and sales action and big records create excellent road conditions. After a gold record and number one hit, we were greeted with loving pandemonium. Everyone adored us—the long-haired hippies, the frizzy, muumuu-draped earth mothers, the stoned free-lovers, young straight kids, and even some "far-out" parents trying to stay young with the hip counterculture.

One problem we soon discovered on the road was that, behind the "family" aura of the Mamas and the Papas, we still weren't all that happy being together in such close company. Denny and Cass drew their own entourages from city to city, and Michelle and I suddenly went from being separated to inseparable. Given the high-voltage lines connecting Denny and Michelle, Michelle and Cass, Michelle and *me,* *Cass* and me, and, as the perfectionist taskmaster, me and *everyone,* we *were* a round-the-clock party all by ourselves.

During this time, an exciting element was added to the equation: Cass got pregnant and was expecting in the spring. She was elated. Though there was mounting pressure for us to stay on the road, Cass had other designs—and a new life ahead of her as a single mother.

Mitch and I lived, worked, recorded, performed, flew, ate, and slept together for months without a break. No marriage is so perfect that it can't benefit from a *little* space now and then. We had none but, fortunately, it did bring us closer together as friends. Long road tours have kept more than a few rock stars' marriages alive by building in plenty of distance and easy sex on the run. You can have it both ways— the stable hearth, the endless, obedient harem. But when your wife is in the band with you, you try to make life easy and not suffocate each other.

After shows, we'd order up the best dinners and champagne we could find from room service, hang out in a hotel suite and get high, then head out to the airport to fly the Lear to the next city in the middle of the night. We'd collapse at dawn in the next hotel and awake the next afternoon to get to the sound check. It can be a vicious, exhausting cycle—from limo to tarmac to plane to tarmac to limo to lobby to suite to stage to limo to lobby, etc., etc. It was a blur to me then and still is.

And it was all for less than ninety minutes onstage. But once out there in the lights and hysteria, it seemed worth it. No drug ever made us feel that kind of power and love. We couldn't have done any of it without Peter Pilafian, our road manager and our former drowsy drummer at Duffy's. Peter was still living with Michelle's sister, Rusty, and they had had their child, a boy named Damian, right at the same time we had "California Dreamin'." Peter was the fifth passenger in the Lear and doubled as our electric violinist every night for "Spanish Harlem."

The absurdity of performing was that we couldn't hear anything out there. It was just a din. John Lennon once told me that when the Beatles took the stage he sometimes just kept singing "She Loves You" through their forty-minute sets. No one ever knew; no one ever heard. We just shouted back into the mikes without hearing the monitors. No one seemed to care.

From the looks of it, we weren't the headline act for many of our fans anyway—their drugs were. We merely supplied the soundtrack for the movies playing on the acid trippers' interior screens. It was just as well. I was always stoned and at the movies the whole time myself.

I volunteered my body as a human test tube for anything I could get my hands on—mescaline, Black Beauties to keep going, Reds to come down, hash and grass for any occasion. A friend of ours once brought over a box of free drug samples he had taken from a doctor's office. I went through everything in there, including the female hormone, estrogen. Michelle was horrified at some of my drug experimentations. She asked me if I was preparing to go through menopause. "No, but there's probably a little downer buzz in there," I said.

I would have disgraced myself to go out onstage straight in the sixties. It was unthinkable with all that zonked-out energy out front. You needed a buffer to survive. One of Peter's key duties was to make sure several large cups filled with Crown Royal were strategically placed onstage for Denny and me during shows to keep us on an even keel. *Someone* had to be in charge.

Kids didn't come to hear live re-creations of radio hits

that had been market-tested and pre-formatted. That sort of vain self-consciousness was the "Me Decade" stuff of the seventies, still a long way off. In the more innocent sixties of Flower Power and "Make Love, Not War," the wasted warriors of the counterculture showed up to feel the tingly rush of transcendence, to tune in, freak out, to do their own thing. To be, and to be with thousands of others freaking out in synergy. The whole point was not to define the ego but to dissolve it and go with the flow toward the jet stream of cosmic bliss.

As rock stars, we witnessed the flowering of a new consciousness founded on sex, drugs, rock, and the renunciation of Americana.

Free Love! Turn On! Drop Out!

What we saw before us was a bizarre, almost primitive ritual of tribal communion. The unifying force among the youth culture was a crude religion. Or antireligion. If there was a Paradise, it was the drug-induced state of holy oblivion. To roll a joint was to strike another morally right, smirking blow against the Empire. Rallies against Vietnam and the draft were the Crusades. As antistars of the sixties, we created music that helped guide a lost generation during its spiritual catharsis through chemistry.

We saw them in city after city, the glazed, unfocused eyes, sucking on one joint after another from total strangers who became their loving, giddy brothers and sisters for a smile and a peace sign. For this Communion, the offering was not wafers and red wine, but Window Pane acid and hits of Ripple.

The rituals were always the same. Peter's advance work set up the subterranean escape route by limo. As the crowd howled for another encore, we raced offstage and into the car idling somewhere in the backstage bowels of the arena. The soundproofed car would scorch some rubber on the concrete and wind through a tunnel, up and down ramps and out into town, leaving the Peace and Love Generation in the dust. Then, it was upstairs to the suites for four-star dinners, the dope, and Dom Pérignon, and on to another smooth night flight over America in the private jet.

The commute was jarring. We achieved joyful kinship

with the dropouts in their funky rebel trenches one moment; then, the next moment, we were spoiled by our elitist splendor, safely insulated from their world.

Though we were conservative compared to the later, more notorious pillagers, a little road madness went a long way toward keeping your sanity. Acid, the great equalizer, broke down the barriers between Them and Me and eased my passage across the widening void separating the two realms. You could almost do no wrong when everyone was letting it all hang out. One night we were playing the Hollywood Bowl. Cass came out backstage looking so dolled up, like she was heading for the Polo Lounge at the Beverly Hills Hotel. Her silky gown billowed generously, her hair was all pinned up, and she had false eyelashes.

Moments before we ran out, Denny and I filled a bucket of water and dumped it on her head. Cass went crazy and would have tried to kill us if it wasn't showtime. Her eyes glared like a wild bull's and she was thrashing and raving as we ran out. Her screams soon faded into the din of the audience as we hit the stage running. Cass's dress was soaked and clinging—she never wore bathing suits for this reason—and she was enraged. Then she still got a roaring, standing ovation, as if Cass's wet look was a carefully launched fashion trend. The crazier we got, the more they embraced us. Cass, who had been plagued with self-doubt before we ever hit the road, was now in her glory as a heroine for hippie America.

At the Sherry-Netherland Hotel in New York, some of the other backup musicians went a little too far. There were groupies in the rooms and things got out of hand. Hunks of crystal were torn off the chandeliers. The rowdies made too much noise. We were asked never to show our faces there again.

In Rochester, New York, we played a veterans' memorial hall and I took that opportunity to make some rare anti-Vietnam remarks in public. A stage manager type told Peter during the break before the encore that if I didn't retract my statements in a hall dedicated to the memory of our fallen soldiers, then he would pull all security and police protection for us. Peter relayed this and I said, "Nothin' doin'."

That night we found out how much we needed security. Even the limo driver refused to work. Peter drove the limo out of the hall. By the time we got to the street, scores of wild-eyed fans with easy access had us surrounded. They rocked the limo, banged on the hood and roof, climbed on the fenders, and knocked and scraped the windows with their rings. Peter finally navigated us out of danger, but it was a scary brush—our only one—with mob craziness.

It was a thrill to perform in Washington with the whole family in the audience. DEL RAY LOCAL MAKES GOOD! So I *wasn't* Annapolis material. I was sorry my father didn't get to see me in my pop-star uniform.

I got to visit with my mother, Rosie, Susie, and the kids and some of the old buddies like my Linton Hall and Del Ray Local pal, Jimmy Shortt. It was wonderful to see them all and to have a couple of hit records behind us. We talked vaguely about their moving out to the West Coast to be closer to me. It was freezing and snowy, and my mother was getting on in her years. The last crazy idea I presented to the family had something to do with going to the Caribbean to get a band off the ground. That was two gold records and about a million dollars before. Now she tended to listen. Susie was aloof. She had once agreed to move west for me and the kids and came back a single mother of two.

At Susie's apartment, I turned her on to grass for the first time. It turned out she had had a harmless little affair with Scott McKenzie since I had gone out west. It was no big deal. We got incredibly high and ended up in the kitchen with the munchies. We were so stoned we could barely talk. Susie tried to make tuna sandwiches, but ended up fingerpainting in the mayonnaise. It was fascinating to watch her. I never did get to eat. I passed out. Shortly thereafter, she crashed too.

I got to see Scott in D.C. He had tried to get a solo singing career going after the Journeymen broke up and had performed quite a bit at the Shadows and at the World's Fair in New York. Then he came out to hang around with us in L.A. but had been back east a while, visiting with his mother. Now he wasn't singing much at all. Scott was treading and needed a push one way or the other. I told him he should come with us to New York, finish the tour in Texas, and try to get something together in L.A. That was always the answer—head west.

When we had to head north to New York to play Carnegie Hall, a blizzard closed down the airports. We waited for the roads to get cleared and Scott, Michelle, and I rode in a snug, cushy limo with the radio blasting and a bottle of Wild Turkey to keep us warm as we stared out at the driving snowstorm. You couldn't have it any better than that.

It wasn't as if we didn't look for new and better kicks all the time. The plane was usually an eight-seater and the marijuana cloud cover would be pretty heavy inside at cruising altitude.

"What's that funny smell back there?" the pilot invariably asked.

"Ohh, just some awful French cigarettes we picked up in Paris last time," Denny always said.

We would ask the pilot to climb several thousand feet above our flight pattern until a red DANGER light would go on. Then, at the peak of the parabola, he pushed the stick forward for a nosedive that made us feel weightless for half a minute or so as the gravitational force shifted from heavy to nil.

We had Laura with us on one trip and, as we were strapped in, she got herself into a tiny ball on my lap as the jet made its dizzying climb. As we hit the top and veered down, I released her like a beach ball and she floated off, screaming her lungs out with delight, over to Cass and Denny, then Michelle, back to me. A short but exhilarating game of catch.

Cass loved this. She always wanted to trim down. "I'm weightless," she'd scream proudly. "I'm light as a feather."

Along with floating, another wonderful, light-headed rush on the road was cash. Our road trips never made us any money because we worked so hard to spend it. We lived lavishly and no one ever said no to anything. Cass was always inviting hordes of people to her suite for room service breakfasts and dinners. Sometimes she'd book one of the convention rooms for all the local friends she could make in a night.

I never was part of the groupie scene because Mitch was always with me—and I'd never find a beauty like her in the crowd anyway. We drank champagne or carried our little sacs of Crown Royal. We were stoned on something all the time and that tends to mellow you out and keep down the squabbling. Get on the Learjet, take a few hits off a joint, settle back with the juice. In the morning sometimes, Peter Pilafian would come in the hotel room and wake us by playing an electric Brahms violin concerto through his portable amp. Peter was a true Renaissance Roadie. Mitch and I were riding the crest of a spectacular dream wave; we had everything we could have wanted.

By the end of our tour, "Words of Love" and "Dedicated to the One I Love" were getting big airplay. The royalty checks were coming in big—$5,000 here, $20,000 there, a fifty-grander every couple of months. So to get a more tangible sense of what was happening—and to cut the chances of skimming by promoters—I asked to be paid in small bills.

In Denver, we asked and the promoter agreed. Peter hauled the money—somewhere between $60,000 and $80,000 in $100 bills—up to the hotel suite in a suitcase. We covered Cass with the bills. She lay still on the floor until she was entirely covered.

"You always wanted to see yourself rolling in it, honey," I'd say. "Start rolling!" And Cass started to gyrate and roll. Then we put on some music and danced on our cash, scooping up handfuls of bills and tossing them around the room, giggling hysterically until we just couldn't move anymore. As usual, the night ended shortly before dawn, with all of us on the floor, crashed out and clothed, unable to make it back to our own rooms. In the air or on the floor, there was always some way to defy gravity and feel utterly weightless.

Michelle and I came off the road and started work on our dream house. We had gigantic, overstuffed burgundy velvet couches and armchairs made for the living room. We rolled in a grand piano. We bought some beautiful Tiffany lamps, including one with an extremely rare series of zodiac signs on the shade. There was an immense blue oriental rug to cover the floor, and we had a huge marble fireplace built. We filled the main rooms with huge tropical plants. We started throwing names around like Lalique and Limoges. A spectacular French crystal chandelier hung in the foyer. Every now and then, one of the many little bulbs would go out and Mitch would ask me repeatedly to get a ladder and replace it with a new one—if we had a new one. "I will, I will," I'd say. Then another would go out a couple of weeks later and she'd ask me again. "It looks so tacky in a mansion like this," she'd say. "There shouldn't be any burned-out bulbs in a chandelier like that." I assured her I'd replace them. "John," she'd say, "you know, when the last bulb up there goes out, and it's all dark, THAT'S when I leave." There were so many bulbs that I never took her too seriously.

Eventually, we converted the sedate and elegant library in the east wing into our hashish den, complete with a tent, Indian bedspreads draped from the ceiling, bulging, ornately embroidered Berber pillows from Morocco on the floor, and an imposing handtooled six-foot-high hookah in the center of the room. A room worthy of a pasha and his favorite wife.

A pool table occupied the dining room, observed by a gallery of peach-skinned cherubs who were hanging in frames on the walls. Incense burned through the mansion. For the bedroom, I had, specially made, an oversized bed constructed from the same material NASA used for its spacesuits. It had to resist quite intense heat some nights. Michelle wanted to design a Mexican-style kitchen, so we went to Guadalajara and she picked out all sorts of delicate, elaborately handpainted tiles.

One of our early guests at the house was Leonard Goldenson, who was then head of ABC Records, which was distributing Dunhill Records. Leonard was quite the art collector, and a generous one at that. "I've got scores of great paintings from all over the world," he told us once. "They're all museum-quality pieces, just sitting in crates in some dungeon somewhere. Why don't I send you some of them and see if they hang well in your house. Consider them a housewarming. I'd rather see them with young people than going to waste."

Ten crates arrived, along with a little history of each painting from Leonard. It was a magnificent gesture.

Lou Adler contributed his bit, too, a pair of gorgeously

plumed pet peacocks. We hired a gardener to landscape the grounds and terrace the gardens. The birds would strut through the gardens and orchards and bowers and at sunset go to the stone terrace to fan their dazzling plumage. It was quite a spectacle.

We had no problem figuring out how to spend our money and live out all our material fantasies. Before we knew it, five Rolls-Royces were in the driveway. By the time we settled in at 783 Bel Air Road, Rusty's son Damian was a year old. Rusty once went to a pet store with Michelle to buy some food for Damian's little goldfish. When they came back to the house, Rusty was almost in shock. "I went in there to buy 15¢ of fish food," she said, "and Michelle walked out with $500 worth of equipment!" A large aquarium had caught Michelle's eye—along with some equipment.

"That's nothing," Rusty went on. "We went to a book-store last week so I could buy this ninety-cent play and Michelle dropped a thousand bucks on old books! You guys are unbelievable."

"Hey," I said, "a library's got to have books, right?"

"Did she tell you about her new $600 pajamas?"

We collected expensive toys like telescopes and more paintings. We spent thousands of dollars on clothes and walked around the house in Indian robes and sandals. Michelle once expressed an interest in learning to play the cello, so I bought a handsome old cello. We'd go to auctions and buy antiques. I got the idea to transform the attic into my own recording studio, so I could stay high all the time and never have to worry about studio time. I began assembling the state-of-the-art equipment and ran the cost up to about a hundred grand.

We never thought of tomorrow. We were too busy entrenching ourselves in opulence and hedonism *for now*. It was an ambiance that would draw people to us. With the studio upstairs, and less and less interest among us for touring, we were digging ourselves in. It was open house around the clock. We loved being part of the scene in Bel Air. Some uptight Bel Air snobs were afraid their property values would plummet with the rockers' arrival up the street. Did we care? We had our dream home, our music, our friends,

our drugs. We were pushing our quest for pleasure to the
hilt, and life was too sweet to blow much time on the road.

And yet, I was looking for more from the sexual revolution. I found it beyond marriage—a way to gratify my need
to experiment with my more erotic fantasies. In the era of
free love among the rich in Hollywood, all sorts of barriers
were crumbling. It wasn't hard to find beautiful partners
who were willing to explore new directions in lovemaking
with me. Drugs—pot, uppers, acid, mescaline—could break
down almost any inhibitions and hang-ups.

I was into scarves and tying women up. I would watch my
partner for the evening slowly remove her clothes and move
to the bed. There, as she lay on her back, I would bind her
ankles with a silk scarf—without hurting her. This was all in
the spirit of playful and tender foreplay. It was Designer
Bondage, and my lovers often found it highly arousing.
Then, with her feet bound, I sometimes knotted another
scarf around the wrists over her head. The sensations—even
fantasized—of domination and helplessness can be powerfully stimulating to both men and women, though I never let
my lovers tie *me* up. I probably missed out there.

Other times, the turn-on was to bind my partner's wrists
together and then knot the scarf to a bannister with her
hands over her head.

I was never into pain. The paddle-whomping nuns of my
parochial school days may have instilled a hatred of authority and regimentation in me, but they didn't leave me *that*
twisted. But, of course, spanking could be a sexy turn-on.
Once again, my lover that night would give it a try. After
undressing, she'd lie facedown on the bed or across my knees
on the edge of the bed. Then I would lightly slap her until
she began to feel the heat of friction and very slight sting. I
always felt that it was the rhythm and the repetition of the
spanks—not the intensity or force of the hand itself—that
was so hot. Whatever it was about the spanking fetish—
provoking subconscious and forbidden "bad girl" images,
the tantalizing buildup of sexual tension, the heat, the
naughty novelty of it all—it often worked as a turn-on.

Then there was whipped cream. It was part of the sixties
scene to come up with new recipes for the sexually adventur-

ous. Squirting and spreading whipped cream—sometimes
with cherries—over a lover's naked body and then licking it
off seemed to be quite the rage on grass.

I also found out that I liked to watch—or at least discovered a certain taste for instant replay, once the first portable
video cameras hit in the mid-sixties. With a tripod, I could
tape my lover and myself as we made love. Then she and I
could later watch the sexy videos to turn ourselves on.

These escapades never seemed perverted to me. They were
superficial and fleeting and I knew all along that my life with
Michelle was what I really wanted.

She and I did have quite an extraordinary time together as
the success of our career brought our dreams to life. For one
thing, our parties at 783 were incredible, freewheeling open-
house affairs. We must have been among the first pop groups
to mingle socially with the Hollywood film crowd. That was
one aspect of our life together that distanced us from Cass
and Denny. We went Hollywood, so to speak, and, through
Lou Adler and Steve Brandt, the gossip columnist, and others, our friends came to include directors, writers, and actors
like Warren Beatty, Jane Fonda, Jack Nicholson, Candy Bergen, and Terry Melcher, the record producer and son of
Doris Day. We also got to know the Beach Boys and just
about every other musical act in the L.A. area. It was not
uncommon for our house to bring together in one evening
dozens of celebrities from rock and film.

We threw a birthday party for Tommy Smothers one night
and had three hundred people over. As a prank, I ordered a
giant Styrofoam cake on rollers from one of the film studios.
A stripper, all oiled up, was to pop out and kiss him or
something like that. A mariachi band was playing and the
cake was in the taproom. There was lots of fanfare, everybody waited, but no cake rolled out.

Mitch and I went back to check on the problem. I pulled
off the top of the cake and looked inside. The stripper was
inside, all right, and so was Warren Beatty, hunched down,
putting a heavy make on her as he oiled her up. Warren and
I first met in Hollywood, only to find out we had both come
from Alexandria and gone to rival schools. He was Mad
Dog Beatty back then, a rugged footballer.

There was never a shortage of stimulation. Drugs were rampant. Our grass was everyone's grass. I once had so much dope around that I stashed it in a pillowcase. Scott lived with us for a while and he came up to me before some friends came over. "John," he said, "there's some guy here holding a large jug and he says he's a friend of yours. Looks pretty weird to me."

"Great. Tell him to go to the pool table."

It was a friend of mine from back east who worked for one of the major pharmaceutical companies. Scott watched intently as he unscrewed the lid of the large brown plastic jug and emptied thousands of pills onto the green felt of the pool table. He spread them out evenly until there was no green felt visible.

"Go," he said. I started picking out the colors and sizes I wanted from his pharmacological arsenal. I scooped up my handful and lost a few pills. "Black Beauty in the side pocket," I said. Scott grabbed his Rx, then other friends came in and helped themselves to theirs. The dope was out on the tables, in vases and bowls, and money never seemed to change hands. That's how I wanted it in my house. We were there to share and party. And the partying never let up. I just had one hard rule: no heroin, no hard-drug cases, no junkies. They weren't allowed in. Drugs were for living well and having fun, not for dying.

One night Scott and I were on a real tear and in walked Paul McCartney and some friends in the Beatles organization. Paul was in town in connection with "Penny Lane" and "Strawberry Fields Forever." They were the Beatles hits in the early months of 1967. Scott froze in mid-shot. It must have been the first time he had met Paul. Paul was always so nonchalant and disarmingly modest. He just waved casually and, not wanting to disrupt the game, said to Scott, "Eh, mate, don't let me throw you off your game. Just keep playing." Scott shook his head, leaned over the table, and lined up his next shot.

We sat in front of the fireplace and heard all the latest Beatle adventures and folklore from Paul. The grass and pills had been passed around and I was flying. Then Paul spotted Michelle's cello standing in a corner. He had never played one before, but he started plucking away at it as if it were a giant bass guitar. I sat down at the grand piano in the living room and we began noodling around. Then I got up and turned off the lights to show cartoons.

We were all laughing our heads off as Paul walked to the piano. He played the keys and plucked the strings inside the piano, simultaneously watching and scoring music for the cartoons. It was an impressive display of composing genius. By daybreak I had crashed out in the living room. Scott came into the house and woke me to tell a story. He had given Paul, Mal Evans, a Beatles executive, and an L.A. groupie a ride to where they were staying. "It was amazing," Scott said in his boyish drawl. His eyes were widening with excitement. "We get up into Laurel Canyon and stop at this gas station. I'm in the front with Mal and Paul's with the chick in the back. The morning traffic's already on its way down towards Sunset. On the radio, would you believe it, is 'Strawberry Fields' and the guy's standing there with the pump in his hand, singin' along—no *idea* there's Paul McCartney in the backseat. So we drive some more and Paul leans up and taps me on the shoulder real gently and asks, 'Oh, I meant to ask you. What is it exactly you do?' What was I going to say, 'I used to be a Smoothie'? 'I'm an ex-Journeyman'? 'I'm a singer,' I said. Then he asked me what I sang. And I was so out of it and confused I said I didn't really know what I sang. I'll never forget that. It was so *weird,* but he was cool about it." Scott scratched his head and cocked it sideways, full of sudden curiosity. "What *do* I sing, anyway, man?"

"Scott," I said sleepily, "it's time you figured it out. I guess we'll have to come up with something for you to sing."

13

WHO WOULD EVER have imagined that a few months later Scott would be at the top of the charts with what became, in effect, the national anthem for the Summer of Love in 1967? The original idea for the Monterey Pop Festival came to me from an L.A. impresario and friend of ours named Alan Pariser. Alan and an associate wanted to put together a one-day profit-making outdoor concert at the Monterey fairgrounds. He wanted the Mamas and the Papas to close the show and figured we could get other acts to perform with us. "We'll cut you in as partners," he assured me. "You can invest your own money if you want—do whatever you want to do. We'll give you a cut of the gate action. There could be a hundred grand in this for you."

"I'll think it over," I said.

There were a couple of other moneymen involved at the beginning. Pariser already had the venue rented for a couple of months ahead. It sounded like a terrific concept, but I knew it could be improved on and kicked up to another dimension. I talked it over with Lou Adler and he immediately went for it.

I awoke in the middle of the night once and discussed my idea with Michelle. I told her I thought we should buy out

Pariser's idea—and the fairgrounds date—and change the gig to a larger nonprofit festival.

"We really ought to give something back, you know what I mean?" I told her. "Look, we have everything we've ever wanted and much more. Here we are, living in an incredible mansion with all this *stuff*. We could use this festival idea to gain exposure for new artists, and raise money for musical scholarships. We'll be able to attract the very best musicians in the world today. We'll get them to perform for free and we'll call it the Monterey Pop Festival. No one'll get a dime profit."

Michelle agreed that I should buy out Pariser. We decided to ask some of our friends to be on the board of directors. At one of our first meetings in early April, Paul Simon and Art Garfunkel showed up along with Cass, Lou, and Terry Melcher. They were all in. Soon Lennon and McCartney were on the board of directors. Eventually, everyone came to the house for meetings to map out a strategy. It was agreed early on that we didn't want to go on with Pariser's plan. I called him and paid him twice what he had already put up.

Paul Simon was over at 783 several times during the planning stages. We threw a baseball around. He had played in college and we both missed the sound and feel of the game. Besides, no one played stickball in Bel Air, with balls disappearing down those deep ravines. I played him the tapes of our third album and showed him around.

The opulence and spectacle of the place shocked him. He and Artie had spent very little time in L.A. and because they were on the road constantly with so many hits, he was still living in the same modest Manhattan apartment he had had for years. Their music was so good they were already seeing *cover* records become hits. At that time, Harper's Bizarre had a big hit with "59th Street Bridge Song." Still, Paul was a kid from Queens and Bel Air was new terrain for him. "This is, like, the first *real* money we've seen," he said with his wry deadpan humor. "You'd have to say this is a very big house you've got here, John." Paul kidded me by saying that Lou and I were more businesslike and sophisticated, whereas he and Artie were "like, out of England. We're folk. We're pure."

All board members put up enough money to set up offices on Sunset Boulevard and create the Monterey Pop Festival Foundation. We went to work on getting other acts and establishing guidelines for the charitable uses of revenue— mostly music scholarships. Simon, for example, wanted to earmark $50,000 for a ghetto music workshop in Harlem. We rescheduled the event for a three-night, two-day poprock blowout. In between the livestock and zucchini contests, we got the three-day weekend of June 16–18.

It wasn't hard getting acts to play for free. We offered only to cover production costs and provide airfare from the last gig before the festival and to the first one after. I called Phil Walden in Macon, Georgia, who was then managing Otis Redding. "Count on us," he said. Once we got Otis, we had our three closing acts: Simon and Garfunkel, Friday; Otis on Saturday; and us on Sunday night. The rest fell into place easily. Jimi Hendrix was popular in England and Lou had played me "Hey Joe" and other cuts he had out in Europe and I thought we should have him on the bill.

The Beatles had urged us to ask Ravi Shankar. Ravi had played on the *Sgt. Pepper* album, which McCartney had just sent to my home. It was due for release two weeks before the festival and I knew it would have a profound impact on the counterculture. I had tried out the album on all sorts of drugs in my studio and it worked on everything. Ravi would add something special. The Beatles wouldn't come and play because they had retired from live performances, but they were sending their own small film crew so they could see what they missed.

Ravi was the only performer who asked to be paid. He wanted $3,500 for his afternoon ragas—assuring us that it would all go directly to his famous music school in India. We went along.

Lou had the idea to get a hard-rocking London act and we got the Who. They hadn't toured much in America yet and had managed only minimal radio airplay with "I Can't Explain" in 1965 and "My Generation" in 1966. Their newest hit was "Happy Jack" that spring and we figured they would add some tough London rock edge. We also pinned down Eric Burden and the Animals.

The Beach Boys were invited, but turned us down because they felt the hippie crowd would be too drug-oriented for their image.

After much discussion, it was decided the Monkees would *not,* after all, be right for the festival.

Then we turned to the emerging Bay Area music scene. So many groups were coming out of the San Francisco area that we had to open the weekend up to some of them. There were the Dead, the Airplane, Janis Joplin with Big Brother and the Holding Company, Country Joe McDonald and the Fish, Quicksilver Messenger Service, Canned Heat, Electric Flag, a dozen others. There was a definite rivalry and antagonism between the L.A. and San Francisco camps. We had trouble getting them to even talk to us.

To the suspicious Bay Area rockers, L.A. was Star City—slick, moneyed, plastic, and elitist. Haight-Ashbury was becoming the universal hippie mecca for both the drug and rock cultures. Musicians saw themselves as organic postcapitalist advocates of "power to the people." I felt they were out to defeat the purpose of the festival. They wanted to co-opt—that was the word then—the event to feed "their" people in the Bay Area. We had a state charter already that prohibited such limited and specific allocation of the charity. The Dead had been giving free concerts for a while and we respected what they were doing. But we wanted them to understand this was different, much bigger. This was global. Rock stars had never been flown in from all over the world for a single charitable event on this scale.

We set up a summit conference between the two California factions of rock and I asked Paul Simon, a neutral New Yorker, to act as our emissary. The Grateful Dead and "their people" agreed to talk to Paul.

Paul and Artie went up to San Francisco and visited the "Dead House," the band's Victorian commune and base of operations on Haight Street. "It's the spookiest place I've ever seen and these people are the strangest people I have ever encountered in my life," Paul reported. "Jerry Garcia, Bob Weir, Pigpen—man, it's strange up here. I'm sure they're all stoned. They sit around and riff all day. The girls do the chores and the guys work on the music. It's like they're suburban kids underneath it all. Which is mysterious enough for us *right there.* Artie and I are, like, New York City kids. This stuff hasn't hit the City yet. We got picked up by Rock Scully, their manager, and they took us around to the park, to Haight-Ashbury. People gave us joints out in the open. Everybody's smokin' right on the street. Hey, when *we're* on the road in hotels, if we smoke we drape towels in the doorway to keep the fumes in so we won't get busted. This place is unbelievable."

"What about the vibes up there?" I asked him.

"They hate the L.A. groups. Too show-bizzy. And they know the L.A. people don't love them, either."

"What do they want?"

"The Dead want Janis on the bill; they want Big Brother and the Airplane and Quicksilver; they want their own night to do their thing—the final night."

We reached some tentative compromises about the acts and left the scheduling to later. I nominated Paul for a Nobel prize and they split for the road.

Once word got out about the festival, every major and minor agent and manager in the world was calling to get his act on the bill. Nothing of this scale had ever been attempted in rock and roll. Alan Freed had his touring shows in the great glory days of fifties rock, but they weren't for charity and they were usually one-nighters. We knew we were breaking new ground and just feeling our way through. But the enthusiasm was building. Everyone wanted a piece of the action. A big break came when the ABC Network bought rights to the festival for a TV special. It got so hectic in the office that we changed phone numbers a dozen times. Though it was hardly in keeping with the spirit of the event, we eventually had to get the Monterey Pop Festival Foundation office an unlisted number.

The only people who voiced resistance and trepidation were the citizens of Monterey. Their serene Peninsula of Paradise was facing an invasion of rockers and druggies and they were frightened that life as they knew it might rock and roll to a thunderous 120-decibel extinction. They were especially apprehensive about security, violence, lodging, sewage, noise, and pillaging. It hardly helped that the local press predicted that a quarter of a million hippies would descend on Monterey and pick it clean.

Lou and I went to Monterey in the Learjet at least a dozen times to meet with civic, political, zoning, and housing groups. We tried to reassure them that hundreds of extra cops would be hired, that the kids who were coming would be peaceful and gentle. It was a delicate bit of diplomacy. I had to present an image of straight efficiency, and tripping on acid during most of these speeches definitely helped. My pitch sounded right and seemed to do the trick. Before long, we had hired local carpenters as planning began for the stage, lighting, sound, and backstage tent. We booked every hotel and motel room within miles. Lou, Michelle, and I rented a beautiful house right along the water a short hop from the festival site. There was a Monterey buzz in the air all up and down the coast.

Michelle was working constantly in the festival offices as well, either in L.A. or up in Monterey. We were both committed to making it work and it was all we did for three or four months. We also saw our own relationship come together as it never had before, away from the band's infighting.

I thought we should somehow put the word out to the kids that if they were going to San Francisco, they should come in peace and stay cool during the festival. We did not want riots and violence and insanity on our hands there. At the same time, Lou had asked me to write nothing short of a number one hit for a new label he created, Ode Records. He had sold out his share of Dunhill to Bobby Roberts and Jay Lasker and needed to debut on the charts with his usual Midas touch. Lou had always displayed an incredible knack when it came to picking hits, from Sam Cooke to Jan and Dean to Barry McGuire's "Eve of Destruction," the Mamas and the Papas, and Johnny Rivers.

Scott was the first artist signed to Ode and was hanging around with me everywhere I went. It was assumed that I would write Ode's first hit for Scott, rather than for the Mamas and the Papas. Lou didn't want Cass and Denny to try to stand in his way and claim that I wrote only for Dunhill. So we knew we had to work fast and quietly. It was getting pretty cutthroat. We knew a big hit would rankle not only Lasker and Roberts but Cass and Denny as well.

Scott came up with a brilliant idea for a lyrical theme: "Why don't you write a song about all the kids coming west for Monterey, about what they could expect and how they should handle the whole thing?"

It was a perfect promotional hook that would draw immediate worldwide attention to the benefit, *and* help make peace with the good people on Monterey Peninsula.

We sat down with our 12-string guitars one night and the first image I had was "If you're going to San Francisco, be sure to wear some flowers in your hair." Then it was "You're gonna meet some gentle people there." This was the dominant image I had of the Flower Power generation. The song fell into place, like many others, in about half an hour. I didn't want to be so transparent as to name Monterey, but we did get the point across: "All across the nation, there's a strange vibration/There's a whole generation with a new explanation. . . . For those who go to San Francisco, summertime will be a love-in there."

We cut the song in a night at the Sound Factory in L.A. I played guitar and coproduced the track. I kept forgetting the peculiar chord sequences and the key change to the song because I was speeding my brains out. We finally got into a warm, folky groove backed by the 12-string guitar rhythm chords. Fortunately, Scott had leaned on a RECORD button for one of our better versions and we could repeat it until we had it right.

By dawn "San Francisco (Be Sure to Wear Flowers in Your Hair)" was done. Scott's voice—rich and smooth, with a slight drawling edge to it—had never come through with more conviction and power. Lou had it on radio stations along the coast within days. Disc jockeys went berserk over the song. KRLA played it six times in a row the day they got it. It was released the last week in May and suddenly Scott McKenzie—ex-Abstract, ex-Smoothie, ex-Journeyman —had himself not only one of the certified blockbusters of the year, he had sung the anthem of the Peace and Love Generation. Lou was thrilled. Lasker and Roberts were pissed. Scott was stupefied.

That spring Cass found a new kind of joy in her life. Her daughter, Owen Vanessa, was born weeks before Monterey and Cass was thrilled to be a real mama. She spent most of her time at home with Owen and her friends and, like us, seemed to enjoy a new life away from the group.

The money was continuing to pour in—$150,000 or so during the two months before Monterey. And I had two hits moving together up the charts: Scott's and our own "Creeque Alley." Mitch and I had put it together because Lou never could get it straight how we all knew each other in the Village days.

So we told the story with the song titled for the narrow street at Duffy's in the Virgin Islands. The song starts when "John and Mitchie were gettin' kinda itchy just to leave the folk music behind." It winds up with us down by Duffy's: "Broke, busted, disgusted, agents can't be trusted/And Mitchie wants to go to the sea/Cass can't make it, she says we'll have to fake it/We knew she'd come eventually/ Greasin' on American Express card/Tents, low rents, and keepin' out the heat's hard/Duffy's good vibrations, and our imaginations can't go on indefinitely/And 'California Dreamin'' is becoming a reality."

Sure enough, when *Sgt. Pepper* came out, it blew everyone's minds. Now there was an album that proved to the masses what musicians had believed for years: that music and drugs work wonders together. The nationwide hunt for rock-enhancing psychedelics had begun. And the festival was just a couple of weeks away. We were riding the high blissful energy of the counterculture just at the right time.

There were a few minor hitches at the end. We had hired virtually every police and fire department for miles, and built a modest infirmary on the grounds which would become generally known as "the bummer tent." We had managed to appease the Monterey people by sparing no expense for peace and order. But the town demanded we put up a $100,000 security bond against damages and we refused. That became a deal-breaker and we were ready to blow the whole gig. But they backed down. Hiring lots of local citizens to work round-the-clock and with overtime—plus licensing local food vendors to work the festival—smoothed out more than a couple of diplomatic rough spots.

We never thought we'd have the stage and technical side done in time. We hired D. A. Pennebaker to do the *cinéma vérité* feature and everything had to be right for *that* as well. We flew in Chip Monck from the East Coast. He was the best in the business for rigging sound and light systems. He came out and looked over the lay of the land. "It'll take a month," he said. "Gotta build the whole stage from scratch." The dates were locked in. Miraculously, the last nail for the stage was driven about half an hour before show-time Friday night. The last electrical connection was made, someone threw a switch, and—BINGO!—the place lit up like magic.

There was almost no power-tripping by anyone, but we had a few testy exchanges with Albert Grossman, the big-time rock manager from Woodstock, New York. Grossman managed Dylan and Peter, Paul, and Mary and seemed to be making an inroad with the Bay Area acts. He seemed to want to use Monterey as a showcase for his clout and needed to pick some bone of contention with me. It turned out to be the release form for the Pennebaker movie. He came to my office and told me, "Quicksilver, the Dead, Janis, Big Brother, the Airplane—they're not giving away any theatri-cal or recording rights whatsoever."

"Then they're not in the show," we said. All acts were signing release forms to be in the movie. "We don't need them and, besides, nobody outside San Francisco knows who they are anyway. This concert's about getting new acts expo-sure and raising money for scholarships to help musicians. No one's going to get pushed around here. Do it our way or not at all."

We gave him twenty-four hours to send us a letter of con-firmation. Five hours later, it was all worked out.

There was another snag as the first concert crowd arrived like a giant caravan of dropouts around the fairgrounds. Denny was still in the Virgin Islands. Cass arrived Friday night and held court under the backstage tent. But we had no idea if Denny was going to make it. We had seen less and less of him as he retreated into life on Appian Way with his girlfriend Linda. We only saw him for rehearsals or sessions. I spoke with him a couple of times by phone to the Islands and managed to shout the date and hour he'd be needed for our set to close the festival Sunday night.

The fans filled the fairgrounds Friday night, arriving in convoys of jalopies, bikes, cycles, wagons, pickup trucks, vans, and sports cars. They pitched tents all over the place and we knew then that we had made one major mistake. The fairgrounds held only five thousand for each show—twenty-five thousand tickets in all for the five shows. We could have sold out a football stadium. But it was too late. We were locked in—literally—imprisoned by the hippie hordes.

The townspeople responded like true heroes. Everyone pitched in at the last minute as we saw tens of thousands of kids arriving with no tickets, no place to sleep or eat. They were allowed to camp out on people's lawns; then the board of education came through and let them use local football fields as campsites. Monterey was turning into a celebration, an exhilarating coming-together.

We wanted to turn Monterey into a sort of modern-day Renaissance fair. Peter Pilafian worked hard and creatively to set up scores of booths for handmade leather and jewelry, silk flowers, tattoo artists, head shop owners, candlemakers, and every kind of hippie craftsperson imaginable. He coordinated all the activities, concessions, and decorations around the fairgrounds.

There was no expected violence. Just in case, I had my own private bodyguard to shadow me, keep an eye on the Monterey offices backstage, and protect the performers backstage from hassles with cantankerous fans. Or with other cantankerous performers. Anything could happen. My old school buddy from Linton Hall and George Washington High, Jimmy Shortt, had come west through Vegas and then stayed at our Bel Air place while attending a friend's wedding. I asked him to come see us at Monterey while on vacation. I gave him a job that allowed him free access. I felt more secure having a Del Ray Local on hand—particularly one with the grizzly toughness of a fire department sergeant and the diplomatic skills of karate.

I gave Jimmy an all-access badge that let him move where

he pleased, backstage and out front. Then I gave him a hat.
"What the hell's this for?" he asked in his good-ole-boy
drawl. I looked at his head, which was nearly shaved. Jimmy
was six feet tall and a strapping 180 pounds. His hair was in
a fresh marine cut. "Look at your hair, man," I said.

"I ain't got any left," he grinned, smoothing the fuzz on
top with his hand.

"Precisely. Now you know why you better wear the hat.
The long-hairs'll get scared to death you're the heat."

"I ain't no narc."

"With that head you could fool a lot of people out there
and backstage. Wear the hat, man."

The first night went beautifully, despite the chilly fog that
closed in on the open field. Simon and Garfunkel closed the
concert with a sequence of delicate, crafty folk rock harmonies. Their voices floated gently through the low swirls of fog
rolling in off the ocean and got the festival off to a classy,
mellow start.

On Saturday the pace picked up with some hard-rocking
San Francisco blues rock and acid rock acts. People were
getting stoned and making love on the grass. Others were
freaking out on weird drugs and making war in their heads.
The bummer tent soon filled up. Word went around that a
notorious West Coast dealer, a colorful fixture in the San
Francisco drug-rock underground for years, was walking
through the crowd and backstage, like some schizzed-out
Johnny Appleseed, passing out bad acid to kids. He had
thousands of hits on him. I had met him a couple of times in
San Francisco and I had to get him out of there before he
turned the fairgrounds into the world's first and largest
open-air psychiatric facility. I got my guys to track the
dealer down and haul him backstage to the tent so he could
observe just what he had done. For an instant, Peace and
Love gave way to anger.

"You fucking asshole, man," I said. "We've put months of
hard work and hundreds of thousands of dollars into this
and you're running around dosing kids on bad acid. These
kids are fourteen, fifteen. They'll take anything. They could
get loaded just being here at the event, man. That's the
point. Do you realize what you've almost done?"

I led him into the tent. "Isn't that a beautiful sight? Look, some of them are gaining consciousness." A kid on an acid bummer was a grotesque spectacle. They were writhing and thrashing and screaming from their hallucinated horror. The medics were trying to take them down with Thorazine. Some who were recovering just sat and stared like zombies. Then some of them recognized their enemy and started freaking all over again. "There he is. He's the one who dosed me!" they screamed, pointing at us. "Get him outta here. Don't let him near me."

The dealer told me this special batch was known as Monterey Purple. He had whipped it up just for the festival. He made it sound like he was working with the caterers. He said each hit contained an overpowering one thousand micrograms of LSD. I almost strangled him. Jimmy lifted him off the ground with one hand and asked, "What'll I do with'm, buddy?"

"Throw him out," I said. I asked Jimmy to stay close to the bummer tent, to keep any *real* narcs out.

The pace picked up fast. I got a phone call in the makeshift offices backstage near one of the entrance gates. It was Susie, back east. She was serving me with papers requesting back alimony and child support. I was dumbfounded and this news rattled my head. It was like a reel from another movie had suddenly been threaded into my brain's projector. I told her we should maybe talk some other time.

"I sit here and see this article all about how you and Michelle have your his-and-her's Jags and you're setting up this wonderful benefit to help save the world. Oh, that's so cute I could barf." She was obviously not caught up in the Monterey spirit. "I'm the charity case you have to help, honey. I'm struggling and working my ass off at the goddamn Pentagon to support your two kids and you can't come up with $250 a month? I'm down to borrowing bus tokens from your mother and Dottie Blondheim. I'm up for a GS 11 and more money, but I can't work any more overtime than I already do because I'd be away from the kids. And I had to let the maid go."

She then laid into me for not discouraging Jeffrey's $200 in monthly phone calls to L.A. so he could feel he had more of a father. Susie had given Jeffrey the master bedroom and he had plenty of privacy—until the phone bill came.

I told Susie there was only one answer to all this: "Move out here. When the festival's over, we'll make arrangements to move you all out here. It's ridiculous for us to go through this. The kids are too far away. I don't want to put Jeffrey through this anymore."

Jeffrey was having school problems. He was very emotional and kids teased him because his father was "a Mama and a Papa." Susie and Jeff were seeing a psychologist through the Alexandria school system. He felt I had turned away from him when I moved west. "I'm ready," she said. "I've had it with East Coast winters and shlepping through fifteen inches of snow. I'm sick of my job. I want to relax by a pool in California."

Then I got a call from our housekeeper in Bel Air. She said that our home had been burglarized just after Jimmy left to come up north. Mostly cash and some musical equipment. The burglars apparently just backed a truck up to the door and loaded stuff in. "Can't deal with it now," I told her. "Call the Bel Air police."

I walked out of my office back into the euphoria of the festival and saw Jimmy standing over five limp forms on the ground. "What is this, a karate clinic?"

"Had to put 'em down quickest way possible, man," Sergeant Shortt said with a job-well-done smirk. He wasn't even breathing hard. "These gents tried to kick down the gate and enter the premises without proper authorization. I wasn't rilly tryin' to kill 'em, y'unnastand, just throw 'em down."

Eric Burden came up to me before he was scheduled to go onstage with the Animals. "Look," he said in his thick cockney accent, "you got to get me two 'its of acid from out there, man. I never go out onstage if I 'aven't got 'em." I sent out for it to keep Eric and his Animals 'appy.

The Bay Area groups whipped the crowd up fast: the Dead; Country Joe and the Fish, with their hilarious antiwar song "I-Feel-Like-I'm-Fixin'-to-Die Rag"; Quicksilver; Canned Heat; the Airplane; Steve Miller. The Dead also played an all-night alternative concert for the kids in vans, trucks, cars, sleeping bags, and tents at the local football field. The Airplane's nighttime set made spectacular use of the Joshua Light Show, projected on a large screen behind the stage. This was pure head music—set to an endless flow of abstract images that resembled throbbing microscopic protozoa moving through membranes enlarged to twenty feet.

The scene-stealer among the Bay Area bands was Janis Joplin with Big Brother and the Holding Company. I had met her a couple of times in San Francisco and she had shown up at 783 during a party one night weeks before Monterey. She was quiet and shy and awed by the grounds, the pool, the stables, guesthouses, the size of the home. She was carrying her bottle of Southern Comfort with her. "Give me a hit off your Southern Comfort, Janis," I asked as I was showing her around. "It ain't Southern Comfort," she whispered with a sly grin. "It's codeine cough syrup made to *look* like Southern Comfort." That was how she stayed stoned all day. It was high-powered stuff.

She definitely wasn't coughing up there that Saturday afternoon. Or shy. She was radiant and blitzed and belted her brains out with a fierce anguished power that brought the audience completely under her spell. We decided to let her go on again at night.

I let her know backstage. "I think all the audiences should have a chance to see you," I said. "You were fantastic. We'll find another spot."

She held my hand and started crying. "Oh God, that's sweet," she said tearfully. "What can I ever do to thank you?"

I looked down at the bottle in her fist. "How 'bout a big gulp of that Southern Comfort?" I winked and she laughed.

The town's chief of police, who was at the site all day, came by the office and threw me a look full of trouble. "Got some bad news," he said. *Must be Denny,* I thought. *Fuckin' guy's still snorkeling his way in.* I was sure we would have to close the first rock festival in history as the Mamas and the Papa.

"We're gettin' reports from our highway guys that a whole gang of Hell's Angels is massin' a coupla miles outsida town and they're on their way here. Whatta you intend to do?"

I scratched my head on this one. All I wanted to do was make love with Michelle right about then. "Well," I said, "you're the chief of police here. I intend to let you intend to do something about it."

"I can't prevent them from comin' into the city. I can only get involved after they break the law."

"Well," I said, "why don't we drive out to the city limits and talk to them and see what they want?"

As we drove out there, I was very high and very nervous. I wanted no fuckups at this point. We were halfway home and just hitting our stride. It turned out they really only wanted tickets. I told their leader, "I can't give you tickets. The shows are sold out. The whole fucking *peninsula* is sold out, man. If you'd contacted us earlier as an organization . . ."

"Look," the police chief butted in sternly, "if you guys screwed up one time in there—if anything went wrong— we'd bust you, send you all to the state pen." And that was it. They were real cool about it. They made a last-ditch appeal to become our security guards, but we told them we had taken care of that. And then they roared off peacefully.

That night Janis found me and was crying again. "Grossman won't let me go on tonight. He says I'll get overexposed. He told me you had to pay me for the evening performance."

I told Janis she would either have to fire Grossman, go onstage and take him to court, or convince him to let her go on. Then I decided to try to convince him myself.

I found Grossman sipping hot coffee in the brisk air under the tent. "What's up, Al? Give the kid a break. Is your coffee hot enough for you?"

"Yeah," he said.

"Good." I tipped the cup and it spilled over his hands. It was a ridiculous way to express myself and he didn't deserve that. He had, after all, done impressive work handling Dylan and his other acts in the past. But his bluster and power plays had no place at Monterey. "Al," I said, "she is dying to go on again. Janis *is* going on again. I'll spend every dime I've got to sue you, for being detrimental to her career, for misrepresenting yourself . . ."

"She'll go on again," he said.

"Thank you, Al. Now, how about a refill of that coffee?"

By Saturday night the momentum and anticipation were building. The show opened with Hugh Masekela and his thundering African percussion pop sound. Otis would close.

Paul Simon found me backstage. He was having himself a great time. "I've been walking around outside," he said, "and it's incredible. It's a jubilee. You see the tepees and tents all over out there?"

I nodded. "I saw you and Hendrix sitting together with guitars a while ago. That must've been interesting."

He rolled his eyes. "He's amazing, an unbelievable player."

"You and Jimi Hendrix jamming—that must've been a trip."

"Yeah."

"What were *you* playing?"

"Not lead," he said in his great deadpan delivery. We shook our heads and laughed. "Did you see that chick walking around backstage who looks just like Brian Jones?" he asked.

"Yeah, you mean the one with the lipstick and mascara and the frock that looks like a Moroccan caftan?"

"Caftan, *shmatte,* what do I know? I'm from the City. I don't know from caftans. You saw her too?"

"Oh yeah. That *was* Brian."

Janis did her second set Saturday night and again tore the house down with "Ball and Chain."

Before Otis Redding went onstage, Phil Walden and I helped him into his orthopedic-style corset. Otis was such a sweet, lovely man that it moved me to think he might be self-conscious about looking too heavy. This was a major breakthrough for him before a mostly white audience. I had to plant my foot on Otis's broad, thick back and pull the laces in toward me to get the corset real tight, just the way he wanted it. I didn't see how he could breathe and do his set.

He did both—and got the crowd so stirred up that everyone left their seats and pushed forward. "I've Been Loving You Too Long" was slow and soulful and had the females swooning out front in the cold. During "Shake," the police chief came to me and pulled me away from the sound system so I could hear him.

"Hell's Angels again?" I asked. He shook his head.

"That's it. We're closing you down. They're out of their chairs, pushing forward. If they don't immediately get back in their seats, I'll order fire, police, and sanitation to close the house down. I'll pull the plug on ya."

"You pull the plug, my man, and we got no sound, no light, and a lotta kids out there on a lotta drugs with nowhere to go but crazy. Then you really *will* have a problem."

"Got a point. Try to get your man out there to calm them down."

I yelled to Otis to keep the peace in the audience. To try a little tenderness. So Otis went back to the mike and said sarcastically, "So this is the Love Crowd, huh? Well, you better start lovin' your seats and sit down 'cause they gonna take away all our electricity and we all do wanna have ourselves a good time, don't we? So let's all relax and stay cool."

It was the festival's only tense moment and Otis had handled it masterfully.

By noon Sunday, I was sure Denny was a no-show and I started thinking about what we'd do. The afternoon concert belonged largely to Ravi Shankar and his hypnotic, meditative ragas. I was meditating on Denny's absence.

Ravi gave one of the most remarkable performances I have ever witnessed. Within the past year, the exotic sitar sound had wafted into the mainstream of rock. I had visited Ravi at his family's home in L.A. and discussed paying him for his music school in Delhi. I met his wife, his sisters, and their children. They were the most gentle people. We ate curried dishes with our fingers. Incense burned throughout the simple, modest house in the Hollywood Flats. It was unpretentious and suburban and about fourteen people lived in it.

When Ravi visited 783, we stayed up and cut some demos of us jamming together. Ravi exuded a simple joy when playing and he seemed blessed by supernatural stamina and discipline.

And that day, June 18, he was supernatural. The power of

his art had blown out a wall between two civilizations and joined them for a searching, restless generation. At the breathtaking climax of his final raga, he and his tabla player earned a long and rapturous standing ovation.

There was only one technical snag that day. Peter had arranged for 90,000 orchids to be brought in from Hawaii. They were to be lifted inside a hot-air balloon, then dropped all over the fairgrounds. But a shift in winds made this impossible. The orchids would have landed somewhere closer to Alcatraz. Instead, they were spread out on every seat for the afternoon ragas.

The hypnotic serenity created by Ravi's music exploded into rock bedlam Sunday night. After sets by the Dead and the Blues Project, the Who took the stage and tried to blow up the Monterey Peninsula. I didn't like the Who from the start. They were snotty, arrogant, and demanding. Pete Townshend was surly and impossible to talk to. He thought he was the only true musician in the world. Everyone else was "pussy," as he put it. They had wanted to close a night. They wanted a longer set than anyone else. They wanted a special introduction. And I kept telling Pete, "No no no. You can't have that. You can't do that. You can back out and we'll fly you home, but if you go on, you go on like everyone else, in the time slot allotted. You agreed to all this before you left England and I'm not changing anything now."

Every act knew precisely where in the bill it was scheduled so the lighting guys could simply follow their lighting charts, page by page, and know exactly what to do with each performer. There were about thirty acts. The technicians were tightly coordinated. The Who wasn't about to fuck with our system.

Then they went out and, at the end of "My Generation," all hell broke loose. Smoke bombs blew up. Townshend rammed the amps with the neck of his guitar. Explosions went off onstage. Keith Moon kicked over his drums and Townshend totaled his guitar.

After the Who, the war for the hearts and minds of America's rock infantry escalated when Brian Jones came out and took the mike. "I want to introduce you," he said, "to a very good friend of mine and a countryman of yours—Jimi Hendrix—the most exciting performer I have ever seen."

By the time Jimi took the stage, the festival's collective energy was peaking. Understandably, no act familiar with Jimi's performances in Europe that spring had wanted to go onstage right after him—not even the Who. As it was, Townshend, Keith Moon, Roger Daltrey, and John Entwistle had done everything in their power to be a tough act to follow. But Monterey—and America—were just discovering the Jimi Hendrix Experience. Pilafian came backstage. "This should be interesting," he yelled over the din as we watched Hendrix launch into the dense, thundering power chords of his finale, "Wild Thing."

"Yeah. Jimi's out there, all right."

"He popped two hits of Monterey Purple before going on."

"Wild Thing" heralded Jimi's arrival on the acid rock moonscape with a genuinely boggling fusion of space guitar flash, blues funk, pelvic lewdness, and pyromaniacal lunacy. No guitarist had ever worked a one-handed version of "Strangers in the Night" into the power chords of a heavy metal rampage. And chew gum at the same time. His act cut across everything: It was white, black, tender, savage, flamboyant, daring, brooding, cosmic, orgasmic, and scary. Jimi was sheer rock incandescence.

I loved it when he played his Fender behind his back, and when he performed cunnilingus on the strings. I loved it when he did a backward roll and stood up again without missing a lick. I loved it when he humped the amps until they came with an elephantine feedback wail.

Just when it seemed that he couldn't take it any farther, Jimi grabbed a can of lighter fluid. No other guitarists had ever violated local fire codes just to get through a solo. I did not believe it when I saw Jimi lay the Fender down, sacrificially drop to his knees, and squirt lighter fluid on the guitar.

We were raising money for music scholarships and equipment and Jimi was barbecuing a Fender. I couldn't take my eyes off this wildman weaving back and forth across the line separating genius and madness.

Then he tossed a match and created a legend. The flames

danced several feet in the air and died down. Jimi stood and
swung his Fender like an axe until it splintered into kindling
wood. By then, we all sensed that Monterey was making
history. The spectacle was unsettling but spellbinding: the
Who and Hendrix were committed rockers who had pushed
their art over the edge and given destruction a good name.

As Jimi played out his orgy of demolition, I went backstage to see if the Mamas and the Papas were, in fact, ready
to close rock's first three-day festival.

I saw Michelle and she was muttering, "That fucker's not
gonna show. He's not gonna show." Just then I spotted a
long red Caddie convertible pull up near the rear gates backstage. It could only have belonged to one person. "Denny," I
shouted. "Over here." He made it by ten minutes. It was
unreal.

"What the fuck is going on here?" he asked. His eyes were
intense and beady, sweeping over the scene, taking it all in.
Smoke was rising from the stage area. The noise was awful.
"I woke up this morning in the Virgin Islands," he said,
"and I fly to L.A. and drive like a rocket for seven straight
hours to get here in time. I pull up, nobody knows who the
fuck I am, I ask this cop for directions to the stage area, and
he turns around and he's got a fuckin' flower and stick of
burning incense in his helmet. 'Who are you?' he asks me
and I say, 'I'm the next act.' So he lets me in. Then this
speed freak walks up to him and screams, 'Anybody got any
SPEED?' The cop doesn't even give a shit anymore, just
sittin' on his huge chopper. And some guy comes over and
sells the freak a hit of speed right in front of the heat and he
doesn't do shit. Now what the fuck is going on here, man?
It's a zoo."

"I don't know," I said. "Welcome to Monterey. I could
have used five heads and six arms just to keep all this shit
together."

"I could use a hit of speed myself just to get through this
set, eh?"

"No sweat."

We ran out onstage and did our songs completely out of
tune from start to finish. In parts, we weren't even close. We
hadn't sung in months. We hadn't rehearsed at Monterey

because Denny wasn't around. Cass had been partying all weekend. Mitch and I were too busy at the site to worry about harmonies and arrangements. I was fried on speed. I had been up for most of the past week.

Scott came out during our set to do "San Francisco" and *he* was so off and out of it that he sang in a chord sequence that was the reverse of what the band was playing. We stared at each other. As he had done as a Smoothie on "American Bandstand," Scott still closed his eyes when he was nervous. That was why in the Pennebaker film, we had to use Scott's recorded version for the opening credits and not the live one.

The performance was the least of it. It was an extraordinary dreamlike moment frozen in time that left us weary but proud. Michelle and I had been too busy to make trouble for each other. We had worked incredibly hard with so many others to pull off a show and we ended up with a remarkable cultural event. Ravi, the Who, Janis, Jimi, and Otis were all "discovered" at Monterey. It was the first global rock benefit and it ended up raising millions of dollars. There had been no political rip-offs of the festival. There had been no violence and only one arrest. And a parking ticket backstage. The drug victims recovered and limped away. Hendrix proved to the world that amplifiers have sexual organs and that electric guitars *are* sexual organs. And that they are flammable. The L.A. and San Francisco factions had come together for the first time. The hippies had spent three days camping out on the Establishment's front lawn and they all got along like brothers and sisters. For that one brief, glorious time, Monterey showed how peace and harmony could thrive and triumph amid social and cultural gaps, political upheaval, great rock, and weird drugs.

The partying went on all night at the Highlands Inn in Carmel. Pete Townshend got himself another guitar and the Who blasted live music through town from a flatbed truck. By daybreak some of the performers, roadies, hangers-on, and groupies were babbling and nearly catatonic as they cleared out.

Denny came roaring by in his red Caddie convertible, followed by a screeching Porsche manned by David Crosby. They both looked slightly deranged. Denny had Linda with

him and a navigator in the backseat. She was a gorgeous
spaced-out angel of acid huddled over a scented candle balanced on her knees. Her hands curved around it to protect
the flame from the wind. Denny looked back at her, then to
me, and pointed down to the candle with his thumb. "She
says it's been going since the opening act of the festival.
Needs a ride to L.A. We found her at the hotel. Crosby and I
are racing down the Coast Highway to Nepenthe, that restaurant on the mountain. We'll make a pit stop, then next
stop—Sunset Strip. That's where she wants a lift."

The acid angel's candle had in its sixty-hour life unfolded
and bloomed like a squat, shiny plant. The wax was thick on
the dish at its base. Reefer roaches, pills, and matchsticks
were trapped in the hardened wax. She stared down into the
burnout void, guarding Monterey's Eternal Light. I was glad
someone was. Denny roared off and soon we were on our
way, too, looking down at the debris of the fairgrounds from
the Learjet. The festival was ending and the Summer of Love
had begun.

14

WE WEREN'T HOME long before Michelle and I got the wonderful news that she was expecting a baby, conceived, obviously, during the Monterey project. The spirit of the love-in was indeed still alive with us. The time was right. The festival had brought us closer together, the group was beginning to record its fourth album, and we weren't doing any more major tours.

The distance among the four of us was clear during the sessions, which were often tense and unsatisfying. One time, in the studio upstairs at 783, we took a break and Cass called Denny into a small room. She took out a packet and opened it up. Inside, he later told me, was a small quantity of Mexican brown heroin. That freaked him out. Smack killed.

She told Denny that David Crosby had given it to her. She had apparently been snorting smack. This seemed incredible, since she was so dedicated to her baby daughter. She offered Denny a couple of hits in each nostril and he immediately began retching. Mexican brown scorched his nasal membranes. Denny had tried acid a couple of times and backed off. He was the Crown Royal King and he mixed his booze only with smoke and ups. "This is the real thing, eh?" he said to her. "I'm deathly fucking ill. Thank you very much.

This is quite a lot of—*eugghhhhaaa*—fun. I think I'm gonna die now."

Susie moved to California that summer with Jeff and Laura, who were then eight and six years old. She rented a modern condo in Tarzana at the Casa Caballero complex in the San Fernando Valley. By the end of July, she and the kids were settled in.

For them it was a major readjustment. The first time Laura set foot in the mansion at 783, she looked around and —being used to apartment living—said, "Wow, Dad, this place is huge. Which room is our house?"

"It's all our house," I said. Her jaw dropped and her eyes bugged in amazement. They both loved to stare at the peacocks and roam the grounds, lost in make-believe jungles and forests. Laura always had on her turquoise canvas go-go boots, which she called "the love of my life." The kids were often picked up and dropped off by limo and attracted plenty of teasing attention from friends at school and around the condo: They were suddenly children of a famous pop star. Michelle was very attentive and generous with the kids and treated Laura to dresses from a Beverly Hills kiddie boutique.

In the middle of August, we played the Hollywood Bowl. It turned out to be one of the last shows we did, but it was a great way to go out. I sent first-class plane tickets to my mother and Rosie. Her daughters, Patty and Nancy, were already out visiting at Susie's. The whole family came for the show and a big bash at 783 afterward. I called Jimi Hendrix to be our opening act.

Before we left for the Bowl, Michelle pierced Laura's ears, using a needle, pink thread, peacock feathers, and ice cubes for anesthesia. At the same time, Rosie got in a limo at the airport and heard KRLA play fifteen minutes of our music. It was her first trip to California and this really blew her mind.

It was quite a glorious evening: my mother, sister, ex-wife, two nieces, son, daughter, and pregnant wife all together and peaceful under one roof. They were in the front row as Hendrix came out and got hooted at by the Mamas and the Papas fans. He did "Purple Haze," "The Wind Cries Mary," and "Foxy Lady"—but these were our fans and they weren't ready for the Jimi Hendrix Experience.

The party afterward was one of our best and most memorable. The house was jammed with famous names and faces. One of our friends then was a Hollywood gossip columnist named Steve Brandt. Steve and Mitch became rather close and he was a link between our rock world and Hollywood's film crowd. He helped us with party lists and introduced us to everyone. He also encouraged Michelle to think about "going Hollywood" and becoming a starlet, though I didn't agree and felt she should stick to her raw street instinct for rock. In any event, parties were a good way into the business and that night was hot.

All the great songs of the day were playing on the giant stereo system. I brushed past Rosie, the small-town Virginia girl who had been in California maybe five hours, and she was chatting with her number one screen idol Steve McQueen. Rosie worshipped McQueen. She struggled not to faint.

"Oh, so you're John's older sister," he said.

"Yes, that's right."

"He really is such a wonderful talent. It's amazing he wasn't discovered earlier."

"Yes, yes, that's true, isn't it," she said without really knowing what was coming out of her mouth. This was her big moment to ask him everything she ever wanted to know about "Wanted: Dead or Alive."

My mother had a chance to meet *her* hero Lee Majors and ask him all about "The Big Valley." She was weak with excitement. She still felt that tie to the Old West. Rosie's and Dene's heads were swiveling so fast they probably missed a few faces. Warren Beatty and Jack Nicholson were there. Marlon Brando, who lived near Jack in the Hills, showed up briefly. Sonny and Cher floated through the living room. He was buried inside something hip and furry that looked like it crawled off the endangered species list. Cher was the ultimate hippie Pocahontas in beaded headband, long black braids, and hip-hugging bell-bottomed jeans.

Hendrix's entrance was nothing short of heart-stopping, as he glided through the door in his classic Brooding Buccaneer getup—the three-cornered hat, ruffled shirt with french cuffs, skintight black-velvet bell-bottoms and boots. He was also wearing a gorgeous young long-haired blonde on each arm. I caught a glimpse of Rosie catching a glimpse of Hendrix. A racially mixed *couple* would have been scandalous enough for her. A *trio* bordered on mortal sin.

I milled around and made sure everyone had enough of everything. I tried to keep the kids away from the bags of grass and pills lying around. I spent a good amount of time conversing—if that's the word—with Joe Cocker. That was quite a moment. "This is great, this is great," he kept muttering in his hoarse cockney accent as he looked over the room, tugging at his scraggly beard. "But where are we?" he asked.

"The state of California, Joe."

He growled with curiosity. "Hmmmm. California. What city?"

"L.A., Joe."

"Oh yes. Yes, of course, L.A. That's great, man. What a trip. Great house. You're a great friend, you really are. Thank you."

"You're welcome, Joe. You're a great friend too."

"Yeah, yeah," he mumbled between his bizarre jerking tics. He teetered and looked at me strangely, working his eyes into focus. "But, like, who *are* you, man?"

Susie was not having the time of her life and I understood. She told me that she had stayed as late as she could for the kids' sake, but that she had to go. "You were wonderful," she said. "The show, the limos, the house, the party, everything's been just wonderful." Not even her warm, congratulatory tone could mask her anger and envy.

To soften the transition to life out west for Susie—I did want her to stay this time—I bought her the place at Casa Caballero in Tarzana. But, clearly, it was Michelle and I who found the best ways to enjoy our money. We loved the exquisite luxury of being able to pick up and go anywhere.

We spent lots of weekends up in the mountains at Lake Arrowhead and Big Bear. We always stayed in the same place. The cool clean air helped us relax and get away from it all. We made a couple of treks through Mexico. We rented planes to spend weekends in Vegas with Lou, Scott, Keith Richards, and Anita.

Just before Susie moved out, we took one wild trip I would almost care to forget. The group had a standing contract for Learjet service, so we called the charter firm in Columbus, Ohio, and within hours we were on our way to Nassau in the Bahamas. I stuffed a green overnight bag with cash—there must have been close to a hundred thousand bucks. I prevailed upon Susie to let us take the kids. We picked them up at the airport in D.C. at 5 A.M. A well-known London record producer laid some drug on me for the trip. It was, I now suspect, Angel Dust. The effects lasted two weeks, but only kicked in at exactly two o'clock in the afternoon. It was like a psychedelic laxative.

I wanted to take care of the kids and go island-hopping on boats and do regular vacation things. But at two o'clock every afternoon, the drug sickness returned. It was some great high: I'd get the sweats, diarrhea, the shakes, I stuttered and couldn't focus my mind. It was like clockwork. The symptoms lasted a couple of hours. Michelle stayed off the nasty powder. We tried to find a nanny for the kids. This went on for days. I could not get this awful drug out of my blood.

Jeff was calm and stayed around the hotel pool and beachfront much of the time. Laura was Miss Personality, winning limbo contests on the hotel lawn. Once she disappeared for such a long time that we had to go to the police and describe her.

"Your girl is the drum majorette for the local marching band that's in the political demonstration today. She's leading the band."

Sure enough, we found her a couple of hours later, highstepping and twirling in front of a marching band. The Islands always brought out the best in Laura.

When the Angel Dust finally settled, we went out to the casinos. Michelle put a dime into a slot and yanked the lever. Three cherries popped into the windows. There were no lights and bells, but we knew she had hit the jackpot. We called over the manager and he opened the slot and told us we had just won $20,000.

After flying to D.C. to drop off the kids, we went to New York and stayed in a suite at the Sherry-Netherland Hotel. Then we went on a buying spree with our green bag of cash. I felt like we were gangsters on the run, hitting Bendel's, Saks, and Bergdorf's. We got some furs and jewelry for Michelle and suits for me.

I got in touch with our old friend Hugh Duffy, who was in New York. I invited him up. Duffy told us his hard-luck saga of bankruptcy in Creeque Alley. He had been following our careers with keen interest. And he needed a $20,000 loan to open a joint on the Costa del Sol in Málaga.

"Easy come, easy go, Duff," I said. I reached into the green bag and tossed a couple of packs of bills to him. He didn't believe what he had just experienced. He dropped to the floor and picked up the money. "Thanks a lot, man," he said, and walked out the door.

I heard later that Duffy's dream bar in Málaga folded and that he was a short-order cook somewhere.

Right after Monterey, we got to work on our fourth album. It wasn't so easy any longer to bring the four of us together for long stretches of time. We cut most of the tracks upstairs in the eight-track studio at home. The two Mamas had become a little chummier since they could talk about being mamas. The Papas were spaced out on one thing or another most of the time.

The schedule was rough for a pregnant woman. Peter would start setting up the studio in the afternoon and Mitch and I would wake up and have breakfast at about the same time. The studio had a fancy lounge and reception area, with a desk, phones, plush couches, and three banks of colored overhead lights with dimmers. You could adjust the look and mood of the room as if it were a stage—or a giant color TV screen. The entrance to the recording room was behind a concealed panel in the wall.

Cass and Denny would arrive for drinks and hang out until the early evening and then the musicians would arrive so we could begin by nine or ten. The booze and drugs usually came out by midnight and by 2 or 3 A.M., as Peter put it, "the separation from reality" among the users would take hold. The sessions would then trail off as we fell into stupors.

The last track we would record for that album was a re-make of an old Frankie Laine hit from the early fifties called "Dream a Little Dream of Me." One night Michelle's father was at our house for dinner and he heard me humming the jazzy riff as I picked it out on the guitar. It turned out that he had known one of the song's writers, Favian Andre, in Mexico City. "Put it on the album," he said.

I cut it with Cass in the studio upstairs and she com-plained that it sounded dated and campy. I had to make her whistle at the end and do the "ba-dah-dah's." She rolled her eyes and shook her head. *"Really* corny, you know," she *kvetched.* "Next we'll be in blackface. Get out the burned corks."

Perhaps it was the routine of recording, the prospect of fatherhood for a third time, the confinement of living and working at home. But I got restless. As had happened earlier with Susie, some deeply ingrained fears surfaced. I handled them as usual: I ran. This time, though, I didn't run to Cuba. I ran to a willowy black groupie who had gone out with Mick, Scott, and Denny. Hendrix wasn't far behind.

I saw her at her place, in a suite at the Château Marmont Hotel, or if Michelle was asleep, she'd come by 783 late at night. We'd go through a bottle of wine, smoke some dope, and make love. Quietly. I couldn't believe I would be doing this, that I could set Michelle up for that kind of hurt. She had behaved herself in the fifteen months since the Gene Clark crisis and we had survived Monterey. Then it started to fall apart all over again. More bulbs in the french chande-lier were going out without being replaced. It became a standing joke.

One night I came home from the groupie's place. We had driven in my Jag all through the canyons over L.A., staring at a bright moon. I pulled off the road, we got out of the car and threw ourselves to the ground and made love. When Michelle asked me where I had been, I said, "I've been out for a drive."

"Why are there leaves all over your back?" She seemed to

welcome the confrontation to clear the air and vent her anger.

"Have you ever seen a full moon over Benedict Canyon in your Jag, as the light drips through the sycamores?" I asked wistfully. I watched her and knew I was dead meat. "I was moonstruck, so I got out of my car and I hiked to the top of the hill for a better view of the moon, and for a few hours I felt total peace, lying there staring at the moon. It was a really beautiful experience."

"BullSHIT!" she squealed. She knew this wasn't the first time I had cheated on her while living together. I always thought our connection was resilient and durable, that Michelle would be willing to forgive the odd lapse. I had—three times. By then, maybe we were confusing resilient with convenient. Having an affair during her pregnancy was certain to test her threshold. I was obviously sending her a message. The fact that she accepted it only meant, I later realized, that she had probably known that the marriage was doomed. Life went on. I wasn't leaving. We still had to work and have a child together. The groupie faded away.

But the foursome was proving to be unworkable. We just didn't want to be together. Michelle was beginning to devote more time to planning for the baby and was taking much better care of her body. The LP wasn't my top priority anymore, either. I was running around too much and the concentration was gone.

Cass was always itching to get on the road. She knew her greatest strength was her live work and she needed that rush of adulation. She was also chafing for a solo career beyond the shadow of the group.

At home, she was surrounded by losers and cruel users. I added to the equation a teasing, sparring sort of affection that flared up now and then. She was regularly checking in to Cedars of Lebanon for diuretic treatments that could drain twenty pounds of fluid from her body in a weekend. Then I'd kid her that every time she went to a fat farm and lost weight, her value went down by a dollar per pound lost. And her eyes looked closer together. It was nasty banter, but rooted in respect and genuine fondness. I always felt we were intellectual equals—sometimes rivals. She was fast and sardonic and I liked to think I could hold my own with her.

But as for her crowd and Denny's crowd, I was a snob. They were less "literary," and they weren't even top-of-the-line street people. In Cass's case, they were just hustlers, music industry leeches, and I had no time for them. I felt it degraded us all that Cass indulged them so generously. If she came to visit us, she came alone, without her retinue. If I saw her up on Woodrow Wilson, they would leave. I became grim around them. They were sometimes drugged-out, belligerent dealers, in leather with weapons, chains, and cycles.

I loved Cass for her irrepressible buoyancy and decent heart. She was flippant and sharp. These people were neither. They were like muggers. She deserved better.

What was saddest about Cass was that she was a beautiful free spirit imprisoned within her body. That was bondage for Cass. She often felt very alone and essentially resorted to renting friends. She provided shelter, loans, food, drugs, and understanding to a crowd of people who were vastly inferior to her, spiritually and intellectually. It made me angry. It was upsetting to see how men fed off her—and how she went along. Cass's most famous line about her love life was: "It's easy to find boyfriends. I buy them a motorcycle, a leather suit, and put them in acting school." It was always the same guy with a new name. Cass had no illusions about herself, and for that alone she towered over most of the people clinging to her. It was all about buying and selling.

The one close friend she adored—Denny—was out of reach as a lover. The scars from Denny's fling with Michelle were still deep and raw. Denny was retreating from us and hanging out with his more surly gang. When he returned from Monterey, he found his house still crowded with hangers-on, though the cast had changed since his trip to the Islands.

Denny was being ripped off too, and he had grown disenchanted with the sycophants feeding off him. While he was away in the Islands, the muffler and bottom end of his red Caddie convertible had been ruined by a boyfriend of Cass's, a jet-setting rich kid whose father was in the diplomatic service. There were rumors that the Feds suspected him of using secure diplomatic pouches to move drugs between countries.

The repairs had been completed just before Denny arrived in L.A. to drive to Monterey. But the aggravation lingered. When he got back home after the festival, Denny felt like a party-crasher in his own home. He eventually began renting the house next door for some peace and quiet.

The recording sessions finally came to a halt. We just didn't have it. I called a press conference at the Beverly Wilshire Hotel in late September 1967 and said we would be temporarily breaking up. We were going to head for Europe and cool out, put things in perspective. Only three tracks for the album had been completed and we were scrapping the rest for now. "We're just grinding the songs out," I told the music press. "We're not in any kind of groove. We're beginning to feel phony as artists."

At the end of that week, we had to honor a prior booking to appear on "The Ed Sullivan Show" in New York. We had done the Sullivan show a couple times before and Ed really liked us. He and Cass got along famously. We were outrageous on "Sullivan." Michelle once sat in a tub for one skit, peeled a banana, then sucked on it. It was a *rrreally* big show that night.

Ed always seemed to flub part of our introduction. He'd call us the Mamas and the Poppers, or the Mummers and the Papas. He'd lose sight of his cue cards in the spotlights and forget what to say next. Once he completely lost track of what to do. He stood next to me and muttered without moving those iron jaws of his, "For God's sake, *say something.*"

Cass once said, imitating his clenched-jaw staccato, "Say, Ed, how's your little mouse friend, Topo Gigio? We have to follow the mouse again, Ed, and we're not happy about that."

We knew this was our last Sullivan show—the end of an era—and I was depressed. The Sullivan show was an American institution. The Sullivan show was how Elvis got launched, the Beatles, and so many major music acts. It was how Topo Gigio got launched, along with Señor Wences. And us. And now we were on the show saying good-bye to America, announcing that we were going our separate ways.

The following week we sailed the *France* to Southampton, England. We were supposed to play the Royal Albert Hall and promote Scott's new record, "Like an Old-Time Movie." The timing was fortunate. Michelle would have been too far along a month or two later to travel like that. We all had first-class tickets and the giant liner left New York on September 29.

We woke up in Boston and sent a roadie to score a pound of grass in Harvard Square for the crossing. He made contact with some meth monster who took him through every subway stop in Boston for the buy. He just made it back in time. That chilly damp night we cruised past Cape Cod, ordered champagne, and had a dope-cleaning party in our staterooms, tossing the strainers, seeds, and stalks overboard as we pared our stash down to a manageable twelve ounces or so. A Boston Tea Party—1967 style.

The *France* was as elegant as you could get. We had our own wine stewards and did our best to consume as much of the dope as possible. We swam, read, sunbathed, drank, and I stayed high the whole time.

We had to dress for dinner every evening and we never did. The men had tuxes and the women had beautiful gowns, but we dressed like slumming L.A. rock stars. We'd wear raggedy coats; I'd wear a shoelace for a tie. To enter the glittery sunken first-class dining room, there was a spiral staircase. It was bad enough that we didn't care if we looked like stowaways, but we had to make an entrance every time we went to eat. We never went in there without getting a roomful of raised brows and snobby stares.

There was a storm at sea that ruined *Dr. Zhivago* in the theater. It got real choppy and the projector was jerking all over the place. A crew member walked onstage and announced, "We've lost one of the stabilizers and we might lose the other, so we're in for a pretty rough night. Would all the passengers kindly return to their rooms, put on their life jackets, and await further instructions?" It was just like a disaster movie on TV.

"Hey," I yelled, "we're first-class passengers. You can't do this. You don't drop a stabilizer in the fucking Atlantic."

We heard screams from Cass's cabin. We ran in and she

was in a wrestling match with the life jacket. She couldn't buckle it around her middle. The liner was pitching from one side to another, people were yelling from their state-rooms, the smell of first-class barf started wafting through the long passageways as more and more people started to lose their first-class dinners. Bodies were slamming into walls. Tears were streaming down Cass's face as she fought to buckle up and keep her balance. She looked scared to death.

"Don't worry about a thing," Denny said. He was in con-trol of the situation. He grabbed another life jacket off the wall and lashed it to the first one with an intricate nautical knot. "This'll do, mate. It's got to. I'm a sailor from Hali-fax." He strapped her into a bright orange diaper.

Then we tried to take as much of our drugs as we could, just in case we went down. We didn't get too far. We passed out first, then awoke a day later in calm waters. I walked out to the deck and leaned against the railing and smoked a joint with the bracing, salty ocean breeze and bright sun in my face. It was smooth sailing again.

The last night at sea we played dress-up and entered the dining room decked out in all our loveliest duds. The whole dining room rose as one and greeted us with a standing ova-tion and choruses of "BRAVO! BRAVO!"

Just as the *France* pulled into Southampton on October 5 and passengers prepared to leave, our passports were seized and we were told to be patient when disembarking. We were the last ones to be allowed off the ship—out of 1,700 passen-gers.

We hadn't known it, but we were told there was an out-standing warrant for Cass's arrest. They had us trapped. With almost half a pound of grass.

Cass came to me on deck. She was white as a sheet. "They're going to search us," she said. Adrenaline shot through me. Panic set in.

"What the hell is this about? They couldn't have known we scored in Harvard Square. Unless they're tailing us. We don't have much time. We gotta ditch the dope fast. They're already moving off the ship. Pretend you're sick and throw-ing up and run to the ladies' room."

"Honey, I don't have to pretend."

We moved quickly through the narrow corridor toward our staterooms to coordinate the dumping operation.

"They're trying to nail me for a hotel bill from six months ago," she said shakily. I had never seen her move so fast.

"Cass, you ran out on a hotel bill? What do you think record company advances are *for?*" I was trying to keep her afloat with humor.

"I didn't, but a friend of mine probably did." She was breathing hard, brushing her hair off her face as she walked. "It was the guy who's the diplomat's son and we stayed at Queens Gate Terrace, this ritzy suite run by the Embassy House Hotel. I gave him a couple of hundred pounds to pay the bill and I assumed he paid. But I took two blankets for the flight home, I guess. I don't know any more."

Cass got the dope and stuffed it—loose—in her bra. Denny and I tried to distract and amuse the Customs and Immigration people while Cass and Michelle went to the head. The stewards and porters were all mumbling that Scotland Yard was after her. Michelle waited for Cass, then walked in on her. Cass had tried to flush the grass down the toilet without bothering to wrap it in anything. Most of it just backed up in the toilet. Cass had then apparently tried to scoop it out and dump it somewhere else because there was wet, clumpy grass clinging to everything.

The agents were getting restless and suspicious and headed off to find the Mamas. Denny and I gasped with tension. There was no one left on the *France*.

They banged on the door. "Come out immediately. Open this door. We must search this room!"

The door opened; somehow they had cleaned up the bathroom and flushed it all down.

We walked off the liner and Cass was promptly arrested. A brawl broke out at the docks in front of hordes of reporters, TV crews, and photographers. I spotted Andrew Oldham standing next to the Stones' limo, waiting to pick us up. We tried to get in, but the cops yanked Cass from the limo and we were in a tug-of-war.

Only months earlier, Mick and Keith had had their own drug trials dragged through the Fleet Street scandal sheets.

There wasn't much sympathy left in straight London for the rock and roll devils. It didn't look good. The cops slapped the cuffs on Cass and hauled her away as the crowd hooted and jeered.

Then I realized Cass had a couple of hash cookies and roaches in her purse. I thought we were goners.

Michelle, five months preggers, went crazy. She wound up and slugged a policewoman. "They can't take her away! They can't take her away!" she screamed.

"I'll get you for this, honey," the lady cop shouted at Mitch. "Oh yeah," Mitch spat back. She was fired up for more, fists cocked in front of her swollen belly. "You want some more, come on, I got some more," she said. I tried to hold her back. Then she nearly collapsed as the police van moved away.

Cass was strip-searched in the police car. We got into Oldham's limo and smoked some fat hash joints riding into London.

Cass was charged with stealing two blankets and a hotel room key, worth about $28. We missed by *seconds* getting busted for possession because she had taken two blankets. Incredible luck.

We went to the police station and posted bail to get her out of jail. Then we found out what the real story was. Scotland Yard was not, in fact, interested in two blankets. The Yard was hoping to squeeze Cass for information about her boyfriend's suspected international smuggling maneuvers.

We immediately drove in the limo to an art supplies store. We bought posters and paints and made our own FREE MAMA CASS posters. We picketed the police headquarters and made the news and papers all over London.

The courtroom was noisy and packed to the rafters for Cass's case before a magistrate. It looked like a scene from a Charles Dickens novel. Cass had already met with Scotland Yard and convinced them she had no idea where the guy was and how or where and with whom he operated—if he operated. They were satisfied and halted their pursuit.

"Madame," the judge proclaimed with his learned Oxford lilt, "we find you not guilty—and you may leave this courtroom with your honor unsullied."

Cass threw her arms up triumphantly, rolled her eyes with relief, and mugged as cameras clicked and the room buzzed with approval. Then she bellowed like a trucker, "I don't like da way doze woids sound, Judgie. But tanks anyways."

As we were walking out, a court officer handed Cass her purse. "Got any cookies?" I asked Cass. She said the cops had found them in the strip-search but let it go. They really were after bigger game. Now the TV and print press were after us for comments. She opened her purse when we stepped to the sidewalk and took out the hash cookies. I ate one and gave one to Denny. "Here," I said, winking. "Eat up."

"I understand completely," he said, and stuffed it into his mouth, right on camera, as we got into a limousine. Then we swallowed the roaches. We weren't taking any more chances. "There goes the last of the evidence, guys," I said.

There was a press conference in the hotel with some of the Stones on hand and we all wore shades and answered questions with witty, cryptic remarks. Afterward, at a party, Cass was telling Mick the story of her bust off the *France* and I brushed by and said something like, "Oh, Cass, that wasn't how it went," or "Mick, she's got it all wrong." I was just joking around, but Cass flew into a rage. "Well, fuck you," she shouted angrily and stormed off to her room.

Denny intercepted her in the hallway and they went to her room. I had humiliated her in front of her idol Mick. She couldn't tolerate being upstaged like that. And this had been one of Cass's finest hours. She was a national hero in England and didn't want anyone—least of all me—ruining her moment.

"That son of a bitch," she yelled, waving her arms wildly. "Who the hell does he think he is, telling me how to tell my own goddamn stories? Well, FUCK HIM! And FUCK ALL OF YOU! I've had it. This is the straw breaking the camel's back. I march to a different drummer from now on. I've fucking HAD IT with this group. I'm out. Finished."

The trip to London offered all sorts of surprises. At one point, Michelle told me she was in love with Lou Adler. Just like that. I never took it too seriously. By this time, she was in her fifth month and knew I was running around on her.

She was not happy with that, but we knew we were no longer at our best. Still, it was provocative and added a little more excitement to the trip.

We were planning to play Royal Albert Hall at the end of the month, but we canceled to protest our shabby, disrespectful treatment at the hands of the cops. Then we all went our separate ways. Denny and Cass went home; Michelle, Scott, Annie Marshall, and I stayed briefly in London to help Scott promote "Old-Time Movie." Columbia Records International, which was distributing Ode throughout Europe, was picking up part of the travel tab. I had originally wanted to give Scott "Twelve-Thirty (Young Girls Are Coming to the Canyon)" as a follow-up hit. I had written it during the Monterey work. The instrumental tracks were done. Scott was to sing the vocals when we got back from some shows in the midwest. But Lasker was pressuring us to get out another single after "Creeque Alley." I called Scott and asked him if it was all right for me to record the song with the Mamas and the Papas. He was at Lou Adler's office. Adler wanted another number one hit for Ode. Scott owed me one after "San Francisco" and said sure. Adler said no. We did it for Lasker anyway because it was my song and Scott did "Old-Time Movie."

In London, we stayed on at the Hilton and Scott was clearly a hippie idol in Europe. Fans gathered outside the hotel and chanted his name, lit candles, and sang the anthem as they tossed flowers toward the suites. Scott admitted he was "half-cracked" under the strain of stardom. He cowered in his closet. "I'll never forgive you for this," he muttered. "How'd I ever let you get me into this?"

"Grab it while it's hot, man. You got the largest single in Columbia's history."

"Can't handle it, man."

Mitch, Scott, his date, Annie Marshall, Peter Pilafian, and I moved on to Paris and into a magnificent suite at the eleganzo George V hotel on the Right Bank. Scott was big stuff in Paris—he had lip-synced on color TV, one of the first acid-rockers to appear on the tube there. One French kid saw us on the Champs-Élysées and threw himself to the ground to genuflect. "I can't handle this either," Scott said as we watched the kid bow. "Okay, Scott," I said. "Then we're getting out of Paris and going to Switzerland to get drunk."

Before we hit the road, I told Mitch that Scott and a friend of ours were going to do a little *cherchez les putes* in the tawdry Pigalle section. I didn't want to miss out on anything great, so she let me go—reluctantly. We found a joint that didn't look too bad and went in. The girls lined up in the red glare and we each picked a favorite. It was pretty racy, though my girl was young, wholesome, and pigtailed— she could have been a Bavarian "werchin" for all I knew.

We met outside half an hour later, bought a bottle of champagne, and decided to go back and get *all eight* of the girls. It was closing time, they could use the overtime. When we got in, we forked over the francs. Scott promptly went to his girl, I followed his cue and went back to my peasant girl. In no time the girls were giving rather sincere lip service to our needs on the bed. Scott and I were lying next to each other. In a ceiling mirror, we saw our buddy surrounded by the other six hookers. His eyes were glassy and he was smiling as his clothes came off. He was massaged and caressed by twelve hands, twelve lips, twelve breasts.

"We're so dumb, Scott," I whispered, "we really are. What *are* we doing wrong?"

"Don't make me laugh," he grunted. "It's late. We haven't got much time in here."

We all drove southeast to the spectacular snows of Mont Blanc to take in the Alps for a few days and stayed at a lovely inn. One night at about ten o'clock, we decided to go hike up a mountain behind our quaint inn. We had three bottles of brandy and we were so drunk that we kept slipping down and rolling over the hard-packed snow, laughing our asses off. We almost lost it from frostbite. We got down the mountain by three in the morning, only by forming a human toboggan and sliding together.

The rugged, parched terrain around Marrakesh was an exotic change. Marrakesh was a stucco and stone city with a salmon-colored glow to its ancient structures. Much warmer, sunnier, and better drugs. We befriended a carpet

merchant who sold us some rugs and he invited us for dinner. The door to his home was one of dozens along a crusty
stucco wall of a twisting alley in the medina, the section of
the old city walled in by medieval ramparts. Inside, though,
was a veritable pasha's palace, with a large courtyard, fountain, and his own small orange grove. No plumbing, just a
squat pot, bucket, and spigot.

He served us cous-cous, with an appetizer of sheep stomach lining. We sat around a huge brass serving platter and
ate with our fingers. Then he was good enough to spin the
platter around and offer the sheep's eyeballs. "National tradition for guest of honor," he said proudly. "First say,
'Bs'millah'—in the name of Allah."

"Right. Bs'millah," I said. Then I took a breath and down
went the slippery treat.

He introduced us to another local delicacy, a brown, seedy
paste made up of hash and two dozen herbs, nuts, and
spices. It was called maajoun. Street vendors sold chunks of
it—as well as maple candy laced with hash—for a quarter.
You didn't need a tour guide after that.

"Maajoun good for you," he said. "National tradition."

"I can imagine."

I rolled up a glob of it in my fingers. "Bs'millah," I said.
He laughed. "Bs'millah," he repeated. I popped it on my
tongue and washed it down with sugary mint tea. Maajoun
was very strong. There was a lot of crazy laughter for a
while, then I don't know what went down, except that by
morning I was still extremely stoned out in a grove, shaking
olives, oranges, and figs off trees.

We stayed in the King's Suite of the famous Mamounia
Hotel, with beautifully patterned ceramic tiles six feet up the
white wall, a gushing fountain in the center of the courtyard,
everything blinding white and clean. And the ubiquitous
sound of the Egyptian singer Oum Khaltoum's sinuous
quiver on the radio. We'd walk around the native medina
and wind through a disorienting maze of alleys and
crowded, dusty markets. It was utterly hypnotizing.

Morocco is a place that can be lyrical and brutal at the
same time. Many English rock stars of the sixties like the
Stones, particularly Brian Jones, had vacationed and ex-

plored Berber music and indigenous mind-expanders in Morocco. Hip jet-setters and expatriates then attracted kids from the ever-spreading dropout circuit, and cities like Marrakesh and Tangier received the counterculture's stamp of altered-consciousness approval.

Marrakesh was a city that altered consciousness whether you took drugs or not. Michelle and I saw a man beating a camel with a large stick around the eyes and nose while casually talking to a friend. Michelle begged him to stop. Our guide, Mohammed, tried to tell us that this was one of those everyday folksy things Westerners don't understand. "Many people are beating the camels," he said in fractured English. "Camel is food for people Moroccan."

"Well, then ask him to stop hitting his food. It's making me ill to see blood all over this poor helpless camel's face."

"I can not to ask him to stop." The camel's face was gruesomely bruised and pained.

"Then how much would it cost to buy the camel?"

"Monsieur want to buy camel?" Mohammed asked, slightly offended. He asked the food-beater for a price, looking back at me. At least the beating stopped.

"Okay, you can to buy the camel. For you, one hundred dirhams. Twenty dollars. But, John, my brother, tell me, what you will do with this camel?"

"Let me buy it first." I pulled out a wad of Moroccan funny-money. On the bills, there were colorful drawings of King Hassan II and loyal workers digging a ditch. My head was throbbing in the blinding sun and choking dust. I was tripping.

I handed over the money and the man gave me the rope attached to the poor beast's neck. Then he gave me the stick. I snapped the stick in two, and released the rope from around the camel's neck. Then I set the camel free and we wandered toward the carpet suq.

We walked through the markets and past the long rows of handicrafts booths in the sprawling Jemaa el-fna square just outside the medina walls. One rickety old man with a bare, waxy brown chest and huge white turban sat with a primitive lathe attached to his foot by a string around his big toe. With a tireless sawing action of his foot, he carved beautiful foot-long hash pipes. His son sat next to him and painted intricate designs. They never spoke.

The Muslims, we were told, were celebrating their holiest day of the year, the last day of Ramadan, Aid-el-kbir. The streets were more crowded than usual, with everyone buying food for the big family feast. My eyes stopped blinking altogether on the *maajoun*. The endless onrushing images, scents, and sounds just poured through, unfiltered, frighteningly vivid.

Then we walked back to the Mamounia at sunset for a Moroccan feast in the dining room. A brilliant, gleaming full moon rose through a deep and clear azure sky. Soft clouds seemed to shred into pink and lavender wisps as we watched them sail by overhead. The sensuous pounding of the G'naoua drummers in their white robes and caps never let up from the frantic pulsing heart of Jemaa el-fna. The walls and towers of Marrakesh gave off their rosy tint at dusk.

At dinner I glanced up and thought I was hallucinating. I was sure I spotted Candy Bergen and Terry Melcher, two of our friends from Bel Air, outside the hotel. I shook my head and blinked hard. I went to the front desk and asked if a Terry Melcher or Candice Bergen was registered.

It was them, all right. I ran out and flagged them down. We sat around together and shared our adventures. I had trouble sleeping all night because of all the *maajoun* and the sensory overload of Morocco. I went to Terry's room.

"Got any Valium?" I asked him.

"Sure," he said.

He gave me a yellow five-milligram Valium, but back in my room what I took was a tab of Sunshine without thinking. The pills looked similar. An hour later, the words of the *International Herald Tribune* started sliding off the front page. The sun was coming up. I went into an adjoining room and switched on the light and felt an explosion go off in my head. Mitch was fast asleep. Very few women five months pregnant had been running around like she had and she was exhausted. And she was drug-free.

I walked down to the lobby and colors flooded out of the fountain in the center of the courtyard and washed over the white tiles. In the deserted streets I heard the haunting call to prayer from the top of a nearby mosque. Now, from all corners of the city, men in long white robes, yellow slippers, and turbans were sleepwalking toward the mosque with prayer mats rolled under their arms.

I couldn't sit still, so Scott was my guide through the medina. It was one jarring image after another. We went down to the suq, with its crippled, maimed children crouching with their bony hands extended, fire-eaters, kids with shaved heads and flies stuck in the ointment covering their open impetigo sores, stiff, green-skinned syphilitics with collapsed saddle noses, gaping eye sockets, cataracts, and gnarled hands. We walked past toothless wonders, leprous beggars, snake charmers, Blue Men from the Sahara, sword swallowers, Berber women with their hands and faces tattooed with blue tribal markings, workers from the tanneries whose arms were dyed the color of their vat.

A couple of sadistic kids tortured a cat to death by tying a wet cord around its neck and one of its hind legs. The cord was wet so it wouldn't slip. Every time the doomed, snarling cat tried to free itself by kicking, the knot tightened around its neck until it slowly strangled itself, letting out a horrifying death gasp at the end. A group of stoned-out locals silently grinned and applauded.

We met an American expatriate drunk who had lived in the medina for years. "You know, a lot of the families cripple one of the children on purpose—and that's the beggar of the family," he said. "He supports the family. Bind the feet, twist the legs like licorice sticks." The wonders never ceased.

Aid-el-kbir came and I was finally crashing—just in time for the religious sacrifice of thousands of sheep and lambs in the homes of the medina. By nightfall, a stream of animal blood was running down the narrow dirt alleys. Little girls walked through the medina lugging water buckets and stone pots filled with white-hot coal embers used to cook the animals' flesh, organs, organ linings, brains, and eyeballs. This annual sacrifice symbolized the Muslims' humble submission to Allah for ruling and ordering their lives.

I eventually came down and we got back to Bel Air. It was nice again to walk through a marketplace and not see any moist animal organs. It was time for us to begin ruling and ordering our own lives again.

15

THROUGH THE END of 1967 and the early months of 1968, Michelle and I were witnessing the beginning of one life— our baby—and the end of another—the Mamas and the Papas.

It was clear that we were on the ropes when the label released *Farewell to the First Golden Era,* a greatest hits collection, in November 1967. It was as if the label was already saying good-bye.

While I was discovering the surreal Third World mystery of Morocco, "Glad to Be Unhappy" sluggishly ran up the charts to the mid twenties and swiftly dropped out of earshot after less than two months. The title was ironic. That record signaled the beginning of the end for us. It was a badly timed slump. Right after Monterey, the group's royalty rate was doubled from 5 to 10 percent—pending delivery of our troubled fourth album by mid-September. That one was still in the works.

Though four of our first five releases had made it into the Top 5, our record sales had been erratic for a year. "Dancing in the Streets" had vanished somewhere in the seventies on the charts. But two months later, "Dedicated to the One I Love," which featured Cass and Michelle, hit Top 3 and stayed there almost a month. "Creeque Alley," boosted perhaps by Monterey and "San Francisco," made it to Top 5 in the spring. But "Twelve-Thirty" and "Glad" fell short of the Top 20. We had lost momentum. "Dancing Bear" came out before Christmas and was gone by New Year's.

There were other bothersome signs of trouble. ABC Television had bought rights to broadcast a documentary on the Monterey Pop Festival for $500,000. Then the network yanked it because it was apparently too controversial and anti-Establishment, even though there were no political speeches or overt protest songs performed. We also learned that $50,000 had been ripped off from the Monterey Foundation account by a little old white-haired bookkeeper from Scotland. She had a police record as long as a Fender Stratocaster. She'd make you coffee, give you aspirins, chat about the bank account, pat your head, and then forge Lou Adler's signature on the Foundation's checks. The bank nailed her and she did time. The Foundation was later credited with the stolen $50,000.

On January 2, 1968, our accountant, Don Sterling, sent something of a New Year's wish to Jay Lasker at Dunhill. "We appear to have been able to get through 1967 by the skin of our teeth," the note read, "for which we thank our lucky stars. However, we can't go very much longer without an infusion of funds for our prized clients."

Sterling's letter was a request for advances and they were issued within a week. Michelle and I were in good shape, considering how fast we went through our small fortunes. I got the songwriting royalties and we pulled down half the group's artist royalties. Close to a half million dollars had rolled in since the trip to Europe. Not even we could spend it that fast.

But Cass and Denny were having trouble staying ahead, and Cass was getting itchy to launch a solo career. Denny seemed to go through money with great ease and had a year-round party to bankroll up at the Astor mansion. There were stories that Cass was deep into debt and had blown everything on an extravagant life-style of fast cars, furs, jewelry, and her unstinting generosity toward her spongy retinue. She knew our fans adored her and that her vocal "hooks" on songs like "Dedicated" had plenty to do with their success. She was certain she could sell records and book a lucrative tour on her own without us. She was the one with all the charisma and she had a daughter to support.

Our daughter, Chynna Gilliam Phillips, was born on February 12, 1968—also my mother's birthday. Except for her visits to L.A. and the odd trip to Washington, I hadn't seen much of Dene since the Mamas and the Papas hit. She had been drinking a lot, her blood pressure was up, and she was alone much of the time. She retired from her job with the government and came to stay with us for a few weeks after Chynna's birth. There was nothing tying her down to Washington any longer. Some of the Gaines Boys, like Uncle Orbie and his wife, Aunt Frances, and Uncle Hoyt, were living out west, as were Susie, Jeff, Laura, and Rosie's two daughters. We decided she should move too.

Every morning she helped Michelle with the baby, then got in a limo and rode all through the Valley, Bel Air, and Beverly Hills to look for a home. She finally settled on a lovely house in the Valley, but she said, "I'm afraid it's just too much money. It's really sweet and has a pool and it's just what I'm looking for, and it's in a place called Tarzana. But it costs forty grand. That's a bit high, don't you think?"

"Sold!" I said.

We got the place for $37,500 and I threw in a Lincoln Continental. She loved the sunny weather and western terrain. She bought a wardrobe of muumuus for the pool, dyed her hair pale blue, and made new neighborhood friends. And, of course, she played with her infant granddaughter.

Michelle adored the baby and relished her new life as a mother. But the marriage was crumbling as fast as the group. I was beginning to see more of Mia Farrow, though Michelle and I hadn't openly discussed the situation. Mia came with us to Palm Springs for a rest when Chynna was less than a month old. Michelle was nursing and weary and going through the postpartum blues. I didn't make them any better. Mia and I took off for Joshua Tree and left her behind. It was a low blow. Then I came back and wanted everything to be right again. That was out of the question.

A while later, as Mitch rebounded from the strain and
exhaustion of the baby's infancy, she pursued an affair with
an English documentary filmmaker named John Shepherd.
She had met him in London. He had won awards for films
on Biafra and Vietnam and she made it clear that she found
him worldly and stimulating. She told me about him and I
was skeptical about its working out. I didn't see them lasting. That only seemed to make the fling more alluring.

I was truly taken by Mia. Our first "date" was at a dinner
party arranged by Steve Brandt. Mia was estranged from
Frank Sinatra and sharing her time between Sinatra's Bel
Air house and her brother John's house at the beach. Mia
had recently finished shooting *Rosemary's Baby,* which was
directed by Roman Polanski. She had spent a month with
her sister Prudence meditating with the Maharishi in Kash-
mir.

Mia was gentle and flighty, but she was also very bright
and outspoken and loving. She was a real Flower Child. She
took her business meetings barefoot and on the floor, usually
decked out in beads and wild clothes. Sinatra lived mostly in
his Palm Springs compound, with a twenty-four-hour guard
on duty at his house. Every time I arrived to pick Mia up,
the guard took the license number and name and listed it.
That didn't deter me from leaving well into the night or
early morning. I really was crazy about Mia.

Mia was lots of fun. We went to the movies together, spent
time at the beach, and had dinners with Roman and his new
wife, Sharon Tate, the gorgeous actress. I met dozens of
Hollywood people through Mia's group of friends. When the
movie came out, she and I went to see it three or four times,
sneaking into the theaters five minutes after the opening
scene so no one would recognize the star. Mia had played
Allison MacKenzie for two years in "Peyton Place" on TV.
The big screen truly fascinated her.

Mia and I once took mescaline and had a great pillow
fight. While tripping, Peter Sellers, who had dated Mia and
was still in love with her, dropped in. He was upset that we
were so stoned. "I'll get you down from that drug," he said
angrily, "if I have to pull you down by the pubic hairs."

We would later spend time at the Joshua Tree Inn in the

desert. We shared an intense passion, but Mia always had her own piece of the world all to herself, where no one got in. It simply wasn't available and could not be reached. In that sense, she was unlike Michelle, who gave herself totally and never left any doubt as to what was on her mind. That was part of Mia's beauty. Behind her keen, questing intelligence lay another aspect—elusive, spiritual—that belonged only to Mia.

I was always fearful that Old Blue Eyes might think *he* belonged only to Mia and seek some sort of reprisal. We were once pictured on the cover of some fan magazine, arm in arm, leaving the Candy Store nightclub. Above us, on the cover, was a superimposed Sinatra glowering down at us. The caption read: WHAT DOES PAPA JOHN HAVE THAT DADDY FRANKIE DOESN'T? I figured it wouldn't be long before I'd be knocked off. Riding an elevator in Beverly Hills once, a big thug in a dark suit elbowed me in the ribs and whispered, "Why don't you stick to your own wife and leave other men's ladies alone?"

This happened a few times while we dated, but I was able to find out that Sinatra had nothing to do with these goons. They apparently took it upon themselves to intimidate me, without getting any "orders" from the Chairman of the Board. But I did hear that one of his security men was relieved of his duties for failing to snitch on us.

Later on, when Mitch traveled to New York and Washington to be with Shepherd while he was filming the Doors on tour, I tried to cast the situation as badly as I could to deter her, even though I knew almost nothing about him. "Mitch," I said, "look, we're sort of through. That much is clear. But I hate to see you or me or both of us taken in by somebody flattering us to death when all they're out for is your money and fame."

She was sullen and defensive. "Never," she snapped.

She called me from Washington and sounded quite upset. She told me she was going to be staying at my sister Rosie's for a few days before heading back to L.A. "You were right," she said, "it was just like you figured. It didn't work out. I'm so sorry. Please, can I come back?"

"I'm in love with Mia Farrow," I said. It was my first chance ever at revenge. I loved it.

"How could I have been such a fool? I want to come back."

She marched back into the house and tossed her bags down. I was glad to have her back, but I was still seeing Mia. One night I was preparing to go out and Michelle asked, "Where are *you* going?"

"I have a date with Mia, as a matter of fact."

"Oh, is that right? Well, get over here." She was reading a novel in bed. Her tone was unusually playful, since we weren't exactly sharing a bed as man and wife in those days. Things were pretty strained. We often just lay there in stony silence or exchanged terse, clipped sentences. Michelle spoke mostly in Spanish when she was really upset.

"You're probably going to sleep with her, aren't you?" she said teasingly.

"Probably." That got her going. She tugged at my belt and pulled me close to her. Then she went for my zipper. All of a sudden, we were going at it pretty good. Who was I to resist? She was still incredibly sexy to me. By the time we stopped, I was, to say the least, in no condition for a date. Mitch still had that kind of power over me.

"Now," she murmured, "you can go out if you like."

Mitch had once asked me to make a choice between her and Mia, but they became friends and it didn't seem to matter as far as our marriage was concerned. There were only a few bulbs lit in the chandelier by the time *The Papas and the Mamas* came out in the middle of 1968.

The mood of the LP and, in fact, the country itself were both dark. With titles like "Midnight Voyage," "Safe in My Garden," and "Mansions," the album came off as a melancholic meditation on a life of insulated unreality, fame, money, and drugs. It was, in a word, about me.

What was happening on the front pages of the papers seemed all too real. Martin Luther King, Jr., had been killed in April. Vietnam had split the country into Hawks and Doves. The Generation Gap split parents from their rebellious youth. The Credibility Gap split reality from govern-

ment deception. Campuses had become the hotbed for the
sexual revolution and the battlefield for the antiwar movement. Bombings by anarchistic lunatic fringe groups were
becoming more frequent; there were more National Guardsmen than students on some campuses. Columbia University
was a combat zone. Grungy student radicals seized adminis-
tration buildings all over the country and dropped acid in
the deans' armchairs. The peace marches on Washington
were drawing hundreds of thousands of dissidents who
raged against the war effort, the military draft, police brutal-
ity, and the policies of Lyndon Johnson. Getting clubbed by
a helmeted, face-masked cop in a cloud of tear gas was becoming a popular college spectator sport on TV. LBJ
wanted to send half the nation's able-bodied young men over
to pacify and defoliate Vietnam.

We kept our distance politically. The Black Panthers in
California had tried to recruit us to do some work for them,
but we never made a commitment. We had gotten to know
Jane Fonda, Peter Lawford, and other politically active celebrities, but I never felt comfortable with political advocacy. I attended marches only as a private citizen. I was too
safe in my garden.

I was interviewed on Dick Cavett's show once, along with
Pierre Salinger and Arthur M. Schlesinger, Jr. I was supposed to mouth the sentiments of the youth culture. I said I
was against the body counts, the secret wars, government
deception, etc., etc. That's where my sympathies lay, but I
felt I was merely parroting what I had always heard Jane
and other politicos say far more persuasively at rallies.

Then, when Bobby Kennedy was running for the Demo-
cratic presidential primary race in California, his people,
through my friend Peter Lawford, had asked me to write a
Mamas and the Papas song for his campaign in California. I
was having enough trouble creating music for the president
of my record label, much less for the most likely candidate
for the White House. I never did write one, but we did meet
Bobby and rode through L.A. on the back of a flatbed truck,
singing songs for his rally that day just before the primary.

"Safe in My Garden" hit the charts the same week Sirhan
Sirhan assassinated Bobby Kennedy. Like millions of other

Americans, I was watching TV as Bobby made his way toward the podium in L.A. to make his victory speech. Again the country went into shock, then mourning. The two political conventions that summer were shaping up to be violent, chaotic watersheds. The Summer of Love had given way, only a year later, to violence and hatred.

"Safe in My Garden" stalled out somewhere in the fifties on the charts after about a month. It was the group's fourth stiff in a year. Cass was already making TV guest appearances on variety shows and was shooting for a long engagement in Vegas.

Dunhill decided to release another album cut right away and went with "Dream a Little Dream of Me." The only twist was that the label chiefs released it as a Cass Elliot single.

I felt stung and insulted. They were acting out of self-interest by virtually "stealing" the song from the group. They must have felt that it was Cass's popularity that was keeping us alive at all, that she alone could survive. In pushing to have "Dream" included on the album, I inadvertently came up with the song that cut her loose from the Mamas and the Papas.

We had lost the touch. Our time had come and gone. That's what they must have presumed. It hurt me that Cass went along with it. And this was a song Cass had hated at first. I had taught her to sing the song, worked hard on the arrangement, and gotten her to *whistle* at the end. Now it was a Cass Elliot hit. And a big one. The song lingered on the charts for close to three months and got to the Top 10. Cass finally had the solo acclaim she had craved so long. I could hardly blame her, but it was hard not to feel resentful and depressed.

That fall the Beatles turned out their epic *White Album* and had the biggest hit of their career, "Hey Jude." The song stayed at number one for over two months running. Times had changed. The Beatles showed the way. Music itself was heading toward a technological and compositional complexity that would leave many of us behind. It was tough to keep up. If there had been an innocent, sunny spirit to the sixties, it was fading fast. The Mamas and the Papas were being driven from power in the counterculture and drowned out on the radio.

We tried two more times for a hit record in the final months of 1968—the last of a dozen or so singles we released in the sixties. The results were grim. Between Thanksgiving and Christmas, "For the Love of Ivy" and "Do You Wanna Dance?"—our slow-motion cover of Bobby Freeman's great fifties hit—both spent little more than a month on radio playlists and hardly broke into the Top 80.

Cass smartly tried to cash in on "Dream" with "California Earthquake" and an album of new material. Then she got herself booked for a highly publicized stint at Caesars Palace. She signed for three weeks at $40,000 a week, with another three weeks a year later.

While Richard Nixon was winning the White House in early November, Cass was losing Vegas. Her opening night proved to be a catastrophe. The Earth Mother of hippiedom had been ill with nervous cramps and an ulcer for a couple of weeks prior to opening night in the extravagantly tacky Circus Maximus room.

I got a call that afternoon from Bobby Roberts, our group's manager. I had not seen him or Cass for months. He was with Cass at Caesars and had a major crisis on his hands.

"John, she can't sing. Nothing comes out," he said anxiously. "We rehearsed this afternoon and she sounds terrible. I don't know what to do. If you guys are able to get her to sing, if you can possibly come to Vegas before the show, see what you can do, I'll send a plane to get you here."

"I'll be there. I'll do anything for Cass." Mitch and I were there in a couple of hours. Cass's elaborately produced show was to be a slick blend of pop, soul, rock, schmaltz, and Cass's self-mocking stage shtick. But by showtime opening night, she still had hardly been able to get through a rehearsal. She had a fever, a chill, and kept herself wrapped inside her massive new sable coat.

When we got to Cass's room at Caesars, it was clear that she was fucked up. There were a few hangers-on, as usual, guys I didn't care for and who didn't care for me. They were part of a clique that hung out around Cass in the hills or

around the house that Terry Melcher sublet to Roman Polanski up on Cielo Drive in Bel Air. Melcher had nothing to
do with them. It was hardly his kind of scene. Among them
were Jay Sebring, who was a popular hairdresser to the stars;
Wojtek Frykowsky, a longtime friend of Roman's from Po-
land; and the same boyfriend of Cass's who had been sought
by Scotland Yard a year before.

Roman and his stunning wife, Sharon Tate, had become
good friends of ours. She had lived with Jay Sebring until
she met Roman in London when he directed her in *The
Fearless Vampire Killers* earlier that year. Jay and Sharon
had stayed close friends, despite his heartbreak. It was not
unusual for all of us to be at the same parties several nights a
week.

There were rumors that Wojtek, who often stayed at the
Cielo Drive home, had some unsavory connections involving
drugs and that this crew was given to kinky sexual practices.
When I got to Cass's suite at Caesars, a couple of these
goons were already there.

I noticed one of them, named Billy, sitting over this immense block of Iranian hash. It was the size of a wheel of
cheese. It had the words GIFT OF GOD stamped on it in Farsi.
The block was at least eighteen inches wide and four inches
thick and they had been chipping on one large wedge of it. I
was enraged. This was the night Cass had been dreaming of
all her life. She was paralyzed. Her concentration was shot,
she couldn't remember the lyrics to "Dream," and she was
messed up.

I tried to work with Cass, but she couldn't sing. She
gasped and croaked when she opened her mouth. For the
first time since I had known her, Cass looked wasted.

"I've lost over a hundred pounds in five months," she
muttered. She had been fasting half the week for months,
eating a meal a day the other days. She told me at rehearsals
she had had to wear her new sable coat to keep from shivering in 100-degree heat. She was a sick woman. She could not
get a note out. Her throat sounded clamped. Now she was
sweating profusely and the air conditioning was keeping the
room temperature down to 65 or 70 degrees.

"Help me, help me," she begged. I tried to get her to do

vocal exercises to loosen her voice. She told me her vocal
cords had been hemorrhaging.

Billy watched me as I moved around the room. I wanted
to kill him. I felt the situation was hopeless. I called Bobby
Roberts, who was her manager now.

"She can't go on," I said. "You should bail out now. She's
sick. Get a private ambulance and get her out of town.
Reschedule the date. Tell the press she's got peritonitis—
anything."

"I can't, John," he said. "It's too late for that."

"Bobby, it's never too late. Just do it. Get her out of
here."

Cass went out for the first of two shows and bombed miserably. It was sad and painful to watch. Mitch and I were at
a table up front, along with all of her closest friends and a
table full of press. Cass's voice was dull and throaty. There
was no pace, no kick. The energy was way off. She looked
lost onstage in her flowing chiffon. She missed her cues,
threw the band off, flubbed her lines, blew lyrics, and generally looked lost. I was dying for Cass.

The first set was a disaster. Some fans walked out midway
through. These were not Cass's constituency of Flower Children, but rough-edged gamblers and high rollers accustomed
to brassy dance numbers offering tits-'n'-ass and feathered
headdresses. Vegas was Monterey Pop for Middle America.

Cass sang a tone to a half tone flat the whole show. It
would take much more than a blow to the head with a lead
pipe to get her voice back up there now.

Between shows, we went backstage. I was angry. I
couldn't help but assume that these leeches around her had
been feeding her drugs.

Michelle sat beside Cass and consoled her. There were
bouquets of flowers and telegrams from Cass's famous
friends wishing her well from all over the country. I went to
Billy and backed him against a wall. He warned me that he
was a karate killer. "I can destroy you in ten seconds," he
said.

I pushed harder. "That's good, man. 'Cause you got five
to get the fuck outta here."

Cass was distraught, sobbing, sweating between shows.

The mood in the dressing room was gloomy. Cass didn't seem to know where she was. She did a second show and went to bed afterward.

Cass got out of her engagement and another act was flown in to replace her. I had never done any opiates, heroin, or morphine back then and I had never used a needle. I had gone through the usual assortment of highs—grass, hash, acid, speed. But now, looking back and contemplating Cass in her room, after having gone through much worse later on, I know that I got to the same place and looked the way she did that night.

The rumors spread like crazy all over Vegas about Cass's condition. The wire services ran items in early November about Cass's admission to Beverly Glen Hospital for treatment of tonsillitis and hepatitis. We were all heartbroken for her, but we knew she was far from through.

The year ended on more of an upswing. We hosted a free-swinging party on New Year's Eve and invited all our Hollywood friends, plus the cast of the new L.A. production of *Hair*. Many of the cast members showed up in costume—nude. That certainly got the party going around midnight.

It was one of our wilder affairs. A good number of the actors and actresses were strutting around naked, making conversation, pouring drinks, smoking grass. Well after midnight, at least one couple started making love on a couch in the living room in front of our guests. I had to go over, tap the guy on the back, and ask them to cool it. Scott was getting hornier by the minute and told me he hadn't had any luck. Meeting women still brought out his shyness and insecurity. "I've had my eye on that chick from the show all night," he said, looking at one of the naked beauties. "It's hard to imagine a great-looking chick like that walking around naked and NOT wanting to get laid, wouldn't you think?"

"*There must* be an explanation for why she's naked, right?"

"Right. I was hoping you'd say that."

Then I broke into the *Hair* theme about a new age of interplanetary peace and harmony: "This is the dawning of the age of Aquarius, age of Aquarius—"

"Later, man," he said, moving away slowly, tracking the chick's long dancer's body as she made her way across the room.

Scott caught up to her as she grabbed her raincoat. She slipped it on as they talked. Then he followed her outside to her car. The negotiations broke down in a hurry and he was back, confused as ever. He was shaking his head in bewilderment.

"She wouldn't have it," he said. "Struck out."

"What'd you say to her?"

"I watched her go to the car. The raincoat was wide open. Man, did you see her bod? I couldn't think of anything clever to say and I didn't have a lot of time. I just said, 'Wouldn't you like to make out with me a while in your car?' " I winced. "And that *didn't* work? I find that hard to believe." Scott was perplexed and began sweeping his eyes over the room for his next move. I knew what he was thinking: *Christ, I blew it. I wouldn't have even had to take her fucking clothes off.*

He threw me a hard-luck smirk and mumbled: "Age of Aquarius, my ass."

IV

MAN ON THE
MOON

16

I KNEW the final year of the sixties was getting off to a bad start when the last bulb in our crystal chandelier went out. Not long after, in January—as she had facetiously predicted —Michelle decided she had had enough and moved out to Malibu. Our marriage had simply burned out and she needed a new life for herself with Chynna. I don't know that I would have been able to do the leaving. The electricity was weakening and we were bored, drifting apart. We had lived fast and hard; in seven years, we squeezed in enough love, passion, glamour, adventure, pain, triumph, and indiscretion to keep most other marriages going strong for twenty years. We had simply been through too much and left too many scars.

The magic of the music no longer tied us together. I was hardly a mentor anymore. Mitchie had grown up. She had developed a wonderful hardness, a formidable temper, and a fast, cutting sense of humor. Part of her, though, remained out of reach. That too was part of the bond: I was driven by a need to crack that feisty exterior and, being a Virgo perfectionist, to master her. But Michelle proved unconquerable in the end. I could love her, lose her, forgive her, hurt her, yes —but conquer her, never.

Now, perhaps, with Chynna, our marriage had achieved a completeness that could lead only to greater independence. We knew, as most parents do, that we would remain attached by our child even through our split. Michelle needed to move her life beyond me and share experiences with other kinds of people.

That didn't take her too long. Once in her place up Pacific Coast Highway, she began seeing the French director/actor Christian Marquand. Mitch had wanted to play the title role in *Candy* in Marquand's racy film, but she was pregnant with Chynna when the film was cast. I was still not beyond intense jealousy.

I soon found myself with more than a comfortable amount of time for solitary self-examination. The mansion was painfully vast and empty and I missed her terribly. I was often down at the Whiskey and hanging out with my niece Nancy, who worked there and had plenty of girl-friends. I needed stroking; I needed change. I decided to try scoring soundtrack music for films. I needed a new creative outlet and, with Lou Adler moving into film production, the time seemed right.

I started partying harder to cut the loneliness, and I fell in more with a Hollywood crowd. I ran around town with a casting director named Mike McLean. He had just finished working on *Patton* and was about to cast *Myra Breckinridge*.

Through McLean, I met a young London screenwriter/director named Michael Sarne, who asked me to host a premiere party for the Westwood opening of his new movie, *Joanna*. He heard that 783 was the perfect house for a big Hollywood party. The film caused quite a scandal in London. The starlet in the title role, a South African girl named Genevieve Waite, was highly controversial back home because she took a black lover in the film. The storm caused by the film's ban in her country, plus its cult following, turned it into a major London hit. I was, naturally, quite eager to meet the young starlet.

I said yes to Sarne. Unfortunately, she never showed for the party, but Sarne and I became fast friends when he came to L.A. to begin preproduction on his next film, *Myra Breckinridge*. The mysterious Miss Waite, they told me, was inter-

ested in the lead role, but she would have to audition, along
with Raquel Welch, among others. I still looked forward to
meeting her. McLean, Sarne, and I hung out together all the
time. Fortunately, with them around, there was no shortage
of stunning young starlets who were always available for
small parties and dinners at the night spots.

Michelle wasn't the only loss in my life in early 1969. The
Mamas and the Papas, after three and a half years and four
gold albums, made it official before spring. Dunhill released
us from our contracts and we were history, though we still
owed the label another album.

Now that Michelle and I were ex-spouses *and* ex-partners,
we found that we could be around each other as friends—
and occasional lovers. The pressure to make the marriage
work and the feeling of being trapped were gone.

I didn't realize just how much vulnerability and passion
were still there until I drove past Michelle's house and saw
Scott McKenzie's car. I saw the same car several times and
came to the plausible conclusion that my hometown buddy
Scott McKenzie and Michelle were getting it on. Scott had
been best man at our wedding. He had had a brief affair with
my first wife, Susie. This one would be harder to forgive.
Looking at it from another angle, Michelle was having an
affair with a *second* close friend of mine—after Denny. My
feeling of betrayal cut deep and left nasty scars: I wouldn't
speak to Scott for the next fifteen years.

Michelle, however, was locked in my life.

We went drinking one night at Daisy, on Rodeo Drive in
Beverly Hills, and for once we turned loud and nasty on
each other. We yelled insults and accusations at each other
as my anger and sadness came to the surface. There was
some scuffling and I tried to get her into the car. An actor
friend of ours passed by and halted. Thinking the scene was
under control and she was in no danger, he moved along.

"Wimp," she muttered. "If you had an ounce of balls,
you'd *stop* this maniac."

Back at the house, the arguing escalated and I finally lost
it. Shortly before sunrise, I smacked her hard across the
face. It was the first time that I had ever broken through the
barrier between rage and violence. I was smashed. Mitch

saw that her nose was bleeding and she came at me wild-eyed and full of fury. I was looking for a swinging fist, but she caught me instead with a rising foot right between the legs, lifting me off the ground in pain.

As a reflex, I swung and knocked her across the bed with a closed fist. There was blood. The low, dull pain spread from my groin into my stomach. I whacked her one more time and she fell to the bed again. She slumped over and looked up at me.

"I know what you're doing," she said, breathing hard.

"Yeah?" I said, dropping to the bed.

"You're murdering me, aren't you? You're going to kill me, aren't you?"

Those words shocked me back to my senses. "My God," I said, seeing what I had done to her, "I'm so sorry. Did I do —I don't know why . . ."

"Yeah," she said softly, "you did it."

"I've got to drive you to the hospital. Now. You look pretty bad." I couldn't believe how I had lost control.

"I'll drive myself, thank you. You'd probably drive us off the road into a ditch and kill the two of us, just to make yourself happy." Michelle got to the hospital and claimed I had given her multiple concussions.

A few weeks later, in April, Denny, Lou, and I attended a record industry convention down in the Bahamas. I needed to get out of town and cool it, even though the group wasn't really in the business any longer. Cass was busy with her solo act after Vegas and Michelle had decided to spend a couple of weeks in Europe with Chynna and Marquand. She was renting a house for a month or so and told me they were planning to go to Paris and Russia. She would leave the baby with a nanny.

Denny and I scored big at blackjack in the casinos and drank like fish. We were invited to a party at the mansion owned by one of the wealthiest scions of American industry, a middle-aged and slightly eccentric playboy. We met the captain of his powerful speedboat at the casino and roared and bounced over the water to the mansion on a canal. It was some party.

We walked across the perfectly groomed lawn and went

in. Denny scanned the huge living room and sized up some
of the guests. It must have looked like his own scene at the
Astor mansion. "Speed freaks and down monsters."

"Think he knows who they are?" I asked.

Denny shrugged. "Maybe. Maybe not."

I never saw people shoot drugs before that weekend.
Denny pried open a locked liquor cabinet and we helped
ourselves.

They could have been heirs and heiresses whose idea of a
good time was to slum it in the Bahamas and finance their
drug habits with trust funds. They mainlined downers with
broken eyedroppers instead of syringes. It was so gloriously
decadent. I was sick.

They were shooting Seconals and nodding out. We were
told by some of the stoned guests that they were using the
Seconals as hamburger helper for the tycoon's lunch. They
would crack open four or five of the Reds and sprinkle the
powder on some raw meat, then fry it. They'd watch him eat
and turn drowsy. Then he'd pass out upstairs in his palatial
bedroom so the party could go another twelve hours.

I was content with a more bourgeois kick: a great-looking
young woman who worked for the man. She and I were
making love at one point at night in a bedroom and I noticed
one slat of the venetian blinds was crooked. This bothered
the perfectionist in me. I interrupted our passionate writhing
and got up. "It's bugging me," I whispered. "I've got to fix
it. Why is it crooked?"

"Don't worry about it," she said. "I always leave it like
that."

I paused, then got up and walked to the window. I spread
open the slats and almost had a stroke when I stared straight
into the tycoon's face. He had been watching us make love
through the space created by the crooked slat. I mouthed the
words "FUCK YOU" with a smile on my face through the
window. He hardly flinched. Then I shut the blinds and
returned to bed.

"Your boss," I said, "was watching us."

"I know. He likes that," she sighed casually as we picked
up where we left off. "Now we can't disappoint him, can
we?"

The party ended for me when I got a disturbing phone call from a friend in L.A. who had just gotten a call from an Englishwoman in London. The woman in London needed to speak with me right away. I got the phone number and called. She told me that Chynna was with her, but that she didn't know exactly where Michelle was. She claimed she had not heard from Michelle in days and was getting concerned because Chynna was coughing. She didn't want to take the responsibility for the baby anymore and asked if I could fly into London and take Chynna.

I left on the next plane for Heathrow.

When I landed, I bought a knapsack and filled it with anything I figured the baby would like—rattles, stuffed animals, whatever I could find at the airport gift shop.

I taxied to the address. Chynna didn't look well. It was a foreign country, she was a year old and with a woman she didn't know. I left Michelle a note explaining the circumstances. I grabbed Chynna and took off. She was so happy to see me that her little hands clutched me tightly.

Back in Bel Air, my mother arranged for Chynna to stay with two of her sisters living near Anaheim. I didn't want Michelle to know where the baby was.

When Michelle called the nanny in London, she was shocked to hear that I had come and taken Chynna. She was in Morocco and she was livid.

She said later that she immediately drove from Marrakesh to Casablanca, flew to Paris, then to L.A.

She called my mother, figuring I wouldn't have Chynna myself. "Where is she, Dene?" My mother stonewalled and Michelle tightened the screws. "I know you know, Dene," she said. "It is utterly INCONCEIVABLE that John still has her."

"I really don't know, Michelle," my mother said.

Michelle was outraged and turned threatening. "Dene," she said, "when all this is washed over, I'll have Chynna and you know it. We'll get divorced and go through the whole thing, this week, next week, whenever. I assure you, I will have custody of my daughter. And once I do, I will decide if you EVER have a relationship with her. COUNT on it. So if

On August 1, 1980, above, having spent a dismal night in custody following my arrest on federal drug trafficking charges, I was led to my arraignment in Lower Manhattan.

At left, Laura and I were windblown but invigorated at Bill Cleary's house on the water at Newport Beach in the summer of 1979, shortly before Laura's wedding.

At right, after the cross-country drive with Tam in the fall of 1979, Gen and I retreated to this lovely rented home tucked away in Old Greenwich, Connecticut, on Long Island Sound.

Inside Mediasound Studios on West 57th Street, I couldn't tell day from night in late 1977, even with the help of a wall clock, as Keith Richards and I worked to complete tracks for my solo LP begun in London with Mick and Keith. It was a heavy drug phase for both of us and the LP never came out.

Mick Jagger and Mama Cass didn't throw rice when Gen and I got married—they ate it, with chopsticks. The wedding ceremony and feast afterward were at the Golden Dragon restaurant in downtown L.A. on January 31, 1972.

I let my beard grow out for my "Jesus Christ Superstar" phase in 1971, while we recorded our *People Like Us* album.

In 1975, Gen and I got to know Princess Margaret and her boyfriend at the time, Roddy Llewellyn, shown between the princess and me, at the castle in the Scottish Highlands of Lord Colin Tennant, the third Baron of Glenconner, left. We all went to the Edinburgh Music Festival in September that year.

The faces, names—and couture—that made rock history during the festival: clockwise, Rolling Stones guitarist Brian Jones, who did not perform but was a main backstage attraction, Otis Redding, Janis Joplin, The Who's Pete Townshend, and Jimi Hendrix.

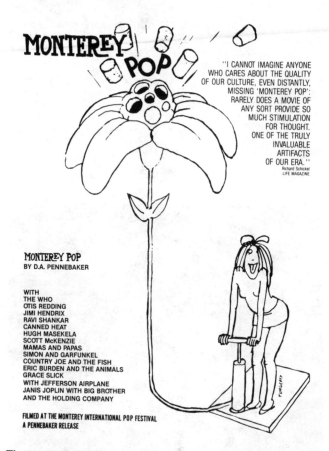

The poster heralding D. A. Pennebaker's film of the Monterey Festival, above, offered only a partial list of acts on the three-day bill in June 1967.

Left, Mitch and I had plenty to celebrate with Cass Elliot and Denny Doherty at our communal Green House in L.A., September 1965; we had just come to town, auditioned for Lou Adler, and within a month, signed a deal with his Dunhill Records label.

Below, we expanded our free-swinging philosophy to clothing—go where you wanna go, do what you wanna do, and wear what you wanna wear.

the development with long-term loans.

If the three or four companies can devise means to work at one studio in harmony, it's possible that a brand-new Hollywood will arise among the shaded acres of the Malibu Mountains. It may not be as glamorous as the old one. But it will be built to last.

The Smoothies had it all in 1960—matching plaid blazers, snap-on ties, plenty of teeth, and a killer wingspan. I'm in the upper right corner, next to Mike Boran. Bill Cleary, left, and Phil Blondheim are in front. Phil later changed his name to Scott McKenzie and sang "San Francisco (Be Sure to Wear Flowers in Your Hair)" for the Monterey Pop Festival in 1967.

Opposite, by 1963, Phil/Scott and I had barnstormed the campus and club folk circuit for two years as the Journeymen with banjo virtuoso Dick Weissman, in this Washington newspaper advertisement, above. When the Journeymen broke up, I formed the New Journeymen in 1964, below, with a folk banjo picker named Marshall Brickman and a gorgeous twenty-year-old blonde named Michelle, who also happened to be my wife.

I stood still long enough for a proud cap-and-gown shot at St. Stephen's School after eighth grade—my one and only such pose.

Though Jeffrey was born on Friday the thirteenth in December 1957, Susie and I, at left, were quite lucky to have such a handsome, healthy boy with us in our first apartment in Alexandria.

I was proud to be my mother's little soldier boy during my five years —second through sixth grades—at Linton Hall in Manassas, Virginia. Looking forward to her Sunday visits and a picnic lunch with my pals got me through the dreary weeks. She never let me down. My sister Rosemary, right, was at college by the time I could spit-shine my Linton Hall Military School belt buckle—but she always came back to see how well my other "sisters" were keeping me in line.

Marine Corps Captain Claude Andrew Phillips was proud, happy, and victorious when he returned home from France after World War I. He was in his early thirties and he wasn't about to stick around Watertown, New York. He made his way to Okmulgee, Oklahoma, where he took over a hotel and saloon he had won in a card game on the cruise home. The real prize turned out to be my mother—a teenage Cherokee girl who helped her mother with the housekeeping.

Gen looks more glamorous than ever in 1981 with Chynna, a stunning thirteen-year-old, and Tam; and, below, in 1984, with Tam at age thirteen.

In March 1982, almost fifteen years after the Mamas and the Papas ceased performing, it was time for me to leave Creeque Alley, put the group back together, and hit the road—with my old friend Spanky McFarlane, left, taking on Cass's vocals; Denny; Laura, handling Michelle's vocals and her own solos; and Papa John doing what he always loved best—making music, having fun, not taking anything too seriously.

you don't tell me—RIGHT NOW—where she is, you'll never have a life with your granddaughter—born on YOUR birthday. So it's up to you. I wanna know where she is."

There was a long pause. My mother was quivering. "Michelle, I really don't know."

That was it. Michelle blew. "Well, dammit, may God strike you dead, Dene," she said, and hung up.

When she drove to 783, I met her outside. She demanded Chynna back. "Where the hell were you?" I asked.

"You knew fucking *well* where I was," she snapped back. "I told you on the phone exactly where I was going to be. I was at the Mamounia in Marrakesh. I want my baby— NOW!"

"Chynna's not here," I said.

We had and still have completely different versions of whatever it was that happened. She didn't believe the nanny had ever called L.A.; she accused me of "kidnapping" Chynna out of jealous rage. Chynna, she said, was fine with Annie the nanny, as she called her. The nanny knew exactly where she was all the time, she claimed, and said she had checked in every day. She and Marquand had gone to Morocco, she said, because their visas for Russia had gotten lost in the mail when they were in Paris. "You knew all this, dammit," she screamed. "I gave you the nanny's number and address. And we went over it all on the phone when you were still in L.A. AND, you called me a trollop, if you recall."

I didn't budge. The baby was left with a strange woman in a foreign country and Michelle was thousands of miles away. The nanny had called to say that she didn't know what was going on. It was incredible how far apart we were. I told her I had gone to a lawyer to let him know that I was considering going away with Chynna. He strongly urged me to rethink it. "They'd nail you for kidnapping."

"I want my baby," she insisted.

"Uh-uh. She isn't here."

Michelle stepped forward and slugged me with all her strength, right in the mouth. We were at it again. This was getting crazy. She jumped on top of me and bashed me again in the jaw as I tried to get a grip on her forearms. I was barely conscious after the blows to the face. My head throbbed. I could hardly see. She was over me, kicking my neck, stepping on my groin, trying to wedge her heels in my eyes.

I spun away and stood up and then we went at it toe-to-toe like two sluggers. She was incredibly tough. Finally, this insanity ended and she took off.

Days later, Michelle got a court order requiring me to surrender Chynna to her within seventy-two hours. In the first week of May, I filed divorce papers.

But Michelle and I could still have fun together as ex-spouses. We were both invited to a party that spring by Roman Polanski and his wife Sharon Tate. It was a sort of housewarming party. In February they had moved in and taken over the lease at 10050 Cielo Drive, the house Terry Melcher and Candy Bergen had lived in way up in the hills off Benedict Canyon. Terry and Candy left Cielo Drive to stay at Doris Day's weekend retreat at the beach.

The party was one of those everyone-is-here-tonight affairs. When she lived there with Terry, Candy had strung up an elaborate array of lights along the rail fence, then left them up outside the house. The imitation French country house, set back off Cielo Drive and obscured by tall trees, leaned against a steep hillside. The brightly lit pool glowed like a giant turquoise stone set in the soft lawn. The scent of pines and cherry blossoms in the night air brought back sensations of spring fever as a teenager. I had a pocketful of drugs and Michelle looked great to me.

I was chatting with the French film director Roger Vadim, who had done *Barbarella* with his wife Jane Fonda the year before. Vadim and Jane had a place on Old Malibu Road. Then Vadim asked, "Why don't you and Michelle come over from this party tonight and meet us at the beach?"

"Sounds perfect," I said. "I'll ask Mitch."

"That way," he went on, "you wake up by the ocean, go for a swim, we have breakfast together, spend the day in the sun at the beach. Yeah?"

"Yeah."

Mitch said yes. Vadim told us he would leave on the parking lights of his car so we would find the house. An hour later, we left Cielo Drive for the beach.

Mist and salty air were rolling in over the rocks along Old Malibu Road. It was a gorgeous night. We found Vadim's car with the lights on. As arranged, we turned the lights off, found a note on the front seat that said, PLEASE COME IN, and entered.

Warren Beatty was sitting across the spacious living room, leafing through a magazine. Vadim greeted us and poured some wine. Vadim had such charm and style. Their home was soothing inside. I remembered the time Vadim came to our house when loud rock music was playing and a weird cast of characters was wandering in and out. He said, *"This is the way to live. It's so American!"*

After a while, I asked, "Where's Jane?"

"Upstairs in the bedroom, reading," he said. "Why don't you go up and say hi."

I crept up the steps and turned into the bedroom. The lights were dim. Jane was under a sheet. I had always admired Jane as a gifted, highly intelligent actress and, by that time, for her daring antiwar stance. She was also one of the world's greatest-looking women. "Pretty interesting situation," I said. I lit a joint. She smiled. Moments later, we heard footsteps up the stairs. For a flash, I wondered if I had made a big mistake. But there was no problem. Before we knew it, all five of us were together and loosening up fast. I was lit. This was just too good to be true.

Looking back, it seems hard to believe it could have actually happened the way it did. So hard, in fact, that some of the people in that room now prefer not to remember. After all, these are far more conservative times today. Maybe they're embarrassed. But that was a different, more innocent and permissive era—California Dreamin', vintage 1969. The possibilities seemed limitless. That night they *were,* for sure. We all got a second wind and came to life. Another party was starting up and we would go for it all the way till dawn.

17

I SPENT much of that summer working out of a small bungalow on the 20th Century-Fox lot where *Myra Breckinridge*
was in preproduction and where it would be filmed. I was
hired to write some music for the movie. I hoped the new
medium would give me a much-needed creative lift. Mike
Sarne was cowriter and director. The bungalow had everything a composer might need: grand piano, couch, kitchen-
ette, recording equipment, shower, and a bed. I really didn't
need the piano. I was too busy trying to get laid to ever
actually write anything in there.

You'd peek your head out and see a group of girls in grass
skirts or nursing whites from some other set walk by—out
there among the Roman soldiers and cattle rustlers heading
for the commissary in costume. Who could write music with
distractions like that outside your door?

I was living in a guesthouse behind the house Sarne was
renting at Malibu Colony. I also began work on my first solo
album. Lou Adler was helping me produce it for my own
label, Warlock Records.

The highlight of *Myra* for me was working with Mae
West. Her apartment in Hancock Park, in a building she
owned, was entirely white. The carpet, the piano, the walls,

everything was white. Her skin was pink and heavily made up. I was in awe. The first song I tried out for her there was too tame, she sneered. It was called "Hollywood's a Honky-Tonk Town." She heard the chorus and stopped me.

"Look, sonny, come over here," she said. She sounded tough, just like in her movies. She edged close to me and whispered confidentially, "The song's okay, but the thing is, see, Hollywood is *not* a honky-tonk town."

"No sweat," I said quickly. "We'll just change it." So I started the song on guitar again in her living room, then went into the new chorus. "Hollywood's not a honky-tonk town/Gotta find someone to show you 'round."

Only one tune, "Secret Places," got in the film and Rex Reed sang it. The film turned into a total fiasco. The cast, which included John Huston, Rex Reed, Raquel Welch, Mae, a young Farrah Fawcett, and a pre-mustache Tom Selleck as the Stud, split into nasty factions. Everyone got cranky and petty. There was constant warring over what the film was supposed to be about. Even the teamsters on the set seemed to have script approval. There were rewrites of the revised rewrites. The actresses all seemed to have costume, even color, approval. If two actresses emerged from their trailers in the same color, they'd retreat until one would give in and change.

There was one amusing hassle with casting. McLean was impressed with a young black actor and hired him for the part of the outrageously swishy Irving Amadeus. It was the guy's first major film role. Sarne wanted him fired in favor of his friend Calvin Lockhart, who'd starred in *Joanna.* The head of Fox, Richard Zanuck, called McLean and backed Sarne. McLean broke the guy's heart and fired him, hiring Lockhart. Years later, McLean met Sarne in London and asked him if he remembered the incident. Sure he did. The actor McLean fired was Richard Pryor.

Sarne went through hell to finish the picture. People had warned him not to take on the project—a high-camp sex farce based on Gore Vidal's novel—after his success with the more arty *Joanna.* But he wanted to go for it. He turned down other film offers to work with this diverse cast. He was on a big rush—first Hollywood film, a budget soaring past

$20 million, lots of stars with sky-high salaries, an office on the Fox lot, and, as writer and director, a hefty paycheck.

It was an eye-opener for me. Too much input and ego. It degenerated into composing by committee. I tried to get my name off the credits.

Myra was the last picture Sarne directed in Hollywood. It was way ahead of its time. It was then about the biggest box office failure in history.

By the time Sarne, McLean, and I got away from that madness and made it out to the beach or up to 783, there was plenty of steam to blow off. Dope, coke, and mescaline around a crackling bonfire on the cool sand at night usually did the trick.

By Sunday night each weekend, there always seemed to be a dozen people on or near the NASA bed—an eight-by-nine-foot monument to aerospace R&D and the sexual revolution. Drugs were rampant; everyone naked, everyone doing everything to everyone else.

I reconnected that summer with my old New Journeyman friend Marshall Brickman. He was then a head writer for Johnny Carson. Marshall still liked to give me a hard time over the New Journeymen's three-way credit card I used to finance the trip to the Islands. He joked that he was still having trouble getting credit. We had quite a few laughs over that.

"I'm sitting there, back in '65, '66," he'd say, "in the office I shared with Joan Rivers at 'Candid Camera' and some guy named Feeney would always call looking for you. 'If we can't find him, we'll come after you,' he'd say. He was from the dunning department at AmEx. God, John, they won't give me another card in my own name until I have fifty grand in cash and a net worth of a *quarter million.* What did you DO with that card? So I'd say to Feeney, 'Come and get me. I make three-ten a week.'"

Being head writer for Carson's "Tonight Show" was so Middle American for Marshall's New York wry intellectual taste that he'd have to come up to 783 every now and then, sink into our huge couches, and decompress. He was a riot. He absorbed enough of L.A. life to cowrite those great L.A.

scenes in *Annie Hall* with Woody Allen and win an Oscar for best screenplay.

"I swear I'm afraid I'll turn into flocked wallpaper if I stay at the show too long," he'd say. Sometimes he'd ask if he could "borrow one of those great sleeping pills." He meant Doriden. Marshall was in his mid twenties and coping admirably with the pressures of writing nightly gags for America's most popular TV personality. He was living in a suite at Gene Autry's Continental Hotel on Sunset Strip, which later became the notoriously raunchy Continental Hyatt (or "Riot") House for rock and rollers in the seventies. It was pretty tawdry back then.

Marshall never arrived in his rented Mustang without describing the dramatic border crossing between the tacky neon Strip and the lush, fragrant wilds of Beverly Hills as he headed west on Sunset past Doheny.

"That smell," he'd say, "honeysuckle, bougainvillea, what *is* it? It hits you just as you get to Beverly Hills. It just starts there. And the mists rising off the pools in spring, outdoor lights bouncing off the rhododendrons? My God, it's so Proustian, I'll always remember that smell, that light. It's like the Planet Venus. I leave the Carson show, then I come up here to that huge Rolls, a Jag, three peacocks, and these freaky people carrying sacs of Crown Royal and stashes of white powder and all this. From the hotel to here, I've got the best—and worst—of both worlds." Marshall couldn't have been straighter. He didn't need drugs to unwind, just a long walk along the beach to clear his feverishly inventive mind.

Once, just before daybreak, he must have been really overworked. Or homesick for New York. He walked out to the beach and said he wanted to see the sunrise. I watched him from the deck as he assumed a yoga-type position and began to groove on the horizon ahead of him. "Marshall," I yelled, "you're never gonna see the sunrise like that. You're facing Hawaii. The sun rises in the east back here—*behind* you."

At the end of June, Mike Sarne asked me to pick up a friend of his at the airport. I asked him who she was. "Genevieve Waite," he said, "you know . . ."

"Joanna," I interrupted. "How will I know her?"

"You'll know her."

He was right—enormous green eyes; sharp, upturned nose; high cheekbones; sensuous mouth; and a shock of tightly frizzed blond hair. With those giant, bright eyes, her stunning face looked frozen in an expression of constant amazement.

She was wearing a very Mod leather mini and boots. She free-associated in a high, breathy doll's voice. She had grown up in Capetown, South Africa, and studied science and psychology at Johannesburg University. She made one film in her country, then she split for London and did some modeling. She walked into an audition for *Joanna* and beat out three hundred and fifty other actresses for the part. She had been married to a Brooklyn-born poet she met in London. She was just barely nineteen; they forged consent papers and used a cigar band as her wedding ring. She told me she had always wanted to marry a Brooklyn Jew. That was her American Dream—a Brooklyn poet.

When they met, she said, he told her he had just gotten out of Bellevue and Genevieve thought that it was a university for poets. He was a couple of years older and looked just like Montgomery Clift.

"I have all your albums, you know, in South Africa, but aren't you the one who's married to Mama Cass?" she asked.

"Uh-uh," I shrugged. She spoke in a well-articulated stream of consciousness that was like nothing I had ever heard. For their honeymoon, she and the Brooklyn poet moved into a suite at the Chelsea Hotel, she said. He locked her in the room for a month, stuffed a pillow down the back of his shirt, and called himself Quasimodo. I presumed she played Esmeralda to his Hunchback of Notre Dame. They only lived together for a couple of months once he let her out of the bell tower.

Back home, Gen's father, a manager for an engineering firm, took his son-in-law fishing and hunting. Manly things. The city kid didn't take well to the bush. He always held a handkerchief across his mouth and choked, "The dust. Oh God, the dust."

The *Joanna* experience had been wonderful, she said, especially the promotion tour, the film festivals throughout Europe, the critical acclaim in London, the big dinners.

But he resented all the attention she got. He threw food at banquets. He wrote one song for her, she told me, called "Sixteen-Millimeter Baby."

Then in Sicily, she said, she was sexually attacked at the film festival by Mayor Daley.

"There's a Mayor Daley of Sicily?" I wondered.

"No, of Chicago," she said. I knew right there that this lean, beautiful waif's flair for storytelling was a match for my own.

So she brought the poet back home to Durban, hoping her father would line him up in the cross hairs of one of his hunting rifles. They were getting divorced when she left for L.A. to find her mentor and onetime lover Michael Sarne. But there would be no audition for the lead role in *Myra Breckinridge*.

"It's already gone to Raquel Welch," I said.

"Oh," she said casually. The affair, she said, had ended when Sarne married Tanya, a schoolteacher he had been seeing for years.

We all drove out to the beach and the three of us took mescaline together. She saw the knots in the table begin to move and told me it was the same image Aldous Huxley had described in *Doors of Perception.* I had the impression she had read almost every book printed in the English language. She was remarkably learned and we discovered that we had several common interests, ranging from romantic poetry to James Taylor's new albums. She had always wanted to try hallucinogens ever since reading Huxley. We spent the night running and howling along the surf, making home videos, and dancing around a bonfire.

Genevieve got the idea that we should film the story of Byron and Shelley because Michael looked like Shelley, with blue eyes and blond hair, and I looked like Byron, with my beard and long hair. We discussed shooting a sixteen-millimeter film on the life of those two poets. Gen and I began reciting their works. Her favorite poem was *Tamerlane.* Romantic verse was all I ever retained from high school and finally it was coming in handy for something—a trip on mescaline with a stunning young actress at Malibu.

Gen offered to read the Tarot cards for me. She opened her eyes wide and said there would soon be a new woman in my life—and she found it particularly bizarre and auspicious to learn that her birthday was the same day as my mother's and my daughter Chynna's.

Gen and I went to bed the following afternoon and made love through the night, then slept off the mescaline for another day. There was something wonderfully unique about her—a keen intelligence mixed with an otherworldly airiness. The blend kept me on my toes. I never knew what to expect and there was never a dull moment. It was similar to the way Michelle was a mixture of intensity and elusiveness. If Michelle was tough and unapologetic in her independence, Gen was vulnerable and wondrously bonkers. Naïveté was a key element in her spacey charisma. She was quite the eloquent romantic herself. Later, she admitted that she wrote a London friend about those first twenty-four hours together. In the letter, she said that she felt as if her whole life—from boarding school to her dramatic training and film work—had been leading up to the moment of our first meeting. She had been waiting for that moment all her life and, she added, she felt she had been born again.

We spent the next two weeks together until she had to leave for New York. She was beginning to shoot *Move* with Elliott Gould and Paula Prentiss. She took an apartment in the Chelsea Hotel and hung out with Andy Warhol's Factory crowd, whom she had gotten to know in London. I had a strong sense that Gen would be back in my life before too long. She was, without question, an original.

A month later, I watched the *Apollo XI* moon landing at Sarne's beach house. We videotaped it and showed it dozens of times for friends. I was as mesmerized as anyone by the incomprehensibility of it all. I began to kick around some ideas about a musical or film set in space. I already had a female lead in mind.

I moved from Sarne's guesthouse to the house next door to his at the beach. In early August, on a Friday night, I went out to a Japanese restaurant in Century City with Steve

Brandt, Mia, and a few other friends and we all got smashed
on sake. We had to remove our shoes. As a prank, we
dumped Steve's shoes in the trunk of his car. As we were
leaving, Steve went crazy, prancing barefoot all over the
place, screaming, "The Japs have stolen my shoes!"

We stopped off at Daisy for a few drinks and I made my
way home to 783. I heard from Marshall Brickman and I
told him to come by and we'd get something going. Marshall
drove out, deeply inhaling the Proustian jungles of Bel Air,
and I told him, "There's a message on my service from
Sharon Tate. She's having a few people over. Roman's still
away. It's just Jay Sebring and a few others. Or we could go
out to the Colony and hang out at Sarne's."

"I hear this is the right time to see the phosphorescent
plankton in the Pacific," he said. It sounded like a straight
line for one of Carson's gags.

"No, really," he said. "In my constant and fruitless quest
for new material, I read every newspaper in America. I read
about this the other day. You know when the wave breaks,
you can see that neon tube flashing along the beach? Let's go
up there. That's what I need."

"Phosphorescent plankton."

"I'm that type of guy."

"Let's go."

Marshall and I went out to the beach in my '52 Rolls after
picking up some friends at Sarne's. We all built a fire on the
sand. Marshall wanted to experiment with mescaline for the
first time that night. I told him he didn't have the type of
personality to handle a personality-altering drug.

"You're too introspective and analytical to begin with," I
said.

"Will I lose my sense of humor?" he asked me.

"Marshall, you will lose your sense of *reality!* This will
tighten the microscope on yourself," I jokingly warned him.

Once his hand started to strobe in front of the fire—and
he started to fear he might never come down—he decided,
"This is NOT the type of life I want to live." I got real tired
and passed out.

Marshall called a woman friend who picked him up and
drove him back to his hotel after we were all asleep. He told

the hotel switchboard operator not to put any calls through unless it was Johnny Carson himself.

I made it home somehow myself and was awakened by a call Saturday morning from Joyce Haber, an L.A. newspaper columnist.

"Thank God you're alive," she said. I sat up in the dark with a sharp jolt of adrenaline.

"What the hell are you talking about? What's wrong?"

All hell had broken loose, she said. Bodies were littered all over the place at 10050 Cielo Drive. She was apparently calling Roman's friends to see who might have been involved.

The victims were soon identified as Sharon Tate, who was eight months pregnant; our hairdresser friend Jay Sebring; Roman's Polish friend Wojtek Frykowksi; his girlfriend, the coffee heiress Abigail Folger; and Steven Parent, a single man none of us knew, who was found shot to death in a Rambler. The dream of Peace and Love had turned into a living nightmare with real demon killers stalking the hills.

We didn't know then, but they had been senselessly sacrificed by the slaves of Charlie Manson. The maniac Manson ordered his worshippers to kill anyone living at the Cielo address. He assumed that Melcher—the man he believed, in his paranoid psychotic derangement, had kept him out of the music business—still lived there.

All of us who were friendly with Roman and Sharon were saddened and stunned beyond words. It was impossible not to be haunted by the agony and horror of the doomed victims' last desperate moments at the hands of their demented killers. My heart broke for Roman. He was still in London working on *The Day of the Dolphin.* He flew home right away.

By midmorning, as news spread through town and across the country, I got dozens of frantic calls from friends and family, wondering if I could have been at Roman's, as I often was. I quickly reassured Susie, Michelle, my kids, and Mother.

In the aftermath of the Tate murders, paranoia swept through Beverly Hills and Bel Air. Rumors of a "hit list" began to spread and the investigation heated up. There were bizarre theories that attempted to link the murders to LSD and Satanic rites, kinky and deadly sexual perversions, and, somehow, to Polanski's own penchant for violence in movies like *Knife in the Water, Repulsion,* and *Rosemary's Baby.*

You had to wait on line at sporting goods stores to buy guns. I immediately went out that Saturday and bought a nine-millimeter Browning at Kerr's Sporting Goods on Wilshire Boulevard. I already packed a twenty-five-year-old Beretta. I concealed knives all over the house. It was a great time to be in the attack dog, bodyguard, electronic alarm, or armed security business.

Michelle and Chynna promptly moved back in with me at 783 Bel Air Road. That same night a single woman friend of ours called and asked to stay with us. Everyone was terrified, waiting to see who would be sacrificed next. No one felt safe. We were afraid to fall asleep. Tequila took care of that.

The demand for security guards was so great that I think the security firms were hiring Eagle Scouts. We went to a party several nights later and left this young kid with a gun and holster and uniform in the house with Chynna. When we came home, the kid was out cold on the couch with the TV on. He was flat on his chest and snoring. The door was unlocked. I delicately removed the gun and silently pushed open the french doors to the living room. Then I fired three shots into the garden and the kid practically plastered himself to the ceiling out of fright as he searched for his gun. When he saw it was me, I tossed him the gun. "Get outta here, you punk," I said.

Over the next few days, it was hard to keep from selfishly retracing my steps that night—thinking how close I had come to going up there. If anything had gone differently—if we hadn't pulled the prank on Steve, I'd have missed the call from Marshall, Marshall wouldn't have come to see his plankton, etc., etc.—we might have been up there. It occurred to me that Mike Sarne had almost moved in to that house before Roman and Sharon had.

In the absence of facts, my mind skipped wildly to all sorts of weird scenarios. I recalled incidents that I previously disregarded as trifling.

Several days earlier, Wojtek Frykowski had come to my

door unexpectedly and demanded to be let in. He seemed slightly incoherent and had a bizarre presence about him. I wouldn't let him in, but he insisted. I just didn't feel right about it. He was rumored to have had weird drug connections and was part of the crowd that had been feeding off Cass. I apologized and closed the door in his face.

I recalled strange conversations I had had with Dennis Wilson about a year earlier. He and Melcher had talked of this wild-eyed self-proclaimed "god" who tripped on acid and imposed absolute control over a harem of hippie chicks. They had all pulled up to Dennis's house toward the beach on Sunset in a psychedelic bus and moved in.

"This guy Charlie's here with all these great-looking chicks," he told me once. "He plays a guitar and he's a real wild guy. He has all these chicks hanging out like servants. You can come over and just fuck any of them you want. It's a great party."

Terry called me once or twice about the same guy and said he had some songs. He played me a tape once of his music and I wasn't particularly impressed. Terry was apparently at one time considering giving the guy a break and producing a song but had rightly changed his mind. I never went out there. It sounded a little too crazy and cosmic for me.

Then I heard "Charlie" and his sex slaves moved out of Dennis's house and took $10,000 worth of recording equipment and personal belongings.

A guitarist friend of mine told me about a horrifying night he had spent out in the desert among a bunch of acid-crazed hippies who worshipped their leader. He had described the guru again as a wild-eyed hippie who had a beard and played a guitar.

"The guy tries to steal your soul," my friend told me. "He sucks it out of you through your eyes when you're tripping with him around the fire and he knows your thoughts. He has the craziest look in his eyes and it's really terrifying. Then he says you can screw all his girls. So I did. Then I tried to drive a pitchfork through his heart I was so freaked out. But his goons stopped me and I left."

Another aspect that bothered me was that I had invested $10,000 in Sebring International, Jay's new business venture, a line of designer grooming products for men that was to be marketed a few months later. Some of his other friends had backed him as well and I wondered, stretching to make sense of this ghastly act, if that was relevant.

The L.A. police came to my house and quizzed me about that night and what I knew of the victims. I helped them all I could, but it wasn't much.

Roman returned to L.A., and in the subsequent weeks, he, Mike Sarne, Mike McLean, other friends, and I did some investigating of our own. I consulted a numerologist, who told me a Satanic cult of killers had used animal blood for the ritual murders. Roman allowed the Dutch psychic Peter Hurkos to visit Cielo Drive and take photographs for *Life* magazine. We went though our phone books and speculated about an "inside" job among our circle of friends.

In the midst of the wave of paranoia, the Woodstock Nation was born in upstate New York, three thousand miles away. It was Monterey all over, but this time with half a million people. I had had no interest in working with the producers. At Woodstock, kids were blissing out on drugs and rock for three days. I knew that we had helped pave the way for Woodstock, but it seemed to be a long way off now. In L.A., the savagery of the killings had become a morbid obsession. The sixties' myth of peace, harmony, and free love had been shattered by a blood-soaked orgy of murder and mutilation.

Life went on. Genevieve telephoned me from New York one night to tell me that she had seen a rock concert and was in her Chelsea Hotel suite having sex against her will with the members of a well-known West Coast band—and tripping on acid. "One right after another!" she screamed. She asked me to call the front desk and send somebody up to call them off. I was neither jealous nor convinced. I told her to get out of the room. She said she was taking an apartment in Gramercy Park and that our friend Steve Brandt would share it with her. She would be out west soon and wanted to rent a room at 783.

I went out for dinner one night and got so wrecked that I took a ride home with friends and forgot about the Rolls I had left with the valet parking attendant. Six weeks later, the

LAPD called me and said the car was still there. The restaurant was getting concerned. But I had lost my parking ticket. "Just bring your license and I.D.," they said. There was no registration in the glove compartment, but there was an uncashed royalty check for about $25,000 in there. I had forgotten about that too.

As the weeks wore on without a break in the case, it seemed that Roman would crack. Then the case—Roman's anyway—took on its most bizarre twist: Roman began investigating *me* as his prime suspect.

Apparently he had gotten a criminal test kit from the police and sneaked into my garage to check the car for any blood or fiber samples that might connect me to the victims. He peeked in the trunk of my Rolls and found a machete that belonged to a friend of mine; it was, of course, clean. He was able to rummage through my green stash bag, but he was interested only in my address book. He sent a handwriting sample to a graphologist. He wanted to check my large block lettering against the word PIG scrawled in blood at the site of the murders. I knew nothing of these attempts to implicate me at the time—and learned about them only later.

Roman's fevered and macabre rationale for suspecting me hinged on a motive of insane sexual jealousy and revenge. It was a little distressing to imagine a friend thinking you capable of such madness. But he had his reasons.

Earlier in the year, he and Michelle had had a brief affair in London. He knew that I knew about it. She had also had an affair with Beatty in London, too. I had phoned Warren once and, like the thugs in the elevator warning me about Mia, I warned him, in a drunken, stoned stupor, to lay off other guys' wives or he'd get himself seriously injured. Warren must have related that conversation to Roman, who must have been impressed with my anger and potential for violence. So Roman now knew that I was aware of *both* affairs with Michelle and he might have concluded that I could have been enraged and unstable enough to seek revenge by committing—or orchestrating—a mass murder.

If this, indeed, was part of Roman's torment, it came to the surface one night at Sarne's beach house, where some friends gathered weeks later for dinner. Gen was back in town for work on *Move* on the Fox lots.

Gen was almost unrecognizable now. While in New York, she said, she had hung out with the Factory types, spent summer weekends in Woodstock, chopped off her hair, lost weight for modeling jobs, and taken a number of acid trips. "I'm totally Americanized," she boasted with a smile. She was very upset about Sharon's murder. Steve Brandt had had a violent flipout in her apartment and she had had to call police and have him taken away. But Sharon haunted her. They had met a year earlier at the Cannes Film Festival, before it was shut down by the student riots in the spring of 1968. "Sharon," Gen pointed out with sadness in her thin voice, "was an Aquarian and had been helpful with clothes and things and so sweet."

The lights had been turned off and the house was candlelit with glowing lanterns. We had hung long swatches of muslin so it would blow in the ocean breeze. There was a full moon. We were all helping to prepare dinner. Roman was chopping vegetables with a cleaver. I was sitting on the couch, still in my bathing trunks.

Suddenly I felt a powerful hand clutch my hair from behind and yank my head back with a violent jerk. I felt the razor-sharp edge of the cleaver pressed against my throat. I recognized the shape and strength in the hand from countless arm wrestling bouts. Roman grunted, "Did you kill Sharon? Did you?" I stayed calm and didn't flinch.

"No, Roman, I didn't, I didn't." The grief and strain had finally pushed him over the edge. I thought it might be one of his macho pranks, a test of strength and nerve. He kept applying pressure. "Roman," I said, "this isn't funny. What are you talking about? Of course I didn't kill Sharon, and if you don't take that thing off my neck, we're going to have a major problem here."

Roman eased his grip and backed away. Then he flung the cleaver into the wall. That ended his suspicions.

In December, Charles Manson was charged with the five murders at Roman's house—and with the two La Bianca murders committed the night after Cielo Drive. By then, life was more or less back to normal.

Gen and I got to spend time together on the lot. We'd eat in the commissary, I'd show her around the elaborate *Myra* sets, and we'd make love in the bungalow. Sarne gave her a scene in the film—sitting in a cigar-smoking dentist's chair while he talks on the phone and works over her teeth. She had one line, spoken to his well-endowed hygienist leaning against her: "Oh, you've got such lovely boobs. They're *such* a comfort to me."

While she was in New York, Gen had read a script called *The Telephone Book,* written by Nelson Lyon, who would be directing the film. He and a producer at Rosebud Films, Merwin Bloch, wanted Gen for the female lead role. She was intrigued by the story line and discussed changes she would like to have made. In late September, she signed a contract for the film at her agency. At the time, as she would later say, Gen's agent told her he thought it was a "skin flick" and he didn't understand why she would want to do it. She was confident that it was being changed more to her liking.

One sunny fall afternoon I bought some fresh lobsters and asked Gen to whip up a lobster salad for some guests of ours who were spending the day with us at the beach house. It was as if Gen had never *made* lunch before. Her eyes widened with panic. "I don't know how," she whined. She had been feeling weak lately.

"It's not hard," I said. "Just do your best."

An hour later, I was sitting outside on the deck with friends and she tried to make it down the steps in her underwear with this mess on a tray. She stumbled and dumped the tray in the sand. I felt horrible for her, then realized she was out cold. I couldn't believe she had tried to overdose because I had asked her to cook lobsters. "What's wrong?" I asked, slapping her to keep her awake.

"I don't know how to cook lobsters," she mumbled groggily.

I worked hard to keep Gen awake and got her to Malibu Hospital. Her stomach was pumped and she had, in fact, taken a few Seconals, but not because of the lobsters. I had been taking them in the mornings when I awoke, she explained. I always told her they were vitamins. That morning she tossed a couple down, thinking they were vitamins. By the time I asked her to whip up lunch, she was ready to pass out—and didn't know it. It was a close call that, among other things, hinted at the power of Gen's commitment and unquestioning faith in me as a force in her life.

In November, Gen and I threw a party for Laura's tenth birthday and she was a perfect hostess. I showed the kids a rather eclectic triple feature—the film of the Monterey Pop Festival, *Dumbo*, and *Willie the Whale*.

They were in Summerhill by then and they were a precocious pair. Summerhill was ultraprogressive, the kind of place where instead of textbooks they give kids pets. That was my impression of the place. The projects were a goat, a mouse, a rat. And some storybooks. They didn't miss the structured classroom setting of more conventional schools.

My kids were growing up fast. I knew Jeffrey was beginning to smoke dope and toot on coke whenever he could get his twelve- or thirteen-year-old hands on some.

In November, Gen read a second draft of the *Telephone* script and was disappointed that few—if any—of the expected changes had been made. She was supposed to show up for wardrobe meetings in December. She rewrote some scenes on her own and called Lyon to tell him the rather lurid ending was unsatisfactory—that the Pig Man and Alice characters shouldn't have orgasms in separate phone booths. Gen said Lyon told her the script was perfect as it was. Now, when she wanted out, the film was going into production with her name on a Fox contract as the female lead. A showdown was ahead.

By the time the sixties drew to a close, Gen—wild, sexy, delightfully unpredictable Gen—and I were together and often hanging out at Bumbles, a posh private disco on La Cienega in which I had staked ten grand. It was owned by a friend of mine who also had a famous London disco. Some of my film and music industry cohorts went in on it too, and it became one of our watering holes.

The Manson arrest had ended the paranoia, but I still packed a gun at times. I had one last bizarre encounter that justified arming myself. One night I was driving around town with Sharon Tate's younger sister, Patricia. I stopped at a traffic light on Sunset and, out of nowhere, my Rolls was

bumped hard and menacingly several times from behind. I
sped on, but was clearly being pursued. It appeared as if four
men were in the other car. The gun was in my green drug
bag on the floor of the car. I had never even aimed the
damned thing.

I raced up into the hills, imagining there might be some
connection to the Manson affair. I pulled into a familiar
driveway in Bel Air—belonging to the tough Italian-born
manager of a Vegas star. The car slowed behind mine. I
raced out with Patricia, holding the gun. "Joe, Joe," I
screamed, "I'm being followed!" He came to the door. The
goons were still in the car on the road, casing the place.

"Shit," he said. "I'd blow 'em away if I had a piece right
now."

"Great!" I said. "Try this one." I tossed the loaded gun
and his face lit up. "ALL RIGHT!" he said. Joe went right
into a military crouch, steadied the gun with both hands,
and fired a warning shot right over their car. He fired twice
more—and the car screeched away.

At home, Laura and Jeff were spending more time with
me because the new man in Susie's life was having trouble
handling them. My *Wolf King* album was in the can for a
spring 1970 release. Gen and I were beginning to put together our *Space* musical. Cass had revived her solo act.
Denny was planning to clear out of L.A. and head for Florida. Mitch and I were on more friendly terms and our divorce settlement was in the works.

It had been a painless property settlement. She kept what
was hers; I got what was coming to me. I paid her $10,000
and $250-a-month support payments. I had to give her
credit—she was boldly stepping out on her own and leaving
a lot behind. I stayed in the house and she was at the beach.
She kept her Mercedes, I got the Rolls-Royces, and I learned
in the process that I owed $160,000 in taxes.

Then, in December, Lou dropped the bombshell: He unloaded Dunhill Records for $3 million, selling it to ABC.
The Mamas and the Papas were gone. Now even the place
that had been our record industry home had been torn
down.

The sixties were winding down darkly. Steve Brandt killed

himself, we heard, with an overdose of downers after attending a Stones concert at Madison Square Garden in late November. Steve had been despondent over Sharon Tate's murder. She was one of his dearest friends. He was getting messed up on drugs. The story we heard was that he tried to run onstage during the show and was punched in the face by a guard. He went home and OD'd.

Then, less than two weeks later, the Stones gave their free concert at the Altamont Speedway. Right in front of the stage, a Hell's Angel stabbed to death a fan who had been seen waving a gun just seconds before. The savage act was captured on film by Albert and David Maysles for *Gimme Shelter*. Three other fans died in connection with that concert.

The holiday season was dampened by the *Telephone* affair. Right around Christmas, Gen got a two-page telegram from the producer, in which he said that, despite Gen's reluctance to go ahead, he was "banking on" her. "It is all up to you." She was feeling cornered and becoming accident-prone.

She had sustained third-degree burns on her leg in an accident while shooting *Move* weeks before. She needed four stitches when she sliced a knuckle in the kitchen. She slipped in the mud along the roadside in Malibu and dropped into a ditch, hurting her leg. While frying some chicken at home, grease splattered and singed her face.

I took her away to a cottage in Lake Arrowhead for New Year's Eve. I thought we both needed the change. We built fires, lit candles, sipped wine, and sang songs together. We brought with us some of the rare first editions of romantic poetry that we had found together in Beverly Hills bookshops. Some of them cost hundreds of dollars, but that never mattered to me. It was a passion we shared and we loved to sit by a candle and read works by Keats, Byron, or Shelley to each other. Gen began writing fiction herself at the lake and displayed a seemingly effortless knack for graceful prose in her stories. But, despite this interlude of peace and relaxation, Gen's bad luck still seemed to follow her. That night she was lighting a gas oven with an apparent leak and a flame shot out and burned her hair, eyelids, and lashes.

Just after New Year's Day, 1970, I found out that my modest investment in Bumbles was in trouble. It had opened only months earlier, but business was already sagging. I never made back my investment after the place finally went under. Then again, I never settled up my bar tab or paid for all the dinners I signed for, so I probably broke even. Money wasn't the issue. I was never one to dwell on the cash flow.

The critical fact behind what was happening as the decade drew to a close was not that a club—conceived as a private nocturnal refuge for the hip, creative elite of L.A.—was in trouble. It was rather that my outrageous freewheeling odyssey as the "patriarch" of a musical family through the sixties was over and I was on my own. Looking back now at the turn of the decade, Gen's troubles with Rosebud and mine at Bumbles were symbolic. On the last night of the sixties, Gen had been singed and very nearly disfigured. I had invested ten grand in a rock club and got burned as a backer. We couldn't know it then, but these events foreshadowed for us a slow, irreversible descent into a living hell.

18

GEN AND I saw Elvis Presley perform at the International
Hotel in Vegas and visited him backstage. His performance
was amazing. Afterward, Gen's voice was shot from screaming during "Suspicious Minds." He hadn't played any shows
in nearly a decade, but he was still the King. We stood at the
door of the dressing room and watched the noisy entourage
mill around and protect him.

We moved forward slowly, through clusters of well-con-
nected fans, friends, and the good ole boys of Graceland.
Gorgeous women stood and gaped, ready to throw themselves at Elvis. I was escorting one of them, to be sure. "He's
so exquisitely beautiful," she whispered. We were both in
awe.

Up close, he was as handsome and charismatic as a man
could be. His slick black hair was still wet, a towel was
draped around his neck, and he sat calmly, saying very little.
We moved closer and caught his eye. We jockeyed to a spot
just beside him. His father, Vernon, was nearby.

"Elvis looks like my cousin Hadley, the Afrikaans tank
commander who died after playing water polo, doesn't he,
John?" Gen said softly. I nodded, then stepped forward and
shook his hand. He acknowledged who I was and said he

liked our music. Then he noticed Gen and whispered to Vernon, "My God, it's Joanna."

He smiled at Gen and told her it was one of his favorite movies. This was all she needed to hear. The flattery broke the ice and started a brief but heady friendship with Elvis around his home in Palm Springs.

In Palm Springs, we usually stayed at the Joshua Tree Inn or rented someone's house. We got in touch with the Colonel and tried to see the King. He and Priscilla were living apart then.

The first time I saw him in the desert I was on my Triumph 750. I almost crashed into another biker, a dangerous-looking thug in black leather on a monster Harley chopper. There were a dozen other bikers a hundred yards behind him. They all seemed to be saddled in identical Harleys. I was outnumbered.

He flipped up the visor of his helmet and smiled. "John?" he said. "Elvis?" I laughed. We shook hands again and rode off back to his house, followed by the Graceland Angels.

The Colonel never took to us. We would usually stop there first and he would get on the intercom and tell Elvis, "The hippies are here." But Elvis and the gang saw me as a southern boy. I was from Virginia, after all. He had heard a demo of my solo album before its release and liked it. It had a country edge to it, with steel guitar ace Buddy Emmons on most cuts, as well as Elvis's own hot lead guitarist, James Burton. He and the guys liked to tease me when I'd walk in by singing one of the album cuts, "Mississippi"—about the bayou country. So if I was a hippie, at least I was a southern hippie.

Gen used to say that the mere sight of Elvis walking out to receive guests bordered on the orgasmic. He'd emerge silently in some gaudy jewel-studded white jumpsuit with a wide belt and stop, feet apart. He sometimes looked as if he was about to go right into "Don't Be Cruel." He'd shake his shoulders and mumble hello under his breath, flash those sheepish, sexy eyes, and Gen would gasp. When he pinched her cheek and muttered, "You pretty lil' thang, you," Gen swooned. Her face froze, her body shivered with delight, and she very nearly dropped dead.

It was the decor that almost did me in. Real tacky stuff. Rugs on the walls with matadors and bulls woven into them, harsh colors—red, blue, purple—everywhere. The worst. Elvis grabbed me by the arm once and said, "Look, I wanna show you somethin', man, that's fuckin' incredible. Come on out by the pool." We got outside. "There," he said, "look."

"What?" I asked dumbly, looking around.

"It's all AstroTurf, man," he said. He had surrounded the pool with it. Artificial turf was still a new and ingenious creation. "It's great, ain't it?" he boasted. "Never have to mow it—ever. It don't grow, man."

The three of us were always excusing ourselves to the bathrooms with suspicious frequency, and though drugs were never discussed or displayed in Elvis's home, it was safe to assume we were not all suffering from the same intestinal disorder.

Gen came home one evening from her work at Fox on *Move* and launched into one of her animated tales. "Elvis has been following me, John. He found out that the Fox limo picks me up here at six in the morning and we got to this traffic light and Elvis was in this car with all these guys and they were out all night carousing and I leaned out and said, 'Wow, Elvis!' and he followed me all the way to Fox and stayed with me while I was getting into makeup."

Elvis once took a bunch of the guys in a limo and drove through Palm Springs until they came upon a group of gorgeous women in bathing suits crowded inside an El Dorado convertible. He rolled down the darkly tinted windows and whispered, "Hi, ladies." I never heard ear-splitting squeals like those. Total madness wherever he went.

There were always parties going on. The sexual energy in the air around Elvis was intense. You could sense it in the women who got close to him. They were always being flown in from all kinds of places and practically carried out on stretchers. It would not have shocked me to hear ladies speaking in tongues in his presence. They were intoxicated. Yet sex seemed just another spectator sport to Elvis most of the time. Often, we'd just end up taking out a guitar and singing together. He was rather subdued around his guests.

Elvis once asked me if I knew any women that I could fix

him up with. I flew in a woman I had dated in L.A., a sharp-witted aspiring actress with a big-city sort of sophistication. They hit it off well enough, but no sparks landed on his jumpsuit. He liked his women simple and docile, and even then he wasn't into sex for the sheer sport of it—from what I could see.

Whenever a sexual subject came up, Elvis would pick up his Bible for moral guidance and quote something. "Better to plant your seed in the belly of a whore than to waste it on the ground," he'd say right before a party. And who was I to disagree with the King on *that?* Then he'd slap the Bible shut and say, "Let's hit it!"

Gen always found Elvis something of a flirt. "He loves to tease and make me giggle," she would say. He especially liked to give her a hard time for having a black lover, Calvin Lockhart, in *Joanna.*

He and Gen took trips into the desert on his cycle. She came back once with another story. "We were out in the middle of nowhere, just us and the cactuses, and he said all of a sudden, 'Get off my back, man. I don't want people on my back who have been screwin' niggers.' He likes to tease me so much. And I said, 'Elvis, I'm South African! How can you say this to me?' I thought he was going to leave me there. I said, 'Elvis you can't strand me here.' So I said to him, 'I swear to God I never screwed a nigger.' He smiled and said, 'Get down on your knees and kiss my boots if you haven't screwed a nigger.' "

He told Gen he drove by the house in L.A. and waited outside for her, but she never showed. He'd say it was God's will that he and Gen kept crossing paths. She'd tell me Elvis made it plain to her that if she left me and came to live with him it would be fine with him and Vernon and that she'd be welcomed in Graceland anytime.

At the end of the summer of 1970, we learned that Gene-vieve was pregnant.

A few weeks later, we were sued for breach of contract over the *Telephone* affair by Rosebud Films. Rosebud charged Gen with breaking her contract to do the film and claimed the delay in production caused by her refusal cost Rosebud $250,000. Mike Sarne and I were named as codefendants for allegedly advising Gen not to do the film. The case left both of us disillusioned and Gen came to the realization during her pregnancy that she did not want to pursue a career of acting in films. We eventually settled with Rosebud for $15,000.

I worked on my solo LP and original music for *Brewster McCloud,* which Lou and I co-produced. I wrote some music to helicopter sounds and things like that, as well as a couple of songs. We got to see the film being shot in the Houston Astrodome—Elvis would have loved the wall-to-wall.

The so-called *Wolf King* album, from Gen's nickname for me, came out in the middle of the year. It was an instant collector's item. Which is to say it was DOA in the record stores. So few of them, in fact, made their way into the American economy that when they do pop up at rock and roll flea markets, they now sell for about $40 a shot.

I hated performing as a solo artist. There aren't many things I have ever enjoyed doing alone. I have always hated performing alone, creating, sleeping, traveling alone, *being* alone. I never had the front man's ego and that LP proved it. I nearly mixed my vocals off the album. I sounded seriously depressed. The songs were fine, the backup vocalists and musicians were fine, but the lead singer seemed groggy. All I ever wanted to do was dissolve into a vocal group, do the writing, lyrics, arrangements, tinker with the sound at the mixing board, and hide my voice in the harmonic flow. The idea is to remain invisible. That work sounded lethargic, the voice disembodied.

I did a brief tour of clubs to help salvage the solo album late that summer—places like the Bitter End in New York and the Cellar Door in Washington. One nonpaying gig on the itinerary was L.A. County Courthouse, where Michelle and I met to finalize our divorce. Gen came along to make it interesting. They were getting along well then.

Michelle had recently shot *The Last Movie* in the Peruvian Andes and was in an intense new love affair with Dennis Hopper, the mad genius behind *Easy Rider.* Hopper was the film's director and star. After the divorce, the three of us went to the Bel Air Hotel for a celebration breakfast of eggs

Benedict and champagne. Then we all came back to 783 and
everything seemed under control. As we were walking down
the stairs into the living room, Michelle fainted backward
into my arms. She came to ten seconds later and she was
trembling. I realized it had finally hit her—that it was over
and we were divorced.

"We should get back together," she said softly. "We
should get back in the car, go downtown, get a license, and
get married all over again. We're really going to blow this if
we don't. Immediately."

Gen glanced away and seemed awkward and wary. This
was the scenario she feared the most—a reconciliation. It
may have occurred to her that my hunt for one-night stands
was a smoke screen to obscure my more genuine desire to
rekindle with Michelle.

Michelle had been to the house numerous times to drop
Chynna off, pick Chynna up. Gen always imagined that she
and I were still getting it on during the lulls between Michelle's boyfriends.

Gen moved quietly across the room and sat down on a
couch. Her hair was all chopped off and she wore a dark
green miniskirt and knee-high boots of soft hide. This was
her Peter Pan look.

"Gee, Michelle," I said, "I don't know. I just can't do it,
darling."

"If you don't want to do it right now, then let's forget it,"
she said decisively. "I'll marry you again right now if you
want to."

"Mitch, darling, we've only been divorced *an hour and a
half.* Everything's been divided up. We've gone through
months of pain. I'm just not going to do it."

"I guess that's that," she said. And it was.

One dramatic reunion—if not quite a rekindling—was set
in motion around the same time. Dunhill Records threatened to sue all of us if we did not deliver one last album on
our contract that had been extended to September 1971.

We were all struggling to make it on our own: Denny was
working on a solo album, eventually entitled *Watcha Gonna
Do,* that would come out in early 1971; Cass had an anthology due out and was doing TV guest appearances and solo

concerts; I had the *Wolf King, Space,* and Byron and Shelley projects; Mitch was making her move to film. A season together in the studio seemed incongruous now, but I started writing material in a hurry.

It was a confusing time, pulling me back to the past, toward an uncertain future. The prospect of one more child made me wonder. Gen and I had been together less than a year and our relationship was sometimes tenuous. Gen felt lost much of the time, marooned at the beach house without a license while I would spend two or three days in town. Her career was at a turning point. We had *plans* to work together, but a child would *commit* us to stay together and it just seemed too soon. There were vague, ambivalent suggestions of "an alternative"; appointments were made and broken, money rounded up and forgotten. Gen and I both loved the idea of kids. But I was turning thirty-five, I was father to three, an ex-husband twice, my career was in a lengthening lull, I was behind on payments to *two* women, and the IRS was threatening to lien on me, so to speak. I felt we needed more time, but we were running out of it.

We spent many evenings in late summer at Larry Hagman's house up the beach. He had a great hot tub and I got to know Jack Nicholson. Jack was breaking up with a girlfriend and was brokenhearted. One night, when Gen was at Hagman's, I met a woman walking along the beach. Twenty minutes later we were in my bedroom making love.

Gen left Hagman's and strolled home. She opened the bedroom door and went wild when she spotted us under the sheet—raving all over the house, screaming, and slamming doors. My track record with affairs during pregnancies wasn't improving. I quickly escorted the woman outside. When I came back, Gen was on the deck, screaming and hurling all my belongings onto the sand. "John Phillips," she wailed, "you cruel bastard, get out of here!"

I later found out that the woman I had met on the beach and taken home to bed was Jack's heartbreaker. Maybe I started to feel I owed him one.

While in New York for the Bitter End gigs, I got on Dick Cavett's interview show and popped a tab of acid before the taping. I saw myself on the tube that night and I looked ninety-five years old.

Gen was the hot, glamorous property, not me. *Move* came out that summer and she earned herself solid reviews. She was booked for a ten-page *Vogue* spread with Richard Avedon. Not even morning sickness could diminish her delicate elfin beauty.

Once we secured a $50,000 commitment from a film producer, we got to work on our *Byron and Shelley Experiment.* Mike Sarne was directing us and he put together a small cast that included Jimi Hendrix, who was living at a hotel on Central Park South with two women, and a striking Nicaraguan woman named Bianca. Jimi was acid rock's Voodoo Child extraordinaire, and the sultry, mysterious Bianca was living in Paris, dating a prominent French record mogul named Eddie Barclay. She had done some modeling in Paris and had been hanging around with Hendrix and his crowd in New York.

Gen, Bianca, and I shared one suite at the Plaza and Mike took another. Gen would come home from her shoot and accuse me of sleeping with Bianca during the day. I denied it. Gen was so prone to jealousy that she claimed Bianca was dosing her coffee with acid in the morning before the Avedon sessions.

We took Bianca to a dinner at Diana Vreeland's home and introduced her to all the top fashion people like photographer Francesco Scavullo and jewelry designer Kenny Lane. Gen put the idea in Bianca's head that when she returned to Paris she should make a move on Mick Jagger. It was one way to get her away from me, in Gen's mind. "If I didn't have John," she told Bianca, "I would try for Mick. He's broken up with Marianne Faithfull and he's available."

There was a thirty-fifth birthday party for me in our suite at the Plaza and Gen invited Andy Warhol's entire crew from the Factory. Never in my life had my birthday been celebrated by people with names like Divine, Ultra Violet, and Diva. Sarne's London crowd showed up, along with Gen's poet and actor friends. It was an insane mix and we tore the place apart. We got it all down on film.

The movie was to be shot in a *cinéma-vérité* style, with

Mike and I playing Byron and Shelley as modern men—a musician and film director—and then as themselves, in period. Bianca was to play Teresa, Byron's mistress. Gen was to play Mary Shelley, the novelist and wife. We weren't sure exactly where the Voodoo Child fit in but Richard Leacock, who did *Monterey Pop* with Pennebaker, was the cameraman whose crew followed us everywhere.

In the few weeks we worked on the project, we shot scores of hours on sixteen-millimeter film. I remember mostly the numerous takes we did snorting coke in gram lines off peacock feathers. One long sequence was shot among Warhol's people at the Factory. And we visited my father's grave at Arlington when I played in D.C.

Through the film, I finally got a chance to get to know Jimi as a gentle, remarkably delicate man. We often went to Hippopotamus in the Village and sat in a dark back booth. We talked about fame, how quickly it can come and go through your life. *Electric Lady* had just come out and it was his most spectacular album. We talked about the hangers-on, the rip-off artists who come out of the woodwork once you've struggled to the top. I remember Jimi looking up behind him, at a tiger skin nailed to the wall. "That's where they want me, man," he mumbled cynically, "on the wall like a trophy."

"The way you're living, man," I said, "they might bag you sooner than you think."

"I can handle it."

A month later, Jimi was dead. Janis and Jim Morrison weren't too long after him.

Bianca was in Paris, looking for a street fighting man; Sarne was back in London; Byron and Shelley were in turnaround.

We heard a chilling tale that one of the girlfriends living with Jimi overdosed shortly after his death. It was apparently suicide by hotshot—a fatal load of coke and smack. The story went that the last despairing moments of her life, including the fatal injection, were filmed by a friend of hers. The new decade was getting off to a sick and ominous start.

Back in Bel Air, little had changed. I was visited one day by a middle-aged acid queen who was known in drug-rock circles as Princess Leyda. She just walked out of the woods one day and came to the door. She flitted around in white robes and metallic belts and sandals and looked like she was ready for the Olympics—the original games in ancient Greece. I had only heard of her, but she knew a lot about me.

She had "Satellites"—younger, but no less eccentric girls with names like Venus and Neptune—and they were rumored to engage in bizarre sexual practices. One story had them using live swans in autoerotic rituals back at their Hollywood mothership. She and her girls would hypnotize the swans and use their downy soft necks as sex aids.

Princess Leyda was good enough to tell me that she had become fixated on my dog, a golden retriever named Trelawny, named for the friend of Byron and Shelley. How did she know about Mr. T, I started to ask, getting a little paranoid. She then informed me that the dog collar around her neck was Mr. T's. He had been abducted while I was out.

"That's impossible," I said.

"I am your dog now," she said.

"Don't take this wrong, Princess, but I'd rather have Mr. T." I was furious—and losing patience with this hippie acid case. Was this the legacy of the sixties—the great artists dying young and the aging survivors using swans as vibrators and abducting dogs? Leyda got upset and disappeared into the Bel Air bushes around our house.

One hour later, she came back lugging a huge pillowcase. Peter Lawford was at the house now. I asked her in so he would believe what I had just told him. She dropped the pillowcase on the floor. The dog collar was attached to it and inside I could tell a live animal was trying to escape. There was a crude hand-drawn map on the pillowcase that indicated the path to Princess Leyda's palace up in the hills.

I assumed it was my beloved Mr. T in the sack, but it was a live swan. When I let it out, the swan broke into a brisk waddle through the house, looking either for a body of water or the body of a female. Leyda made a now-predictable mysterious departure.

My limo driver, Little Joe, came in and got the swan back

in its pillowcase. "Who the hell has swans in this city?" I
asked Peter. We both came up with the same answer.

I called the Bel Air Hotel. "Is one of your swans missing
from the pond outside?" I asked.

"Funny you should ask," the front desk told me. "We
happen to be one swan short at the moment."

I told him of the swan-napping and suggested they put the
Bel Air Patrol on the case. They came and picked up the
swan. Then Peter and I went to the Hollywood precinct
house of the LAPD and said we wanted protection when we
went up there to liberate Trelawny. They refused, then sent
two cops to shadow us.

We lurked in the bushes up at Princess Leyda's and I
called out Trelawny's name as the cops crouched down,
ready for a firefight. Manson *was*, after all, still on the collective L.A. mind. Suddenly Mr. T made his break—through a
screen door window—and jumped in my arms, unhurt.

A month later, I played the Troubadour on Santa Monica
Boulevard and the whole balcony was taken over by Leyda
and the Satellites. They could have cut a record with that
name. They lit candles and chanted weird black magic doo-
wop vocals during the set. I didn't mind. I always hated
singing by myself anyhow.

I was entering the East Gate of Bel Air only days after the
show when my boyhood friend and ex-Smoothie, Bill
Cleary, noticed from the passenger window the Satellite Venus walking Trelawny on a leash. This was too much. I got
out of the car and slugged her. She dropped for the ten-
count and I took back my dog.

It wasn't over yet. I received in the mail a square cardboard box that was ticking upon arrival. I was seized with
terror. I called the bomb squad and they sent over a trio of
experts in high-tech jumpsuits and a lead-reinforced con-
tainer for the delicate defusing operation. They managed to
pry the box open and view its contents without leveling Bel
Air. Inside was an oversized Mickey Mouse alarm clock and
a senseless note from Princess Leyda: I THOUGHT YOU
WANTED TO PLAY.

We went to Washington for more dates in the fall. It was
strange to play Washington with most all of my family out

west. Gen was nearly three months pregnant. After a show,
Bill Cleary, Gen, and I had one final discussion about "the
appointment" we had been avoiding. The time had come to
move on it.

I drifted off to sleep. All of a sudden, I'm at a hotel front
desk with a newborn baby in my arms. I'm starting to check
in and the baby starts to squirm and choke. He can't
breathe. He makes these awful noises and turns scarlet. I
panic. I ask the hotel manager for a doctor. "Take the child
to the top floor of the hotel and, if you hurry, you can get to
the doctor in time."

I race through the lobby, slapping the baby's face as I feel
the air slipping out of him. I'm crying and screaming and
pounding the elevator door. "The elevator's broken," I'm
told. I run up all fifteen flights of stairs and I choke and gasp
for air. The muscles in my legs feel engulfed in flames.

I get to the top floor and the baby is a lump of soft flesh in
my arms. Tears run down my face. I push open a door and
suddenly I'm standing in a vast tropical rain forest on the
roof of the hotel. A wide raging river cuts through the forest.
I try, but I can't revive the baby. I don't know where I am
and I can hardly breathe.

There is no raft, so I start to wade across. I lose my foot-
ing and go under with the baby. I struggle to tread across
the powerful current and almost drown five or six times. I
gag on water and try to hold the baby high over my head in
one hand.

I make it to the other side, soaked and exhausted. The
baby is barely breathing. The forest stretches on forever in
all directions. The sky above is blue, but the tops of the trees
are so dense that night has fallen where I stand. Sunlight
hangs trapped in the tall trees like a brilliant orange
spiderweb. I aim my body and break into a blind, desperate
sprint, cutting my arms, legs, and feet on sharp branches. I
feel the warm trickle of blood down my limbs as I move. The
baby's face is turning gray.

In the middle of the forest, I come to a small clearing and
a pagan temple with a thatched roof that glows in the sunlight. The solemn, unforgiving faces of primitive icons stare
out at me from around the temple as I approach.

I enter the temple, and seated on a crude throne made of limbs, bark, and vines is a shriveled-up Holy Man with brown leathery skin and shocking white hair. He is wearing only a loincloth and a religious talisman against his waxy, skeletal chest. He must be two hundred years old.

He can barely move his hands, but he gestures for me to surrender the baby. I hand the baby to him and watch the Holy Man's face. He looks down and waves his long bony fingers over the baby and from the absolute silence in the heart of the forest comes a screeching wail of life as the baby begins to twitch again. The Holy Man rocks slowly in his throne and hands me the baby. "You have saved the baby's life," he tells me.

I feel sharp, persistent taps on my arm. I wheel around to look behind me in the temple, expecting to see a tribe of ancient men. But as I turn, I see only the face of Bill Cleary. He is kneeling next to my bed in a hotel room in Washington, tapping my arm to wake me. I stare at him; Gen is standing behind him, looking down at me. I am bathed in sweat. The sheets are soaked.

"Come on, let's go," Bill said quietly. "You must have had one helluva dream. The limo's downstairs, the money's ready, we're gonna be late."

"Where are we?" I was floating out of the ozone. No forest, no river, no pagan temple. I blinked hard several times.

"Washington. You grew up here."

"Jesus," I said. "I don't believe what just happened. Forget the limo. Cancel the appointment. There's no way we're not going to have this child."

19

DURING HER PREGNANCY, Gen mellowed out and stopped taking acid and mescaline. She spent a lot of time by herself at the beach house. She had little choice. She couldn't drive and I divided my time between the beach and 783. There, I could retreat to the soundproofed, womblike insulation of the studio and noodle around with new tunes for the album. The baby was due around the same time we were aiming to begin rehearsals for the "reunion" sessions, just before spring.

Gen soon began to feel more lost than serene. After three frivolously campy and creative years among the stoned avant-garde of theater, rock, and film in South Africa, London, New York, and L.A., life by the ocean became rootless and dreamlike. She had one trusted confidante, a woman photographer friend of ours, who would talk with her for hours.

We would occasionally take leisurely strolls along the beach. We'd stop to collect shells and talk. "It's like I'm not even in California," she would say. "I knew lots of people in South Africa, I had a very nice agent in London at International Famous, and I made movies and I ate lunch at White Elephant, but I can't function here." Gen's imagination always needed space. When she wasn't creating, she devoured literature. Sometimes just talking about art, books, and her feelings brought her spirits up.

"I don't have a license. I walk to the library here and I read Virginia Woolf, and Aleister Crowley's huge autobiography about all that black magic in the English countryside, and he put a lot of women in the loony bin, you know. That can't happen to me," she said. "But I'm very attracted to men like that—powerful and physical and charming. I feel isolated. Nothing seems real to me except my reading. Which is fine. I never really wanted to be a model or an actress. I wanted to be a writer—sort of like Hannah Arendt, with lots of ideas and philosophies. I don't have to worry about this deal or that script or screen tests. I can just sit and read and educate myself out here and watch and feel the baby grow. And so in a sense I suppose I really *am* quite happy."

Michelle's life, meanwhile, was far from placid. She had been spending a lot of time with her *Last Movie* mentor and lover, Dennis Hopper, at his house in Taos. She and Chynna went there after the shoot. She married Hopper sometime around Halloween and the marriage barely lasted a week. I called it the Six-day War.

Gen and I gave them a reception at the big house after a Leonard Cohen concert at UCLA's field house. The tickets for Hopper and some friends weren't at the window and the show was sold-out. Michelle was performing as Cohen's backup vocalist. Hopper got surly and loud and took a swing at the usher. We all got into a brawl in the lobby. I had to pull the guy off Dennis.

Hopper bullied his way into the hall as Cohen sang and we all sat on the floor in front of the front row. Dennis then kept up an obnoxious running commentary that clearly disturbed Cohen. "That's great, Leonard!" he'd call out. "Loved that one, baby! Keep it up!"

The lights went up for the intermission and I felt embarrassed for Michelle, or Holly Hopper, her new married name. I persuaded Dennis to come back to the house and prepare for the party. The police were waiting for him in the lobby, but they didn't press charges.

Scores of friends showed up. Dennis was pissed off at me. He told me I had ruined his evening out. He thought I was trying to steal Michelle back and accused me of not paying the caterer. I was sorry I didn't let the usher pulverize Dennis when I had the chance.

They went to Taos—to the house once occupied by D. H. Lawrence—and fought the Six-day War. A week later Mitch called. She wanted to get away from the guy. She was afraid to have Chynna around him. She asked if I would pick her up at the airport and if she could stay with us.

She cried as she told us about her turbulent week of marriage in Taos. How Hopper had been firing guns in the house. He had handcuffed her a couple of times to keep her from running away. He thought she was a witch. There were fights. He was stoned and out of control. She impulsively decided to leave while Hopper was asleep. She grabbed Chynna and made it to her car and was well on her way when he awoke.

As I heard the story, he raced to the airport in a pickup truck and drove onto the runway in a futile attempt to block the plane. She was relieved now to be safe.

Michelle stayed in the guesthouse and we all got along quite peacefully. She and Gen became good friends. They lunched in Beverly Hills and Gen was happy to participate in little Chynna's care. Michelle was stronger, more independent. She was going through a lot with single motherhood, her movie career, and Hopper. Gen kept the lid on her jealousy and suspiciousness, though she always assumed Michelle and I were still getting it on. We weren't—for the most part. One night, though, I did make love to Michelle in the library while Gen waited for me to come to bed in our room.

The Mamas and the Papas were just beginning to rehearse at Cass's house in the hills. Michelle was soon back in circulation. She moved to another place in Malibu and started dating Jack Nicholson as we got going with the album. I was all for it and encouraged Jack.

Michelle gave Gen her baby shower at our beach house. "John," Gen said to me as we looked around at all the women on hand, "this is such a lovely day, isn't it? It's quite a guest list." She was moved by Michelle's generosity, and the gifts suddenly made motherhood seem more real. It hadn't diminished Gen's sardonic comic timing. "I think you've been to bed with every woman in this house."

Terry Melcher called me and said that Sly Stone was interested in buying the house at 783 Bel Air Road. He brought Sly over and we stayed up all night and played music. He loved the grounds, the furniture, the studio, the whole shot. Sly wanted to make an album there. But he didn't have enough money to make the buy. I was ready to give up the house and shuttle between the beach and a bungalow at the Château Marmont. Even I could see I needed a better cash flow after the failure of the solo album. The IRS was still sniffing and circling around my ASCAP royalties.

So we agreed that he could rent the house for about $12,000 a month—with unlimited use of the studio—while recording his album. Originally, the lease was for three months, and at the end of that period he had to come up with $25,000 to be placed in an escrow account to be credited—along with the rent—toward the eventual purchase price of $250,000. If he failed to close the deal for the house, that money was nonrecoupable.

Sly kept coming up with the escrow payments and then was unable to close the deal. With penalties, Sly lost well over a hundred thousand dollars in escrow payments for the times he defaulted on the balance of the purchase price. This must have been a real estate first for Bel Air. I was making a killing on not selling the house.

Gen gave birth to our son, Tamerlane, on March 14, 1971. By then, we were living at the beach most of the time and I was rehearsing with Cass, Denny, and Michelle. Tam was a beautiful baby with plenty of hair and Gen's giant green eyes.

That same month the IRS went ahead and put a lien on ASCAP, tying up my royalties so I could make a dent in my $160,000 outstanding tax bill.

When Sly failed to come up with a $50,000 payment at the end of another three-month period in 1971, I had to evict the forty or so Family Stone members who had settled in. I went up to the house and saw that it was in bad shape. They were

partying and rocking pretty hard. Sly wasn't around. He was
in New York. His goons were sullen, unfriendly, and armed.
I spoke with them and told them they had twenty-four hours
to come up with the money or split. These people were
rough. They laughed at me. There were lots of guns, rifles,
machine guns, big dogs. These people didn't screw around.
"Fuck off, man," they said. "Just get out."

They had until midnight the next night. I called a Mexican friend, and I told Chico what was going on.

"They're awfully tough," I said.

"No problem." He smiled, savoring the challenge. "I'll
take care of it. Chico's got many friends."

Gen and I went up there to resolve the issue. It probably
didn't help to bring with me a woman known to be from
South Africa. The Family was dancing and cooking in the
kitchen and teasing Gen. Every fifteen minutes, I went to the
chief bodyguard and warned him time was running out and
I needed Sly's answer. I looked out the window and heard
rustling noises in the bushes below the bedroom where Gen
and I waited. Outside, Chico and about forty of his gardener
friends were lurking in the bushes. They all seemed to have
machetes, chain saws, and nasty gardening implements. This
toughened my bargaining position with the dude.

"I'll call Sly again," he mumbled, "but who the hell do
you think you are, man, and who do you think you're dealin'
with? Ain't no one pushin' us round here."

"Well, look, a deal's a deal, man. If you want to trash my
house and assault me, I'll come down on you as hard as I
can, to the full limit of the law. Maybe even harder, to protect my property and family." I paused, then asked him to
come with me to the front door. We walked outside. That
was the cue for Chico's battalion to creep forward out of the
garden mist into plain sight. "And besides," I said, as I
proudly watched the men move forward wielding trowels,
hedge clippers, whirring curb cutters, and spades, "I've got
about forty gifted landscape artists of Mexican extraction
who are right this minute sharpening their machetes and
chain saws. They're a little messed up on Cuervo and beer
and this private army of mine has been watching this whole

thing go down and they're looking for a little action—just to work off the tequila."

The dude got Sly on the phone and I grabbed it.

"I've laid all this *bread* on you, man," Sly pleaded.

"It's not enough," I answered sharply. "We had a deal."

"My tapes are all hidden up in the studio . . ."

"I'll respect all your property. Just get your fucking people out of my house or come up with the fifty before midnight." I handed the phone over to the dude. He listened for a few seconds, then hung up.

"Okay," he said to me.

"Okay, someone's gonna give me fifty grand?" He shook his head. "Okay, we outta here in a half hour."

We moved back in briefly while Sly continued his efforts to buy the house. We would finally unload it to him by the end of the summer, but not before his defaulted payments had pushed the total price of the house to about half a million dollars. It was better money and far less work than working the road.

The *People Like Us* sessions were efficient but perfunctory. It was rare we were all together. Most tracks were dubbed, one vocal at a time. The material was too laid-back and failed to make maximum use of Cass's voice. I spent hundreds of hours splicing tape together and creating an illusion of "live" harmony. We had been apart now for as long as we had been together. The elegance, the fire, the graceful union of our voices were long gone.

Dunhill ABC interpreted a lot of the studio charges as waste and indulgence on my part and they nailed me for $40,000 in overages against royalties. The album cost $125,000 and stiffed. We managed to make it on the charts for three weeks with one cut off the album, "Step Out"—it got to about Top 80 and vanished.

We certainly were no longer the same stoned, carefree innocents we had once been. Cass had a full-time uniformed nurse assigned to watch her and she would sit there, hour after hour, knitting and reading in the control booth. We never did know what exactly was wrong. She was such an integral part of the sessions, Nurse Regina earned herself a credit on the album for "Medical Aid."

Michelle—the ex-Mrs. Holly Hopper—showed up now
and then with Nicholson, who just watched and listened,
and we recorded a song of mine called "Grasshopper" in her
honor.

Denny had been moving between Carmel, Halifax, L.A.,
and Florida. His girlfriend Linda had given birth to a daughter. He had done his solo country-style album and been back
home after the death of his mother. He had rented out the
Astor mansion and stayed in the house next door when in
town. Denny was pretty much out there. One night he was
dehydrated and drunk and grabbed an ice pop from the
freezer. He chewed it right off the stick. Half an hour later,
Denny realized that the colors were running off the rug into
the corners of the room. The ice pop was laced with acid.
Denny freaked and ended up calling a taxi to Michelle's. She
was alone. He stayed in a guest room and stared at the TV
all night. At dawn, he couldn't recall that he had slid his
boots under the bed. He went poking around in Michelle's
room and found a pair of boots. It was dark and he tried not
to disturb Michelle. He tried the boots on. They didn't fit.
They were Nicholson's. Jack had come home in the middle
of the night and Denny hadn't heard or seen him. Jack
awoke, saw what he thought was an intruder's silhouette
hunched over the bed, and went berserk. Denny didn't know
it was Jack. Each man almost frightened the other to death,
literally.

Doing the album put Mitch and me into close quarters. It
wasn't long before there was sexual teasing during playbacks
or downtime if Jack wasn't around. She'd sit on my lap and
we'd nuzzle off in a corner. Michelle was still a fox; nothing
would ever change that.

We went to my rented bungalow at the Château and I
poured us some shots of tequila. Gen was at the beach with
our newborn baby. Sly was gettin' down at 783. We started
to giggle and snuggle and throw down more shots of tequila.
Then we dropped some acid and I realized that we had never
made love right after taking acid. This was obviously the last
chance and we made the most of it all through the night.
The paths of our lives were stretching wider apart as time
went by. We both realized that it was time to finally let go.

The solo album and *People Like Us* made me come to grips with the fact that I had lost the drive, the knack for writing Top 40 songs. I dreaded performing as a solo act. I needed a new medium for my muse. The *Byron and Shelley* project was defunct and composing for films had left me cold.

Gen took Tam home to South Africa for a couple of weeks in the fall, and when she came back we threw ourselves into work on our *Space* musical. We brainstormed together, revised and rewrote, she adapted the play to a screenplay format, and we discussed male leads like Elvis and Jack Nicholson. I wrote more than a dozen songs and we searched for a production deal as a musical or a feature film. Suddenly we were animated and charged up again. We were more excited by *Space* than about any other project since we had met. We knew we were onto a winner.

I was also into large amounts of cocaine through the day and night. I weaned myself from acid and snorted coke, which I found to be a source of powerful, lucid energy. It was rightfully called a "hard" drug. Grass, downers, and acid were "soft" drugs that expanded and mellowed consciousness. The sparkling crystals of pure coke focused and intensified it, honed the inner edge until you felt, in a soaring heart-pounding rush, that your creative blade could slice through anything.

We tossed around all kinds of wild concepts and plot lines. One of them involved getting married. Of course, we ruled out any conventional scenarios. On January 31, 1972, we took our vows in a Chinese restaurant in downtown L.A. But we kept our guests—who included Warren Beatty; Jack and Michelle; Mick and his recent bride, Bianca Jagger; Cass and Denny; and California Lieutenant Governor Jerry Brown—waiting over an hour at the restaurant. We were holed up in a penthouse at the Château Marmont Hotel, working out the last details of a prenuptial agreement. We had to wait while a lawyer tried to photocopy Mick's prenuptial agreement with Bianca. It turned out that neither agreement was legal or binding because neither listed the spouses' assets.

A one-legged Buddhist priest presided over the brief cere-

mony. He wore a kimono and Gen wore a dress loaned to
her by a Chinese woman we knew then. The dress had been
in her family for generations. She also arranged for the ceremony and the elaborate traditional ornamental touches. Her
three stunning young daughters all arrived as dates of a
roguish film director friend of ours. That was a most decora-
tive sight.

Then we feasted on a delicious Chinese banquet. Gen and
I received some novel gifts, like the open plane tickets and
hotel reservations for a honeymoon to Bora Bora from
Mick. We never got around to going. I was too busy honing
my edge. But Mick called a couple of months later and
asked if we had gone. I said not yet. He wondered, since all
the arrangements had been made, if he could get the tickets
back. "You're going on *our* honeymoon?" I asked. Ten minutes later, some guy was sent over to retrieve the gift.

Later that night, the director friend stopped by our place
in Malibu and offered me a rather unconventional gift: his
trio of slinky foxes. I politely declined and asked him to go
away. I had enough on my hands as it was. But it was a nice
touch.

By spring, there was another kind of treat: Michael Butler, our polo-playing socialite friend from Chicago who had
turned *Hair* into a pop-culture legend, decided to option
Space. He advanced us $50,000 to come up with a final
script and score. We were on a roll.

In the first few months of 1972, I recommended to Mick
Jagger that the Stones rent a fabulous mansion near 783 in
Bel Air. It was a pink Italianate palace at 414 St. Pierre
Road that looked like one flank of a great château. They
needed an L.A. base to rehearse for a U.S. tour. William
Randolph Hearst built it for his mistress Marion Davies.
There was an enormous ballroom downstairs, a guesthouse,
fourteen-foot-high ceilings in the front entrance, a glittering
mirrored hall, a gigantic pool fed by a 150-foot electrically
operated waterfall, ponds, gardens, stone walks, and precious oriental art, rugs and antiques and knickknacks all
through the interior.

We got to see a lot of Mick and Bianca. Mick had been out
at the beach for a while, and then, when he moved to Bel

Air, he and I would go out at night and cruise. Gen and Bianca would try to find my blue Rolls limousine and catch us in a lie. Gen had figured out how to drive in from the beach. I had switched from the bungalow to a three-bedroom penthouse suite at the Château, the same one used by Sarne in *Myra* that looks right into a giant billboard on Sunset. One night Gen the supersleuth and Bianca found the limo and scaled the balconies along the outside of the Château, hoping to nail us in the act. As usual, though, the limo was just a decoy. We had taxied to parts and parties unknown.

I felt everything going our way again. When the Stones left 414 and went on the road, I decided we needed a home base that would immediately deliver the message to any and all prospective backers, directors, producers, and friends that we were making it big, that we were a creative force to reckon with. In June, we moved into the house the Stones vacated at 414 St. Pierre Road on a $3,000-a-month lease. One thing hadn't changed from the sixties: my belief that if you wanted other people to treat you like a star, you had to treat yourself like one first. The Pink Palace at 414, high above Bel Air, would prove to any visitors that I was doing just that.

20

SHORTLY AFTER we moved in and went into high gear with *Space,* Jeffrey and Laura came to live with us at the Pink Palace. Susie had recently remarried a businessman who moved into her condo in Tarzana. "Straight" life in the Valley suburbs made both kids rebel. They had spent weekends with us at 783, the Château, and in Malibu. They ran in a fast crowd and were already past booze, pot, and acid before high school.

If they found drugs on their own, I hardly steered them away by my actions. Visits to our homes were like "Father Knows Drugs Best." They saw what went on at the parties. We became synonymous with escape and freedom. Actually, anarchy was closer to it.

They were both talented, creative kids who were turning toward music and acting. Drugs seemed built-in. Jeff was sensitive, physically large, and, though given to brooding, easygoing and relaxed. He wanted to study the sax. Laura was skinny, wild, and theatrical. A natural for the stage. She was a live wire. They complemented each other perfectly.

First, Jeffrey left the Valley. He planned it more like an escape. He was fourteen. He struggled with school and never pushed himself. He knocked on Laura's bedroom window in the middle of the night. His albums were tucked under one arm and a sax was hung around his neck. He told her he was leaving. She sat up, startled. "Shhh," he said, "you'll wake up Mom and Len. Come on, get a taxi and come. I hate to leave you, kid, but I'm gettin' outta here." He moved into 414 that night.

Laura, who wasn't even thirteen yet, was miserable and torn. She stared at the cottage cheese soundproofed ceiling and cried all night. Her closest ally had abandoned her, but she loved Susie. She couldn't just walk out. She had to be tossed out.

Laura began misbehaving. She was leaving the house at night, crawling out the window and down the fire escape to meet friends and drop acid, then would show up for homeroom in the morning. She made noise while Susie talked on the phone; she irritated Len. Len once tore the phone out of the wall while she was speaking. No one would have been able to handle those kids. Laura finally had what she wanted. She stuffed her clothes and makeup in shopping bags, filled a shopping cart one night, screamed and cried to them in their bedroom, then proclaimed her independence.

She wheeled the cart down the block to my mother's. Dene was always great to Laura. Gave her beers after school. She called her a taxi and Laura arrived at 414 the same night.

We tried to set rules. "What's my curfew?" Jeff asked.

"December," I said glibly. I didn't want to seem unreasonable.

"And me?" Laura asked, her huge brown eyes bulging with anticipation. I sensed from her outrageously provocative getups that there was no stopping Laura—rules or no rules. She had grown up *awfully* fast.

"One A.M. on school nights. Five A.M. weekends, with one all-nighter a week. Weekends are all yours—and never *ever* come home in the morning in the same clothes you left in the night before." Her eyes rolled and her jaw dropped. "Dad," she said, "those aren't rules."

"Exactly. That's rule number one. You're on your own." They had it made.

She shaved off her eyebrows, frizzed out her hair, sprinkled her long, stretching body with glitter, tattooed her arm, used a skintight tank top as a miniskirt, wore black lipstick, learned to balance herself in six-inch platform shoes, and played at being Ziggy Stardust's kid sister every night at Rodney Bingenheimer's English Disco on the Strip. I had seen it coming ever since our trip to the islands, when she was barely out of a stroller. This kid was a star.

The huge closet in her room became the headquarters for a dozen of her spangled, glittered-up girlfriends. One of them repeatedly made it clear to me, as she'd strut around in a mid-thigh mini and nasty high heels, that a couple of toots and a quick fuck just might get her through algebra homework. I resisted.

Jeff got stoned, wailed on the sax all day, and blasted his BB gun at anything that moved outside or cost over $500 inside. He took out a color TV and a museum-quality vase one night and fired a few rounds into the priceless antique beveled-mirror panels of the great hallway.

I had the feeling Jeff was dipping into the coke stashes left lying around in bags and bowls. I never permitted the kids to use coke—that was where I drew the line. But I hardly made it impossible. It was going for about $30 a gram back then. Still, they never had to leave the house to score. I caught Laura making off with a fistful of sticks of Panama Red. "There goes the little thief," Gen would seethe and the two of them were at war.

Soon Jeff moved to the guesthouse by the pool and Laura had her own wing at 414. Jeff would scoop out some coke from a bag or vial and toot his brains out by the pool. One afternoon I slid a bowl of coke under the TV cabinet in the living room and told Jeff we were going to take a nap. It was one temptation after another; it would have taken quite a kid not to give in.

When Laura asked Jeff what a coke high was like, Jeff had an ingenious explanation. He found a battery-powered vibrator. "Here," he said, "switch it on and put it between your jaws sideways and clench your teeth. Coke makes you feel like that."

She tried it and went buzzing around the room with her

teeth clamped down on the vibrator. "So?" he asked, "whad-dya think?"

"Hell," she said, "let's give it a try."

Jeffrey soon got to the point where he could barely roll out of bed and take a leak without his wake-up toot. Jeff's idea of a pick-me-upper was about three-fourths of a gram to greet the day. Then he started missing school and telling me it was because he couldn't find the school bus.

Laura found the bus. She also once found a little silver box with a coke spoon attached to the lid by a short silver chain. She filled it up with coke and never had to worry about lunch. She sat in the back row with a girlfriend and tooted behind the girl's open briefcase. Once, the box fell and coke spilled all over the rug. The teacher asked what it was and, as the girls mashed the coke into the rug with their heels, Laura calmly explained, "It's talc . . . for my hands . . . uhhh, on the parallel bars . . . in gym class. Yeah, that's what it is." It was clear she had Del Ray Local blood in her. She was learning, as I had at the same age at the downtown Alexandria hardware store, that there was a way out of anything. Except this was getting into narcotics, not penknives. The edge was even sharper now.

Soon Laura didn't have to get her allowance from me. She was her own boss, with her own career. She was the lead singer in a rock group called CLAS—for Chris, Laura, Adam, and Scott, her three schoolmates in the band. They would do amateur nights at the Troubadour and after one set she was introduced to a casting director, and then to Fred Roos, a film producer. Michelle started taking her around to some agents and auditions and the next thing she knew, she was up for the part—along with about two hundred other girls—of a big mouthed lovable brat who hops a ride on a chopper in *American Graffiti*. A month later she had the part, at $500-plus a week for the shoot during the summer of 1972.

If Laura got a little cocky from her first whiff of stardom, Jeff was getting more paranoid. They were still partners in crime. Jeff was never afraid to steal drugs and Laura never hesitated to ask me for a few bucks.

When I began stashing the drugs in a safe, Jeff would

kneel down and listen to the tumblers, trying to crack it. If I left the room, he'd dash in after me and search around for a hit. He would sweat and start thinking that people were following him. I warned him that he would end up an addict, that he was on his way out, that he had a week to shape up. I knew Jeffrey was afraid of me but that I couldn't control him. I was in no shape—nor was I willing—to give up my drugs and set a sincere example. He and his sister must have sensed that I could never get them to stop until I stopped doing drugs myself. Until then, I was deluding myself—and failing them.

Gen and I once started to pull out of the drive and head for Palm Springs. Gen went back in to get something she had forgotten. She found Jeff standing on a chair, poking around the top shelf of the closet. "Oh, hi, Gen," he said. Gen later threatened him: "We'll send you to a boarding school in Hawaii where they make you run around a track all day with Dobermans snapping at your heels if you don't stop this."

I warned him myself and threatened something almost as dreadful: deportation to Tarzana.

Jeff once thought he saw the silhouette of an intruder behind the drawn shade of the pool house. He jerked the door open and sprinted up to the house and told me someone was after him. I was with a friend of mine, a Mexican named Yippie, and we armed ourselves and prowled around the pool house to prove to Jeff that there was no one around.

Later that night I went into the kitchen to grab a cold beer. Out of the corner of my eye, I saw a figure crouched in the corner. He lunged at me and put a stranglehold from behind. Maybe Jeff *had* seen an intruder. I wrestled the guy to the ground. It was Jeff—in his underwear. He still thought he was being followed and jumped me without knowing who I was. I had had it with him and cold-cocked him on the spot. Then I got my beer and went upstairs.

Yippie and his girlfriend Marsia Trinder had become two of our close friends at 414. He had been in the Mexico City production of *Hair*. Marsia was a beautiful and well-bred designer from London with dazzling blue eyes and wavy red hair. Marsia's father had been the lord mayor of London

and she had come to L.A. in the late sixties to design ul-
trahip leather and suede clothes for the stars. I met her while
I was writing for *Myra* and she told me she had helped
design the costumes for *Hair* in London and Mexico City. I
asked her to make Gen a leather coat while she was in New
York.

Marsia and her boyfriend moved in with us for about
three months in the early 1970s. She became Gen's best
friend. As Gen had done with Bianca, she now recruited
Marsia for her snooping expeditions, hoping to catch me
"with my pants down," as Gen laughingly put it. They once
even rigged up a wild booby trap for Yippie and me after we
left for a late party at the Playboy mansion. There was a
string, wet sponges, lightbulbs unscrewed. Whatever the
contraption was, it all depended on us flicking the switch
when we arrived. We got home at ten in the morning and
never even needed the lights. But we got a good look at their
crude booby trap. They were *so* embarrassed.

Marsia was a devout health nut who avoided drugs. I was
always afraid she wasn't having enough fun at our parties.
Not that I didn't strive to be the perfect host. There was
always a pretty mound or two of coke lying around for my
friends whenever they stopped by. It was right there on a
small mirror or marble slab, with the razor and straw. Eventually, though, she began making clothes in exchange for
drugs. She did white leather pants, a chamois shirt, wide
belts with rhinestones. I paid her in coke and that may have
explained why she did such fast and inspired work. She was
usually one garment behind, but I never minded advancing
her a gram here or there on credit.

Coke was fast becoming the hip social drug of choice for
the new decade. There was always plenty around. For any
deal larger than a couple of grams, I insisted on testing the
coke with a flame or Clorox. Sometimes, when it was an
offer I simply could not refuse, I left the testing and ex-
changing to a pro.

I was brought in on one group deal by a close friend—a
celebrated Hollywood screenwriter—that must have made a
whole bunch of people happy for weeks. It sounded so good
that even his dealer was tense as he collected our cash before

making the buy. He went to the airport and, by cryptic pre-
arrangement, scored behind a locked men's room stall with a
pair of arriving passengers from New York—burly thugs in
dark suits carrying aluminum attaché cases. We were content to stay at the beach, snort what we had, and pray for his
safety. He made it back unscathed. The thugs left the men's
room and boarded the next flight back to New York.

The rock I ended up with was one awesome glacier. It was
larger than a golf ball, diamond-hard, lumpy, and pure. It
was so pure that my friend and I chipped in and treated
ourselves to a microscope, just so we could get high and
behold its magical snowflakes on a slide. I even kept it in a
velvet, satin-lined box used to protect precious gems.

Another friend once ventured reluctantly into the Sierras
for a score involving a new and mysterious source. Again, I
was one of many "backers." He smelled a setup; it seemed
too good. This friend had a serious problem with trust. So in
case the new contacts gave him a hard time, he carried in his
attaché case the agreed-upon $50,000 in cash and a hand
grenade.

He met three men in a remote hilly area. They demanded
to inspect the cash; he demanded to test the rocks. When
they closed in on him, he unlocked the attaché case, grabbed
the grenade, and pulled the pin. The guys panicked and
raced off screaming, hands over their heads. He casually
lobbed the grenade off into the distance. It exploded as they
hit the dirt and rolled, unharmed.

But his faith was quickly restored. In their panic, the
plastic bag packed with coke fell to the ground. He swiped it
and raced off to his car, the fifty grand untouched. That
blow was definitely worth going to war for.

Occasionally we lost track of our drugs, too. One day
Trelawny gobbled up a bag of mescaline caps and ran in
circles for three days without stopping. He was crazed and
needed to run, so I drove him out to the beach. He ran like a
greyhound for hours until he was exhausted. Then he just
stared at himself in the mirror for twelve hours. Trelawny
spanned the genetic gap. He was never quite the same. He
was more human than anything else after swallowing all that
mescaline.

After a few months under the Butler option, we began to feel like we were running in circles too. I wasn't sure whether it was a necessary business move for the project or merely a grandiose cocaine side effect, but I bought my own Telex machine for the magnificent library at 414. I had played with Butler's Telex in his Chicago mansion and office and decided that no one should be without one. When workers came to install it, they had to run wires into a secret room off the downstairs ballroom. The room had long been sealed off by an impenetrable steel door. I had been warned by the owners never to try to enter that room. Mike McLean and I were in the house when the hardhats somehow got the door open and entered the forbidden sanctum. Minutes later, all hell broke loose down there. I learned that I was, in a sense, sharing the place with Howard Hughes.

A pack of grim security men swarmed into the house and raced into the room, ordering the workers out immediately. By prying open the metal door, the workers had set off a silent alarm that brought the private security force. The room was crammed with stacks of documents apparently belonging to Hughes. I could only assume that he must have known one of the owners at one time or another and used the little room to stash his papers.

We did eventually get to poke around in there. There were some homemade records on flimsy red vinyl. On one of them, we heard a woman coquettishly ask Howard, "Tell me, Howie, what's the secret to making lots of money?"

Over a scratchy surface noise, Hughes answered: "Well, it's simple. It's like fishing. You need a net with really big holes in it. That way you let all the little minnows and small fish swim through and get away. They don't matter. But the big ones get caught—and all you need's four or five really big catches and you're on your way."

Howard's priceless wisdom really fired me up. I turned the library at 414 into my own private *Space* command center. I don't know what Howie would have said about my secret for entrepreneurial success. I'd get wired on coke or speed and fire off dozens of Telexes all day and night. I loved the library, with its fireplace, oak paneling, oriental rug, built-in bookcases, and long conference table. There was no quicker way to feel a rush of omnipotence than to sit there with all those drugs and instantaneous global communications at my disposal. When the *Space* staffers came over for a brainstorming session, a pile of coke in the middle of the table helped to keep the ideas flowing.

The project, though, began to bog down with creative, financial, and organizational hassles. The original synopsis centered on a humanoid thermonuclear "little red box" left on the moon by an Apollo crew. It may detonate a nuclear explosion in space, destroying the universe. It must be defused. An Andy Hardy character is chosen to go from Earth and the Intergalactic Commission selects representatives from planets and stars to help Andy on his risky mission. This was the Space Chorus and one of its members was Angel, from Canis Major. She was wild-looking, childlike, out-of-step, and out-of-tune—and capable of immaculate conception in space, merely by falling in love. This was the part for Gen. It was a touch bizarre, but people got hooked. Because of the Apollo moonwalk, outer space was in.

The songs stretched me far beyond the Top 40 format. There were titles like "Last of the Unnatural Acts," "Yesterday I Left the Earth," "Von Braun's Blues," and "Speed of Light." It was a great step for myself in composition, arranging, and lyrics.

The manic energy behind the project got scattered over direction, casting, design, and logistics issues. I tried to get Columbia Records interested in a soundtrack and sent Clive Davis a script. Butler and I agreed that Michael Bennett would direct. Bennett considered the project for many weeks. I had in mind a hip, campy "street" cast. We worked with Toni Basil on choreography—and she turned us on to the entire dance crew at "Soul Train." People put themselves on the line, rehearsing and working without formal contracts and for no money. But we all believed in it and people like Marsia, who designed some fabulous costumes, were willing to wait until we went into production to get paid. As Marsia once said, "John, this is so wonderful. The energy is so *there,* it's like *Hair* all over again."

Under the agreement with Butler, I received $10,000 a month for five months while we tinkered with changes and revisions. When I wasn't revising or composing, I was Telexing Butler about every little hassle that came up. One Telex to 414 from Butler's office informed me that typing the manuscript was my expense, not the producer's. And yet, Gen and I were constantly pushing ourselves harder and harder to create the ultimate space fantasy.

I sent a long Telex detailing my idea for a fairyland decor at the Aquarius Theater. The box office would be the pearly gates. There would be an Astroflash horoscope computer at the box office. Each ticket taker would be in a white beard and flowing robe like St. Peter. The lobby would be "a tunnel of infinity, representing elevation to higher thought," with angels, harpists, flowers, vapors, mists—and ushers bearing angelic wings and gowns. Artistically, we were shooting for the moon.

Meanwhile, Angel was having trouble staying alive on the planet Bel Air. Gen had a tendency for fender benders at the wheel of the custom-built, beige cat-eyed Park Ward Bentley I bought her after Tam was born. It cost about twenty grand then.

Gen was sure the car was haunted. She would turn the radio on and the windows would go down. Or she would press the window button and the brakes would catch. She would put it in DRIVE and the trunk would pop open. Once she cracked up the Bentley in a parking lot right after gum surgery because she was still mildly anesthetized.

Then there was the one where Gen came running into the house, crying. "Oh, John," she sobbed, "the most awful thing's happened. I was leaving a parking lot and I was driving and I hit a pole."

"Is there a lot of damage?" I asked.

"No," she said, "just a slight dent." She hesitated and looked around with her big girlish eyes. "But you just had the car fixed and I feel so badly." I shrugged it off. I was used to this.

A couple weeks later, I got a phone call from a man identifying himself as a Beverly Hills attorney. "Mr. Phillips," he said sternly, "I was in a parking lot in Beverly Hills a few weeks ago and my car was rammed broadside by a Bentley. I've traced the car by getting half the license number and piecing together car types and it leads to your name. Do you happen to have such a plate number?"

"Yup," I told him, "that's mine, but there has to be a mistake."

"Do you have a blond wife with a very high voice?"

"Yes," I sighed, "I'm afraid I do. Why?"

He told me he approached her to exchange insurance policy numbers and told her his name. Suddenly she must have gotten scared and drove off through the underground lot. He chased the Bentley, but only got half of the plate number. He had been tracking me for weeks and was furious and insulted.

"Geez," I said, "that's awfully weird. I just remembered something. She did say a few weeks back that she hit a pole in a parking lot, but nothing about hitting—"

"For Christ's sake!" he shouted. "My name's Rozanski and I'm from Warsaw. She DID hit a Pole. ME!"

He was livid now. He threatened to press felony charges, hit-and-run. "I'm willing to prosecute the bitch," he said. "If I don't have ten grand in cash down here at my office by the end of the day, I'm going to the police. I'm sure she doesn't have a license. No woman could drive like that and have a license."

I went to Gen. "You remember the pole you hit in the lot?"

"Umm-hmm. Why?"

"Well, the Pole called today and squeezed me for ten grand."

Angel raced upstairs, embarrassed.

In September Michael Bennett came to the conclusion that he was "wrong" for the show. He envisioned a splashy, polished Broadway production with glossy staging and high-kicking dance numbers. I had a funkier vision. On Broadway, he felt, you do it a certain way with certain people or it doesn't work. I had to admit that I was out of my league. I had only seen one musical in my life—*West Side Story*. I still held to my concept of using rock and rollers instead of stagey, mannered Broadway performers. I didn't want to work with so many narrow constraints on my ideas. I thought that *Hair* was but the first of its kind for a musical, and that *Space* could well be its successor in the seventies.

Bennett sent us a letter in which he cited "artistic impasses," the fight for ultimate control of the show, the "inefficiency and inexperience" of the staff. He went on: "You are a genius, John, and see the show in your head better than I do. . . . I know at this point in your life your ego will not allow you to be anything but the boss, and at this point in my life I'm in the same position. . . . As you know, I love the material, and I'm sure you will have a terrific show."

I was glad he was so sure. He went on and directed *A Chorus Line*. We were devastated. We wondered if we should try for a film option instead. At one point, Ray Stark, a producer, was interested in the project for Hollywood, but he wanted to pick the star. We didn't know which direction to head for, but I was committed to bringing the project to a stage one way or the other. Marsia and other friends were generous in letting me know that there was still a mystique —a belief in my vision—that pulled them through the long and complicated preparations.

We were about to begin rehearsals, the cast was ready to sign contracts for their first week's pay. We were at one point going to sign a young unknown named Don Johnson for the cowboy-astronaut lead. This was more than a decade before "Miami Vice." The staff and crew contracts were ready, Marsia's drawings and fabrics were in the costume shops. Disney Studios and the Ice Capades were all set to begin designing some of the elaborate props, like the walking furniture. Butler was due to show up for final cast approval, but he sent a telegram saying he wasn't coming. He tried to delegate cast approval to Marsia, but Marsia told him she felt unqualified as a designer to take on the responsibility.

Then Butler pulled out altogether and the financing was shut off. We were all in shock. We had all killed ourselves for this project for close to a year. He never even told me directly; he just must have lost faith—or interest. He eventually sued to recoup his advance and block me from moving ahead with the project.

Meanwhile I signed with CBS Records to cut a solo LP with the Jazz Messengers and got a $50,000 advance to be-

gin work on it in the second half of 1972. A single titled
"Revolution on Vacation" was released around Christmas
and failed miserably. One report from the label's West Coast
promotion man said: "Unintelligible lyrics can't seem to be
overcome. Looks like lost cause at this point. No nibbles.
Sales nil." That hurt, though the sessions continued into the
early part of 1973. In all, we cut about a dozen tracks with
titles like "Marooned," "Too Bad," "Devil on the Loose,"
and "Bandit."

Columbia was going through some major executive shake-
ups that spring. The recording industry was becoming big
business, with slicker studio techniques, bigger budgets, and
monster profits. The phenomenal inflation that turned pop
music into a $4-billion a year industry in the mid-seventies
made sixties rock look like a mom-and-pop operation. With
an industry known for its massive cash flow, egomania,
greed, hard drugs, and soft bookkeeping, it was inevitable
that the ghost of fifties payola would come back to haunt
rock and roll again—this time as "drugola" or the higher
math of creative accounting.

At Columbia, the head of artists relations was dismissed
for overcharging outside contractors and pocketing the difference. Then the label's internal investigation turned on
Clive Davis, the president. Davis was fired in June. He was
accused of using $54,000 of Columbia's money to decorate
his apartment, another $13,000 to rent a home in Beverly
Hills, and a whopping $20,000 for his son's bar mitzvah.
The charges led to a tax case that was settled on a plea. My
"case" at Columbia, however, was not. Somewhere in the
upheaval, I had to assume, my album lingered in the cans
and the most prestigious pop label never released it. "No
nibbles" had turned into a hunger strike.

The Davis affair foretold other scandals at my own former
label, Dunhill. A bookkeeper who worked for a New Jersey
pressing plant happened to see Cass on "The Tonight
Show." Johnny Carson facetiously asked her something
about her wealth and Cass replied, more seriously, that she
wasn't rolling in it by any means.

The bookkeeper felt badly for Cass, but he had good reason. He called ABC, which had bought Dunhill, and asked

for Cass. I happened to be in Bobby Roberts's office when he took the call. Bobby passed the phone to me.

"I know where all the money is," the guy said mysteriously. I betrayed no emotion and got his number back east. After a lengthy chat by phone about what was going on at the manufacturing plant, I flew the scrupulous bookkeeper in and took an affidavit from him. What I heard was so shocking and upsetting to me that I took the material to a Senate subcommittee headed by New York Senator James Buckley, who was already investigating the recording industry.

When investigators for the subcommittee raided the plant, they confirmed the bookkeeper's claim that a double set of books was being moved from city to city, plant to plant, to hide the actual size of the pressings. In fact, an entire set of books was hidden exactly where he had claimed: in the ventilation ducts. When the books dropped out, according to the story I heard, the owner of the pressing plant dropped dead on the spot from a heart attack.

The scheme was simple enough: The plant was cranking out hundreds of thousands of new LPs for shipment and sale abroad but not reporting them to the label. Hence, we received zero royalties on those sales. The plant operated around the clock to keep up the supply. Dunhill, in turn, claimed that those records were "cutouts" that could be resold at greatly reduced prices. We got almost no points on cutouts. The royalty payments for me as songwriter on even tens of thousands of LPs at retail would be in the six-figure range. I decided to pursue a lawsuit against the companies involved. I was outraged. It seemed like we were being ripped off—and the scheme had been going on since our heyday in the late sixties.

I felt safest with my Telex, spending days and nights wired on coke, thumbing through my Telex worldwide directory with all the code names so I could stay in touch with friends, corporations, senators and congressmen, foundations, universities, and Kings and Queens all over the world. I could sit there at the big desk for hours at a stretch, pecking out messages to keep the White House and NASA on top of every new development in our own moon landing, dealing with Butler and his production staff. I signed all communications SPACE. The flow of information and drugs both seemed endless.

The Telex machine was also the perfect machine for sending party invitations. I threw a *Gone With the Wind* theme party, where everyone was to be dressed up in costume. I invited the L.A. Lakers organization, the Dodgers, the Wells Fargo Bank, the Stones, the "Soul Train" dancers. It was unbelievable. I think everyone showed but the bankers. Mike Sarne and I went out and stocked the 150-foot electric waterfall cascading down to the 100-yard-long pool with live trout. We needed a guest list and security men at the gates. Cass showed up in a hoop skirt as Scarlett O'Hara. Roman Polanski arrived dressed as a Confederate soldier.

The next move on *Space* was to sign an option with Lenny Holzer. I had met Lenny in New York through Gen and the Warhol crowd when he was married to Baby Jane Holzer. Baby Jane was one of Andy's main stars of the day. Lenny was an entrepreneurial genius; his family was in real estate and he had made a few major killings in investment banking and shopping malls and he was worth many millions. I always had this impression of Lenny flying his helicopter out of La Guardia Airport at night and looking down for any large area in Jersey or Connecticut with no lights. Then he'd buy up the land and build a mall with the best architects and place great art in them. That's how I always imagined Lenny's genius worked. He had *lots* of money and class.

Lenny was now living with a stunning young actress named Julia Robinson, who had been "discovered" by Jack Nicholson when she was seventeen. Jack helped get her a brief tap dancing sequence in *The King of Marvin Gardens.* Lenny and Julia stayed at the Château, where we had stayed, and one night I walked into a closet and stepped on something that stung my foot. I looked down and there were needles all over the floor. I soon learned that Lenny was shooting coke around the clock. His one venture into film was to produce *Gimme Shelter,* the Stones film about Altamont. Lenny had failed to pay out royalties to the Stones and other co-owners of the film and they sued. He settled up by giving them back their money and the film.

The problem, he explained later, wasn't deceit or greed but coke. He was becoming careless in his tangled, high-rolling business interests. He would stay up for five days straight and then crash for two. He was always going to the bathroom to shoot up.

Lenny saw the project as a film rather than on Broadway, but he agreed to front me close to $100,000 to get the show off the ground. He was thinking of a film with Nicholson, Streisand, Fred Astaire, Jackie Gleason. Lenny wasn't convinced that Gen could carry a big-budget film. "The name Streisand," he said, "is just better sounding than Genevieve. But I'm not setting myself up as a judge of talent."

Once the four of us became close social friends, another complication threatened to get in the way: Gen and Julia revealed to Lenny and me that they had been carrying on a secret and emotionally intense love affair. It was Gen's only such affair, but she later told me, "You never realized how deep my love for her was. It was physical and intellectual and I identified with her. She was the first person who ever satisfied me sexually. It was very romantic."

They would get together almost every afternoon when they were in the same town, usually meeting in Lenny's suite at the Château. When Lenny found out, he was quite upset. Here was a new friend in my life who was about to lay about a hundred grand on me to option the musical. And now the two ladies in our lives were lovers. I tried to maintain a sense of humor and detachment about the situation. I said to Gen one day: "You know, I'll give you the same brilliant advice I always used to give Mike Sarne. It's the first rule of Hollywood and you should obey it. DON'T FUCK THE PRODUCER'S WOMAN!"

We both had a great sardonic laugh over that one. As it turned out, Lenny turned the money over and the affair carried on anyway.

The reality was that Lenny had deeper problems. He was elegant, handsome, and worldly. But he was beginning to see that his addiction to coke was distorting his judgments and leaving him wasted. Still, the rush, the grandiose visions had hooked him. "The feelings of power are enormous," he would say. "The euphoria, the urgency, the grandiosity are enormous. Streisand, Nicholson, the fabulous film—see, that's a fantasy. The reality is that we've got a story that isn't worked out and finished and that no one to whom I have spoken about investing in the show takes it very seriously."

Mostly, Lenny seemed to be talking to himself about the project; as he would put it, he was thinking more of retiring than recouping his investment. In the middle of the option, he split L.A. and headed back to New York to deal with financing *Space* there. The fate of the universe was on hold.

Laura and Jeff had both failed school at Colin McEwen High in Santa Monica that spring. I didn't know what to do with them so I sent them away. Maybe I was punishing them. Jeff went to the Isomata music camp up in the mountains at Ojai, where he was to study the saxophone in the summer. He visited after three weeks and seemed to be doing well. I was so proud. I rewarded him with a few lines of coke in a small jar and a couple of joints to take back with him for the rest of the course.

He got back to camp, and at a dance he started handing out sleeping pills and collapsed on the dance floor. The next morning he surrendered his drugs and asked to be sent home. I was truly disappointed in him.

Laura was sent to a girls' finishing school in Switzerland just before the premiere of *Graffiti*. The school was called La Châtelainie and it looked like a spectacular place to spend a summer. Gen and I picked it out for her after we saw it featured in a fashion layout for *Vogue*. But Laura was furious that she was missing all the excitement. I kept her posted on the film and our musical via Telexes from the library, signing them all: THE KING OF CONSCIOUSNESS.

We sent Laura all the wonderful reviews and she was clearly an actress with a future. None of her new friends believed she was a movie star. She was enraged to be missing her moment of glitter and glory on the Strip. Her whole life had been a rehearsal for that moment and she was blowing it in the Alps. She would sneak out windows and skip classes; I failed to make a couple tuition payments and they took away her horseback riding privileges.

She came home to L.A. and before she was unpacked, a girlfriend pressed into her palm a bluie, a hypnotic downer on the order of a Quaalude. But life back on the Strip, despite her newly won stardom, soon turned into a terrifying bummer.

She and two friends hitched a ride home late one night from Rodney's with a powerfully built black man they thought they recognized from the club. She sat up front with him. He offered them a joint, then fumbled around and showed them a gas cap. He told them he had forgotten to twist it back on the last time he filled the tank.

At Sunset and Fairfax he somehow got the others out to check for him and put it on. That was the ruse. Laura sensed danger and she lunged for the door. He suddenly flashed a knife and pressed it against Laura's neck and sped off. The door was still open and one of her platform shoes was dragging on the pavement. He almost chopped her foot off when he pulled her in and slammed the door.

He drove her up into the hills and raped her at knifepoint in an empty lot overgrown with weeds at the rim of a ravine. Bleeding and hysterical, she ran back down to Sunset. By that time, her two pals had called the police and me and I got my childhood pal Bill Cleary to go over to Rodney's with me.

My heart broke for Laura. She was in agony—sobbing, injured, and frightened. She was all messed up with blood and dirt. Her rhinestoned mini and red halter top were bloodied and torn. I put my arms around her to comfort her and realized how, beneath her precocious posing and smartass edge, she was still just a vulnerable little girl.

The cops took her to the hospital for tests to verify that she had been raped. The wary and jaded detachment of the processing made her feel worse—Laura picked up their suspicion that she had either asked for it by hitching in a rather provocative outfit or that she had exaggerated the incident. I knew better.

Cleary and I organized our own task force over the next two weeks—staking out various locations on the Strip, hunting down thugs and cars matching the kids' descriptions. We got nowhere and time had its way of smoothing things out.

It was a brutal and traumatic episode for her, but if there was an up side, it was that she saw—she said for the first time—that I really did love her and wanted to protect her.

In the middle of the year, Michelle and Chynna came to live with us and stayed at the guesthouse. Michelle was breaking up with Jack Nicholson after two years and Chynna had to have surgery to remove a huge but benign growth in her thigh. Michelle didn't want to bring her home to an empty, unfamiliar home, so she took the guesthouse. She planned on just staying for a few weeks, but got so comfortable around the place that she stayed for three months. We all got along quite peacefully.

In July I once again contacted the office of Senator James Buckley and told him that we were going ahead with the lawsuit. Michelle was with me all the way on the case. We appeared together at a news conference in Century City in early August and I announced that we were filing a $9 million civil lawsuit against ABC-Dunhill for fraud, breach of contract, and copyright infringement. I also named my two publishing companies. I was seeking $6 million in punitive damages and another $3 million in lost income from the fraudulent accounting practices. The suit would stretch on more than a decade before a settlement could be reached—in which MCA, which acquired ABC Records, paid us back close to half a million dollars in 1985.

Gen and I gave one last party at 414 before going to New York to help Lenny get *Space* going. One of our friends, the promising country-rock cowboy Gram Parsons, was at the party and behaving unusually melancholic. Gram had grown up in New Orleans and was a genuine outlaw-poet with a powerfully moving voice for country rock. His *Grievous Angel* LP was a killer and he had worked with the Flying Burrito Brothers. He and Emmylou Harris were together all the time and sang harmonies that took your breath away. They had come over to 414 to rehearse and hang out several times.

I had met Gram years earlier backstage at some of the Journeymen concerts down south when he was a teenager. Then he found Mitch and me on Charles Street and stayed on our floor for a couple of weeks when he was about nineteen. I helped buy him his ticket to L.A.

Once we took a motorcycle ride through Bel Air while Gen and I were still at 783. Gram's chopper was pure redneck—buckskin seats, fringe hanging down. He was the real item. The front fender was loose and he had rigged it together with a coat hanger or something like that. All of a sudden we realized that we didn't hear his chopper behind us. We turned around and went back about a mile and found Gram and his new friend Maggie lying on the road, the chopper on its side. There was blood all over. Gen was hysterical and I kneeled beside Gram and thought he was gone. He looked up at me and squeezed my hand. "John," he said, semiconscious, "take me on that long white ride."

The ambulance took him to the hospital and he recovered slowly but was never the same. When he came to our party at 414, he brought a friend and a bottle of Jack Daniel's and talked to me about labels, contracts, and about Merle Haggard producing his new album. He got very stoned and sat down at the piano and began playing all kinds of tunes. It was amazing. He just wouldn't stop until his hands were dragging across the keys. Then he passed out and slumped off the piano stool.

He left at dawn and returned to his home in the desert at Joshua Tree. A week or so later, Gram went on that long white ride. We heard the awful news that he had been found dead of a drug overdose at home.

Ray Stark's daughter Wendy, who had become a good friend of mine in L.A., decided to go to New York with Gen and me to work with Lenny. Marsia had spent a week in New York and met with Lenny about costuming before returning to L.A. She said she had gotten along real well with our new producer and it was clear that something had clicked between them, though Marsia still had Yippie and Lenny had Julia.

Marsia had helped look after Tam on weekends in L.A. and whenever things got out of hand at home. So Marsia watched closely over Tam, who was two. She knew what she was doing. She offered to come to 414 and keep an eye on him.

"We'll be back in four days," I assured her.

"Is there a phone number?" she asked, responsibly.

"Don't sweat it. We'll call when we have one," I promised. We never came back.

We stayed in a sprawling suite at the Alray Hotel in the East 60s. We were having a wonderful time, shuttling back and forth to Lenny's fabulous home in Connecticut by helicopter. Then he'd drive into town at 2 or 3 A.M. in his big Cadillac and call a meeting. He'd take us to "21" for lunch and order caviar by the pound. Lenny loved backgammon and he'd go to the bathroom and then come out and play for a while until he had to go back and shoot up again.

I called weeks later to let them all know we were alive. The news from 414 wasn't good. Jeff had racked up his car on ludes and the cops had called Rosie from the station house. They didn't book him, but she was losing patience. Then Michelle, who had encouraged Laura's move into films, took her for a ride through town for a heart-to-heart talk. Michelle had observed close up what was going on with the kids when she stayed at 414. In her tough, well-intentioned way, she warned Laura that she'd be the next Judy Garland-type star-casualty if she didn't get her act together. And Rosie would call and remind me that the owner of 414 was after the overdue rent. All in all, I was better off not staying in touch. We were in New York to conquer Broadway.

The campaign wasn't going too well. Wendy Stark had helped us set up meetings and brunches with Broadway backers in New York. Lenny's condition on drugs didn't always help the cause. At one meeting in Wendy's Park Avenue apartment with a group of important Hollywood people, Lenny leaned forward and a number of syringes slid from his shirt pocket.

The next time we spoke to Marsia was six weeks later. I just never bothered to check in after the early calls. I was getting sucked deeper into the vortex of cocaine myself and my obsession with *Space* was growing more intense all the time.

Gen and Julia continued their affair in New York, usually at the Plaza, where Julia would book a room. By now she and Lenny were on the rocks and there seemed to be some interest in Marsia on his part, though she was baby-sitting for our kids in L.A.

Around this time I took the next inevitable step with drugs: I experimented with skin-popping coke. I'd load a syringe with a solution of coke and water and shoot into a soft, fleshy muscle, much the way a doctor innoculates a patient in an arm or buttocks. I dreaded needles and was squeamish. But soon I realized that intramuscular shots of coke were a waste. The rush wasn't worth it. But I had gotten past my fear of needles and crossed the line into shooting hard drugs. I went back to snorting, but I snorted more. Marsia was at the end of her rope with life at 414. "Jeffrey and Laura are getting drunk and taking Tuinals every night and going dancing," she said. "They call at four in the morning, screaming, 'We're getting attacked by colored guys! Come and pick us up!' Then I go and find out they've driven my car, so I have to find Yippie or get a taxi and drive all over the Strip to find them. And they drink this awful cheap wine. It's crazy."

"We've got tickets for you and Tam to come here. We'll get this musical to Broadway one way or the other. We need you."

Marsia came east with Tam. By then, my sister Rosie, who had suffered her first heart attack on the previous Christmas night, retired from the Pentagon after twenty-seven years and finally joined the rest of our family in L.A. Short, stocky, and resolute, Rosie moved in to 414 to be "the Enforcer," to impose some discipline over Jeff and Laura.

Laura was beginning to get calls for guest appearances on sitcoms and to read scripts for features. The law required an actor under eighteen to be accompanied by a guardian, so Rosie began taking Laura around to agents, producers, and directors. She got Laura back in a Hollywood school for professional high-school-age kids and talked with Susie constantly about Laura's drug use. Laura reveled in her new celebrity as she strolled down Sunset and into Beverly Hills shops and restaurants, where everyone recognized her from *Graffiti* or "Baretta" or "The Mary Tyler Moore Show." She

had been a star for a decade. Now she finally had fans of her
own.

Then Rosie's stunning daughter Patty moved in. She and
Laura made quite a pair. Rosie was in way over her head,
but she stood her ground with a mixture of love, discipline,
and, in her dealings with me, amused resignation. Nothing
much had ever changed there.

But not even Rosie could ward off the fury of the woman
who owned 414 St. Pierre Road. I was faltering in my rent
payments and Rosie had to take most of the heat concerning
eviction. When the owner saw what condition the Pink Palace was in, she threw everybody out shortly before the end
of 1973. She also kept thousands of slides and Laura's volu-
minous diaries and personal effects and refused to return
them until I covered the back rent and the damages to her
home. She eventually assessed damages at close to $12,000
in a report that was prepared for the lawsuit seeking recovery of the money. That report was an alarming inventory of
drug-related demolition and havoc. Or, as she put it, "extensive vandalism."

She cited close to ninety specific items for repair on the
furniture and *objets d'art* inside the house and another sixty
for the painting and replastering of walls, resurfacing of
floors, repairing and replacing of windows, and tidying up
the house itself.

By her account, virtually everything—a teakwood hand-
carved Chinese loveseat; a marble table; a prayer mat; a wal-
nut dresser; a Florentine set of tables; a china lamp; an oriental rug; a hand-painted silk screen; an amber glass chandelier; a Venetian antique dining room table; silver
candelabras; silk pillows; Wonda Weave wall-to-wall carpet-
ing; an upholstered cherrywood sofa; an inlaid Spanish
chest; a mattress and box spring; an antique phonograph;
even the porcelain bidet—that could be stained, discolored,
torn, scorched, chipped, gouged, shattered, scuffed,
scratched, and cracked made it into her report.

By the time 414 was restored to its former state of ritzy
old-world splendor, we were renting an elegant townhouse
on East 77th that Stanford White had built in the twenties. I
was still determined to treat myself like a star at any cost.

The cost was beginning to skyrocket. What happened at 414 was regrettable. We couldn't see it then, but our lives were already out of control. And yet the wake of material destruction we left behind us would later seem calm and glassy compared to the cold, dark, churning river of madness ahead.

21

ONCE IN NEW YORK, our luck seemed to improve with the change of scenery and fresh contacts. We met an aggressive young businessman named Dan Broder at a party. He had just closed a lucrative deal, had some capital, and was looking to invest in a record industry venture. I mentioned to him my interest in going into the studio with Gen and recording a solo LP with her. Through Broder, who seemed to be about thirty at the time, we met with a commercial lawyer named Bob Tucker and he helped set up a deal in which Broder would finance the LP for my own label, Paramour Records. Gen was thrilled.

We moved around the Upper East Side, living briefly in a townhouse owned by the dancer Edward Villella on East 68th Street, then in an apartment owned by the actor Richard Benjamin in the 70s. By spring, we settled into the unusually narrow Stanford White townhouse on East 77th that was owned by a member of the Rockefeller family at the time. We worked nonstop on the sessions while entrusting the musical to Lenny. We believed an album that proved Gen could sing would only increase our bankability at backers' auditions.

Broder soon learned it didn't take much to kiss $100,000

good-bye in the record business. At $175 or so per hour at Mediasound, it was costing $400 or $500 just for Gen and me to settle a fight over vocal or instrumental arrangements. Relations with Broder rapidly deteriorated as he saw the budget soar. On some sessions we had twenty-five musicians for a string orchestra fill. We plodded on and finished the tracks. I was happy to get back into the studio, where I often spent the night toying around with sounds and mixes. We got a great sound from the band Elephant's Memory.

The songs showcased Gen's unique *vocal sound—a breathy, delicate whisper that recalled Marilyn Monroe. I wanted to have the album distributed by a major label and for a while Mo Ostin, the president of Warner Bros., sounded interested. But Warners wouldn't let me release it on a Paramour specialty label. Gen begged and pleaded with me, but I wouldn't give in and the label took a pass. I had pulled a power play and lost. Gen was crushed that I was so stubborn and had turned my demand for my own label into the deal-breaker with a major label.

We had to make the rounds until we ended up settling for a distribution deal with the old bandleader Enoch Light and his little known Project Three Records. This didn't exactly knock us out. Here we had music geared to the booming mid-seventies market of urban hipsters—the dressy, upscale, campy, gay, bi-, and straight lounge lizards of the disco revolution—and the man responsible for tapping that market was last heard on "I Want to Be Happy Cha Cha" in 1958 and the follow-up a year later, "With My Eyes Wide Open I'm Dreaming," which carried Enoch Light and the Light Brigade to number ninety-nine on the pop charts.

But we spared no expense to put together a classy album and drew, it seemed, enough publicity to make it succeed. We made the scene on the party circuit all around town. Our names were always popping up in the gossip columns. Laura came into town after wrapping her next film, *Rafferty and the Gold Dust Twins,* in Arizona and ended up with her picture as an up-and-comer in one of the very first issues of *People.*

Michelle spent some time in New York with us and we all went out together. We worked on some demos in the studio

and discussed doing *her* solo album. We fell in with the
Warhol crowd at his Factory in Union Square, and people
like Peter Beard, Paul Morrissey, Mick, Bianca, and Dick
Cavett were crossing our path as we did Manhattan by night
after the sessions.

In May, Michelle, Gen, and I showed up as a trio at one
of those "everybody's somebody" screening parties for *Andy
Warhol's Frankenstein* at an Upper East Side cinema. Morrissey directed the film. The guest list mixed names like Kennedy, Lawford, Buckley, Yasmin Khan, Holly Woodlawn,
Elliott Gould, Diane and Egon von Furstenberg, Andy
Warhol, and Monique Van Vooren, who starred in the 3-D
horror spoof. There were four hundred people on hand and
the New York *Times* reporter covering the event managed to
spot us and ask me facetiously how I *dared* bring both a
current and an ex-wife. "How do I dare *not* bring both of my
wives," I told her. A picture of me with my two dates made
its way into *People* as well. It felt good to be back in the
public eye and to be busy on a couple of new projects.

Gen and I also worked out a cabaret act and performed it
many times over several months at Reno Sweeney's in the
Village. We even went out and did it in the Hamptons one
summer weekend and stayed at Lenny's place. Lenny saw
past the slick veneer, the witty repartee, and the clever tunes
and felt we were faking it. He knew I dreaded feeling so
exposed out there onstage. Audiences ate the show up, but
close friends who had known me in the sixties couldn't help
but see that the spark was gone.

Like the album, we did the cabaret act to attract attention
to Gen's unique and theatrical vocal style and improve our
chances with backers. The gags were fast-paced and sardonic, in a mid-seventies Burns and Allen vein. "This is my
wife and I love her," I'd say. "Yes," Gen would reply with
her eyes bugging satirically, "I eat right, I keep fit, and I
shoot Geritol every day." We did some of the album tunes
and created others for the act.

One night Nick Roeg, a film director, came down to hear
the show and afterward he told me he wanted to test Gen for
a female lead in *The Man Who Fell to Earth,* a movie he was
about to shoot in London with David Bowie. I told him that

Gen would be tied up with the Broadway show for months
and unavailable. He didn't want to hear that, so we ended up
in a shoving match and knocked over some tables and
glasses. He left and got Candy Clark for the part.

The cover of the *Romance Is on the Rise* album showed
Gen from behind, bending over and looking back in beige
silk shorts and shirt and glass shoes. It was shot by Richard
Avedon, who had been our neighbor when we first came to
New York and lived in Richard Benjamin's apartment. Gen
and Paula Prentiss had become friends during *Move*.
Avedon's place was adjacent and he was good enough to
shoot the cover for no fee.

We spared no expense to make the art work. The shot we
used perfectly conveyed Gen's desire for a forties glamour-
queen pinup look. Marsia Trinder designed the outfit for
$700. Gen's glass shoes cost $400. The hearts in the picture
cost $300. *Newsweek* and other major publications ran the
sexy shot when the album came out in July. There was
enough PR and industry buzz, we hoped, for a sleeper hit.
We got Gen's other friend from *Move,* Elliott Gould, to be
the "host" of a $5,000 bash at Le Club, at which we per-
formed some of the album cuts.

The album barely sold ten thousand copies. It was so
poorly distributed that record stores were calling *us* to find
out where they could buy it. Harvey Goldberg, the album's
young and talented engineer, personally delivered copies to
DJs who were playing cuts at gay and straight discos.
Broder at one point explored getting a 1–800 number to help
sell it through a late-night TV ad campaign. The decision to
walk away from Warners and go with a small distributor
proved to be catastrophic. It killed any chances Gen's LP
had of making it. If we had scaled the records from rooftops
in half a dozen major cities, we'd have had more effective
distribution. Despite the first-class art, the support of all our
friends, despite the publicity, class packaging, and some generous reviews in the music press, *Romance* immediately
joined the *Wolf King* album in the $40 cult-record bins of
America.

The scale of this failure stunned us. Broder was not
happy. He took a financial beating behind the scenes. We

took ours in public. John Rockwell of the *Times* covered Le Club and wrote a rather ungracious thank-you note in his "Pop Life" column a couple of days later.

He said Gen "mewed out her songs in a childishly nasal whine, booping along with the beat with loose-limbed twitches. Mr. Phillips accompanied on the guitar with a look of fixedly amused adoration on his face. Music," he went on, "is not the point of Miss Waite's latest career venture, however." Gen was not only "aimlessly giving glamour a bad name," Rockwell concluded in his graveside eulogy, "it was just kind of dumb."

Less than two weeks later, Rockwell was burying another member of my "family" in an obit—this time, tragically, for real. It was the end of July and we had been at Warhol's magnificent country house along the rocks above the Montauk shoreline. I had just come in for some iced tea after an invigorating ride on horseback with Dick Cavett through piney trails and open fields by the ocean. The phone rang and it was Lou. Right away, this seemed strange—that he would track me down to Warhol's after a couple months' silence. "I'm having a great time," I said. "Weather's lovely. Why? What's going on?"

"Who are you with?" he asked.

"Dick Cavett and Gen."

"Put him on." I was worried now.

Cavett took the phone and I saw his face tighten as his eyes locked on mine.

"What's going on here?" I asked impatiently. Cavett hung up. "Lou can't do it. He can't tell you . . ."

"Jesus, man, what IS it?"

"Let's sit down and talk," he said solemnly. He took me into the living room. My heart was pounding and I was practically gasping for air. There was bad news. Real bad.

"Cass is dead," he said softly.

The words just bounced off me. It wasn't real. Mitch and I had been working together on some demos and wondering if we would invite Cass in for some vocal tracks. She was due in from London, where she was performing, and we were worried that she might be hurt if we didn't ask her to sing along.

It didn't hit me when we flew to L.A. for the funeral. It didn't hit me when I saw all the old faces. Mitch was there; Denny flew in from Carmel, where he had been living with his young daughter Jesse. My mother came with us to the funeral, along with all the musicians, the friends, and three hundred people who showed up for Cass's final appearance. There was a wake with a closed casket and I wouldn't let myself believe that Cass was inside. I was sure that Cass would pop out of the casket and come up with some great zinger about what a joke all this was.

When I saw Cass's mother, I knew from the grief in her face that it was real, that Cass was gone. I was numb. Denny, Mitch, Ann Marshall, and I rode together in a limousine from the funeral service at Hollywood Memorial Park Cemetery. We were moving and talking about Cass in a heavy, slow-motion haze of sorrow. The next day I completely fell apart and surrendered to the grief, crying and reminiscing among friends or by myself. Gradually the pieces of Cass's life began to fall into place.

She had just made it on her own after a tough struggle that began after the fourth album in 1968. She was on her way up after the Vegas disaster that year and had tried to put the rest of her life together too.

In 1971 she married her friend "the Baron," whom we had seen hanging around the sessions. Baron Donald von Weidenman had no great wealth and introduced himself as a writer. Evidently Cass wanted to have a man around the house. She went into therapy and realized that she had made a mistake. They stayed together for about a year, but we were hardly in touch. Alan Carr took over her management and got her back on her feet. In 1972 she divorced the Baron, cut two LPs for RCA, and worked hard for the George McGovern campaign through the fall right up to Election Day.

She went on with her TV spots, returned to a triumphant comeback in Vegas, and released her *Don't Call Me Mama* album at the end of 1973. She sang a theme song for a Warhol/Morrissey film called *L'Amour* that year and had been up for a summer series just months before she died. She had been on and off a variety of prescription drugs, was in and out of "fat farms," and had had to cancel some shows because of fainting spells and other ailments. But she always stormed back, irrepressible and irreverent as ever. Nothing would ever keep Cass down for long.

She was in good enough health and spirits to take on a demanding and important two-week engagement at the Palladium in London that month. The shows were sellouts and London was all hers. She had finally achieved the solo acclaim she had craved for so long. But Cass paid the ultimate price for making so remarkable a comeback. Two nights after her Palladium engagement ended, she went to sleep and died in the Mayfair apartment she had taken for the London run.

While an autopsy dragged on, cruel and ludicrous stories had Cass choking on a ham sandwich and OD'ing on heroin. A week later the coroner's report, prepared by Britain's leading pathologist, found that neither ham nor heroin had killed her. Obesity had, in effect, killed her. She weighed 225 pounds at her death, nearly twice the average weight for a woman her height. There were no traces of either alcohol or drugs in her blood, the report stated, and no food was found blocking her esophagus. According to the pathologist, some of the muscle tissue in her heart had turned to fat and weakened it. Her heart had just given out after thirty-three years. And that was some big heart.

I ran into Andy Warhol at a party and I mentioned to him that I had written fifteen tunes around a story concept for a Broadway musical set in outer space. Lenny Holzer's option was running out, I told him. Before long, I was playing the music and talking through the story with Paul Morrissey, the imaginative avant-garde director of Warhol films such as *Flesh, Trash,* and *Heat.* I showed him the musical's "book" —the script—and he said, "I like all these tunes. It's real Broadway stuff. You're a fine composer. And it should be a great vehicle for Genevieve."

Morrissey's reaction proved to me that with *Space* I had pushed myself beyond the limits of pop-rock clichés. "These tunes," he said, "are much closer to Tin Pan Alley, really. They're pleasant and cute, lyrically clever. I like them." He was excited, he said, by the idea that a sixties rock composer was finally going to make the transition to Broadway. It was a tremendous step for me, he felt, and he wanted to get behind it.

Morrissey said that he was sure he could get backing. *Frankenstein,* his high-camp horror spoof for Warhol, had cost under $500,000 and was making big bucks. *Dracula* was already shot. Paul was bankable.

His "bank" turned out to be a former Manhattan lawyer who left a firm to become, as I referred to him, a coal baron. His name was John Samuels and I got the impression that he owned half of the coal in America at the time of the oil crisis in the early seventies. Two years earlier, Morrissey had tipped him off through a mutual friend to a tiny twenty-five-acre island in Long Island Sound with a mansion and a dozen guesthouses on it. It was on the block for an incredible $350,000 and it belonged to one of America's wealthiest families. Samuels rented a helicopter, checked the place out, and bought it on the spot.

Morrissey went to Samuels, played him the tapes, and talked the story through. He ended up with a $300,000 production deal. We went right to work. Gen was cast as Angel and Paul got Monique Van Vooren, his *Frankenstein* star, to play her mother, Venus. I asked Marsia to do the costuming and called in Denny to play the part of a Werner von Braun-type German scientist. He had done a second solo album, *Waiting for a Song,* and was living in Big Sur. It was a great support to have Denny, a link to the good old days, on hand for the new venture.

Denny's early skepticism about the whole thing was soon broken down when he met a production assistant named Jeannette Chastonay. They fell in love and started living together.

Pat Burch, a much-sought-after choreographer who had worked in feature films, on Broadway, and in television, was brought in for the dance routines. Morrissey said that one of her gifts was to work with nondancers and make them move like dancers. Paul hired a public relations man, Bobby Zarem, to make sure the show was always getting mentioned in the columns and to create a media buzz all over town among New York's show business élite. No one was better at that than Zarem.

Richard Turley, a lawyer with the same firm Samuels had worked for, left his practice to be the producer in charge of overseeing the budgeting and day-to-day production.

All the players were in place, but there were obvious artistic and personality clashes from the time we began rehearsing in Warhol's Factory downtown. Though he sincerely liked the music, Morrissey was continually toying with the book, making or asking for changes in the story line and concept that conflicted with my ideas. He was never wild about the concept that we had created in L.A. He envisioned a much campier, unsophisticated production that would look like a childish fantasy. I was still shooting for a musical that combined the best elements of *Hair* with those of the Apollo moonwalk.

Rehearsals through the fall and right up to Christmas were often tense and chaotic. We did get the music and dance numbers down, but there were endless script changes. Gen and I would sometimes work through the night to come up with new lines for Morrissey. And then he'd just toss them out. But Paul thrived on improvisation and spontaneity in his film work. He had written his horror satires by dictating dialogue to a secretary in a car as he was driven to the set. The lines would be typed up and brought to actors minutes before the cameras rolled.

That method may have worked in film, where a director can shoot ten takes of a scene and choose the one he likes best. But I didn't feel you could do that to stage actors. They need a script and direction. They need structure and their performances have to be right the first time. They don't get a second crack out there in front of a demanding live audience. My experience as a rock performer told me that spontaneity worked best when you had a set format to play with. As I told Paul once, "If it's not on the page, it's not on the stage." Neither of us had ever done Broadway before. If Paul began to feel he had no real "book," I felt he wasn't on top of directing actors and dancers in a Broadway musical. Our differences grew sharper and more bitter.

We rented the Little Theater for rehearsals the last two

months before opening night. This gave everyone a chance to get used to the actual stage they would perform on. But by then, it didn't matter where we did it; I saw that I had lost control of the project. It wasn't even *Space* anymore, but *Man on the Moon*.

In my anger and dejection, I began dabbling with snorts and skin-pops of heroin at home. Gen picked up on the changes when she saw me sitting around lethargically, staring at TV shows like "Gilligan's Island." I soon had another, more arousing, kind of escape at home.

One of Gen's longtime friends, a tall, voluptuous, and ravishing ex-model, came to New York and ended up staying with us. She and Gen had been best friends in London years earlier and Gen had always said that I'd fall in love with her if we ever met. She was right.

She had come to New York in the sixties as a teenager and sought out Warhol to become one of his starlets. The rumor was that he put her in a couple hard-core films that were never released. She went on to become a top international cover girl.

She got messed up on Angel Dust out in L.A. in the early seventies and ended up back in New York, running wild, modeling, hanging around with Lenny Holzer and Julia and their crowd in New York again. Gen had always teasingly asked why I didn't make a move on her. When she came back into our lives during the Broadway rehearsals, I finally did make my move.

Gen went into the hospital for a few nights to check out some pains she was having in her abdomen. While I was visiting Gen, the ex-model walked into the room and joined us. She was staying with Lenny and Marsia uptown. She was still breathtaking.

We left, had dinner together, went dancing downtown at a tough East Village rock club, and polished off a couple of bottles of champagne together. Her long, shapely body was shrink-wrapped in a slinky dress and when she started to move, the dance floor cleared and people just gaped. We decided to leave and go uptown.

As we left to get a cab, a small wiry foreigner followed us

out. He stepped in front of me. "I take the lady home, okay, and we hab no problem."

I thought he was joking. I was a foot taller than he was. *She* was half a foot taller than he was. "What are you, from Spain or something? What is this shit?" I asked with a contemptuous shrug.

"My freng and me, we takin' the lady home."

"Isn't that up to the lady?" I said calmly.

"Bitch!" he said. Then his hand went to his back pocket and I saw the blade come up and catch the light from the street lamp overhead. I had a shoulder bag and I grabbed the strap in my fist and wailed down on the guy. He staggered back, then a squad car turned down the street and headed for us. The little turd took off into the shadows.

"Jesus, you saved my life," she said to me with one hand over her heart, the other on my shoulder. The scare really got our hormones flowing.

Back at East 77th, we promptly tore each other's clothes off. She was even more magnificent in the dark. The next time we got together was at the East 92nd Street place Lenny was renting—one of the last original farmhouses from the prehistoric time when Manhattan still looked like the eastern fringe of the Great Plains.

Gen was upstairs asleep in the guest room. We were staying over at Lenny's that evening and all of us had gotten smashed. After Gen crashed, her friend and I found some creative ways to amuse ourselves downstairs. We made a fire, got even more drunk, took off our clothes, smashed glasses and bottles on the floor for no reason, and danced nude all around the shattered glass. Lenny came down at 3 A.M. in his robe, asking us what the hell we were doing. We didn't even cut our feet. He went back upstairs.

She eventually moved in with us and when Gen was at rehearsals in the afternoon she and I would stay home together, sniff smack, and make love.

During the end of rehearsals, everything fell apart. Turley had to take charge and make some big decisions. Morrissey was suddenly out as director and a new guy was brought in from the provinces to glitz-up the dance numbers and the whole look of the show. Three gag writers, one of them a newspaper gossip columnist, were brought in to punch up the script with tacky one-liners between the tunes. New dialogue was added and the chorus was beefed up. A new actor was thrown in. Most of Pat Burch's nifty dance routines were thrown out. Most of my book was thrown out. *I* was thrown out as an actor in the role of King Can and Denny was given the part. More palm trees and more planets were added to the stage design. Morrissey was banned from the theater for the last weeks of rehearsals.

Panic spread among the cast. At a cast meeting, Turley called us "a bunch of sybarites." Everyone listened and nodded and then went home that night and looked up the word in the dictionary.

Gen freaked out from all the confusion. She consulted a psychic who wrote horoscopes for *Vogue*. The woman said the show would not be a success. Gen's vehicle on Broadway was stalling out.

Even Bobby Zarem, the PR wizard, privately told me, "It doesn't look good. See if you can get your name off the credits."

But there was no turning back. Fortunately, Gen's brother Warwick arrived from South Africa the last week before opening night and she had a sounding board in the kitchen until all hours of the morning. She was ready to tear her hair out, writing me long letters that detailed her hassles with the show. I was floating away toward Gilligan's Island. I had let the damned thing slip right through my fingers.

Jeffrey, Laura, Rosie, Michelle, and Warren Beatty, her boyfriend at the time, were all in town. Jeff helped us out at the theater with stage production chores and Laura was at the Sherry-Netherland Hotel with Rosie to promote her new film, *Rafferty*. Her career, at least, was riding high.

The panic finally got to be too much for Gen. Two nights before the opening, Jeff, Laura, and I found her unconscious in the townhouse on East 77th Street. We got her to Lenox Hill Hospital and she came to after her stomach was pumped clean of whatever it was she had taken. *Poor Gen,* I thought. There were tears in my eyes at her bedside. She was forty-eight hours from her Broadway debut and she was lying in Lenox Hill with a tube up her nose. *What have we done to her?*

She rallied bravely for opening night, January 29, but nothing could have saved the show by then. Her voice was still hoarse from having that tube down her throat. She had to sing over the orchestra and she was weak from her hospitalization.

I took it all in from midway up the balcony, sitting on a step in the aisle. I wanted to die. For three years, this had been my baby. Now the show was a colossal bomb. I saw all of New York "society" there, out for an evening at the theater, struggling out of politeness to sit through it.

Palm trees fell onstage. Denny limped stuporously on a sprained ankle, dreaming of Nova Scotia. Actors dropped their lines. Denny saw Gen onstage and said in a tense whisper, "For God's sake, help me!" Gen must have thought he was feeding her a line *she* didn't even realize she had blown. So she repeated aloud, "For God's sake, help me!"

I felt like screaming the same line myself from the back of the house. Instead, I left halfway through the show, walked outside to Times Square a couple blocks away, and bought myself a three-piece $40 corduroy suit for the big bash afterward at Sardi's. It felt more like a wake.

I could hardly wait for the reviews to hit the street the next morning. The first paragraph of Clive Barnes's review in the *Times* ended: "It is the kind of show that can leave a strong man a little numb and a little dumb." That was John Rockwell's word for our cabaret act material—"dumb." Barnes did commend the music, but attacked Warhol for producing "works of art so inept that their ineptitude becomes their value." That wasn't all. "Thus, for the connoisseurs of the truly bad," he went on, *"Man on the Moon* may be a small milestone." Only Gen among the performers came out unscathed, for her "waiflike charm" as Angel.

I got a call from my attorney Bob Tucker. "Congratulations," he said from out of town. He obviously wasn't reading the same paper I was. "I had some work to do," he assured me, "but I'm coming back to town and I got tickets for the weekend. Can't wait."

Tucker never saw the show. There *was* no weekend. Samuels pulled the plug after two or three performances—I don't even remember. I was in shock. Three years of hard work, heady dreams, business deals, creative compromises, and God knows how much money had all come down to one "dumb" evening of theater on the Great White Way.

The coal baron at least could go back to the energy industry, but I felt strip-mined as an artist by the disaster. Gen and I were both wickedly disillusioned.

The eulogy this time appeared a week later and was delivered by Brendan Gill of *The New Yorker.* He left early, he said, to maintain his sanity. That was the good news. He said the show "came as close to being totally mindless as any stage work that I can recall, and to its mindlessness was coupled an inexplicable self-confidence; nobody engaged in the enterprise appeared to have the slightest notion of how boring it was."

We all dug out from the rubble on Broadway. Michelle had a lot going for her—a promising film career and Warren; Denny went on to collect a $2,500 BMI check and took Jeannette to his beloved homeland for some salmon fishing along the rugged coastline; Laura's strong notices for *Rafferty* got her to Norman Lear, who was putting together a sitcom called "One Day at a Time" for ABC.

The ravishing model left us and headed west to become a stockbroker somewhere in the Rockies.

Gen and I stayed in New York and wondered what to do next. "The world of Broadway," she said resentfully, "has nothing to do with you and me. Those who survive on Broadway are the people who really *are* Broadway."

I retreated farther into the comforting rituals of cocaine, a mistress who never failed to flatter, excite, and satisfy. We *weren't* Broadway; Gen was so right. But what *were* we? Our solo recording careers had failed; Gen had given up films and modeling; cabaret was an awkward *shtick* for me to pull off; scoring soundtracks by committee left me cold; and our breakthrough on Broadway had turned into a fiasco. All we ever wanted out of *Space* was to work together and have some fun with it. I was furious at myself for letting it get out of control. If only we had stuck to one of those early hunches and done it as a movie for Disney, filled with special

effects, we could have beaten *Star Wars* by five years. I really
came down hard on myself for blowing it.

I had one last plan to salvage some fun and self-respect
from the catastrophe. I called Zarem. "You know, Bobby," I
said, "that guy Tom Snyder's got that controversial late-
night talk show, right? Why don't you call him and get us on
there one night this week. I mean, here's the hook. We've
just gotten the absolutely *worst* reviews in the *history* of show
business. No one has ever gotten reviews like these. It's a
great hook. No one else can make that claim."

Zarem mulled it over and reluctantly said he'd call Tom.
He called back a few days later. I was all ready. I had in
mind a great sardonic bit with Snyder all about the collapse
of the show. "I spoke to Tom," he said. "I told him what
you had in mind."

"Yeah, so? When are we on?"

"He turned it down."

22

WE DECIDED to go to Mustique, an island in the British West Indies. The night before leaving town, Gen and I had dinner at Elaine's. Elaine Kaufman was seated at the table next to us with a dapper, cultivated Englishman who looked something like David Niven. Elaine introduced us and said the gentleman's name was Colin Tennant. Elaine asked how we were doing. "Fine. Give my regards to Broadway. We're heading for Mustique tomorrow, as a matter of fact," I said.

They looked at each other and smiled. "That's fabulous. What a lovely coincidence. Colin *owns* Mustique."

"What flight are you on?" he asked. We were on the same plane to Barbados.

It was curious—I was still meeting the right people at the right time. Colin was a wonderful and elegant travel companion for Gen, Tam, and me. His family had owned a vast petrochemical conglomerate called Imperial Chemical, once one of the largest privately held corporations in the United Kingdom. Colin was an aristocrat who really knew how to live well.

Still, I got into the spirit of the trip and offered to split the charter flight to St. Vincent, and then we took yet another charter to the landing strip on Mustique. We didn't have to pass through Customs. This was one situation where the guy floating through the place like he owned it really did.

We stayed for six weeks. I was in bed much of the first week with what I thought was the flu and sun poisoning. It was, in fact, a mild withdrawal from the heroin I had been snorting. Within a week my body settled down. We stayed in an elegant hotel and did very little but relax by the ocean. Mustique was an extraordinary place, an island consisting primarily of millionaires. No blacks were allowed to stay overnight on the island unless they worked there. Otherwise, they had to ferry to St. Vincent for the evening. When we first arrived and settled in, Colin came by to check on us. I asked Tam, "So, Tam, what do you feel like doing now?"

Tam looked around at the dreamy surroundings. "Let's have a party."

I looked at Colin, who smiled at Tam and threw up his arms obligingly. "And why not?" he said with his effervescent good cheer.

Colin flew in the renowned British set designer Oliver Messel from his home in Barbados. Messel designed sets and costumes for many important plays, operas, and ballets for over thirty years. He dressed all the waiters at our party as moonmen and painted coconuts silver. Some of the other staff painted their *own* coconuts silver and strutted around naked. The makeshift stage was lit by Jeep headlights in a circle on the sand beneath a full moon. Then Gen did some of the tunes from the Broadway show for all of Tennant's elite circle of friends on the island and we had ourselves a wonderful time. We met his lovely wife, Lady Anne, and Bianca Jagger showed up as the Moon Goddess. Mick was working with the Stones on a U.S. tour and she was alone. They often vacationed on the island and were friends of the Tennants.

We swam, lay in the sun, walked along the beach, and behaved ourselves.

Upon leaving Mustique from the airstrip, Colin said we would *have* to join him and Lady Anne at the upcoming Edinburgh Music Festival in September and visit his castle called Glen. *Sure,* I thought. *Visit my castle. Right. Let's have lunch.*

We left New York to put on the cabaret act in L.A. at the Roxy. We rented a house at the beach in Malibu next door to David Geffen and Cher. I had known Cher for years, ever since we did the 1965 benefit at the Hollywood Bowl with her and Sonny. Chastity and Chynna were about the same age and we had gotten together a couple of times with the kids on weekends in Bel Air. Now, though, she was in the throes of a turbulent on-off marriage to Gregg Allman and had sought some refuge with David. The media blood-hounds were on her trail, but no one could find her.

I had met David around town in the late sixties through Lou's network of record industry executives. Cultured and gentle, David believed in Genevieve as an artist. He said he was shocked and disappointed by the failure of Gen's album; he said he might want to buy up rights to it and re-release it himself. David had the Midas touch in the mid-seventies with the rare artists he found classy enough to warrant his backing and guidance at Elektra Records—artists like Jackson Browne and Joni Mitchell.

Our own act was getting quirkier every time we performed it—but more fun. ABC approached us for a summer replacement series and that had us scratching our heads. After a Roxy show in June, Lou came back and said, "You know, I'm sure it could be successful, but you have to ask yourself if you want to be a *comedian.*"

"No, Lou," I said without hesitation, "I do not want to be a comedian."

"Then maybe you shouldn't be part of a comedy act."

"Exactly." He had a point there.

Dennis Hunt, the L.A. *Times* critic, would have agreed. He described our humor as "awful" and the act "lusterless." "With better material and a straight man more sensitive to her wacky style," Hunt speculated helpfully, "her scatter-brained character could be effective."

Was there a man alive more sensitive to her wacky, scatterbrained ways than me? I was losing my sense of humor about getting beaten up in print.

Such disappointments and criticisms were taking their toll. Gen began drinking more heavily and was prone to impulsive and violent outbursts. She got herself into fights.

A woman photographer friend of hers scaled the rooftop and, using infrared film like some CIA spook, clicked off a daring scoop of Cher in Geffen's home through the window. Geffen caught her in the act and was enraged. He blamed Gen for her *chutzpah*. Gen thought Geffen was unfairly harsh and accepted no responsibility, but we prevailed upon the woman to not publish the pictures.

Gen, who had always gotten on fine with David and respected him, insulted him at one point and they never spoke to each other again. Needless to say, Geffen never did acquire rights to Gen's album.

Gen stormed into Michelle's acting class one day, called her male instructor a tramp, and punched him. I found a different way to express my frustration: I started skin-popping heroin. We were both unraveling.

I had been oblivious to money for my whole life, but I soon learned that it was much more fun to be oblivious when I had plenty of it than when I had none. Our cash flow had shrunk because my assets from ASCAP were temporarily tied up in litigation. Drugs were eating up whatever was left after taking care of survival. But by then, drugs and survival were becoming more closely unified.

In the summer, Colin Tennant somehow found our address and sent a telegram that simply said he was expecting us in early September for the Edinburgh Music Festival. A man of his word and quite the gent, after all. I had so little cash that I asked Lou to loan me $5,000 and he told me to have a good time partying among the English aristocracy.

Colin picked us all up at the airport and drove deep into the lush English countryside into a small, quaint village to post some letters at his own post office and pick up some items at the pharmacy. He was still gliding about as if he owned the place and we soon found out that he did: every house, shop, plot of land, and restaurant.

We drove all the way up into the chilly Scottish Highlands to his immense Victorian castle called Glen. It had been built by Colin's grandfather, who was knighted and became Lord Glen Connor. The castle was phenomenal. The NCAA basketball championships could have been played in some of the rooms.

A rolling meadow rose all around Glen, setting it off in a soft heather pillow of deep green. Shepherds, clutching staffs, dropping out of the distant mist, walked among their flocks of sheep on the steep hillsides. It could have been a dream.

Inside, the vast dining room was dominated by a magnificent crystal chandelier and endless bookcases containing priceless first editions. The works of art on the walls would have looked right at home in the British Museum. Servants, livery boys, and staff in uniform busily criss-crossed the dining room. Colin showed us the music room, and it seemed as large as Carnegie Hall. "Come," Colin said, all in tweeds and silk, "I want you to meet some friends of mine. Our other houseguests." We were exhausted.

"John Phillips, Genevieve Waite," he said ceremoniously as we approached the familiar-looking woman awaiting us in the living room, "I present to you Her Royal Highness Princess Margaret." I almost told her that the Queen Mother had almost ruined me twenty years earlier by wiping away all my plebe demerits at the Naval Academy. The other guests included her boyfriend, Roddy Llewellyn; Rupert von Lowenstein and his wife, and various other lords and ladies. Colin and Margaret had been friends for twenty years and he had given her some land with a house on it in Mustique and that's where she and Roddy escaped to get away from the sniping press and paparazzi.

Every day we lunched in someone else's castle. All the patricians ever moaned about was taxes and selling their centuries'-old paintings. The new Labour government was killing the rich with taxes. Colin and I planned a little variety show for all the neighbors in the other castles. I was sure that it would cheer them up.

We hit it off immediately with Princess Margaret, the Queen's sister, and Roddy. She had stirred up a scandal years earlier when she divorced her husband, the photographer Anthony Armstrong-Jones, Lord Snowden. Roddy was something of a playboy, a member of the Welsh upper classes, and they were a constant target of the Fleet Street gossipmongers. I taught Roddy to sing like the Wolf King of Wales. Margaret needed no musical instruction. She turned out to be a first-rate pianist and vocalist with an impressive repertoire of American show tunes from the forties and fifties and a flair for boogie-woogie.

I almost broke my back showing off for the princess when I tried a one-and-a-half flip with a half-twist off a low diving board into the pool. It was hard to concentrate with the flocks and shepherds in the background and those impassive judges, the Greek statues, all around the pool.

I took her and Colin to see Tim Hardin's set at the festival. I thought they'd enjoy some authentic American folk rock music from an original artist who had written some wonderful songs in the sixties. I stopped backstage before the show to say hi after so many years and tell him about his special visitors. We had known each other from the Village folk days. Tim was in a long slide with his career and seemed in pretty bad shape. He said it would be fine to bring my guests backstage after the show.

We never made it backstage after the show. He passed out onstage while playing some Wurlitzer or electronic piano. He was doing fine, sounding soulful and poetic as ever with songs like "Don't Make Promises," "If I Were a Carpenter" and "Lady Came from Baltimore"—until he slumped over and his head hit a chord that sustained for a minute and a half. A roadie had to help Tim off the stage. Colin perked up with what he imagined was a nifty bit of showmanship. "That's simply *fascinating* the way he ended his performance," Colin gushed.

We prepared quite a show ourselves. I phoned Wendy Stark in L.A. and she sent us a bunch of T-shirts with tuxedos printed on the front for everyone to wear. Margaret went into Edinburgh to rent costumes for the evening and Gen took on the role of her lady-in-waiting. Margaret was far from stuck-up on herself and seemed quite knowledgeable about many subjects. After choosing an outfit in a shop, Gen came out and whispered, through a mischievous smile, "My God, John, who would ever imagine that Princess Margaret is wearing woolen undies?"

The show went beautifully. The élites loosened up and got friendlier once Margaret launched into her spunky rendition of "Chattanooga Choo-Choo."

We returned to London and visited Margaret at her home in Kensington Palace. Security was extra-heavy, with a new wave of IRA bombings in the news. We would party until four or five in the morning, Margaret on piano, me on guitar. Then she'd get weary and say she had a busy workday in the morning, with her official receptions, openings, and goodwill visits.

We drove out to Roddy's family home in Wales, which was filled with trophies, photographs, oil portraits, and mementos of a thoroughbred racehorse, Fox Hunt, owned by the family. We visited the old town of Bath, where 150 years earlier London's aristocrats would "take the waters," which were believed to have healing minerals. The baths were now just museums. Roddy owned an experimental farm and a restaurant in the area, but Margaret had never been there. We were chauffeured in her official royal family car with her Secret Service-type bodyguards following us.

We were cruising along quite frivolously on the M-1 highway outside London when we suddenly heard a sharp and loud pop. The car swerved crazily and came to a stop on the shoulder of the road. We all hit the deck and thought the same thing: that the IRA had snipers shooting at the car or that a small bomb had been planted underneath the car. The agents certainly had made that assumption and quickly surrounded the car and led us away.

A tire had blown. No terrorist attack.

"This is so exciting!" Gen sighed.

But when our adventures with royalty ended, we flew back to L.A. and felt deflated. It was quite a comedown. The money problem was still there and I didn't know what to do next. The star system in America can really churn you up, like a powerful wave at high tide that you thought you could ride safely in to shore. I was depressed. Maybe I hadn't deserved it all in the first place. Maybe it was all a fluke. I must have mistrusted my success because I had thrown it all away. I turned away from a solo career despite promising reviews; I got into artistic ego clashes over the musical with a brilliant and committed director who finally backed off and went on to do *A Chorus Line* and, later, *Dreamgirls* with Geffen; I pulled a power play with Warners so I could have

my own label for Gen's album and got nailed when they
refused; my obsession with *doing* the musical blinded me to
the way it was being done; the cabaret act exposed us to
more critical meanness; under all this pressure, Gen and I
both found ourselves resorting to one drug or another. To
top everything off, the new musical revolution of the seventies was passing me by.

It had come so damn easy the first time through. A month
in L.A. and we were on our way. We had the magic touch
then. All I had to do was look down at the Hollywood Bowl,
want something badly enough, make a promise, *and make it
happen.* That inner, natural power, I began to fear, was now
gone, replaced with the short-lived molecular dynamics of
cocaine. For the first time since I left Alexandria twenty
years earlier, I felt that I couldn't figure out some way to fit
in. I was on the outside and I was beginning to feel alone on
the fringe. I felt creatively stagnant; I was blocked but too
burned out to work my way through it. I realized how much
I needed Gen and Tam around me, as tough as I made it for
them.

The good news for my family was that Laura was just
debuting as the smart-ass, slinky teenage daughter Julie on
Norman Lear's sitcom "One Day at a Time," which also
starred Valerie Bertinelli and Bonnie Franklin. From the first
show, it was clear she was going to make it big in Hollywood
—the issue wasn't talent and drive. Laura, at sixteen, had
been a celebrity in her imagination for half of her life already. The problem was that she would have to *slow down* to
survive in the fast lane. But during that first season, she was
terrific, week after week, and she made all of us quite proud.

The lease was ending in Malibu and I said to Gen, "It's
time you get out of town." We were struggling to live on my
dwindling finances. It had all just vanished. She took Tam
back to her parents' in South Africa in the late fall for three
months and I moved in with my old friend Wendy Stark. She
had been so helpful in introducing us around New York and
trying to get the musical off the ground. She was still there
for me as friend.

The British director Nick Roeg was in town and got in

touch. The tone of belligerence that brought us to blows at Reno Sweeney's a year earlier was gone. His movie was completed and due out in half a year. He was with Candy Clark, the female lead in *The Man Who Fell to Earth,* the movie for which Gen had been unavailable.

Roeg said he wanted to screen the film for me at Candy's house and asked if I would consider writing the score. I asked him why David Bowie, who was making his debut as a feature film actor, didn't write it. Roeg wanted banjos and folk music and Americana for the film, which was about an alien who drops from the sky into the southwest. "David really can't do that kind of thing," Roeg said. "We asked him who he thought he would like to do it and you were the first name that popped out of his mouth. 'Ask John Phillips to do it,' he said."

Roeg then showed the film with just the dialogue—no music—and I was knocked out. I loved it. A movie about a spaceman—a subject I had some interest in. I was flattered and delighted to participate and we worked out a quick deal with British Lion Films for $50,000 to create the original music in the film and help put together the soundtrack album.

He later played me Bowie's score, which I thought was haunting and beautiful, with chimes, Japanese bells, and what sounded like electronic wind and waves. Very spacey and meditative. "I got to be honest with you," I told Roeg, "I think this stuff is gorgeous and fits the film perfectly. I don't see how I could ever match it. Think it over." I didn't want to start another pushing and shoving match by telling him now that *I* would be unavailable, but Bowie's music seemed perfect. By then, it was clear that my self-confidence as a composer was on the shaky side.

"No," he reassured me. "We want Americana. Five-stringed banjos. That's you. You've got that feel."

I left for London in mid-January 1976 and met Gen and Tam, who had returned from South Africa. We were registered at the London Hilton, but when we arrived we found out that the IRA had recently bombed the hotel. Two people had been killed, dozens more had been injured, and the lobby was mostly boarded up and blasted out. So we moved into Blake's, a hotel popular with rock and Hollywood types. I was happy to throw myself into the film score work.

Our arrival in London wasn't a day too soon. I needed the money and I was grateful for Roeg's much-needed vote of confidence. This film would draw a lot of attention because David Bowie was starring in it and because Roeg was gaining a reputation as an artful and cerebral *auteur*.

We left behind us a stack of unpaid bills that ranged— rather indiscriminately—from our *Times* subscription to Gen's dentist; the parking garage; the pharmacy; the food market; the Rainbow Bar and Grill; the dry cleaners; dues for Lou's private rock club, On the Rocks; Manny's music store in New York. There was just no money to pay out. I felt alive in London, where I had nothing but vivid memories of good times with old and new friends. I quickly got in touch with Keith Richards and Mick Jagger. The Stones were preparing for a major European tour in the spring, but we found time to hang out at night and jam together. I was energized and in better shape all the time. I was trying to push drugs out of our lives and I believed that things were finally beginning to turn around for the better.

London was the last place on earth that I would have expected the nightmare to begin.

V

ROLLING STONED

23

ONE OF THE first things that I did for the film was to find Mick Taylor, the shaggy blond blues-rock guitarist who replaced Brian Jones in the Rolling Stones. To me, Mick didn't just play guitar; he performed 12-bar ballet on guitar. I was told he had become a recluse while battling heroin. Mick had left the Stones abruptly a couple of years earlier and had been replaced by Ron Wood. There was, I heard, no love lost.

I got his address from a friend, went over to Taylor's place, and knocked. He peeked through a hole in the door. We had met before, but he didn't recognize me. I told him what I wanted, but he snapped, "I haven't played a guitar in two years," and shut the peephole. I pleaded for him to open up. He bruised his eyes on the light. "Which one were you?" he asked crankily. "The tall skinny one with the funny hat and beard?"

It took me three hours, but I persuaded him to help me out and work on the soundtrack sessions. "All right," he shrugged, "I'll do it."

Doing the score was fascinating. Mick headed the four-piece group I put together. I stayed in the booth as producer. I did the vocals and created all the music, while a copyist translated it to score sheets because I still could not write music. I hardly had to with Taylor. He was an incredible quick study and a true virtuoso.

We moved into a great loft-type duplex on Glebe Place, right around the corner from where Mick Jagger and Keith Richards had homes. The upstairs was a studio for artists, a large open room with a huge skylight. Shortly after we settled in, I got a strange call from a young London guy who said he was a friend of a small-time dealer from whom I had bought small amounts of heroin for skin-pops and snorting. I still believed that I could walk away from smack anytime. The kid sounded nervous. He was in a subway station.

"I got Merck," he said in a flat conspiratorial voice, knowing I'd understand—and be curious. I waited, listened. A train rolled by, stopped, took off again. He was still there. "Two bottles," he went on.

"Big or small?"

"Big." Two ounce bottles of pure glistening pharmaceutical coke manufactured by Merck Sharpe & Dohme for clinical testing. There may have been other brands, but Merck was the word on the street for synthetic and uncut blow. Merck meant never having to worry about the economy of Colombia. Merck was so powerful that psychologists used it on monkeys. In a famous series of tests, laboratory monkeys repeatedly injected themselves with coke, ultimately forsaking food, water, and sex until they mainlined themselves to death. Merck was ridiculously cheap. The kid said that he had to leave England fast and needed to unload. He wanted about $30 a gram.

"Sold."

I called Keith. He had just come back into town from the countryside and called earlier in the day. I told him what was happening. "I'll be right over."

It was a sight that took my breath away—a great pile of fine, snowy Merck on a large mirror, a gleaming razor blade, a gold straw, a full bottle of iced Stolichnaya, and a pair of custom-built Gibson 12-strings. The night was ours.

Keith and I now had an ounce of coke each and he started to hang around Glebe Place. He lived with Anita Pallenberg just around the block on Cheyne Walk, but they were staying at Claridge's. The Merck made us soar for hours. We were just snorting then. Keith never shot coke, never mainlined smack. He always seemed to know what he was doing.

Snorting and skin-popping heroin was a high that started with violent puking within fifteen minutes, as my body adjusted to the toxins. Then I'd get a woozy, euphoric rush and feel like nodding out. After an hour or so, I was able to carry on. I thought there was no withdrawal from snorting and skin-popping, even though I had been sick in Mustique. I refused to see the connection.

One night he came by and Mick Taylor was there. It had been almost three years. They were a bit cool at first, then warmed up when the guitars came out. Guitarists become different people with a Gibson or Fender in their hands. We all played blues and rock through the night and nothing else mattered.

The film score was completed by April and the Stones hit the road for the tour. Gen persuaded me to join her and Tam in Mustique for some rest. They had flown ahead during Easter two weeks earlier. We stayed in a beachfront cottage at the Plantation Hotel, then moved in with some friends to a spacious villa by the water.

For me, it was worse this time than sun poisoning. The second day there, I was pale as a corpse and shivering among the sun-bronzed jet-setters. I stayed in my room alone and played guitar, screaming to the walls. I was desperate, edgy, and depressed. This wasn't the flu. I was detoxing from heroin.

There were no drugs on Mustique, so I flew to another island and got the name of a yacht in the marina. Posing as the yacht's captain, I went to the town pharmacy and told the druggist, "I need medical supplies, sir. Shippin' out. Someone might get sick."

I scored vitamins, morphine, and syringes and the morphine gradually began to deaden my libido and pull me away from Gen. The sexual urge gave way to an affair with smack.

When the morphine was gone, days later, I started shooting Vitamin C, just to have something to do, sort of like target practice. Anything to distract me from the pain ravaging my body. It didn't get me high, but I didn't get any colds, either.

My body came back to life and we were treated to a quick, luxurious trip to Caracas with a playboy we met through Bianca on Mustique. I brought my guitar and we all sang songs. When we returned to the island villa, Gen and I were happier together than we had been in weeks—more seductive, more mentally and physically alive with each other.

We came back to New York and stayed at Lenny Holzer's huge apartment over Central Park West in the 70s. Lenny and Julia Robinson had broken up the year before and Marsia Trinder had moved in. They married and had a son, Chayt.

Julia moved to L.A. and her affair with Gen trailed off. She then went home to Oregon to straighten out her life and died from smoke poisoning from an electrical fire in an apartment next to hers as she slept. Gen was devastated when Marsia called with the grim news.

Lenny was still shooting coke. The temptation was too much to handle and I lapsed back into it. The drug's hold on me didn't seem overpowering as long as I snorted it. It gave me an instant blast of energy without the miserable side effects of smack.

As June approached, I had a wonderful idea. Michelle was sailing for London on the *QE 2* for a plum film role as Rudolf Nureyev's lover, Natasha Rambova, in *Valentino*. I thought it would be fun if a bunch of us surprised her and hitched a ride over to England with her. I had to return for additional work on the soundtrack album for *The Man Who Fell to Earth*.

I decided to fly in Jeff and Laura. Lenny and Marsia agreed to come, along with Chayt. I bought the tickets and got everything arranged. I spoke to Michelle when she was in town and we decided to have a champagne send-off for her on deck. Gen, Tam, and I took a room at the Park Lane Hotel for a week. While we were there, a $20,000 royalty check popped up out of nowhere and I celebrated by skipping out on a $2,000 hotel bill. My values were beginning to corrode under the prolonged influence of hard drugs.

Whatever qualms I may have had hardly got in the way of

the party in Michelle's stateroom with my four kids, Gen, Michelle, Lenny, and Marsia. Michelle was thrilled about *Valentino*. It was a risky and challenging breakthrough for her. Ken Russell was the director and Nureyev was the star. Mitch was still with Warren Beatty, but her traveling companion was her ballet coach for the film.

"Time to go," Lenny said after an hour or so and we all put our champagne glasses down, wished Michelle and Chynna "bon voyage," and appeared to leave the liner. Michelle and Chynna went to the deck to wave to us as the ship pulled out. We had actually just hidden long enough to sneak up behind them. As they scanned the families and friends waving to the other passengers, I heard Chynna say, "I don't see them. Where are they?"

"Here we are!" I said, and they whipped around, just as the liner pulled out. The surprise worked perfectly.

At dinner that evening, the eight of us all found each other in the first-class dining room. Michelle and Chynna looked magnificent, all dolled up in the swanky dining room. Chynna was eight, with long blond hair way down her back and big blue eyes.

The rest of the cruise was wonderful. We met every evening for dinner and, unlike 1967, I now insisted on dressing up. We all looked healthy and quite elegant and I had grown back my beard and let my hair grow to my shoulders, my "Jesus Christ Superstar with a tan" look. Gen looked gorgeous and we all wore light-colored clothes and felt hilariously out of place among the more sedate Beautiful People. When Laura saw me in a perfectly tailored white suit, standing on the deck at sunset before dinner, she smiled and said, "You gorgeous, brilliant, well-mannered rock and roll sleazeball."

Lenny came prepared. He carried on board a bottle of liquid coke in a water solution all ready for injection. Marsia, always trying to get him straightened out, dumped scores of syringes out through a porthole.

Laura had a shipboard romance with a young guy who was lucky enough to have his own room, since she and Jeff shared a small room with narrow beds.

Once we had disembarked in the middle of a rare heat

wave, we wished Michelle well with her film. The kids, Lenny, and Marsia moved in with us at Glebe Place. Laura's suitor kept calling, but she had to break it to him that there were certain flings that are meant for land, others for water, and some for both. Theirs was "water only."

Laura was on hiatus from her show and she had plenty of money to blow. She hung around with a friend from L.A., Lorna Luft, and got to be friends with J. Paul Getty III, the teenage grandson of the oil billionaire. I, too, had a Getty friend in London, the teenager's father, J. Paul Getty, Jr., whom I had met socially through Mick Jagger. Jagger and Getty both lived on Cheyne Walk near our place.

Laura's pal J. Paul III had been kidnapped in 1973 by terrorists who cut off his ear and sent it to an Italian newspaper in Rome. The ear took three weeks to arrive, we had heard, because of a postal strike. He was freed after the family paid a ransom approaching $1 million. He later worked in oil fields around Bakersfield and wrote a slim volume of poetry. He gave it to me to read and asked my opinion. I read it and suggested he give it the title *Lend Me Your Ear.* He told me all about the terrorists, how he got drunk with them every night and played cards in the mountain cabin he was thrown in. They treated him decently until they tied him up for the mutilation.

Paul Jr. was an eccentric, sometimes amusingly decadent friend. For a time, he was a registered morphine addict who could fill prescriptions for coke and smack. London had a typically civilized approach to narcotics addiction. Those junkies with habits too big for the street could score from the government.

Paul Jr. almost never left his mansion on Cheyne Walk. His art collection was spectacular and he was something of a connoisseur when it came to rare and antique erotic literature. He loved old movies starring Fred Astaire, Gene Kelly, and Humphrey Bogart. There were always checks lying around for millions of pounds. He was one of the very few people in the world who could have a Rembrandt messengered over after acquiring it on the phone.

On the cocktail table, there would be a pile of heroin on one side, coke on the other, and a check for $4 million from some Getty enterprise that he hadn't gotten into the bank yet. Moving men would come through—"Where would you like the Rembrandt, sir?"—and he'd motion vaguely to a corner where other masterpieces piled up.

He had been married twice and his second wife, Talitha, had died of a heroin overdose several years earlier. He had become a recluse, but with all the drugs and money floating around, there was never a shortage of stunning, classy ladies passing through the place, ready for anything.

He and I never shot up together; we only snorted. His morphine came in pills and he crushed them up. He had grandiose schemes on drugs, like going around the world with his friends—in his own nuclear-powered submarine. He was a sweet and easygoing man. He sent Bianca as his representative for his father's funeral because the bureaucrats wouldn't let him travel with his drugs. Almost nothing could get him out of the house. He would spend his days and nights doing coke and heroin, indulging his sexual whims, watching his old movies, and planning a cruise in a nuclear sub. It was an extraordinary scene inside that mansion. It would have taken a lot to get *me* out of that kind of home life. I loved the man.

I completed the soundtrack album that summer. The film and the music both were quite well received by the critics and I felt like I had the touch again.

One day Jeff walked into the bathroom and saw a number of syringes lying around. He went to Lenny and confronted him. "You know," he said, "you really shouldn't leave that stuff around with all these little kids in the house. They might get hurt."

"What stuff?" he mumbled curiously.

"Come on, man, the syringes, the spikes, the ones I almost cut myself with in the bathroom just now." I heard the voices and walked into the other room.

"Jeff," Lenny said, "that's not my stuff in there. We aren't using that bathroom."

Jeff looked stunned. "Then . . . wait . . . whose is it?" They both looked at me and at that point Jeff and Laura knew.

Lenny and Marsia left for the country home of her parents to get out of the heat and took the kids. Marsia was always generous and sensitive to the kids' needs whenever we were out of commission and she was especially warm toward Tam, her godson.

We got to see a lot more of Mick and Bianca in London. Not necessarily at the same time. They often seemed apart. Mick developed a crush on Michelle. He would ask me how he could get her to take him seriously as a suitor. He said, "I love that woman. I want to be with her. How can I do it?" I've always had the impression that he figured out a way while she was filming *Valentino*.

One night I figured out a way to be with Bianca. I ended up in Mick's bed with her. I knew Mick was out of town. I took a four-hour break from my studio work and went to see her. We got smashed and went to bed. I didn't show for the early morning session, but twenty-six members of an orchestra did and the studio called Glebe Place. Gen was sure I was there, the studio was sure I wasn't. Gen's first hunch proved correct. She charged over to Mick's place around the corner. Her timing couldn't have been better. She was in a rage.

She somehow got into the house, talked herself past their maid, and blew open the door to the bedroom and went wild. She sure ruined a deep sleep. In her rage, she impulsively split for Paris to cool out with Jack Nicholson and Ann Marshall, who was then working for Jack. The story kept Fleet Street busy for days. The press had their dream scandal. By the time we read about it, Gen had *broken into* the house, *slugged* the maid, flown into a violent rage, and *left me* for Jack. It was *almost* that exciting, but not quite.

Mick called when he returned to London from their tour. This was not a great scene for him to come home to. I expected him to explode with jealous anger and call me a rotten, disloyal bastard.

"Would you like to go to see some tennis at Wimbledon?" he asked gently. "I've got some *excellent* seats for the next match. I'll pick you up at one-thirty."

He never mentioned the affair and was a total gentleman about it. Gen was always taking off for the countryside to get away. She went north to Shropshire, to the beautiful farm owned by her friend Francis Ormsby-Gore. She would always find the rural life calming and inspiring. She would take long walks, visit small seacoast towns, and read every novel, biography, or volume of poetry she could get her hands on. She was an insatiable reader and always had a wealth of new information to discuss.

Later in the summer Mick called again, this time for cricket about two hundred miles outside of London in Old Trafford. He picked me up in a shiny new Ferrari. He said we were in a rush, that we had to get to this old castle before the evening sitting or we would miss a great dinner. Mick was always, as he sang, "a man of wealth and taste." He seemed to do this regularly. The castle was halfway to Old Trafford and we were to stay in an old country inn that night and see the match the next day. It was wonderful how, after playing to millions of hysterical, worshipful fans in hundreds of cities all over the world, that Mick's idea of a good time could still be a drive into the country for cricket. He had this all worked out, down to the meals.

I had heard about cricket matches and came prepared; I brought my guitar and a few books. Mick drove like he performed—on the edge. We were shooting to arrive for dinner. I think we made it by lunch. We got there in about eight minutes. Everyone at the castle and in Old Trafford knew Mick and treated him with a dignified sort of reverence suited to a true folk hero.

We shared a large two-bedroom suite in a hotel in Old Trafford. That night there was a party in the hotel for members of the Dance Theater of Harlem. The company had performed in town. Mick and I got some champagne and walked in. The room was loaded with gorgeous, long-legged black dancers who were so sexy they drove us nuts. A good number of the men in the troupe could definitely have been gay. We tried our best, but couldn't get anywhere. Finally Mick mumbled, "Let's split. We ain't gettin' laid tonight. Fags won't let us. They ain't gonna leave till we leave. That's the deal they worked out with the girls. They stick together as a group."

"Well, I guess we could always get a couple of the fags, eh?" Mick's face wrinkled into his twinkly, rubbery grin.

We spent three days at the matches and I had no idea
what was going on out there despite Mick's patient attempts
to explain. It didn't matter. It was just lovely to sit with
Mick in the late-summer country tranquility and go back to
the hotel, drink a bottle of good wine, and play guitar.

I sang a bunch of songs, some from the cabaret act, others
from the Roeg film, some new ones. He seemed to enjoy
what he heard.

"You really ought to do an album with all these tunes,
man," he said. "They're great."

"I'll make you a deal. You produce it, I'll record it."

"Okay, we'll start next week."

It was incredible. I thought he was joking. By the end of
August, after the Stones played one last outdoor gig in the
natural amphitheater at Knebworth, we were in Olympic
Sound Studios on Church Road to record the first track,
"Zulu Warrior," a song inspired by a marathon discussion
with Gen about some racial bombings in South Africa.

The song had a fierce, primitive kick to it. It was about the
proud and beautiful Zulus and Bantus in South Africa who
ride rickety trains from their unspoiled tribal lands into
Capetown to find work in the cities. They arrive with tiger
and leopard skins draped over their shoulders, bearing tribal
scars and wearing native dress—and emerge from the diamond and gold mines, their spirits broken, their bodies bent
and sick with tuberculosis, wearing shiny, worn-out blue
business suits and clutching transistor radios.

Gen had caused a scandal in the sixties for her daring and
bold antiapartheid views. In *Joanna,* she bore a child by her
black lover. The film was banned there, but played in underground clubs for the antigovernment intellectuals. When she
was sixteen, she had letters to editors published and she was
placed under house arrest several times. Her father went to
France because she kicked up such storms in the South African press.

"Zulu" was a power-packed song and by the time it all fell
into place, the rhythm section and voices just about lifted
the roof off the studio. Michelle was still doing the film and
wanted to keep her voice in shape, so I asked her down.

Laura was over for a visit and they filled in the backing chant.

The studio rocked with amazing energy. Mick acted as a producer and before long we had Mick Taylor on slide guitar and Rebop playing a huge hand drum. Keith dismissed the project as a joke at first and thought Jagger was wasting his time. But when he came down to hear the track, he was knocked out. Soon Keith was at the sessions, playing alongside Mick Taylor, the first—and last—time since Taylor left the group. Ron Wood came down and played some bass. This wasn't like the other projects; this one was *hot,* it couldn't fail. Mick and Keith believed in it and soon we had a verbal commitment from Ahmet Ertegun at Atlantic, which distributed Rolling Stones Records, to finance and release the LP.

Late that summer, Keith called and sounded deeply troubled. He said he and Anita had to get out of their hotel in London. "We can't do without drugs. She's trashing the place, tearing the walls down and tossing things out the window. I don't know what to do."

They had closed down their Cheyne Walk apartment and had been back and forth to Switzerland. They were having some grave personal problems. They were at Claridge's.

They were in real bad shape. Anita had given birth to a son who had died in infancy.

Keith had also been picked up by the police and charged with possession of coke. They were paranoid about staying at the hotel and Anita was a wreck. They were both better off with others around to help look after them and their son, Marlon. He was a couple of years older than Tam, but he hardly ever went to school. He was always worried about his parents and seemed afraid to leave them home alone. It was a terrible burden for Marlon. There was no question. They moved into Glebe Place.

They took Tam's room and Tam slept in our closet. Keith moved in his state-of-the-art sound system and they ate tons of sweets like most junkies—candy, baby food, custards, and cereal.

While Keith and I were spending more and more time at the studio, Anita rarely emerged from her room. She lit can-

dles, sobbed, snorted coke, cooked shots of heroin, and was
in agony.

Keith and I would jam for hours in the upstairs loft,
mostly country and blues classics. There was a steady supply
of high-grade China white heroin and we shared everything.
There was no organized crime controlling heroin in London.
Junkies ruled the heroin trade and they were registered with
the government and put on methadone. The smack was better and cheaper than in the States. Keith had his habit under
control; he knew how to maintain.

For six weeks during the sessions, I had been snorting and
skin-popping heroin—convinced that I had it under control,
too.

Some tracks sounded like killers and we worked with unusual efficiency. No one was shooting up anything at the
studio. Some grass, some snorts, but no two-hour delays to
shoot and recover from smack. Shooting in the studios is
dumb. You puke, then you're manic and wired and incapable
of playing. Then you go out for a half hour into a half-dream
state. You can talk, but you can't open your eyes; you can
see, but you can't speak. You can see *and* speak, but you
can't play. Or you can play, but it's at half speed. Finally, an
hour or two later, you're maintaining and cool for six or
eight hours.

One favorite tune was a country ballad called "Oh Virginia" and I never heard an electric and 12-string guitar
sound like Taylor's did. We were creating something great
and I was very lucky to be working with some of the great
masters of rock.

One late morning Keith and I staggered in after an all-
night session. I had the most severe flu I could remember.
My eyes burned, my head throbbed, my nose was running,
every joint and muscle ached, and I shivered with fever.
"Oh, man," I groaned to Keith, "I'm sick. I've got the flu. I
need a doctor." I was high on denial.

Keith sank back in his chair and his eyes blinked slowly,
knowingly. He shook his head. "What doctor, man? You're
not sick," he said almost angrily. "You're a junkie. You've
got junk flu. You need a shot. You're hooked."

At that point, I had a choice before me: conquer smack or

surrender to it. I tried to get up and walk, but I was dizzy and my body trembled painfully with fever. I was covered with sweat. I got to the bedroom and called Gen in. I made myself believe that I was still guided by reason, that I still had a choice. I did. I went for the syringe.

Gen came in and sat beside me on the bed. Candlelight filled the room with a warm amber glow. She knew precisely what was going on.

She knew it in Mustique the first time. She knew it in New York during the musical. There was some white stuff right there. I was about to submit to my mistress.

Gen grabbed my hand and bent my arm. "Just squeeze your fist tightly. Try this cocaine first. It'll help. I'll do it for you."

"I've never done this before," I said softly. She said she had been around shooters and knew what to do. I was a little tense, but far too sick to hold back now.

I held my arm bent and clenched my fist while she drew the shot up through a cotton ball to catch any impurities that might cause an embolism.

She bent open my arm. The vein across the crook of my arm was bulging with blood. The needle slid in flat and easy. There was a trickle of blood down my arm, but I felt no pain. In seven seconds, the shot kicked in and spread a warm tingle through my body that was pure, exquisite pleasure—a cardiovascular orgasm before the nausea could worsen. The junk flu symptoms disappeared immediately afterward.

Gen looked at me and smiled. "Anita gave me a shot of dope in the butt and I cleaned the whole house and took Tam and Marlon to school and felt like Superwoman. I didn't get sick for once. I had amazing energy. And then I woke up the next morning and almost immediately I knew I could function better with it."

The days of late fall were getting shorter, colder, and wetter and I was getting in deeper. Gen knew a source of small amounts of heroin, but I told her I wanted my own contact —a junkie with a constant supply. I didn't want to score through Keith. I had been burned a few times with bad shit from the street and had gotten real sick and angry. I was still a perfectionist: If I was going to do this, I had to do it right.

Gen had a woman friend who used junk. She offered to line us up with her own big-time source. She also sampled the smack when it arrived at her posh hotel suite. It was good, all right: The friend turned pale and passed out, but we got her up and moving and to a hospital in time.

Once I had my own source set up, it didn't take long for our friends to pick up on what was happening. Jack Nicholson visited Glebe Place one evening from Paris. I had just snorted a few lines about ten minutes before he arrived. When he got there, I was vomiting in the sink and sitting on the toilet. He had to wait downstairs alone for a long time before I was able to get past the initial sickness and feel the high. He must have seen that it wasn't the flu.

Michelle lived less than a mile away and came over to pick up Chynna after a visit. She went back into Anita's bedroom to find Chynna's shoes. She found Anita giving herself an injection. I swore to her that we were not junkies. She later bought Chynna a doll for that Christmas and hid it on a shelf in our closet. When she came back to look for it, she reached up and her hand hit a bunch of syringes. Michelle was too sharp to miss the signs. "John's taking Vitamin B-12 shots," Gen told her. Michelle nodded as if she believed it.

When Marsia Trinder stayed with us after her visit to her parents' country home, we saw the look of astonishment on her face. The place was a stinking, chaotic wreck. Anita was out of it much of the time, Keith just wanted to get high, play guitar, listen to Elmore James records, or watch TV with me when we were home. Mostly old American sitcoms and movies. Nothing, though, could separate Keith from his guitars. He'd lie on the couch and play in the flicker of the TV screen or bring his guitar to the table when we ate.

Keith did love his son Marlon and every now and then we'd all pile into his Jaguar. He'd tear through London, swerving and careening wildly as the kids howled with delight and terror in the backseat. The image of an incoherent, stuporous junkie never fit Keith. He was far too smart and sensitive and gifted for that. He was a master at surviving on junk. The pressures of his notoriety as a Stone and their private turmoil had sharpened his instinct to fight back.

Marsia was disturbed by what she saw in the children. Tam, she told us, "was wired." One morning Marsia awoke to the smell of smoke around her bed. She jerked up out of the sheets and saw Tam sitting on the floor, waiting for her to awaken.

"Tam, my God!" she said, reaching for his hand, pulling the sheet around her. "There's a fire under the bed! We've got to put it out! Quick, wake up your parents!"

"I can't," he said, "I tried. I already lit one there and *that* one's going *okay,* but they're still asleep. Can't get 'em up."

"That one? What are you talking about, Tam?" She dropped to her knees and looked under the bed.

"The fire under my parents' bed. I also did one under the rug on the stairs."

"My God." She snuffed out Tam's little fires and woke us up. She said she was taking him out to Kew Gardens, to a park. "Tam and Marlon have nothing to do all day," she said. She was disgusted.

It was not for a lack of toys and games. Keith and I would regularly give the kids a hundred or two hundred pounds to go to a corner toy store and stock up. Sometimes they bought so many things they had to make several trips. When they got bored with those, we'd give them another couple of hundred pounds.

In November I returned briefly to New York for some meetings with Ahmet Ertegun and Earl McGrath about the album deal. I stayed at Earl's place near Carnegie Hall. I wasn't home long before I realized that I was going into withdrawal and had to go out on the street and score junk.

I went up to Spanish Harlem, around 115th Street and Second Avenue, and scored a hundred bags of street shit. I was scared to death. All I could think of was getting knifed and ripped off and ending up on the *Post* front page.

When I got back to Earl's, I lifted a Sterling silver spoon from his kitchen and hid it under my bed. I cooked my shots in the room and blackened the spoon. I was terrified his maid would find it, but I made it back to London two weeks later without getting found out. Or so I thought.

The friend who may have been most disturbed was Mick. One night at Glebe Place, I was skin-popping some junk into my butt. Mick saw what I was doing, then spoke up solemnly. "Don't you think you're doin' a bit too much of that stuff, John?" he asked. Mick's innate cool led him to understatement. I knew he was angry with me and disappointed.

"No, man, it's great. I got it under control."

He stared at me with mild disgust as the poison traveled through my body. I could sense that he was putting some distance between us. Gen told me that he had given her the same look when he stopped over for breakfast several times during my New York visit. She said she had started shooting up while I was away and that whenever she needed a shot, she sweated. Mick noticed the change in the kitchen. "I've made breakfast for Mick and Keith six hundred times and never sweated," she said. "But then I noticed him just staring at me as I was making the eggs and baking the tomatoes and mushrooms. It was because all of a sudden I was sweating and I'm sure he knew then that I was hooked."

Now he was giving *me* the warning and I chose to ignore him. I wasn't catching on. Mick saw it quite clearly. Mick never let drugs take over. He was just too cagey. He never forgot that and never let anyone else forget that. Drugs were fine—a little snort here, snort there, as long as you stayed in control. He told me that he once had to end one of the loves of his life because of heroin. It happened with Marianne Faithfull in the late sixties. He told her she'd have to make a choice between him and smack—she couldn't have both. When she failed to get rid of the drugs, he got rid of her, put her in a limo, gave her $1,000, and told the chauffeur not to drive her back. He saw the same showdown taking shape in my life with Gen.

Mick's growing concern and anger had to do with the album; he had made a verbal commitment to help me while we sat in the tranquility of cricket matches and the countryside in summer, when I was in good shape. He had gone out on a limb for me and helped swing considerable financial support from the label chiefs, Ahmet Ertegun at Atlantic and Earl McGrath, who ran Rolling Stones Records. Both executives long trusted Mick's canny musical and business judgments. We already had joked about a title, *Phillips '77.*

The Stones *never* committed themselves like this to projects with other artists.

There was another problem. Our young and dynamic engineer, Keith Harwood, who had worked with the Stones before, left a session and passed out from drugs at the wheel of his car. The car crashed and he was killed instantly. It was a terrible blow. We all loved Keith. He had just become a father months earlier and he was doing great work for us.

Mick made it clear by his absences that he was pulling back. I knew he loved Keith and Anita and considered me a friend. He didn't want to see anything bad happen to us. Mick trusted me as a friend and artist. Now he saw what had been happening at Glebe Place since Keith and Anita had moved in. I was being drawn away from Mick and drifting toward Keith—and the spell that had always surrounded him and defined the Stones' sound with its dark, menacing, brilliant edge.

Beyond the issue of my physical and emotional health, Mick was quite rightly beginning to worry about me as an *investment*.

Keith and I were arriving at the studio late at night and I'd promptly go into the bathroom and shoot up. Nothing happened until that first shot. Often, nothing happened *after* the first shot, either. Hours went by sometimes with very little music. The $125,000 estimated budget was looking small as it swelled past $50,000. We had three or four songs cut by Christmas and already we were beginning to grind down. As Mick retreated from the sessions, the drive and discipline soon fell apart, leaving Keith and me more on our own. By Christmas, we decided to take a much needed break and head for Redlands, Keith's colossal medieval castle in Chichester, just a few miles from the Channel in the south. I flew in Laura and my mother and they were invited too. Even my mother, whom Laura said had been drinking heavily of late, noticed the changes for the worse. Keeping the secret was impossible.

Before we left, Keith and I found ourselves without smack and going into withdrawal on a cold, bone-stiffening day. Laura was around. Everyone else must have been shopping. We all got on our hands and knees for hours, picking

through the rugs and wiping the floor for dust, rocks, anything that *looked like* smack. We scooped up old cottons and
shredded *them*. Laura knew we were totally mad. We
scraped together half a gram, enough for a weak shot. We
left her alone with her diary and drove around town until we
scored. Then we were ready for Redlands.

The drive out should have been covered for "ABC's Wide
World of Sports." The highway glistened with freezing rain.
Headlight reflections stretched and wiggled ahead of us like
long red and yellow ribbons poking through the fog. Keith
and I were in front. I was in the death seat. Marlon, Tam,
Chynna, and a girlfriend of hers from L.A. were crunched
up in the back of his Jaguar. Keith took that opportunity to
set the land speed record from London to Chichester. I was
so freaked out that I got down on the floor and listened to
tapes. "Oh, come on, man," he grinned cockily, "we done
this a hundred times. You don't trust my driving?"

We skidded and fishtailed and barely missed cars and rail-
ings a dozen times. Finally I reached across and yanked the
keys from the ignition, forgetting that the Jag would lose its
power brakes and steering. Keith was furious. "How dare
you take someone's keys . . ."

Fortunately, we were on a straightaway and caught in
some traffic. I made Keith promise to drive more safely for
the kids' sakes. I don't think he ever forgave me.

Redlands was the ultimate English retreat, set on a vast
stretch of country lushness. We hardly went out and it never
stopped raining. I'd cook a shot of smack every afternoon
and my mother and Laura would prepare tea and cakes on
gorgeous silver trays. Very English. I wanted to believe that
I was fooling them, but I really wasn't. "Dad," Laura whispered once, after a tour of the place, "they've got syringes on
the bathroom sink in a glass like toothbrushes, for God's
sake."

Tam and Marlon were by now soul brothers and inseparable. They slept in a loft. One of the beds wedged up against a
key left in a lock that governed a silent alarm system. It was
in the OFF position and Anita explained to Tam that he
should never, ever, turn it to ON because the police would
come.

Tam translated her warning to mean that the house would be doubly safe if he turned the key to ON. He gave it a twist without letting anyone know.

It didn't sound in the house, only at the local police station. At the same time, Gen and Laura were reading quietly in the living room. The rest of us were scattered all around the house. "Oh look!" Gen said, pointing with childlike wonder as she gazed out the front windows across the field to the country road. "Look at all those lovely white balloons floating by. Isn't that a beautiful sight! It must be the balloon man!"

Laura threw Gen a startled smirk. "The *what*, man?"

"The balloon man, with a fistful of strings for all his balloons." Laura sprang from her chair and went to the window. A jolt of fear shot through her. "Holy shit! Those aren't balloons, dammit, those are cop helmets. It's a raid!"

Laura and Gen raced screaming the news all over the house to give us time to stash everything. She remembered the toothbrush cup and stuck it in a chest. She found Keith calmly alphabetizing about fifteen hundred records on the floor in one room. She told him the local Bobbies were visiting. Keith got up and met them while I gathered my stashes and paraphernalia and hid it all.

The cops told Keith the burglar alarm had been set off and Keith assured them they were mistaken. When they checked, the alarm key had been twisted to ON. False alarm. Close call.

Christmas came and we could have started a nationwide child-care center with the toys Keith and I bought for the kids. By New Year's Eve, Anita and Laura were on warm terms, playing dress-up with shoulder pads, belts, scarves, dresses.

Laura and I both quit smoking that night and tossed out all our cigarettes. An hour later, we were scavenging through the garbage for butts.

My mother, who was in her seventies, stayed several weeks and had vague notions of what was going on. "Oh, he's doing it again now, isn't he?" she'd say whenever Keith would pop up and disappear. "This is when he does it, right?"

She may have been amused by Keith's little rituals, but
she would have been horrified if she ever found out that I
was snorting lines with Laura out at Redlands. We had our
own White Christmas. Yet I didn't see it as sick and reckless.
Laura had been into drugs for years, whether I was around
or not. It was what all of her friends were doing—and all of
mine.

We came back to London to resume the sessions and
Keith and Anita left Glebe Place for their own home. We
had done about six tracks by then. There had been talk of
continuing in New York at Mediasound with Harvey
Goldberg, an engineer who had worked on Gen's album. I
had to get out of there and get to New York. We were both
slipping deeper into heroin. Gen bought an electrical shock
box from Mick Taylor that had been developed experimen-
tally to block opiate addiction. It was a contraption not unlike a Walkman, with electrodes pressed against the temples
and a small box that produced electrical vibrations intended
to block the craving.

At the end of February, Keith, Mick, etc. went to Toronto
a week before an unpublicized show at the El Mocambo
Tavern for a live album. Keith and Anita were arrested at
the airport by the Royal Canadian Mounted Police. She was
charged for possession of cocaine and hashish; he was
charged with possession of heroin with intent to traffick and
possession of cocaine. They were released on bail, the concerts were held as planned, and Keith then lived under a
tense legal cloud for the next eighteen months. (In October
1978, his guilty plea got him a suspended sentence with one
year of probation—and a court-ordered booking to play for
the Canadian Institute for the Blind within six months.)

As the sessions began to fall apart, Gen flew home to New
York and stayed with Lenny and Marsia. I followed a week
or so later, but not before setting up a way to keep myself
supplied with precious China white back home.

I walked off the plane at Kennedy Airport with the shakes
and sweating. The pants I was wearing had been cut open
along the lining of the waistband, all the way around. I
packed coke and heroin inside a yard-long makeshift "belt"
fashioned out of plastic bags, then flattened the belt and slid

it inside the slit of the lining and around the waist. The lining was sewn back up.

I was petrified I'd be caught, but after my one nightmarish foray to Spanish Harlem, I was just as terrified of living at the mercy of killer smack and homicidal dealers. I only knew how to score on King's Road and was used to paying $20 a gram for the best junk. I could barely get off on what I bought in the City and got violently ill from whatever it was cut with. But I also got violently ill without it.

Gen met me at JFK Airport and I made it past Customs.

I went through the smuggled drugs but then went to the next plan. A friend of mine in London hollowed out a volume of romantic poetry and stuffed it with China white. The book arrived and I had another sizable stash. The symbolic irony hit me as soon as I opened the book and saw my stash. Five years earlier, Gen and I had opened the same kind of book and read verse to each other by candlelight at the beach. Now the poetry had been ripped out and replaced with pure heroin. Gen and I were both getting deeper into it. Another package came to keep us going. Finally the flow was cut off.

I was desperate. A friend of mine suggested that I get in touch with a Dr. D on the East Side, a well-known European who catered to a wealthy clientele off Fifth Avenue. "He's got a real Freudian background, old-world type sophistication, and he's the man to see. He'll cure you. It's only $35 a pop," the friend said.

This sounded absurd. Here I was, withdrawing from smack, and this joker was advising therapy. "Hey, man, I haven't got time for fucking psychoanalysis. Do you think I can lie down on a couch in this condition?"

"Who said anything about psychoanalysis?" We were both confused.

"You said he was Freudian."

"He is. At one point in his career, Freud was certain he could cure opiate addicts by shooting them up with coke. Didn't you know that? He was absolutely convinced for years that cocaine was the wonder drug of the future."

"You mean it isn't?"

24

WE LEFT Lenny and Marsia, moved into a hotel on Central Park West in the 80s, and made an appointment for us to see Dr. D across the park near Fifth. It was one of the coldest winters in years in New York. A blizzard had softened and silenced the City with a couple of feet of snow. Just outside our door, frigid, rugged Central Park could just as well have been Wyoming, for all I knew.

The invigorating half-mile hike through the park lifted my spirits as I made myself believe that maybe Dr. D's mysterious cure *could* melt away that other, wicked snow that had fallen so hazardously across the path of our lives.

Two dozen people waited outside his office. They all seemed to have money and early withdrawal symptoms— pacing, moaning, gnashing their teeth, rocking, sweating. His nurse—a rigid, sour-faced middle-aged woman with an accent—sat at her desk and told me to "vait viss everyvone else." She was a real horror show.

Fortunately, it was the end of the day and the overheated reception room emptied quickly. Before I could finish a magazine article, the doctor emerged, looked around to see how many patients remained, and called us in.

He was well into middle age and didn't waste any time.

He explained it was a twenty-cc. shot of B-12 laced with a form of synthetic morphine and a dash of meth. A real one-a-day load. He turned his back briefly and then approached me with the largest syringe and spike I had ever seen. The needle was six inches long and the syringe was two inches fat.

"Jesus, Doctor, I want to kick heroin, not win the Preakness. What the hell *is* that?"

He half-smiled politely, but said nothing—which said to me that this was the universal reaction—then scrubbed the crook of my arm with a cotton ball saturated with alcohol. I took in a deep breath, made a fist to pump up the vein. "This will be an opiate that will satisfy you," he said in a monotone with a thick accent. "Each day you come in the morning. I give you less and less opiate substitute, more and more vitamin. Reduction therapy. It will take a month. Don't move." I gritted my teeth.

He leaned on the syringe and slowly pumped the load. My arm felt like it was going to burst with pressure from the fluid. Within seconds, there was an awesome and ecstatic rush that cleared my head and made me feel indestructible. My mouth dried up and I fell back against the table.

Dr. Feelgood glanced at me a second or two, then tidied up after himself. Gen was next. Her eyes were wide with apprehension and we clasped hands for a second. I gave her a reassuring look. I was still alive. The doctor seemed impatient. "There will be a certain amount of discomfort in several hours." He scribbled on a prescription pad and tore off the top scrip. "Take these when it comes on. You go to K & B Pharmacy over on Madison and 81st. They'll take care of you. Every day this happens. But less and less every day. Please pay out front. I see you tomorrow."

We walked out to Fifth into a whole new world. I was gliding weightlessly on a cloud of white clear energy. A dry taste of ashes lined my mouth. I felt more than a powerful rush; I felt omnipotent. The scrip was for ninety Percodans. I went up Madison to K & B. It was a cramped and tiny pharmacy with a counter just at the entrance. I handed the scrip to the druggist. I struck up a conversation with him and the other pharmacist and found out that they were the

K & B owners: They introduced themselves as Sidney Korn
and Alvin Brod. They recognized me or my name, asked me
all about my daughter the TV actress, and wanted to know
what I was up to. The scrip and the doctor's name should
have told them a lot. But nothing was said. They were very
open and friendly and I liked them.

That night, after the shot wore off, I began writhing and
screaming from muscle and intestinal cramps, nausea, and
sweating. I downed a bunch of the codeine-based Percodan
painkillers.

They cut the edge, but I went out into the icy night winds
blowing across the park to score a quarter bag of smack for
$25. I had some syringes left and came home and hip-
popped to cool down. The street shit was so heavily stepped
on that it didn't work. I swallowed some more Percodans,
lay down, drifted in and out of sleep, and staggered into Dr.
D's office the next morning.

There were two dozen people waiting outside again, all
trying to cajole their way past the receptionist. It couldn't
have been a great job—dealing with Manhattan's A-list
junkies from TV, film, the arts, the *Social Register*—people
strung out on drugs and privilege. Junk was an even heavier
leveler than acid. You could walk away from acid and stay
away. Coke and smack robbed you of any choice. Behind the
furs, the flashing gems, the Hong Kong silks and suits, they
were all junkies. The only distinction was that they didn't
roam the streets and mug people for their hits; they stayed
home and messengered it in. Or they called a Dr. Feelgood
for a $35 appointment.

I told him about crashing the night before. He nodded
with distant sympathy. "This time I put ten milligrams calcium, okay?" he said. He saw his twenty-cc. glass monster
the way a pitcher sees a baseball. The mix of liquids inside
was his grip on the seams of my nervous system and he
could throw fastballs, curves, sliders, sinkers, knucklers,
spitters, change-ups, and scroogies. He scrubbed the crook
of my other arm and the smell of alcohol rose to my face.
The windup . . . around comes the arm . . . the pitch!

Calcium, I found out in ten seconds, as I stared in disbe-

lief at the needle sliding under my skin, was the rising
Heater, a staggering hot-flush 100-m.p.h. strike.

Gen loved to engage Dr. D in brainy discussions about
literature and art while we got our shots. They were both
enormously well-read and Gen had begun an elegantly written and movingly autobiographical novel. She was constantly quizzing him about his experiences in Europe decades earlier. While she flirted and philosophized, I would
walk around to the cabinets and cupboards in his office and
casually rip off syringes, little bottles of opiates with rubber
seals, whatever I could conceal.

His nurse hated us. We would barge in and demand immediate time with him. "We're extremely ill," Gen would say
right in her sullen face, "and we may just die right here in
front of all these people, and what if he finds out we died in
his reception area because of YOU and we have migraines
and we need to go in immediately and we cannot STAND to
be around OTHER PEOPLE!"

Gen never failed to get us in. The doctor had five examining rooms and kept someone waiting in all of them while
shooting people up in his main office. If he knew we were
there, he would see us right away and hang out for twenty or
thirty minutes, talking to Gen about history and literature
while pumping us full of B-12, speed, pharmaceutical coke,
or calcium. The more they spoke, the more I stole. I didn't
feel guilty. He was essentially a quack who fed off people's
habits and cravings.

He gave us scrips for Percodan to kill pain, tincture of
opium, and Tuinal, a barbiturate for sleeping. I went mostly
to Korn and Brod and became friendlier with them over the
weeks.

Gen and I went to Dr. D just about every morning for
more than a month. It was costing us $70 a day, but we were
really paying with our lives. We were living in a hotel and I
was shooting Lenox Avenue street shit with broken eyedroppers now. Still, money was tight. Then Bob Tucker called in
late winter to tell me of a $100,000 BMI check related to
Kingston Trio and Journeymen royalties. It was Susie who
called BMI and found out. Her motives were not humanitar-
ian. She was suing me for $350,000 in back support, based

on estimates—way off—of my gross income over the years. I
got her to settle for $40,000, borrowed the money from
Tucker, Tucker paid her, and, when the check arrived, I paid
Bob.

My other ex-wife, Michelle, was soon waging her own
battle against me. She sent Chynna to us in March after we
told her we wanted to take her and Tam to Disney World for
Tam's birthday. Chynna adored Tam, so she agreed, even
though she was still disturbed by what she had seen of our
drug use at Glebe Place. I don't think she ever went for my
story that the needles were for our B-12 injections. Three
days later, she called and got Gen in a rather woozy moment. We never left. Gen told her that she had water on the
knee and that we were having a little birthday party instead.
Michelle was upset and told Gen that she wanted Chynna
home right after the party.

Days later, Michelle later claimed, Marsia Trinder called
her and said, "Get Chynna out of there. Don't be alarmed,
but get her home."

After Chynna returned home, Michelle later said that she
was waking up in the middle of the night and dressing for
school at 4 A.M. Her whole life was off schedule. Michelle
thought it was jet lag. She was only nine. Michelle sensed
that Chynna had witnessed something while with us that
had left her practically traumatized. After Chynna had a
nightmare and crawled into bed with Michelle, she claimed,
Chynna asked her, "Mommy, do drugs kill you?" Michelle
was enraged and immediately brought Chynna to a child
psychiatrist so she could feel free to describe everything she
had witnessed and understand it better. From that point on,
Michelle was at war with us as parents.

After about two months with the doctor, I realized how
his heroin "cure" worked: He had addicted me to coke. He
cured my heroin habit by indirectly creating a coke habit.
Dr. D was so happy with our progress that he came over on
his birthday and gave Gen a coke shot as a gift to *her*. She
then got so high that she took Tam to a toy store and stayed
there for five hours. I was spending so much time supple-
menting with street coke and in shooting frenzies through

the night at home that there wouldn't have been enough time in the day to stay hooked on smack. I was blowing a ton of money on high-grade coke from a dealer named Ed and mainlining all over my body. As veins got used up, they lost pressure and became harder to find. I was shooting in my hands, groin, arms, calves, and thighs—wherever I could raise a vein. I had multiple track marks and sores on every limb and I was so strung out on coke that I had wasted away to about 150 pounds.

By the time I got down to the juicy vein that stretches across the top of my left foot, I was utterly crazed and out of control. It's a vein women often use because the tracks don't show. I used it because a lot of my other veins didn't show anymore. They had collapsed. I was running out of veins. Then the vein opened up and became infected, but that didn't stop me.

As the pain increased, two oozing ulcers—hot, red, and diseased—began poisoning the vein. I kept jabbing needles into the inflamed blood vessels dying in the ulcer and made myself feel no pain. When I realized I could hardly walk, I called Lenny and moved from the hotel to his apartment. I was referred by a friend of mine to call Dr. Robert Millman at New York Hospital in the East 60s.

Millman was a young, dynamic psychiatrist building a reputation for himself as an expert in treating coke and heroin addiction. I just needed to save my foot. After examining my foot and taking a recent history, he put it bluntly. "You could lose your foot to gangrene. There are needle tracks in the vein itself. The infection could spread. It could get to your heart. You're killing yourself." He ordered me hospitalized the next day, April 27, in a private room in the medical, rather than psychiatric, ward.

Millman prescribed massive doses of antibiotics and Percodan for the pain. The ulcers were weeded and cleansed. He came in every day and spoke with me about the junkie life-style that he said was destroying me. We had some good talks. He told me I needed intensive and long-term drug therapy, and he offered to see me after my discharge. Millman, despite his caring, knowing approach, was not impressed with my motivation to get better. My wall of denial

was higher than ever and I never returned for out-patient
help. "You're charming," he said. "You're quite bright, but
your judgment is completely blown. You're clearly in danger
of killing yourself and you don't know what you're doing."

It was worse than he even knew. While Dr. Millman was
saving my foot—maybe my life—Lenny Holzer was bringing
in coke during visiting hours for me to secretly shoot up in
the bathroom.

There was no question at that point. I had been on the
ledge of sanity, looking straight down, barely holding on.
Millman offered me a strong, secure way back through the
window. I rejected his appeal and inched away along the
narrow ledge. Finally, I leaped into the void of unreality.
When I landed, I was still alive and I was standing in K & B
Pharmacy near the corner of Madison and 81st.

For several weeks, Korn and Brod had been filling my
scrips for Percodans, Tuinals, Seconals, some amphetamines,
and syringes without actually having the white prescriptions.
We had become that familiar and casual. Gen had gone
home again to South Africa to try to clean herself out and
she was due back within a week after my discharge on May
2. By then, I was out of Lenny's because the day I left New
York Hospital, Lenny was admitted for endocarditis and
eventually he needed triple-bypass surgery. Marsia had some
relatives staying with her and it didn't seem right that I
would be around without him there. I moved across the park
into a suite at the Stanhope Hotel at 81st Street and Fifth, a
short crosstown block from K & B.

Gen returned from South Africa, having learned that almost all junkies who clean out end up turning to alcohol. It
had been a rough trip, with lots of phone calls and letters
between us. But she hadn't lost her wit. "John," she said,
"even *you* look good after South Africa." Unfortunately,
drugs were looking good to her, too, and by the time Laura
visited us during her TV series hiatus, she was back into
coke. Laura was booked on various game shows and intended to cut some demos with me at Mediasound for her
own album. I could have used a new musical project. The
Stones sessions were suspended. Michelle and I had gotten
together to do some tracks for her *Victim of Romance* solo

album in New York and later in London. I was originally
going to write and produce the album, but I was no longer in
any shape to finish it off. She and her label, A & M, agreed
to get another producer and another opportunity had
slipped away.

I had just settled in at the Stanhope and needed some
toothpaste, shampoo, shaving cream, and aspirin. Laura
came with me to K & B and we all talked for a while. They
recognized her from "One Day at a Time" and were pleased
to meet a real TV star. I noticed a box of syringes on a shelf.
"Can we help you with anything else?" one of them asked.
"Yes," I said, "a box of syringes." "Where are you staying
now?" I was asked. "The Stanhope."

"We'll have it delivered to you in an hour."

The box of disposable syringes arrived at the hotel with
forty Tuinals thrown in. I had not given the pharmacists a
scrip for either item.

Over the next few weeks during the summer of 1977, my
primary source of coke, the dealer named Ed, noticed that I
had a wide assortment of pills. He asked me where they were
from. "A pharmacy," I said. "Can you get a drug called
Dilaudid?" he asked. "Or Demerol, morphine, things like
that?"

"I don't really know. I'll have to ask them, you know?"

I had heard of Dilaudid, a pure and synthetic form of
morphine that is so powerful it is prescribed almost exclu-
sively for cancer surgery patients. Everyone on the street
wants it because it's stronger and purer. It's like Merck, only
it's heroin.

The drugs Ed named were different from those I had in
one regard: They were all Schedule II narcotics requiring
not the simple white scrip but a New York State triplicate
form. The yellow triplicate was created after a toughening
up of state drug laws several years earlier. The state, the
doctor, and the druggist all kept copies. The closer monitoring of legitimate purchases of narcotic prescription drugs
was intended to deter illegal drug activity. I wasn't even
concerned with opiates and I had not used heroin in months.
I could thank my addiction to cocaine for that.

I went to K & B and asked if I could get the drugs. "You

can't have them," I was told, "without the state triplicate prescriptions. If you get the triplicates, we can get the drugs."

I arranged to meet Ed and tell him the discouraging news. He operated a limousine service and we met in one of his cars and drove through the East Side. "I can't get them, man, without these triplicate forms, you know what I mean? Sorry."

He nodded confidently. "That shouldn't be a problem."

By July, we had left the Stanhope and moved into a rented duplex on East 72nd Street near Park, a spacious, hand-somely appointed sublet owned by an attorney. By now, both Gen and I were shooting coke with alarming frequency; I shot into the back of my hands. I didn't start the day without pumping some coke into a vein somewhere. Thanks again to Dr. D, I had learned how to inject myself. If I was alone, I'd get some rubber tubing, slip it in a knot around my arm, yank a loose end in my teeth with a jerk of the head to raise a vein, then shoot. We were spending less and less time out and around town because we needed to keep shoot-ing. The craving was a desperate, blinding compulsion. I would sometimes have to shoot up every fifteen minutes. Our friends from the *Man on the Moon* days in 1974 were horrified and kept their distance. They knew our demons had finally seized control. The apartment immediately began to deteriorate from our mad cocaine frenzies.

We hired a maid named Versey, an obese, sweet-natured West Indian, to help cook, clean, and look after Tam. It wasn't long before she had to scrub jagged streaks of blood from the bathroom walls and ceiling—the gruesome junkie signature scrawled by unclogging used syringes. One night we tossed out four hundred of them, but not before bundling them up by the dozen in heavy-duty foil so the garbagemen wouldn't stab themselves.

Ed set up a meeting with a friend of his named Andy. They came to the apartment to discuss a new sort of deal: If I could procure narcotics from K & B, they could provide me with all the high-grade coke I would need to feed our habit. At the time I was up to $400 a day. I couldn't rely on finding Merck. Not even at K & B. I still had to score Co-

lombian and at least Ed had class blow. I rarely used heroin
and came down on Tuinals.

Andy then tossed me a new empty book of twenty-five
triplicate forms. We discussed prices and amounts and
agreed to a complicated system of bartering K & B's pharmaceuticals for their coke. The plan was for me to buy coke
with K & B drugs or, if needed, cash. The book of twenty-
five triplicate prescriptions, he told me, counted for as much
as $500 or $600. He would buy the pharmaceuticals from me
in exchange for coke or, if he didn't have it, lead me to it.

In effect, I could end up supplying myself with coke for
nothing. K & B's inventory would, if the system worked,
become the currency of exchange. I would later estimate
that with the wholesale purchase of drugs like Quaaludes for
$1.75 apiece from K & B, reselling them—and others—for
double that price to the dealers earned me an average of
$500 a week from the transactions. This money, however,
was immediately used for the purchase of coke, after the
swap of triplicates and huge amounts of pharmaceuticals
were factored in.

I took the book to the pharmacy and gave it to the druggists, along with a good amount of cash from Ed and Andy.
It was the last time I felt apprehension about this deal. I
struck a drug gusher. They handed over a bag full of bottles
containing Dilaudid, Quaaludes, Demerol, and more. K & B
then had to try to keep track of what went out and how
many scrips came in—and match the flow with bogus names
and doctors.

Everyone had what they wanted: K & B got some extra
cash and the scrip books to make it all look legit; Ed and
Andy had access, potentially, to thousands of sharply dis-
counted pills, which they could then move on the street for a
big markup and profit; and I had a steady source of the best
coke around from top-echelon dealers and the syringes from
the pharmacy.

The shopping list soon included Dexedrine; Benzedrine;
Desoxyn, a synthetic, pure speed; the barbiturate Nembutal;
and Dolophine, which is a rare opiate substitute like methadone that was developed by the Nazis for combat wounds.
The drug was named for the Führer himself.

The one hitch in the triangle trade route was that I immediately had to try Dilaudid for myself. I had turned to Dr. D and cocaine in the first place only because I had come home from London strung out from the China white. The cycle was complete. Dilaudid made me forget China white.

Now there was something even better, purer, stronger—and just up the block. I was soon hooked on Dilaudid and coke and as Andy would give me more hot books, I'd leave K & B with more and more Dilaudid. I was soon handing over up to $1,000 a week to K & B and coming home to 72nd Street with up to 240 pills of any drug.

In early summer, Michelle came to town for some film work. Again, she came by the suite at the Stanhope and did not like what she saw. Gen and I were in horrible condition, with track marks up and down our arms and a tendency to nod out.

We arranged for her to take Tam back to L.A. for a few weeks. When she came over to get the money to buy the ticket, she walked into the bathroom and saw half a dozen used syringes. Her immediate reaction was to get Tam out to the coast for part of the summer.

By August, I was, like many of Freud's patients a century earlier, cross-addicted to cocaine and heroin—or Dilaudid. The deal with K & B fell into place with surprising ease. And it seemed rather ingenious and foolproof. I was soon going weekly, twice weekly, $1,000 a visit. I was a junkie living only for the next shot. We were still visiting Dr. D for his blast of energy through speed and calcium. I was still a perfectionist and, if nothing else, though this bizarre "partnership" with the pharmacy may have been slowly killing me, it was at least a stunning success all the way around.

I did some demos with Laura at Mediasound and asked Harvey Goldberg if he would want to work on the Stones project with me. He was wary. I was going into the bathroom every twenty minutes and shooting up. I hadn't seen Harvey in almost three years and he picked up on the difference right away. He had spent his whole life watching musicians come and go and he knew all the tricks.

But Harvey said sure, he always wanted to meet and work with Mick and Keith. And he respected my songwriting. By

the middle of August, Keith was back in town and living
with Anita and Marlon in an old and quaint country house
outside a rustic town in Westchester County. With close to
$100,000 already spent on the tracks, Atlantic wanted to see
us hit the streets soon. Ertegun was getting restless and
wanted the Stones to get into the studio, turn out a much-
needed killer album, and tour. They had been in a sales
slump over two or three albums and Keith's bust in Toronto
hardly helped.

We scheduled our first session on August 16. It turned out
to be a dark day for rock and roll all over the world, but not
for that reason. I was awakened by a call from Harvey. "Do
you think you'll still come down for the session?" he asked.

"Sure, why not?" I mumbled.

"Didn't you hear what happened?" he asked. I hadn't.

"Elvis died today."

It was impossible to picture Elvis dead. I hadn't seen him
in years, but he was always so handsome and full of life.
There were calls all through the night for Keith, reporters
tracking him down for quotes, people asking if he would go
to the funeral.

Looking back, the irony was that Keith and I already *were*
at a funeral of sorts. I was getting buried alive in junk.
Elvis's death would cast a pall over the sessions for the next
few weeks as we tried to bring the project back to life.
Keith's drug trial in Canada was coming up in the fall and
he knew he'd have to clean out once the case was resolved.
He wasn't holding back, either. Harvey knew right off that
something was wrong. For almost every night during August
and September, Harvey would show up for the 10 P.M. booking with some musicians and wait until we arrived—sometimes not until 2 A.M. He'd call us at home and we were
always "on our way." Keith wouldn't drive down from
South Salem in his Jaguar before seven or eight. By nine or
ten, he'd come to 72nd Street and wait for me while I woke
up with a shot of coke. Maybe he would snort some and then
we'd be ready to rock.

We'd rarely make it to the studio before midnight and
then it was time for me, sometimes Keith, to walk right past
everyone—all the musicians, hangers-on, the small-time

dealers looking to give you a few lines just to be able to stick around, the groupies, engineers, Harvey—and go into the bathroom again for another shot. Maybe it would be Dilaudid for me. Then I'd nod out and get real high for an hour until I could come down and get ready to play. If I was too wasted by then, it would be time to go to the bathroom and shoot some coke to get me rolling again. And this was at $175 an hour of studio time. Sometimes I just wouldn't come out. I'd sit on the toilet seat and keep shooting up, unable to stop. As soon as one shot would start to wear off, I'd crave another, and another. Harvey, Keith, Mick, or someone would knock on the door and listen for signs of life, then tell me to come out.

Harvey came over to me one night after we arrived. A tall, skinny young man with dark sensitive eyes and a gentle manner, Harvey was pushing himself to the limit with us. "John," he said, "this is really getting absurd, man. I've got no life left. The only people I talk to now are junkies and dealers and I don't even do any drugs and it's getting me weirded out. I stopped talking to my own friends. I'm here all the time waiting for you and Keith. The only time you're up and productive is like ten minutes after shooting coke. And this chick's been here night after night hanging out and I'm, like, stuck here waiting for you guys, having to deal with her. She drives me nuts, keeps asking me if I want to see her scrapbook, do I want to see her scrapbook, and so I finally say okay. Well, I thought it would have stars' pictures in it and stuff, but it's all filled with hundreds and hundreds of prescriptions and ads for drugs and potions and bizarre cures from the eighteenth and nineteenth centuries, for Chrissakes. It's a goddamn *drug* scrapbook. These are your new friends."

Harvey came up to Keith's place in the country over a weekend and there were about eight other guests. Harvey, who had managed to avoid serious drugs while establishing himself in late-seventies rock recording, kept walking into rooms where people were sitting there like zombies, shooting up. "Ooops," he'd say politely, "wrong room. Sorry." He walked in on a shouting match between Anita and Gen.

Anita was accusing Gen of stealing drugs. And Keith was depressed because his drug trial was coming up.

Harvey tried really hard to make me see how the drug binges were jeopardizing the album. "The lyrics are becoming too introverted and related to nothing," he said, "if not drugs. That's all that matters," he said. "Can't you see that?" I nodded and told Harvey what he wanted to hear without hearing it myself—that I would get everyone out, leave the City, break off with the dealers.

One night Keith and I got so loaded that we spent the entire night either in the bathroom or tuning our guitars and trying to remember what song we were working on. The other musicians spent the night waiting in an all-night coffee shop on West 57th.

Earl McGrath, head of Rolling Stones Records, lived nearby and came by several times while walking his dog. He tried to give us pep talks, then gave up. Mick was living around the corner from me on East 72nd Street and he had, by then, all but abandoned the sessions. Mick did the backup harmonies to "Just 14," but pulled out when he saw the condition we were in. The writing was on the wall and it was written in blood—all over the bathroom ceiling, walls, toilet, and floor. The sad part was that somehow we *were* getting some great stuff done.

Most of the songs were personal statements about people I knew. One was about the ravishing redhead model. "Just 14" ("She's a movie star queen . . . she's always too high on arrival") was about Laura in her glory days of glitter and platforms. "Mr. Blue" ("elegant Jew") was about Lenny Holzer in the Julia Robinson days. "Oh Virginia" referred to the differences between the Virginia I knew as a kid and Susie's ballet and horsey set outside Washington. "Zulu Warrior" came out of a long conversation about Gen's political passions. "Dread" was inspired by a terrifyingly vivid dream the night Mick cornered me at Glebe Place and told me to lay off the heroin. That was when he told me about making his decision about Marianne Faithfull. In the dream, it's snowing heavily outside and Tam and I are watching Gen through the huge windows of the loft. She carries her suitcases outside and gets in a black London taxi and heads off to a mental hospital as Tam asks me what's going on. The song was about Gen's anguish and our confusion and sadness.

The music ranged all over the place from ballads to country to pop to hard rock. The best tracks were those where Mick Taylor and Keith would trade licks, or Taylor would take your head off with one of his single-note or slide solos and Keith would play his incomparable sharp and hot rhythm chords. Even though the sessions were bogging down fast from drugs, I was still sure that we had ourselves a killer. There *were* times, through it all, when Keith and I *both* felt great together at the same time and could find our groove with the musicians and Harvey at the board. Keith was one guy who could sit there half-asleep, hands still on the guitar, and know exactly what was happening around him and then, from that stupor, roar off into one of his scorching guitar runs.

My voice began to strain and growl in some sort of tribute to Mick. I have always been a vocal chameleon, taking on the colors of whomever I'm around. When I was around Denny, I sang smooth and warm like Denny. When I was around Mick a lot, I sang raw and hard like Mick. That was always one of my problems: I can imitate almost anyone.

We'd leave the sessions in the middle of the night and hang out at Studio 54 or get a late-night Chinese restaurant to stay open for us. By sunrise I'd be home or racing up to Keith's along the narrow, winding Saw Mill Parkway at hair-raising speeds.

We held meetings after about two months of sessions. Pressure—and costs—were both rising fast. We met at Mick's apartment with Earl McGrath and Harvey. It was time to wrap it up. Mick told me—then repeated to Harvey —that I had to lay down all the vocals and get the last tracks done.

There never was a formal contract for the album. Atlantic and Ahmet Ertegun had given Mick the green light to finance the project. Ertegun and McGrath—everyone, in fact —may have been anxious over Keith's legal dilemma. At that time, Keith's trial was scheduled for December 2, 1977, and the Stones had to get a new album—*Some Girls*—and

tour under way. The trial was postponed several times until
Keith entered a guilty plea a year later.

By the end of the sessions, we could hardly get anything
done. Harvey or sometimes Mick would bang on the bathroom door and try to force me out. Mick once talked to me
about my drug craziness through the door, warning me that
the album was never going to get done if I didn't cool out.

I'd shoot up every ten minutes. It was frightening. I could
not stop myself. The shots became a compulsive ritual that
ruled me. A cat was alive and scratching at my skin from the
inside and I had to appease it. I could not bear to look at
myself in the mirror. I was down to 140 pounds. I'd come
out of the bathroom and wipe blood off my hands and arms
before picking up the guitar.

"John, man, you better get it together," Harvey said to me
one night as I came in. "The secretary who works here in the
morning came in today and told the manager she had to
walk past these two awful-looking derelicts together, standing outside the studio at eight when she came in. She said
they were real grungy and she asked her boss how come they
always had to stand *right there* at the entrance."

"Yeah . . . so?" I shrugged.

"Hey, you don't get it, do you? The derelicts were you and
Keith! You walked out of here at eight this morning and
scared her shitless."

Harvey hired an arranger to work on the strings for
"Zulu," a young kid from the midwest, a friend of Harvey's.
He came to the apartment one afternoon for an appointment
and knocked at the door. I was out cold. Gen answered the
door stark naked. The guy looked away, down at the floor—
almost in shock. "Is John in?" he asked. "I'll go see," she
said and asked him in as she wandered through the house
naked. We were totally out of touch. As hard as Versey and
her boyfriend, Frenchie, worked for us, the apartment was
littered with dogshit, week-old Big Macs and Whoppers,
cans, bottles, butts, syringes, baggies, and wet garbage. It
didn't matter where we lived—it was a junkie pad by the
time we left. We were in the swanky Upper East Side gallery
district. Our elegant duplex was a gallery too—a shooting
gallery.

In the middle of November, Atlantic fired off a memo to
Bob Tucker and informed him that the budget for the album
had soared to over $170,000. There were close to a dozen
completed tracks and no one heard any singles in them. The
record industry during the mid-seventies had become a sin-
gles-oriented market dependent on strict radio formatting.
Album sales were soaring. The five-million mark, once a
virtual impossibility except for a handful of the very top
artists, was broken over and over on the strength of one or
two giant hits off an album—and sometimes a *debut* album.
The disco boom was peaking, but turning the pop-R&B
sound into a mindless but simple formula that couldn't miss.
New acts were signed up in great numbers. Having one
dance hit on an album had made dozens of them rich. Rock
had become a fast-buck business for a new rapidly growing
class of slick one-hit wonders, and I was missing all the fun.

Mick and Keith decided, finally, by December, to quit the
project and go to Paris to cut *Some Girls.* Atlantic pulled the
plug on the money and shut us down for good.

It was in my hands now to complete the vocal tracks on
my own—alone. I knew what that meant. It was all over for
me. I would never complete and release the album by myself. I was devastated. I had sabotaged the greatest break of
my career since the Mamas and the Papas split up. The
failure of the album just at the start of the Christmas season
filled me with sad and intense self-loathing.

It was clear that my whole family was beginning to tear
apart as my life disintegrated. Shortly after her eighteenth
birthday, in early December, Laura was out celebrating the
closing deal on her new house in Laurel Canyon. She was
going around town with our old Mexican friend, Yippie, and
was high on Quaaludes. They pulled over on Robertson and
she slid out of the car. She tripped onto the street right in
front of two passing motorcycle cops. She was barely conscious, teetering and slurring as they questioned her.

Fortunately, the ten ludes she was holding fell out of her
purse and rolled under the car seat. But it was bad enough.
They hauled her down to the station and she consented to a
blood test. She said she kept saying, "All I want is a smoke."
They claimed she was saying, "Just give me some coke." In

any event, she was just hitting her stride on TV and making tons of money. Neither she nor the network needed the bad PR and she was charged with a drug misdemeanor that made the L.A. *Times.* TV gossip said that she had taken enough ludes to kill a horse. The network eventually suspended her. She was placed on a year's probation and assigned to a drug-diversion therapy program.

Jeffrey had sunken into a drug-abusing life-style as well and he was beginning to get more into heroin and coke. For a while he moved into Laura's place in Laurel Canyon. We spoke once every two or three months, but the drugs made it impossible to really connect. Unlike his sister, he had very little money to blow on drugs and that may have saved him. He worked for Susie's second husband and learned quite a bit from him about the mechanics and assembly-line production of pumps for hot tubs and whirlpools. With weekly take-home pay of about $200, he wasn't going to get strung out on *anything* but cheap wine. But the desire, the intent, the craving were there. I wasn't seeing much of Jeff then because, while Laura was always coming to New York for her career, Jeff couldn't hop a flight to see us. But there were heartbreaking moments when he admitted his fears and told me that he couldn't survive with drugs and couldn't survive *without* them. He was lost, but I knew exactly what he was going through.

I decided to fly out and stay with Jeff at Laura's because I had to unload my cars and personal property for cash. I was spending close to $500 a week on coke, even with the K & B bartering system. Before I left I persuaded both Mick Jagger and Jack Nicholson to loan me $5,000 each. They agreed. I used most of the money to buy drugs and I headed to L.A.

I had the Bentley, two Rollses and another car, some art, the prized Tiffany lamps with the zodiac signs, a series of Warhol lithographs, and other effects that generated a quick cash flow. I got rid of everything.

I hadn't seen Jeff in months and he was alarmed at my appearance. Laura had rented a limo for herself and Jeff, but she was out of town. "You look green, Dad," he said at the airport. "Skin and bones and the color of guacamole."

" 'Guacamole'? You've been in L.A. too long," I joked.

This was no joke. When we got in, Jeff, just as he had done as a younger kid, poked around to find my stash. He looked inside my suitcase and found about three hundred syringes. He froze in horror and neither of us said anything. The next morning he came into the kitchen while I was preparing to shoot four yellow four-milligram tablets of Desoxyn. I had shaken them up in four cc.'s of water the night before and let them dissolve. Desoxyn is to cocaine what Dilaudid is to heroin—a pure, synthetic amphetamine. I had been getting it at K & B, but I usually gave it over to Andy for coke. When my money ran down, I shot it myself because it was much cheaper than coke. And it was so potent that it lifted my head right off my body.

"I can't believe I'm seeing this," he said emptily. He knew what had been going on, he saw I was gaunt and wild, but he had never witnessed the ritual.

"When you've been shooting coke every fifteen minutes for a year or two, kid, this is nothing. This'll get me through the morning."

"Jesus. A shot like that would blast me through the roof."

"How would you know?"

"I've shot Desoxyn—one at a time." This was the first I knew he was shooting up. I was sick for Jeffrey. I couldn't very well help him while cooking up a $60 shot of pure speed. The visit ended disastrously with a big fight and I told Jeffrey to move out with his girlfriend and leave Laura's. I told him that he wasn't growing up. I told him Laura wanted him out. I had the impression—never proven—that he and the girlfriend were helping to supply Laura with drugs. And Jeff believed that his sister and I had acted together to get him out of the house. We had talked about it. But the issue of Jeffrey's staying or leaving was irrelevant. The fight was really about the slow destruction of the members of my family as the drug plague spread.

At Christmas, Michelle, Chynna, and Michelle's godmother Marika Sail came to a big party celebrating the holidays and Keith's birthday. Her solo album was just out and she was in fine spirits. Chynna was delighted to see Tam and didn't seem upset to be around us. Michelle was planning to go from New York to Haiti with Tam and Chynna for a vacation. Keith and I were so strung out that we could hardly lug a Christmas tree five blocks. Versey worked her heart out washing blood off the bathroom walls before the guests—Ahmet, Earl, Lenny and Marsia, Harvey, Dr. D, Keith and Anita, Mick, Elaine Kaufman of Elaine's restaurant, and many others—showed up.

Then we bought boxes and boxes of decorations, gaily colored balls, tinsel, sets of blinking lights, and candy canes at Lamston's. But we were too fucked up to actually trim the tree. The kids were thrilled and did a beautiful job—on the lower third of the tree. Our guests were due in less than an hour and the upper two–thirds was ridiculously bare. So we just hung the boxes on the tree as they were. We took extension cords and lit the lights in the boxes and did the same with the balls, tinsel, and candy. It looked like something in a hip Soho gallery.

Michelle knew exactly how hip it was and was outraged. I was talking with her and my hand was shaking so hard that she heard the ice cubes rattling against glass. There were other signs. Tam had been running around naked and unbathed. He often didn't go to the Lycée Kennedy, a private school that Dr. D helped him get into. At the party, Tam, Chynna, and Marlon raced around in front of our guests squirting syringes like water guns. My hands were scarred and sores dotted my body.

Michelle's sane, protective instinct told her we could no longer look after our own son and she was right. Tam was not allowed to return to school after I defaulted on the payments. With the help of Marika, with whom I had always shared a mutual affection and respect, Michelle persuaded us shortly before Christmas to let her take Tam to Haiti and then back to L.A., where she would get him into school while we got our lives straightened out. Gen cried and resisted. But we knew it was best for Tam. The next day we packed his clothes and toys and kissed him good-bye.

As the new year began, Gen and I found ourselves alone with each other and our drug madness during another brutally cold and snowy winter. Our world was shrinking fast and we were growing more dependent upon one another for friendship. Our sex life had vanished, as it often does with junkies, and she saw in that a moral superiority toward everyone else with baser, lustier drives. In Gen's wry, facetious vision of things, there was, perhaps, an up side: I wasn't fucking around on her any longer.

"You know, John," she would say with a sardonic smile, "we've settled down more on junk. Maybe this is the answer to my problem. It's taken away your libido, hasn't it? So I don't really have to deal with all the other women anymore. Since you've gotten into junk, you're not that interested in women and we really have gotten much closer, haven't we? I only have to deal with the coke and Dilaudid. I'm sure it's all unconscious, but you know, in a funny way, heroin's sort of saving our marriage, isn't it?"

25

FROM THE MOMENT we were hooked, we *wanted* to clean out but couldn't. Dr. D's "cure" left me cross-addicted and involved in an elaborate dealing scheme with prescription forms and huge cash payments to a pharmacy. The cats under our skin kept scratching for more and we would have to feed them to put them to sleep again. We were paying dearly to keep them quiet: We had signed over temporary custody of our own son to my ex-wife Michelle.

In the heart of the bitterest winter in memory, Denny called and asked me to come to Halifax to appear with Michelle on his new TV variety show. He had come back to New York and worked as a stagehand, loading shows in and out. He married Jeannette, then went back to Halifax to do some local theater. By early 1978, he was hired for a half-hour CBC Network weekly variety show and was taping the first few weeks of material. I agreed to do it, but only if Michelle did it. She agreed, but made me promise to go clean. We all assured each other.

In February, I flew out to L.A. to visit Tam and rehearse some material with her. Tam seemed to be doing great. Michelle and I got along fine and I stayed at her place for a few days. Tam was happy with Chynna around. Michelle may

have believed my claim that I was clean until she, Annie
Marshall, and I went for dinner at Imperial Gardens on
Sunset just below the Château. I nodded out in the moo shoo
pork. They dragged me out and dumped me at the Beverly
Hills Hotel.

Michelle got enraged when I hid a bagful of dirty syringes
at the top of a closet in her house, thinking, in my junked-
out confusion, that I'd pick them up on my way back from
Canada. Her maid got to them first. Michelle yelled at me
about the risks of diseases with Chynna and Tam around.
She felt more determined than ever to keep Tam with her
and out of danger. I was stricken with guilt—for about ten
minutes, until I could take my next shot. I was incapable of
reacting any other way. The drug ruled my mind and emotions.

When I got to Halifax, I realized I had somehow lost my
stash of Dilaudids for the week-long trip. I had enough for
half a day. We were scheduled to tape three shows in four
days. There was no way I was going to live for another
twenty-four hours if I didn't score.

"Denny," I said quietly on the set, "I've got to score Dilaudid or we're done for. Ask around discreetly."

Denny went to his producer and explained the situation.
The guy called a doctor in town and came back to us. He
looked at me in disbelief. "Christ, the doctor says there's
only like thirty Dilaudids in the whole fuckin' country. It's
for terminal cancer patients."

"I'll take them." I got thirty-three. I was shooting an inhuman amount of the stuff—eight four-milligram pills in a
shot, a shot every eight hours. Enough for thirty-six hours. I
was halfway home.

Michelle knew what was happening and hated me for it.
We had adjoining rooms and she came in once after I had a
shower. I was in a towel. She saw the ugly scarred gash on
my calf, an inch wide, where a vein had exploded. "Jesus
Christ, what is that?" she gasped.

"That's where I shoot."

The third day, I was getting the shakes and felt the cat
waking up again. A musician offered me some Percodans.
"Thanks, man, but, like, I come *down* on that shit. I need to

get *high.*" He just stared at me. The tapings had gone well, with each of us singing our own solo songs and some Mamas and Papas medleys as a trio. We were really cooking with "Zulu Warrior" when the drummer in Denny's studio band suddenly stood and yelled, "CUT!" The producer was pissed and barked that he had no right to yell "CUT!" "There's a fuckin' syringe stickin' outta John's pocket, eh?" the drummer yelled back. "You want that to go out on TV?"

The taping bogged down and I pulled Denny aside. I told him that I had to score again or I'd have to split. I was running out of time. "There's one real funky joint by the docks that's so sleazy, man, I wouldn't go there on a bet," he said. "It's called the Rusty Nail and it's in the murder-stabbing district of town. Don't go."

"What's the address?"

We put the taping on hold while Denny drove me there with one of the production assistants, who caught on and gave us a name of a friend who was holding. We were in our stage costumes, pancake makeup, and hair spray. We could easily have passed for drag queens looking for some action.

I went in and it was pretty rough. I milled around, looking for the wild, beady eyes of an opiate junkie, someone I could relate to. The girl found her friend, a local pusher. He told us to drive him to his home in Dartmouth, the twin city across the harbor. "Shit, man," Denny muttered behind the wheel. "I left my fuckin' license, I.D., and papers at the studio."

"No way we'll ever get stopped in a small town like this," I said.

We found the house and he and I went inside. He sold me some Dilaudids and some coke. We got back in the car and took off for the road to Halifax. As we got on the main drag, the car was suddenly swallowed up by vans, police squad cars, flashing lights, and motorcycle cops. All four of us panicked.

"Mounties. SHIT! We're fucked, our ass is burger meat," Denny said, gritting his teeth. "Ten to fifteen in Dorchester Pen, no questions asked. John, toss out your shit now!"

The kid in the back was frantic. "Here," he said to the

girl, emptying pills from his pockets, "take these and shove
'em up your pussy."

She punched him on the head. "Fuck you!" she yelled.
"Shove 'em up your ass!" Denny pulled over. The flashlights
hurt the eyes. Denny slumped down and exhaled gloomily.
"My whole life is passing before me," he mumbled.

The first Mountie painted Denny's face with his flashlight.
Then he jabbed me with the beam of light as icy winds
poured through the car. "Hiya, Officer," Denny said with
hysterical calmness. "I'm Denny Doherty. I have a TV show
over in Halifax and my wallet's in the studio right this minute, as a matter of fact."

Two officers looked at each other and bent over to check
the backseat. "I've never heard of that show," one said to
the other. Denny winced. "It hasn't been aired yet. We're
still taping, see?" I sat on my hands to cover the needle
marks. They paused and mumbled among themselves.
"Hey," one officer said, "aren't you the guy in the Lovin'
Spoonful?"

"There ya go!" Denny smiled.

They looked him over some more. "That isn't the guy we
want," one of them said. "Okay," the Mountie said into the
car, "you guys go on ahead. Sorry for the inconvenience."

We got back to the studio and the producer told us we
were in a big hurry to wrap. I went straight to the bathroom.
Denny came in with me to make sure I didn't fuck up. He
watched in astonishment as I shot a speedball I.M. right
through my pants into my hip, came out, and finished the
taping.

On our way to the airport the next day, Denny asked me
to make sure I didn't have any drugs or syringes on me when
I went through security. I squirmed and was sitting on
something hard. I pulled out a bent, blackened tablespoon
used for cooking shots. "What are you, some kind of psychic
too?" Denny joked.

I rolled down the window and flung the spoon toward an
embankment off the roadside. "No, just some kind of
junkie."

When I got home, Gen had an eerily similar story to relate. I had left her some Demerol, a narcotic painkiller, but

she ran out at about the same time I did up north. A blizzard smothered New York, so she and Versey were stuck in the apartment just when Gen began to withdraw. Gen became delirious, with high fevers and cold sweats. Versey did all she could. She gave Gen her two-milligram Librium "pressure pills," which were useless.

Versey acted with loving antebellum devotion right out of *Gone With the Wind.* She filled the tubs in both bathrooms, one with hot water when Gen got the shivers, the other with cold for when the fevers broke. Then she and her aging boyfriend, Frenchie, carried her back and forth up and down the stairs to the tubs.

Gen showed a gritty courage against the excruciating pain of withdrawal and stayed off. One day she came home with lots of fancy boxes. "I was feeling pretty good," she said breathlessly, looking stronger and more radiant than she had in months. She was not only eating and walking again, she was shopping. "And so I took Versey to Fiorucci and bought her $700 worth of clothes for her family."

But to stay off, we knew Gen had to leave. Heroin may have been saving our marriage because it had deadened our sex drives for over a year. But it wasn't saving our lives.

As the days warmed up, the snow began to thaw and icicles dripped from awnings and overhangs. Gen decided to go live and work on the farm owned by her friend Francis Ormsby-Gore way up near Scotland in Shropshire. She also planned to go out to see Tam, whom she missed terribly. Michelle was seeing a new man in her life, a programming director for a radio network in the southwest named Bob Burch. It was a far more stable and conventional home than we could have given him then.

Gen had visited Frank's farm while we were first getting into drug trouble in London. As it was then, Shropshire was still a peaceful, nurturing refuge. Frank's girlfriend was an old friend of Gen's from Europe and L.A. Gen lived in their farmhouse, worked the land every day, and found some inner peace among close friends in the country. When she needed the buzz and energy of the city, she saw friends like the Sarnes in London. But she started drinking.

Gen stayed for three months through the spring. I spent

most of my time locked inside my shooting gallery at 72nd Street. I had a new pack of friends that came and went at will. They were young, attractive, sophisticated—heirs of some of America's most powerful and wealthy families in politics, industry, and society. I knew them from the neighborhood, from Studio 54, or through their parents. They knew me from the music. Sometimes Mick and Keith would be over. With the Stones and other rockers coming in and out, and the endless supply of drugs, the duplex was the best place to indulge their naughty, preppy decadence. They showed up with their Oxford pin-striped shirts hanging out of their Brooks Brothers suit pants, delighted that they didn't have to go to Harlem to score. Some of them insisted on buying small amounts of coke or heroin or pills, and they paid for them with checks and most often the checks would bounce. These kids were worth millions, but, as I had learned, drugs are great levelers. A junkie heir is still a junkie.

One of my new acquaintances was Bobby Kennedy, Jr. Bobby was brilliant, rugged, ambitious, intensely charismatic, and so handsome it was ridiculous to watch women eyeball him on the street. Bobby was a superb jock and outdoorsman. More than his brothers and cousins, Bobby was, it seemed, genetically selected to bear the colossal burden and promise of the Kennedy mystique.

Bobby would usually come by alone to do drugs. His girlfriend at the time, Rebecca Fraser, stayed clear. Sometimes he would come by several nights a week, hang out, get high, then go out again. The syringes, bandages, cottons, pills, spoons, and lighters were all out on the tables for the young heirs. Dilaudids were going for anywhere between $5 and $15 apiece on the street. I never set a price. We were running a candy store. These kids were sharp; they shot behind the knees and places where no one in their straight day world could see the tracks. It didn't even matter if I was around; I was often locked in the bathroom for hours.

Bobby was always welcome. He seemed to have life in balance. He could shoot drugs intermittently for a week and then shoot white-water rapids in some far-flung wilderness. It angered Bobby that I had a severe habit. He was always telling us to stop, that it could kill us. He was, at that point, still stronger than the drugs. He had enough physical strength, willpower, and self-confidence to stay on top of it.

Bobby was always able to stay away long enough not to get real messed up. This was before he became an assistant district attorney in Manhattan. He had been researching a book in Alabama on Frank Johnson, a federal district judge, and whatever drugs he took never seemed to weaken his dedication to working on his future in the law. We were called a few times by Lem Billings, JFK's college roommate and close family friend, who had become a surrogate father to Bobby after Bobby Sr. was killed ten years earlier. Billings pleaded with us not to indulge Bobby's desires for drugs.

Bobby had a taste for shooting speedballs that mixed the hazy euphoria of heroin with the clearheaded invincibility of coke. He could handle himself quite well. We would sit up for hours and discuss politics, literature, jazz, blues, art. I knew Peter Lawford and Andy Williams and I had met his father once or twice during his primary campaign; we knew some of the same people. He knew Frank Ormsby-Gore at Shropshire, and had even stayed there a while before Gen left. And Gen had met Bobby Sr. in the sixties at a rally in South Africa. Frank's father had been an ambassador during John Kennedy's presidency. Bobby had gotten to know Mick and Keith and when they were over, we would stay up to all hours, take out the guitars, and sing blues songs all night. Bobby loved acoustic-style blues the way Keith and Mick could play them, with the Mississippi Delta influence of Robert Johnson.

Ironically, Bobby and Mick shared an even more obscure field of knowledge: opiate substitutes. He and Mick both—at different times—asked me to supply them with the methadone-like Dolophine. Mick, who was angered that Keith and I were destroying ourselves, said he wanted about four hundred of them for Keith during the Stones' upcoming summer U.S. tour. Keith had to stay straight until the trial later in the fall. Almost no one had even heard of the Nazis' World War II morphine substitute. But then Bobby asked me to get a far smaller supply for a relative who was going off to the wilderness to clean out from drugs. In each case, K & B

stocked up on them and I gave them over. I never knew if
Keith ever got them, but I suspected Mick changed his mind
and thought better of it.

Our old friends from rock and Hollywood gradually faded
away, leaving us alone with our one passion—narcotics. I
ran into Elliott Gould on the street and we started hanging
out and shooting baskets in schoolyards. But he came to the
apartment and immediately saw what was going on and took
off.

The place was a stinking mess. The owner of the apartment and his wife had been sleeping in mechanically adjust-
able twin hospital beds because she had been ill a long time.
When we were high, we would crease the beds into odd
shapes and play around on them. Then, when we failed to
pay the electricity bills, the power was cut off for quite some
time and the beds were locked in lumpy positions.

Laura came out for the annual summer-hiatus-game-show
visit. Her boyfriend, rock producer Peter Asher, was in
town, too. Laura was doing a substantial amount of coke-
snorting and ludes, but was still on top of it. But she was so
shaken by our sordid habits that she returned to L.A. and
sent two of her free-basing friends to visit me and try to
wean me from syringes. It was harder to OD on free basing
and the risks of getting blood diseases from dirty needles
were eliminated.

She also appealed to Mick Jagger, whom she visited at the
Château in L.A. when she learned he was in town that summer. "My dad's going to die and you've got to help me help
him." She was pleading with him. "There's all this shooting
going down there."

"There's nothing I or anyone can do. I've tried. He's a
grown man. I can't tell him what to do. I've shaken my
finger at him in New York, in London, in the bathrooms, at
the studio, in the country. I can't haul him out and toss him
into some rehab. I'd go to the ends of the earth for John and
he knows that. But I don't see how I can help at this point."

I was already at the end of the earth. Laura's friends came
into town. I tried free basing. It brought me down too
quickly after the rush and it wasted a tremendous amount of
good blow. They looked at each other as if something might

have been done wrong. There *must* have been some mistake. I should have been flying. The theory behind basing was to burn out the cut and impurities and reduce your stash to purified coke. Because my access to the pharmacy led me to top sources, my coke didn't *need* to be sterilized first. It was *already* close to pure.

"Here," I said, "I've got an idea. Why don't *you guys* take a shot of *my* shit and make up your *own* minds." It was a taste test for junkies: coke versus coke classic. I cooked a shot for each of them. The seduction took less than a minute. I watched their eyes close and they sank back into the couch, moaning with delight. One of them kicked over the small tank of propane, the dish, and the glass pipe used for free basing. "It's yours, man," he muttered. "Where'd you *get* this shit?"

Mike McLean was in New York to cast a film and he started coming by. I had not seen Mike in a couple years, since he came east and helped out during the musical and Gen's album.

When he walked in the door, a look of shock spread over his face. He saw derangement in my eyes; the place was a mess and I was gaunt and diseased-looking. He would come over after the theater or after a long day of casting. We sat around and talked about the old times from *Myra,* the Château, 414, the beach. The reminiscences were painful and I went to the bathroom a few times. I was by then premixing coke shots in syringes, loading in a quarter or half-gram so I just had to run some water in there and shoot.

He would never shoot anything, so I fixed up a free-base hit. He became gloomy after the rush and pushed the works away.

"John," he said solemnly, "what's going *on?* The magic, the gleam in the eyes, the wild and crazy ideas and schemes, the creative spark—it's all gone, man. You yourself were always the first to say heroin was over the line—you've broken your own first rule." He looked down contemptuously at the propane torch. "What is basing, man? Thirty seconds of an incredible rush and wonderful ideas and then everybody crashes and silently sits there staring at the empty pipe, praying desperately that the host fills it up again. I've seen it out in L.A. I know what it's about. It's the worst drug there is."

Denny came down a couple of times and, after our near catastrophe in Halifax, he tried to get me to stop. He saw that I was racing down a dead-end path. One night he was over with Bobby, Mick, Keith, and some other friends and we were having a great time with the guitars and the drugs. Denny was sticking to Crown Royal. I started teasing him. "You don't know what you're missing," I said.

"I have no idea what the fuck is so all-goddamn-consuming about this shit," he said. "Come on, let me have it." He tapped his bicep.

I poked him with a quarter-gram solution and Denny just sat there, waiting for the Heavens to open up. He was lucky. Nothing happened. He shrugged and looked at us all like we were nuts. "Next!" he yelled and opened up his sac of Crown Royal.

I started to worry about the law when I got a call from a very well-known network TV and Vegas entertainer whose livelihood has always depended on a squeaky clean image for Middle America. "I've heard you can really help me out?" he said and asked at the same time.

I had no idea what he was about to ask. "I can't get you a Christmas special, man," I joked, unaware that he was looking to score.

"No no," he laughed. "I need the *other* thing, you know?"

I knew. I didn't want to discuss anything by phone. I told him to come over, but I didn't like the idea of a reputation. He walked in and had obviously never been to a junkie duplex before. I asked him to have a seat, but he looked around and must have decided not to dirty his velour jacket on a week-old Whopper. "So, what can I do for you, anyway?" I asked, getting down to business. I could see he was tense and embarrassed. I assured him that his secret was safe.

"Do you have, like, one, maybe two I could have?" he asked sheepishly. It seemed like a lot of work for that little coke. I shrugged and said, "No problem." I went into another room, thinking I was the only guy this big star had ever come to. He seemed awkward. I tossed him a packet. He opened it and laughed.

"No, man, I'm sorry. Two *ounces.*" I almost dropped dead.

"You're shitting me," I said. I was a Middle American, too. I watched TV. I couldn't believe this guy was a coke fiend. I did what I could for him and he was forever grateful. But I begged him not to send anyone else to see me. I wanted to keep this in the private sector.

More and more, my family was making it to the public record because of me. Out in L.A. in May, just a few months after Laura's arrest and probation, Jeffrey and a new friend of his were booked by police for attempting to rip off a drugstore. He had met the friend where he was working. He didn't know the kid had an arrest record and was, at that, a bungler. He got Jeffrey roped into getting a car and trying to break and enter a pharmacy for drugs.

The irony was chilling. I was walking into K & B like I owned the place and getting shopping bags loaded with drugs. Jeff didn't have K & B; he resorted to B & E. Late at night, while they were high, they broke in and set off a silent alarm. They never even got into the getaway car; there weren't enough parking spaces for all the squad cars that answered the alarm.

Jeff broke down before the arresting officer. "If you guys hadn't caught me," he said, "I probably would have tried this again. Thank God you stopped me. I'm so sorry." Now another one of my children was sentenced to a year's probation for a drug-related arrest.

Gen flew to L.A. to see Tam in late May. Michelle let Tam stay the night with Gen at my sister Rosie's apartment along Pacific Boulevard in Venice. She got Tam for day visits and spent time with him at the beach, on the colorful oceanfront walk of Venice, or riding bikes together.

She got through it with light painkillers and stayed off hard stuff. Rosie watched the soaps all day and Gen read, waiting for her next visit with Tam. It was important for her to reconnect with her son, but she felt that Michelle and Rosie were working against her as his mother and keeping Tam away. Rosie dispensed some sisterly advice to Gen while she was there. "Leave John," she said flatly. "Give up

drugs, get a job and a place to live and no judge will keep
Tam from you. As it is, no judge will give him to you."

"But I *love* John," Gen answered.

"Yes, well, then you better choose," Rosie said. "I am *not*
letting Tam go back to that life and I'm going to be adamant
about it."

Even Rosie had to see that Tam was happy to spend time
with his mother and missed her terribly. But she and Michelle stood firm and refused to let Tam stay overnight with
Gen alone. Gen came home in despair. When word got back
to Rosie and Michelle that Gen wanted to return to L.A.
and take Tam for good in the summer, Michelle filed papers
in an attempt to get custody of Tam.

Gen went out again and stayed with Rosie. This time she
had had enough of the whole mess. She called and told me
she had decided to leave me. Gen told Michelle she wanted
to take an apartment near Rosie, re-enter Tam's life, and
asked her to help her out financially. Michelle declined. Gen
asked me to send her money. "I'm sitting here looking at
twenty grand in front of me in cash," I teased. "You're coming home." She was enraged.

When she got home, I had a sick little surprise waiting for
her under her pillow on the crooked hospital bed: I had gone
to K & B and noticed an eighteen-inch-long fifty-cc. syringe
used only as a display for the medical supply house. The
pharmacists gave it to me and I set it on the pillow next to a
baggie stuffed with flour. Gen knew she was home.

When she first got in, Bobby Kennedy was there with
some other friends. They talked about Frank Ormsby-Gore
and Shropshire and Bobby Sr. Gen knew that 72nd Street
had become a prison. But now she felt cornered, with no one
to help her. I had stood, with my wad of cash, between her
and freedom. I needed her too much. Selfishly, I panicked at
the thought of being abandoned and left alone with my
junkie horror. She was the last ally left and she knew it.
Feeling trapped and depressed, she took her first shot of
Dilaudid within an hour and surrendered once again.

We were booted from the shooting gallery by the owner
when he came by and saw what was happening to his duplex. Another lawsuit for damages was in the works. The

situation with the pharmacy was out of control. I was losing
stashes. I would lock my green Gucci bag and forget the
variable three-digit combination for a day or so. We left the
City and rented a home for the summer in Darien, Connecticut. We were virtually isolated from everyone now, except
my small band of dealers, who kept the triplicate books and
coke coming in as long as I kept the blue-chip stock of pharmaceuticals going out to them.

Gen's parents came to see us in Darien and helped us
unpack. Their long marriage was splitting at the seams over
our situation. We pretended that we were drug-free and
fooled neither of them.

Her father, Lionel, had it in mind to fly to L.A. to per-
suade Michelle to let him and his wife, Audrey, become
Tam's legal guardians. They saw that we were wrecked. Lionel quickly realized the truth: that his grandson was indeed
better off there, with Chynna, Michelle, her husband, and
Rosie. In fact, Rosie had taken formal steps to assume legal
guardianship of Tam in the state of California. She and Michelle were eager to establish California as the jurisdiction
for Tam's case, where they would have a better chance of
winning.

Lionel and Audrey decided, instead, to take care of Gen
and got her out of Darien. They took her home to Durban
for one more brutal cleanout.

It was the dead of winter there and she had a miserable
time with the shakes and chills. Her beloved grandmother
was suffering from cancer. She stayed in a clinic under the
care of a friendly and sympathetic psychiatrist she had
known years before. He weaned her off morphine, but she
was still wracked with pain and fevers between shots.

Gen endured the difficult cleanout and searched for inner
peace by moving to the country and seeking inner calm
through religion. She read the Gospel, attended church, and
prayed. She was gone for almost two months.

Gen had found God and had a powerful vision of Jesus. I
wasn't that lucky. I found Merck and saw coke bugs. That
was our problem: There was nothing in our lives between
ecstasy and torture. An ounce of Merck turned up through
dealers. I was shuttling into town up to three times a week in

a limousine or in my 1978 white Caddie El Dorado with the red interior.

I was so thrilled about the Merck that I started shooting up with an unprecedented ferocity. I was turning into one of those frantic suicidal monkeys strapped to a syringe. I wasn't eating, sleeping, or fucking. I was shooting.

Most coke addicts experience the same bizarre hallucination: disgusting bugs either crawling over them or, in my case, crawling under my skin all over my body. It was the most harrowing aspect of shooting coke and it blew open the door into the void of insanity. The more I shot coke, the more often I saw them: horrible white bugs, like maggots, that wiggled and crawled just below the surface of my skin. Freud knew of this psychotic reaction and it has since been called formiphobia, from the French word for ant, *fourmi.*

I believed not only that they were real, but that they lived in my eyes. They only came out when I shot coke because they got excited. I got sharp surgical tweezers at K & B and began picking away at my skin to try to capture them and preserve them in alcohol cultures. I saw dermatologists and parasitologists and showed them the cultures.

Keith, Anita, and Gen always assured me that there were no bugs. I once made Bobby Kennedy stare at my eyes for fifteen minutes in the bathroom after shooting up—so he could see them come out.

Just as there are quacks who will cure heroin addiction by hooking you to coke, friends can find you a parasitologist who will reinforce your delusions about coke bugs by diagnosing you as having South Carolina sandworms. I found one of them. I was overjoyed at the news. "They're real! They're real! I really DO have worms!" I mumbled to myself as I breezed past half a dozen bewildered patients in the reception area.

I treated myself with salves, insecticides, ointments, creams, and powders used to kill lice and crabs. I went to K & B and instead of drugs I asked them for Sergeant's flea and tick powder. The bugs never went away and I slowly realized that I had been had. I wondered: Had my friend referred me to a parasi*to*logist or parapsy*chol*ogist? I spent hours in the shower, scrubbing my body with abrasive sponges and anti-lice creams, gouging my tracks and sores with a scalpel to pry out the slimy little fuckers.

I asked Lenny Holzer for advice. "I would get a mucous membrane suit and cover your body with it because they come out of the mucous membranes. I'd cover your whole body except for your face and inject right there. Then, when they all come out, I'd rip off the suit and trap them in it and toss the suit into a furnace."

I never found just the right material, so I decided to go with Saran Wrap. One night I covered my entire body with it. I took a shot and waited for them to get trapped inside the suit. When they started crawling, I waited as long as I could —until I was ready to scream in horror. There were thousands of them. I could feel them all burrowing under my skin. I was in utter agony. I peeled off the Saran Wrap as fast as I could, hoping to wipe them off my body. The next time I shot up, though, they were still there.

The side effects of my drug addictions were costing me almost as much as the drugs. My weekly habit was averaging almost $700—$500 for the drugs and $200 for the medical expertise. I finally saw a psychiatrist friend. He watched me shoot coke after discussing the problem with me for an hour. "Tell me exactly when they come out," he said in a grave clinical tone.

I told him when I started to feel them. "Oh Jesus, this is classic. This is great," he said, scribbling notes as he watched me. "This is textbook shit we got here. John," he said, looking up at me, "there ARE no bugs. NONE! You've gotta believe me. It's a classic case. You're NOT covered with bugs." He was so happy that he got up and did a jig. "I'm so thrilled," he said. "Would you mind if I called some of my colleagues to see you? They've been dying to see a bug psychosis case."

"Sure." I was relieved. I didn't care who saw me. "Now for the bad news," he said. "You're stark raving crazy. You're totally fucking nuts."

The bugs finally went away and left me alone. It was a nightmare. I never knew—or appreciated—what sanity was until I realized that I had slipped over to the other side into mental illness.

The Merck I brought up to Connecticut was so strong that I started hyperventilating after one shot too many. I felt so light-headed I couldn't think. Fortunately, I wasn't alone. Two dealers had come back out to Darien with me and the Merck. My vision blurred and I was sure I was dying. I wandered outside, through the fall leaves on the front lawn. I staggered across several yards, trying to keep alive. I felt like I was burning up with fever. I collapsed and passed out on a neighbor's lawn. The police came and hauled me to New Milford Hospital. The dealers saw me off at the hospital and went back to New York with the rest of the Merck.

Not even an OD on synthetic coke could slow me down. The only visitor I had—Gen was still in South Africa—was a local Connecticut dealer. He sat on my bed beside the I.V. pouch. "You want some blow?" he asked.

"You gotta be kidding!" I said. "I can't shoot up here."

"You don't have to shoot up." I saw him nod silently toward the I.V. stand. "What are you talking about?" I asked.

"They already *have* you mainlining. Here."

He closed the door tightly. I had a private room. He took out a vial of coke. I watched as he opened the clear plastic sac at the top of the stand and shook some coke into the tubing. I shook my head. "I don't *believe* you."

By late fall, Gen was home and shooting Dilaudid again. We were in Stamford. "It's almost like we're a couple from a story by John Cheever," Gen said once with her typical sardonic humor, "only with Dilaudid."

I agreed. We were in the heart of Cheever Country, but my real "home" was the drugstore. I lived for the trip into the City to score. My hands and body were covered with sores and abscesses. I was running out of veins. Our hands were scabbed and swollen. There was no stopping it.

At Christmas, we went to L.A. to visit Tam, but Rosie and Michelle made it clear that they would not let us be around him much as long as we were on junk. They were firm. We brought gifts with us, but it was hardly a joyful trip. We returned to Connecticut aware that we would lose Tam for good if we didn't get our shit together fast. I got in touch with another Dr. Feelgood I had met and seen around the music scene in town. He was a young, hip MD who traded prescriptions for hanging out. That was *his* drug. Access.

He'd get stuff from me, I'd get stuff from him, everyone got something from somebody. There were always rock and roll doctors lurking at sessions, concerts, backstage, parties —true seventies Renaissance figures who had found a way to mix expertise in psychopharmacology with a flair for Air Guitar.

The word on this one was that he had successfully detoxed some well-known rockers. "I've heard great things about your cures," I told him on the phone one day that winter.

"They always seem to work," he assured me. "I've taken people to Europe and done it, I've taken people to the country, to the islands, wherever they want to go." It sounded a bit absurd—he just forced you through cold turkey in isolation with guards around to monitor you. I had no choice. I was afraid to go to a hospital because that might lead to publicity and the police. We had to keep this underground and at least the doctor understood the need for strictest privacy. A lot of record deals and concert bookings had hinged on his ability to maintain strict secrecy for his patients.

"I've got this place way out in the woods near Charlottesville, Virginia," he said. "That's probably the best shot for you and your wife."

"Have you seen the snow we're getting?" I asked.

"That's even better. You've really got to get yourself out of where you're at and break the circuit. *No one's* going to get any drugs to you out there, that's for shit sure."

"Yeah, right."

26

I NEVER IMAGINED doing Virginia on $1,000 a day. Actually, it was $2,000 a day, since Gen and I were both going into the Virginia wilderness for the cure. This was a double-occupancy detox. Nine days, eight nights: $18,000. I placed a lot of faith in the doctor. We had come to the end of the line.

I went in thinking I had an edge on him. I had once persuaded him to write a scrip for twelve Dilaudids, even though he preferred I take Percodans. I agreed to the twelve, then went to a stationery store and bought a pen with an exactly matched ink. I carefully altered the one to a seven, filled the scrip at a pharmacy, and ended up with sixty bonus Dilaudids.

Now he was driving us down I-95 through a gray sheet of snow with a couple of partners who weren't physicians. I assumed that they were homosexuals. The house was near Charlottesville, way out in the sticks. The place was solar-heated, but the hot water wasn't hot and the house chilled the bones. He put us in an upstairs room and we sweated, thrashed, and screamed for three or four days until the worst of withdrawal was over.

The first night Gen had a seizure from her withdrawal

and in her disorientation stumbled down the stairs and almost fractured her leg. No one paid any attention to her, though it swelled and bruised and was killing her. It turned into phlebitis. On the fourth day, I grabbed the doctor and knocked him around. "No violence. No violence," he pleaded.

"This whole scam is bogus, you're a fucking crook and an asshole. My wife's leg is all messed up because of your idiocy . . ."

"Please. I've never been hit in my life. No violence."

He was afraid I'd kill him and at that moment I could have. He packed his bags and left the house. He was terrified that I would expose him to police or medical authorities if I got treatment for Gen's leg injury.

With the doctor gone, we were left alone with the musclemen and our panic. The one who seemed to co-own the house told me that he was addicted to Quaaludes and asked me if I could get him five hundred of them. "You're nuts. I'm paying two grand a day and you want *me* to go to New York and score?"

"I thought you'd like to get out of here for a while. I know about the drugstore. You can do it. I'll give you the money upfront."

This was blackmail. He knew I was like a caged beast. He had been a bodyguard at cross-addiction cures before. He knew I'd score Dilaudids up there.

I called two of our young rich friends from East 72nd Street, a boyfriend-girlfriend team worth millions in department store and auto industry money. They were both from Palm Beach and both of their mothers had committed suicide and they were both on methadone. They were part of the block association of East 72nd Street junkie-heirs. But I liked them a lot and asked them to meet me in New York and come back down.

I didn't know why I asked them, why they'd want to travel ten hours in a blizzard. I was so confused. Someone says "Do this" and you jump, just to have something to do as a distraction from withdrawal, an object tossed across your fixated sightline on junk. I couldn't take being alone on the awful endless trip back through the bitter cold and blinding snow.

She said she'd come, he took a pass.

The lisping bodyguard put me on a plane with the cash for the ludes. In the City, I got my car from a garage and made the buy at the pharmacy. I picked up the young socialite and drove to La Guardia Airport. We missed the flight to Friendship in Baltimore by seconds.

I knew there was a long layover at Friendship, and that the plane to Charlottesville was a milk run that stopped three times, every fifteen or twenty minutes, wherever there's an airstrip in the Virginia farmland.

I drove through a heavy snowfall down to Baltimore. The roads were hazardous and the wipers had me hypnotized, along with oncoming headlights at noon through the slanted waves of snow.

She shot herself up in the car with Dilaudid, but I managed to stay clear. We made it to Friendship as the snow let up, but missed the connecting flight to National and Virginia by seconds. We raced back to the car and had less than an hour to get to Washington National thirty-five miles away. We made it by five minutes, but I had to find a good parking spot. The best and closest one to the terminal was marked PRESIDENTIAL PARKING ONLY. I pulled in and shut off the engine. We made a run for it, as she tried to stash her bag of pills in her jeans and the jug of ludes in her purse. We were a mess. I had no socks, my shirt was hanging out, no luggage, the dead of winter.

My mind was a vacuum in which memories mixed indistinguishably with current experiences. I couldn't separate past and present.

Gen's leg was getting worse when we arrived. The heiress's Dilaudids were gone and we left a couple of days later. The lude fiend had a party.

The other guard drove us to Richmond Hospital and Gen's leg was X-rayed negative. She was in agony, but they wouldn't give her painkillers. The kid agreed to drive us to Alexandria on his way up to Pennsylvania. We stopped at a liquor store and tanked up on Jack Daniel's and vodka. By the time we got to my hometown, I thought I was out in

California visiting my sister Rosie. Past and present were one. L.A. was buried under two feet of snow.

I called my old buddy Jimmy Shortt, the town's fire inspector. I had lost my wallet somewhere along the way. Jimmy came and got us, we drove the heiress to the airport, and, as always, Jimmy was right there for us when we needed him. A Del Ray Local forever.

"Where's your wheels?" he said in his good-ole-boy way.

"National."

"We were just *at* National, man."

"That's true. It's in the President's parking spot."

Jimmy called the cops at the airport and asked them if they had tagged any white Caddies. They had and a squad car met us at the spot. The car was filthy, the hubcaps had been stolen, and the battery was dead. I had left the headlights on. There were twelve inches of snow outside, and about eight inside the car. Because I was sweating, I drove the whole way with the windows open and left them open. Jimmy coaxed the cop into jump-starting my car and we drove back to Jimmy's.

We cleaned up, bathed, and settled down in the comfort of Jimmy's lovely home.

"We got to tidy up that wreck 'a yours," he said. "You drivin' a criminal's car, man. Ain't no way you gonna make it back up nawth. Any self-respectin' officer 'a the law'd haul you over and ask for some I.D."

"Now there's *another* problem."

"Well, I'll fix her up so no one'll even bother."

Jimmy was a true friend and I felt incredibly lucky. He bought new hubcaps, had the car washed and waxed and reamed out from the inside, and wouldn't let me leave until it looked new again. It took two days. He loaned me a grand —after getting an assurance from Bob Tucker in New York that he would wire him the money a day later—and nursed us back to health.

That night Jimmy had his weekly bowling league and left us alone. I went out for a drive and got some dinner. Gen stayed home with her wounded leg. I was so whacked-out that I didn't even know my way around Alexandria anymore. It was every child's nightmare—I couldn't find my way home.

I came back to Jimmy's and found Gen sitting on the stairs, drunk, eyes rolling, waving Jimmy's two loaded .45s in the air. The guns were licensed; Gen wasn't. I walked up the four or five stairs and very carefully sat down next to her and disarmed her. She had found them in his nightstand while rummaging around for pills. I never mentioned this to Jimmy.

Jimmy and his wife waved good-bye to us the next morning and they both must have been relieved to see us go.

We got back to New York and stayed in the Beekman Tower Hotel on the East Side. Keith happened to be staying there too. The next time I stopped by the Connecticut house, I got my 12-string guitar and brought it into town so he and I could jam again. We got in touch with another rock and roll doctor familiar with the Stones, another pill "writer"— the street term for a doctor who will write prescriptions for narcotics and other drugs on demand for a nominal fee. He had been doing it for rock stars for a long time. He gave Gen a couple of downers and then we all went to a party downtown at the club John Belushi owned. When the pills kicked in, Gen spun out and nearly passed out. She was holding on to the bar so hard that she almost pulled it over. She could hardly stand. Belushi asked me to take her home.

At the hotel, I encountered a rock guitarist and his brother who were setting up a drug buy. They came to our room and I got myself a little coke. I didn't notice then, but one of them also made off with the prized Guild 12-string, the one I had used ten years earlier on "Creeque Alley" and "San Francisco" and so many other songs. I felt incomplete without it. It was rare and irreplaceable. I was furious, but the scumbags were long gone by the time I went after them.

We drove to Stamford and when I woke up the next afternoon I realized immediately that I needed to go to the pharmacy. There was just no way I could go on without drugs. I started going back to K & B once, twice a week to load up on Dilaudid and Desoxyn.

We spent our days in seclusion, reading and shooting. We hardly ate; we picked at thawing frozen foods. I was anemic

and in a hazy twilight zone between reality and madness.
Now and then I would shoot some speed or coke to get
moving again. Sex was history. We watched soaps and felt
that all that lusting and sexual intrigue was absurd.

Gen again left for Africa to stay clean. By now, her parents had split up and her father had moved to France.

The deals were as routine as picking up some shampoo
and toothpaste. I'd call, ask if everything was okay, say I
wanted to come by. If there was a special order, I'd have to
give them a couple of days. There were no cryptic codes, no
passwords.

I was meeting the dealers—now it was always the same
two or three men—at their apartments or in a limo somewhere. Often the dealer would give me the cash and wait
down the street from K & B at a pizza joint while I picked
up the shopping bag. Then he'd give me the coke. I was into
shooting more and more Desoxyn—synthetic speed. The
shot lasted for hours, didn't bring back the bugs, and it
spared my veins unnecessary abuse. They were pretty flattened out by now.

When Gen came back, we lapsed again and decided to
clean out away from the City. By now we were desperate to
have Tam back in our lives. He had been with Michelle for
eighteen months. But we had to get—and stay—clean.
When we lost the lease in Stamford in the spring of 1979, we
decided to go to Bermuda and clean out for good.

I took with me only a modest stash of Dolophines to ease
me through cold turkey.

The first few days were hot and dry and we had everything under control. We got a lovely cottage by the deep blue
bay in Bermuda. The owner was a spry, well-traveled elderly
widow who lived across the street and only rented to people
she met and liked. Gen represented us with her charm, girlish naïveté, and brainy wit. They had tea and discussed
Spain and France and South Africa. Gen wrote her a poem
about our little place by the water. She really got over on the
woman. There were no car rentals, so we had to rent mopeds
to get around.

I hid the Dolophines in a mossy hollow under a rock at
the base of a tree. Junkies are notorious for lying and hiding

—even with spouses who are fellow junkies. Gen wouldn't have needed them. She was always less susceptible to the symptoms of cold turkey; she'd drink herself into oblivion and awaken after the pain wore off.

As the withdrawal came on, I'd go out and bite off a chunk of a pill and get by. Then my troubles began. It rained.

I had fallen out and awoke, in some flulike pain, to the light drumming sound of rain against the roof and windows. I wandered out half-naked in the morning downpour and threw myself to the ground at the base of the tree. I lifted the rock and saw nothing but a grayish paste where the Dolophines had dissolved into the dirt. I let out a beastly howl and clawed at the paste and dirt. I dug into the mud and dabbed some on my tongue, tasting for the Dolophines. I gagged on the dirt and spit it out as rain soaked my hair and body.

"Gen," I said as I stomped in, "I'm fucked." I told her what I had done. "You've got to go to the mental hospital on the island and tell them we need migraine medication."

Gen was as committed and willing as ever. "I thought you were really serious about getting off drugs, but if you want some, then let's go."

We made it to a hospital, but it wasn't easy. We had to navigate on mopeds while going cold turkey. Quite a road test. Just before 8 A.M., as the morning shift was taking over from the departing midnight-to-eight crew, we checked into the emergency room. We wore sunglasses, winced a lot, and looked like we were in terrible pain. Some fine acting by Gen. Our nurse was weary and crabby at the end of her night on duty.

"We've got terrible migraines and we're on vacation and our luggage is lost with all our pills," I explained as Gen nodded in support. More wincing, more holding our heads. "Your names?" the worker asked. "Mr. and Mrs. Black."

We got free shots of morphine and names of neurologists. A few hours later we were craving more. It was as if our lives were now being played out as a board game called DETOX and we kept going backward to the big square that read COLD TURKEY. They wouldn't give us a scrip for narcotics until we had one from an MD. "Too much hassle," I said. "We're on vacation." But I had a plan.

The next day we returned to the same emergency room but waited until just after 8 A.M., when the day shift was already on. We told the same story—same glasses, grimaces, and moans. "Your names?" the new nurse asked, filling out the report. "Mr. and Mrs. Green."

We got new patient cards, saw different doctors, and took another round of morphine. "This is the only shot we can give you," the MD said, "until you see a neurologist."

We were beginning to thrash and trash the duplex cottage. It wasn't because we wanted to be destructive; we were out of our minds. We knocked stuff over, smashed things. We were in a lot of pain, but Gen was doing better than me. I could barely walk and I was seeing double and stuttering.

I tried to get to the hospital on the moped, but I almost killed myself half a dozen times, wiping out in the road. My sense of balance was ruined and I had double vision. When the sun went down, we were getting wild. We took a taxi back to the emergency room. This time we waited until just after four in the afternoon; the 8 A.M.-to-4 P.M. nurse would be gone and the four-to-midnight crew, who we hadn't met yet—would be on duty. We went through the charade for a third set of nurses and doctors. "Your names?" we were asked.

"Mr. and Mrs. White." We thought the color-coded system might just keep us on free morphine forever. But the next morning we returned and slipped up. Our timing was off. We saw the nurse who processed us in the morning as the Blacks and told her we were the Greens. That was our 8 A.M.-to-4 P.M. color.

"Just wait here a moment," she said. She got a psychiatrist to come out and see us. He was very serious and firm.

"Obviously," he said, "you people have a problem."

"Yes, we're color-blind." He was in no mood for humor. I admitted we were strung out. He was quite decent. He gave Gen sleeping pills and told her to rest. I was admitted to a fortresslike psychiatric unit way up on a hill. I was the only patient in there for a drug cure. Everyone else there was *really* crazy: paranoid schizophrenics and suicidals and hand-washers all pacing around, drooling and raving. A real snake pit.

They zonked me with a giant load of Thorazine. When I awoke, a huge black native was at the end of my bed, shaking my leg and screaming, "Wake up! They're going to kill you! Get out of here immediately! Your life is in danger!" I told him that would make two of us if he didn't back off.

The withdrawal this time was severe. I hadn't been shot up in sixteen hours. Thorazine was like a sleeping pill for me. I looked around; patients were twiddling thumbs, their eyes and faces twitched, they were clawing their arms, muttering to themselves, and pacing.

I tried to reason with a nurse. "Look, there must be some mistake, miss," I said calmly. "I've been admitted to the wrong ward. A lot of staff here isn't real fluent in English. I said that my problem upon admission was Dilaudid, not *deluded.*"

I called Gen and asked her to come and sign papers releasing me. Once again she came through, even though she thought if I could hang in there for another two days I'd make it. "I won't *make* two days here. I know that."

We got a cab right outside the psychiatric hospital. "Where's the black gambling club in town?" I asked the driver.

His eyes shot back to me in the rearview mirror. He knew I was crazy then. He gave me the name of the place, but shook his head. "No white people ever go there. Police don't even go in there. It's not for tourists. It's for criminals and people like that."

"How fast can we get there?"

He pulled the cab over and refused to drive us. The third driver who stopped agreed to go and I laid $10 on him. The driver introduced me to the thug at the door and said I wanted to play cards. "You got money?" he asked. We were the only whites. All eyes turned to Gen, a slinky, well-shaped blond with wild, kinky hair and huge angelic blue eyes.

I flashed a roll of ten grand. I dropped a quick five hundred at one table, just as a lure. I took one of the card dealers aside, having earned his sympathy. I told him I had a

problem that needed to be solved immediately. He nodded
with complete understanding. "Come on," he whispered.

He and two pals were relaxed as they took us to a house
with some white musicians, fishermen, and rich yachting
types who were hanging out among the blacks. It was a
shooting gallery. Everyone there was hitting up for $25 a
pop.

"Keep hitting me till I tell you to stop," I said. I was too
fucked up to do it myself. I met a young blond kid who
worked on a fishing boat. He gave us each some shots in the
arm and leg. We had to get a shot every fifteen minutes
because it wasn't high-grade smack.

We scored about two grand in quarter bags and a bunch of
syringes. Then the three of us went back to the cottage.

"Holy shit," the kid moaned when he walked in, "this
place has been hit by burglars."

"Wrong, man," I said. "It's been hit by cold turkey." The
paintings faced the wall, lamps were lying across the floor,
glasses were broken, chairs were overturned. I didn't remember doing any of it.

The widow chose the next day to stop by and invite Gen
for tea. She took one look inside, stiffened, clutched her
chest, and nearly had a heart attack. She ran out screaming.

I called my Heir-Head friends in New York, the only two
people I trusted with this request. I instructed the boyfriend
to score some Dilaudid from my dealer and fly down immediately. He was there in a day with his girlfriend, who I had
last seen in the snow at National Airport. We all moved to a
resort hotel and stayed in a big bungalow.

The guy and I went into town and when we came back the
bungalow was jammed with cops. The widow had gone to
the police and trailed us. We were nailed with the drugs and
paraphernalia right there. I thought we were going to be
lifers on Bermuda.

We were brought to a jail and I called Bob Tucker in New
York. He stayed calm and asked to speak to the chief of
police. Tucker told him that we were wealthy, that he
worked for a giant U.S. firm, that he would make contact
with a local law firm and promptly get the bail money to
spring us.

Money talks. A couple grand shrieks. We never made a
court appearance. We could have been looking at forty-eight
years; we ended up with forty-eight hours to leave Bermuda.
As it worked out, when the local lawyer came by and arranged for us to leave the stockade, he read the arrest report
and grinned. "I can't believe people like you went to a joint
like that to shoot up," he said, shaking his head.

"Why?"

"My brother's one of the guys who runs it."

We returned to the City and stayed in a hotel. I made a
trip to the pharmacy and we were back on junk an hour
later, mixing it with barbiturates and coke. We were fugi-
tives, slipping from hotel to hotel, beating the bills when
possible.

The torment of addiction was unbearable. All the attempts to detox had failed and only complicated our lives.
Dr. D got me cross-addicted. Gen's trips to England and
Africa led her to alcohol. We had given up our son. Virginia
was a cruel sham. Bermuda was a close and costly brush
with the law. And wherever we went, we left a wake of
junkie havoc. The cats inside us had ripped through our skin
and grown into angry beasts. We were trapped in their lethal
jaws with no way out.

Several days later, in mid-June, I got a call from Rosie,
who tracked us down somehow. "It's Mom," she said. I
waited, trying to focus my mind. "She's had a massive
stroke. You better come out. They don't expect her to make
it through a week."

It all came to a sudden stop. My mother was dying. We
had to go west, but there was no way we could take enough
drugs with us and I could never set up a good enough contact in L.A. We were going to have to fly once more straight
into the deadly turbulence of cold turkey.

In my panic, I raced to K & B and got all the Dolophines
and Dilaudids they could spare, about a forty-day supply.
Then we left for the coast.

Laura picked us up and took us to my mother's house in
Tarzana. The early withdrawal and the scene there brought
me down in a hurry. Rosie and Michelle were still reluctant
to let us have Tam for more than a day visit. They had been

preparing sworn affidavits and getting medical and psychological "witnesses" to state that Tam was in better shape with Michelle. She, Rosie, and Marika all weighed in with their horror stories—that Chynna and Tam had both seen us or our friends shooting up, that Tam had to be de-liced and innoculated when he got to Michelle's, that he stared at the TV all the time, that Chynna's "jet lag" was in fact part of her traumatic reaction to having stayed with us, that Tam was eating better, enjoying a more normal schoolboy life, and developing new friends. They brought out all the big guns and were hoping to get full custody as long as we were on junk.

Michelle had him during the week so he could be with Chynna. They were both enrolled in the same Montessori school. Tam was seeing a child psychiatrist, the same one Michelle found for Chynna after her nightmares upon returning to Michelle eighteen months earlier.

Tam stayed with Rosie in Venice on weekends to go to the beach, feed the ducks in the Venice canals behind her apartment, and visit with his cousins. He seemed to be healthy and cheerful and they obviously had taken good care of him. But he was still our flesh and blood and we wanted him back.

I saw my mother at the hospital, all hooked up to machines, and I saw that I would never speak to her again or hear her voice. Through the physical symptoms of kicking, I felt an intense sadness, knowing she was already gone. We had drifted farther and farther apart as she grew older and drank more heavily. I sat beside her in gloomy silence and wondered what kind of life she would have had among her Cherokee people in Oklahoma if she had never left that dusty barren town of Okmulgee. Her assimilation had been pretty thorough as she neared seventy-five. She had a home in the Valley, blue hair, a Lincoln Continental, and a couple of hours of soaps every afternoon. I would have wanted to ask her one last time about Roland Meeks, the man she once told me was my real father. But she didn't move, didn't speak. The stroke had left her half-paralyzed, mute, and semi-aware. There would be no deathbed secrets revealed. Rosie said she had become slightly senile, asking if the children were ready for school, if the bus had come yet. She was confusing her poodles with children and probably had earlier, undetected strokes.

After a week in the Valley, Gen and I were getting sicker by the hour and had to get out. We were leaving syringes around and I knew that my nieces, Nancy and Patty, knew the score. The drugs were dwindling fast.

My brother Tommy had been living there with the latest in a string of younger women. I hadn't seen him in years and that was depressing. He was a big drinker and had a fat belly. He had driven a cab and worked as a short-order cook in a Boston hotel. He was divorced, but was still in touch with some of his adopted stepchildren out west.

I hadn't seen him since he showed up in Bel Air in the late sixties. I gave him a car to use and a room at 783. He was a bartender and when he got fired he put on a Lone Ranger mask and tried to rob the bar. "Come on, Tommy," the owner said, handing him the money from the register in the middle of the afternoon. "We know it's you."

"I don't know what you're talking about," he said. "Who's Tommy?" It was so pathetic.

He made his getaway and backed into a cop car leaving the parking lot. I got him out of jail after a weekend and the next thing I knew, the San Francisco cops had him in custody with my wallet. He had checked into a motel, using my credit card, and was so fucked-up he spelled our last name with four *p*'s at the end. The clerk became suspicious.

He moved to San Francisco, then came down to L.A. and moved in with my mother. He drove her nuts. He was a compulsive talker who would rant and rave at her when she went to the bathroom or watched her soaps.

He had even managed to assume control over my mother's finances after her stroke, according to Rosie, cashing in her three monthly government checks—$2,000 total—and signing for her credit cards. The bank didn't spot the forgeries because his handwriting was shaky from booze and he was able to convince the bank that it looked that way because she had a disabling stroke. Tommy had been so badly shaken by what he saw and did in World War II combat that he was never the same once he came home. We were ten years apart and I never felt connected to him as a brother; I was in no shape to make contact now.

We crawled out a window in Tarzana and moved into Le Parc Hotel in West Hollywood with the help—and credit card—of my old friend Mike McLean. We had been off drugs for a week and we were getting wild.

We complained to the front desk about migraines and tried to get Percodans—anything. We got a doctor to write us scrips for the kind of electric shock box Gen had used in London. We fought, we stumbled, we roamed the halls in our silk kimonos and matching electrode sets, we trashed the room and got moved around as guests complained.

Finally, we just snapped one day and started screaming at each other. We were wearing our colorful kimonos. Gen was wearing nothing under hers and the brawl carried out into the hallway, past a couple of housekeeping carts and room service trays on the floor, down the elevator and out. Gen stormed through the lobby and wandered toward Santa Monica Boulevard with the untied sash of her kimono flowing behind her. I ran down after her in mine.

The hotel eventually had enough. Management called McLean because he had checked us in on his card. Mike liked his own house just the way it was; he didn't want us there. We couldn't go back to Tarzana because my brother drove me crazy and we were trying to close up the house. I was down to a couple of thousand dollars in my New York bank. Mike called Tucker in New York, Tucker called Bill Cleary, my Del Ray Local buddy and Smoothie partner, in Newport Beach.

We got a limo to take us down to Bill's big house in the ritzy Balboa Peninsula section on the water. He and his girlfriend Louise were most generous. Bill worked hard to keep us clean. It wasn't easy. I had already called my nephew Billy in L.A. and asked him to score us some Mexican brown and he refused. I knew he would—and I knew he'd report to Rosie.

When we got there, we couldn't write our names. Gen wanted to continue work on her poetry and novel, but couldn't hold a pen. I had the shakes. I was so frail and weak that I could barely cross the street. I had to lift my leg up with my hands to plant my foot on a high curb.

Bill and Louise made us eat fruits and vegetables every day and take vitamins. Bill and I started playing music together. Louise and Gen got along well. Gen read a book every day or so. They had us swimming and riding bikes. I couldn't go ten feet without tipping over at first. My strength and balance were shot. We rented boats and went out in the ocean and slowly worked our way back among the living.

And loving. When a junkie detoxes, the body resensitizes itself as the brain begins to manufacture its own form of natural pleasure-inducing opiates called endorphines. These are the chemicals that give the glowing rush after jogging or sex.

Heroin blocks the brain from making endorphines. You don't want or need sex when you're hooked; you can certainly get by without jogging shoes. When the nervous system reawakens in withdrawal, there are some weird reactions. The binding effects of heroin give way to chronic diarrhea and mighty flatulence. Sexual urges heat up with wilting intensity. Gen said she was having spontaneous orgasms while walking around with her clothes on. And off. After well over a year, we were making love once again.

As we began to repair ourselves, we asked for more time with Tam. Rosie and Michelle still wouldn't let him stay with us overnight. They were both driving down on weekends so we could see him and take him sailing and swimming.

Laura came out a few times in her flashy red Mercedes. She was going through her own hassles over Peter Asher. She had been with him for two years, but he was considering, she thought, reconciling with his wife, Betsy, who lived in their old house in Coldwater Canyon. Laura was tormented. She had been happy with Asher. It went back and forth.

She and Peter went to New York for a James Taylor concert and she met a young hipster named Jeff Sessler who worked as a gofer for Keith and the Stones. I had known Jeff's father, Freddie, for years. He ran weight-loss clinics in

Florida and the Stones seemed to know him well, too. Laura was sure she had fallen madly in love with young Sessler—and at least had some leverage in dealing with Asher.

She hadn't even known Jeff for two weeks when she called me from Florida and impulsively announced plans to elope with Sessler. Everyone tried to talk her out of it. They just didn't seem to be that compatible. It was too rash. We all tried to talk sense into her. Bill and I did; Asher tried. Sessler's own *parents* told her that it would be risky. *Betsy Asher* called Laura and offered *Peter* back if it would keep her from taking the plunge with Sessler. Laura was in a vulnerable spot and her judgment was distorted. She was making well over $30,000 a week from "One Day." She was also doing large amounts of coke and ludes and was being scrutinized by her producers. She didn't need any more bad press.

Bill and I flew to Miami and stayed in the same hotel as Laura and Jeff. The wedding was already planned, so I tried to stall for time and get her to hold off. We met with Jeff's family and they were no happier about the marriage than we were.

"You owe it to your family. Let them meet the guy," I said emotionally. "Take your time and think it over." She wasn't in a thinking mode. The more pressure she got to dump the kid, the deeper she dug in. She was rebellious and headstrong. "You can't come out here," she snapped, "and tell me what to do. Don't tear this apart and fuck up my life, dammit."

"No, kiddo," I said, "I'm trying to *fix* your life." She trusted my intuition enough to come back to L.A. We were in first class, taxiing on the runway. They were across the aisle from me. I gave her a pair of Tuinals. She dreaded flying. She gave one to Sessler. Tuinals are downs that can make you feel okay about air travel. They make you feel even better about sex. Sessler whispered something to her and they got out of their seats. She gave me a naughty look and they headed back to the lavatory. The plane hadn't taken off yet and they were already flying.

She returned to the show for the fall episodes. Asher was calling all the time, trying to head her off and asking her back. They met at his apartment in the Château and she tried to hide her engagement ring. Then she gave in. She decided to go back with Asher and told Sessler it was all over.

When James Taylor played the Greek, she met Asher backstage, but Betsy Asher then called and said *she* was coming down and wanted Laura out of there. Asher sent Laura back to the Château in a limo and she was really freaking out by now. When Asher returned hours later, he tried to wake her and talk.

"Look," he said, "I've been up all night talking with Betsy . . ." She didn't want to hear it and rolled over into a deep sleep. When she awoke, she walked out, found Sessler, and married him in Englewood on August 15. If she had stayed awake long enough to hear Asher out, he would have told her that he and Betsy had decided, after all, to get a divorce.

Despite my hunch about Jeff, I rented John Wayne's yacht, the *Wild Goose,* out of Newport Beach, for a twenty-four-hour wedding party a couple of weeks later. The yacht was a converted minesweeper in Newport Harbor and was available for parties. It was a fabulous affair. We picked up our L.A. guests in Marina Del Ray and plied the harbor all night long. We had two bands on deck. The bride and groom got Wayne's luxurious stateroom and made love on his bed beneath a portrait of the Duke himself on the wall.

Beautiful Hollywood couples were bouncing in and out of the private rooms all night. We got a few tickets for disturbing the peace. I was almost clean. I had a few shots of speed and vitamins, but I felt and looked great, with a tan and a dapper nautical look—white pants, saddle shoes and no socks, white shirt, blue double-breasted blazer with brass buttons, and a captain's cap. Laura was radiant in a white antique dress Peter had bought her in a New York shop.

I stopped her at one point and talked on the deck. We were both happy that night. She was sure she had made the right decision and I gave her my blessings. Tam and Chynna were able to come with Michelle's permission; Rosie came onboard in the spirit of a peacekeeping mission. We were at least talking again.

It was a gorgeous balmy night at sea with a lot of friends.

I told Laura how beautiful she looked. "Where are you going now?" she asked. I wiggled my eyebrows and gave her a sly leering glance. "I'm going to my stateroom to abuse the Zulu."

After the party, Laura and Jeff took off for a honeymoon in Hawaii. While they were away, Laura's house in Laurel Canyon was destroyed by fire. That marriage wasn't meant to be.

Tucker called me and let me know that another one of those mysterious royalty checks had popped up on a computer somewhere and before I knew it I had another hundred grand to play with. Gen and I dressed in style, behaved ourselves, and finally persuaded Rosie to let Tam start spending Sundays with us. Michelle was out of town briefly. So Rosie brought Tam and Chynna for several weekends in a row and we bought them roller skates, boogie boards, and skateboards and had a great time. Tam was clearly happy to be back with his own parents.

By the early fall, we learned that Gen was three months pregnant and the child was expected by April. She was afraid at first because the baby had been conceived in withdrawal when she was drinking and smoking grass. We had both been hooked and mainlining for years. And our marriage was hardly serene. She had asked to leave several times and at one point got out of my Cadillac, which had been driven west by a friend, and crawled on her knees, begging for a divorce.

I had another nightmare about a small child—this time a ship was sinking in a storm at sea. The child was drowning in cold, gray, choppy waters. I was in the water, flailing and lunging for the child with a life preserver and getting closer, closer, as the swells lifted our bodies and pulled us apart.

At the moment I touched the child's desperate hand and pulled it close to me, I awoke—much as I had after the dream when Tam was conceived—drenched in sweat and flushed with the aura of a miracle.

"We're having this baby," I decided, "and you aren't going anywhere. This baby is going to save our lives. Our lives will be horrible if we don't have this baby. Something awful will happen. She will be our salvation." Or at least one part of it. The other part, we realized, was Tam.

Through a local drugstore I had gotten the name of a "writer"—an elderly Chinese physician whom the druggists knew to be prolific in his scrip writing for hire. "He's phasing out his practice," I was assured. "He needs to do a volume business." I met him several times over a few weeks in the fall. He was gentle and sympathetic, with white hair and a sweet wrinkled smile. And he was prolific. I began stockpiling Dilaudids, hundreds of them, along with syringes.

Rosie's trips with Tam had gone well and we were finally ready to take him overnight. Michelle insisted, though, on a meeting beforehand at which Dr. Baker, who was Tam's therapist, Gen, Michelle, and I discussed a gradual and months-long plan to get Tam back into our lives out west. In Michelle's view, the plan was positive, orderly, and fair. But it was in California, where they had papers showing Rosie to be Tam's legal guardian. I wanted any eventual legal action moved to a state where we'd have a better shot.

The endless psychodramas were taking their toll on Rosie. In the midst of all the wrangling about access to Tam, she suffered scary cardiac arrhythmias and was hospitalized for tests and close supervision. It was clear that she had to start taking it easy again.

Just days after she was released, she and Michelle finally consented to let Tam stay overnight with us at Bill's in Newport. By November 11, the day Rosie arrived with Tam and Chynna, we had close to four hundred Dilaudids and boxes of syringes secretly stashed away. We were going to need all of it.

This was our only chance. There was no other way to handle it. We had Tam, we had the car, and we had more than enough pure morphine to survive the drive across America with our boy. We were going to try to make it as a family all over again.

We didn't know they were going to call it kidnapping.

27

ONCE ROSIE LEFT US alone with Tam and Chynna, Gen secretly made it out to the airport and got a flight with Tam to Las Vegas. As the hours wore on, I feigned concern and called Michelle. I told her I was getting worried, that they had gone out shopping and maybe to a movie, then possibly to dinner. I had Chynna with me and she was extremely upset. Jeff, who was visiting me, drove Chynna back to Michelle.

Gen called and was tense about the drugs and the abduction. She took a room at Circus Circus, a hotel oriented to kids and families, with high-wire acts in the lobby, jugglers and magicians in the elevators.

Michelle reported Tam's disappearance to the LAPD and they turned it over to the FBI as a federal child-stealing case because it was assumed that state lines had been crossed. Over several days, I was quizzed by the authorities in L.A. and Newport. I also secretly flew to Vegas twice to drop off drugs and money to Gen.

Finally, I called Michelle to say I had heard from Gen. I said she had taken Tam to Vegas without my knowledge or consent and that I was quite upset with her. I was going to Vegas to retrieve her and Tam.

I drove my Caddie through the desert to Vegas and joined them at Circus Circus. When we were all finally reunited and on our own, Tam looked at us and ran to me. He threw his arms around me. "I'm so happy. It's like a dream that really came true. Do you guys know how many nights I've gone to bed at Michelle's and just dreamed that you would come and take me away."

I had about fifty grand in cash and four hundred four-milligram Dilaudids. We stayed in Vegas for about a week and then hit the road on the lam, heading east. It was like Bonnie and Clyde and Tam. I heard radio reports that we were missing, so I stuck to the back roads. I let Tam help with the steering. He was on a wild adventure. He was almost nine, sitting on my lap, piloting a huge white Caddie. I had to stay on the road eight hours a day and whenever I had to shoot up in the car to maintain, Tam was eager to take the wheel. He wasn't freaked out. He had seen his daddy take his "shots."

"You know," Gen said optimistically, "we could really make it on a maintenance dose of eight milligrams a day, like now. That's all it would take and we wouldn't look stoned and we could function. Why do they have to keep taking our Dilaudids away? Why can't it be civilized like in England, where you register as a junkie with the government. Look at us. We're dressing nicely, we don't have the obvious sores, we're at a good weight. We're going to movies and stuff. That Chinese doctor was such a sweetheart. He really saved our lives."

We took a southerly route through Oklahoma so I could visit my mother's homeland. Okmulgee was still there in the eastern third of the state, just near the border of the Cherokee Nation in the middle of nowhere.

I had never been out to Oklahoma and in my mind I tried to picture the dusty Main Street and saloon where Claude and Edna first set eyes on each other more than half a century earlier. It was all gone now. One old toothless geezer, a half-breed like me, smacked his wind-puckered lips together at his one-pump gas station and vaguely remembered the Gaines Boys were "real bad guys, right? Ain't heard nuffin' 'bout 'em in years." I asked him if he remembered where the saloon once stood in the center of town and he squinted into the hot midday sun and motioned to a busy intersection with stop lights. "That's it," he said. "Long gone."

By the time we got near Manhattan, most of the Dilaudids were shot. New York, with all my drug contacts, was too crazy. We had to get into Cheever Country. Connecticut was revising its child-stealing laws. I had been advised that we had a better chance there. Darien and Stamford were out. We arrived at Old Greenwich, a quaint, upscale Yankee enclave on Long Island Sound. It was just before Thanksgiving. The town was gearing up with its great New England tradition and hot turkey. We were heading toward cold turkey.

We stayed in a Holiday Inn and I remembered a quarter bag of street heroin that had slipped behind the steering column months earlier. I had never been able to pry it out. Heroin proves that necessity is the mother of addiction. I bought a tool kit in a local hardware store and spent the next eight hours in trembling agony, dismantling the Caddie dashboard and steering column. Finally, the packet dropped out.

The phone rang one morning and it was a woman identifying herself as a reporter from *People* magazine. I didn't know how she knew where we were. *This was supposed to be the hotel chain with no surprises,* I thought.

"Michelle says she has charged you with felonious kidnapping," the reporter said. "She also said the two of you are both junkies. Do you have any comment?"

"I remember that we dabbled with heroin once."

We split the Holiday Inn and rented a beautiful haven tucked away on the Sound along Shore Road with top-of-the-line large porches leading from the living room and the bedroom upstairs and a spectacular southeastern view overlooking Long Island Sound.

"We're turning into over-Cheevers," I said. The house was owned by a family named Finch. They had not moved in yet because Mr. Finch was still tied up with his IBM job out of town. We were flanked by Steve and Chris Thurlow and their two beautiful kids on one side and Bob and Joan Blackmore and their family on the other. The house came sparsely furnished.

We introduced ourselves to Steve and Chris Thurlow. They were in their thirties, youthful, and attractive. I had to put on the best possible front. I couldn't exactly say, "Hi, we're your new neighbors. I'm John, this is Gen, and we're heroin addicts from Manhattan who are into trashing and we're on the run from half a dozen homeowners, the state of California, and the FBI and we're facing a federal child-stealing rap. What are *your* names?"

Steve had been a pro running back with the New York Giants and the Washington Redskins in the sixties. We had actually met, he recalled, in Washington in the late sixties through mutual friends and hung out at a couple of bars once or twice. We all hit it off right away and I was able to talk sports for hours with Steve, a tall, muscular guy who had clearly done quite well for himself in investment banking.

More than the other neighbors, I felt that Steve understood the peaks and traps of celebrityhood, the roar of the crowd, the sniping in the press, the pressures of performing in public. They responded to us as friends, not fans.

The Thurlows were devout Catholics, socially active, caring, and warm. Dream neighbors. We went over there and sang along with tapes of the Stones project and Gen's album and had some good times with them over beers and pizzas. Chris, a tall, stunning beauty with short auburn hair and deep blue eyes, had quite a good voice and ear for doo-wop harmonies.

I came into town to see my main dealer, Andy, and K & B in late November. I hadn't seen him in close to half a year and he was edgy. He told me we were going to the apartment of another dealer named George on First Avenue. I had met George once a year earlier through Andy during another buy. At that time, Andy told me George had been the source for his triplicates all along.

Now, as we sat there in George's luxury high-rise apartment, a major change was in the works and it made me nervous. Andy had been busted and was under indictment. He told me he was going to leave the country and go to

London, then Israel, rather than face the charges of trafficking. From now on, it was agreed, I would get books and cash and coke from George and give all the pharmaceuticals to him. George, he said, would give me a dollar more per pill than I had gotten from Andy because the middleman, Andy, was now out of the picture.

One crisp fall weekend, Steve Thurlow and I drove up together into northern Connecticut and cut down our own Christmas trees at a tree farm. We talked about the serene life-style of Old Greenwich. I said we wanted out of the City for Tam's sake, that he needed other kids around, that I was working on an album. He had no idea that I was living a secret life as a junkie and drug dealer. As we drove through the beautiful country in the late-afternoon light, I could feel the pills and syringes in my coat pockets and I thought of my next shot. At night I was always dropping over—their house was no more than fifty feet away from ours across a lawn and driveway—and Steve and I often watched "Monday Night Football."

Chris visited Gen across the way in our kitchen. Gen had wild frizzed-out hair and an outrageous getup. "I'll give you a list," Chris said helpfully, "with the nearest pharmacy, supermarket, pediatrician, dentist, laundry, dry clean . . ."

"You've seen my teapot, haven't you?" Gen interrupted.

"Pardon me?"

"Well it's Art Deco, you know."

"Oh no, I'd love to see it," Chris answered, thrown off course by Gen's non sequitur. She was just getting used to Gen's humor and stream of consciousness. Gen handed her a teapot with a handle fashioned in the shape of a reclining nude woman.

Chris and her local women friends chipped in some furniture—Joan kicked in a dining room table, Chris donated a rocker, some lamps and towels, dishes and silverware.

We tried in vain to stay quiet, not draw undue attention or rock the boat. We were still underground. No one knew where we were. Gen was nervous and always dropping in on Chris and talking her ear off. Chris was overwhelmed.

Tam played with their two children, Katie and Michael, but was always high-strung and watching our every move in and out of the house. I was stopped by local cops when I pulled out of a nearby McDonald's with the headlights off. I had no license on me. The cop followed me home so I could find some I.D. The last thing I needed was a dumb little fuckup with the local cops. My fear—and my assumption— was that they would run a check on me and find out a warrant for my arrest had been issued in California.

It occurred to me that when Rosie and Michelle found out where I was someone might be looking to snatch Tam. And I had a new dealer in the City. A fever started to rise around my brain.

I decided to bring things out in the open and take off the pressure. We went to the court and told the state what had happened. We said we had been away and left Tam, that we had tried to get him back and been refused access to him, and that it had never been our intention that he stay out west. I said we would never have gotten a fair shake in California, where there was testimony from doctors against us, and that we didn't understand the implications of the papers we signed when Michelle took Tam to L.A. I said that we loved our boy and wanted him back. So we did what we did. We knew Rosie had been named Tam's legal guardian in February 1979, though Tam was mostly with Michelle and Bob Burch. Rosie, in turn, had named Michelle as her stand-in if Rosie were ever disabled.

On December 3, we filed a motion in Superior Court in Bridgeport, requesting, first, that Gen and I be awarded custody of Tam as his natural parents and, second, that the guardianship of Rosie and Michelle be immediately terminated. On December 10, the state of Connecticut granted us temporary custody. Two days later, a friend called to tip me off that the authorities were closing in and ready to collar us. I raced to Old Greenwich Elementary School and got Tam out. Gen and I frantically discussed her leaving instantly for Canada with him. Before we could move, plainclothes cops hopped from their car in the driveway, came inside, and slapped cuffs on me.

Gen was pacing and wringing her hands. A social worker with the officers said that Tam would go to a foster home while we posted bond. Gen saw Chris Thurlow. She was standing at the kitchen door, watching in bewilderment. Shore Road had never seen such action.

"They're arresting us. Please don't let them give Tam back to Michelle," she begged.

Chris was in a terrible spot. It was a small town and she knew everyone. She called the local D.A., got the social worker's name, and called her. "I live next door," Chris said. "Tam knows me. He's comfortable around me. He's probably very fearful now. This must be an upsetting ordeal for him. Could you release him in our custody?" She offered to provide church, school, and community references. The answer was no, but the worker suggested that Chris go to the approved foster family's home for dinner. Before she could, we posted the bond and went straight home and got Tam.

A welfare worker notified Rosie of our arrest and advised her to come east and look after Tam. Rosie and Michelle immediately flew to New York and drove to Old Greenwich. They hired a local lawyer and stayed in a motel for the next ten days for hearings in Bridgeport.

We appeared in court for two hearings in Bridgeport. On December 13, Michelle and Rosie filed a motion to dismiss *our* motion—requesting custody—and claimed that California, not Connecticut, was the correct jurisdiction to decide the case. They felt they would win there, since they had their own statements and those from doctors, shrinks, and relatives attesting to our addiction and general recklessness as Tam's parents. They even snooped around on their own and visited the owners of our rented homes in Darien and Stamford. They heard their stories of trashing, syringes, and blood-streaked walls. They heard that we had left a string of unpaid bills all over Fairfield County.

I later learned that between the two hearings, Rosie and Michelle sat up in their motel room and discussed snatching Tam *back* to California. Rosie figured that if she could get him on a plane and back home, she was in the clear as legal guardian in California. They went so far as to drive by and case the house; they knew where Tam's school was. The plan, presumably, would have been to stake him out at either location and grab him.

They abandoned the idea and decided instead to await the second hearing. It would have been far too traumatic for Tam. Besides, they needed to depict *us* as the child-stealers.

The welfare department worker found that image hard to reconcile with what she knew. "Shore Road's one of the best, classiest addresses in the state," she told them. "Only good people live there. All this stuff just can't be true."

Even the lawyer Michelle had retained for the case found it hard to accept the horror stories. He was so insulated from our world that his only contact with a junkie was with a black hooker. As Rosie said later, she felt that the straitlaced Connecticut Yankees were prejudiced against two women they privately saw as just two more kooks from California.

Tam got his own court-appointed attorney and when he called me to discuss the case, we got along well and he was charmed.

We had an attorney who presented us as sophisticated upscale Shore Road types fighting to keep our family intact against a disgruntled older sister and an antagonistic ex-wife. Gen's mother was visiting from South Africa and it seemed as if she was helping us care for Tam in a grandmotherly way while Gen began to show her pregnancy. She stayed with Tam in a hotel room in Bridgeport for the hearings, in case the judge wanted to see him. I hired a former boxer and security man for the Stones named Sal to be near Tam at all times in case anyone *else* wanted to see him. And Sal was going to be our tour guide to Canada—if the court ruling went against us.

I created a debonair country-gentleman look in a tweed sports jacket with suede elbow patches, flannel shirt, scarf, and boots. I swore under oath that I was off drugs. I knew I was perjuring myself and taking a colossal risk with the law. But it was worth it. If we were ever going to pull our lives together, we needed Tam back. Otherwise, we were doomed to an image of ourselves as failures—and an unbreakable vicious cycle as addicts that would only reinforce that image.

A week later, December 21, we returned to court and the judge denied the Rosie-Michelle motion to get a California trial. The court would not hear more of the case until further

evidence from California was presented. For the time, we
had won. They were enraged and disillusioned and out ten
grand in legal fees.

At the end of the day, I asked to speak alone with Rosie in
the cafeteria. Michelle was fuming and thought I was going
to try to get her to drop the case and the charges. She knew
me well.

"Rosie," I said solemnly, "you have to believe me when I
say I am not a junkie, or a dealer anymore. Come live with
us. I'll take care of you. Leave Venice. You won't be a housekeeper or baby-sitter. You're family. I love you and I miss
you so much."

I saw that she didn't know how to react. She was torn
between a reflex of skepticism and a desire, a wish, to believe
me. I had appealed to the part of Rosie that had always felt
deep affection and love for me all my life despite everything.
We were family and there was, essentially, no one left. Dad
was gone; Mom was essentially brain-dead in a convalescent
home; Tommy was way out there, being Tommy.

Between us we had eight kids and a ninth was on the way.
There were strong, durable bonds. Tam had spent summers
playing with his cousins. Another part of Rosie, though—
tough, wise, and less sentimental—heard her inner shit de-
tector go off. She had been through this a thousand times
before. My stories. Her wanting to believe them. Getting
burned.

She sat impassively in the courthouse cafeteria, hands
folded across her lap. It was cold and dark outside and
barely five o'clock. I was sure I had won her over.

"Uh-uh, John," she said sternly. "No. I don't buy it this
time. I just can't. I'm going to stick with Michelle and go
back and keep trying to fight this one. We are both very
attached to Tam. I just feel sorry for the baby you and Genevieve are bringing into this world."

Rosie and Michelle called and asked to see Tam. "You can
come by," I said, "but the fact is, he doesn't want to see
you." They did not believe me.

They arrived that evening during a light snowfall. The
Christmas season had not yet swept through our house. Tam
had built himself a bomb shelter in the basement, taking

canned goods, bread, mayonnaise, luncheon meats, and sodas with him. Then he blockaded the door to the basement.
When they knocked, Audrey, Gen's mother, began screaming for them to go away. Gen and Audrey didn't want me to
let them in, but I prevailed. They walked into the dining
room and saw Sal, the bodyguard. We all went to the kitchen
and Audrey and Michelle got into a verbal spat over Michelle's impact on Tam's life. "He was so unhappy before
they got him," Audrey said. Michelle held her own. "That's
nonsense. He was very popular in third grade out there.
John and Genevieve are still doing drugs, can't you see that?
He's dealing. How do you think they have this house, that
Caddie?"

Rosie asked me to get Tam. I tried to get into the basement. "See if you can get through now," he yelled up from
down below. "They'll never get me."

He finally emerged, hiding behind me. He wrapped his
arms around my leg and I dropped an arm around him.
Rosie was calm and rational. "Tam, darling," she said, "you
know I love you and I'm only interested in what's best for
you."

"I know that, Aunt Rosie," he said. "I know you really
love me and all that stuff. But I really wanna live with my
mom and dad and that's just the way it is. I'd rather be here
than anywhere else." He wouldn't let Rosie go near him; he
was too confused by it all and didn't know what was right. It
was a horrible position to put a nine-year-old in. Michelle
tried to give him a hug and he pulled back. She sensed that
we had somehow brainwashed him into fearing her. Rosie
was smart and protective enough to back off. "Let's go,"
Rosie said gloomily.

Michelle stormed out. "Well, Merry Christmas and fuck
you." She slammed the door, ripped the Christmas wreath
off the front door, and flung it in the snow. Then she got in
her rented car and drove back and forth over the wreath half
a dozen times. She and Rosie then skidded off down Shore
Road toward town.

Rosie and Michelle got back to L.A. just in time for
Christmas at home with their families. Gen and I went for
dinner several times over the holidays with the Thurlows.

Laura flew in and spent some time with us. We opened up a little about Tam's case, our brush with heroin a few years back, but that was all *way* behind us now.

As convincing as I thought I was about having our act together, the lawyer who represented us in Tam's case obviously saw room for improvement. For Christmas, he and his girlfriend gave us $50 toward an est weekend.

On January 20, my mother died in the convalescent home out west. She was buried next to my father in Arlington National Cemetery. Rosie was ill again and did not come to the funeral. Her son Peter made the arrangements. At the end, my mother was being kept alive on machines and fed intravenously. The irony there was eerie.

Gen, Tam, and I went down for the burial, then gathered at Peter's home in Virginia. We stayed at a nearby hotel but brought our overnight bag upstairs into a bedroom. Tam bumped into Patty, the youngest of Rosie's four children, in the kitchen and spilled soda all over both their clothes. Patty was twenty-five and quite beautiful. She went upstairs and looked inside our bag to get Tam a clean dry shirt. She found some needles and what she assumed were narcotics in there. I didn't, of course, hear this from her, but from Rosie, days later when she called me in Greenwich from L.A.

"It's real neat, John," she said bitterly. "The Connecticut Yankee's all cleaned out, but he couldn't even make it to his mama's funeral without his drug kit." "There wasn't anything in there," I told her. I was sure now that she and Michelle would be back any day to battle us in court for Tam.

They decided, however, not to pursue the case because all of their witnesses would have had to come east for depositions and cross-examinations. Whatever they *knew* in their hearts, they would have had to *prove* beyond a reasonable doubt that we were junkies and that I was dealing. They had no idea how hard I would have—and could have—made it for them to prove.

A couple of weeks later, Tam's lawyer and a social worker demanded that I submit to a urine test as part of the welfare department's upcoming home visit to make sure we were all doing well. They had to give you a week's notice. I knew we'd be fine because Dilaudid would get us through. Gen took no chances.

She asked Chris Thurlow next door to come by and help her and a maid fix up the house. Gen went to United House-wrecking, a giant houseware flea market, and bought stained-glass knickknacks, matching pictures of Christ and the Virgin Mary. Gen was careful to leave open books lying around—Dr. Spock, a book on natural childbirth, *Pride and Prejudice* with a bookmark left in it, flowers on the mantel. She dumped some knitting in a basket by the window. She placed Tam's textbooks and some half-completed math homework on the kitchen table, a pad of her own watercol-ors on a chair, and a tea service in the living room. She should have gotten an Oscar for set design. "Oh, of course," Gen asked, "have you got a spare crucifix or a statue of the Virgin Mary?"

Bill Cleary was with us from Newport. There was no way I'd get a clear urine, so the day before the test I bought a yellow plastic lemon filled with lemon juice concentrate in a supermarket. I unscrewed the top, emptied it, washed it *very carefully,* and had Bill urinate into it. I placed the lemon in my underwear and went, most deliberately, to the meeting with the lawyer, knowing someone always *listens* to verify by sound the act of fresh urination.

I locked the bathroom stall, removed the lemon, and, with extreme care, unscrewed the top. Keeping it in my crotch guaranteed secrecy and proper warmth. I aimed the lemon toward the toilet and squeezed, perfectly simulating pissing sounds. I held the sample cup over the toilet and squirted some of Bill's clean urine into it. I screwed the top on, stuffed the lemon back into my underwear, zipped up, and handed over the clean urine sample.

It was, however, getting harder and harder to fool our next-door neighbors. We'd always have to leave several times during dinner and shoot up Dilaudid, coke, or Desoxyn, whatever the cat inside clawed for. "I have to check the phone," I'd say.

"You have the same kind of phone we do," Chris would answer ingenuously.

Chris took Gen around to her dentist when she complained of a toothache, then to Chris's obstetrician, then to the orthopedist to look at Gen's twisted ankle. The plea was always the same: "I need painkillers." These were all friends of the Thurlows. They were suspicious and told Chris.

One day Chris drove up and noticed that a safety drain on the grass just on our side of the common driveway was backed up. Instead of flooding the kitchen or bathroom, the safety drain diverted the overflow to the outdoor drain. Some odd blue objects in the middle of this soggy, stinky mess around the grating caught her eye. She took a closer look and saw a dozen blue syringes. I drove up moments later and she came out to meet me. "You've got a blockage there, haven't you?" she said. She pointed to the drain.

"Sure seems like it."

"Why are you flushing hypodermic needles down the toilet, John?" Her voice was tougher, more accusatory.

"Gen's obstetrician asked me to give her vitamin shots because she's weak. I do it three to five times a day in the behind."

"That's terrible. I'd cancel him, allowing a husband to inject a pregnant woman like that. You could cause an embolism, any number of other things."

"I had some medical training in the Navy . . ."

"What's this guy's name?" She was far too sharp, dogged, and skeptical. "Because I know about every doctor in this town and this one sounds like a quack."

"I'll ask Gen. She'll know."

A landscaper came by to work on the two adjacent yards. He was planting some bushes along the wall of the Finch house. I knew we were running out of luck when, out of all the thousands of square yards to work on, his long spade struck something crunchy but not rock-hard. He bent over and uncovered another two dozen buried syringes and went right to Chris, knowing the owners weren't occupying the house. When she confronted me this time, I said *those* needles were for the shots I was giving to *Trelawny* for the mange.

"The mange?" she snapped back incredulously.

"Yeah, mange. Like mangy. Athlete's foot of the fur for dogs."

"I *know* what it is. I just don't believe this. Your dog looks pretty healthy to me."

"Imagine how bad he'd look without the shots."

I explained that I had to stash and bury the syringes because I was afraid *someone*—acting on behalf of Rosie-Michelle, Tam's attorney, the social workers—might start poking through our garbage for evidence of parental unfitness in order to reopen Tam's custody case.

"As a matter of fact," I said, handing her a fifth of vodka, "would you mind holding on to this for a while?"

Days later, Chris's son Michael and Tam were playing upstairs in Tam's room and a toy race car broke. He got his mom to come over to fix it. She walked into the closet to get a hanger for the repair job. She spotted a paper bag on the floor and looked inside. She saw bloody Kleenexes and more syringes.

The Thurlows' vigorously healthy family life centered on dynamic friends, church, school, and community projects, sports, and culture. It was so far removed from our life-style that they found it all but impossible to believe the mounting evidence of our addiction.

Gen told them that she was leaving in February to visit her mother in South Africa. She was, in fact, going to London for an emergency cleanout with a famous addiction specialist. We were terrified of living the agony of Anita and Keith in London with their newborn. We were scared of birth defects. Gen had been staying on a low dose of Dilaudid and we prayed that she and the baby would pull through with a quickie cure.

Through the winter, I was running up a tab in the thousands of dollars for a limousine service out of Port Chester, New York, to shuttle me to and from the pharmacy and my various drug contacts. The scrip books were going for as much as $500 apiece now, but I couldn't let go. From the time I arrived in Greenwich through early March, I dealt mostly with George in the East 80s. He was short, stocky, fortyish, and bearded. He could have been a Hasidic Jew with a cane.

The modus operandi had not changed. I'd call K & B to check the availability of drugs—usually Dilaudid, Desoxyn,

Quaaludes; I'd call George to check the availability of blank
books. I'd take the limo or Caddie to George's, get his list of
the pharmaceuticals he wanted, the book or books, up to
$1,000 in cash, then head over to K & B. If he—or anyone—
ever accompanied me to make the swap in the limo or Caddie, he waited half an hour down the block from K & B at
the pizza joint. Then, to consummate and cash-out the deal,
once we all knew what we had to exchange, he would give
me either a quantity of high-grade cocaine or cash to even
things up. The precious commodity that fixed all the other
exchange rates was the pharmaceutical load.

I felt uneasy at George's. There were too many people
around. Some of them looked at me and did double-takes.
All I needed was one Flower Power nutcase stuck in the
sixties with a brain basking in Sunshine and a good memory
for album covers—and my cover was blown.

George lived in a luxury high rise and always had a line of
people waiting to score pills and coke from him. They
waited either in the lobby downstairs or in his living room
while he took his clients, one at a time, into the bedroom or
bathroom. These were all white-collar clients, a very attractive group: Yuppies in pin-striped Wall Street suits, hot-looking models, actor-waiter hunks, middle-aged paunchy executives, and tanned Sugar Daddies with their schizzed-out
coke whores sipping champagne in the limousines while they
did their deals with George.

I ran into Jeff there, another dealer and sometime backgammon partner from two years earlier. Around the same
time, in the early eighties, I also met a real estate developer
named Scott at George's. Scott and Jeff seemed to know
each other and said hello. It was getting to be a small world.
I saw George sell Scott some of the ludes I had sold George.
The circle was tightening.

In mid-February, Bill Cleary came to stay with me again
on Shore Road. Over the next couple of weeks, he rode with
me to the drugstore in my Caddie. Right away, he saw I was
in trouble. Suspended license, speeding, erratic behavior,
and, on the way back, a full load of Dilaudids. I broke down
and let him know just how deep it had gotten. Over the next
couple of weeks, we went by limousine and on several occa-

sions George rode with us between the pharmacy and his apartment.

Bill was quite upset. He had tried hard with Louise to get us back into the real world. Now he warned me, "Get out, man. I don't like what I see." No friend went back farther and stuck by me longer than Bill. But I still refused to listen.

Bill had met George once to pick up $500 he owed me. They had talked in the limo. Bill told me George had brought up the possibility of arranging a major cocaine buy several times. "It'll be the best," George assured Bill. "I'll get you a sample."

Bill had tried to lay the guy off. We didn't want samples, he said, we weren't interested. We didn't care how much George may have needed the cash. "Whole thing sounds like a setup," Bill said in his slow, knowing Virginia drawl.

"It is a little strange," I agreed. "George never initiates coke buys. It only comes into play at the end of the swap, when we even up *after* the pills and books get handled."

On March 4, Bill and I decided to stay in the City at the Essex House Hotel. George got in touch with us there in the afternoon. He wanted to talk more about setting up a coke deal. His persistence was disturbing. He knew that I had all the pharmaceutical speed I needed. An ounce of blow for me was a lot. A kilo was ridiculous.

"Okay," I said curiously, drawing him out, "a pound and a half."

"The first price I gave you was $35,000, right?" he said.

At that point I eyed Bill warily and shook my head. "You never gave me a price."

"Thirty-five for a pound," he said. "You get a break if you buy a key. Forty to forty-five thousand."

"It doesn't sound bad."

"I'll see the guy tonight. When should I set it up?"

"Today's Tuesday," I said. "Hold on." Then I related all this to Bill in a whisper with my hand over the phone. Bill's face tightened and he shook his head silently from side to side.

"Bill says don't go any further with this, George," I said. "Bill needs seventy-two hours to line up the money with our people first. And then we'll give you the go-ahead. Don't expend any more effort. Within three days we'll have an answer."

I hung up and we stared at each other. My heart was fluttering. I didn't speak to George again that week and avoided all calls.

Back in Greenwich, Bill and Louise were reading books one night in an upstairs bedroom when Bill put his book down and looked at her. "Let's pack it in. We're just gonna get into a whole lotta trouble here. We can't do anything to stop it." He came downstairs and found me in the kitchen. I asked him what was wrong. "You're violating all kinds of federal laws is what's wrong. I can't be part of this. You shouldn't either."

"Yeah, but . . ."

"I already called the limo, man. We're packin' it in."

I tried to pull back and hide out at home with my stock-pile of Schedule II drugs. I was shooting up constantly, try-ing to maintain and hold it all together.

Laura's life was falling apart and she came to stay with me in March. Days later, Gen returned healthy from her two-month detox and seemed ready to give birth at any moment. Chris threw a baby shower for Gen on the back porch on a warm evening and it was lovely—all these Old Greenwich matrons giving her booties, backpacks, and car seats while Gen had just won her battle to kick narcotics.

Laura's marriage, like her home, was in ashes. I couldn't even have predicted how disastrous it would be. Her man-ager had advised her to get a prenuptial agreement. She didn't bother. She had been fired from the show during her six months of marriage and she had been through the drug therapy program after the police hauled her in.

Laura, prior to her firing, had been staying up all night in a recording studio, trying to get an album off the ground. She was on the sitcom set all day. She was signing checks on her account without knowing what they were for. She was in a haze all the time. "A half a million dollars is gone. That's all I know," she said dejectedly. "I was awfully high the whole time on coke and ludes." Late one morning, Jeff told her to get some money to pick up a coat they had bought. Laura was wearing overalls, a Hawaiian shirt, Capezios, and no socks. She kissed Jeff, said she'd see him in an hour, beeped the car horn twice going down the hill, and never turned back.

She walked off the airplane in New York like a street urchin, lost and disheveled. Kids came up from all sides, wanting her autograph. Laura was the only one who didn't seem to know who she was anymore.

The Thurlows' daughter, Katie, was thrilled to have a real star like Mackenzie Phillips right next door. Katie loved to sing in choir and had been in school plays, so they had *plenty* to talk about. Laura was like an older sister, assuring her that she had potential. Katie was sure this was her big break. They were instant pals.

On March 29, we were invited to the Thurlows' for dinner. The occasion was their son Michael's first Communion. Katie Thurlow was so excited to have Laura coming for dinner that she made sure she was seated next to her famous new friend. Gen arrived first, at around seven, and said we were coming right over. I arrived and said Laura was still in the tub. I asked Steve if I could make a call to upstate New York, to a town ninety minutes away.

Steve must have sensed what was going on. He probably pieced together that this "friend" of ours was to drive down that night to "help Laura out, just like last time."

Gen went back to check Laura. I went back to check the phone. We were coming and going, driving Chris crazy because she wanted the dinner to be perfect. By ten or so, we all got there and sat down. Her kids were pooped.

Laura was in a daze, totally out of it on downers. She could barely sit up in the chair. She looked over the roast beef and mashed potatoes. "I don't eat anything red," she mumbled.

"Well," Steve said sardonically, "there go the beets."

She slowly and humorlessly turned to him and said, "I *hate* beets."

"Just a joke," he said. "You can have all the white food."

Chris handed her a plate of mashed potatoes and gravy. Katie, sitting between her father and her TV idol, stared in amazement at Laura's semicatatonic movements. Laura brought a glass of milk to her lips, but then couldn't decide on the next move—whether to bring her lips to the glass or the glass to her lips. Katie tossed her fork down so she and her father would both bend over to pick it up.

"Dad," she whispered as their heads almost touched under the table, "she's drunk or somethin', isn't she?" Steve nodded silently and handed her the fork.

Moments later, Laura's eyes closed, her head drooped, and her face fell right into the plate of mashed potatoes and stuck there. I was mortified. I leaned over and pulled her face away so she wouldn't choke. Katie was devastated. She had been so excited about telling all her friends the next morning that Julie Cooper from "One Day" had come for Communion dinner. There was Julie, being carried, stuporous, across the way through the cold rain. "Those damned antibiotics," I said. "She's had this awful cold and she's on these powerful drugs and I should never have given her that stiff gin and tonic before dinner."

The Thurlows were appalled that we had made such a travesty of this important religious and family affair. "I'm just glad I didn't invite my parents and the whole family this time," Chris said as we left.

Two hours later, the Mercedes drove in from upstate and took off half an hour later. The Thurlows must have heard the engine. This wasn't like the City. Our anonymity was gone in the suburbs. Our secret life belonged more and more to the community.

The next day Chris walked over with my trenchcoat. I had left it there. A wave of paranoia rolled over me. I was getting sloppy, making mistakes. I knew we had almost identical coats and she said she had tried mine on by mistake. That's all she said. But that's not all she necessarily knew. When she left, I reached inside the left pocket and felt a fat twenty-five-scrip triplicate book and a rubber surgical tourniquet.

On March 31, in the afternoon, I got a call from George, who was still trying to suck me into his $45,000 cocaine clearance sale. "I've retired," I told him. I didn't like this at all.

"I heard you were doing something with Dwight downtown," he said.

"Dwight? I haven't seen him in a year." I knew he was fishing around for something. It stunk.

"John, I got cash, I got books. We never fucked up or had a beef, right?" He wouldn't let go.

"I'm not coming in today anyway," I said. "It's snowing. It got out of hand. Things are a little hot now. The dealings weren't streamlined enough. There was too much waiting."

Hours later, in the middle of a freezing cold night, Gen went into labor contractions. There was no warning and she started screaming. I called the local volunteer rescue squad and helped Gen to the living room couch. Laura was high on something upstairs and I yelled for her to stay up there. We didn't need a gossip sheet scandal, too. I had taken a shot of Dilaudid. I didn't have time to wake the Thurlows and get to a hospital.

I was scared and cursed every minute the rescue van took to arrive. It seemed like an hour. But after only a ten-minute labor, they arrived just in time for Gen's delivery. I held her hand as her face hardened with pain.

She gave birth to a baby girl right on the couch and the rescue volunteers rushed them both to a hospital. The van felt cold inside as our newborn lay across Gen's chest in her arms.

They both made it through the night. It was April Fool's Day as the sky lightened at dawn, but this was nothing to joke about. We named her Bijou, the French word for jewel. She was weak and sick at birth.

Doctors told us that she might not pull through. We prayed. They put her in an intensive care "preemie" unit at Yale Hospital. Her organs were in shock. She went on kidney dialysis right away. She had a chance. But it would be a fight for life.

The doctor at Yale turned out to be an old university chum of Gen's and, after staying up for forty-eight hours to see her through the acute crisis, he promised us that he would personally make sure that Bijou got the best care. Once more I had the amazing good fortune to come across the one person I needed most at that instant.

Gen checked into Greenwich Hospital for a couple of days. Laura considered Silver Hill in New Canaan to detox and get her life in order. She was determined. Silver Hill has long had a fine reputation as a favorite dry-out clinic for the wealthy and famous.

For the next several weeks, I ran amuck just holding everything together. Gen took a room in the Sheraton Park Plaza Hotel in New Haven to be near the baby. Laura got an adjoining room, but she was messed up on drugs. We were allowed to see Bijou any time, day or night, but I was reluctant to leave Laura by herself in the hotel alone.

"There's too much going on now," I said, "for me to give you the kind of time and attention you need. You should get professional help."

A Yale doctor helped arrange her admission to Silver Hill, a renowned drug and alcohol cleanout and rehab clinic in New Canaan. Tam was in Old Greenwich. Gen was in New Haven near Bijou. Laura was in New Canaan.

And my drugs were at the corner of 81st and Madison.

A limousine would pick me up on Shore Road and, if I needed a supply of Dilaudid or Desoxyn, take me to the pharmacy. The rest of the day I spent traveling along a triangle connecting three dots on the Connecticut map. I had to be in Old Greenwich in the morning to see Tam off to school and I tried to see Laura on most days. I often brought some speed into her bathroom and shot up, just to keep pace. If I slept, it was two or three hours a night.

Before visiting Bijou, I applied makeup to my hands to hide my mainline tracks from her nurses and doctors. We had to wear surgical gowns, gloves, and masks to hold her and massage her after the first couple weeks. The heat inside the gloves turned the makeup to paste. But it was an amazing spectacle. She really *was* a miracle baby. Tam was tough through it all too. When he came to stay with us at the hotel, we would just crash from exhaustion and stress and he would wander through the nearby mall. He learned early on to take care of himself.

After a week at Silver Hill, Laura told me that I should check in or she would check out. That was only fair, she said. She had a boyfriend in Silver Hill and she was doing well. I smuggled in some coke in the top of deodorant spray cans.

I checked in and hid drugs wrapped in foil in the woods behind a tree. I'd take walks and find my rock and hit up. I had a little thermos of water, spoon, lighter, and Dilaudid for the shots. I even carried a pack of cigarettes, in case anyone caught me with the lighter. Junkies *have* to be devious. I cooked my shots in the woodsy spring air. I didn't go I.V. then, just shot it through my pants into the hip. Took less than two minutes. After a week I had had enough of the charade and checked out. Laura was soon released.

Tam wanted me to manage a Little League team, so I signed up and got him on my team. I tried this a couple of weekends, hiding my stash behind the dugout. Every other inning or so, I'd wander back there, looking for a foul ball. Then I'd fire a speedball of my own in the thigh and come back and fiercely root my boys on.

By that time, I had gotten George off my back and begun dealing with Jeff, whom I had recently seen at George's. He scored two scrip books, waited in the pizza joint while I went to K & B, and brought me to the West 70th Street apartment of a man he said would help him cash-out a deal with me when he came up short with the coke. The cash, he said, would come from selling the drugstore ludes to the West Side guy.

He turned out to be Scott, the real estate developer and Quaalude addict. I was getting the Quaaludes, in bottles with the manufacturer's lot numbers scraped off by K & B, for $1.75 apiece. Jeff paid me $3.75 per lude and Scott, in turn, paid Jeff $5.00. Jeff also bought some Desoxyn and I kept the Dilaudids. I could usually get something like 20 Desoxyn, 200 Tuinals, 100 Dilaudids, 90 Percodans, 20 Dolophines, and varying numbers of just about any other psychoactive buzz.

Jeff told me during that visit that he was getting his books from George and didn't want me to let George know we were dealing together because it would upset George. I had a feeling George was already upset with me because he had failed to suck me into the coke buy. By now, in my paranoid frenzies, I was pretty sure George was working with new people anyway—the Feds.

We all got back home by the middle of May. We never

imagined that Bijou would pull through the way she did. She was beautiful, with giant green eyes and a tiny upturned nose just like Gen's. Laura was off in the City, hanging out with her new boyfriend, also a Silver Hill graduate. He was teaching her how to mainline coke and heroin.

It was at that time that Gen, coming down off barbiturates, went into the violent, thrashing seizure that landed her in New Milford Hospital. I ended up with sixty milligrams of Dilaudid, which I rationed but used up quickly.

Chris Thurlow visited Gen in the hospital and tried to lighten her spirits by laughing about the baby shower. Chris had always had an open-door policy and Gen had walked through it a fair number of times for tea and commiseration. Chris could never get over how Gen knew the lineage of all the Tudors and the Stuarts, but sometimes couldn't get it together to remember milk at the market. And once she had come over to the house and seen how a beautiful old New England suburban home can be turned into a junkie pad next door. But they never came down on us. By now Steve and Chris knew exactly what was going on. They were too decent to judge us and they still cared.

"Gee, you must have been laughing up your sleeve during that whole baby shower," Chris said to Gen. "Here you were, Mr. and Mrs. L.A., jet-setters, artists, mixing with us straitlaced Greenwich matrons with our baby slings and little booties." There were tears in Gen's eyes.

"What you don't understand, Chris," she said, "is that all I have ever wanted in life was to be just like you—at least to have the kind of life you have here. The little house with the picket fence and the petunias in the garden and a husband with a real job and the family unit. I don't want rock and roll, all those people. It's weird. You were sitting there thinking I saw *you* as all these squares and there *I* was wishing to God I was part of all that—but never will be."

"It breaks my heart to hear you say that, Gen, but you have to know that we do care about you and John and the kids. We do."

I was dropping farther out of touch. It hadn't even hit me how much Laura needed me to be there for her in her worst time of crisis.

She was visiting us from New York and knocked on the door to the bathroom. I said I was busy. She asked me to come out. She was upset and needed to speak to me. "I can't come out, darling. I'm shooting up. I'll be out in a while." I couldn't believe those words when I heard myself say them. It horrified me, but I just kept shooting myself up.

She came with me once to the pharmacy and was amazed at what was going on there. I had lost all judgment as a parent, as far as she was concerned. I was doing what I could for Tam and Bij. I was failing Laura miserably. I knew the full extent of her drug problems and there were times that she was using my drugs. In one instance, we were sitting around stoned and I wanted to do an I.V. hit of coke. Trying to hide it from her just didn't matter anymore. She not only understood, she wanted a shot. I put on my discount store prescription glasses and got a preloaded syringe full of coke and water. I took my shot. Laura sat there, ready. There was another syringe right there. I hesitated, then did it. I took her arm and squeezed it. This was my little girl. It was total madness. The needle went in, my thumb pushed down on the plunger, then I held my breath and pulled the needle away. We both looked down and she waited. She shook her head in her wise-ass way. "Get new glasses. You missed the vein, Pop." I was relieved. It was the last time I ever did that.

The Finches were preparing to build up the attic as a bedroom for their son and a contractor came to the house one afternoon while we were out. He went upstairs and began peeling back rolls of insulation from the eaves of the slanted roof. The foil-covered padding was loose and ill-fitting in one section. He gave it a tug. Out fell hundreds of used syringes from behind the thick roll of insulation.

Nothing was said to me then, but I knew what had happened. The Finch house was turning into a horror movie set. The syringes were popping up everywhere: in closets, bathroom glasses, under sofa cushions, behind the eaves, in the soil along the house, flowing from outdoor drains. The nightmare was spreading to the sane, innocent people whose paths happened to cross ours as our life on Shore Road turned into sheer madness.

Michael and Tam were shooting marbles upstairs one evening and I was shooting Dilaudid in the bathroom. Michael, an adorable, bright kid, raced after a marble and chased it under my bed. When I saw him looking under the bed, I got wild and angry and yelled, "You're spying on me, kid! Get outta here!" I tossed Tam's baseball glove at him and scared him to death. Drugs had seized total control of my personality.

He ran home, flailing his arms, yelling, "Mom, Dad, Mr. Phillips is spazzing out!"

We had to run for our lives. Gen and I made plans to rent a place in the Hamptons from the end of June for the summer. By May, I later learned, the Thurlows were put in an impossible situation: A local detective they knew came by and told them I was being investigated in connection with a drug-conspiracy ring. He pumped them for details of my movements, asked them to pick out familiar faces from mug shots, and asked them what they knew. They were faced with a tough choice: to respond as good friends or as responsible citizens. They managed to do both. They shared what they knew, but also admitted that they had never seen me do drugs. The Thurlows never mentioned it to us. It was already too close to home for them. They knew more about us than they wanted to know and more than they could ever admit knowing. They must have known something was about to blow.

One night a thunderstorm tore across the Sound to the southeast. As it moved overhead, I walked out along the seawall with no shirt on and turned my face to the sky. I raised my arms and opened my palms to the warm torrential rain. My body was soon drenched; the rain trickling down my face and chest made me feel alive and full of childlike wonder at the power and immensity of nature. Jagged, blinding streaks of lightning exploded spectacularly in the dark, revealing thunderheads hovering ominously over the horizon. For an instant, I felt real again.

Then, on the afternoon of June 9, I rolled slowly out of a deep narcotized funk and woke up with a premixed shot of coke. The day was hazy. I drove my Caddie into the City to make one more stop at K & B. I parked my car and went to the drugstore. The door was locked and I phoned from the street. They let me in and wrote me a note: THE DEA WAS HERE THIS MORNING. THEY HAVE YOUR PICTURE AND THEY WANT ALL OUR RECORDS BY MONDAY MORNING.

Late that night, I got a call from my niece Nancy in L.A. She had devastating news. Her younger sister, Patty, Rosie's daughter, a stunning, bright young woman who lived her life to the fullest, was found dead of an overdose in a girlfriend's apartment in North Hollywood. I wanted to die for Rosie. Nancy was strong and trying to hold everything together at Rosie's place in Venice. Rosie was in shock.

There were mysterious questions surrounding her death and an autopsy was in the works. Patty had gotten married two months earlier to a young talented camera operator named Brad May. He had a future ahead of him as a cinematographer. They had been together for almost three years. Right after they married, he left to prepare for a shoot in Arizona but came in on weekends when he could. Patty did not work.

She was a party girl who loved to dance and who was on and off speed to maintain her shapely figure. Rosie was always watching out for Laura around her because they loved to hang out and go club-hopping. The two of them were on everyone's party list around town. Laura was a few years younger and Patty was a sister to Laura.

On Sunday night, Patty dropped her husband at the airport and drove to Rosie's for lasagna with Rosie, brother Billy, and Nancy. She made some phone calls, had a brief spat with May upon his arrival, and went out to the Rainbow with a new girlfriend of hers from the discos whom no one knew. Her name was Nichole.

Police were saying that they left with two men they believed to be small-time dealers. It was assumed the women knew the men, but they hadn't been identified. They went to an apartment in the Hollywood Hills. It all sounded strange. I vowed to hire a private investigator.

Rosie was destroyed. I sadly wondered, *Did I help kill her?* Rosie had looked after me as a child, been a surrogate mother, spent years taking care of Jeff, Laura, and Tam, and was committed to an absolutely straight life as a loving single mother of four. Now one of her girls was gone, while *our* baby, whom we feared didn't stand a chance at a healthy life, was thriving. It all seemed so damned unfair.

The next day, in a deranged flight from reason, I drove up and down Shore Road like a madman, looking for our driveway. I didn't care what happened to me now. The DEA had my picture and was going to pop me any day. I could smell them on my trail. My niece was dead. It was pouring. The circle was drawing tighter by the hour. I was looking desperately for Tam.

I ran up onto a neighbor's lawn and spun out. I floored the car, but it was in reverse. The rear wheels took hold, chewed up some grass, and the Caddie lurched backward. I felt a crunching thud. The car jumped the low concrete seawall ten feet above a sandy strip of beach at low tide behind the house. It perched there, stuck. I thought if I sneezed, the car would spill backward and crush me to death inside.

I slowly extricated myself and began wandering around in a stupor until I found my house. I saw Chris. "My God, what happened?" she asked.

"Long story. Meantime, you know any towing companies?"

We returned to the neighbor's home. The police arrived. I emptied my pockets, looking for I.D. Hundred-dollar bills were flying out of my hands, floating in the low, balmy winds into the Sound.

The local cops went to the owner of the house and asked him *not* to press charges. "This man is under surveillance," they told him confidentially. "We don't want to give him any reason to feel he's being harassed or any excuses to take off."

As the cops wrote up the report and the tow truck lifted my car off the seawall, the driver told me that he didn't have change for a $100 bill, so I asked Chris to loan me the $40 for the towing. She had $39. I asked the owner of the house if he'd lend me the last dollar. He refused. He loaned *Chris* the dollar instead.

On June 26, we left the Thurlows and Shore Road for the Hamptons. Two weeks later, Mick Jagger and Jerry Hall came out for the July Fourth weekend and witnessed my inhospitable heroin cure.

A month later, the private investigator's report arrived. There were still unanswered questions about Patty's final hours. The autopsy revealed traces of heroin, cocaine, speed, and Quaalude. She had been drinking, but Patty was no junkie. There was a fresh needle mark in the crook of her arm. It looked like a deadly hotshot in a Hollywood Hills bedroom.

After Patty passed out on the bed, the two men and Nichole got her to Nichole's place in the Valley. The bastards were obviously too worried about saving their own asses to get her to an emergency room.

They left her on Nichole's couch and split. Nichole crashed. When she awoke, she rushed to arrive on time at her receptionist job. She checked and noticed Patty was still breathing but unconscious—and left her to die.

The two men who last saw Patty alive were never identified. Nichole was too intoxicated the night Patty died to lead police or the investigator to that Hollywood Hills apartment. There would be no justice for Rosie.

The moral irony was excruciating. I was living in the Hamptons and had been spending over $500 a day for years pumping my veins with narcotics; and it was sister Rosie, because of one lethal, reckless five-second injection, who had to pay a parent's ultimate price for the evils of drugs. I felt a terrible grief for Rosie and wondered when and if my time would come. I couldn't expect to beat the odds forever.

A week later, on the afternoon of July 31, I was lying on my bed in the rented house in Water Mill, staring blankly at "Live at Five," when I heard unfamiliar cars pull up and a loud knock at the door. Adrenaline surged through my chest and my heart pounded crazily. I closed my eyes and sucked in a chestful of air. My time had come. I was lucky. Papa John was about to be rudely—but mercifully—awakened from his nightmare. For me, justice would be served.

"John," Gen yelled upstairs with an agitated edge in her voice, "some men are here to see you—and they've all got Hawaiian shirts and guns."

VI

STRAIGHT
SHOOTER

28

EVEN AUGUST in the Hamptons can get you down when you've got forty-five years in the slammer bearing down on you. During the week after the arrest, Bob Tucker and I met several times to gather our wits and prepare a defense. Tucker wasted no time in calling Richard Schaeffer, a crack criminal attorney he had gotten to know professionally. Tucker said that Schaeffer was far more experienced than he was in trial defenses and hoped he would take on the case. With K & B shut down, I tried to maintain and get my last hurrahs on heroin by scoring harsh, granular, low-grade junk from a black dealer in Bridgehampton named Roscoe. His stuff was so bad, it should have been used to *clean* my syringes, not fill them.

Gen got herself into an AA program with an interesting group of artists, painters, poets, writers, and Jesuit priests. The meetings were in old churches in small towns. I gave it a try, but always giggled or passed out drunk on vodka. The sloganeering—"Blossom where you're planted"; "Keep your memory green"; "One is too much, but a hundred isn't enough"—drove me up the walls.

On August 12, I met with Richard Schaeffer, a lean, youthful criminal lawyer with a prestigious midtown firm.

Schaeffer had a narrow face and large, expressive brown eyes and he swept his thick dark brown hair straight back.

I sensed that Schaeffer was taken aback by my gaunt, tense, and unkempt appearance, though we tried to keep things congenial and optimistic. We sat in his conference room high above Third Avenue. Gen napped on the couch in his office.

Schaeffer saw me drop about ten sugars into my coffee, devour candy bars, and leave for the toilet every fifteen minutes. I don't believe he thought I was suffering from some rare blood-sugar disorder. He said he had worked with hundreds of criminals and junkies. He knew the junkie's sweet tooth.

He struck me right away with a blend of warmth, eloquence, bluntness, self-confidence, and sardonic humor. I had no doubt that he was a brilliant tactician in court and he came quite highly recommended by Tucker.

Schaeffer had worked for four years as an assistant D.A. under Frank Hogan in New York after graduating from law school in the late sixties. For the last two of those years, he nailed killers in homicide cases. Then he went to the big firm in 1973 and spent, he guessed, 80 percent of his time on commercial, corporate, tax, and labor disputes.

That left little time or energy for the grit and drama of homicide trials. But rather than become another fat-cat corporate attorney, he voluntarily placed himself on a rotating list of lawyers for assignment, he said, to two *pro bono* murder cases a year involving indigent defendants. The cases were assigned to him—and hundreds of other attorneys—by the Appelate Division of the New York Supreme Court. The Legal Aid Society has traditionally not represented defendants in murder cases, he explained, so he waived even the standard cut-rate $15 hourly fee permitted in those cases.

Going up against the young ambitious prosecutors in court with lives on the line kept not only his trial skills but his ethical edge sharp and gleaming.

"It's a public service," he said with a mix of moral conviction and genuine humility. "I enjoy the process. It's not often that people charged with murder can afford their own lawyers. It's a way to stay active and I enjoy doing it. It's the right thing for lawyers to do."

Then, once we got down to business, he gave me the bad news. He would be meeting the U.S. prosecutor, Mark Pomerantz, and a DEA agent the following day to go over the evidence against me, which would be presented to a grand jury. The indictments were to be handed down in a week. Jeff was under indictment and would be represented by William Kunstler; Korn and Brod, unindicted co-conspirators, were going to plead guilty and would cooperate if I went to trial. The other man facing indictment, incredibly, was my boyhood pal Bill Cleary, who had the miserable bad luck of accompanying me to the pharmacy while I was being tailed, bugged, and photographed. Bill was so freaked out he was already underground.

Schaeffer was digging in for a tough case and he was wary of my wasted look and my sweet tooth. I was a risk. He couldn't gauge my motivation for a cure. He imposed two conditions in accepting my case. "First, John," he said, "you have to be perfectly candid with me, no matter how embarrassing it might be for you, if I am to help you. There is no problem you cannot deal with as a lawyer—IF you know about it in advance and can create a strategy for it."

The other condition cut deeper. "This is going to be a difficult case for both of us," he said gravely, staring right through me with his intense brown eyes. "These kinds of cases take a lot out of your stomach, no matter how much you're paid for them. You can develop great affection for a client, beyond the professional lawyer-client bond. This isn't a commercial case, where all that's at stake is money. We're talking about your freedom and liberty. You're a man with five children whom I'm sure you love and who love you. Look, I'm prepared to undergo the tensions and pressures to do what I have to do to hold up my obligation. But I don't want to do it for a man who is going to die within the next six months to a year. It just isn't worth it for me. And, quite frankly, you could well be on your way."

I listened, nodded, and realized that I was at the most important crossroad of my life. This was for real.

Schaeffer walked me out and looked me over—the worn

jeans, shoulder-length straggly hair, tennis shirt, running shoes, and no socks. "John, the arraignment is coming up," he said. "We're going before a federal judge. Now, it's quite clear, John, that you are *not*, in fact, an investment banker. You are not under indictment for failing to dress like an investment banker. But we *are* going to enter a plea of not guilty and I want you to wear a sports jacket and slacks."

The next day Schaeffer met with Pomerantz and Donald Brown of the DEA. Pomerantz unloaded the goods on me: nineteen trips to K & B between February and April; some fifty calls to K & B from Greenwich; another thirty or so to George; two dozen to Scott, the lude junkie; and another eighteen to Jeff, my onetime backgammon partner, last drug contact, and current co-defendant.

There were dozens of receipts from Freddie's Limousine Service; the drivers and druggists were ready to testify against me and the DEA had my pictures. Schaeffer was shown piles and piles of hastily scribbled triplicate forms from K & B's desperate week of homework.

Pomerantz played for Schaeffer three wiretapped phone calls between George and me, including the suspicious one about the $45,000 coke setup in the Essex House. Bill was right—the call was bugged from George's home for the DEA to flush me out.

Pomerantz and Schaeffer discussed a plea bargain. I asked Schaeffer for an assessment. "The tape recordings," he said with his flair for wry understatement, "will not be helpful to us if we go to trial. That much I know."

My hunch was that George, a top dealer moving 90-per-cent-pure coke, had been squeezed by the Feds to turn over someone big and he had picked me. I figured that he was a professional informant because he was still on the street and had never been prosecuted. It was a bitter lesson in betrayal.

"I don't know," Schaeffer said, "but my impression is that most people in the drug community know him to be some-body you don't talk to except about the weather and the Mets score."

"How does it look?" I asked.

"Short of having the entire crime over three years recorded on videotape, John," he said with a sardonic lilt, "there really *is* nothing to try here. There is essentially no defense or question about the government being able to make its case."

"Where do we go from here?"

"Not to jail. At least, that is the primary objective now. Or, for as little time as possible."

We talked several times about an insanity defense, or diminished capacity—that my desperate addictions ruled my body and my rational processes, that I didn't know what I was doing. He told me that that strategy had never worked in trafficking cases. Schaeffer saw that drugs had caused me to suffer *some* form of insanity and imbalance. But getting a jury to acquit on those grounds was another story. It was time to make a deal.

We agreed on two points: that I had to detox immediately, and, if I made a deal, that I had to use my "celebrity" status to my advantage and wage a sincere antidrug campaign through the media prior to sentencing. And then, at sentencing, pray for leniency.

We met with Dr. Robert Millman, who had saved my foot three years earlier at New York Hospital. He referred me to Dr. Mark Gold, the director of research at Fair Oaks Hospital in Summit, New Jersey. Fair Oaks' highly touted detoxification program was noted for its high rate of lasting success. Gold was the new wunderkind of heroin withdrawal and heroin and coke cleanouts. He had made a name for himself by developing a detox using Clonidine, a well-known antihypertensive medication used to lower blood pressure. He was using Clonidine as an opiate substitute that gets the brain to function as if you are NOT in cold turkey when, in fact, you are. Clonidine is how a detoxing junkie spells relief. The other wonder drug Gold used was Naltrexone, a nonaddicting opiate antagonist that blocks heroin from getting you high. Gold had the situation covered. One drug fooled you into thinking you weren't coming down; the other fooled you into thinking you weren't getting high.

Nobody was fooling Pomerantz into anything. He was young and professional, with a beard and horn-rimmed glasses. He told Schaeffer that in any deal he would ask me to reveal the names of *everyone* I ever gave drugs to. Schaeffer said that was unfair; Pomerantz said I had to go all the way, answer every question, name everyone.

On September 3, the day before the arraignment, Schaeffer called and told me to be at his office at one o'clock. He reminded me to wear a sports jacket. I got there half an hour late and Schaeffer's face registered instant disgust. "John, you son of a bitch," he steamed. His head fell forward into his hands with exasperation.

"I'm sorry I'm late. I . . ."

"Forget the time. I thought I told you to wear a *sports* jacket."

"Whattya mean?" I turned my back to him and showed him what I had on. "This IS a sports jacket, Dick," I bragged. "Look, it's a KNICKS warm-up jacket."

I was glad to see that Dick, who had a flair for witty, sarcastic banter, could laugh and break the tension, even if I looked ridiculously inappropriate.

I pleaded not guilty to all charges and the trial was set for October 27 before Judge Leonard Sand. Dick made me aware that I could switch my plea to guilty any time before that date and enter into a deal.

Gen and I were admitted together to Fair Oaks on September 4 for the standard twenty-eight-day in-patient cure. Junkies tend not to have major medical health insurance and I was no exception. No Blue Cross, Blue Shield. Just bluish-gray hands that were slightly dead to the touch and cross-addictions to opiates and downers, an infected abscess on my left leg where I had been shooting, an enlarged liver, excessive weight loss, anemia, and severe depression.

I was told that the month-long cure would cost close to $30,000. *Apiece.* I promptly signed over an ASCAP advance to the hospital to get in and begin. A bed opened up in the psychiatric ward and I was one of the only drug cases there.

Gen's analytical highbrow grounding in the classics didn't take well to psychopharmacology. "The lab has replaced the couch," she complained. "They don't want to know who raped you when you were eight or what's happened to you. They come in and take your blood and *they* tell *you* whether you're depressed or not and I say, 'Whatever happened to

Freud and Jung and those wonderful people? You can't just throw them out the window.'"

I was more preoccupied with images of a jail cell mattress than an analyst's couch. I had to go clean any way I could. I met with Dr. Gold, the short, boyishly handsome, mustachioed research director. He started me on Dilaudid. My dealer Roscoe would have liked Dilaudid. He had been fooling my brain into thinking I was *buying* smack when I wasn't—at least not pure enough to leave me gravely opiated. My detox had, in a sense, begun under Dr. Roscoe's care. Maybe *that's* why I was paying him $100 a visit. His downtown was so heavily stepped on that I was easier to bring down on Bridgehampton brown than I would have been on Dilaudid. As a consequence, I detoxed rather painlessly and was taken off Dilaudid. Gold then put me on maintenance doses of Methadone and, later, Clonidine and Naltrexone.

I thought it absurd that I was stuck with locked-ward lunatics who were hallucinating and suicidal. But that arrogance wore off and I soon found myself drawing them out and playing shrink with them. It was good exercise for me and enabled me to isolate my own personal strengths and get some perspective from the *real* world of insanity. I had been through all the tricks as a junkie parent of drug-abusing kids. I began to feel that I could really make a difference.

Gold saw me a couple of times in sessions. He never tried to—or let me—turn my past or my inner life into an excuse for addiction. All he wanted, he would say, was a 10 percent motivation the first week, 20 the second, and so forth. At 50 percent, he'd say, it becomes a therapeutic situation. You've got a shot at the goal of going—and staying—straight. Control the drugs first, *then* dig into the underlying problems. A junkie with a lot of Freudian-Jungian insight is still a junkie.

Gold could see, as I sat through long, sometimes tearful silences in his office, that, beyond the hopefulness of the detox, I was overcome with feelings of midlife aimlessness, gloom, and unbearable sadness at what I had thrown away and ruined. I had lost my childhood, my family, my wealth, my career, my stature, *myself.*

"Do you ever wish," he once asked me solemnly, "that you would die?"

"I just think, sometimes, not so much about killing myself but about dying in my sleep. I do wonder at times if it's really worth going on living."

That may have been a useful—if painful—therapeutic breakthrough, but it was hardly the kind of talk Dick Schaeffer needed. In early October I was released from Fair Oaks. Drs. Gold and Millman both felt that an insanity plea was out. "We are not, in fact, going to write new law here," Schaeffer concluded.

He turned his attention to working out a plea bargain on Count One, the conspiracy and trafficking charge. Pomerantz was insisting on a guilty plea to the offense carrying a fifteen-year prison term. Schaeffer was not happy with that. "The best I could do for you on a fifteen-year plea," he told me, "is three, four years inside. I want to plea to the possession counts only, which carry five-year terms. But because of the number and gravity of the offenses," he said, "the court enjoys a tremendous latitude in sentencing."

When we were discharged as in-patients, we moved into a hotel in Summit, New Jersey, and I spent days only at the hospital. Gen's father rented a house nearby on Lake Hopatcong and helped with the children. As soon as I got out, I began to drink vodka. I was tense and fearful about the upcoming trial. There were staggering IRS and financial tangles to sort out. Tucker was invaluable in getting that under way. I walked around adding "45 + 45 = 90" in my head. I couldn't shut it out. The equation of doom: my age plus maximum term equals death.

Through an old Virginia friend, I got in touch by phone with Bill Cleary. He had vanished into the Cascade Mountains. I thought *I* had problems. They named Bill in the indictment and he was just along for the ride. "I was pissed off that they named you, man," I said. "Can you think of two people in the world who'd hate spending forty-five years in the hole more than you and me? Maybe it's a plot to break up the Del Ray Locals."

He laughed, but didn't say much. He was scared. I assured him that I would go all the way to clear him. He knew he was innocent, but he feared that the steamroller of justice would flatten him once they got Jeff, Korn, Brod, and me. *Someone* had to do time for putting a couple of hundred thousand pills on the street. Korn and Brod were making a deal; George was freelancing for the Feds; Andy had chosen Jerusalem and the Wailing Wall over maximum security; I was tending toward a deal; Jeff hired Kunstler to try to win at trial; Bill was out in the cold.

"Can a hot-air balloon make it into Canada from up there?" I asked. He laughed. I told him I was serious. "You know the border."

"Problem isn't the border," he said. "It's passports, man."

"Can we do anything about that?"

"We might make a call or two, you know, see what the situation is, so on and so forth." Bill's amusing flair for the tense, cryptic mumble, which I had known since my teens, was still intact through it all.

I called an old L.A. friend of mine and explained what was going on. He said that he knew some people who did some work with licenses and passports. He said he'd get back to me. I was too keyed up to wait.

Gen was drinking heavily again. We vaguely discussed Canada, exile, disguises, underground albums, coming back in five, six years under a different political sky. I called Denny up in Halifax. He had been reading the papers. "Doesn't look good," I said. "Is there someplace you know of up there that I might need?" I asked.

"Yeah," he said. "It's about fifty miles outside of Halifax. It's a nice little farm. I could get it cheap. All the privacy a man would ever need—and then some. *No one* wants to go up there."

"I'll take it."

Gen handled disguises. She practiced using hair dye on Trelawny. It worked. No one would have ever recognized Mr. T as a black golden retriever.

On October 17, Schaeffer called. I had never heard him so inflamed. "Mark Pomerantz just called me, John, and he says he has received information from three reliable sources that you have been in the market for three passports."

I almost dry-heaved with panic. "Pomerantz," Dick went

on, "is alarmed and he is going into court to have Judge
Sand increase your bail." My mind was racing: *Who turned
me over* this *time? Am I being watched and bugged around
the clock?*

"What does this mean?" I asked shakily.

"It means, effectively," he said, "that you could be dining
this very evening in the slammer. And you don't want to
plea or lose on a conviction while you are incarcerated. If
you stay out of prison prior to conviction by plea or trial,
John, you stand a better chance of doing a lot less time."

Schaeffer got Pomerantz to meet with us later that day,
with the written agreement that nothing I would say could
ever be used against me. I rushed into the City from Fair
Oaks, wondering if I'd be in behind bars by night.

Dick felt thoroughly undermined as I explained what had
happened. I had violated his first condition. "I panicked. I
asked some questions. That's all. Can't you understand? I'm
forty-five now, I've got five kids, I can't bear the thought of
the rest of my life in prison. It was foolish. I won't flee.
Obviously. I'd be gone by now."

"That was very stupid," he said. Pomerantz wouldn't tell
him who the snitches were. L.A. was a small town. I had my
hunches. I had to assume it was a family affair, another
move to prove me an unfit parent. I knew that the arrest
must have left Rosie and Michelle feeling vindicated. Pomerantz was sharp but easygoing. We discussed my career, the
pharmacy, the beginnings of my heroin habit, my dealers,
the rock and roll doctors. I was as frank and thorough as
possible. I apologized for my impulsive call about the passports.

Pomerantz backed down and agreed not to go to Judge
Sand.

A week later, October 24, at Federal Courthouse, I
pleaded guilty to Count One of the indictment, with a possible term of fifteen years. Counts Two through Seven—relat-
ing to the sale of Quaaludes—were dismissed. I agreed to
cooperate with the U.S. district attorney's office in any trial
or grand jury investigation. Part of the bargain stipulated
that the U.S. prosecutor—Mark Pomerantz—would report

to Judge Sand on my role as a government witness, but would not make any recommendations about my sentence.

I had a shot at impressing him—a week later. Pomerantz let me know he would be briefing *me* as *his* star witness against my co-defendant Jeff. I had "flipped" on my gamble for leniency.

Schaeffer got Judge Sand to delay sentencing for three months until January 26, 1981. I was in an out-patient recovery program and working up to forty hours a week as a counselor-in-training, he noted. I needed extensive debriefing as a government witness. I was also beginning to get my life back in shape and work as a drug counselor. I was to use my celebrity status to speak out against drugs. I was to become, in essence, a model ex-junkie.

No one needed me now more than my two oldest children. And I needed them to round out the picture of reform. I called Laura and Jeffrey out west. They were sharing an apartment and drugs.

Back in L.A., Laura went through a detox and twelve days of isolation at St. John's Chemical Dependency Center. She had hepatitis and she was gaunt. The cure didn't take. She moved in with Jeff in West Hollywood. They were mainlining and snorting and staying *just* far enough away to not be clinically hooked. That was close enough for Schaeffer and me.

I called Laura and told her what I had been through and how I had changed. "Come to Fair Oaks and give it a shot," I pleaded with her. "I see now," I said, "that everyone else in the family was getting into it because I was setting the example. If that's the case, fine. Now I'm setting another example. I did it. You can do it. You *have* to do it. Do it for me. For yourself."

"Holy shit," Laura muttered, "you're fuckin' serious, aren't you? Dad, you really *have* cleaned out."

"That's right. They may want to send me to prison, but I'm going to make it as hard for them as possible. Don't you get it? I'm fighting for my fucking life—and so are you and Jeff. Come stay with me."

"Dad," she said, "this is the first time in my life, I think, I really hear something different in your voice."

They arrived for Thanksgiving. Laura started going to the hospital as an out-patient and Jeff was put to work in the hospital lab as a step toward getting him to quit drugs. We rented a rambling nine-room house in New Providence. Sometime around Christmas a couple of ex-addict counselors moved in. Then I started getting the itch to pick up the guitar again for the first time in years.

I called Denny and told him that I thought we could do it again. Denny was drinking heavily. I told him that Fair Oaks South, the alcohol treatment wing, could help him. He came down by Christmas. He was huge, in a long furry wolverine coat. His wife Jeannette came a month later with their small child.

Chynna came to see us over the holidays with a girlfriend. It was really special to have all my children with me and to feel free of the needles. I took them to Newark Airport and noticed that the terminal was loaded with single parents shipping their kids back to their ex-spouses. I felt so frightened for the kids, traveling alone between parents, that I started writing a song in my head called "Three Babies."

It was exciting to hear the music flowing again. It wasn't long before Denny and I discussed finding Mamas. Laura heard us. "No one's heard those harmonies longer than I have," she said. She was right and she was in. I knew she could sing and strut with a natural sexy intensity. Then we thought of our old friend, Spanky McFarlane, who had some sixties hits as Spanky and Our Gang—"Sunday Will Never Be the Same" being the best-known. She was short and large and could hold her own with Cass's parts. She flew in, we made fires, had some fun again, and did some rehearsing.

The drinking got heavier and heavier. Gen went to more AA groups and started going in and out of Fair Oaks for treatment. We were quite sexually aggressive there. We had sex in the bathrooms several times, but we were getting into more brawls than ever before. We had a commune life-style of ex-junkies, friends, and drinkers at home with our two young kids. One night we were so bombed we wanted to build a fire.

"Shit," Laura said, shivering, "there's no kindling."

"You're *sitting* on it," someone else said. We axed a chair into small chunks of wood and got a great fire going.

I took the stand in Jeff's trial as Pomerantz's chief government witness and had to face William Kunstler's tenacious and cagey cross-examination. He wanted to catch me in factual discrepancies and contradictions to discredit my testimony. He hammered away at my perjury in Tam's hearing and I admitted that I had lied—about being drug-free—out of love for my son.

"So if the desire on your part is strong enough, and you want something badly enough," he said, "you have lied in the past, have you not?"

"That's true," I said openly.

"You want your liberty quite badly too, don't you, or as little imprisonment as you can get?"

"That's true," I said. The implication was that I would commit perjury again in Jeff's trial.

He grilled me at length on the call from George for the coke buy. "Who were the people you were going to sell the kilo of cocaine to if you got it?" he asked.

"They were fictitious people," I said. The appearance left me withered. There was a mistrial the first time around, but Jeff was convicted on retrial. Jeff jumped bail and fled justice.

But I had done my part and Schaeffer and Pomerantz both gave me high marks for honesty, accuracy, and the inner strength to hang in there with the great Kunstler. As ambivalent as I had felt about violating a street code of honor, I felt I had no choice whatsoever—and had achieved a personal victory under great pressure in the courtroom. Schaeffer, though, was bothered by the fact that with Jeff's flight I would be facing sentencing as the only defendant who could do time.

Two days before Christmas, Sidney Korn and Alvin Brod were sentenced on their guilty pleas. They had both been cooperative with the U.S. Attorney's office, and had described their lives and careers as having been shattered by their involvement with me. They were both sentenced to twenty-six successive weekends in prison, five years' probation, $7,500 fines, and three hundred hours of drug-related community service. They were allowed to maintain the drugstore, but were prohibited from personally selling or distributing prescription drugs while on probation.

My energy and self-confidence increased from my work at Fair Oaks as well. I had my own keys to the locked ward. I showered schizophrenics, I kept suicide vigils, helped nursing staff put violent psychotics into four-point restraints and body sheets. Some of these guys were huge and convinced by voices in their heads that they were Moses or Samson. Having a barber on the ward would have been a better way of managing the Samson psychotics.

We would drive some of the Jersey junkies through the Holland Tunnel and around the Village, where they used to score heroin. The flashbacks for a junkie reliving his scoring rituals are incredibly powerful and scary. These kids would get halfway through the tunnel and suffer wild anxiety attacks because the nightmare came back with excruciating, often humiliating vividness. It never failed to work as a deterrent.

My drug rituals weren't that localized. There wasn't a season or meteorological condition, ethnic sound or scent, time of day, aspect of sunlight, urban or rural setting that didn't, in some sense, provoke a flashback of addiction madness. I was covered. My entire life had been that nightmare.

At Christmastime, we had three Jesuses and a couple of wise men. We tried not to let them meet each other. I learned some ingenious methods of secreting drugs from our resourceful and wily patients. One came in with a huge bottle of Scope mouthwash. I never saw anyone put away mouthwash on the rocks before—or get off from gargling. I sneaked into his room, took a swig and almost choked. It was straight vodka and food coloring.

Some patients got pills and tablets from visiting lovers and relatives who "gummed" the drugs—hiding them above their teeth—while passing through security. Then they passed them into the patients' mouths while greeting them with a kiss.

A tall wasted blond kid who had been on junk for years came in and continued to have high opiate counts in his urine for the first week of hospitalization. I confronted him about his stash and he denied having one. And he wasn't withdrawing. We searched everywhere—pushed up the ceiling modules and poked around with flashlights, cut up the mattress, searched his clothes—nothing. Another week and the levels were still way up. No visitors. No meals off-ward. No sports. No stash. A true medical mystery.

I had to go through his clothes once more before we would toss him out. I saw a tie-dyed shirt on the rack. It felt starchy in spots. Part of one shirttail was ripped—a little too neatly. And one cuff was just gone. There was a large golden blotch on the back. I asked him how the shirt got ripped and he said basketball. "You don't go out for activities," I answered.

"Beats me," he shrugged. I grabbed the shirt, ripped off part of the sleeve, and licked it. It was laced with Dilaudid. I knew that taste and it explained the color of the blotch. He told me that he had soaked a solution of Dilaudid into the cotton before signing into the hospital. He was eating the shirt piece by piece and staying high the whole time.

Laura and I sat with patients and families and helped discuss complex family problems by referring to my own. Jeffrey did well for a while as a lab technician working on chromotography.

I was also beginning to go out and do interviews with Laura and sometimes Dr. Gold as part of my own antidrug campaign. Schaeffer knew this would have only a positive impact on sentencing. We went around to local schools and spoke in assemblies. There were plenty of phone calls and letters coming in. We seemed to be having an impact. I talked to Gold and his business partner, Dr. Carter Pottash, about forming a therapy-support group called Musicians and Artists Against Drugs—MAAD. We set up a nonprofit organization and a fund to aid in the drug treatment of burned-out musicians.

I was so busy doing interviews with Laura and Gold and working at the hospital that Schaeffer managed, incredibly, to get *another* sentencing delay—this time until April 7, 1981. The theory was working: that a well-known recovering junkie can get kids to listen when others can't. Three more months meant getting many more people to listen. We stepped up the campaign.

I often pointed out with genuine conviction that I finally reached two kids—my own—whom I thought never had a chance. That seemed to have the most impact—that Laura and Jeffrey had come in, along with Gen, and worked through their drug problems as a family. And we were still going back for therapy sessions.

The big push (mostly arranged by *People* magazine) came in the six weeks leading up to sentencing. Gold and I did numerous network and local talk shows together. We did "Good Morning America," "Live at Five"; we did an exhaustive three-part "Dick Cavett" on PBS, which was exhilarating; we did "A.M.-this," "P.M.-that," John Davidson's daytime show in L.A. We did local newspaper interviews. I appeared before a New York State panel on heroin and alcohol abuse.

But it was the cover photo and story of Laura and me in *People* magazine the last week in February and a full-hour appearance with Dr. Gold on "Donahue" the following week that seemed to have maximum reach. The *People* piece —HOW THEY KICKED THEIR $1-MILLION HABIT ONE DAY AT A TIME—was sensitively reported and written by a hard-digging *People* staffer named Mary Vespa. She covered plenty of ground in a week, talking to Gold and Pottash, following us around the hospital and to the big house. Hers was the most detailed account to date of our "drug ordeal," as the cover copy put it. Laura and I looked happy and healthy in the cover shot.

The magazine's own PR department then went to work to promote the issue. We ended up on "Donahue." The first few minutes of the show were fed to "Today" from the Chicago studio, so we hit the morning network TV daily double. It was one of my strongest moments on the leniency-campaign trail. I laughed and rolled with it when Phil—winding up for a "You had it all"-type question—committed a classic Freudian faux pas, saying, "Most people don't *get* to be Papa John Mackenzie."

I admitted I felt "guilty" and had been an "awful" father when my daughter needed me most as a drug-abusing teenager. I described the agony of sharing "mirror addictions" with my wife over the years. Phil, going in for the kill, asked the camera to pan in on my tracks. "This is a lovely thing to do," I said. "No," Laura said, "don't do that to my poor dad."

He cynically likened me to John Dean, who he said got rich off his Watergate memoirs and lectures. "It doesn't make me a whole lot of money to be able to shoot up," I snapped back.

He got more provocative, almost accusative, when he said I was exploiting the media to get off light, that street junkies with no money can't do magazine covers and network talk shows. Phil didn't mention that he was using *us* too. It wasn't my idea to zoom in on my needle marks for Middle America. I felt ripped off and I blew up.

"Yeah, I understand your problem," I snapped back. "You see, I personally have no influence over the judge. Whatever he wants to do he can do. If I have to go to jail, I think it's an understandable situation. That's not something I would consider to be an awful thing to happen. Being on the cover of *People* magazine, you know, saying you're an ex-drug addict and you've spent a million dollars on drugs and being here and showing my arms to the public and so forth is not my idea of show business. It's not my idea of getting back into the limelight again. It's something that's very embarrassing and something that I don't relish doing. But I do feel a great responsibility to my family and to all the people here, as a matter of fact. To try and keep other families from going through what I've been through."

The studio audience stood and erupted in wild applause and shouts for me; chills swept up and down my spine from their support and admiration.

The real moment of triumph, however, may have occurred ten minutes before airtime. A young woman who had escorted us backstage to or from makeup came to me while I was alone. She was skinny and speedy-looking. "I wonder if you could help me," she said. "My husband's a drug addict. He's hooked on cocaine." I had heard these words hundreds of times by then. I bent over toward her with more concern. "Yeah, yeah," I said. "Anyway, we have to split up because of that, you know, but he left me with, like, an ounce of coke." Her voice was getting softer. She looked around the halls.

"Yeah. So?" I didn't get it.

"So it's in my purse right this minute as we speak and I thought maybe you'd like to have it."

I panicked. Mark Gold was off in another room. I was breathing hard and sweating through the makeup. I walked away and found Gold. I was trembling and weak and I told him what had happened. I wasn't sure Mark really believed me. He may have thought I had made it up or exaggerated the incident—as a way to arm myself with some spontaneous paranoia before facing Phil and the heartland.

A lot was riding on my appearance and he could have been gunning for me. The sentence was a month off. I wondered whether she was looking to entrap me into buying or snorting a few lines early in the morning as a friendly wake-up. Or was she asking me simply to *relieve* her of the coke and destroy it? Was it all scripted? Would Phil have then interrupted one of my impassioned antidrug remarks by bringing out his star witness to put me away for good?

We never found out. The good news was that I had said no.

On the morning of the April 7 sentencing, Gen and I met Shaeffer and Tucker at an East Side midtown hotel and traveled by cab to Federal Courthouse. My nerves were raw. I felt resigned as we rode down the FDR Drive. I looked across the East River to the dreary warehouses and factories of Long Island City. The early-spring air coming in off the murky brown river was warm and humid and somewhat foul from the river and exhaust. And yet it smelled sweet to me for a good reason: I was still free.

I wondered for how long—if at all—this air might not be mine to breathe. I chewed hard on my lip and said nothing. It is an American cliché, but it is probably impossible to fully grasp and understand freedom until you are on the verge of losing it. *If nothing else,* I thought, *I've learned* that.

Laura and Jeffrey, Spanky and Denny, Mark Gold and Carter Pottash were there, as were Schaeffer's tireless and cheerful assistant, Maureen Kenniff, and some other office staffers.

Gold, Schaeffer, Tucker, Gen, Jeff, Laura, Millman, Pottash—everyone involved had done his or her best for me. I was expecting the worst as we walked inside. Several reporters lurked by the entrance. The courtroom was empty but for several agents and officials involved in the case and my cheering section.

Dick, who never once complained of overwork and stress, had lost twenty-five pounds and hundreds of hours of sleep since taking on my case. But he was as buoyant and dynamic as ever, perfectly at home in the spacious wood-paneled courtroom, wearing a natty dark-blue suit.

"Judge Sand," he said to reassure me, "is a very thoughtful and intelligent judge. Pomerantz is sensitive, bright, and he did as much as he could. Hopefully, it will turn out right."

"I guess it's not like TV."

"That is correct. It is quite unlike TV, John, in that you can't turn it off or change channels or get up in the middle and come back later." The quiet creaky courtroom was incredibly charged with electricity.

Dick tried to snap the tension. I had dressed up for the occasion and he noticed. "Let the record reflect," he said with an approving smile, "that I'm glad to see we now have some agreement on what exactly constitutes a sports jacket. We have certainly made some progress there. I would *not* have been pleased to see a Philadelphia 76ers warm-up suit today."

Dick explained that Judge Sand had read all the related documents of the case. Gold and Schaeffer had prepared lengthy and detailed pre-sentence reports for Judge Sand. Gold's dense six-page single-spaced letter covered all the medical and clinical aspects of my in-patient, out-patient, and "on-staff" experiences at Fair Oaks. He attached an eleven-point treatment plan involving individual and group therapy, twenty-hour volunteer work weeks, maintenance on Naltrexone, and monitoring urine for opiates. He recommended against imprisonment and wrote that "at the present time, John is our most effective peer ex-addict drug

counselor. He is also the most credible and articulate spokes-
man for recovering artists and other addicts."

Schaeffer's pre-sentence report and his statement before
Judge Sand were eloquent and, at times, almost poetic pleas
for probation. Even on TV I had never seen a trial lawyer
with such a remarkably fluid and self-assured delivery. In
arguing that a jail term for me would not serve to rehabili-
tate, deter, or punish me, he wrote movingly that my "tortured existence during the period of [his] drug addiction,
1976 through mid-1980, constituted a continuous course of
devastating punishment."

After some opening formalities, Dick stood and addressed
the judge. Gen was praying to herself. I was trying to stay
calm, but I thought everyone could hear my heart pounding.
Laura and Jeff kept their eyes on me for support.

Whereas I dealt drugs to procure *more drugs* for myself,
Dick pointed out, other dealers were, he said, "salesmen of
death," operating strictly for greed and profit. I was different
from typical dealers; if I hadn't been a user, I'd have never
been in the conspiracy.

Schaeffer said that Michelle had made "unreliable," "ven-
omous and untrue" comments about me to probation officers
in their report. He said that her remarks—that Gen and I
were using drugs four months after my bust, that I had once
given her a brain hemorrhage, that Tam hated Gen, that I
was "the devil incarnate," as she told Pomerantz by phone
—were motivated by vindictiveness and bitterness. Urine
tests at Fair Oaks would prove, he said, that her claim about
drugs was false.

He referred to Pomerantz's own generously supportive
letter to the judge, in which my roles as government witness
and antidrug activist were praised as genuine and honest.

Judge Sand then asked me if I had any comment to make.
I stood at the table before the judge. I wanted desperately to
appear sincere without stuttering, freezing, losing it. No
public appearance in my life would ever top this for tension.

"Yes, your honor," I began, "being in this court this
morning, in front of my wife, and my two eldest children,
my friends, is probably the most real moment in the last five
years of my nightmare of addiction we have all been

through. I am sincerely sorry for everything that has happened and hope I will be able to make amends for it as much as possible.

"Drugs have torn my family apart. My wife, my son and my daughter and myself were all addicted. It was a horrible thing. No one was able to accept treatment until I was first able to accept treatment."

The adrenaline was surging. The back of my shirt was cold and sticky. I was thinking about how long fifteen years would be. I'd be sixty. I looked over at my family and friends and swallowed hard. I sat down and Dick gave me a quick nod of support. He and I stood for the sentencing.

My heart was bursting. "It is the judgment of this court," Judge Sand announced, as my neck and chest throbbed with a frantic pulse, "that you be sentenced to a term of eight years . . ."

Nerve endings exploded. I went numb. The judge spoke on. I heard nothing. "FUCK!" I seethed to Dick. My fists hardened to stone. "EIGHT YEARS!"

". . . of which thirty days are to be spent in incarceration in such facility as the Bureau of Prisons shall determine . . ."

"Eight years," I said, dazed. "No no, John," Schaeffer said, "not eight years . . ."

It was all slow-motion, hazy, voices, stares. Gen dropped to her knees in the aisle. "Our Father who art in Heaven, hallowed be Thy name, Thy Kingdom come, Thy will be done . . ."

". . . that the execution of the sentence is suspended and that you be placed on probation for five years."

"Eight years." I repeated. Schaeffer grabbed my elbow. "No no, John. Thirty *days*. You didn't hear the rest."

I looked around and saw their faces.

Overjoyed. Astonished.

It was over.

We had done it. It slowly sank in. The judge went on about the conditions of probation, a $15,000 fine, two hundred and fifty hours of public service, thirty days in prison.

Dick had pulled off a miracle. He, Gold, the DEA, the man who turned me over—they had all done their part to give me back my life. I was looking at forty-five years and got thirty days.

Schaeffer wasn't done yet. He asked Judge Sand for my prison term to be served on weekends and requested a thirty-day delay of imprisonment to put my affairs in order. The judge said no to weekends and granted a shorter delay.

A month-long delay, the judge said, "simply prolongs the morbid anticipation of the event." And besides, he noted, "thirty days' incarceration is not forever."

That was the understatement of the century. I wanted to fly. We were all stunned and elated as we hugged and kissed and shook hands and patted backs. This was better than TV. I never wanted this scene from the movie to end.

Reporters crowded around and I answered some questions. Abbie Hoffman had just gotten three years for a drug bust. They had a hook for a column or editorial: The celebrity had gotten off light.

Dick and I went to the probation department to take care of details of my surrender. Then we rode uptown together. There was so much to say to Dick, but I kept it simple. "Thank you for saving my life." I was so relieved that I was nearly in tears. "I just hope that at some point in my life I can repay you for your kindness and hard work."

"I was happy to do it," he said. "We all were. I hope you can now devote your life to making up for all those years you lost. I view you not only as a client but as a dear friend. I hope your life continues on the same track it has been on."

Days later, Schaeffer had news of yet another—if smaller —victory. He had persuaded the Bureau of Prisons to let me do my time at Allenwood Federal Camp, the notoriously laid-back minimum-security facility in rural Pennsylvania. He was concerned that I might be branded as a "snitch" and be subjected to harassment or violence in rougher joints. Allenwood became facetiously known as the Watergate Country Club in the mid-seventies because several of the key figures involved in the White House scandal did time there.

"What's it like?" I asked Dick.

Dick paused and prepared his reply. He tried to keep a

straight face, but couldn't keep a slight grin out of the corner
of his mouth.

"John," he said, "I think you'll find that Allenwood is a
lot like Aspen—only not quite as chilly this time of year."

29

GEN AND LAURA cried all the way to Allenwood on the morning of April 20, when my prison term began. "Everything is going to be all right," I assured them. "I got the lightest imaginable sentence." We got to the front gate an hour early and drove into the nearest town. A bar was open and I drank four doubles of vodka and orange juice. Then I was ready. When some time was lopped off for the two days at MCC after the arrest and for good behavior, I was in for twenty-four days.

An ABC-TV news crew out of New York was there to film my arrival and the poignant last kisses before my surrender. We got it in just a few takes.

No massive iron bars slammed shut behind me with a terrifying crash of finality. Allenwood looked more like a rural state university campus. No high barbed-wire stone walls, only four identical dorms on a hillside, with walks leading to the building that housed the visiting center, commissary, and offices. There was a furniture workshop and a farm up the road. And activities included basketball, aerobics, softball, tennis, archery, and golf. The prison officials treated most "residents" with unusual decency.

I was assigned to grounds maintenance. Visitors were allowed every day from nine to five. Along with a warden, the place could have used an executive headhunter. Among the cons were racketeers, an ex-mayor, a bank executive, a town prosecutor. The wealthy ones made sure their families visited by buying homes in the township during their terms.

I had a fifty-square-foot cubicle in a dorm containing about a hundred and sixty men. It wasn't uncomfortable. Plastic partitions, chair, bed, desk, lamp. There was no curfew, but if you wanted to stay up late you had to go to a common room to watch TV or read.

There were about twenty-five guards and they told you at the beginning: "If you wanna go, just go." The guards didn't carry guns. The prison librarian spoke to me before I went to my dorm. "Expect some razzing, man. They all saw you at the gates this morning before breakfast on TV. They all saw you and Phil Donahue. They saw you and everybody, man. They been watchin' you for months. They seen you get thirty days, man. They hate you ass."

If they read the *Daily News,* they probably did. An editorial the day after sentencing—titled A DISGRACE AND AN OUTRAGE—denounced Judge Sand's courageous and light touch as "indefensible." No paper got as pumped up as the *Daily News.* "Reserve a niche for Leonard Sand in the judicial hall of shame," the editorial began. My sentence was compared to Abbie Hoffman's three-year term for trying to sell $36,000 of coke to a narc. I was referred to as a "missionary" and my case was cited as evidence that a double standard existed for the poor and the rich and famous. Allenwood was angrily called a "posh federal lockup." I just seemed to be on a big roll of bad press. Didn't seem to matter *what* I did; I always drew the critics.

That night I had on my prison greens and a group of black prisoners approached me. "You Phillips, right?" one of them said.

Fuck, I thought. *Problems already.*

"Yeah, that's right."

"You the one who sings, right?"

"Yeah, that's right." I saw everyone else nearby stop and listen. The guy was tall and wiry and real cocky.

"Okay, muthafucka," he said, angrily jabbing a finger at

me, "sing a song." He looked at his cronies and they all
burst out laughing. "You all right, man. Relax, we just
fuckin' witcha."

I gulped and half-smiled. "Love your sense of humor."

A short Italian thug in the corner caught my eye and
waved me over with a nod. He was stocky and dim, with a
basketball-cut undershirt and a hairy chest, wavy slick hair,
and small dark, glassy eyes. "Hey, Johnnyboy," he said,
"you okay kinda guy. We gone take carea you. I likea you
daughter. Just stick to da rules and everybody we make
friends."

"Rules?"

"Yeah. Our rules. When you go to meals, you go wid us,"
he said. Each rule had a new finger springing from his fist.
"We walk togedda. You tall, you stand in *damiddle*. When
we get up, you get up. When we sit down, you sit down. We
go to sleep, you go to sleep. You suit don't fit right, we fix,
makea nice. Twenty-tree days you go home, we stay. Whattya gone do, eh? Have a good time and don't worry about
nuttin'."

It was a safe place. I worked out and played basketball
games every night after dinner, mostly with blacks and
Puerto Ricans. No one was out to hurt anyone else because
most Allenwood inmates were short-timers—cons with brief
sentences or transfers from federal lock-downs, serving out
their time before parole and *not* looking for trouble. Anyone
insane enough to provoke fights that close to release *should*
have been locked up.

I learned very few names and stuck to myself. No one
hated me. The warning from the librarian about hazing *was*
the hazing. I never picked up any of the guitars lying
around. I just wanted to shut down for twenty-four days and
get out.

My probation officer, Phil Albertson, helped me a great
deal. He was shrewd and wise enough to warn me about the
snakes who might bait me over the light sentence—just to
sucker me into a punchout that would get me heavy time in
a lock-down.

And there was the standard prison wisdom: Do not under
any circumstances tease the homosexuals. I showered before

sunrise, just to get in there by myself. Residents tended to shower in special-interest groups. The blacks showered with blacks. Puerto Ricans with the Puerto Ricans. Gays with the gays. Politicians with the politicians. Same seat, same people at every meal. It wasn't too different from life on junk in one sense: Rituals blinded you to the outside world, shaped your time, and gave life purpose.

The chatter never drifted far beyond the present, the chores, books, food, sports, TV. Very few conversations centered on the past, home, work, the outside, the Big Fuckup that got you inside. They tell you to forget it. It drives prisoners nuts to have to talk about it, to have a past and broken dreams. They focused on tomorrow, the prison as microcosm. This is My World now. The only reality. Visitors came and went.

More than menacing or hostile, the atmosphere was gray and solemn. For the first time in longer than I could remember, I felt—and often was—alone.

I read mysteries, escapist novels. Erle Stanley Gardner, Dashiell Hammett. Gen came three times a week with Laura and they behaved like ladies. Tam came three times, Jeff once. The day room for visits was large and barren, with plastic chairs, tables, and big windows.

The food was a pleasant surprise, with a delicious kosher kitchen, an elaborate salad bar, and a tasty brunch on Sundays at ten-forty-five, four hours later than usual.

Three and a half weeks was enough time to get depressed and reflect on what had happened and what lay ahead. Ironically, some of the men inside said they preferred lockdowns with high walls, armed guards, and killers on the loose. They looked at minimum-security not as a privilege but as a threat. Some had been so cooped up and demoralized for so long under duress that they didn't trust themselves any longer. They couldn't risk even *seeing* the wideopen spaces until they were out. They were afraid of panicking, they'd snap, run for it, throw it all away just as their hard-won liberty was within reach.

At Allenwood, I came to understand with greater clarity that dread of freedom and what, in my case, lurked behind it —a destructive self-loathing unleashed on my life's accomplishments and joys. That's what was so overwhelming. I could clean out, I could do time for trafficking in painkillers. But the underlying crime for which I had *really* been nailed was trafficking in pain. I had committed a felony of the heart. And there was no way to cop a plea on that charge. I just had to start living again.

When I was released, the TV crews were waiting for me at the Big House in Jersey. Having paid my debt to society, I now faced—sobered and trim—the staggering debts to just about everyone else. There was close to $150,000 to pay out —not counting back taxes, fines, and penalties. I owed $8,000 to two hotels; $18,000 to hospitals for Gen, Laura, and Bijou; $10,000 to Dick Schaeffer's firm; another $35,000 to Tucker's for contractual haggling he had done since Gen's solo LP in 1974; $4,000 for the limousine firm that got me to and from the pharmacy—and, inadvertently, to and from Allenwood, traveling by plea bargain; another $20,000 or so in outstanding claims and judgments for bloody walls and unsolicited interior design as a tenant. Then there was Fair Oaks.

I had racked up a massive bill in the $60,000 ballpark for in-patient and out-patient therapy, laboratory and other charges for all of us. The services covered me and all my treatment and related work, Laura's evaluation and treatment, Jeffrey's two hospitalizations, Denny's evaluation and hospitalization, Gen's evaluations, emergencies and three lengthy hospitalizations, and outpatient treatment of friends and family.

Gold's "forensic" work for me as an expert witness came to more than $10,000—all of it related to my campaign for leniency. He charged $750 an hour—his standard fee for such work—to write his letter to Judge Sand. There was a three-hour, $2,250 meeting with Schaeffer about the letter. On two occasions, he billed me for "continuous psychiatric supervision"—once for two days, once for three days—at $1,000 a day. These were for trips we made—I recall it was Chicago and Houston—for lesser media appearances, when I wanted him to be on hand for support. On those days, Gold felt our TV appearance, because of brevity, local rather than network viewership, or focus on me, offered him a more limited opportunity to present his own expertise on drug prevention and detoxification. So he billed me for his time. However, there was no charge for, say, our higher-profile appearances with Dick Cavett in New York, John Davidson in L.A., or Phil Donahue in Chicago.

Gold had told Schaeffer that he would not want to take the stand and offer testimony under oath before Judge Sand at my sentencing hearing. So they agreed that Gold would prepare a letter in which Gold would recommend probation.

Pottash and Gold showed up for the trial and the sentencing as observers at my insistence. (My attorney and I had asked them to cancel appointments for the entire day).

I never doubted that Gold's caring, active presence in my life was critical to me and the family—for my medical and legal rescue. I was just broke and uninsured and I felt I had, after all, helped put Fair Oaks on the national map through my appearances on TV and in the press, although the hospital was filled both before and after I went there.

It was soon clear that I had to make a choice between becoming a professional patient or a professional musician. The spring and summer of 1981 was a difficult time of readjustment. Gen was in and out of Fair Oaks for months that year, part of the time at Fair Oaks South, the alcohol treatment center in Lakehurst, where the *Hindenburg* went down. We seemed unable to live together straight. While I had been in prison, she went to numerous AA meetings. Once I got out, I too was lapsing fast into the only "drug" available to me—booze. We were both battling for our sanity all over again. "You were a prince on junk," she said, "compared to how you are on vodka."

She was on Thorazine some of the time and we attended marital counseling sessions with her therapist. It was painful for her to sometimes see Laura and me do a talk show on a TV set in the dayroom.

By then Denny, Jeannette, their young child, and new baby had taken their own place in a nearby town. Denny, bloated and drinking heavily, agreed to go to Fair Oaks South. Laura and Spanky moved out and shared another place. Gen's mother Audrey was with me at the house to help with the shopping, cooking, and the kids.

While I was in Palm Beach for a media appearance, Gen tried to escape Fair Oaks as an in-patient. There were suggestions in therapy that she leave me, that she could never have her own independent personality around me. She fought the idea. "Marriage is a sacrament," she said.

She started running past staffers and down hallways. "DR. STRONG! DR. STRONG!" resounded over the hospital's P.A. system—the code for an emergency. She ran like a frightened deer, colliding with patients and staff, kicked in a door, and raced into the residential street. A passing car struck her and knocked her to the ground. She was, fortunately, not seriously injured.

In the summer we started rehearsing as the new Mamas and the Papas. I had to get on the stick. I hadn't picked up the guitar in three years. As luck would have it, my prized guitar turned up in a Manhattan pawn shop after its disappearance from my hotel room. The kid who bought it was later told it had once belonged to me. He was sensitive and honest enough to track down Bob Tucker. The kid thought it was only right that I get it back, and we made him a solid offer for the guitar. I had played for cancer ward patients and the elderly as part of my public service and those moments inspired some new tunes. Soon I was cutting demos at Mediasound and it felt great to be involved with music again.

Gold and Pottash, despite my unpaid bills, floated me personally loans of $7,000. I owed Psychiatric Associates another $13,800 for services to myself, members of my family, friends, and relatives of friends. The money was used to set up a new band and to cover living and moving expenses. We talked about a business deal with them and Tucker. We would call it Four Point Management, a reference to a means of restraining patients. Tucker would do the day-to-day management of the band.

The idea was abandoned before it got very far. Gold and Pottash grew concerned about the ethical issues of entering into a business venture with an ex-patient—one whom Gold had ignored at first to shake out any smug superiority. Now I owed the hospital a fortune, had borrowed close to $7,000 from Gold and Pottash, and was discussing a business deal with them. I was reentering the music industry, but it did not fly.

Before sessions at Mediasound, I liked to come in from Summit and hang out at the rooftop pool of the Sheffield, a high rise across the street from Mediasound on West 57th Street. I was dating a woman who lived at the Sheffield, but began flirting with a lively bright-eyed University of Pennsylvania student named Jane. Jane was the Sheffield lifeguard. She always had a cheerful smile, a great sense of humor, and she loved to laugh. She was a foot and a half shorter than me. She had dark wavy hair and big sparkling green eyes.

I stood against the rail, looking west over what once was known as Hell's Kitchen, past the Hudson into Jersey. I motioned for Jane to come over. I told her to give me a kiss. She laughed.

"Give me a break," she said.

"Let's go."

"Ahhh," she sighed sarcastically, "you're SO charismatic."

My Sheffield girlfriend turned out to be as big a drinker as I was and not much fun in the sun up there. Or in the bar on the street. She knew every guy. So I flirted with Jane in her Speedo suit and whistle. In fact, we spent so much time together by the pool that Jane felt sorry for the woman.

Someone else must have, too, because one night I left a bar after visiting her on West 57th and headed over to Mediasound across the street. I was carrying my guitar. I had a vague feeling that someone had followed me out, someone who had seen us. I ignored him. As I stepped on the curb, I felt a push, then a mild twinge through my neck. I saw someone in the corner of my eye and I instinctively swung my guitar case and caught him in the head. He took off. I was smashed.

I felt no pain, just faintness. I walked back to the Sheffield. The doorman went crazy. "What's all this blood from?"

"Blood?" My leather jacket was ripped near the collar and I had pools of blood at my feet. My clothes were soaked. I dropped to a chair and felt numb. I tasted blood. I started to panic. The nudge I had felt on the street was a knife going into my shoulder and neck area, right toward my lung. The leather saved me. The cops arrived and took me down the street to Roosevelt Hospital. I was lucky. "Another inch either way and . . ." they told me.

Gen and I spent one weekend that summer with Carter at his rented place in the Hamptons. I had gotten to like both Gold and Pottash. Mark was the dedicated clinician and family man who wanted to be at home after work. Carter was the crack administrator, a bachelor with a busy social life.

It was great fun. After ordering dinner at Melon's in Bridgehampton, I left Gen and Carter at the table and drove to my dealer Roscoe's for some moonshine. He also bootlegged. I finally found Carter's house at four in the morning. They had hitched home from the restaurant with my doggie bag.

The next day I took Carter over to meet Roscoe. He asked Carter if he wanted anything to drink. I told him to give Carter some vodka. Carter must have been expecting a glass. As a host, Roscoe didn't pour vodka from the bottle but *into* the bottle. He walked into the kitchen and got a bottle from a case of empty fifths under the sink. "Be right back," he said. Then he went to his vats and returned with the bottle filled with his homemade vodka. Carter shook his head, wouldn't touch the stuff, then lectured me about my drinking all the way back.

He and Gold both knew I was getting into trouble and they used their leverage. In August, they sent a blunt letter to Schaeffer. I had violated my eleven-point treatment program. I was not sticking to Naltrexone as scheduled, they said; I had failed to continue therapy sessions; I had dropped the ball on MAAD; my antidrug work was petering out: I was "in bad standing" with Fair Oaks, Mark wrote, and "leading an erratic, unstructured, and irresponsible life which will certainly lead [me] to re-addiction." They threatened to inform the court of my behavior within ten days if I didn't shape up.

We stepped up the rehearsals and demos and started falling into place as a foursome. Bob Tucker was our manager and he had begun managing Laura's career. She got a film

part for *Love Child,* about a woman who fights to bear her
child in prison. Laura spent close to two months around
Fort Lauderdale and was excited about working again. Because she kept clean off coke—which cuts the appetite—she
put on weight. She had dropped to under 100 pounds when
she came east to get help. Now she looked clearheaded and
wanted to work. She had a friend named Sue Blue down
there to look after her, as well as a Fair Oaks drug counselor
named Karen. After the shoot she rented herself a spiffy
Mercedes 450SL.

Life at home with Gen was turbulent. She had tried to
stay off booze for months and was going to AA meetings.
Jeff and I were drinking heavily and we both ballooned to
250 pounds. I was out of the house for days on end and
having an affair with the next-door neighbor. Gen let me
know she was still in love with me and plagued by jealousy
and anger.

Susie came in to visit Jeff and Laura and stayed with
Spanky and Laura in their own place. Susie and Audrey,
Gen's mother, got along quite well. With Denny and Spanky
and their family ties, counselors dropping in and out, Gen,
my kids, and me, we had one big happy family.

While we were all out of the house shortly after my birthday, Gen took a bottle of Scotch into the bathroom, locked
the door, and chugalugged it until she went into a blackout.
She slashed up her arms and wrists with a dull knife and was
bleeding heavily when we found her, conscious and hysterical, in the kitchen. Sue, Susie, Laura, and I restrained her,
tied up the arteries to cut the flow of blood, and got her to a
hospital. She was in Regent Hospital in New York for a
couple of months, right up until Christmas Eve, 1981.

In early 1982, Audrey left for South Africa, Sue Blue
moved in from the City to help with the chores and kids,
and we began putting together a road band at SIR studios in
the West 50s. Our first bookings were for March. When Gen
got word that her grandmother had died and left her a small
inheritance, she used the money to move into her own apartment in Summit by late winter. Weeks later, we were legally
separated. While at the Regent, she had come to the conclusion that she had no other recourse.

The music made me feel alive again, though it was peculiar to hear the old harmonies with Cass gone and Michelle
accusing me of being the devil incarnate. The wistfulness
soon fell away. Denny was still a bond to past glories.
Spanky was a close friend of Cass's and, like Cass, had a big
contralto voice. And, to Laura, I *was* Papa John.

We had a hot band behind us, led by a slightly built,
gently mannered South African keyboardist/composer
named Arthur Stead. I had met Arthur at Mediasound when
I was doing demos and he was with Peter Frampton. We hit
it off and I offered him a gig as leader of the road band.
Arthur had blond curly locks, big blue eyes, he wore tight
pants and T-shirts, and was a true rock and roll road warrior. Arthur also seemed to have a taste for imaginative
partying. I had never been on the road for more than a week
at a time, except as a Journeyman in the Ice Age of acoustic
folk. My backup musicians looked like they were *teething* to
"Monday Monday." I was ready for the road after four
years of staring at "General Hospital" and "All My Children" on junk. I needed some air.

My probation officers needed to make sure that was *all* I
needed to get through a tour. I was frank with them. I was
not a gospel act. There would be drugs around. "Give me all
the urine tests you want," I said. "I can't guarantee you a
drug-free band. I just don't want to be popped for this," I
said. I had to check with my P.O. at least once a month—
but he could see me whenever he wanted. And Probation
could administer a spot urine on me anytime, anywhere. If I
had a "dirty" urine with opiates, I'd be thrown in the slammer to serve out every day of my eight-year suspended sentence. And not in Aspen.

There were very precise ground rules. Every time I left the
Southern District, I was to let Probation know and they'd
call ahead to where I was going. If I crossed state lines, there
were calls to make on both sides of the border.

On the eve of the tour, I wanted to get the band into the
proper spirit of debauchery, so we all went to a live sex show
in Times Square with unbelievable S&M stunts having to do
with naked girls holding dripping candles over guys
strapped down on wooden beams in leather jockstrap-like

harnesses. "What's supposed to happen after all this?" Laura asked me, peeking squeamishly through her hands.

"I guess the guy wax off."

We did an unannounced gig at the Other End on March 3, which was a strong show that built our confidence. Then we opened the tour on March 5 in Princeton.

It was the day John Belushi was found dead in his suite at the Château Marmont. For two hours before the show, we sat in a hotel room and watched the evening news reports. That had once been my home. So had the speedballs. The sad, grisly tale cut awfully close. Belushi was alone in a hotel room. So was Cass. So were countless others. I had a hundred and fifty nights alone in hotel rooms stretching ahead of me. I always dreaded being alone. I hated hotels. My mind wandered. The only drug to cut the loneliness would be booze.

The first week went great and the music was hot. After a Philadelphia show at the Ripley Music Hall, one of our road managers handed me a paper towel backstage with a note scribbled on it: HI! DO YOU REMEMBER ME? I WAS THE LIFEGUARD AT THE SHEFFIELD LAST SUMMER. I'M STILL AT PENN AND CAME BY TO SEE THE SHOW. IT WAS TERRIFIC. I'M AT THE BACKSTAGE ENTRANCE AND I TOLD THE BIG GUY OUTSIDE I WAS AN OLD FRIEND OF YOURS AND WANTED TO SAY HI. FIFTY OTHER PEOPLE SAID THE SAME THING AND WE'RE ALL STILL OUT HERE. I'D LOVE TO SEE YOU. JANE.

I was delighted to see a familiar face on the road at Penn. Jane was as cheerful as ever. Her spring break was starting the next day and she was driving up to the City to see her family.

"Great," I said, "I'll get you tickets for the show tomorrow at the Savoy. Better yet," I said, "come by the St. Moritz in the afternoon and we'll hang out and go over there together."

Jane saw the show with her two sisters. She came backstage afterward and so did Gen. It was uncomfortable. By then Gen had a new boyfriend from AA and was settled in her small apartment in Summit. I secretly held Jane's hand whenever Gen was out of sight. I was being cute. "I guess it

never really hit me that you're actually married," Jane said.
She was a bit uneasy.

"I haven't really lived with her much since you and I met."

"That's true."

We spent the next day together, brunching on eggs Benedict, strawberries and cream, and brandy. We had the *Times* sent up and read a brief review by Stephen Holden together on the bed. I wanted to get New York out of the way early. My feeling was that if the *Times* liked us, we were in the clear. If they killed us, why go on? Before commenting on the music, Stephen Holden felt compelled to remind readers of my media tour in the early spring as a "shamelessly self-promoting press blitz as he avoided a jail term." Then despite his dark suspicions about a "quick money" motive, he conceded that we came across with "a surprising amount of verve and expertise." He said we had a future. "The feeling onstage was one of genuine celebration rather than fake camaraderie."

We got an even better rave from Wayne Robins in *Newsday* after a show in Glen Cove on the Island. "It is with some astonishment," he concluded, "and a good amount of glad-heartedness that it can be said that not only did the songs and singers sound terrific, in most cases they never sounded better."

The band had a few more dates in the metropolitan area and I saw Jane again a week later on St. Patrick's Day, just after her twenty-first birthday. I was at the St. Moritz. We got totally wild, hit all the Irish bars, and ordered up champagne. Jane threw up three times and passed out.

We were inseparable for the next four days. We went out for dinner, slept off the mornings, had dinner at Elaine's, lunch at Maxwell's Plum, caught an act at the Lone Star Café, hung out with Laura, walked all over town from the Village to Central Park. We were both quite happy. It meant so much to have someone with me who lived for the brighter side of life, rather than a morbid fixation on drugs, booze, and escape. Jane was just what I needed.

In March and April we played New England, Ohio, Denver, Chicago, Minnesota, Texas, Louisiana, and Washington.

At our gig in Boulder, Colorado, Denny and I met backstage
with Dick Weissman, my Journeyman banjo-picker. It
seemed so far back. He had his dream house in the Rockies,
a lovely family, and a thriving academic career at the University of Colorado–Boulder with the Music Department.
We loved reliving the old folkie days.

Arthur helped guide me through the new funky days. In
our regressive and decadent road mode, we christened the
band members' cocks—the Educator, the Destroyer, the
Spoiler, the Crippler, the Terminator. Arthur taped photos
of nude women on the hard plastic flip-down window shades
on planes.

I bought him plastic handcuffs as a gag birthday gift and
he slapped them on a gorgeous woman on a flight to New
Orleans. She was happy to sit with him as his prisoner. She
worked a topless joint in the French Quarter and knew dozens of dancers and party girls for the band. She took Arthur
home and showed him her set of steel cuffs on a chain bolted
to her four-poster bed.

"Let's see if you're ready for the real thing now, hotshot,"
she bragged.

We carried ridiculous sex aids with us, like the inflatable
date whose brief virginal life ended noisily when she sat on a
lit cigarette in my hotel room and flew all over the room
until she was a rumpled wad of plastic. I was drinking,
searching for new improved female companionship to cut
the loneliness. Arthur and I joked about the S&M fetishists
who asked women to crawl around with leather-studded dog
collars and leashes in foreplay. I had to give it a try. I met a
woman after a show and she wanted to party.

She was bright, playful, and rather stunning. Her parents
used to like the Mamas and the Papas. I didn't know how to
get things going. I asked if she could bark. She seemed not to
understand.

"You heard me right. Do you like to bark?"

"Of course not. I don't *bark.*"

"Can you meow, make cat noises?"

"No way. What is this, a pop group or 'Wild Kingdom'?"

I got upset and took charge. "Gee, I don't know what
kind of party this is going to be. I thought you wanted to

have fun. You don't bark, you don't meow, what the hell *do* you do for kicks?"

She seemed offended. "For Pete's sake, John, you haven't asked me if I could *quack!*"

When I wasn't on the road, I came back home to a room at the Gramercy Park Hotel. Jane came up for as many weekends as possible, bringing her heavy texts and papers while she finished out her junior year.

I was flunking out at Fair Oaks. In early May, Gold sent off a succinct, critical letter to Schaeffer, to the effect that I was still "in bad standing" with the hospital, I was "an alcoholic in need of detoxification and intensive psychiatric treatment," and "a major relapse risk." Again Gold noted my failure to keep up with the treatment regimen. "I have no other choice," he wrote, "but to terminate John from our program."

Pottash then wrote Tucker explaining that I was not terminated for failure to ever pay anything for my aftercare; that was my "smokescreen" excuse in avoiding therapy. I met with Pottash over lunch and he told me to tell him which bills I thought I ought not to have to pay and he would simply cancel them. I set aside the media-related continued supervision charges and he agreed to lop them off the total. I set up a schedule with Tucker for repayment of the loans and for payments of the bills that were left. Carter also urged me to come back into treatment and resume the probationary regimen.

The band was on the road through the summer. Jane and I were at the Gramercy and she worked as a lifeguard again a couple of days a week. Gen moved to a house in Short Hills, New Jersey, and was constantly fighting with her mother, whom she felt always took my side and condoned an "Edwardian," sexist marriage.

Whenever I visited her and the kids, we would get drunk and she would be consumed by her deep hatred for me and would sometimes go after me. It was an ugly scene.

"You know," Gen would say, "Old Greenwich on Dilaudid was sane compared to this."

Jane came with me for a lovely stretch of the road through New England in late summer. We recorded more demos near Silver Lake in Plymouth, Massachusetts. We returned several times in the fall. She was in her senior year and would fly up on weekends. She was lucky enough to schedule all her classes on Tuesday.

The band was running into financial trouble by then. The hotel and travel expenses were soaring. Bob Tucker had staked a lot of money for the tour and it didn't look good.

Laura made it back to "One Day" for a few episodes in the early fall. Gold had helped negotiate her return by stipulating to her producers that a drug counselor be with her at the studio at all times. She had been off drugs for most of two years. She did two or three shows, then returned to the road.

Tucker and I were notified in October by attorneys for Gold and Pottash that repayment of the $7,000 I owed them should be made immediately or they would initiate legal action to recoup their money, since I had failed to honor the payment schedule that Tucker and I had set up with them. Repayment of the $13,800 owed to Psychiatric Associates was also due, since I had defaulted on that payment schedule as well.

The bills just kept mounting. In the fall, my son Jeffrey was going back on downers and having trouble staying awake at the lab job. He went into the City and swapped his tape recorder for a quarter ounce—seven grams—of coke. He shot it all in one frenzied fifteen-hour binge and nearly went out of his gourd. He was fired by Fair Oaks and narrowly avoided a catastrophic head-on car crash with Laura's friend Sue Blue. He spent three months at Fallkirk Hospital near Bear Mountain. It was a sad period for Jeffrey, but it shook him up, scared him, and got him on the road to recovery.

In November 1982, Jane and I, during one of her visits from Penn, moved into a quaintly furnished one-bedroom place on Hudson Steet in the West Village. The apartment had a working fireplace and terrace over a garden and saved us a fortune after the hotel. Tam visited on weekends from his boarding school in Jersey. We got to relax and have peaceful dinners by the fireplace. Jane always handled the time with Tam beautifully.

Christmas, again, was difficult. Gen and her mother fought until Gen threw Audrey out. I grabbed Bijou and brought her to Hudson Street through the holidays over Gen's protests. Gen left for England and Audrey stayed with Tam and Bijou in Jersey. Audrey and Jane were getting along rather well—despite the potential for awkwardness.

In January we played the first of several successful extended bookings in the casino rooms in Nevada. We had a week at the Sands and a week at the Imperial Palace in Vegas. It was a rush to drive down the dazzling Strip in Vegas at night and see THE MAMAS AND THE PAPAS on a huge marquee, knowing the big rooms and meals were comped by the hotel. It really *was* like we were back.

But Vegas was also the first time I was required by Probation to register with local authorities as a federal drug felon. All felons have to do this in cities with legalized gambling and ports of entry for drug smuggling. You have twelve hours from the time of your arrival in town. It was strange. I had to apply for permission to travel abroad, too. We had lucrative bookings in Israel, but the Probation people turned me down. Then they *granted* permission to play a three-month tour of Australia and the Far East and *Australia* turned me down.

Checking in with the sheriff was humiliating. It was the only time since the sentencing and prison term that I was made to feel like a criminal. I had to pass a urine test, then get fingerprinted and photographed for a laminated I.D. card that branded me a CONVICTED FELON. KNOWN DRUG ADDICT.

When I checked into the hotel, Arthur asked me what was wrong. I said nothing.

"Hey, man, you been crying or what?" He was right. I wiped away a tear and toughened up.

"Nothin', man, I guess if I liked goin' by the rules I wouldn't have this problem to begin with, would I?"

In April I invited Gen out with Bijou—her third birthday was coming up—and Tam stayed in school. Gen looked wonderful. She had stayed off booze for a couple of weeks. We had a large suite with the mirror over the bed, the big sunken tub, the works, Vegas-style. We swam and had a good day together.

Then at night everything went haywire. Gen started drinking as we waited backstage. She got tanked up and wandered through the casino, swiping gambling chips off the felt tables and tossing them into the air. When we took the stage, she started screaming wildly—"1976! 1976! DAMMIT!"—and throwing glasses and ashtrays toward us. I could only assume she was referring to the year we got hooked on smack in London. One glass struck a pregnant woman in front, but she wasn't cut.

The show went on, but Gen was finally hauled off by security guards. Gen was in a blackout state and didn't know what she was doing. No charges were pressed. She left Vegas the next day and flew back. We sent Bijou off to be with Audrey, who was visiting my sister Rosie in L.A.

Jane graduated in May, signed a lease for her own apartment in Brooklyn, and took off for a six-week jaunt through Europe in early June. She had been accepted to a medical school for the fall and she had to get on with her life.

Gen and I tried something of a reconciliation at Hudson Street. Jane was furious. Hudson Street was *her* place, too. She left for Europe with pneumonia and was down to 100 pounds.

Gen had taken a loft a mile uptown at 26th and the Avenue of the Americas. We tried living under one roof. By the end of that sometimes brutal month, we were lucky there was a roof at all.

Jane called every four or five days from Europe and was miserable. It took her two weeks to stop crying. She called from the only phone on a Greek island and Gen accepted the collect call—only to scream at her six thousand miles away.

"John doesn't love you! He never wants to see you again! Stop calling him!" Gen yelled.

When Jane called from the next island, Gen got on the second phone and starting insulting Jane again. Jane screamed back this time, "Get off the FUCKING PHONE, dammit! John, if you don't do something about her, I'm never going to see you again!"

We got into a furious screaming brawl. Neighbors called
911 and the police arrived. I put Jane on hold thousands of
miles away and shoved Gen out of the apartment. She
started pounding on the door and shrieking. I told Jane to
come back early. I was black and blue. Vases were broken. I
told Jane I needed her. The cops came and made me let Gen
in. She grabbed her shoes and returned to her apartment.

"You're drinking two fifths of vodka a day and abusing
me all day long and you haven't given me any money. You're
a savage and an Indian," Gen yelled.

The band left days later, in the middle of July, for a week
at Harrah's Marina in Atlantic City. I was feeling depressed
and hopeless. After a show, I went out looking for oblivion.
The summer air was still and humid. I asked a taxi driver to
take me to the sleaziest bar in town. I didn't give a fuck
about anything anymore. The driver did what I asked. I was
the only white man inside. The place looked like an unem-
ployment office for terrorists. I downed five screwdrivers and
got numb-drunk.

The bartender was tough and black. I asked him to crack
a fifty and I walked to a pay phone across the street to call
the cab company. I was followed out of the bar by three guys
who asked me for my wallet. They were dark, with foreign
accents. Before I could think about it, I kicked one of them
in the crotch and dropped him. I took the other one out with
an elbow to the nose-eye region. The third one and I went
toe-to-toe until I collapsed and lay still, moaning.

When he reached down for my pocket, all my pent-up
fury erupted and pumped a ferocious strength back into my
arms. I wasn't going to take this shit from anyone. I grabbed
his hair in my two fists, rose up off my back, and steered his
face flush against the rough concrete pavement. Twice. He
howled in pain, went limp, and rolled over.

Jane arrived the next night and when she saw the bruises
and the blood in my ears she got me to a doctor. We went
back to New York for a much-needed week's rest. I was
taking a beating on the road. I wasn't the only one.

Laura signed a new contract with the show for the fall
1983 season. She was elated. She wanted nothing more than
to work her way back into the TV industry. She was strug-

gling with the crazy pressures and pitfalls of the road. I didn't want to see her fall into any traps that would threaten or stop the progress she had made since she came east in 1980. She was giving it everything she had. Besides, the way the finances were going, we *all* could have used some moonlighting gigs.

The band had lost more than $150,000 in a year and a half. I was thinking of cutting an album, but I just couldn't bring myself to commit to it. There was new music, but we were turning into a nostalgia act. The real risk, though, was that Laura and I might wind up gambling our lives just to keep on the road. No gig was worth that.

Jane and I decided to get away from it all during my week off. We saw Bill Cleary in Ocean City, Maryland, for a day or so, but the resort area was too crowded and commercial. We asked Tucker's secretary to find us a quiet spot on a lake somewhere. Days later we pulled into the Colonial Court Motel on Lake George in the tiny upstate New York village of Bolton Landing.

The place was owned by Dan Towers, an entrepreneur who had been the executive vice-president of the real estate division of Fuqua Industries in Phoenix. He then left the huge multinational firm and bought up small, sometimes run-down buildings and businesses—liquor stores, restaurants, motels—and refurbished, renovated, and expanded them. Then he would sell them and look for something else.

Jane and I stayed in a two-room cabin with a fireplace, a creaky wide-plank floor, and old furniture. We loved roughing it. Behind the cabins, a cold, clear stream fed into the lake. We took long walks and went boating. I was drinking so heavily that I couldn't stay out in the lake for more than an hour without having to go back to a lakeside bar to tank up.

Gen put Tam on a bus at Port Authority and went back to her apartment. I knew Tam, who was thirteen, would love the clean, woodsy air and the boating. Audrey had taken Bijou on to South Africa. Tam's departure left Gen all alone and despondent. She felt she couldn't make it on her own.

Tam called her from a bus station upstate and told her, "I love you, Mom."

Gen was coming apart fast. "I love you, Tam," she cried, "but I can't go on living and I want you to remember all the good times we've had. But I can't go on being tortured like this."

Tam was so afraid for Gen that he called from every bus stop to see if she was okay. She wasn't—and the phone kept ringing.

She had gotten a prescription filled for antihistamines, swallowed thirty pills, and collapsed. A plumber who had been working in her apartment returned and got in. When he bent over her limp body, her heart had stopped. By the time she was rushed to Bellevue, emergency medical workers had brought her back to life.

Every day up in Bolton Landing, I would walk the hundred yards from our cabin to see Dan Towers and his wife Betty. I told them all kinds of weird stories about what had been happening with my life since the Mamas and the Papas of the sixties. Dan was more of a Vic Damone–Big Band buff. I told him the band was getting killed on the road. I mentioned my long-standing unresolved business with ABC/MCA. I said the IRS had frozen my ASCAP income.

In August I decided to disband the Mamas and the Papas and catch my breath. Laura went straight from our last show into rehearsals with no break. She was burned out and not ready to jump in. She needed a week's break, but she was locked in. She struggled through three episodes of her show, but she was irritable and distracted. She was fired again.

Later in the fall, I got a long, long-overdue call from an old friend who finally tracked me down—Scott McKenzie. He was living in Virginia Beach, playing the odd local gig, living the ambiguously distinguished life of a true One-Hit Wonder.

"It's amazing, man," he laughed. "If I had a dime for every Vietnam vet who comes up to me and told me how 'San Francisco,' like, got him through the war because it made him dream of the Summer of Love, his girlfriend, making it in the woods on acid, man, I'd be . . ."

"Scott," I said, "that's the problem. You *do* get a dime. That's *all* you get, Scott. The problem is you don't get a *dollar.*"

We joked about the past. He opened up and told me about Michelle and the brief affair at the beach in 1969 after we split. We caught each other up. I told him Denny had dried out. Scott had too. He had been messed up for years, but had finally gotten the kind of help he needed all along. I told him I had recently seen Weissman out in Boulder. He knew all about my case from the papers and had seen me on TV. He had never met Gen. It was the first time we had spoken in fifteen years.

Scott came up to see me several times at the end of the year. He looked weathered but healthy—long, bushy salt-and-pepper hair, a thick mustache, and clear blue eyes. We sat up all night and wrote a song called "Kokomo." We called Denny together and talked about getting a trio going. Then I went down to see him at the beach. It was great to have an old friend from home back in my life.

Jane was under great pressure at med school in the city and had her own problems. I had lost the Hudson Street place and, if I wasn't floating between hotels, I was at Jane's apartment. I didn't exactly fit in. There were two roommates. She was fed up with my drinking and finding pint bottles of vodka in her shoes and in her dresser. We broke up a couple times—for a week breather each time—through the winter months.

The probation department got me a court-appointed Irish shrink whose office was on 42nd Street and Eighth Avenue above a porno palace. It was bitter cold. I had on a Robert Hall coat and a pint of whiskey in my pocket as I'd walk past the hookers, pimps, junkies, and peep-show perverts. I had ugly stubble, my face was turning Bowery purple, I had wild gray hair, and I didn't give a shit about anything anymore. Before and after my appointments, I wandered around Times Square in a double-vision funk, deciding whether or not I *should* live in the Bowery.

"What's your problem?" he asked.

"They want me to give up drinking."

"Now why would they want you to do that?" he asked, as if he had never heard a more preposterous demand. He said the state provided tokens for the sessions; he handed me packs of four.

I returned to Bolton Landing for a visit in the early spring of 1984. This time Dan Towers told me that he would be interested in managing my career—*if* I agreed to quit drinking altogether. His plan was to settle all the outstanding legal tangles, get the band shaped up again with tighter management, and get me healthy.

"If you don't agree to all this," he said, "fine. Betty'll give you ten dollars and you can take off. Because you can't even get out that door by yourself—and it'd be your last ten."

"Gimme the ten and I'm outta here," I said, holding my palm out with a grin.

He took me up on the dare. I grabbed the money and walked out the door.

"Where's he going like that?" I heard Dan ask Betty as they watched me head toward the lake drive from their kitchen window. Then I stopped. Where *was* I going to go?

I turned around and walked back into their kitchen.

Dan laughed and extended his hand. "Who are you kidding? I knew you'd be back. Now let's stop cockin' around and get to work, whattya say?"

Dan and Betty set me up in their largest unit at the resort and I worked on getting into better shape as the spring thaw brought movement and color back to drowsy Bolton Landing.

In the spring, Tam came up to visit at Dan's during a school break. Gen came up once, during one of my brief breakups with Jane. But she and I didn't get along very well and she took a bus home.

Later in the spring, Dan and Betty stayed at the St. Moritz and Dan and I drew up some papers to begin a management deal. Dan set high goals for me. He isn't the kind of man who wants to hear no for an answer. He doesn't let you off the hook that easily. All of his goals for me depended on my drying out.

I was wetter than ever. Dan and I had an appointment with one of New York's most powerful and best-known talent agents. I had tanked up secretly at the hotel. We walked into the agent's plush office high over Madison and I started sweating and panting. My hair was matted down, I was dressed like a midtown messenger boy, I couldn't focus on the conversation, and I looked awful. Dan did all the talking for me and it was clear that I was an alkie. Needless to say, my shabby performance up there blew any chances I had of interesting the hotshot agent in my career.

It was most fortunate that Jane decided to stay with me in the hotel. When I awoke, I was violently ill. Being a med student, she knew exactly what to do.

She took my pulse. Her big green eyes betrayed real fear. "Orthostatic hypotension," she said. "It's like shock. You can end up brain-damaged from this."

I was severely dehydrated and disoriented, with an erratic pulse. Jane got me to New York Hospital. I was hooked up to an I.V. unit, checked out, and released. The next morning I was still vomiting, with diarrhea, and I was still dangerously dehydrated. Jane called doctors for an hour until I said she should call Carter.

It was an awkward call to make. Gold and Pottash were bringing suit against me for the loans now. But the problem at hand transcended money. And, as a friend and physician, Carter was there when I needed him. He arranged to get me to see a colleague of his.

"You're an alcoholic," the doctor said flatly. "You are going to die if you don't stop drinking immediately. You could die in the next few days if you don't stop."

Going to Dan and Betty was out because I could not have made the four-hour trip. I didn't want a hospital. Jane took me home with instructions to call him if I had hallucinations —the classic "pink elephants" vision—or the DTs.

Hours later, I was experiencing both and Jane got me to Lenox Hill.

She stayed with me all night there and they shot me up with Valium. I asked to leave the next day. Jane agreed to take me to her place for a week. We went to a grocery store to buy juices and food that I could eat and keep down. We split up and I promptly found the beer cooler. I cracked open a can of beer and guzzled it right in the aisle. Jane found me and was furious.

"You're just hurting yourself," she said. When we got to her apartment, she put me in bed and locked the gate in front of her brownstone from the outside to keep me in.

Her air-conditioning unit wasn't working yet and I had to take four cold baths a day. I screamed and sank toward DT hell. It was early June. Jane's first-year finals were approaching. After a week, she shipped me off to Dan and Betty upstate.

Scott came up to visit and work on some new songs. Chynna and Tam were with me at the motel. I had some long talks with Chynna. She begged me to stop drinking. She was just sixteen, but she understood the dangers. She asked me to go into a hospital and get better. I told her I would, that I'd be fine. As I said good-bye to her before seeing her off at the airport, she put her arms around me. "I love you, Daddy."

Dan asked Scott to stay with me up at the motel, rather than in the cabins a hundred yards closer to the stream and lake. He was keeping a close watch on me. Still, I was tying bottles of vodka to rocks in the clear stream, so it looked like they were empty, in case anyone caught me fishing around for them. I stashed six-packs in the woods.

Jane came to visit before going to work on a kibbutz for the summer. She had been fantastic to me and my kids. But she needed time away from the madness. We moved down to one of the larger cabins in the wooded area a hundred yards from Dan's motel.

Several days after Jane left, I finally pushed it all too far. I lay awake as Scott, my new bodyguard, fell asleep at midnight. I walked fifty yards along Route 9N and turned left toward the cluster of cabins where Jane and I were staying. I got to the cabins and wandered through the woods, measuring my steps in the dark, and found my stash. I had a couple of beers and was smashed. The stream was rushing high.

I tried to find the seven-horsepower motorboat tied up along the stream, but it was pitch black. I was dizzy and faint, but I wanted to ride up the lake a mile, tie up at a Bolton public beach dock a hundred yards away, and walk over to the late-night bar there for a long lineup of screwdrivers.

I slipped and fell into the rushing water and bounced along the moss-covered, ice-smooth rocks. My body twisted in the current like a puppet. I had no control. My arms were useless to break my slide. Water came up over my head and I gasped for air. I could see nothing. I felt the rocks—round ones, sharp ones—pounding against my back, legs, and arms. I tried to protect my head. I sucked in water, choking and gasping.

I suddenly felt no more rocks. I had been carried into a waterfall that spilled me ten, fifteen feet into Lake George. I paddled around for the dock where Dan kept his small outboard.

I found the boat, but it conked out offshore. I paddled with my arms in the dark until I hit the dock near the bar. I had five triples, then staggered out until a couple drove me to Dan's. My body ached from crashing against the rocks. I found the cabins, but passed out in the wrong one—the one I had stayed in the summer before.

Three days later, over the July Fourth holiday, I was lying across the backseat of Dan's plush Cadillac with my head on Scott's lap. He was stroking my sweaty head and pouring shots of vodka into a cup for me. I was getting the shakes, trying hard not to barf on the slick interior, and breaking into fevers. The doctor said I should drink to prevent a severe withdrawal. It was getting worse by the minute. I thought the end might come at any second.

I never saw any pink elephants, but I did believe that I was a camera flying over Spain. We were actually flying down the interstate, heading south to the Conifer Park drug and alcohol rehab center near Albany. My friends were trying to keep me awake—and alive.

After the madness of thousands of needles jabbed into my veins, I couldn't believe it was all going to end because of goddamn *vodka*. What a fucking punch line. All the windows were open and the wind whipped around the speeding Caddie like a hurricane. I concentrated on every breath and forced myself to stay alert. This was the time to pray for one last chance.

Scott stroked my hair, patted my sweaty back—anything to comfort me. "Thirty years ago," Scott yelled over the wind, "if we were just a couple of local jackasses sittin' in the Hot Shoppe in Alexandria and you told me that over the

Fourth of July 1984, you and I would be sittin' in this car doin' what we're doin' right this second, I swear, man, I'd have said you were completely outta your fuckin' mind."

I motioned for the bottle and Scott gave it to me. I raised it to my lips and downed another shot. My arm fell limp to the floor of the speeding Caddie and I twisted my head around to see him. I could barely manage a slurring retort.

"And see how wrong you'da been?"

30

BY THE TIME I began my fiftieth year of life on August 30, 1984, I was out of Conifer Park and dried out from alcohol. My head was finally beginning to clear after nearly a quarter of a century of substance abuse. Back at Dan's house, I joked that my next career move would be to write a Michelin-type international guide for abusers, called *The Top 100 Rehabs Handbook*. Instead of stars, my guide would use cold turkeys to rate the centers. Who among the living knew the field like I did?

When you kick alcohol or junk, your senses are reawakened and heightened. The mind and body both undergo an amazing process of clarification. I heard and felt and smelled and saw life all over again. It was as if I had had bypass surgery and my arteries had been cleansed and opened wide. I was moved by a spirit of renewal and incredible luck.

My two youngest children joined me at Dan Towers's resort along the western shore of Lake George. Scott stuck around part of the summer and we picked up where we had left off in the late sixties, playing guitars, fooling with harmonies, telling each other outrageous stories. He watched over me like a brother and there was no lingering resentment over Michelle. Friends are too important.

I swam in the pool every day, played one-on-one basketball on the parking lot with Dan's rugged eighteen-year-old son Danny, caught plenty of sun, and dropped ten, twenty, then forty pounds. After the ravages of addiction and the grotesque bloat of booze, my body was starting to belong to me again.

In the fall, I decided that we should hit the road one more time. Music was what I did best and I had to keep doing it to stay alive. Denny, Spanky, and Laura were all game. I continued to pass all my urine tests in Albany, sixty miles south. Promoters were always fair to me—they never stigmatized me as an ex-con, a junkie, or a felon. They were willing to give me a chance and we always delivered.

Jane returned to medical school after her summer in Israel and, though we saw less of each other, we kept in touch. She had been there with me through so many bad moments and close calls. Jane was always unselfish and giving. I certainly came to feel that she was a devoted friend and that I was most fortunate to have her in my life.

I moved into a spacious and modern four-bedroom house with a large deck and big windows overlooking the lake. Autumn was a crisp and invigorating spectacle of colors and woodsy smells rising off the water's edge into the mountains for miles in either direction. Tam started public school and Bij was in a nursery school. It would have been impossible not to feel optimistic in that pure bracing air. I was meeting all sorts of new people who lived very different lives from mine. In fact, up in Bolton by early October, virtually every conversation turns to the stocking of logs for the long, harsh winter. The simple, rugged life was for me.

"Got yer wood in?" the owner of the one-pump general store would ask every day. He was already in his scratchy wool hunter's jacket and thermal undershirt.

"Nope."

"Want some?"

"Y'bet. Got some?"

"Could be. How much y'need?"

"Donno."

"Prob'ly take a half-cord f'now, eh?"

"Y'bet. Sounds 'bout right."

Gen came up at Thanksgiving to see the kids and stayed through Christmas. We discussed giving it another chance. We got along peacefully for a couple of weeks.

Denny came in from Halifax in January, as did Jeffrey from L.A. They were both trimmed down and in real good shape. Life at home was a bit frenetic with all of us together again after so much coming and going. But when we stayed clear of booze, we did okay. Gen was cooking and caring for the kids and they seemed to take to the cold winter wonderland terrain. The Lake George region is a summer vacationland with few major ski resorts. The area is deserted through winter. Most restaurants and shops are shut down until spring.

On Super Sunday, 1985, Denny, Scott, and I performed a benefit concert as a folk trio for Caffè Lena, a hallowed coffeehouse in Saratoga, half an hour south of Lake George. The night was bitter cold and snowy. We packed the creaky, cozy, slightly tilting second-floor café with two hundred die-hard folkies affiliated with Skidmore College. The swirling snow and Super Bowl game emptied the streets, but we filled Caffè Lena with warm three-part harmonies and an intimate feeling for a long-gone era. We sang the Mamas and the Papas hits and some new songs. Scott did "San Francisco" and brought tears to more than a few eyes. Denny whistled —with perfect pitch and phrasing—Bud Shanks' famous flute solo in "California Dreamin'" and killed the crowd with it.

There we were, in our mid- to late forties, eight kids among us, three rehabbed alcoholics still making music for the fun of it. I was surprisingly nervous up there. It was the first time I could recall performing totally straight since I sang in choir as an altar boy.

I kept the patter loose and personal and I grew more comfortable as the evening wore on. Scott and I had performed on that stage with Dick more than two decades back, before there ever was a Super Bowl, before color TV, before the Mamas and the Papas. I remembered back to the more innocent winter of 1965, when Denny and I had it all in front of us down in the Village, heading for the Islands. Scott and I had already sung together for seven years then and he was moving into the apartment when we left.

Everything since had gone or changed, but the music was still alive.

Spanky, Laura, Denny, and I went to Reno for two weeks in February and played Harrah's. We had an even hotter road band this time. I wasn't getting drunk and the music was as tight as it had ever been. The days were hot and dry; the town was surrounded by the snow-covered Sierras. My head kept clearing.

Gradually, the pieces fell into place. I came alive. I had a past; I had a future. I tried to find a life for myself in the present. There was plenty of partying, but no craziness, no barking or quacking, no double-donged sex aids. I was breaking my ass trying to behave myself and stay out of trouble.

It wasn't easy at home, though. We just couldn't be together without brawls and blackouts. Gen and I slowly sank into the same old traps. There were nasty, often violent fights. I did some drinking, but didn't let it get out of hand. Something in the bond itself between Gen and me was tearing us up. That was our fundamental paradox.

We had become a drug to each other—first intoxicating, then habit-forming, finally destructive. We loved each other and, most likely, always would. As artists who shared ideas and created together, we taught and stimulated and gave each other so much over our fifteen years together. As the parents of beautiful children, we were blessed as a genetic team.

But we had been paying a terrible price to make it work. It was bringing in too many other people. "You two can't stay together," our friends had told us for years. It wasn't even drugs any more. It was just the volatile meshing of personalities.

I've spent a lot of time wondering exactly why I gave in, gave up for so long. If the motive was to foster marital torment, then drugs allowed us to sink deeper toward a state in which Gen was a slave, I was a master. Perhaps that was our ultimate high. Sometimes we reversed roles, sometimes I was my own slave. Before the arrest, we never analyzed, discussed, visited therapists. It never occurred to us that we were together for any other reason but to be man and wife and, later, parents. Whatever the motives, somewhere along the line drugs stopped being an escape and turned into a cage.

Gen saw it more clearly than I did. We both tried many times to free ourselves of drugs. Only Gen had the instinct to get out of the marriage, but I held on and always got her back.

Finally, we broke apart in the spring and tried to live without each other. Gen went to L.A. and got started on a screenplay. She had a gift that needed to be salvaged and nurtured—her witty, elegant writing. The kids stayed with me.

The year marked the twentieth anniversary of the Mamas and the Papas' arrival on the pop culture scene. Denny and I found ourselves returning to many of the old haunts and landmarks. We played at a fairgrounds outside San Francisco in Mission Vallejo and Scott and I rode over to the North Beach Strip.

Where the Hungry i once stood, there was now nothing but an excavation pit. This was where the Journeymen got their big break, where I met Michelle. It was just a gaping hole in the ground. The Vesuvius Coffee House was still there, as was the City Lights bookstore. The Purple Onion looked deserted. The Jazz Workshop, where Lenny Bruce and Jerry Mulligan made names for themselves, was gone.

In L.A., a favorite Italian restaurant was now a radio station; a well-known sixties hangout is gone and a parking lot has taken its place in Beverly Hills. The Candy Store had moved to another spot and a hair salon is in its place.

We played a couple of sets on a cruise ship from Miami to St. Thomas, Nassau, and Barbados. "This is a very *large* cruise ship," I said to Denny. "And familiar, eh?" It turned out the ship was the converted liner the *France*. We had all taken the *France* in late 1967, when Cass was busted upon arriving in Southampton.

In St. Thomas, Denny and I saw an old friend of ours who had been there twenty years earlier as a hippie. He now had teenage kids. We walked by Duffy's old place and the upstairs seemed gutted by fire. Creeque Alley was still buzzing with outdoor stalls, shops, and vendors. The harbor was still as beautiful and inspiring as ever; the memories, the sounds of the summer of 1965, Denny's flirtation with Michelle, the crazy fascination with acid, Cass's obsession about joining up, "Like a Rolling Stone," "I Got You Babe," "Help!," "Satisfaction," "Mr. Tambourine Man"—every note, smell, rush, color, and taste came alive again with each foamy, salty crash of the surf.

I remembered too the sensations of love and passion and potential I felt with Michelle. I was, then, as happy as I imagined I could ever be. I heard the words. "I saw her again last night. . . ." I could see her standing there at the water, her long blond hair blowing in the breeze as she twisted her body and face into the sun. They were poignant, haunting, and vivid recollections.

Laura was just over five years old when we arrived at Camp Torture and she hustled the sailors for breakfasts. I had Tam and Bijou with me this time. Bijou was, within weeks, exactly Laura's age in 1965.

Bijou had a terrific time on the cruise. She can be a holy terror when she gets going. She has great big deep-blue eyes, soft rosy cheeks, an upturned nose, and golden hair. She is a precious little girl; except for the straightness of her hair, she is a miniature Gen.

Tam formed a gang and I saw him three or four times during the cruise—whenever he needed money. Tam was turning into a rugged, bright, and handsome teenager who could make friends wherever he went.

The Mamas and the Papas played the Bottom Line for four nights in the summer, all standing-ovation sellouts. We always got up for New York and we were hitting our stride. The music seemed to pack greater wallop in the Village—right down the block from where I once took the stage at Gerdes Folk City. That tradition—early sixties folk—is still so alive for thousands of fans and you can still feel it on Bleecker and Macdougal.

It was great to be with Jane again. She saw all the shows and stayed with me at our hotel. She was working hard and I hadn't seen her in eight or nine months while Gen came back. But the awkwardness soon fell away and we felt as relaxed as ever.

We spent that Sunday afternoon up in Old Greenwich visiting my former neighbors from Shore Road—Chris Thurlow and Joan and Bob Blackmore. Steve Thurlow was away for work. Bijou had always wanted to see her birthplace, so we took her inside the Finches' home and I pointed to the couch in the living room.

"There, Bij. Right there. That's where you were born." It could have been the same couch, reupholstered and in the same spot. She hopped up, patted the cushion with her little hands, and looked around to take it all in. I watched her and shuddered as images of that cold horrifying night came back —how close we had come to losing her.

It was a warm, sunny day and we swam. The kids all planned to go speedboating with Chris, but Jane and I stayed at the Blackmores' with Bob and Joan. I told Bij to put on a light sweater before going out on the boat. She resisted and I got firm. I grabbed her, gave her a little spank, and told her to do as I said. She sulked and went shuffling off to get her sweater from a chair. She brought it to me, I slipped it over her, and she ran off.

Chris gave me an incredulous look and shook her head. I was playing Daddy. "It's just amazing," Chris said, looking to Jane. "I'm sure John's told you about what went on up here five years ago." She nodded. "We just can't believe how great he looks and how wonderful he is with the kids. It's a remarkable transformation."

Before an early evening barbecue, Jane and I took a stroll down Shore Road, past all the fine homes with their cool shaded lawns at dusk, the outboards rocking by the docks at sunset. There was one more local sight to see.

We walked past the home of the neighbor whose lawn I tore up with the Caddie the day after K & B closed and my niece Patty died. I saw the low stone seawall that ran along the far edge of the property above the private strip of beach. Clouds streaked with scarlet and pink floated across the clear evening sky over the Sound toward nightfall. But I was thinking back to a deranged and mournful rain-swept afternoon in 1980, to a car dangling perilously on that wall and the madman behind the wheel.

It had been a long and tortuous route back to Shore Road. The body needs months—sometimes years—to recover. The brain doesn't immediately begin to produce the endorphines that are suppressed by long-term opiate addiction. It can take a long time. I ached for a year. I felt like I had arthritis through my entire body. I know why junkies plunge into booze.

I had countless dreams of shooting up and feeling the rush again—only to awaken with a desperate craving for a shot of coke to get me in gear.

I was haunted by nightmares in which the Rockettes at Radio City Music Hall came out in their kick line, except that each dancer's long legs were transformed into loaded syringes that high-kicked across the stage. And there were scores of anxiety attacks triggered by a flashback while walking down some side street—and I'd immediately want to score heroin and shoot up. I'd want it so badly, but I knew I couldn't go near it. Those cravings often left me disoriented and upset for hours.

Looking back, I am absolutely certain I would not be alive now if I had not been arrested. As strange as it sounds, the dealer who turned informant on me saved my life. I could never have stopped by myself. The prosecutor helped save my life. Facing forty-five years in prison would give any hard-core addict a reason to defeat his addiction to smack and coke.

I was never allowed to fall back, but I got much more help and support than I felt I might have deserved. I hit the criminal justice system, the detox, prison, and probation systems just right. I had always managed to meet people at the most opportune moments, whether the connections involved sex, drugs, rock, travel, or money.

When nothing short of my survival and freedom were on the line, I had a charmed life. I had the best kind of help you can have. I met intelligent and decent men like Dick Schaeffer, Mark Gold, Mark Pomerantz, Judge Sand, and my probation officer, Phil Albertson. They were always willing to

encourage me to do my best and tell the truth, to make me
feel that I was going to make it if I just played it straight for
once. I had trusting and caring friends like Bob Tucker,
Denny, and Jane. I had my family. Genevieve showed remarkable courage in joining me at Fair Oaks; she had no
self-serving motive. She wasn't under indictment or facing a
jail term. She went through the agony of withdrawal a dozen
times, not just for her own survival but for mine and our
children's.

I've looked back for the turning point when it all started
to go out of control, when I began shredding apart the fabric
of my life with needles. Without question, it was the demise
of the Broadway musical. It made me doubt, then hate, my
true successes and feel that I had never deserved them to
begin with. I was nothing but a shooting star that had flared,
then faded.

Maybe I had made it too easily. I wasn't in L.A. a year yet
when I had a top song and album, a Grammy-winning song
at the top of the charts, more money—well, *almost* more
money—than I knew what to do with, I was married to one
of the most beautiful women in the world. Then we had a
beautiful daughter. I was stoned all the time and what else
was there? That was supposed to go on until I was forty and
then I would die. It scared me. I didn't die. I had to *throw* it
all away. I couldn't keep it going. When I got to London and
discovered mainlining, I sacrificed everything—my health,
my art and music, my possessions, my freedom, my family—
to punish myself.

I wasn't ready to stop until Mark Gold made me admit
that my family was dying with me. I had put them in a
precarious position. Only by saving myself could I save
them. "There will be a lot of accidents, maybe some fatali-
ties," he made me see, "because they are all trying to live
just like you. Why you're even here, alive," he said, "I don't
understand. Very few people get away with the shit you
pulled. Many of your friends are dead. You aren't *supposed*
to be alive. You're sick. You are not immortal or indestructible and you need help."

That was the other turning point. I've beaten incredible

odds. I'm not proud but humbled. I know rock and roll's list of casualties, from friends like Elvis and Mama Cass on down: Hendrix, Morrison, Janis, Brian Jones, Keith Moon, Belushi. Once Dr. Gold had me, I realized what he was saying. I was impossibly lucky. I saw that I could die in prison without ever having my family back. It was time to clean out and move on.

As a drug counselor, I was always asked how to get off drugs. The best way to stay off drugs is to never get *on* them. I don't blame anybody else for what happened. Not friends, not "hangers-on," not the American "star system" that makes and breaks its heroes with such swiftness. If anyone claimed me as their victim, it was me.

My values were totally turned upside down. The normal human's priorities—what to eat; where and with whom to sleep; who to love and why; social, family, and professional goals; the pursuit of money and material comforts—are abandoned for the maniacal quest for drugs. No task was more overwhelming than turning my value system right side up again. But none was so rewarding, either.

Junkies tell a joke about the addict who shoots up and drops dead in a shooting gallery. Two of his friends slap him around and try in vain to revive him. Two other junkies walk by and look down and say to the dead one's friends: "Man, that musta been some good shit. Where'd you score it?"

Junk turns you into a beast. It takes a long time to believe there is a life worth living again after drugs and alcohol. I fought it for years. I'm just glad I woke up in time.

There are gnawing regrets that will be with me forever. So many illicit drugs made it to the street and into young people's bloodstreams as a result of my connection to K & B. I was just so far under the ether myself that I wasn't aware of those consequences.

I cheated three of my children out of having a real father with them when they were young and I will always be sorry for that. I let them down when they were teenagers because of the example I set. I have little doubt that, in the case of Jeff and Laura, their own drug abuse was a twisted way for them to reach out and connect with me, get my attention, win my love and approval through emulation. It took a decade to turn my example around for them, but it has been, finally, well worth the struggle.

I recently said to Laura that I was sorry I could never replace or redeem those lost years. I wanted to let her know that I knew how hard it had been for her and Jeff. It hurts to admit that I cannot retrieve what I threw away.

Michelle has always been an active and loving parent with Chynna. I never wanted to get in the way. Since Chynna was a child, we have connected best around creative endeavors—singing and writing music together, poetry, teaching her guitar. I have always cherished the gentleness and calm of my relationship to Chynna. Michelle was wise enough to insulate her from me during the worst drug years—and to take Tam over to her and Rosie's side. Painful as it is to acknowledge, I was grateful for what she and Rosie did, but sorry it ended in a Connecticut courtroom with a bitter accusation of federal child-stealing. I imagine that Michelle will always believe that I should be in jail.

The fact that I am not has given me a rare chance few men get: to watch two more young children grow up while piecing a shattered career back together. I am writing music again. Who knows? Maybe I'll give Broadway another shot.

I would like to stay on the road with the foursome, but I draw the line at recording with—and as—the Mamas and the Papas. I can't arm wrestle with the legend. I love those songs and will perform them onstage anytime, anywhere. They will live with me—I hope with all of us—forever. There is a deep sense of fulfillment for having accomplished *that* and I feel extremely lucky for it. But it's time to move into the next half century of my life.

One key to my finding myself again at fifty was finding my two little ones, Tam and Bijou. I don't know where I would be without them at this time in my life. Laura came to visit us in Lake George recently and, like the Thurlows, she had to wipe her eyes to make sure she wasn't imagining that I was giving Bij a bath. "It's so weird to see you being Daddy," she said.

"It's so painful," I answered, "to realize that I never did this for you and Jeff and Chynna."

The hard work of parenthood day in and day out often leaves me tired but content. I stick with it. I look forward to taking the kids to the mall on Saturday afternoons for pizza, to let them run loose and check out all the stores. It's part of a life that I've never known before—the normal, sane part. It's time I learn to fit in there.

Is there a better test of that than refereeing a dispute between siblings over control of the airwaves on Saturday morning? Bijou ran to me in bed, cheeks red and puffy, her bloodshot green eyes watery with tears. "You know what Tam is?" she asked, grimacing and clenching her fists. "He's just a sad jerk, a *really sad jerk.*" It was a moment that made me realize just how much I had missed and there were tears in my eyes too.

Tam, of course, is neither sad nor a jerk. In fact, since he's gone off to a first-rate prep school, he isn't even *Tam* anymore. After some research, he's changed his name to Mike. Tall, wiry, wily, and handsome, he's got a bit of the rebel in him already. He always hated the name Tamerlane Orlando. He discovered something awful.

"Dad," he said, running up to me with his finger still on a page in an open book of names, "I'm the only person in the world with the name Tamerlane."

"Just think how lucky and unique that makes you."

"WRONG! Michael's, like, the most common name, so from now on I'm Michael and every time you call me Tam, or Tamerlane, or anything that even *sounds* like it, you're fined 75¢."

Single fatherhood also means waking up each morning at 7 A.M. to fix a provolone-and-boloney sandwich for Bijou's lunch at nursery school. That's the high point of my day. Bijou's got to have *everything* just right in her little lunchbox before Mr. Mom's off the hook. There's got to be just the right amount of Miracle Whip, enough peanut butter cookies to fill Bijou's two fists, and her one and only favorite juice, a carefully blended mixture of orange and cranberry.

I always know when I've screwed up the mixture with too much of one and not enough of the other: Bij chucks it in my face. And the napkins have to be placed in the lunchbox just right, along with the plastic cup of juice. *And* if she's been a

Good Bij, she gets chocolate pudding. If I've been a Good Dad, I get a kiss good-bye when I drop her off and a nap when I get home.

As busy as she keeps me, I am prone to feeling very lonesome without a woman around. No matter how hard I try to be Mr. Mom, I'm not Mom.

Out in the country, sound travels. I hear doors shut and distant voices and expect someone I love to walk in. I hear the wind slam the bathroom door upstairs and think someone's in the shower. I wake up out of a dream and reach over and no one's there.

There's still so much to unravel and understand—parenting, career, finances, the separation, custody, living without drugs and booze, restoring a social life based on friendship rather than drug frenzies. My psychiatrist upstate, a soft-spoken Korean, is fond of saying, with his accent, that the secret to my survival is "setting rimits on yourself because you never set rimits before." I always had "rimits" imposed on me—and I grew up in a constant state of sullen revolt toward authority and regulations.

I was the product of a marine and a Cherokee squaw steeped in prairie mysticism and legends. Maybe it was fated that my life, which began during a tropical storm, would turn into my own one-man Trail of Tears.

I grew up at a Catholic military boarding school where a nun blew a bugle every morning, where the cadets wore uniforms, carried toy wooden guns, and marched in lock-step to class. The drill master wore a habit; the penguins watched us shower and hit us when we were naughty. Who wants "rimits" after four years of *that?*

I have no second-guesses about leaving the seminary studies and Annapolis behind. I'd have been about as good a priest as a naval officer. I have been able at time to steer aircraft carriers and men's souls—but with my own private compass.

I needed a way out—or around. The Locals taught me everything I needed then. I got by; I hid a lot behind my cool until my music expressed my emotions for me. I rarely ever felt close to my father. My mother held me together, then drifted away. I had to find myself through music and I woke up one morning at the top of the mountain. It happened so fast. When I abused, then abandoned, my own creative gifts, I lost the way out; I lost the magic and I lost myself. I lost the respect and affection of my peers and the public—and myself—and there was nothing to replace it until I found smack. It was a long and brutal trip down from the mainstream of pop to the mainline of junk.

I was a crazy man when they slapped those cuffs on me. But that signaled the beginning of my liberation. I had developed a sociopathic personality disorder. Any number of friends, hotel owners, landlords, and ex-wives would be happy to tell me that for free. I believe that all drug addicts are sociopaths. They lie and destroy and swindle and posture and do anything to stay high. I had to be incarcerated to set myself free.

Ever since I went on probation I have done everything in my power to stay straight. The toughest and truest test of my commitment to sanity will prove to be not life on probation but *after* probation. The lesson of Allenwood stays with me: Freedom is a double-edged sword that can cut you loose or cut you down. Some cons need the bars.

My five-year probation was lifted on May 8, 1986. The jail cell of my probation was my bladder. You are a prisoner to your own urine as a convicted narcotics felon. You aren't truly free until the urine tests end with the lifting of probation.

At that point—when the cloud of criminality passed over, then the test of freedom was for real. No one was watching over me.

My oldest friend in life, Bill Cleary, wryly suggested not long ago that I petition the court for another five-year stint on probation. Bill was being facetious, but I know there was some truth in what was passing through his mind. No one has known me better or longer than Bill.

"You're doin' too well, man," he said. "I'd hate to see ya blow it now."

"I'll take my chances and go free," I told him. "I feel more optimistic about the future as I get to know myself all over again. I think it's a good time for my family and me. I need my freedom now to live the way I want to."

Dick Schaeffer put it best before Judge Sand: I started serving time the moment my first shot of heroin flowed into my veins. Now, with any luck, the punishment is over and Hurricane John will blow out to sea. I welcome the calm and the clearing, the ultimate challenge of freedom.

"Ya sure it doesn't scare ya?" Cleary asked sympathetically, with a wary little twist of his head, a gesture I've known all my life. "Don't ya think you might feel the temptation to go back, do a little this, a little that, get back into things, so on and so forth, and . . ."

"Hey, wait." I cut him off with a shake of the head and two palms raised in his face. "I'll be happy just not peeing into a bottle with my felony I.D. number on it. I have no idea how I'll live as a free man. I don't wanna even *think* about it. I'll just have to cross that bridge when it burns."

Index